Middle School 3-1
학교시험 완벽대비

KB100523

1학기 전과정
적중 100 plus
영어 기출문제집

중3
동아 | 이병민

Best Collection

구성과 특징

교과서의 주요 학습 내용을 중심으로 학습 영역별 특성에 맞춰 단계별로 다양한 학습 기회를 제공하여
단원별 학습능력 평가는 물론 중간 및 기말고사 시험 등에 완벽하게 대비할 수 있도록 내용을 구성

Words & Expressions

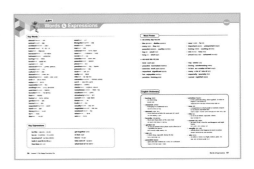

Step1   Key Words 단원별 핵심 단어 설명 및 풀이
          Key Expression 단원별 핵심 숙어 및 관용어 설명
          Word Power 반대 또는 비슷한 뜻 단어 배우기
          English Dictionary 영어로 배우는 영어 단어

Step2   실력평가 단원별 수시평가 대비 주관식, 객관식 문제풀이

Step3   서술형 대비 학업성취도 및 수행능력평가 대비 서술형 문제풀이

Conversation

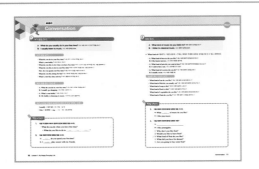

Step1   핵심 의사소통 소통에 필요한 주요 표현 방법 요약
          핵심 Check 기본적인 표현 방법 및 활용능력 확인

Step2   대화문 익히기 교과서 대화문 심층 분석 및 확인

Step3   교과서 확인학습 빈칸 채우기를 통한 문장 완성 능력 확인

Step4   기본평가 시험대비 기초 학습 능력 평가

Step5   실력평가 단원별 수시평가 대비 주관식, 객관식 문제풀이

Step6   서술형 대비 학업성취도 및 수행능력평가 대비 서술형 문제풀이

Grammar

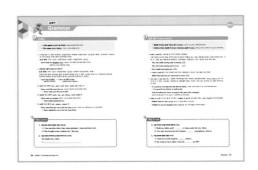

Step1   주요 문법 단원별 주요 문법 사항과 예문을 알기 쉽게 설명
          핵심 Check 기본 문법사항에 대한 이해 여부 확인

Step2   기본평가 시험대비 기초 학습 능력 평가

Step3   실력평가 단원별 수시평가 대비 주관식, 객관식 문제풀이

Step4   서술형 대비 학업성취도 및 수행능력평가 대비 서술형 문제풀이

Reading

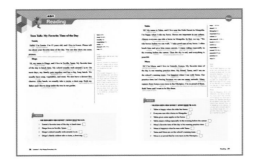

Step1   구문 분석 단원별로 제시된 문장에 대한 구문별 분석과 내용 설명
          확인문제 문장에 대한 기본적인 이해와 인지능력 확인

Step2   확인학습A 빈칸 채우기를 통한 문장 완성 능력 확인

Step3   확인학습B 제시된 우리말을 영어로 완성하여 작문 능력 키우기

Step4   실력평가 단원별 수시평가 대비 주관식, 객관식 문제풀이

Step5   서술형 대비 학업성취도 및 수행능력평가 대비 서술형 문제풀이
          교과서 구석구석 교과서에 나오는 기타 문장까지 완벽 학습

Composition

|영역별 핵심문제|

단어 및 어휘, 대화문, 문법, 독해 등 각 영역별 기출문제의 출제 유형을 분석하여 실전에 대비하고 연습할 수 있도록 문제를 배열

|단원별 예상문제|

기출문제를 분석한 후 새로운 시험 출제 경향을 더하여 새롭게 출제될 수 있는 문제를 포함하여 시험에 완벽하게 대비할 수 있도록 준비

|서술형 실전 및 창의사고력 문제|

학교 시험에서 점차 늘어나는 서술형 시험에 집중 대비하고 고득점을 취득하는데 만전을 기하기 위한 학습 코너

|단원별 모의고사|

영역별, 단계별 학습을 모두 마친 후 실전 연습을 위한 모의고사

on the textbook

교과서 파헤치기

- **단어Test1~3** 영어 단어 우리말 쓰기, 우리말을 영어 단어로 쓰기, 영영풀이에 해당하는 단어와 우리말 쓰기
- **대화문Test1~2** 대화문 빈칸 완성 및 전체 대화문 쓰기
- **본문Test1~5** 빈칸 완성, 우리말 쓰기, 문장 배열연습, 영어 작문하기 복습 등 단계별 반복 학습을 통해 교과서 지문에 대한 완벽한 습득
- **구석구석지문Test1~2** 지문 빈칸 완성 및 전문 영어로 쓰기

Lesson 1

I Can't, but We Can

의사소통 기능

- 안부 묻고 답하기
  A: How have you been?
  B: I've been good.
- 기쁨 · 유감 표현하기
  A: I came in first in the marathon.
  B: I'm happy to hear that.

언어 형식

- It ~ for ... to부정사
  It was not easy **for us** to choose the best idea.

- 관계대명사 what
  We finally made **what** we wanted.

Words & Expressions

Key Words

- **again** [əgén] 부 다시
- **as** [əz] 전 ~로서
- **bad cold** 독감
- **base** [beis] 명 (사물의) 맨 아래 부분
- **busy** [bizi] 형 바쁜
- **by** [bai] 전 (정도·차이) ~의 차(이)로, ~만큼
- **call** [kɔːl] 동 전화하다, 부르다
- **challenge** [tʃælindʒ] 명 과제, 도전
- **close** [klous] 형 막상막하의, 우열을 가리기 힘든
- **competition** [kàmpətíʃən] 명 (경연) 대회, 시합, 경쟁
- **creatively** [kriéitivli] 부 창의적으로
- **detail** [ditéil] 명 세부, 상세
- **divide** [diváid] 동 나누다
- **each** [iːtʃ] 형 각각의 대 각각
- **go** [gou] 동 (일의 진행이 어떻게) 되다
- **improve** [imprúːv] 동 개량하다, 향상시키다
- **instead** [instéd] 부 대신에
- **later** [léitər] 부 후에
- **lose** [luiz] 동 (시합에서) 지다

- **marathon** [mǽrəθàn] 명 마라톤
- **mess** [mes] 명 엉망인 상태
- **number** [nʌ́mbər] 명 수, 전화번호
- **point** [pɔint] 명 (경기 등에서) 점수
- **pretty** [príti] 부 꽤, 매우
- **relationship** [riléiʃənʃip] 명 관계
- **role** [roul] 명 역할
- **same** [seim] 형 같은
- **score** [skɔːr] 명 (경기 등에서) 득점
- **stick** [stik] 명 지팡이, 막대기, 막대기처럼 기다랗고 가는 것
- **still** [stil] 부 여전히
- **string** [striŋ] 명 끈, 줄
- **stuck** [stʌk] 형 움직일 수 없는
- **suggest** [səgdʒést] 동 제안하다
- **teamwork** [tímwərk] 명 팀워크, 협동 작업
- **tent** [tent] 명 텐트, 천막
- **triangle** [tráiæŋgl] 명 삼각형
- **upset** [ʌ́pset] 형 속상한, 기분이 상한
- **wrap** [ræp] 동 감다, 싸다

Key Expressions

- **be busy at 명사**: ~으로 바쁘다
- **be good at (동)명사**: ~을 잘하다, ~에 능숙하다
- **by itself**: 홀로, 저절로
- **divide up**: 분담하다, 분배하다
- **get well**: 병이 나아지다
- **have a cold**: 감기에 걸리다
- **have a fight with ~**: ~와 싸우다
- **in a hurry**: 서둘러, 급히
- **in detail**: 상세하게
- **in first**: 처음으로, 최초로

- **in the end**: 마침내
- **Long time no see.**: 오랜만이야.
- **look like+명사**: ~처럼 보이다
- **lots of**: 많은
- **right away**: 즉각, 곧바로
- **so so**: 그저 그런, 평범한
- **spend A on B**: A를 B에 쓰다
- **such as**: ~와 같은
- **try to 동사원형**: ~하려고 애쓰다

Word Power

※ 형용사와 부사

(1) 형용사는 명사를 수식하고, 부사는 명사 이외의 것들, 즉 형용사, 동사, 부사, 문장 전체를 수식한다.
- □ **different**(다른) – **differently**(다르게)
- □ **quick**(빠른) – **quickly**(빨리)
- □ **slow**(느린) – **slowly**(느리게)
- □ **happy**(행복한) – **happily**(행복하게)
- □ **possible**(가능한) – **possibly**(가능하게)

- □ **sudden**(갑작스러운) – **suddenly**(갑자기)
- □ **easy**(쉬운) – **easily**(쉽게)
- □ **careful**(조심하는) – **carefully**(조심스럽게)
- □ **true**(진짜의) – **truly**(정말로)

(2) 형용사와 부사의 형태가 같은 경우도 있다.
- □ **early**(이른) – **early**(일찍)

- □ **late**(늦은) – **late**(늦게)

(3) 주의해야 할 부사
- □ **hard**(열심히) – **hardly**(거의 ~ 아니다)
- □ **near**(가까이) – **nearly**(거의)

- □ **late**(늦게) – **lately**(최근에)
- □ **high**(높은) – **highly**(매우, 높이)

English Dictionary

□ **base**: (사물의) 맨 아래 부분
→ the lowest part or surface of something
어떤 것의 가장 낮은 부분이나 표면

□ **call**: 전화하다
→ to telephone someone
누군가에게 전화하다

□ **challenge**: 과제, 도전
→ something that needs a lot of skill, energy, and determination to deal with or achieve
어떤 것을 해결하거나 달성하기 위해 많은 기술, 에너지, 결정들이 필요한 것

□ **close**: 막상막하의, 우열을 가리기 힘든
→ finishing or being played, fought, etc. with both sides almost equal
양쪽이 거의 같게 끝마치거나 경기하거나 다투는

□ **detail**: 세부, 상세
→ a minor point or aspect of something, as opposed to the central ones
중심이 되는 것과는 대조적으로 어떤 것의 사소한 점이나 양상

□ **divide**: 나누다
→ to separate people or things into smaller groups or parts
사람이나 사물을 작은 그룹이나 부문으로 나누다

□ **improve**: 개량하다, 향상시키다
→ to make better
더 좋게 만들다

□ **lose**: (시합 · 싸움 · 선거 등에서) 지다
→ to not win a game, argument, election, war, etc.
경기, 논쟁, 선거, 전쟁 등에서 이기지 못하다

□ **mess**: 엉망인 상태
→ a state of confusion and disorderliness
혼돈과 무질서한 상태

□ **pretty**: 꽤, 매우
→ fairly or more than a little
꽤 또는 상당히

□ **relationship**: 관계
→ the way in which people feel and behave towards each other
사람들이 서로에 대해 느끼고 행동하는 방식

□ **role**: 역할
→ the actions and activities assigned to or required or expected of a person or group
사람이나 모임에게 할당되거나 요구되거나 기대되는 행동들

□ **stuck**: 움직일 수 없는
→ impossible or unable to move from a particular position
특정한 위치에서 움직이는 것이 불가능하거나 움직일 수 없는

01 주어진 문장에서 밑줄 친 point의 뜻으로 사용된 것을 고르시오.

> We lost by one point.

① He noted down the main points of the lecture.
② David has the greatest number of points in Math.
③ I missed the point of his speech.
④ The woman is pointing at the computer screen.
⑤ The point is simple: Don't worry too much.

02 다음 밑줄 친 부분의 의미로 알맞지 않은 것은?

① They can also help them think creatively. (창의적으로)
② Only one hour was allowed for each presentation. (각각의)
③ Teens will face new challenges and learn skills including teamwork, leadership and planning. (과제)
④ The surfing competition was for dogs. (대회)
⑤ It had been pretty warm till yesterday. (예쁜)

03 밑줄 친 부분과 바꿔 쓸 수 있는 말을 모두 고르시오.

> In the end, the love story won't come to a happy ending.

① Finally   ② Besides
③ In particular   ④ In addition
⑤ At last

04 다음 빈칸을 〈보기〉에 있는 어휘를 이용하여 채울 수 없는 것을 고르시오.

> ┌─── 보기 ───┐
> busy   instead   same   upset

① Sorry for being late. I got _____ in a traffic jam.
② I'm very _____ because of my sister.
③ After all, children eat the _____ way as their parents.
④ I'll have tea _____ of coffee, please.
⑤ Rachel said she would be too _____ to come.

05 빈칸 (A)와 (B)에 알맞은 말로 짝지어진 것을 고르시오.

> • Jamie looked upset this morning. Maybe she had a fight (A)_____ her mom.
> • They spend too much time (B)_____ computer games.

   (A) (B)　　　　　(A) (B)
① with – of　　　② with – in
③ with – on　　　④ of – in
⑤ of – on

01 다음 밑줄 친 부분의 쓰임이 자연스럽지 <u>않은</u> 것을 찾아 고치시오.

> ⓐ It is <u>early</u> morning.
> ⓑ I always get up <u>lately</u>.
> ⓒ It is too <u>late</u> to cancel the party.

➡ _____

02 밑줄 친 부분과 바꿔 쓸 수 있는 말을 주어진 철자로 시작하여 쓰시오.

> We went to the theater <u>fairly</u> often.

➡ p_____

03 다음 괄호 안의 단어를 문맥에 맞게 고쳐 쓰시오.

> I've been told that there is a fair _____ here. (compete)

04 다음 빈칸에 공통으로 들어갈 말을 쓰시오.

> • You'll make mistakes if you do things _____ a hurry.
> • She talked _____ detail about future plans for the school.

05 다음 영영풀이에 해당하는 말을 주어진 철자로 시작하여 쓰시오.

> the lowest part or surface of something

➡ b_____

06 다음 빈칸에 알맞은 단어를 〈보기〉에서 골라 쓰시오.

> ┌── 보기 ──┐
> have   see   spend   try

(1) Always _____ to do your best.

(2) How much time do you _____ on homework?

(3) When I _____ a fight with my younger brother, my mom is always on his side.

(4) Long time no _____.

07 다음 우리말에 맞도록 빈칸에 알맞은 말을 쓰시오. (철자가 주어진 경우 주어진 철자로 시작할 것)

(1) 나는 지금 매우 바쁘다.
➡ I'm p_____ _____ right now.

(2) 나는 네가 발목에 얼음을 조금 놓을 것을 제안한다.
➡ I s_____ that you put some ice on your ankle.

08 다음 우리말에 맞게 주어진 단어를 바르게 배열하시오.

(1) 나는 곧바로 두 골을 득점했고 우리 팀이 한 골 차이로 게임을 이겼다.
(game, goals, one, two, and, the, by, won, right, goal, scored, team, I, my, away)
➡ _____
_____

(2) 그들은 아직도 이야기 중이다.
(still, are, they, talking)
➡ _____

Conversation

교과서

1 안부 묻고 답하기

A: How have you been? 어떻게 지냈니?
B: I've been good. 잘 지냈어.

■ 'How have you been?'은 '(그동안) 어떻게 지냈니?'라는 뜻으로, 오랜만에 만난 사람에게 안부를 물을 때 사용하는 표현이다. 'What have you been up to?'로 바꾸어 말할 수 있다.

■ 'How have you been?'과 'How are you?' 둘 다 안부를 묻는 표현이지만, 'How have you been?'은 한동안 만나지 못했던 사람을 오랜만에 만났을 경우에 사용하고, 'How are you?'는 자주 만난 사람에게 사용할 수 있다.

안부 묻기

- How have you been doing?
- How's everything?
- What's going on?
- What have you been up to?
- How have you been getting along these days?
- What's up?

■ 안부를 묻는 말에 답할 때는 상태를 나타내는 다양한 형용사를 사용할 수 있으며 구체적인 이유를 덧붙여 말할 수도 있다. 또한, 안부를 물어봐 줘서 고맙다는 의미로 'Thanks.'를 덧붙인다.

안부 묻는 말에 답하기

- (I'm) Fine, thank you. / I've been fine[good]. Thanks. / Pretty good. / Great. / Good. / Not bad. (잘 지내.)
- So so. (그럭저럭 지내.)
- Not so good. (별로 안 좋아.)

핵심 Check

1. 우리말과 일치하도록 주어진 단어를 배열하여 문장을 만드시오.

A: _____ (어떻게 지냈니?) (been, have, how, you)
B: I've been fine. Thanks. (잘 지냈어. 고마워.)

2 **기쁨 · 유감 표현하기**

> A: I came in first in the marathon. 마라톤에서 1등으로 들어왔어.
> B: I'm happy to hear that. 그 말을 들으니 기쁘구나.

■ 상대방이 한 말에 대하여 기쁨을 표현할 때 'I'm happy to hear that.'이라고 말할 수 있다. 'happy' 대신에 'glad', 'pleased' 등을 쓸 수 있다.

■ 상대방에게 좋지 않은 일이 있을 경우, 'I'm sorry to hear that.'을 사용하여 유감을 나타낼 수 있다.

기쁨 표현하기

- I'm glad to hear that. (그 말을 들으니 기뻐.)
- I'm happy for you. (잘 되었구나.)
- I'm pleased to hear that. (그 말을 들으니 기뻐.)
- That's wonderful[great]. (굉장하구나.)

유감 표현하기

- I'm sorry to hear that. (그 말을 들으니 유감이야.)
- What a pity! (안됐구나!)
- That's a pity[a shame]. (정말 안됐다.)
- That's too bad. (정말 안됐다.)
- That's terrible. (끔찍하구나.)

핵심 Check

2. 대화의 순서를 바르게 배열하시오.

> (A) That's great! I'm happy to hear that.
> (B) What's up?
> (C) I finally got on the school basketball team!
> (D) Thank you.

➡ _____

3. 우리말과 일치하도록 주어진 단어를 배열하여 문장을 만드시오.

> A: What's up, Chris? You look upset.
> B: I can't find my bicycle. I think I lost it.
> A: _____ (그 말을 들으니 유감이야.) (that, sorry, hear, I'm, to)

Listen and Speak 1 A

B: Amy, ❶how have you been?

G: ❷I've been great. ❸How about you, Mike?

B: Not so good. I ❹have a bad cold.

G: Oh, no! ❺Get well soon.

B: Thanks.

B: Amy, 어떻게 지냈니?
G: 잘 지냈어. 너는 어때, Mike?
B: 별로야. 독감에 걸렸어.
G: 어, 저런! 빨리 나아.
B: 고마워.

❶ 'How have you been?'은 '어떻게 지냈니?'의 의미로 오랜만에 본 상대방에게 그동안 어떻게 지냈는지 안부를 물을 때 사용하는 표현이다. 비슷한 표현으로 'What have you been up to?', 'How have you been doing?', 'How have you been getting along these days?' 등이 있다.

❷ 'How have you been?'에 대해 응답을 할 때 'I've been ~.'은 생략되기도 한다. (I've been) Good., Fine., Great., Busy. 등을 쓸 수 있다.

❸ 안부를 대답한 사람이 안부를 물어봐 준 상대방의 안부가 어떤지를 묻기 위해 'How about you?(넌 어떠니?)'를 이용해서 질문하고 있다.

❹ bad cold: 독감   have a cold: 감기에 걸리다

❺ get well: 병이 낫다

Check(√) True or False

(1) Amy is sick now.   T ☐ F ☐

(2) Amy hopes Mike gets well.   T ☐ F ☐

Listen and Speak 1 B

G: Hi, Jinsu! We're in ❶the same class again!

B: Yeah! ❷It's good to see you, Sora. ❸How have you been?

G: I've been great. How about you?

B: I've been ❹pretty busy. I have a piano ❺competition next week.

G: Oh! ❻I didn't know you played the piano.

B: Really? ❼I've played the piano for 5 years.

G: You ❽must be good at it. ❾Good luck in your competition!

B: Thanks.

G: 안녕, 진수야! 우리 또 같은 반이구나!
B: 응! 만나서 반가워, 소라야. 어떻게 지냈니?
G: 잘 지냈어. 너는 어때?
B: 난 좀 바빴어. 다음 주에 피아노 경연이 있어.
G: 오! 네가 피아노를 치는지 몰랐어.
B: 정말? 난 피아노를 5년간 쳤어.
G: 넌 분명 피아노를 잘 치겠구나. 경연에서 행운을 빌어!
B: 고마워.

❶ the same: 같은

❷ It은 가주어, to see you가 진주어이다.

❸ 'How have you been?'은 '어떻게 지냈니?'라는 의미로, 안부를 물을 때 사용하는 표현이다.

❹ pretty는 형용사로 '예쁜'의 의미로 사용하지만, 부사로서 형용사를 수식할 때는 '아주, 매우'라는 의미이다.

❺ competition: 대회

❻ know 다음에 명사절을 이끄는 접속사 that이 생략되었다.

❼ 현재완료의 계속 용법이다. 과거부터 지금까지 계속된 행위를 표현하며, '~해 왔다'의 의미이다.

❽ must는 '~해야 한다'의 의미가 아니라 '~임에 틀림없다'의 의미로 사용되었다.

❾ 'Good luck in ~'은 '~에서 행운을 빌어.'의 의미로 좋은 일이 생기도록 기원하는 표현이다. 'Good luck to you.(행운을 빌어.)', 'I'll keep my fingers crossed for you.(행운을 빌어.)'로 바꾸어 말할 수도 있다.

Check(√) True or False

(3) Sora has played the piano for 5 years.   T ☐ F ☐

(4) Jinsu has been busy because of a piano competition.   T ☐ F ☐

Listen and Speak 2 A

B: Susan, you ❶look excited. Do you have any good news?

G: Our team ❷got an A on the science project.

B: That's great!

G: Our team had the best teamwork.

B: ❸I'm happy to hear that.

B: Susan, 신나 보이네. 좋은 소식이 있니?
G: 우리 팀이 과학 프로젝트에서 A를 받았어.
B: 잘됐다!
G: 우리 팀은 팀워크가 최고였어.
B: 그 말을 들으니 기뻐.

❶ look+형용사: ~하게 보이다 excited: 신이 난, 흥분한 감정을 나타내는 동사의 경우 현재분사는 '~하게 하는'의 뜻으로 감정을 유발하는 대상에 쓰이고, 과거분사는 '~하게 된'의 뜻으로 감정을 느끼는 대상에 쓰인다.

❷ get an A: A 점수를 받다

❸ 'I'm happy to hear that.'은 '그 말을 들으니 기쁘구나.'의 의미로 상대방이 한 말에 대하여 기쁨을 표현할 때 사용한다.

Check(√) True or False

(5) Susan got an A on the science project. T ☐ F ☐

(6) Susan thinks that her teamwork was good. T ☐ F ☐

Listen and Speak 2 C

A: Bob, you ❶look happy.

B: I came ❷in first in the marathon.

A: ❸I'm happy to hear that.

A: Bob, 너 행복해 보인다.
B: 마라톤에서 1등으로 들어왔어.
A: 그 말을 들으니 기뻐.

❶ 동사 look은 '~해 보이다'라는 의미의 2형식 동사로, 뒤에 상태를 나타내는 형용사가 온다. 부사처럼 해석되지만, 형용사를 보어로 취함에 주의한다.

❷ in first: 처음으로, 최초로 marathon: 마라톤

❸ 상대방의 좋은 소식을 듣고 기쁨을 표현하는 말이다. 'I'm glad to hear that.', 'I'm pleased to hear that.', 'I'm happy for you.'로 표현할 수도 있다.

Check(√) True or False

(7) Bob is planning to run a marathon. T ☐ F ☐

(8) Bob is happy now. T ☐ F ☐

Listen and Speak 1 C

A: Mina, ❶how have you been?

B: ❷I've been good. ❸How is everything?

A: ❹Pretty good. My new classmates are nice.

❶ 'How have you been?'은 안부를 물을 때 사용하는 표현이다. (= What have you been up to? = How have you been doing? = How have you been getting along these days? = What's up? = What's going on?)

❷ 안부를 묻는 말에 대답할 때 상태를 나타내는 형용사를 사용할 수 있는데 여기서는 good(좋은)을 사용해 자신의 상태가 좋다고 대답하고 있다.

❸ 'How is everything?'은 '어떻게 지내니?'라는 의미로 안부를 물을 때 사용하는 표현이다.

❹ pretty: 아주, 매우

Listen and Speak 2 B

G: Andy, ❶how did the basketball game ❷go?

B: Our team ❸lost.

G: Oh, ❹I'm sorry to hear that.

B: It's okay. It was a great game.

G: What was the score?

B: It was 80 ❺to 79. We lost ❻by one point.

G: That was really ❼close!

B: Yeah. We played really well as a team.

G: That's wonderful! I want to watch your next game.

❶ 특정한 경험이 어땠는지를 'How did ~ go?'로 물어볼 수 있다.

❷ go: (일의 진행이 어떻게) 되다

❸ lose: 지다 (lose-lost-lost)

❹ 좋지 않은 소식에 대해 유감을 나타내는 표현으로 'That's too bad.', 'That's a shame.' 등으로 표현할 수도 있다.

❺ '(점수가) A 대 B'의 뜻으로 말할 때 대조, 대비의 의미를 가진 전치사 to를 사용하여 'A to B'라고 표현한다.

❻ by: (정도·차이) ~의 차(이)로, ~만큼

❼ close: 막상막하의

Real Life Talk Step 1

Minho: Linda! Is that you? ❶Long time no see.

Linda: Minho! It's been a long time.

Minho: ❷How have you been?

Linda: I've been good. How about you?

Minho: I've been really busy at school. ❸How's your new school?

Linda: It's wonderful. I've made many new friends.

Minho: That's great! ❹I'm happy to hear that.

Linda: Thanks. Oh! I ❺have to go to my violin lesson now.

Minho: You still have my number, right?

Linda: Yeah. I'll call you later. Have a good day!

Minho: You, too. Bye!

❶ '오랜만이야.'라는 의미로, 한동안 보지 못했던 상대방에게 반가움을 나타내는 표현이다. 'It's been a long time.', 'It's been ages[a while].', 'I haven't seen you for a long time.' 'I haven't seen you recently.' 등이 있다.

❷ How have you been?: 어떻게 지냈니?[안부 묻기]

❸ How is[was] ~?: ~은 어떠니?[~은 어땠니?]

❹ 'I'm happy to hear that.'은 '그 말을 들으니 기뻐.'의 의미로, 상대방의 좋은 소식을 듣고 기쁨을 표현하는 말이다.

❺ have to 동사원형: ~해야 한다

Real Life Talk Step 2-1

A: How have you been?

B: I've been great.

A: ❶How was your vacation?

B: Wonderful. I ❷joined a ski camp.

A: That's great. I'm happy to hear that.

❶ 'How was ~?'는 묻는 사람이 상대방의 경험에 대해 알고자 할 때 쓰는 표현으로 '~가 어땠니?'라는 의미이다. 'How did you like ~?'로 바꾸어 쓸 수 있다. vacation: 방학

❷ join: ~에 참가하다 / 타동사이므로 목적어가 전치사 없이 연결된다.

Real Life Talk Step 2-2

A: How have you been?

B: ❶Not so good.

A: ❷How come?

B: I lost my dog.

A: Oh, no! ❸I'm sorry to hear that.

❶ 'Not so good.'은 '좋지 않아.'의 의미로, 안부를 묻는 말에 자신의 상태가 좋지 않을 때 대답하는 표현이다.

❷ 'How come?'은 '왜?'의 의미로, 이유를 물을 때 사용하는 표현이다.

❸ 'I'm sorry to hear that.'은 '그 말을 들으니 유감이야.'의 의미로 좋지 않은 소식에 대해 유감을 나타내는 표현이다.

교과서 확인학습

● 다음 우리말과 일치하도록 빈칸에 알맞은 말을 쓰시오.

Listen and Speak 1 A

B: Amy, _____ have you _____?

G: I've _____ great. How _____ you, Mike?

B: _____ so good. I _____ a bad cold.

G: Oh, no! _____ well soon.

B: Thanks.

B: Amy, 어떻게 지냈니?
G: 잘 지냈어. 너는 어때, Mike?
B: 별로야. 독감에 걸렸어.
G: 어, 저런! 빨리 나아.
B: 고마워.

Listen and Speak 1 B

G: Hi, Jinsu! _____ in the same class again!

B: Yeah! _____ _____ to see you, Sora. _____ _____ _____ been?

G: _____ _____ great. How about you?

B: _____ _____ _____ busy. I have a piano _____ next week.

G: Oh! I _____ know you _____ the piano.

B: Really? _____ _____ the piano for 5 years.

G: You _____ be good _____ it. Good _____ _____ your competition!

B: Thanks.

G: 안녕, 진수야! 우리 또 같은 반이구나!
B: 응! 만나서 반가워, 소라야. 어떻게 지냈니?
G: 잘 지냈어. 너는 어때?
B: 난 좀 바빴어. 다음 주에 피아노 경연이 있어.
G: 오! 네가 피아노를 치는지 몰랐어.
B: 정말? 난 피아노를 5년간 쳤어.
G: 넌 분명 피아노를 잘 치겠구나. 경연에서 행운을 빌어!
B: 고마워.

Listen and Speak 1 C

1. **A:** Mina, _____ have _____ _____?

   B: I've _____ good. How is _____?

   A: Pretty good. My new classmates _____ nice.

2. **A:** How _____ _____ _____?

   B: I've been good. How _____ _____?

   A: _____ so. I _____ a bad cold.

3. **A:** _____ _____ _____ been?

   B: _____ _____ good. _____ is everything?

   A: _____ good. My new classes are exciting.

4. **A:** _____ _____ _____ _____?

   B: _____ _____ good. How is _____?

   A: So so. I _____ lots of homework.

1. A: 미나야, 어떻게 지냈니?
   B: 잘 지냈어. 어떻게 지냈니?
   A: 잘 지냈어. 나의 새로운 반 친구가 좋아.
2. A: 어떻게 지냈니?
   B: 잘 지냈어. 어떻게 지냈니?
   A: 그저 그래. 감기에 걸렸어.
3. A: 어떻게 지냈니?
   B: 잘 지냈어. 어떻게 지냈니?
   A: 좋아. 내 새로운 수업이 재미있어.
4. A: 어떻게 지냈니?
   B: 잘 지냈어. 어떻게 지냈니?
   A: 그저 그래. 숙제가 너무 많아.

해석

Listen and Speak 2 A

B: Susan, you look _____ . Do you _____ _____ _____ news?

G: Our team _____ an A on the science project.

B: That's great!

G: Our team _____ _____ _____ teamwork.

B: _____ happy _____ _____ that.

B: Susan, 신나 보이네. 좋은 소식이 있니?
G: 우리 팀이 과학 프로젝트에서 A를 받았어.
B: 잘됐다!
G: 우리 팀은 팀워크가 최고였어.
B: 그 말을 들으니 기뻐.

Listen and Speak 2 B

G: Andy, _____ _____ the basketball game go?

B: Our team _____ .

G: Oh, I'm _____ _____ _____ that.

B: It's okay. It was a _____ game.

G: What _____ the _____ ?

B: It was 80 _____ 79. We _____ _____ one point.

G: That was really _____ !

B: Yeah. We _____ really well as a team.

G: _____ wonderful! I want to watch your next game.

G: Andy, 농구 경기는 어땠니?
B: 우리 팀이 졌어.
G: 오, 그 말을 들으니 안타까워.
B: 괜찮아. 정말 좋은 경기였어.
G: 점수는 어떻게 되었니?
B: 80 대 79였어. 우린 1점 차이로 졌어.
G: 정말 막상막하였네!
B: 응. 우린 하나의 팀으로 경기를 정말 잘했어.
G: 정말 멋지다! 너희 다음번 경기를 보고 싶어.

Listen and Speak 2 C

1. A: Bob, you look _____ .

   B: I came _____ _____ _____ the marathon.

   A: I'm _____ _____ _____ that.

2. A: Ann, you look _____ .

   B: I _____ _____ _____ _____ my friend.

   A: I'm _____ _____ _____ _____ .

3. A: Tom, you _____ _____ .

   B: I _____ the school dance contest.

   A: I'm _____ _____ _____ that.

4. A: Bomi, you look _____ .

   B: I _____ my dog.

   A: I'm _____ _____ _____ that.

1. A: Bob, 너 행복해 보인다.
   B: 마라톤에서 1등으로 들어왔어.
   A: 그 말을 들으니 기뻐.
2. A: Ann, 너 속상해 보인다.
   B: 나는 내 친구와 싸웠어.
   A: 그 말을 들으니 안타까워.
3. A: Tom, 너 행복해 보인다.
   B: 나는 학교 춤 경연대회에서 이겼어.
   A: 그 말을 들으니 기뻐.
4. A: Bomi, 너 속상해 보인다.
   B: 난 개를 잃어버렸어.
   A: 그 말을 들으니 안타까워.

5. A: Jim, you _____ _____.

   B: I _____ a new bike.

   A: I'm _____ _____ _____ that.

6. A: Jane, you look _____.

   B: I _____ my new smartphone.

   A: I'm _____ to _____ that.

5. A: Jim, 너 행복해 보인다.
   B: 새 자전거를 샀어.
   A: 그 말을 들으니 기뻐.
6. A: Jane, 너 속상해 보인다.
   B: 나의 새로운 스마트폰을 떨어뜨렸어.
   A: 그 말을 들으니 안타까워.

Real Life Talk Step 1

Minho: Linda! Is that you? _____ _____ no see.

Linda: Minho! It's _____ a long time.

Minho: _____ have you _____

Linda: I've _____ good. How _____ you?

Minho: I've _____ really busy _____ school. _____ your new school?

Linda: It's wonderful. I've _____ _____ new friends.

Minho: That's great! _____ _____ to hear that.

Linda: Thanks. Oh! I _____ _____ go to my violin lesson now.

Minho: You still _____ my _____, right?

Linda: Yeah. I'll _____ you later. _____ a good day!

Minho: You, _____. Bye!

민호: Linda! 너구나? 오랜만이야.
Linda: 민호야! 오랜만이야.
민호: 어떻게 지냈니?
Linda: 잘 지냈어. 너는 어때?
민호: 난 학교에서 정말 바빴어. 새 학교는 어때?
Linda: 정말 좋아. 새 친구들을 많이 사귀었어.
민호: 잘됐다! 그 말을 들으니 기뻐.
Linda: 고마워. 오! 난 지금 바이올린 수업에 가야 해.
민호: 아직 내 번호 가지고 있지, 그렇지?
Linda: 응. 내가 나중에 전화할게. 좋은 하루 보내!
민호: 너도. 안녕!

Real Life Talk Step 2

1. A: _____ _____ _____ _____?

   B: I've been great.

   A: _____ was your _____?

   B: Wonderful. I _____ a ski camp.

   A: That's great. I'm happy _____ _____ _____.

2. A: How _____ _____ _____?

   B: _____ so good.

   A: _____ come?

   B: I _____ my dog.

   A: Oh, no! _____ _____ to hear that.

1. A: 어떻게 지냈니?
   B: 잘 지냈어.
   A: 방학은 어땠어?
   B: 좋았어. 난 스키 캠프에 들어갔어.
   A: 잘됐네. 그 말을 들으니 기뻐.
2. A: 어떻게 지냈니?
   B: 좋지 않아.
   A: 왜?
   B: 난 개를 잃어버렸어.
   A: 어, 저런! 그 말을 들으니 안타까워.

01 대화의 빈칸에 알맞은 것을 고르시오.

> B: Amy, _____
> G: I've been great. How about you, Mike?
> B: Not so good. I have a bad cold.
> G: Oh, no! Get well soon.

① how did you like it?
② what did you do?
③ what happened?
④ how have you been?
⑤ what have you been to?

02 주어진 문장 이후에 이어질 대화의 순서를 바르게 배열한 것을 고르시오.

> How have you been?

> (A) How was your vacation?
> (B) Wonderful. I joined a ski camp.
> (C) I've been great.
> (D) That's great. I'm happy to hear that.

① (B) – (A) – (C) – (D)   ② (B) – (C) – (A) – (D)
③ (C) – (A) – (B) – (D)   ④ (C) – (B) – (A) – (D)
⑤ (C) – (D) – (B) – (A)

03 대화의 빈칸에 들어갈 수 있는 것을 <u>모두</u> 고르시오.

> A: Jane, you look upset.
> B: I dropped my new smartphone.
> A: _____

① I'm sorry to hear that.
② I'm pleased to hear that.
③ I'm happy to hear that.
④ That's too bad.
⑤ I'm afraid to say that.

01 다음 대화의 빈칸에 들어갈 말로 알맞지 <u>않은</u> 것을 고르시오.

> A: Jim, you look happy.
> B: _____
> A: I'm happy to hear that.

① I came in first in the marathon.
② I bought a new bike.
③ I won the school dance contest.
④ I had a fight with my friend.
⑤ I got an A in the math test.

 다음 중 짝지어진 대화가 <u>어색한</u> 것은?

① A: Long time no see. How have you been?
　 B: Good. How about you?
② A: We haven't seen each other in ages.
　 B: I know. I've been busy a lot.
③ A: I haven't seen you recently. How have you been?
　 B: I'm sorry to hear that.
④ A: How have you been?
　 B: I've been fine, thank you.
⑤ A: My grandmother is sick now.
　 B: I'm sorry to hear that.

서답형
03 대화에 나온 단어를 이용해 빈칸을 채우시오.

> A: Bob, you look happy.
> B: I came in first in the marathon.
> A: I'm _____ to hear that.

➡ _____

[04~06] 다음 대화를 읽고 물음에 답하시오.

> G: Andy, how did the basketball game (A) _____?
> B: Our team lost. (①)
> G: Oh, I'm sorry to hear that. (②)
> B: It's okay. (③) It was a great game.
> G: What was the score?
> B: (④) We lost by one point.
> G: That was really close!
> B: Yeah. We played really well as a team. (⑤)
> G: That's wonderful! I want to watch your next game.

 위 대화의 ①~⑤ 중 주어진 문장이 들어갈 알맞은 곳은?

> It was 80 to 79.

①　　　　②　　　　③　　　　④　　　　⑤

05 빈칸 (A)에 알맞은 말을 고르시오.

① go　　　② make　　　③ do
④ have　　⑤ get

위 대화를 읽고 답할 수 <u>없는</u> 질문을 고르시오.

① Did Andy's basketball team win?
② When was the basketball game?
③ What was the score of the basketball game which Andy took part in?
④ How many points did Andy's basketball team lose by?
⑤ How did Andy feel about the basketball team?

[07~09] 다음 대화를 읽고 물음에 답하시오.

> G: Hi, Jinsu! We're in the same class again! (①)
>
> B: Yeah! It's (A)[bad / good] to see you, Sora. (②)
>
> G: I've been great. How about you?
>
> B: I've been pretty busy. (③) I have a piano competition next week.
>
> G: Oh! I didn't know you played the piano. (④)
>
> B: Really? I (B)[played / have played] the piano for 5 years.
>
> G: You must be good at it. (⑤) Good luck in your competition!
>
> B: Thanks.

 위 대화의 ①~⑤ 중 주어진 문장이 들어갈 알맞은 곳은?

> How have you been?

①   ②   ③   ④   ⑤

서답형

08 위 대화의 괄호 (A)와 (B)에서 적절한 것을 골라 쓰시오.

➡ (A) _____ (B) _____

09 위 대화의 내용과 일치하지 <u>않는</u> 것은?

① 진수는 피아노를 5년 동안 연주해 오고 있다.
② 소라는 요즘 잘 지내고 있다.
③ 진수는 요즘 꽤 바빴다.
④ 진수는 피아노 대회에 출전했다.
⑤ 진수와 소라는 전에도 같은 반이었다.

10 다음 대화의 빈칸에 들어갈 말을 〈보기〉에서 골라 순서대로 바르게 배열한 것은?

> Minho: Linda! Is that you? Long time no see.
>
> Linda: Minho! It's been a long time.

Minho: How have you been?

Linda: _____

Minho: _____

Linda: _____

Minho: _____

Linda: Thanks. Oh! I have to go to my violin lesson now.

Minho: You still have my number, right?

Linda: Yeah. I'll call you later. Have a good day!

Minho: You, too. Bye!

> ┤ 보기 ├
>
> (A) That's great! I'm happy to hear that.
> (B) It's wonderful. I've made many new friends.
> (C) I've been good. How about you?
> (D) I've been really busy at school. How's your new school?

① (B) – (A) – (C) – (D)
② (B) – (C) – (A) – (D)
③ (C) – (A) – (B) – (D)
④ (C) – (B) – (A) – (D)
⑤ (C) – (D) – (B) – (A)

 빈칸에 알맞은 말이 〈보기〉에서 <u>모두</u> 몇 개인지 고르시오.

> A: Mina, how have you been?
>
> B: I've been good. _____
>
> A: Pretty good. My new classmates are nice.

> ┤ 보기 ├
>
> • How is everything?
> • How have you been doing?
> • How's it going?
> • What are you doing?
> • What have you been up to?
> • How have you been?

① 2개   ② 3개   ③ 4개   ④ 5개   ⑤ 6개

[01~03] 다음 대화를 읽고 물음에 답하시오.

G: Andy, (A)_____ did the basketball game go?

B: Our team ⓐ[lost / won].

G: Oh, I'm sorry to hear that.

B: It's okay. It was a great game.

G: What was the score?

B: It was 80 (B)_____ 79. We lost (C)_____ one point.

G: That was really ⓑ[big / close]!

B: Yeah. We played really well as a team.

G: That's wonderful! I want to watch your next game.

01 빈칸 (A)에 알맞은 의문사를 쓰시오.

➡ _____

02 빈칸 (B)와 (C)에 알맞은 전치사를 쓰시오.

➡ (B) _____ (C) _____

03 위 대화의 괄호 ⓐ와 ⓑ에서 적절한 것을 골라 쓰시오.

➡ ⓐ _____ ⓑ _____

04 빈칸 (A)와 (B)에 공통으로 들어갈 말을 쓰시오

A: (A)_____ have you been?
B: Not so good.
A: (B)_____ come?
B: I lost my dog.
A: Oh, no! I'm sorry to hear that.

[05~06] 다음 대화를 읽고 물음에 답하시오.

Minho: Linda! Is that you? (A)_____

Linda: Minho! (B)It's been a long time.

Minho: How have you been?

Linda: I've been good. How about you?

Minho: I've been really busy at school. How's your new school?

Linda: It's wonderful. I've made many new friends.

Minho: That's great! (C)그 말을 들으니 기뻐.

Linda: Thanks. Oh! I have to go to my violin lesson now.

Minho: You still have my number, right?

Linda: Yeah. I'll call you later. Have a good day!

Minho: You, too. Bye!

05 빈칸 (A)에 밑줄 친 문장 (B)와 같은 의미가 되도록 쓰시오. (4 단어)

➡ _____

06 밑줄 친 (C)의 우리말을 주어진 단어를 이용하여 영작하시오.

➡ _____ (happy)

07 be동사를 빈칸 (A)와 (B)에 알맞게 고쳐 쓰시오.

A: How have you (A)_____ ?
B: I've been great.
A: How (B)_____ your vacation?
B: Wonderful. I joined a ski camp.
A: That's great. I'm happy to hear that.

Grammar

교과서

1 It is[was] ~ for ... to부정사

- **It** was not easy **for us to choose** the best idea. 우리는 가장 좋은 아이디어를 고르는 것이 쉽지 않았어요.
- **It** is necessary **for him to do** the work by tomorrow. 그는 내일까지 그 일을 할 필요가 있다.

■ 비교적 긴 to부정사 부분이 문장의 주어로 쓰일 때 보통 그 to부정사 부분을 문장 제일 뒤에 두고 주어 자리에 가주어 it을 넣어준다.
- **It** is interesting **to play** soccer. 축구하는 것은 재미있다.
  = **To play** soccer is interesting.
- **It** is easy **to read** the book. 그 책을 읽는 것은 쉽다.
  = **To read** the book is easy.

■ to부정사의 의미상의 주어
to부정사의 동작을 실제로 하는 주체를 to부정사의 의미상의 주어라고 한다. to부정사의 의미상의 주어는 to부정사 바로 앞에 'for+명사[대명사]의 목적격'으로 나타낸다. 이때 문장에 쓰인 형용사가 nice, kind, rude, polite, careful, smart, wise 등과 같이 사람의 성향이나 성격을 나타내는 말일 때는 'for+명사[대명사]의 목적격'이 아니라 'of+명사[대명사]의 목적격'으로 쓴다.
- **It** is important **for you to deliver** it. 네가 그것을 전달하는 것은 중요한 일이다.
- **It** was nice **of you to deliver** those papers to him. 네가 그 서류들을 그에게 전달해 준 것은 친절한 일이었어.

■ It ~ to부정사 구문에서 to부정사의 의미상의 주어가 일반적인 사람일 경우는 보통 생략한다. 또한 to부정사의 부정은 to부정사 앞에 not이나 never를 써서 'not[never]+to부정사'로 나타낸다.
- These days, **it** is difficult **to live** without a cell phone. 요즘은 휴대전화 없이 살아가는 것이 어렵다.
- I prefer **not to think** about it. 나는 그것에 대해 생각하고 싶지 않다.

핵심 Check

1. 다음 빈칸에 알맞은 말을 어법에 맞게 쓰시오.
  (1) It is exciting _____ learn English.
  (2) It is boring _____ me to watch baseball games.
  (3) It was wise _____ you to say so.

2 관계대명사 what

> - We finally made **what** we wanted. 우리는 결국 우리가 원하는 것을 만들었어요.
> - That is **what** I wanted to say. 그건 내가 말하고 싶었던 것이다.

■ 관계대명사 what은 다른 관계대명사와 다르게 선행사를 포함한 관계대명사로 '~하는 것'으로 해석하며, the thing(s) which[that]의 의미를 나타낸다.
  - Don't be shy about telling me **what** you want. 수줍어하지 말고 원하는 것이 있으면 말해라.
  (= Don't be shy about telling me the thing(s) which[that] you want.)

■ 관계대명사 what이 이끄는 절은 명사절로 문장에서 주어, 보어, 목적어의 역할을 한다.
  (1) 주어 역할
    - **What** you did was wrong. 네가 한 일은 잘못된 것이야.
  (2) 보어 역할
    - This is not **what** I asked for, I'm afraid. 이것은 제가 주문한 것이 아닌 것 같습니다.
  (3) 목적어 역할
    - You'll never guess **what** she told me. 넌 그녀가 내게 무슨 말을 했는지 절대 알아맞히지 못할 거야. (동사의 목적어)
    - I don't agree with **what** you said. 저는 당신 말에 동의하지 않습니다. (전치사의 목적어)

■ 관계대명사 what의 관용적인 표현
  - Most planets are started from **what is called** star dust. 대부분의 행성들은 소위 성진으로부터 시작된다.
  - He is content with **what he has** although he is very poor. 그는 비록 매우 가난하지만 자기가 가진 것에 만족하고 있다.
  - **What's worse**, he didn't even call. 설상가상으로 그는 전화까지 하지 않았다.

핵심 Check

2. 다음 우리말과 일치하도록 빈칸에 알맞은 말을 쓰시오.
  (1) 저는 제가 뭘 하고 싶은지 몰랐습니다.
    ➡ I didn't know _____ I wanted to do.
  (2) 그건 내가 찾고 있는 게 아니야.
    ➡ That's not _____ I'm looking for.
  (3) 그녀의 행동은 쇼가 아닌 것 같다.
    ➡ _____ she's doing doesn't seem like a show.

01 다음 빈칸에 알맞은 것을 고르시오.

> A: Isn't it important _____ ?
> B: Sure.

① exercise regularly

② exercises regularly

③ to exercising regularly

④ to exercise regularly

⑤ of you to exercise regularly

02 다음 중 어법상 <u>어색한</u> 문장은?

① Tell me what you did yesterday.

② What she bought yesterday was a book.

③ Let me tell you that I think.

④ Remember what I said before.

⑤ This is what I thought.

03 다음 중 생략할 수 있는 것은?

> ①It is not ②good ③for you ④to make a noise ⑤in the library.

①   ②   ③   ④   ⑤

04 다음 괄호 안에서 알맞은 말을 고르시오.

(1) It is interesting (talk / to talk) about the past.

(2) (This / It) is important to study English.

(3) It will be helpful (for / of) you to read the book.

(4) It was foolish (for / of) you to call her.

(5) (What / That) he wants is to drink cool water.

(6) Don't put off (what / it) you can do today.

01 다음 중 어법상 올바른 것은?

① It's so kind for you to help me.
② It isn't easy teaches music to little children.
③ It's good hear your voice on the phone again.
④ It is a pleasure to talk with you.
⑤ That's necessary to know when to draw the line.

02 다음 중 어법상 올바르지 <u>않은</u> 것은?

① We finally made what we wanted.
② Do you always believe that you see?
③ What are the things that are in your pocket?
④ What was considered good may become only partly true.
⑤ Let me check the report which you handed in yesterday.

03 다음 빈칸에 알맞은 말이 바르게 짝지어진 것은?

> • It is important to listen carefully to _____ others say.
> • It is necessary _____ me to sleep more.

① which – for
② that – for
③ what – for
④ that – of
⑤ what – of

04 다음 괄호 안에서 알맞은 말을 고르시오.

(1) It is exciting (fly / to fly) kites with friends.
(2) It is impossible (of / for) Bella to do as you wish.
(3) It was wise (of / for) you to provide for a rainy day.
(4) The shop doesn't have (that / what) I need to buy.
(5) I do not believe all (that / what) he said.

05 다음 대화의 빈칸에 들어갈 말로 알맞은 것은?

> M: I heard a very strange story from Ted yesterday.
> W: Oh, did you? Tell me _____ you heard from him.

① it   ② that   ③ this
④ which   ⑤ what

06 다음 문장의 빈칸에 들어갈 알맞은 것은?

> It was easy _____ me to get here.

① for   ② of   ③ at
④ with   ⑤ on

07 다음 중 어법상 옳은 것은?

① It's impossible to live without water.

② It is very important of us to study foreign languages.

③ It was silly for me to believe what he said.

④ It was careless for her to open the door for the stranger.

⑤ It is difficult of us to swim in this river.

08 다음 주어진 문장의 밑줄 친 what과 같은 용법으로 쓰인 것을 모두 고르시오.

> I don't believe what cannot be seen.

① What did you do last night?

② I understand what you did.

③ What made me smile was just looking at the pictures.

④ I'm not sure what to do after school.

⑤ I wonder what that sign means.

서답형
09 다음 문장에서 어법상 틀린 부분을 찾아 바르게 고쳐 쓰시오.

> The exercise he is doing is that is called yoga.

_____ ➡ _____

서답형
10 주어진 어휘를 이용하여 다음 우리말을 영작하시오.

> 운전자는 운전 면허증을 휴대하는 것이 필요하다. (drivers, a driver's license, it, carry, necessary, to)

➡ _____

11 다음 두 문장을 한 문장으로 바르게 연결한 것은?

> • He was eager to see the things.
> • They were under the Christmas tree.

① He was eager to see were under the Christmas tree.

② He was eager to see they were under the Christmas tree.

③ He was eager to see which were under the Christmas tree.

④ He was eager to see what were under the Christmas tree.

⑤ He was eager to see that were under the Christmas tree.

12 다음 우리말과 일치하도록 빈칸에 알맞은 단어로 묶은 것은?

> 오늘 제가 이 자리에 서게 된 것을 기쁘게 생각합니다.
> = _____ is a pleasure _____ me to be here today.

① This – at   ② That – of
③ That – for   ④ It – of
⑤ It – for

13 다음 빈칸에 들어갈 말이 나머지 넷과 다른 하나는?

① This is the house _____ Mariel lives in.

② Do you understand _____ Andy is talking about?

③ You'd better go over _____ you learned in class.

④ Let me know _____ you want.

⑤ You are not paying attention! Please listen to _____ I'm saying.

14 다음 문장의 빈칸에 들어갈 말로 알맞은 것은?

> It was brave _____ to speak on behalf
> of the people.

① of he
② of his
③ of him
④ for him
⑤ for his

15 다음 문장에서 어법상 어색한 것을 바르게 고쳐 다시 쓰시오.

(1) It was very hard of me to concentrate
on the story because of the noise.

➡ _____

_____

(2) It was rude for you to ignore the elderly.

➡ _____

(3) It is difficult for the little girl reading
this book.

➡ _____

(4) I will read the book what you bought
last Saturday.

➡ _____

_____

(5) Tell me which you learned in class
yesterday.

➡ _____

(6) Slaves were expected to do that they
were told to do.

➡ _____

16 다음 중 어법상 <u>어색한</u> 것을 고르시오. (2개)

① It's nice of her taking care of the poor
people.
② It is a lot of fun to work with the
students here.
③ It was possible for us to build a beautiful
and tall tower.
④ Lots of people do that they suggest and
find happiness in their relationships.
⑤ What I said was that I was sure that he
would not want to do that.

17 다음 우리말에 맞게 영작한 것을 고르시오.

> 저는 아이들이 예절을 배우는 것이 매우 중요하
> 다는 것에 동의합니다.

① I agree that it is very important for kids
learn manners.
② I agree that it is very important for kids
learning manners.
③ I agree that it is very important for kids
to learn manners.
④ I agree that is very important for kids to
learn manners.
⑤ I agree that is very important for kids
learning manners.

18 다음 중 빈칸에 들어갈 말로 알맞은 것을 고르시오.

> So why don't you just tell me _____
> was really going on?

① when
② which
③ who
④ that
⑤ what

01 다음 두 문장이 뜻이 비슷하도록 빈칸에 들어갈 알맞은 말을 쓰시오.

(1) He rarely gets an A⁺ in math.

= It is hard _____ get an A⁺ in math.

(2) She nicely offered me a ride.

= It was nice _____ offer me a ride.

02 다음 우리말에 맞게 주어진 어구를 바르게 배열하시오.

(1) 저는 100년 전에 일어난 일이 잘못되었다고 믿습니다. (I, 100 years, happened, believe, was, ago, what, wrong)

➡ _____

(2) 가장 중요한 건 내면의 아름다움과 자신감이다. (most, beauty, self confidence, matters, is, inner, and, what)

➡ _____

_____

(3) 그 유기견을 입양하다니 너는 정말 착하구나. (the abandoned dog, you, adopt, nice, it, very, is, of, to)

➡ _____

_____

(4) 그가 아침 일찍 조깅하는 것은 정말 멋지다. (him, in the morning, jog, it, really, wonderful, early, is, for, to)

➡ _____

_____

(5) 오늘 3시에 저와 만날 수 있으세요? (today, three, you, me, it, meet, is, possible, for, at, to)

➡ _____

03 그림을 보고, 주어진 어휘를 이용하여 빈칸을 알맞게 채우시오.

(1) Could you tell me _____?
(what, want, drink)

(2) The Eiffel Tower is _____ to visit. (I, want, what)

04 괄호 안에 주어진 말을 이용하여 어법에 맞게 문장을 완성하시오.

(1) It was thoughtful _____ the flowers to Mike. (you, send)

(2) It is dangerous _____ alone. (a child, swim)

05 주어진 두 문장을 what을 이용하여 하나의 문장으로 쓰시오.

(1) • This is different from the things.
　　• I expected the things.
　　➡ _____

(2) • Bob couldn't accept the thing.
　　• Theresa offered it.
　　➡ _____

(3) • The thing was said by Tina.
　　• It was surprising.
　　➡ _____

(4) • Something is important.
　　• It is present, not past.
　　➡ _____

06 다음 문장에서 어법상 어색한 것을 바르게 고치시오.

(1) It is exciting of me to watch the soccer game.
　　_____ ➡ _____

(2) It is rude for you to talk like that to your elders.
　　_____ ➡ _____

(3) It was careless for them to not do test marketing.
　　_____ ➡ _____

(4) This is the book what I wanted to read.
　　_____ ➡ _____

(5) That I like to do most in my free time is playing baduk.
　　_____ ➡ _____

(6) This bag is that I want to buy.
　　_____ ➡ _____

07 다음 주어진 표현을 사용하여 문장을 완성하시오.

(1) (the argument, careful, avoid, her)
　　➡ It is _____.

(2) (children, dangerous, home, alone, walk)
　　➡ It is _____.

08 다음 우리말을 괄호 안에 주어진 어휘를 이용하여 영작하시오.

(1) 네게 서울에 살고 있는 친척이 있는 것은 다행이다. (you, have, living, it, lucky, a relative, 12 단어)
　　➡ _____

(2) 밤에 거리를 혼자 걸어다녀도 안전한가요? (the streets, it, walk, safe, alone, 10 단어)
　　➡ _____

(3) 경찰이 성난 군중을 진정시키기는 쉽지 않았다. (the police, the angry crowd, calm down, easy, it, 13 단어)
　　➡ _____
　　_____

(4) 어제 우리가 했던 이야기 기억하니? (remember, talked about, 8 단어)
　　➡ _____

(5) 우리는 남아 있는 것들 중에서 골라야만 했다. (choose, had, from, remained, 7 단어)
　　➡ _____

Reading

Try the Marshmallow Challenge!

You need:

20 sticks of spaghetti, 1 marshmallow, 1 meter of tape, 1 meter of string

Rules: Each team has four people.
each는 '각각의'라는 뜻으로, 단수 명사와 함께 쓴다.
You have to build the tallest tower in your class.
have to '~해야 한다' '의무'를 나타내고, 뒤에 동사원형을 쓴다.   tallest: 형용사 tall에 –est가 붙은 최상급. '가장 높은'. 형용사의 최상급 앞에 the를 씀.
The marshmallow must be on top.
must: ~해야 한다(조동사). '의무'를 나타내고, 뒤에 동사원형을 쓴다.
The tower must stand by itself.
'홀로, 저절로'. 탑이 다른 버팀목에 의해 지탱되는 것이 아니라 '홀로' 서 있어야 함을 의미함.
The time limit is 15 minutes.

This activity is good for: Building Relationships, Solving Problems, Thinking Creatively

How did you do the marshmallow challenge? Every team does the
every+단수명사
marshmallow challenge differently. Let's look at some examples.
각 팀이 수행한 marshmallow challenge의 몇 가지 예
Which one do you like best?
some examples 중 하나.   '가장'(well의 최상급). 동사 like를 수식함.
TEAM A: Think before you act.

We had many good ideas. We talked about each idea in detail. It
가주어
was not easy for us to choose the best idea. Suddenly the teacher
의미상의 주어   진주어
said, "Five minutes left." In a hurry, we taped the sticks of spaghetti
셀 수 없는 명사 spaghetti가 stick과 함께 쓰여 스파게티 면이 여러 개임을 나타냄.
together. Then, we wrapped the string around them. The string got
'함께, 같이'(부사). 동사 tape를 수식.
stuck to the tape and it was a big mess. With one second left, I put the
~에 붙었다   답을 만드는 과정을 묘사한 전체 상황을 가리킴. 엉망진창인 상태   과거분사
marshmallow on top!

---

challenge 과제, 도전
stick 막대기처럼 기다랗고 가는 것
string 끈, 줄
relationship 관계
creatively 창의적으로
in detail 상세하게
in a hurry 서둘러, 급히
wrap 감다, 싸다
stuck 움직일 수 없는
mess 엉망인 상태

📎 **확인문제**

● 다음 문장이 본문의 내용과 일치하면 T, 일치하지 <u>않으면</u> F를 쓰시오.

1   When you try the marshmallow challenge, the marshmallow must be on top. ☐

2   After you finish building the tower, you can hold the tower with your hand. ☐

3   Team A talked about each idea in detail. ☐

4   Team A had no difficulty in choosing the best idea. ☐

5   It was very easy for Team A to build the tower. ☐

TEAM B: Just do it.

We didn't spend much time on planning. All the members started
spend A on B: A를 B에 쓰다. B에 명사나 동명사를 씀.
building the tower right away. Our first tower looked like a tent.
start+동명사/to부정사: ～하기 시작하다. right away: 즉시, 곧바로   ～처럼 보였다
It wasn't very tall. We tried again. The next tower was tall but it
couldn't stand by itself. After many tries, it was possible for us to
가주어   의미상의 주어
build a beautiful and tall tower. It looked like the Leaning Tower of
진주어
Pisa. We finally made what we wanted!
선행사를 포함한 관계대명사

TEAM C: We're one team.

We didn't try to choose the best idea. Instead, we took a good
try to부정사: ～하려고 애쓰다   '최고의'(형용사 good의 최상급)
idea and improved on it. One student said we needed a strong base.
a good idea   팀원 중 한 학생, said 뒤에 접속사 that이 생략되어 있음.
Another student suggested a triangle shape for the base. We all agreed
팀의 다른 학생
and divided up the roles such as time checker and tape cutter. We
divide up: 분담하다, 분배하다   ～와 같은,
worked together as a team. In the end, we built our tall tower!
～로, ～로서(전치사).   마침내(= finally, at last)

tent 텐트, 천막
instead 대신에
base (사물의) 맨 아래 부분
suggest 제안하다
triangle 삼각형
divide 나누다
role 역할

확인문제

● 다음 문장이 본문의 내용과 일치하면 T, 일치하지 <u>않으면</u> F를 쓰시오.

1 Team B didn't spend much time on planning. ☐

2 Team B's first tower looked like the Leaning Tower of Pisa. ☐

3 After many tries, Team B could build a beautiful and tall tower. ☐

4 Team C tried to choose the best idea. ☐

5 The members of Team C all agreed on a triangle shape for the base. ☐

6 Team C worked together as a team without dividing up the roles. ☐

● 우리말을 참고하여 빈칸에 알맞은 말을 쓰시오.

1 Try the _____ _____!

2 _____ _____ : 20 _____ of spaghetti, 1 marshmallow, 1 meter of tape, 1 meter of _____

3 Rules: _____ _____ four people.

4 You _____ _____ _____ the tallest tower in your class.

5 The marshmallow _____ _____ _____ _____.

6 The tower must stand _____ _____.

7 The _____ _____ is 15 minutes.

8 This activity _____ _____ _____ : _____ Relationships, Solving Problems, Thinking _____

9 _____ did you do the marshmallow challenge?

10 _____ _____ _____ the marshmallow challenge _____.

11 Let's _____ _____ some examples.

12 _____ _____ do you like best?

13 TEAM A: _____ before you _____.

14 We had _____ _____ _____.

15 We talked about each idea _____ _____.

16 It was not easy _____ _____ _____ _____ the best idea.

17 Suddenly the teacher said, "_____ _____ _____."

18 _____ _____ _____, we taped the sticks of spaghetti together.

19 Then, we _____ _____ _____ around them.

---

1 마시멜로 과제를 해보세요!

2 여러분은 필요해요: 스파게티 면 20개, 마시멜로 1개, 테이프 1미터, 끈 1미터

3 규칙: 각 팀은 4명입니다.

4 반에서 가장 높은 탑을 만들어야 합니다.

5 마시멜로는 꼭대기에 있어야 합니다.

6 탑은 스스로 서 있어야 합니다.

7 제한 시간은 15분입니다.

8 이 활동은 여기에 좋아요: 관계를 맺는 것, 문제를 해결하는 것, 창의적으로 생각하는 것

9 마시멜로 과제를 어떻게 했나요?

10 모든 팀은 마시멜로 과제를 다르게 해요.

11 몇몇 예들을 살펴봐요.

12 어떤 예가 가장 마음에 드나요?

13 A팀: 행동하기 전에 생각해라.

14 우리에겐 좋은 아이디어가 많았어요.

15 우리는 각 아이디어에 대해 자세히 이야기했어요.

16 우리는 가장 좋은 아이디어를 고르는 것이 쉽지 않았어요.

17 갑자기 선생님께서 "5분 남았어요."라고 말씀하셨어요.

18 서둘러서 우리는 스파게티 면들을 테이프로 붙였어요.

19 그리고 나서 끈으로 스파게티 면 둘레를 둘렀어요.

20 The string _____ _____ _____ the tape and it was a big mess.

21 _____ _____ _____ _____, I put the marshmallow on top!

22 TEAM B: _____ _____ _____.

23 We didn't _____ _____ _____ on planning.

24 All the members started building the tower _____ _____.

25 Our first tower _____ _____ a tent.

26 It wasn't _____ _____.

27 We _____ _____.

28 The next tower was tall but it couldn't _____ _____ _____.

29 _____ _____ _____, it was possible for us to build a beautiful and tall tower.

30 It looked like the _____ _____ _____ _____.

31 We finally made _____ _____ _____!

32 TEAM C: We're _____ _____.

33 We _____ _____ the best idea.

34 Instead, we took a good idea and _____ _____ it.

35 One student said we needed _____ _____ _____.

36 Another student suggested a triangle shape _____ _____ _____.

37 We all agreed and divided up the roles _____ _____ time checker and tape cutter.

38 We worked together _____ _____ _____.

39 _____ _____ _____, we built our tall tower!

20 끈이 테이프에 붙었고 엉망진창이었어요.

21 1초를 남기고 제가 마시멜로를 꼭대기에 꽂았어요.

22 B팀: 그냥 해라.

23 우리는 계획하는 데 많은 시간을 보내지 않았어요.

24 모든 팀원들이 바로 탑을 만들기 시작했어요.

25 우리의 첫 번째 탑은 텐트 같았어요.

26 그건 그다지 높지 않았어요.

27 우리는 다시 시도했어요.

28 다음 탑은 높았지만 스스로 서 있지 못했어요.

29 많은 시도 후에 우리는 아름답고 높은 탑을 만들 수 있었어요.

30 그것은 피사의 사탑 같았어요.

31 우리는 결국 우리가 원하는 것을 만들었어요!

32 C팀: 우리는 한 팀이다.

33 우리는 가장 좋은 아이디어를 고르려고 하지 않았어요.

34 대신에 우리는 좋은 아이디어를 골라 발전시켰어요.

35 한 친구가 우리에겐 튼튼한 기반이 필요하다고 말했어요.

36 또 다른 친구는 기반으로 삼각형 모양을 제안했어요.

37 우리 모두는 동의했고 시간 점검하는 사람과 테이프 자르는 사람과 같이 역할을 나눴어요.

38 우리는 하나의 팀으로 함께했어요.

39 마침내 우리는 높은 탑을 만들었어요!

● 우리말을 참고하여 본문을 영작하시오.

1 ▸ 마시멜로 과제를 해보세요!

➡ _____

2 ▸ 여러분은 필요해요: 스파게티 면 20개, 마시멜로 1개, 테이프 1미터, 끈 1미터

➡ _____

3 ▸ 규칙: 각 팀은 4명입니다.

➡ _____

4 ▸ 반에서 가장 높은 탑을 만들어야 합니다.

➡ _____

5 ▸ 마시멜로는 꼭대기에 있어야 합니다.

➡ _____

6 ▸ 탑은 스스로 서 있어야 합니다.

➡ _____

7 ▸ 제한 시간은 15분입니다.

➡ _____

8 ▸ 이 활동은 여기에 좋아요: 관계를 맺는 것, 문제를 해결하는 것, 창의적으로 생각하는 것

➡ _____

9 ▸ 마시멜로 과제를 어떻게 했나요?

➡ _____

10 ▸ 모든 팀은 마시멜로 과제를 다르게 해요.

➡ _____

11 ▸ 몇몇 예들을 살펴봐요.

➡ _____

12 ▸ 어떤 예가 가장 마음에 드나요?

➡ _____

13 ▸ A팀: 행동하기 전에 생각해라.

➡ _____

14 ▸ 우리에겐 좋은 아이디어가 많았어요.

➡ _____

15 ▸ 우리는 각 아이디어에 대해 자세히 이야기했어요.

➡ _____

16 ▸ 우리는 가장 좋은 아이디어를 고르는 것이 쉽지 않았어요.

➡ _____

17 ▸ 갑자기 선생님께서 "5분 남았어요."라고 말씀하셨어요.

➡ _____

18 ▸ 서둘러서 우리는 스파게티 면들을 테이프로 붙였어요.

➡ _____

19 ▸ 그리고 나서 끈으로 스파게티 면 둘레를 둘렀어요.

➡ _____

20 끈이 테이프에 붙었고 엉망진창이었어요.
➡ _____

21 1초를 남기고 제가 마시멜로를 꼭대기에 꽂았어요.
➡ _____

22 B팀: 그냥 해라.
➡ _____

23 우리는 계획하는 데 많은 시간을 보내지 않았어요.
➡ _____

24 모든 팀원들이 바로 탑을 만들기 시작했어요.
➡ _____

25 우리의 첫 번째 탑은 텐트 같았어요.
➡ _____

26 그건 그다지 높지 않았어요.
➡ _____

27 우리는 다시 시도했어요.
➡ _____

28 다음 탑은 높았지만 스스로 서 있지 못했어요.
➡ _____

29 많은 시도 후에 우리는 아름답고 높은 탑을 만들 수 있었어요.
➡ _____

30 그것은 피사의 사탑 같았어요.
➡ _____

31 우리는 결국 우리가 원하는 것을 만들었어요!
➡ _____

32 C팀: 우리는 한 팀이다.
➡ _____

33 우리는 가장 좋은 아이디어를 고르려고 하지 않았어요.
➡ _____

34 대신에 우리는 좋은 아이디어를 골라 발전시켰어요.
➡ _____

35 한 친구가 우리에겐 튼튼한 기반이 필요하다고 말했어요.
➡ _____

36 또 다른 친구는 기반으로 삼각형 모양을 제안했어요.
➡ _____

37 우리 모두는 동의했고 시간 점검하는 사람과 테이프 자르는 사람과 같이 역할을 나눴어요.
➡ _____

38 우리는 하나의 팀으로 함께했어요.
➡ _____

39 마침내 우리는 높은 탑을 만들었어요!
➡ _____

[01~04] 다음 글을 읽고 물음에 답하시오.

Try the Marshmallow Challenge!

You need:
- 20 sticks of spaghetti • 1 marshmallow
- 1 meter of tape • 1 meter of string

Rules:
- Each team has four people.
- You have to build the tallest tower in your class.
- The marshmallow must be on top.
- The tower must stand ⓐ_____ _____.
- The time limit is 15 minutes.

This activity is good for:
- Building Relationships
- Solving Problems
- Thinking Creatively

서답형

01 주어진 영영풀이를 참고하여 빈칸 ⓐ에 들어갈 알맞은 단어를 전치사를 포함하여 두 글자로 쓰시오.

> 1. without being directly controlled by a person
> 2. with nothing nearby; alone

➡ _____

02 다음 중 마시멜로 과제에 필요한 준비물에 속하지 <u>않는</u> 것을 고르시오.

① 끈 ② 테이프
③ 핀 ④ 스파게티 면
⑤ 마시멜로

서답형

03 다음 문장에서 위 글의 내용과 <u>다른</u> 부분을 찾아서 고치시오.

> You can put the marshmallow on any place of the tower.

➡ _____

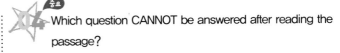

04 Which question CANNOT be answered after reading the passage?

① How many members are there in each team?
② What do you need to do to win the marshmallow challenge?
③ Where do you have to put the marshmallow?
④ What is the best way to do the marshmallow challenge?
⑤ What is this activity good for?

[05~07] 다음 글을 읽고 물음에 답하시오.

TEAM B: Just do it.

  We didn't spend much time on planning. All the members started building the tower right away. Our first tower looked ⓐ<u>like</u> a tent. It wasn't very tall. We tried again. The next tower was tall but it couldn't stand by itself. After many tries, it was possible for us to build a beautiful and tall tower. It looked like the Leaning Tower of Pisa. ⓑ<u>우리는 결국 우리가 원하는 것을 만들었어요!</u>

05 위 글의 밑줄 친 ⓐlike와 같은 의미로 쓰인 것을 고르시오.

① We had a chance to meet people of <u>like</u> mind.
② No one sings the blues <u>like</u> she did.
③ He's very <u>like</u> his father.
④ I <u>like</u> to read this book.
⑤ Hemingway wrote many wonderful novels <u>like</u> 'A Farewell to Arms' and 'The Old Man and the Sea'.

서답형
06 위 글의 밑줄 친 ⓑ의 우리말에 맞게 한 단어를 보충하여, 주어진 어휘를 알맞게 배열하시오.

wanted / we / finally / made / we

➡ _____

_____

중요
07 Which question CANNOT be answered after reading the passage?

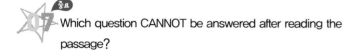

① Did Team B spend much time on planning?
② What did Team B's first tower look like?
③ Was Team B's first tower very tall?
④ How long did it take for Team B to build a tower?
⑤ What did Team B's final tower look like?

[08~11] 다음 글을 읽고 물음에 답하시오.

TEAM A: Think before you act.
  We had many good ideas. We talked about each idea in detail. (①) It was not easy for us to choose the best idea. (②) Suddenly the teacher said, "Five minutes left." (③) In a hurry, we taped the sticks of spaghetti together. (④) The string got stuck ⓐ the tape and it was a big mess. (⑤) ⓑ one second left, I put the marshmallow on top!

08 위 글의 빈칸 ⓐ와 ⓑ에 들어갈 전치사가 바르게 짝지어진 것은?

	ⓐ	ⓑ		ⓐ	ⓑ
①	to	With	②	on	For
③	on	In	④	for	With
⑤	to	For			

중요
09 위 글의 흐름으로 보아, 주어진 문장이 들어가기에 가장 적절한 곳은?

Then, we wrapped the string around them.

①　　②　　③　　④　　⑤

10 According to the passage, which is NOT true?

① Team A talked about each idea minutely.
② Team A had difficulty choosing the best idea.
③ Team A taped the sticks of spaghetti together in haste.
④ The string that Team A wrapped around the sticks of spaghetti got stuck to the tape and it was a big mess.
⑤ Team A couldn't do the marshmallow challenge in time.

서답형
11 다음 중, 위 글의 전반부에 어울리는 속담과 후반부에 어울리는 속담으로 알맞은 것을 각각 고르시오.

① A friend in need is a friend indeed.
② Haste makes waste.
③ Birds of a feather flock together.
④ A bird in the hand is worth two in the bush.
⑤ Too many cooks spoil the broth.

➡ 전반부에 어울리는 속담: _____ 번
후반부에 어울리는 속담: _____ 번

[12~14] 다음 글을 읽고 물음에 답하시오.

How did you do the marshmallow challenge? Every team does the marshmallow challenge differently. ⓐLet's look at some examples. Which ⓑone do you like best?

서답형

12 위 글의 밑줄 친 ⓐ를 다음과 같이 바꿔 쓸 때 빈칸에 들어갈 알맞은 말을 네 단어로 쓰시오.

➡ Let's _____
some examples.

서답형

13 위 글의 밑줄 친 ⓑone이 가리키는 것을 본문에서 찾아 쓰시오. (형태 변형 가능)

➡ _____

중요

14 위 글의 뒤에 올 내용으로 가장 알맞은 것을 고르시오.

① the introduction about the materials for the marshmallow challenge
② the explanation about the rules of the marshmallow challenge
③ the description of the advantages of the marshmallow challenge
④ the description of the disadvantages of the marshmallow challenge
⑤ some examples of doing the marshmallow challenge differently

[15~16] 다음 글을 읽고 물음에 답하시오.

Try the Marshmallow Challenge!
You need:
• 20 sticks of spaghetti • 1 marshmallow
• 1 meter of tape   • 1 meter of string

Rules:
• Each team has four people.
• You have to build the tallest tower in your class.
• The marshmallow must be on top.
• The tower must stand by itself.
• The time limit is 15 minutes.
This activity is good for:
• Building Relationships
• Solving Problems
• Thinking Creatively

중요

15 다음 중 마시멜로 과제의 규칙을 옳게 이해하지 못한 사람을 고르시오.

① 상미: 각 팀은 4명으로 구성해야 해.
② 현경: 목표는 반에서 가장 높은 탑을 만드는 거야.
③ 영훈: 마시멜로는 꼭대기에 있어야 해.
④ 수철: 탑이 쓰러지지 않도록 잘 잡아주어야 해.
⑤ 규진: 제한 시간은 15분이야.

서답형

16 본문의 내용과 일치하도록 다음 빈칸 (A)~(C)에 알맞은 단어를 쓰시오.

The marshmallow challenge can be helpful in improving the ability to (A) _____ _____ , (B) _____ _____, and (C) _____ _____ .

[17~20] 다음 글을 읽고 물음에 답하시오.

TEAM C: We're one team.
We didn't try (A)to choose the best idea. ⓐ_____, we took a good idea and improved on it. One student said we needed a strong base. Another student suggested a triangle shape for the base. We all agreed and divided up the roles such as time checker and tape cutter. We worked together as a team. In the end, we built our tall tower!

17 위 글의 빈칸 ⓐ에 들어갈 알맞은 말을 고르시오.

① Therefore
② Instead
③ Similarly
④ For example
⑤ In other words

18 아래 〈보기〉에서 위 글의 밑줄 친 (A)to choose와 to부정사의 용법이 같은 것의 개수를 고르시오.

┌─── 보기 ───┐
① It is not always easy to choose the best idea.
② They met yesterday to choose the best idea.
③ We were happy to choose the best idea.
④ She must be clever to choose the best idea.
⑤ I think it difficult to choose the best idea.
└──────────┘

① 1개   ② 2개   ③ 3개   ④ 4개   ⑤ 5개

19 위 글의 주제로 알맞은 것을 고르시오.

① It is important to choose the best idea.
② So many men, so many minds.
③ It's all a castle in the air when you don't have a strong base.
④ A successful team needs division of roles and cooperation.
⑤ A triangle shape is a perfect structure for the base.

서답형
20 본문의 내용과 일치하도록 다음 빈칸 (A)와 (B)에 알맞은 단어를 쓰시오.

┌──────────────────────┐
The members of Team C took (A)_____ _____ _____ and improved on it instead of trying to choose (B)_____ _____ _____.
└──────────────────────┘

[21~23] 다음 글을 읽고 물음에 답하시오.

TEAM B: Just do it.
We didn't spend much time on planning. All the members started building the tower right away. Our first tower (A)[looked / looked like] a tent. ⓐIt wasn't very tall. We tried again. The next tower was tall but ⓑit couldn't stand (B)[by itself / of itself]. After many tries, it was possible (C)[for us / of us] to build a beautiful and tall tower. ⓒIt looked like the Leaning Tower of Pisa. We finally made what we wanted!

서답형
21 위 글의 괄호 (A)~(C)에서 문맥이나 어법상 알맞은 낱말을 골라 쓰시오.

➡ (A)_____   (B)_____   (C)_____

서답형
22 위 글의 밑줄 친 ⓐIt, ⓑit, ⓒIt이 가리키는 것을 각각 영어로 쓰시오.

➡ ⓐ Team B's _____ tower
   ⓑ Team B's _____ tower
   ⓒ Team B's _____ tower

서답형
23 다음 빈칸 (A)와 (B)에 알맞은 단어를 넣어 Team B가 마지막 탑을 만든 과정에 대한 설명을 완성하시오.

┌──────────────────────┐
Team B's final tower looked like the (A)_____ _____ _____ _____. Although the members made mistakes, they kept trying, and they finally made (B)_____ _____ _____ after many tries.
└──────────────────────┘

[01~04] 다음 글을 읽고 물음에 답하시오.

TEAM A: Think before you act.

We had many good ideas. We talked about each idea in detail. ⓐIt was not easy for us to choose the best idea. Suddenly the teacher said, "Five minutes left." In a hurry, we taped the sticks of spaghetti together. Then, we wrapped the string around ⓑthem. The string got stuck to the tape and it was a big mess. ⓒ1초를 남기고, I put the marshmallow on top!

01 위 글의 밑줄 친 ⓐ를 다음과 같이 바꿔 쓸 때 빈칸에 들어갈 알맞은 단어를 쓰시오.

➡ We had _____ choosing the best idea.

02 위 글의 밑줄 친 ⓑthem이 가리키는 것을 본문에서 찾아 쓰시오.

➡ _____

03 위 글의 밑줄 친 ⓒ의 우리말에 맞게 4 단어로 영작하시오.

➡ _____

04 본문의 내용과 일치하도록 다음 빈칸에 알맞은 단어를 쓰시오.

> Team A spent more time _____ the best idea than actually building the tower.

[05~07] 다음 글을 읽고 물음에 답하시오.

TEAM B: Just ⓐ_____ _____.

We didn't spend much time on planning. All the members started building the tower right away. Our first tower looked like a tent. It wasn't very tall. We tried again. The next tower was tall but it couldn't stand by itself. After many tries, it was possible for us to build a beautiful and tall tower. It looked like the Leaning Tower of Pisa. ⓑWe finally made that we wanted!

05 위 글의 빈칸 ⓐ에 알맞은 말을 넣어 Team B의 특징을 묘사하는 문장을 완성하시오. (2 단어)

➡ _____

06 What was the problem of Team B's second tower? Answer in English in a full sentence. (5 words)

➡ _____

07 위 글의 밑줄 친 ⓑ에서 어법상 틀린 부분을 찾아 고치시오.

➡ _____

[08~09] 다음 글을 읽고 물음에 답하시오.

TEAM C: We're one team.

We didn't try to choose the best idea. Instead, we took a good idea and improved on it. One student said we needed a strong base. Another student suggested a triangle shape for the base. We all agreed and divided up the roles such as time checker and tape cutter. We worked together as a team. In the end, we built our tall tower!

08 다음 문장에서 위 글의 내용과 다른 부분을 고쳐 두 개의 문장으로 다시 쓰시오.

> Team C tried to choose the best idea instead of taking a good idea and improving on it.

➡ _____

_____

서답형

09 다음 빈칸 (A)~(C)에 알맞은 단어를 넣어 Team C가 그림의 탑을 만든 과정에 대한 설명을 완성하시오.

The members of Team C all agreed on (A)_____ _____ _____ for the base. They divided up (B)_____ _____, worked together (C)_____ _____ _____, and finally built their tall tower!

[10~12] 다음 글을 읽고 물음에 답하시오.

TEAM A: Think before you act.

ⓐWe had many good ideas. We talked about each idea in detail. It was not easy for us to choose the best idea. Suddenly the teacher said, "Five minutes left." In a hurry, we taped the sticks of spaghetti together. ⓑThen, we wrapped the string around them. The string got stuck to the tape and it was a big mess. With one second left, I put the marshmallow on top!

10 위 글의 밑줄 친 ⓐ를 다음과 같이 바꿔 쓸 때 빈칸에 들어갈 알맞은 말을 두 단어로 쓰시오.

➡ Many good ideas _____ us.

11 위 글의 밑줄 친 ⓑ를 After를 사용하여 고치시오.

➡ _____

_____

12 본문의 내용과 일치하도록 다음 빈칸에 공통으로 들어갈 알맞은 단어를 쓰시오.

The members of Team A didn't use their _____ limit wisely. They came near exceeding their _____ limit, but they managed to complete their challenge in time.   *exceed: 초과하다

[13~14] 다음 글을 읽고 물음에 답하시오.

TEAM C: We're one team.

We didn't try to choose the best idea. Instead, we took a good idea and improved on it. One student said we needed a strong base. Another student suggested a triangle shape for the base. ⓐWe all agreed and divided up the roles such as time checker and tape cutter. We worked together as a team. In the end, we built our tall tower!

13 위 글의 밑줄 친 ⓐWe all agreed 뒤에 생략된 말을 쓰시오. (on 포함 7글자)

➡ _____

14 Team C가 마시멜로 과제를 수행한 과정을 4단계로 나누어 우리말로 설명하시오.

➡ 1단계: _____

_____

2단계: _____

_____

3단계: _____

_____

4단계: _____

Think and Write Step 2

My Best Group Project

My best group project was making a video to introduce our school. The
동명사 보어(= to make)   to부정사의 형용사적 용법

name of our group was 'The Stars' and we had four members. First, we wrote
단수명사 The name이 주어이므로 단수 동사 was가 쓰였다.   = there were four members in our group

a dialogue together. Then, we divided up the roles. I took the role of reporter.
= After we wrote a dialogue together.

It was difficult for us to set the meeting time. But our video turned out to be
가주어   의미상의 주어   진주어   역접의 연결사   = proved

great! I learned that many heads are better than one.
learned의 목적어인 명사절을 연결해 주는 접속사 that이다.

구문해설 • introduce: 소개하다 • dialogue: 대화 • divide up: 나누다, 분배하다 • take the role of:
~의 역할을 맡다 • turn out: ~인 것으로 드러나다, 밝혀지다

해석

나의 최고의 모둠 과제
나의 최고의 모둠 과제는 우리 학교를 소개하는 비디오 만들기였다. 우리 모둠의 이름은 'The Stars'였고 4명의 모둠원이 있었다. 먼저 우리는 함께 대화문을 썼다. 다음으로 우리는 역할을 나누었다. 나는 리포터의 역할을 맡았다. 우리는 만나는 시간을 정하는 것이 어려웠다. 하지만 우리 비디오는 훌륭하게 만들어졌다! 나는 여러 사람이 한 사람보다 낫다는 것을 배웠다.

Think and Write Step 2

My Best Group Project

My best group project was making a travel brochure about Paris. The
동명사 보어(= to make)

name of our group was 'The Travelers' and we had six members. First, we
= there are six members in our group

researched Paris together. Then, we divided up the roles. I took the role of
= After we researched Paris together.   동격의 전치사

drawing a map of Paris. It was difficult for me to draw a map. But one of my
가주어   의미상의 주어   진주어

team members helped me. I learned that teamwork makes better results.
one+of+the+복수명사: ~ 중의 하나   협동 작업   형용사 good의 비교급

구문해설 • travel brochure: 여행 안내 책자, • research: 연구, 조사; 연구[조사]하다, • teamwork: 협동
작업, • result: 결과

나의 최고의 모둠 과제
나의 최고의 모둠 과제는 파리에 대한 여행 안내 책자를 만드는 것이었다. 우리 모둠의 이름은 'The Travelers'였고, 여섯 명의 모둠원이 있었다. 먼저, 우리는 함께 파리를 조사했다. 다음으로 우리는 역할을 나누었다. 나는 파리의 지도를 그리는 역할을 맡았다. 나는 지도를 그리는 것이 어려웠다. 하지만 모둠원 중의 한 명이 나를 도와주었다. 나는 협동 작업이 더 좋은 결과를 만든다는 것을 배웠다.

Project Culture Step 2

In Korea, it is natural for us to ask someone's age. But in western countries,
가주어   의미상의 주어 진주어

asking someone their age is rude. So be careful when you travel.
동명사로 주어   동명사가 주어일 경우 단수 취급   결과를 이끄는 연결사

구문해설 • rude: 무례한 • be careful: 조심하다

한국에서는 누군가의 나이를 묻는 것은 자연스러운 것이다. 그러나 서양의 국가들에서는, 누군가에게 그들의 나이를 묻는 것은 무례하다. 그러므로 여행할 때 조심하라.

Words & Expressions

01 다음 밑줄 친 부분의 의미가 다른 하나를 고르시오.

① They arrived <u>early</u> at the party.
② They were having an <u>early</u> supper.
③ The <u>early</u> morning is the best time of day.
④ It's pretty <u>early</u> to go to school.
⑤ We had an <u>early</u> breakfast.

[02~03] 다음 빈칸에 공통으로 들어갈 말을 쓰시오.

02
- Are you busy _____ the pump?
- I'm not so good _____ sports.

03
- I can't smell because I _____ a cold.
- I don't want to _____ a fight with you.

04 다음 빈칸에 들어갈 말을 〈보기〉에서 찾아 쓰시오. (단어는 한 번씩만 사용할 것.)

┌─── 보기 ───
call   go   lose   wrap
└─────────────

(1) _____ it up carefully to protect against breakage.
(2) I hope he doesn't _____ the election.
(3) What time did Tony _____ ?
(4) How did your French test _____ ?

Conversation

[05~06] 다음 대화를 읽고 물음에 답하시오.

> B: Amy, (a)<u>어떻게 지냈니?</u>
> G: I've been great. How about you, Mike?
> B: Not so good. I have a bad cold.
> G: Oh, no! (A)_____ well soon.

05 빈칸 (A)에 알맞은 말을 고르시오.

① Find   ② Stay   ③ Grow
④ Get   ⑤ Make

06 밑줄 친 (a)의 우리말을 4 단어로 영작하시오.

➡ _____

[07~08] 다음 대화를 읽고 물음에 답하시오.

> B: Susan, you look (A)_____ . Do you have any good news?
> G: Our team got an A on the science project.
> B: That's great!
> G: Our team had the best teamwork.
> B: (B)_____ (to, happy, that, I'm, hear)

07 빈칸 (A)에 알맞은 말을 고르시오.

① scared   ② excited
③ disappointed   ④ bored
⑤ anxious

08 빈칸 (B)를 괄호 안에 주어진 단어를 알맞게 배열하여 채우시오.

➡ _____

09 빈칸에 알맞은 말이 〈보기〉에서 <u>모두</u> 몇 개인지 고르시오.

> A: Bomi, you look upset.
> B: I lost my dog.
> A: _____

> ┌─ 보기 ─┐
> • I'm glad to hear that.
> • I'm sorry to hear that.
> • What a pity!
> • I'm pleased to hear that.
> • I'm happy for you.
> • That's a pity.
> • I'm happy to hear that.
> • That's too bad.

① 2개   ② 3개   ③ 4개   ④ 5개   ⑤ 6개

[10~12] 다음 대화를 읽고 물음에 답하시오.

> Minho: Linda! Is that you? (a)<u>Long time no see</u>.
> Linda: Minho! (①) (A)_____
> Minho: How ⓐ_____ you been?
> Linda: I've been good. How about you?
> Minho: I've been really busy at school. (②)
> Linda: It's wonderful. I've made many new friends. (③)
> Minho: That's great! I'm happy to ⓑ_____ that.
> Linda: Thanks. (④) Oh! I ⓒ_____ to go to my violin lesson now.
> Minho: You still ⓓ_____ my number, right?
> Linda: Yeah. I'll call you later. (⑤) ⓔ_____ a good day!
> Minho: You, too. Bye!

10 ①~⑤ 중 주어진 문장이 들어갈 곳은?

> How's your new school?

① ② ③ ④ ⑤

11 빈칸 (A)에 밑줄 친 문장 (a)와 같은 의미가 되도록 대화에 나온 단어를 이용하여 5 단어로 쓰시오.

➡ _____

12 빈칸 ⓐ~ⓔ 중 들어갈 말이 <u>다른</u> 하나를 고르시오. (대·소문자 무시)

① ⓐ   ② ⓑ   ③ ⓒ   ④ ⓓ   ⑤ ⓔ

Grammar

13 다음 문장의 빈칸에 알맞은 말은?

> It is quite silly _____ to accept his invitation.

① for him   ② for you
③ for our   ④ of you
⑤ of your

14 다음 그림을 보고, 괄호 안의 단어들을 의미가 통하도록 바르게 배열하시오.

(I, what, there, expected, see, was, to) Stone Henge.

➡ _____

15 다음 빈칸에 알맞지 <u>않은</u> 것은?

> It's _____ for him to follow her advice.

① possible   ② safe   ③ fun
④ silly   ⑤ easy

16 다음 두 문장의 의미가 같도록 빈칸에 알맞은 말을 쓰시오.

(1) The thing that I bought for her was a nice smart phone.

     = _____ for her was a nice smart phone. (3 단어)

(2) He will bring his daughter something that is really valuable. (6 단어)

     = He will bring _____

     _____.

(3) Some people do anything to get things that they want.

     = Some people do anything to _____

     _____. (4 단어)

17 다음 빈칸에 들어갈 말이 나머지와 <u>다른</u> 하나는?

① It was not easy _____ us to choose the best idea.

② It was foolish _____ him to buy that expensive house.

③ It was exciting _____ her to sing the song with her friends.

④ It's difficult _____ her mom to climb the mountain.

⑤ It can be dangerous _____ children to swim across the stream.

18 다음 ⓐ~ⓖ 중 어법상 옳은 것을 <u>모두</u> 고르시오.

> ⓐ Do you understand that I'm saying?
> ⓑ What make me happy is my family.
> ⓒ I have a sister that studies English every day.
> ⓓ It is bad of your teeth to have too many sweets.
> ⓔ It's a lot of fun for me to learn about different cultures.
> ⓕ It is important for you being careful when driving.
> ⓖ It is a pity to be kept in the house in good weather.

➡ _____

19 다음 우리말을 주어진 어휘를 이용하여 영작하시오.

(1) 그건 내가 말하고 싶었던 것이다. (that, wanted, say, is)

     ➡ _____

(2) 내가 무엇을 하고 있는지 거의 의식하지 못했어요. (aware, doing, hardly, of)

     ➡ _____

(3) 우리는 수업 시간에 배운 것을 반드시 기억해야 한다. (in class, must, learned)

     ➡ _____

(4) 당신과 다시 일하게 되어 기쁩니다. (you, it, a pleasure, work, to, with)

     ➡ _____

(5) 우리가 어려움에 처한 사람들을 돕는 것은 중요하다. (it, in need, important, to)

     ➡ _____

(6) 네가 그의 초대를 무시하는 것은 실례다. (invitation, it, impolite, ignore, to)

     ➡ _____

20 다음 중 어법상 바르지 <u>않은</u> 것은?

① When your mom sees what you did, she will be happy.
② Love is that helps mend a broken heart.
③ What they need is not wealth but health.
④ It is impossible to cross this river by swimming.
⑤ It is easy for my mom to make a cake.

Reading

[21~23] 다음 글을 읽고 물음에 답하시오.

TEAM A: ⓐ_____

We ①had many good ideas. We talked about each idea ②in detail. It was not easy for us to choose the best idea. ③Suddenly the teacher said, "Five minutes left." ④In a hurry, we taped the sticks of spaghetti together. Then, we wrapped the string around them. The string ⑤got stuck to the tape and it was a big mess. With one second left, I put the marshmallow on top!

21 다음 중, Team A의 특징을 묘사하는 문장으로 위 글의 빈칸 ⓐ에 들어가기에 가장 알맞은 문장을 고르시오.

① Just choose the best idea.
② Act before you think.
③ Just do it.
④ We're one team.
⑤ Think before you act.

22 위 글의 밑줄 친 ①~⑤와 바꿔 쓸 수 있는 말이 <u>아닌</u> 것을 고르시오.

① came up with   ② briefly
③ All of a sudden   ④ In haste
⑤ became

23 Which question CANNOT be answered after reading the passage?

① How many good ideas did Team A have?
② Was it easy for the members of Team A to choose the best idea?
③ Why did the members of Team A tape the sticks of spaghetti together in a hurry?
④ What did the members of Team A do with the string?
⑤ Where did the string get stuck?

[24~25] 다음 글을 읽고 물음에 답하시오.

TEAM B: Just do it.

We didn't spend much time on planning. All the members started building the tower right away. Our first tower looked like a tent. It wasn't very tall. We tried again. The next tower was tall but it couldn't stand by itself. After many tries, ⓐit was possible for us to build a beautiful and tall tower. It looked like the Leaning Tower of Pisa. We finally made what we wanted!

24 위 글의 밑줄 친 ⓐ를 we를 사용하여 바꿀 때, 빈칸에 들어 갈 알맞은 말을 쓰시오.

➡ we _____ build a beautiful and tall tower (한 단어)

= we _____ build a beautiful and tall tower (3 단어)

25 다음 중 위 글의 내용을 바르게 이해하지 <u>못한</u> 사람을 고르시오.

① 나리: Team B는 계획보다 행동이 앞선 팀이야.

② 보미: 응, 맞아. 그래서 모든 팀원들이 바로 탑을 만들기 시작했지.

③ 이슬: 그들이 만든 첫 번째 탑은 텐트 같았는데, 스스로 서 있지 못했어.

④ 여름: 그래도 많은 시도 후에 그들은 아름답고 높은 탑을 만들 수 있었어.

⑤ 슬기: 응, 그들은 결국 그들이 원하는 것을 만들었어!

[26~28] 다음 글을 읽고 물음에 답하시오.

TEAM C: We're one team.

We didn't try to choose the best idea. (A)[In addition / Instead], we took a good idea and improved ⓐ it. One student said we needed a strong base. (B)[Another / The other] student suggested a triangle shape ⓑ the base. We all agreed and (C)[decided / divided] up the roles such as time checker and tape cutter. We worked together ©<u>as</u> a team. In the end, we built our tall tower!

---

26 위 글의 빈칸 ⓐ와 ⓑ에 들어갈 전치사가 바르게 짝지어진 것은?

	ⓐ	ⓑ		ⓐ	ⓑ
①	for	from	②	on	from
③	in	for	④	for	to
⑤	on	for			

27 위 글의 괄호 (A)~(C)에서 문맥이나 어법상 알맞은 낱말을 골라 쓰시오.

➡ (A)_____ (B)_____ (C)_____

28 위 글의 밑줄 친 ©<u>as</u>와 같은 의미로 쓰인 것을 고르시오.

① I acknowledge him <u>as</u> my superior.

② <u>As</u> she is honest, she is trusted by everyone.

③ This is twice <u>as</u> large as that.

④ She came up <u>as</u> I was speaking.

⑤ His anger grew <u>as</u> he talked.

[29~30] 다음 글을 읽고 물음에 답하시오.

My Best Group Project

(A)My best group project was making a video to introduce our school. The name of our group was 'The Stars' and we had four members. First, we wrote a dialogue together. Then, we divided up the roles. I took the role of reporter. It was difficult for us to set the meeting time. But our video turned out to be great! I learned that ⓐ_____.

---

29 위 글의 빈칸 ⓐ에 들어갈 알맞은 속담을 고르시오.

① a stitch in time saves nine

② strike while the iron is hot

③ many heads are better than one

④ birds of a feather flock together

⑤ better late than never

30 위 글의 밑줄 친 (A)를 다음과 같이 바꿔 쓸 때 빈칸에 들어갈 알맞은 말을 두 단어로 쓰시오.

➡ My best group project was _____ a video to introduce our school.

출제율 90%

01 다음 밑줄 친 부분의 의미로 알맞지 <u>않은</u> 것은?

① He shook his head <u>slowly</u>. (느리게)
② The book must be handled <u>carefully</u> because of its age. (조심하여, 주의 깊게)
③ Is it <u>possible</u> to get tickets for the game? (가능한)
④ The bus came five minutes <u>early</u>. (일찍)
⑤ I could <u>hardly</u> understand you. (어렵게)

출제율 90%

02 다음 그림을 참고하여 빈칸에 알맞은 단어를 고르시오.

When I got home, the house was a complete _____.

① clean   ② tidy   ③ mess
④ disease   ⑤ mass

출제율 100%

03 다음 빈칸에 들어갈 말을 〈보기〉에서 찾아 쓰시오. (단어는 한 번씩만 사용할 것.)

┌─ 보기 ─
relationship   role   score
└─

(1) The _____ between the two has changed dramatically.
(2) The final _____ was Southampton two, Leeds United nine.
(3) It played a significant _____ in the recent debate.

출제율 95%

04 다음 빈칸에 들어갈 말을 고르시오.

Since there are a lot of things to do, we'd better divide _____ the work.

① of   ② at   ③ with
④ for   ⑤ up

[05~08] 다음 대화를 읽고 물음에 답하시오.

B: Yeah! It's good to see you, Sora. (A)_____
G: I've been great. (①) How about you?
B: I've been (a)pretty busy. (②)
G: Oh! I didn't know you played the piano. (③)
B: Really? (④) I've played the piano ⓐ[during / for / while / when] 5 years. (⑤)
G: You must be good ⓑ[at / for / in / of] it. Good luck in your competition!
B: Thanks.

출제율 100%

05 ①~⑤ 중 주어진 문장이 들어갈 곳은?

I have a piano competition next week.

①   ②   ③   ④   ⑤

출제율 90%

06 빈칸 (A)에 알맞은 말을 <u>모두</u> 고르시오.

① How have you been?
② How's everything?
③ What have you been up to?
④ What do you like?
⑤ What is it going to be?

07 밑줄 친 (a)pretty와 같은 의미로 쓰이지 <u>않은</u> 것을 <u>모두</u> 고르시오.

① I'm <u>pretty</u> sure he'll say yes.

② I felt <u>pretty</u> nervous when I was going into the exam room.

③ We walked down the <u>pretty</u>, tree-lined road.

④ I thought the test was <u>pretty</u> easy.

⑤ A very long time ago, she must have been <u>pretty</u>.

08 위 대화의 괄호 ⓐ와 ⓑ에서 적절한 것을 골라 쓰시오.

➡ ⓐ _____ ⓑ _____

09 다음 빈칸 (A)와 (B)에 들어갈 말이 알맞게 짝지어진 것은?

> A: How have you been?
> B: (A)_____
> A: How come?
> B: I lost my dog.
> A: Oh, no! (B)_____

	(A)	(B)
①	I've been great.	– I'm sorry to hear that.
②	I've been great.	– I'm happy to hear that.
③	So so.	– I'm happy to hear that.
④	Not so good.	– I'm sorry to hear that.
⑤	Not so good.	– I'm happy to hear that.

[10~12] 다음 대화를 읽고 물음에 답하시오.

> G: Andy, how did the basketball game go?
> B: Our team lost.
> G: Oh, (A)_____
> B: It's okay. It was a great game.
> G: What was the score?
> B: It was 80 to 79. We lost by one point.
> G: That was really (B)<u>close</u>!
> B: Yeah. We played really well as a team.
> G: That's wonderful! I want to watch your next game.

10 위 대화에서 다음 영영풀이에 해당하는 단어를 찾아 쓰시오.

> to not win a game, argument, election, war, etc.

➡ _____

11 빈칸 (A)에 주어진 단어를 이용하여 유감을 표현하는 말을 쓰시오.

➡ _____ (to, sorry)

12 밑줄 친 (B)<u>close</u>와 같은 의미로 쓰인 것은?

① Beth <u>closed</u> her eyes and tried to sleep.

② Susan sat on a chair <u>close</u> to the window.

③ It was a <u>close</u> game from start to finish.

④ My brother and I are very <u>close</u>.

⑤ The man moved <u>closer</u>, lowering his voice.

13 다음 빈칸에 알맞은 말이 순서대로 짝지어진 것은?

> • Playing the guitar in my free time is _____ I like most.
> • It is important _____ them to do their homework.

① what – of
② that – of
③ what – for
④ that – for
⑤ which – for

14 다음 중 어법상 적절한 문장은?

① It is boring of me to fish in the lake.
② It's great to hears that you received the award.
③ It's fun to doing different things.
④ It is better for you to eat healthy food.
⑤ It was exciting of him to ride a boat.

15 다음 두 문장이 같도록 할 때 빈칸에 알맞은 말을 쓰시오.

> • It is beautiful! You have the thing that I'm looking for.
> = It is beautiful! You have _____ I'm looking for.

[16~18] 다음 글을 읽고 물음에 답하시오.

TEAM A: Think before you act.

　We had many good ideas. We talked about each idea in detail. ⓐIt was not easy for us to choose the best idea. Suddenly the teacher said, "Five minutes left." In a hurry, we taped the sticks of spaghetti together. Then, we wrapped the string around them. ⓑ끈이 테이프에 붙었고 엉망진창이었어요. With one second left, I put the marshmallow on top!

16 위 글의 밑줄 친 ⓐIt과 문법적 쓰임이 같은 것을 모두 고르시오.

① I make it a rule to get up early.
② It is important to choose good friends.
③ How long does it take from here to the station?
④ Is it possible to master English in a month or two?
⑤ It was raining this morning.

17 위 글의 밑줄 친 ⓑ의 우리말에 맞게 주어진 어휘를 알맞게 배열하시오.

> and / a big mess / got stuck / was / the string / it / to the tape

➡ _____

18 다음 문장에서 위 글의 내용과 다른 부분을 찾아서 고치시오.

> There was enough time left for the writer to put the marshmallow on top.

➡ _____

[19~21] 다음 글을 읽고 물음에 답하시오.

TEAM B: Just do it.

　We didn't spend much time ①on planning. All the members started ②building the tower right away. Our first tower looked like a tent. It wasn't very tall. We tried again. The next tower was tall but it couldn't stand ③by itself. After many tries, it was possible for us to build a beautiful and tall tower. It looked like the Leaning Tower of Pisa. We ④finally made ⑤what we wanted!

19 위 글의 밑줄 친 ①~⑤와 바꿔 쓸 수 있는 말이 아닌 것을 고르시오.

① in
② to build
③ alone
④ at least
⑤ the thing which

20 위 글에 어울리는 속담으로 가장 알맞은 것을 고르시오.

① It is no use crying over the spilt milk.

② The end justifies the means.

③ All that glitters is not gold.

④ Never put off till tomorrow what you can do today.

⑤ Look before you leap.

21 try를 알맞은 형태로 변형하여, 다음 빈칸 (A)와 (B)에 들어갈 Team B에 대한 선생님의 피드백을 완성하시오.

> **Team B:**
> It was wonderful that you (A)_____ many times. I'm sure you learned a lot from (B)_____ and error. Finally, you built a beautiful and tall tower. You finally made what you wanted! Good job!

➡ (A) _____ (B) _____

[22~23] 다음 글을 읽고 물음에 답하시오.

> **TEAM C:** ⓐ_____
>
> We didn't try to choose the best idea. Instead, we took a good idea and improved on it. One student said we needed a strong base. Another student suggested a triangle shape for the base. We all agreed and divided up the roles such as time checker and tape cutter. We worked together as a team. In the end, we built our tall tower!

22 다음 중, Team C의 특징을 묘사하는 문장으로 위 글의 빈칸 ⓐ에 들어가기에 가장 알맞은 문장을 고르시오.

① Try to choose the best idea.

② Focus on the strong base.

③ Just do it.

④ We're one team.

⑤ Think before you act.

23 Which question CANNOT be answered after reading the passage?

① Why did Team C take a good idea and improve on it instead of choosing the best idea?

② On what shape did Team C agree for the tower base?

③ Did the members of Team C perform the same task?

④ Did Team C succeed in working together as a team?

⑤ Was it possible for Team C to build a tall tower?

[24~25] 다음 글을 읽고 물음에 답하시오.

> **My Best Group Project**
> My best group project was (A)making a travel brochure about Paris. The name of our group was 'The Travelers' and we had six members. First, we researched Paris together. Then, we divided up the roles. I took the role of drawing a map of Paris. It was difficult for me to draw a map. But one of my team members helped me. I learned that ⓐ___ makes better results.

24 위 글의 빈칸 ⓐ에 들어갈 알맞은 말을 모두 고르시오.

① cooperation ② teamwork

③ competition ④ responsibility

⑤ collaboration

25 위 글의 밑줄 친 (A)making과 문법적 쓰임이 다른 것을 모두 고르시오.

① Did you finish making a travel brochure?

② He was making a travel brochure.

③ I'm good at making a travel brochure.

④ I saw him making a travel brochure.

⑤ Making a travel brochure is not easy.

01 다음 대화에서 흐름상 또는 어법상 <u>어색한</u> 것을 찾아 바르게 고치시오.

> **A:** How have you been?
> **B:** I've been good. How is everything?
> **A:** Pretty bad. My new classes are exciting.

➡ _____

02 밑줄 친 문장과 바꿔 쓸 수 있는 문장을 주어진 조건에 맞춰 쓰시오.

> **A:** Jim, you look happy.
> **B:** I bought a new bike.
> **A:** <u>I'm happy to hear that.</u>

➡ (glad, 5 단어) _____
(pleased, 5 단어) _____

03 대화의 흐름상 빈칸에 들어갈 말을 주어진 단어를 이용하여 완성하시오.

> **G:** Hi, Jinsu! We're in the same class again!
> **B:** Yeah! It's good to see you, Sora.
> _____
> **G:** I've been great. How about you?
> **B:** I've been pretty busy. I have a piano competition next week.
> **G:** Oh! I didn't know you played the piano.
> **B:** Really? I've played the piano for 5 years.
> **G:** You must be good at it. Good luck in your competition!
> **B:** Thanks.

➡ (been, 4 단어) _____
(up, 6 단어) _____
(doing, 5 단어) _____

04 관계대명사 what을 사용하여, 주어진 두 문장을 한 문장으로 바꾸시오.

(1) • I cannot remember the thing.
   • It happened last night.
  ➡ _____

(2) • Mina liked the dish.
   • I cooked it for her yesterday.
  ➡ _____

(3) • Tell me the work.
   • You want me to do it.
  ➡ _____

05 괄호 안에 주어진 단어를 활용하여 빈칸을 채우시오.

(1) It is not safe _____ to live there. (they)
(2) It was easy _____ to cook camping food. (she)
(3) It was very smart _____ not to miss the chance. (he)
(4) Was it wise _____ to come to the hotel? (you)

06 다음 두 문장의 의미가 같도록 문장의 빈칸을 완성하시오.

(1) Korea is safe and convenient to live in.
  = It is safe and convenient _____.
(2) Matthew was wise to stay under the protection of Rome.
  = It _____ under the protection of Rome.
(3) He was hardly aware of the thing that he was doing.
  = He was hardly aware of _____ _____.

TEAM C: We're one team.

We didn't try to choose the best idea. Instead, we took a good idea and improved on ⓐit. One student said we needed a strong base. Another student suggested a triangle shape for the base. We all agreed and divided up the roles such as time checker and tape cutter. ⓑ우리는 하나의 팀으로 함께했어요. In the end, we built our tall tower!

07 위 글의 밑줄 친 ⓐit이 가리키는 것을 본문에서 찾아 쓰시오.

➡ _____

08 위 글의 밑줄 친 ⓑ의 우리말에 맞게 주어진 어휘를 이용하여 6단어로 영작하시오.

as

➡ _____

09 다음 빈칸 (A)와 (B)에 알맞은 단어를 넣어 Team C에 대한 선생님의 피드백을 완성하시오.

Team C:
You chose (A)_____ _____
_____ and improved on it. Also, I was impressed that you (B)_____ _____
the roles and everyone had a role. Your tall tower looked strong.

[10~12] 다음 글을 읽고 물음에 답하시오.

TEAM A: Think before you act.

We had many good ideas. We talked about each idea in detail. It was not easy for us to choose the best idea. Suddenly the teacher said, "Five minutes ⓐ____." In a hurry, we taped the sticks of spaghetti together. Then, we wrapped the string around them. The string got stuck to the tape and it was a big mess. With one second left, I put the marshmallow on top!

10 위 글의 빈칸 ⓐ에 leave를 알맞은 형태로 쓰시오. (1단어)

➡ _____

11 Why did the members of Team A have to be in a hurry at the end of their challenge? Fill in the blanks with suitable words. (2 words)

Because they spent too much time choosing the best idea at the beginning, they had to complete their challenge within _____ _____.

12 Team A가 마시멜로 과제를 수행한 과정을 우리말로 설명하시오.

1단계: _____
2단계: _____
3단계: _____
4단계: _____

01 다음 〈조건〉을 보고 주어진 상황에 대해 기쁨을 전하는 문장을 넣어 대화를 완성하시오.

┌─ 조건 ─┐
- first place / the singing contest
- to부정사를 한 번은 꼭 사용할 것.

A: What's up? You look e_____.
B: _____
A: That's great. _____

02 A와 B에 주어진 것 중 각각 하나씩과 가주어를 이용하여 어법에 맞게 3 문장 이상 쓰시오.

A : he/easy   we/necessary   he/careless   difficult/she
B: ride a horse   learn Greek   make a wise decision   leave her alone

(1) _____
(2) _____
(3) _____
(4) _____

03 다음 내용을 바탕으로 기억에 남는 모둠 활동 경험을 쓰시오.

My Best Group Project
The project we did: making a video to introduce our school
Group name: The Stars
Steps: 1. writing a dialogue
       2. dividing up the roles
My role: reporter
Difficulty: setting the meeting time
Things I learned: Many heads are better than one.

My Best Group Project
  My best group project was (A)_____ to introduce our school. The name of our group was (B)'_____' and we had four members. First, we (C)_____ together. Then, we divided up (D)_____. I took the role of (E)_____. It was difficult for us to set (F)_____. But our video turned out to be great! I learned that (G)_____ are better than one.

단원별 모의고사

01 다음 짝지어진 단어의 관계가 같도록 빈칸에 알맞은 말을 쓰시오.

(1) pretty : quite = bottom : b_____
(2) happy: happily = early : _____.

02 다음 밑줄 친 부분의 의미로 알맞지 <u>않은</u> 것은?

① A few days <u>later</u>, Jinho gave me a letter. (후에)
② I'm too <u>upset</u> to eat. (기분이 상한)
③ Can you tell me your <u>number</u>? (전화번호)
④ It was a <u>close</u> contest between two teams. (가까운)
⑤ He lost <u>by</u> less than 100 votes. (~의 차이로)

03 빈칸 (A)와 (B)에 들어갈 말로 알맞은 것끼리 짝지어진 것을 고르시오.

• He is busy (A)_____ work.
• He liked taking things such (B)_____ radios apart and putting them back together.

	(A)	(B)		(A)	(B)
①	at	as	②	at	of
③	at	in	④	on	as
⑤	on	of			

04 빈칸을 주어진 영영풀이에 해당하는 말을 이용하여 채우시오.

> something that needs a lot of skill, energy, and determination to deal with or achieve

> Riding a bicycle for three days was a big _____.

[05~06] 다음 대화를 읽고 물음에 답하시오.

G: Hi, Jinsu! We're in the same class again!
B: Yeah! It's good to see you, Sora. How have you been?
G: I've been great. How about you?
B: (a)<u>나는 매우 바빴어.</u> I have a piano competition next week.
G: Oh! I didn't know you played the piano.
B: Really? I've played the piano for 5 years.
G: You (b)<u>must</u> be good at it. Good luck in your competition!
B: Thanks.

05 밑줄 친 (a)의 우리말과 일치하도록 주어진 단어를 이용해 문장을 만드시오. (4 words)

➡ _____ (pretty, been)

06 밑줄 친 (b)must와 같은 의미로 쓰인 것은?

① This box <u>must</u> be moved carefully.
② You <u>must</u> stop at the red light.
③ You <u>must</u> not walk on the grass.
④ She <u>must</u> be very happy, for she is singing.
⑤ I <u>must</u> do my homework first.

[07~08] 다음 대화를 읽고 물음에 답하시오.

A: Ann, you look (A)_____.
B: (B)나는 내 친구와 싸웠어.
A: I'm sorry to hear that.

07 빈칸 (A)에 대화의 흐름상 알맞은 말을 주어진 철자로 시작하여 채우시오.

➡ u_____

08 밑줄 친 (B)의 우리말과 일치하도록 주어진 단어를 이용해 쓰시오.

➡ _____ (a fight)

[09~11] 다음 대화를 읽고 물음에 답하시오.

G: Andy, how did the basketball game go?
B: Our team lost.
G: Oh, (A)_____
B: It's okay. It was a great game.
G: ⓐ[What / How / Which] was the score?
B: It was 80 to 79. We lost by one point.
G: That was really close!
B: Yeah. We played really well ⓑ[as / such as / without] a team.
G: That's wonderful! I want to watch your next game.

09 대화의 흐름상 빈칸 (A)에 들어갈 알맞은 말을 주어진 단어를 이용하여 쓰시오.

➡ (sorry, to) _____
(bad) _____
(a pity, 감탄문) _____

10 위 대화에서 다음 영영풀이에 해당하는 단어를 찾아 쓰시오.

finishing or being played, fought, etc. with both sides almost equal

➡ _____

11 위 대화의 괄호 (A)와 (B)에서 적절한 것을 골라 쓰시오.

➡ (A) _____ (B) _____

[12~13] 다음 대화를 읽고 물음에 답하시오.

Minho: Linda! Is that you? Long time no see.
Linda: Minho! It's ⓐ_____ a long time.
Minho: How have you ⓑ_____?
Linda: I've ⓒ_____ good. How about you?
Minho: I've ⓓ_____ really busy at school. How's your new school?
Linda: It's wonderful. I've ⓔ_____ many new friends.
Minho: That's great! I'm happy to hear that.
Linda: Thanks. Oh! I have to go to my violin lesson now.
Minho: You still have my number, right?
Linda: Yeah. I'll call you later. Have a good day!
Minho: You, too. Bye!

12 ⓐ~ⓔ 중에 들어갈 말이 나머지와 다른 하나를 고르시오.

① ⓐ ② ⓑ ③ ⓒ ④ ⓓ ⑤ ⓔ

13 위 대화를 읽고 답할 수 있는 질문을 고르시오.

① How many new friends did Linda make at new school?
② How long has Linda taken the violin lesson?
③ Does Linda have Minho's number?
④ When will they meet after the conversation?
⑤ How long haven't they met each other?

14 다음 중 어법상 <u>어색한</u> 것을 고르시오.

① It is important for him to take care of his family.

② Was it clever for him to solve the problem so quickly?

③ It is difficult for me to take note of what my teacher tells us in class.

④ Let me see what you bought.

⑤ What I like most is playing computer games.

15 다음 빈칸에 들어갈 말을 순서대로 묶은 것은?

• Laura is proud of _____ she did.

• The movie _____ she watched last night was good.

① that – that　　② that – what
③ what – that　　④ what – what
⑤ which – what

16 다음 문장에서 어법상 <u>어색한</u> 것을 바르게 고치시오.

(1) That he did with the experiment was quite unique.

_____ ➡ _____

(2) We have to decide which we will do in the near future.

_____ ➡ _____

(3) This computer is not the thing what I wanted to buy.

_____ ➡ _____

(4) I don't think it's necessary of you to buy a new computer.

_____ ➡ _____

(5) It was brave for you to speak on behalf of the people.

_____ ➡ _____

17 다음 중 밑줄 친 부분의 쓰임이 〈보기〉와 같은 것은?

┌─ 보기 ─┐

We finally made <u>what</u> we wanted.

① He can remember <u>what</u> she did last year.

② <u>What</u> do you like to do when you are free?

③ I don't know <u>what</u> to say.

④ Can you imagine <u>what</u> these students can do next?

⑤ I wonder <u>what</u> cold noodles taste like.

18 〈보기〉와 같이 문장을 바꿔 쓰시오.

┌─ 보기 ─┐

You should remember to buy a new dress for the party.
→ It is important for you to remember to buy a new dress for the party.

(1) You should listen carefully to what your teacher tells you.

→ It is important _____

_____ .

(2) He kindly delivered those heavy boxes to my house.

→ It was nice _____

_____ .

[19~20] 다음 글을 읽고 물음에 답하시오.

TEAM A: Think before you act.

We had many good ideas. We talked about each idea in detail. It was not easy for us to choose the best idea. Suddenly the teacher said, "Five minutes left." In a hurry, we taped the sticks of spaghetti together. Then, we wrapped the string around them. The string got stuck to the tape and it was a big mess. With one second left, I put the marshmallow on top!

19 주어진 영영풀이에 해당하는 단어를 본문에서 찾아 쓰시오.

> an untidy state

➡ _____

20 다음 빈칸 (A)와 (B)에 알맞은 단어를 넣어 Team A에 대한 선생님의 피드백을 완성하시오.

> **Team A:**
> You had many good (A)_____! You built the tower (B)_____ _____ _____, but everyone worked hard. Nice work!

[21~23] 다음 글을 읽고 물음에 답하시오.

> **TEAM B: Just do it.**
> We didn't spend much time on planning. All the members started building the tower ⓐ right away. Our first tower looked like a tent. It wasn't very tall. We tried again. The next tower was tall but it couldn't stand by itself. After many tries, ⓑ우리는 아름답고 높은 탑을 만들 수 있었어요. It looked like the Leaning Tower of Pisa. We finally made what we wanted!

21 위 글의 밑줄 친 ⓐright away와 바꿔 쓸 수 없는 말을 고르시오.

① at once
② right now
③ exactly
④ immediately
⑤ in no time

22 위 글의 밑줄 친 ⓑ의 우리말에 맞게 주어진 어휘를 이용하여 12 단어로 영작하시오.

> it, for, build

➡ _____
_____

23 Team B가 마시멜로 과제를 수행한 과정을 4단계의 우리말로 설명하시오.

1단계: _____
_____
2단계: _____
3단계: _____
4단계: _____

[24~26] 다음 글을 읽고 물음에 답하시오.

> **TEAM C: We're one team.**
> We didn't try to choose the best idea. Instead, we took a good idea and ___ⓐ___ on it. One student said we needed a strong base. Another student suggested a triangle shape for the base. We all agreed and divided up the roles such as time checker and tape cutter. We worked together as a team. ⓑIn the end, we built our tall tower!

24 위 글의 빈칸 ⓐ에 improve를 알맞은 형태로 쓰시오.

➡ _____

25 위 글의 밑줄 친 ⓑIn the end와 바꿔 쓸 수 없는 말을 모두 고르시오.

① In advance
② Finally
③ At last
④ Above all
⑤ In the long run

26 According to the passage, which is NOT true?

① Team C didn't try to choose the best idea.
② Team C took a good idea and improved on it.
③ The members of Team C agreed on a square shape for the base.
④ The members of Team C divided up the roles.
⑤ The members of Team C worked together as a team.

Lesson 2

Go Green

의사소통 기능

- 걱정 표현하기
  A: I'm worried about global warming.
  B: Me, too. It's terrible.
- 방법 묻기
  A: Do you know how to do a team project well?
  B: Yes. You need to listen carefully to others' opinions.

언어 형식

- 부분을 나타내는 말의 수의 일치
  About **a third of the bee population dies** every year.
- 조동사가 있는 문장의 수동태
  Honey from ancient Egypt **can be eaten** today.

Words & Expressions

Key Words

- **adventure**[ædvéntʃər] 명 모험
- **advise**[ædváiz] 동 충고하다
- **almost**[ɔ́:lmoust] 부 거의
- **ancient**[éinʃənt] 형 고대의
- **around**[əráund] 부 약 ~, 대략
- **bee**[bi:] 명 벌
- **brush**[brʌʃ] 동 양치질하다
- **carefully**[kéərfli] 부 조심스럽게
- **chemical**[kémikəl] 명 화학 물질
- **climate**[kláimit] 명 기후
- **condition**[kəndíʃən] 명 상태, 조건
- **crop**[krɑp] 명 곡식
- **deliver**[dilívər] 동 배달하다
- **disappear**[dìsəpíər] 동 사라지다
- **donate**[dóuneit] 동 기부하다
- **extreme**[ikstrí:m] 형 극심한
- **extremely**[ikstrí:mli] 부 극심하게
- **fine**[fain] 형 미세한, 섬세한
- **forever**[fərévər] 부 영원히
- **global**[glóubəl] 형 전 세계적인
- **global warming** 지구 온난화
- **harm**[hɑ:rm] 명 해로움, 피해
- **harmful**[hɑ́:rmfəl] 형 해로운
- **health**[helθ] 명 건강

- **honey bee** 꿀벌
- **insect**[ínsekt] 명 곤충
- **last**[læst] 동 지속하다
- **opinion**[əpínjən] 명 의견
- **pencil holder** 연필꽂이
- **plant**[plænt] 동 심다
- **plastic bag** 비닐봉투
- **pleasure**[pléʒər] 명 즐거움
- **polar bear** 북극곰
- **pollen**[pálən] 명 꽃가루
- **pollination**[pálənèiʃən] 명 수분작용, 꽃가루 옮기기
- **pollution**[pəlú:ʃən] 명 오염
- **powder**[páudər] 명 가루
- **process**[práses] 명 과정
- **produce**[prədjú:s] 동 생산하다
- **provide**[prəváid] 동 제공하다
- **public transportation** 대중교통
- **environment**[inváiərənmənt] 명 환경
- **recycle**[rì:sáikl] 동 재활용하다
- **reduce**[ridjú:s] 동 줄이다
- **seed**[si:d] 명 씨앗
- **survey**[sərvéi] 명 설문조사 동 설문조사를 하다
- **survive**[sərváiv] 동 살아남다

Key Expressions

- **a quarter of** ~의 4분의 1
- **a sheet of paper** 종이 한 장
- **A such as B** B와 같은 A
- **a third of** ~의 3분의 1
- **be worried about** ~에 대하여 걱정하다
- **because of** ~ 때문에
- **break down** 분해되다
- **by oneself** 혼자서
- **have gone** 사라지고 없다
- **in fact** 사실

- **in the process of** ~하는 과정에
- **less than** ~보다 적은, ~ 이하
- **let ~ down** ~을 실망시키다
- **not only A but also B** A뿐만 아니라 B도
- **pick up** 뽑다, 집다
- **slow down** 속도를 늦추다
- **take a shower** 샤워하다
- **take part in** ~에 참가하다
- **throw away** 버리다
- **turn off** 끄다

Word Power

※ 서로 비슷한 뜻을 가진 어휘

- □ **deliver** 배달하다 – **convey** 전달하다
- □ **forever** 영원히 – **eternally** 영원히
- □ **harmful** 해로운 – **toxic** 유해한
- □ **let** 허락하다 – **permit** 허가하다
- □ **carefully** 조심스럽게 – **attentively** 주의 깊게
- □ **donate** 기부하다 – **contribute** 기여하다

- □ **fine** 미세한, 섬세한 – **minute** 미세한
- □ **global** 전 세계적인 – **worldwide** 전 세계적인
- □ **last** 지속하다 – **continue** 계속하다
- □ **provide** 제공하다 – **supply** 제공하다
- □ **reason** 이유 – **cause** 원인

※ 서로 반대의 뜻을 가진 어휘

- □ **ancient** 고대의 ↔ **modern** 현대의
- □ **carefully** 조심스럽게 ↔ **carelessly** 부주의하게
- □ **global** 전 세계적인 ↔ **local** 지역적인
- □ **later** 나중에 ↔ **earlier** 이전의
- □ **disappear** 사라지다 ↔ **appear** 나타나다

- □ **forever** 영원히 ↔ **temporarily** 일시적으로
- □ **harm** 해로움, 피해 ↔ **benefit** 이득
- □ **leave** 떠나다 ↔ **arrive** 도착하다
- □ **pleasure** 즐거움 ↔ **sorrow** 슬픔

※ 명사 – 형용사

- □ **adventure** 모험 – **adventurous** 모험심이 강한
- □ **condition** 상태, 조건 – **conditional** 조건적인
- □ **harm** 해로움, 피해 – **harmful** 해로운

- □ **climate** 기후 – **climatic** 기후의
- □ **globe** 지구 – **global** 전 세계적인
- □ **health** 건강 – **healthy** 건강한

※ 명사 – 동사

- □ **advice** 충고 – **advise** 충고하다
- □ **donation** 기부 – **donate** 기부하다
- □ **production** 생산 – **produce** 생산하다

- □ **delivery** 배달 – **deliver** 배달하다
- □ **pleasure** 즐거움 – **please** 기쁘게 하다

English Dictionary

- □ **adventure** 모험
  → an exciting experience in which dangerous or unusual things happen
  위험하거나 특이한 일이 일어나는 흥미로운 경험

- □ **ancient** 고대의
  → having existed for a very long time
  긴 시간 동안 존재해 온

- □ **bee** 벌
  → a black and yellow flying insect that makes honey
  꿀을 만드는 검고 노란 날아다니는 곤충

- □ **crop** 곡식
  → a plant such as wheat, rice, or fruit that is grown by farmers
  농부에 의해서 재배되는 밀, 쌀, 과일 같은 식물

- □ **deliver** 배달하다
  → to take goods, letters, etc. to a particular place
  상품, 편지 등을 어떤 특정한 장소로 가지고 가다

- □ **donate** 기부하다
  → to give something to a person or an organization in order to help them
  돕기 위하여 사람이나 단체에 무엇인가를 주다

- □ **fine** 미세한, 섬세한
  → very thin or narrow
  매우 가늘거나 좁은

- □ **insect** 곤충
  → a small creature such as a fly or ant, that has six legs
  모기, 개미와 같이 다리를 여섯 개 가진 작은 생명체

- □ **pollen** 꽃가루
  → a fine powder produced by flowers
  꽃에 의해서 생산된 미세한 가루

01 접미사 '-ful'을 붙여 형용사로 만들 수 없는 것을 고르시오.

① harm ② condition ③ use
④ care ⑤ help

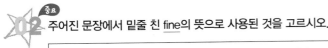
02 주어진 문장에서 밑줄 친 fine의 뜻으로 사용된 것을 고르시오.

> They allow seeing fine details and faint objects.

① If it's fine tomorrow, we'll go out.
② Many people regard Beethoven's fifth symphony as his finest work.
③ Even a professional couldn't pick out the finer points.
④ If you want to use cheese instead of chicken, that's fine.
⑤ It was chosen for its good food and fine wines.

03 주어진 두 문장이 같은 의미가 되도록 빈칸에 알맞은 말을 고르시오.

> The families of the victims feel that the justice system has made them disappointed.
> = The families of the victims feel that the justice system has let them _____.

① out ② off ③ over
④ up ⑤ down

04 빈칸 (A)와 (B)에 알맞은 말로 짝지어진 것을 고르시오.

> • His actions put the child's life (A)_____ danger.
> • I didn't know what "loquacious" meant and had to look it (B)_____ in a dictionary.

　　(A)　(B)　　　　　(A)　(B)
① with – up ② with – over
③ in – up ④ in – over
⑤ in – around

05 다음 빈칸에 공통으로 들어갈 말을 고르시오.

> • Could you help with the preparations? I can't do it _____ myself.
> • The boy attempted to deceive his father _____ telling a lie.

① on ② for ③ by
④ in ⑤ with

06 다음 빈칸에 알맞은 단어를 고르시오.

> She is bored not only with music _____ also with arts.

① and ② except ③ but
④ when ⑤ only

07 다음 영영풀이에 해당하는 말을 주어진 철자로 시작하여 쓰시오.

> a plant such as wheat, rice, or fruit that is grown by farmers

➡ c_____

01 다음 밑줄 친 부분과 바꿔 쓸 수 있는 말을 주어진 철자로 시작하여 쓰시오.

> The hot weather <u>continued</u> for the whole month of June.

➡ l_____

02 다음 괄호 안의 단어를 문맥에 맞게 고쳐 쓰시오.

> Doctors have warned against the _____ (harm) effects of smoking.

➡ _____

[03~04] 다음 빈칸에 공통으로 들어갈 말을 쓰시오.

03

> • Talking can help slow _____ one's eating pace.
> • I have trust in her and she won't let me _____.

04

> • I suddenly felt sorry for him and my anger melted _____.
> • Do not throw _____ glass bottles, cans, and newspapers.

05 다음 우리말에 맞도록 빈칸에 알맞은 말을 쓰시오. (철자가 주어진 경우 주어진 철자로 시작할 것)

(1) 친구에게 보내는 편지와 반친구들에 관한 이야기와 같은 어떤 기사라도 환영한다.

➡ Any articles _____ _____ letters to friends and stories of classmates are welcomed.

(2) 영어 시험이 걱정되니?

➡ Are you w_____ _____ the English test?

(3) 약 반 이하의 학생들이 그 규칙에 반대했다.

➡ About _____ _____ half of the class voted against the rule.

(4) 대중 앞에서 얘기하는 것이 나를 너무 스트레스 받게 해서 나는 시합에 참가할 수 없었다.

➡ I couldn't _____ _____ _____ the contest because speaking in public is too _____ for me.

(5) 나는 검은 차가 사라져 없어진 것을 알았다.

➡ I found out the black car had g_____.

(6) 도로가 젖어 있기 때문에 너는 조심스럽게 운전해야 한다.

➡ You should drive c_____ b_____ _____ the wet road.

06 다음 빈칸에 알맞은 단어를 〈보기〉에서 골라 쓰시오. (형태 변화 가능)

┌─ 보기 ─────────────────────┐
  participate   pick   take   turn
└────────────────────────────┘

(1) Don't forget to _____ off the light.
(2) He _____ up the letter and read it.
(3) Everyone in the class is expected to _____ actively in these discussions.
(4) We need more time to see how things develop before we _____ action.

Conructor 교과서
Conversation

① 걱정 표현하기

> A: I'm worried about global warming. 나는 지구 온난화가 걱정 돼.
> B: Me, too. It's terrible. 나도. 그건 끔찍해.

- 걱정이 된다는 것을 나타내는 표현은 'I'm worried ~.' 또는 'I'm concerned ~.'라고 한다. 걱정이 되는 것은 불안하거나 문제가 있는 것을 나타낼 수 있으므로, 걱정을 나타내는 nervous나 문제를 나타내는 trouble을 써서 'I'm nervous ~.', 'I'm in trouble ~.'이라고 할 수도 있다.

- 걱정이 되는 것이 두려움이나 무서움을 포함하고 있을 때는 scared, frightened, terrified 등을 써서 'I'm scared ~.', 'I'm frightened ~.', 'I'm terrified ~.' 등으로 나타내기도 한다. 이 말에 공감할 때는 'Me, too.(나도 그래.)'라고 한다.

- 걱정이 되는 내용을 덧붙일 때는 전치사 about나 접속사 that을 써서 'I'm worried about ~.' 또는 'I'm worried that ~.'이라고 한다. about 뒤에는 명사, 동명사를 쓰고 that 뒤에는 주어, 동사가 있는 절을 쓰도록 한다.

걱정 표현하기

- I'm worried about ~. (나는 ~가 걱정 돼.)
- I'm nervous about ~. (나는 ~가 불안해.)
- I'm concerned about ~. (나는 ~가 걱정이야.)
- I'm anxious about ~. (나는 ~가 걱정이야.)

핵심 Check

1. 다음 우리말과 일치하도록 빈칸에 알맞은 말을 쓰시오.

> A: _____ (나는 지구 온난화가 걱정돼.)
> B: Me, too. It's terrible.
> A: What can we do to help?
> B: We can use less plastic.

2. 다음 대화의 순서를 바르게 배열하시오.

> (A) Do you know how to reduce air pollution?
> (B) What do you think of this picture?
> (C) I think it's terrible. I'm worried about air pollution.
> (D) Yes. We need to use public transportation.

> ➡ _____

② 방법 묻기

A: Do you know how to do a team project well? 어떻게 조별과제를 잘하는지 아니?

B: Yes. You need to listen carefully to others' opinions. 응. 너는 다른 사람들의 의견을 주의 깊게 들을 필요가 있어.

■ '~하는 방법'은 'how to ~'라고 한다. 방법을 물어볼 때는 'Do you know ~?', 'Would you tell me ~?', 'Could you show me ~?' 등에 'how to ~'를 목적어로 더해서 'Do you know how to ~?' 또는 'Could you tell me how to ~?', 'Would you tell me how to ~?', 'Would you explain to me how to ~?' 등으로 할 수 있다.

■ 대답하는 사람은 방법을 알 때는 'Yes.'라고 한 다음 이어서 방법을 설명해주고, 모를 때는 'No, I don't know.'라고 할 수 있다.

■ 방법을 물어볼 때 좀 더 직접적으로 표현하는 경우에는 'How do I ~?', 'How can I ~?'라고 하거나 'How did you ~?'라고 상대에게 물어볼 수 있다.

방법 묻기

- Do you know how to ~ ? (너는 어떻게 ~하는지 아니?)
- Would you tell me how to ~? (어떻게 ~하는지 말해 줄래?)
- Could you tell me how to ~? (어떻게 ~하는지 말해 줄 수 있니?)
- How do I ~? (어떻게 ~하니?)
- How can I ~? (어떻게 ~할 수 있니?)
- How did you ~? (너는 어떻게 ~했니?)

 핵심 Check

3. 다음 우리말과 일치하도록 주어진 어구를 적절하게 배열하시오.

> A: Can I ask you something?
>
> B: Of course. What is it?
>
> A: (know, how, do, well, a team project, to do, you, ?) (어떻게 조별과제를 잘
> 하는지 아니?)
>
> B: Yes. You need to listen carefully to others' opinions.

➡ _____

Listen and Speak 1 A

B: Jane, ❶what's the matter?

G: My brother ❷broke his leg.

B: Oh, ❸I'm sorry to hear that.

G: ❹I'm worried about him.

B: ❺Don't worry. He'll be okay.

B: Jane, 무슨 일 있니?
G: 내 남동생이 다리가 부러졌어.
B: 오, 그 말을 들으니 안타까워.
G: 동생이 걱정돼.
B: 걱정하지 마. 동생은 괜찮을 거야.

❶ 상대방의 슬픔이나 불만족, 실망의 원인에 대해 물을 때 사용되는 표현으로 'What's the matter?'가 쓰이며 '무슨 일[문제] 있니?'라는 뜻으로 'What's wrong?', 'What's the problem?', 'Is there anything wrong?' 등으로 바꿔 쓸 수 있다.

❷ broke는 break의 과거형으로 '부서지다, 부러지다'의 뜻이다.

❸ 어떤 상황에 대하여 유감이나 동정을 표현할 때 'I'm sorry to hear that.'이라고 말할 수 있다. 이럴 때의 sorry는 미안하다는 의미보다는 '~하게 되어 유감이', '~해서 마음이 아프다' 등의 의미를 가진다.

❹ 어떤 것에 대한 염려나 걱정을 표현할 때 'I'm worried about ~.'으로 표현할 수 있다.

❺ 상대방이 낙담하지 않도록 위로할 때 'Don't worry (about it).', 혹은 'Don't worry too much.' 등으로 말할 수 있다. 'Take it easy.'도 같은 상황에서 사용할 수 있는 표현이다.

Check(√) True or False

(1) Jane's brother hurt his leg.   T ☐ F ☐

(2) The boy is not worried about Jane's brother.   T ☐ F ☐

Listen and Speak 2 A

B: My neck ❶hurts.

G: ❷Be careful not to get text neck.

B: ❸Do you know how to ❹prevent it?

G: Yes. You ❺need to stretch your neck often.

B: Okay, I will. Thanks.

B: 목이 아파.
G: '텍스트넥'이 되지 않도록 조심해.
B: 너는 그걸 막는 방법을 아니?
G: 응. 너는 목을 자주 스트레칭해야 해.
B: 응, 그럴게, 고마워.

❶ hurt: 다치다

❷ 'Be careful not to 동사원형 ~.'은 '~하지 않도록 주의해라'라는 의미로 상대방이 잊어버리지 않도록 중요한 일에 대해 강한 당부 또는 경고하는 의미를 나타낼 수 있다.

❸ 'how to 동사원형'은 '~하는 방법'으로, 'Do you know how to 동사원형 ~?'은 '~하는 방법을 아니?'라는 의미로 상대방에게 방법을 물을 때 사용하는 표현이다.

❹ prevent: 예방하다 / it은 여자아이가 말한 text neck을 받는 대명사이다.

❺ 상대방에게 어떤 것을 하라고 조언할 경우에는 'You need to 동사원형 ~.'으로 말할 수 있다. need to 대신에 should나 had better를 사용할 수도 있다.

Check(√) True or False

(3) The boy's neck is broken.   T ☐ F ☐

(4) The boy will stretch his neck often to prevent text neck.   T ☐ F ☐

Listen and Speak 1 B

G: ❶Are you ready for our soccer game today, Sam?

B: Kathy, didn't you see the news?

G: No, I didn't. What did it say?

B: The yellow dust is terrible today.

G: Oh, no. ❷Yellow dust can cause many health problems.

B: Yeah, ❸I'm worried about our health.

G: We can play another day.

B: ❹You're right. I'll ❺text the other team members ❻right now.

G: Great idea.

G: 오늘 축구 경기를 할 준비가 됐니, Sam?

B: Kathy, 뉴스 못 봤니?

G: 응, 못 봤어. 뉴스에서 뭐라고 했니?

B: 오늘 황사가 정말 심각하대.

G: 오, 안 돼. 황사는 많은 건강상의 문제를 일으킬 수 있어.

B: 응, 나는 우리의 건강이 걱정돼.

G: 우리 다른 날 경기를 할 수도 있잖아.

B: 맞아. 내가 당장 다른 팀원들에게 문자를 보낼게.

G: 좋은 생각이야.

❶ ready: 준비된 'be ready' 다음에는 'to 동사원형'이나 'for (동)명사'가 주로 나온다. ready 대신에 prepared(준비된)로 바꿔 사용할 수도 있다.

❷ yellow dust: 황사 cause: 유발하다

❸ 'I'm worried about ~.'은 걱정을 나타내는 표현으로 전치사 about 뒤에는 명사나 대명사, 동명사를 써서 '나는 ~에 대해 걱정한다.'라는 의미를 나타낸다.

❹ 상대방의 의견에 동의하는 말로 'I feel the same way.'로 바꿔 말할 수 있다.

❺ text: (휴대전화로) 문자를 보내다

❻ right now: 지금 당장

Check(√) True or False

(5) After the conversation, they are going to play soccer.　　　　T ☐ F ☐

(6) The yellow dust is not good for the health.　　　　T ☐ F ☐

Real Life Talk Step 2

A: ❶What do you think of this picture?

B: ❷I think it's terrible. ❸I'm worried about air pollution.

A: ❹Do you know how to ❺reduce air pollution?

B: Yes. We ❻need to use public transportation.

A: 이 그림에 대해 어떻게 생각하니?

B: 끔찍하다고 생각해. 나는 공기 오염이 걱정돼.

A: 공기 오염을 줄이는 방법을 아니?

B: 응. 우리는 대중교통을 이용할 필요가 있어.

❶ 무언가에 대하여 상대방의 의견을 물을 때 'What do you think of ~?'를 사용할 수 있다. 'of' 대신에 'about'을 사용할 수도 있다.

❷ think와 it's 사이에 접속사 that이 생략되어 있다. it은 this picture를 받는 대명사이다.

❸ be worried about: ~에 대해 걱정하다 pollution: 오염

❹ 상대방에게 방법을 물을 때 'Do you know how to 동사원형 ~?'을 사용하여 물어볼 수 있다.

❺ reduce: 줄이다

❻ need to(~해야 한다)를 이용해 조언을 하고 있다. need to 대신에 should를 사용할 수 있다.

Check(√) True or False

(7) To use public transportation can reduce air pollution.　　　　T ☐ F ☐

(8) B knows how to reduce air pollution.　　　　T ☐ F ☐

Listen and Speak 1 C

A: ❶I'm worried about global warming.

B: Me, too. It's ❷terrible.

A: ❸What can we do to help?

B: We can use ❹less plastic.

❶ be worried about:: ~에 대해 걱정하다 global warming: 지구 온난화
❷ terrible: 끔찍한, 좋지 않은
❸ 지구 온난화를 돕기 위해서 무엇을 할지 충고를 구하는 말이다. 'What can we do to help?' 대신에 'What should we do to help?'나 'What do you think we should do?' 등을 사용할 수 있다.
❹ less는 여기서 plastic을 수식하는 형용사로 사용되어 '더 적은'의 의미다.

Listen and Speak 2 B

G: Jinsu, ❶did you know that polar bears are ❷in danger?

B: Yes. I read about it in an ❸article. ❹It's because of global warming.

G: Right. Their homes are ❺melting away and their food is disappearing.

B: We should do something about it.

G: ❻Do you know how to ❼slow down global warming?

B: Well, we can start ❽by saving energy.

G: Right. We need to turn off the lights when we leave the room.

B: That's a good idea.

❶ 상대방에게 아는 내용을 확인하는 표현으로 'Did you know that ~?'은 '너는 ~를 아니?'의 의미이다. that은 접속사로 뒤에 주어와 동사가 온다.
❷ in danger: 위기에 처하여
❸ article: 기사
❹ 'It's because of ~.'를 이용해 앞에 말한 북극곰이 위험에 처한 이유에 대해 말하고 있다.
❺ melt away: 차츰 사라지다
❻ 'Do you know how to ~?'는 '너는 ~하는 방법을 아니?'의 의미로 상대방에게 방법을 물을 때 사용할 수 있다.
❼ slow down: [속도·진행]을 늦추다
❽ by 동명사: ~함으로써

Listen and Speak 2 C 1

A: Can I ask you something?

B: Of course. What is it?

A: ❶Do you know how to do a team project well?

B: Yes. ❷You need to listen ❸carefully to others' opinions.

❶ 'Do you know how to 동사원형 ~?'은 '~하는 방법을 아니?'라는 의미로 상대방에게 방법을 물을 때 사용하는 표현이다. 바꿔 쓸 수 있는 말로 'Would[Could] you tell me how to ~?(어떻게 ~하는지 말해줄래?)', 'How can I ~?' 등이 있다.
❷ need to 동사원형: ~할 필요가 있다
❸ carefully는 '주의하여, 신중히'의 의미로 동사 listen to를 수식하고 있다.

Real Life Talk Step 1

Minho: Linda, did you see the TV program, *The Sick Planet*?

Linda: Yes, I did. ❶I'm worried about our planet.

Minho: Me, too. We should ❷take action to save the Earth.

Linda: You're right. Hey! ❸Why don't we ❹participate in Earth Hour?

Minho: Earth Hour? What's that?

Linda: It's a world ❺movement for the environment.

Minho: Sounds great! ❻Do you know how to take part in it?

Linda: Sure. We ❼turn off our lights together for an hour.

Minho: That's so simple! So, when do we do it?

Linda: I'm not sure. It's different every year.

Minho: Let's ❽look it up on the Internet.

❶ 어떤 것에 대한 염려나 걱정을 말할 때 'be worried about(~에 대해 걱정한다)'을 이용하여 말할 수 있다. worried 대신에 concerned, nervous, anxious를 사용할 수 있다.
❷ take action: [~하기 위한] 조치를 취하다, 행동을 취하다
❸ 상대방에게 '함께 ~하자'는 표현으로 'Why don't we 동사원형 ~?'을 사용할 수 있다.
❹ participate in: ~에 참가하다
❺ movement: (~을 위한) (정치적·사회적) 운동
❻ 상대방에게 방법을 물을 때 'Do you know how to 동사원형 ~?'을 사용하여 물어볼 수 있다. take part in: ~에 참여하다
❼ turn off: [등불·라디오·텔레비전을] 끄다 for an hour: 한 시간 동안
❽ look something up: (사전, 컴퓨터 등에서 정보를) 검색하다, 찾아보다

● 다음 우리말과 일치하도록 빈칸에 알맞은 말을 쓰시오.

Listen and Speak 1 A

B: Jane, _____ the matter?

G: My brother _____ his leg.

B: Oh, _____ _____ to hear that.

G: I'm _____ about him.

B: _____ worry. He'll be okay.

 해석

B: Jane, 무슨 일 있니?
G: 내 남동생이 다리가 부러졌어.
B: 오, 그 말을 들으니 안타까워.
G: 동생이 걱정돼.
B: 걱정하지 마. 동생은 괜찮을 거야.

Listen and Speak 1 B

G: Are you _____ _____ our soccer game today, Sam?

B: Kathy, didn't you see the news?

G: No, I _____. What did it say?

B: The yellow dust is terrible today.

G: Oh, no. _____ _____ can cause many _____ problems.

B: Yeah, _____ _____ _____ our health.

G: We can play _____ day.

B: You're right. I'll _____ _____ _____ team members _____ now.

G: Great idea.

G: 오늘 축구 경기를 할 준비가 됐니, Sam?
B: Kathy, 뉴스 못 봤어?
G: 응, 못 봤어. 뉴스에서 뭐라고 했니?
B: 오늘 황사가 정말 심각하대.
G: 오, 안 돼. 황사는 많은 건강상의 문제를 일으킬 수 있어.
B: 응, 나는 우리의 건강이 걱정돼.
G: 우리 다른 날 경기를 할 수도 있잖아.
B: 맞아. 내가 당장 다른 팀원들에게 문자를 보낼게.
G: 좋은 생각이야.

Listen and Speak 1 C

1. A: _____ _____ about global warming.

   B: Me, too. It's _____.

   A: _____ can we do to help?

   B: We can use _____ plastic.

2. A: I'm _____ _____ _____ bees.

   B: Me, too. It's _____.

   A: _____ _____ we do to help?

   B: We can _____ _____ trees for them.

3. A: _____ _____ _____ hungry children in Africa.

   B: Me, too. It's terrible.

   A: _____ _____ _____ _____ to help?

   B: We can _____ money _____ them.

1. A: 나는 지구 온난화가 걱정돼.
   B: 나도. 그건 끔찍해.
   A: 우리가 돕기 위해 무엇을 할 수 있을까?
   B: 우리가 플라스틱을 덜 사용할 수 있어.

2. A: 나는 사라지는 벌들이 걱정돼.
   B: 나도. 그건 끔찍해.
   A: 우리가 돕기 위해 무엇을 할 수 있을까?
   B: 우리가 더 많은 나무들을 심을 수 있어.

3. A: 나는 아프리카의 배고픈 아이들이 걱정돼.
   B: 나도. 그건 끔찍해.
   A: 우리가 돕기 위해 무엇을 할 수 있을까?
   B: 우리가 그들에게 돈을 기부할 수 있어.

Listen and Speak 2 A

B: My neck _____.

G: Be _____ _____ _____ get text neck.

B: _____ _____ _____ _____ _____ prevent it?

G: Yes. You need _____ _____ your neck often.

B: Okay, I will. Thanks.

Listen and Speak 2 B

G: Jinsu, did you _____ _____ polar bears are in danger?

B: Yes. I read about it in an article. _____ _____ _____ global warming.

G: Right. Their homes _____ _____ _____ and their food is _____.

B: We should do _____ _____ it.

G: Do you know _____ _____ _____ _____ _____ _____?

B: Well, we can start _____ _____ energy.

G: Right. We _____ _____ _____ _____ the lights _____ we _____ the room.

B: That's a good idea.

Listen and Speak 2 C 1

A: _____ I ask you something?

B: Of course. What is it?

A: _____ _____ _____ _____ to do a team project well?

B: Yes. You need _____ listen _____ to others' _____.

Listen and Speak 2 C 2

A: Can I ask you something?

B: Of course. What is it?

A: Do you _____ _____ _____ _____ water?

B: Yes. You _____ _____ _____ the water _____ you brush _____ teeth.

해석

B: 목이 아파.
G: '텍스트넥'이 되지 않도록 조심해.
B: 너는 그걸 막는 방법을 아니?
G: 응. 너는 목을 자주 스트레칭해야 해.
B: 응, 그럴게. 고마워.

G: 진수야, 너는 북극곰이 위험에 처해 있다는 걸 알고 있었니?
B: 응. 기사에서 그것에 관해 읽었어. 그건 지구 온난화 때문이야.
G: 맞아. 그들의 서식지가 녹아 없어지고 있고 그들의 먹이는 사라지고 있어.
B: 우리는 그것과 관련해 뭔가를 해야 해.
G: 너는 지구 온난화를 늦추는 방법을 아니?
B: 음, 우리는 에너지를 절약하는 것부터 시작할 수 있어.
G: 맞아. 우리는 방을 나올 때 불을 꺼야 해.
B: 좋은 생각이야.

A: 뭐 좀 물어봐도 되니?
B: 물론이지. 뭔데?
A: 어떻게 조별과제를 잘하는지 아니?
B: 응. 너는 다른 사람들의 의견을 주의 깊게 들을 필요가 있어.

A: 뭐 좀 물어봐도 되니?
B: 물론이지. 뭔데?
A: 물을 절약하는 방법을 아니?
B: 응. 양치질을 할 때 물을 끌 필요가 있어.

Listen and Speak 2 C 3

A: Can I _____ you something?

B: Of course. What is it?

A: Do you know _____ _____ _____ healthy?

B: Yes. You need _____ _____ _____ fast food.

A: 뭐 좀 물어봐도 되니?
B: 물론이지. 뭔데?
A: 너는 건강하게 먹는 방법을 아니?
B: 응. 패스트 푸드를 덜 먹을 필요가 있어.

Real Life Talk Step 1

Minho: Linda, _____ _____ _____ the TV program, *The Sick Planet*?

Linda: Yes, I _____. _____ _____ _____ our planet.

Minho: Me, too. We _____ _____ _____ _____ save the Earth.

Linda: You're right. Hey! Why _____ _____ _____ _____ Earth Hour?

Minho: Earth Hour? What's that?

Linda: It's a world _____ for the environment.

Minho: Sounds great! _____ _____ _____ _____ _____ _____ _____ _____ it?

Linda: Sure. We turn _____ our lights _____ _____ an hour.

Minho: That's so _____! So, _____ do we do it?

Linda: I'm not sure. It's _____ every year.

Minho: Let's _____ _____ _____ on the Internet.

민호: Linda, '병든 행성'이라는 TV 프로그램 봤니?
Linda: 응, 봤어. 나는 우리 지구가 걱정돼.
민호: 나도. 우리는 지구를 구하기 위해 조치를 취해야 해.
Linda: 맞아. 얘! 우리 'Earth Hour'에 참여하는 게 어때?
민호: 'Earth Hour'? 그게 뭐니?
Linda: 그건 환경을 위한 세계적인 운동이야.
민호: 좋을 거 같아! 그것에 참여하는 방법을 아니?
Linda: 물론이야. 한 시간 동안 전등들을 함께 끄는 거야.
민호: 정말 간단하네! 그러면 언제 그것을 하는 거니?
Linda: 잘 모르겠어. 그건 매년 달라.
민호: 인터넷에서 찾아보자.

Real Life Talk Step 2

A: _____ _____ _____ _____ of this picture?

B: I think it's _____. _____ _____ _____ air pollution.

A: _____ _____ _____ _____ _____ _____ _____ air pollution?

B: Yes. We _____ _____ use _____ _____.

A: 이 그림에 대해 어떻게 생각하니?
B: 끔찍하다고 생각해. 나는 공기 오염이 걱정돼.
A: 공기 오염을 줄이는 방법을 아니?
B: 응. 우리는 대중교통을 이용할 필요가 있어.

01 다음 대화의 밑줄 친 부분과 바꿔 쓸 수 있는 것은?

> B: My neck hurts.
> G: Be careful not to get text neck.
> B: <u>Do you know how to prevent it?</u>
> G: Yes. You need to stretch your neck often.
> B: Okay, I will. Thanks.

① What do I need to prevent it?

② Could you tell me how to prevent it?

③ Do you know if it is possible to prevent?

④ What do you think of preventing it?

⑤ Can I teach you how to prevent it?

02 다음 밑줄 친 ⓐ~ⓔ 중 흐름상 또는 어법상 어색한 것을 고르시오.

> A: ⓐ<u>Can I ask you something?</u>
> B: Of course. ⓑ<u>What is it?</u>
> A: ⓒ<u>Do you know</u> ⓓ<u>why to save</u> water?
> B: Yes. ⓔ<u>You need to</u> turn off the water when you brush your teeth.

① ⓐ   ② ⓑ   ③ ⓒ   ④ ⓓ   ⑤ ⓔ

03 다음 주어진 문장 이후에 올 대화의 순서를 바르게 배열한 것을 고르시오.

> What do you think of this picture?

> (A) Do you know how to reduce air pollution?
> (B) I think it's terrible. I'm worried about air pollution.
> (C) Yes. We need to use public transportation.

① (A) – (C) – (B)   ② (B) – (A) – (C)   ③ (B) – (C) – (A)

④ (C) – (A) – (B)   ⑤ (C) – (B) – (A)

[01~03] 다음 대화를 읽고 물음에 답하시오.

G: Are you ready for our soccer game today, Sam?
B: Kathy, didn't you see the news?
G: No, I didn't. (①)
B: The yellow dust is terrible today.
G: Oh, no. Yellow dust can cause many health problems. (②)
B: Yeah, I'm (A)_____ about our health. (③)
G: We can play another day. (④)
B: You're right. (⑤) I'll text the other team members right now.
G: Great idea.

01 위 대화의 ①~⑤ 중 주어진 문장이 들어갈 알맞은 곳은?

> What did it say?

① ② ③ ④ ⑤

02 빈칸 (A)에 알맞은 말을 고르시오.

① popular ② excited
③ pleased ④ embarrassed
⑤ worried

03 위 대화의 내용과 일치하지 <u>않는</u> 것은?

① 뉴스에서 오늘 황사가 심하다고 말했다.
② Kathy는 뉴스를 보지 않았다.
③ Sam은 다른 축구 구성원들에게 전화를 해서 다른 날 축구하자고 말할 것이다.
④ 오늘은 원래 축구 경기를 할 예정이었다.
⑤ 황사는 건강에 해로운 영향을 끼친다.

04 다음 대화의 빈칸에 알맞은 것을 고르시오.

A: Can I ask you something?
B: Of course. What is it?
A: _____
B: Yes. You need to turn off the water when you brush your teeth.

① How did you save water?
② Should we save water?
③ Do you know how to save water?
④ Have you ever saved water?
⑤ Will you save water?

[05~07] 다음 대화를 읽고 물음에 답하시오.

G: Jinsu, did you know that polar bears are in danger?
B: Yes. I read about it in an article. (①)
G: Right. Their homes are melting away and their food is disappearing.
B: We should do something about it. (②)
G: Do you know how (A)_____ global warming? (③)
B: Well, we can start by saving energy. (④)
G: Right. (⑤) We need to turn off the lights when we leave the room.
B: That's a good idea.

05 위 대화의 ①~⑤ 중 주어진 문장이 들어갈 알맞은 곳은?

> It's because of global warming.

① ② ③ ④ ⑤

06 빈칸 (A)에 알맞은 말을 고르시오.

① to cause ② causing
③ to speed up ④ to slow down
⑤ slowing down

07 위 대화를 읽고 답할 수 없는 질문을 고르시오.

① Why are polar bears in danger?

② What will they do to save water?

③ Does Jinsu know the way to delay global warming?

④ How did Jinsu know that polar bears are in danger?

⑤ How does global warming affect polar bears?

08 다음 중 짝지어진 대화가 어색한 것은?

① A: Do you know how to take this medicine?

B: No, how should I take it?

A: Take the medicine after a meal with water.

② A: Do you know how to take part in this competition?

B: Sure. Go ahead.

③ A: Do you know how to open this can?

B: Let me try.

④ A: Do you know how to ski?

B: No, I don't. But I want to learn.

⑤ A: Do you know how to read ten books a month?

B: Well, I guess it depends on how difficult the books would be.

서답형
09 다음 대화의 빈칸에 들어갈 말을 〈보기〉에서 골라 순서대로 바르게 배열하시오.

> Minho: Linda, did you see the TV program, *The Sick Planet*?
>
> Linda: Yes, I did. I'm worried about our planet.

Minho: Me, too. We should take action to save the Earth.

Linda: _____

Minho: _____

Linda: _____

Minho: _____

Linda: _____

Minho: That's so simple! So, when do we do it?

Linda: I'm not sure. It's different every year.

Minho: Let's look it up on the Internet.

┤ 보기 ├
(A) Earth Hour? What's that?

(B) Sounds great! Do you know how to take part in it?

(C) Sure. We turn off our lights together for an hour.

(D) You're right. Hey! Why don't we participate in Earth Hour?

(E) It's a world movement for the environment.

➡ _____

 10 다음 대화의 빈칸에 알맞은 말을 고르시오.

> A: _____
>
> B: Me, too. It's terrible.
>
> A: What can we do to help?
>
> B: We can use less plastic.

① I'm scared of polar bears.

② I'm nervous about my English test.

③ I'm worried about global warming.

④ I'm nervous of the next soccer game.

⑤ I'm concerned about health problems.

[01~02] 주어진 단어를 문맥에 맞게 고쳐 빈칸을 채우시오.

01

A: I'm worried about _____ (appear) bees.
B: Me, too. It's terrible.
A: What can we do to help?
B: We can plant more trees for them.

➡ _____

02

B: My neck hurts.
G: Be careful not (A)_____(get) text neck.
B: Do you know how (B)_____(prevent) it?
G: Yes. You need (C)_____(stretch) your neck often.
B: Okay, I will. Thanks.

➡ (A)_____ (B)_____ (C)_____

[03~04] 다음 대화를 읽고 물음에 답하시오.

G: Jinsu, did you know that polar bears are in danger?
B: Yes. I read about it in an article. It's because (A)_____ global warming.
G: Right. Their homes are melting away and their food is disappearing.
B: We should do something about it.
G: ⓐ_____ (down, warming, know, global, do, slow, to, you, how)

B: Well, we can start (B)_____ saving energy.
G: Right. We need to turn off the lights when we leave the room.
B: That's a good idea.

03 빈칸 (A)와 (B)에 알맞은 전치사를 쓰시오.

➡ (A) _____ (B) _____

04 빈칸 ⓐ를 괄호 안에 주어진 단어를 알맞게 배열하여 채우시오.

➡ _____

[05~06] 다음 대화를 읽고 물음에 답하시오.

A: (A)_____ do you think of this picture?
B: I think it's terrible. 나는 공기오염이 걱정돼.
A: Do you know (B)_____ to reduce air pollution?
B: Yes. We need to use public transportation.

05 빈칸 (A)와 (B)에 알맞은 의문사를 쓰시오.

➡ (A) _____ (B) _____

06 밑줄 친 우리말을 주어진 단어를 이용하여 영작하시오.

➡ _____ (worry)

Grammar

교과서

① 부분을 나타내는 말의 수의 일치

- About **a third of the bee population dies** every year. 벌 개체 수의 약 3분의 1 정도가 매년 죽는다.
- **Half of the teenagers in the U.S. have** their own bedrooms. 미국의 10대들 중 반이 자신의 침실을 갖고 있습니다.

■ 부분을 나타내는 말은 뒤에 오는 명사의 수에 따라 그 수가 결정된다.
※ 부분을 나타내는 말+단수 명사: 단수 동사
　부분을 나타내는 말+복수 명사: 복수 동사

- **Some of the milk was** spilled. 우유가 조금 엎질러졌다.

- **Some of Beethoven's early works are** an echo of Mozart. 베토벤의 초기 작품의 어떤 것들은 모차르트의 모방이다.

■ 부분을 나타내는 말에는 most of, some of, the rest of, part of, half of, one-third of, two-thirds of 등이 있다.

- **Most of my friends are** married. 제 친구들 대부분은 결혼했어요.

- **The greater part of the land** still **lies** waste. 그 토지의 대부분은 아직도 황무지이다.

cf. 1. many of/(a) few of/a number of+복수 명사+복수 동사
　　　much of/(a) little of/+단수 명사+단수 동사
　　　the number of+복수 명사+단수 동사

- **Many of the seats are** unoccupied. 많은 좌석이 비었다.

- **Very little of the furniture was** saved in the recent fire. 최근의 화재에서 건진 가구라곤 거의 없다.

cf. 2. one of+복수 명사+단수 동사

- **One of the boys is** hurt. 그 소년들 중 한 명이 다쳤다.

핵심 Check

1. 다음 괄호 안에 주어진 어휘를 빈칸에 현재형으로 알맞게 쓰시오.

(1) The rest of the animal's coat ＿＿＿＿＿ white. (be)

(2) A few of them ＿＿＿＿＿ it. (know)

(3) Two-thirds of an apple ＿＿＿＿＿ smaller than three-fourths. (be)

② 조동사가 있는 문장의 수동태

> • Honey from ancient Egypt **can be eaten** today. 고대 이집트 때의 꿀은 오늘날에도 먹을 수 있다.

■ 수동태는 행위자보다는 행위의 대상에 중점을 두고 말할 때 쓰며, 조동사가 있는 문장의 수동태는 '조동사+be+과거분사'의 형태로 나타낸다.
- She must write the report by tomorrow. 그녀는 그 보고서를 내일까지 써야 한다.
  → The report **must be written** by her by tomorrow. 그 보고서는 그녀에 의해 내일까지 쓰여져야 한다.

■ 부정문은 '조동사+not+be+과거분사'의 형태로, 의문문은 '조동사+주어+be+과거분사 ~?'의 형태로 쓴다.
- The product **must not be reused**, **cleaned**, or **reprocessed**. 그 제품은 재사용, 세척 또는 재처리되어서는 안 됩니다.
- **Can** it **be supported** both in theory and in practice? 그것은 이론과 실제에서 둘 다 지지될 수 있나요?

cf. 1. 수동태 구문에서 행위자가 일반인이거나 강조할 필요가 없을 때에는 'by+행위자'를 생략하고 쓸 수 있다.
- It **can be used** as a pillow. 그것은 베개로 사용될 수 있습니다.

cf. 2. 수동태로 쓰지 않는 동사
  자동사는 목적어가 없으므로 수동태로 쓸 수 없으며 '상태'나 '소유'를 나타내는 타동사도 수동태로 쓰이지 않음에 주의해야 한다.
- The accident **happened** last night. 그 사고는 어젯밤에 일어났다.
  The accident was happened last night. (×)
- He has a nice smart phone.
  A nice smart phone is had by him. (×)

핵심 Check

2. 다음 우리말과 일치하도록 주어진 어휘를 이용하여 빈칸에 알맞게 쓰시오.
  (1) 우리들의 권익은 보호되어야 한다. (must, protect)
   ➡ Our rights and interests _____ _____ _____.
  (2) 그 일을 즉시 하도록 권합니다. (should, do)
   ➡ I recommend that the work _____ _____ _____ at once.

01 다음 빈칸에 알맞은 것을 고르시오.

> Some of her family members _____ angry.

① being   ② to be   ③ is

④ are   ⑤ been

02 다음 문장을 수동태로 고쳤을 때 알맞은 것은?

> He can finish a full marathon.

① A full marathon can finish him.

② A full marathon is finished by him.

③ A full marathon be finished by him.

④ A full marathon can finished by him.

⑤ A full marathon can be finished by him.

03 다음 중 어법상 <u>어색한</u> 것은?

① Most of the world uses the metric system of measurement.

② Only the half of it has been sold.

③ One third of all votes was left blank.

④ What two things should be done at the same time?

⑤ The school year book will be published soon.

04 다음 괄호 안의 어휘를 바르게 배열하시오.

(1) Supplies for use at home (purchased, be, must).

➡ _____

(2) People (be, not, should, allowed) to watch TV while driving.

➡ _____

(3) (disease, cured, can, the, be)?

➡ _____

 01 다음 중 어법상 바른 것은?

① Part of that apple are rotten.
② Two thirds of the length of your tooth is in the gum.
③ Twelve percent of all Internet sites uses pop-up ads.
④ About one third of the milk were spilled.
⑤ Most of the earth's surface are water.

02 다음 중 어법상 바르지 <u>않은</u> 것은?

① Many weather effects have to specially created.
② School fees should be paid by the due date.
③ Honey from ancient Egypt can be eaten today.
④ Supplies for use at home must be purchased.
⑤ Agricultural products will be used in many ways.

03 다음 대화의 빈칸에 들어갈 말로 알맞은 것은?

> M: Their homes are melting away and their food is disappearing.
> B: Something _____ .

① does
② is do
③ should do
④ should done
⑤ should be done

04 다음 괄호 안에서 알맞은 말을 고르시오.

(1) About a third of the bee population (die / dies) every year.
(2) A quarter of a dollar (are / is) 25 cents.
(3) Only a few of us (know / knows) them all.
(4) One of my friends (try / tries) to bring disgrace on me.
(5) This ensures that your entire collection (will is / will be) protected.
(6) It (can be not / cannot be) completed in an ordinary way.
(7) Please don't forget that you must (appear / be appeared) tomorrow.
(8) She (resembles / is resembled) her mother in some way.

05 다음 우리말에 맞게 괄호 안에 주어진 어휘를 이용하여 영작하시오.

> 이 여자들의 4분의 3 이상이 20대였습니다.
> (quarter, women, their 20s, more, these, be, in)

➡ _____
_____

서답형

06 다음 우리말과 일치하도록 주어진 어휘를 이용하여 빈칸에 알맞게 쓰시오.

(1) 그는 여생을 안락하게 보냈다. (be)
➡ The rest of his days _____ spent in comfort.

(2) 옆방에서 사람들의 말소리가 들려온다. (can, hear)
➡ The voices of people in the next room _____ _____ _____.

(3) 한 번에 두 계단씩 올라가야 한다. (should, climb)
➡ Stairs _____ _____ _____ two at a time.

07 다음 빈칸에 알맞은 말이 바르게 짝지어진 것은?

> • Around half of Cambodia's population _____ under the age of 15.
> • Any remains of Navajo settlement should _____.

① are – not be disturbed
② are – be not disturbed
③ is – not be disturbed
④ is – be not disturbed
⑤ be – disturbed not be

08 다음 우리말에 맞도록 빈칸에 들어갈 알맞은 것은?

> 도서관은 깨끗하게 유지되어야 한다.
> = The library _____ clean.

① keeps   ② should keep
③ should kept   ④ should be kept
⑤ should be keep

09 다음 우리말을 바르게 영작한 것을 고르시오.

> 건물들 대부분은 페인트 칠을 다시 해야 합니다.

① Most of the buildings needs repainting.
② Most of the buildings need repainting.
③ Most of the buildings need to repaint.
④ Most of the buildings needs to repaint.
⑤ Most of the buildings needs repaint.

서답형

10 주어진 어휘를 이용하여 다음 우리말을 영작하시오.

> 사람들은 대부분의 주에서 일하기 위해서 면허를 취득해야만 한다. (have, be, work, license, in most states)

➡ _____

11 다음 두 문장을 한 문장으로 연결할 때 가장 적절한 것은?

> • He made a visit to many cities.
> • He visited Seoul.

① He made a visit to Seoul is one of the cities.
② He visited Seoul that he made a visit to the cities.
③ He made a visit to many cities that Seoul is.
④ One of the cities he made a visit to is Seoul.
⑤ One of the cities which he made a visit to are Seoul.

12 다음 문장을 수동태로 바르게 바꾼 것을 고르시오.

> They will finish another connection to Seoul by 2025.

① They will be finished another connection to Seoul by 2025.

② They will have finished another connection to Seoul by 2025.

③ Another connection to Seoul will finish by 2025.

④ Another connection to Seoul will have finished by 2025.

⑤ Another connection to Seoul will be finished by 2025.

13 다음 빈칸에 들어갈 말이 나머지와 다른 하나는?

① Half of the money _____ stolen.

② About 23 percent of the lost items last year _____ handbags.

③ Some of the parking lots _____ under construction.

④ Most of the houses _____ burnt down in a big fire.

⑤ The rest of the passengers _____ missing.

14 다음 문장의 빈칸에 들어갈 말로 알맞은 것은?

> Last night not a few of the members _____ present.

① has been   ② had been

③ were   ④ was

⑤ is

15 다음 중 어법상 어색한 것을 고르시오. (2개)

① My e-mail address will be remained unchanged.

② Please wait. Your dish will be served soon.

③ These homeless children must be looked after.

④ Three fifths of the money are paid wrongly.

⑤ The greater part of the students have gone home.

16 다음 문장에서 어법상 어색한 것을 바르게 고쳐 다시 쓰시오.

(1) Two-thirds of the country are covered with forest.

➡ _____

(2) Much of the country are covered by forest.

➡ _____

(3) About a quarter of the callers is female.

➡ _____

(4) This homework must finish by tomorrow.

➡ _____

(5) The change will be occurred in April next year.

➡ _____

(6) The word is can find in the dictionary.

➡ _____

01 다음을 수동태 문장으로 바꿔 쓰시오.

(1) All participants should hand in the report by May 18.

➡ _____

_____

(2) They may hold the event at a school or in a park.

➡ _____

_____

(3) We must eat a lot of vegetables and fruits.

➡ _____

_____

(4) I have to walk my pet dog after supper.

➡ _____

_____

02 다음 우리말에 맞게 주어진 단어에 한 단어를 추가하여 바르게 배열하시오.

(1) 인생은 항해에 비유할 수 있다. (life, a voyage, may, compared, to)

➡ _____

(2) 그것은 언제 출시될 예정이죠? (going, when, on the market, it, be, is, put)?

➡ _____

(3) 주요 등장인물들은 다음과 같다. (some, here, main characters, the, of)

➡ _____

(4) 인터넷 사용자 수가 정말로 증가하고 있습니다. (number, growing, the, Internet users, really, of)

➡ _____

03 그림을 보고, 주어진 어휘를 이용하여 빈칸을 알맞게 채우시오.

(1) Some _____. (the water, spill, of)

(2) It _____ in secret. (must, keep)

04 괄호 안에 주어진 말을 이용하여 어법에 맞게 문장을 완성하시오.

(1) Much of the time _____. (waste)

(2) The bottom half of the fifth inning _____. (have, begin)

05 다음 문장에서 어법상 <u>어색한</u> 것을 바르게 고쳐 다시 쓰시오.

(1) A quarter of the money were spent on books.

➡ _____

(2) A number of fish was flopping on the deck.

➡ _____

(3) A little of her personal touch were needed to him.

➡ _____

(4) The field might destroy because of the cold.

➡ _____

(5) Cultural change can be happened for three different reasons.

➡ _____

_____

(6) The fact has to treat as a top secret.

➡ _____

06 다음에 주어진 어휘를 이용하여 문장을 완성하시오.

(1) (spend)

➡ The rest of his life _____ in wandering about Europe.

(2) (will, send)

➡ Catalogs of our books _____ on request.

07 다음 우리말을 괄호 안에 주어진 어휘를 이용하여 영작하시오.

(1) 대부분의 학생들은 귀가했다. (greater, the, student, part, go, have, the, 9 단어)

➡ _____

(2) 그들 대부분은 하루 종일 책상에 앉아 있다. (a desk, most, behind, sit, 9 단어)

➡ _____

(3) 그들이 먹는 음식의 약 절반이 몸을 따뜻하게 하는 데 사용됩니다. (the food, eat, keep, use, be, warm, about, 13 단어)

➡ _____

(4) 병은 초기에 치료하여야 한다. (beginning, disease, should, very, treat, the, at, 8 단어)

➡ _____

(5) 그의 침묵은 동의하는 것으로 보일 수 있다. (silence, agreement, read, can, as, 7 단어)

➡ _____

08 주어진 두 문장을 〈보기〉처럼 하나의 문장으로 쓰시오.

┌─ 보기 ─┐

• Charles ordered an apple juice.
• Dan drank about half of it.
→ About half of the apple juice Charles ordered was drunken by Dan.

(1) • Emily bought a potato pizza.
• Hannah ate about two thirds of it.

➡ _____

_____

(2) • Tom has story books.
• Bob can read some of them.

➡ _____

_____

Reading

Disappearing Bees

Where have all the honey bees gone? It is really hard to see them
these days. The bees are disappearing! About a third of the bee
population dies every year. This is bad news for bees, but it's even
worse news for people.

Bees are very helpful to humans. First, bees give us honey.
Honey is a truly wonderful food. It is good for our health and tastes
great. Honey can last almost forever. In fact, honey from ancient
Egypt can be eaten today! Second, bees help produce many crops
such as apples and strawberries. These crops cannot be produced by
themselves. They need the help of bees. Bees help in the process of
pollination.

How bees help pollination

• **What is pollination?**

It is moving pollen from one flower to another to make seeds.

• **What is pollen?**

It is a fine yellow powder produced by flowers.

these days 요즘
helpful 도움이 되는
last 지속되다
forever 영원히
population 인구, 개체 수
ancient 고대의
produce 생산하다, (식물이 열매 등을)
맺다
crop (농)작물
process 과정
pollination 수분 (작용)
pollen 꽃가루, 화분
seed 씨, 씨앗

📎 확인문제

● 다음 문장이 본문의 내용과 일치하면 T, 일치하지 않으면 F를 쓰시오.

1 About a third of the bee population dies every year. ☐

2 Bees are very harmful to humans. ☐

3 Honey is good for our health and tastes great. ☐

4 Many crops such as apples and strawberries can be produced by themselves. ☐

5 Pollination is moving pollen from one flower to another to make seeds. ☐

6 Pollen is a big yellow powder produced by flowers. ☐

Why are bees disappearing? One of the reasons is climate change.
Global warming has brought extremely hot and cold weather. Bees cannot survive in these conditions. Another reason is the harmful chemicals farmers use on crops. These chemicals kill not only bad insects, but also good insects, like bees.

Then what can we do to help our little yellow friends? First, we can plant more flowers and trees. This will provide a good environment for bees to live in. Also, trees help slow down global warming.

Second, the use of harmful chemicals on crops must be stopped. These chemicals are unhealthy for bees and people. Our little friends need our help. Let's not let them down!

climate 기후
extremely 극단적으로, 극도로
survive 살아남다, 생존하다
conditions (복수형으로) 환경, 상황
harmful 해로운
chemical 화학 물질[제품]
provide 제공하다, 주다
unhealthy 건강에 좋지 않은
let ~ down ~를 실망시키다

확인문제

● 다음 문장이 본문의 내용과 일치하면 T, 일치하지 않으면 F를 쓰시오.

1 One of the reasons bees are disappearing is climate change. ☐

2 Bees can survive in extremely hot and cold weather. ☐

3 The harmful chemicals farmers use on crops kill not only bad insects, but also good insects, like bees. ☐

4 There is nothing we can do to help bees. ☐

5 Planting more flowers and trees will provide a good environment for bees to live in. ☐

6 The harmful chemicals are unhealthy for bees, but not for people. ☐

● 우리말을 참고하여 빈칸에 알맞은 말을 쓰시오.

1 _____ Bees

2 Where _____ all the honey bees _____?

3 _____ is really hard _____ _____ them these days.

4 The bees are _____!

5 About _____ _____ of the bee population dies every year.

6 This is _____ _____ for bees, but it's _____ _____ _____ for people.

7 Bees are very _____ _____ humans.

8 _____, bees give us honey.

9 Honey is a _____ _____ food.

10 It _____ _____ _____ our health and tastes great.

11 Honey can _____ _____ _____.

12 In fact, honey from ancient Egypt _____ _____ _____ today!

13 _____, bees _____ _____ many crops _____ _____ apples and strawberries.

14 These crops cannot _____ _____ _____ _____.

15 They _____ _____ _____ of bees.

16 Bees help _____ _____ _____ _____ pollination.

1 사라지는 벌들

2 꿀벌들은 모두 어디로 갔을까?

3 요즘 꿀벌을 보는 것은 정말 어렵다.

4 벌들이 사라지고 있다!

5 벌 개체 수의 약 3분의 1 정도가 매년 죽는다.

6 이것은 벌들에게 나쁜 소식이지만, 사람들에게는 훨씬 더 나쁜 소식이다.

7 벌은 인간에게 매우 도움이 된다.

8 첫째, 벌은 우리에게 꿀을 준다.

9 꿀은 정말 굉장한 음식이다.

10 그것은 건강에 좋고 맛이 좋다.

11 꿀은 거의 영원히 상하지 않을 수 있다.

12 실제로 고대 이집트 때의 꿀은 오늘날에도 먹을 수 있다!

13 둘째, 벌은 사과와 딸기 같은 많은 농작물을 생산하는 데 도움이 된다.

14 이 농작물들은 스스로 생산될 수 없다.

15 그들은 벌의 도움이 필요하다.

16 벌은 수분 과정에서 도움을 준다.

17 How bees help _____

18 _____ is pollination?

19 It is _____ _____ from one flower to another _____
_____ _____.

20 What is _____?

21 It is a _____ _____ _____ _____ by flowers.

22 Why are bees _____?

23 One of the _____ is _____ _____.

24 _____ _____ has brought extremely hot and cold weather.

25 Bees _____ _____ in these conditions.

26 _____ _____ is the harmful chemicals farmers use on crops.

27 These chemicals kill _____ _____ bad insects, _____
_____ good insects, like bees.

28 Then _____ can we do _____ _____ our little yellow friends?

29 First, we can plant _____ _____ _____ _____.

30 This will _____ a good environment _____ bees to live in.

31 Also, trees help _____ _____ global warming.

32 Second, the use of harmful chemicals on crops _____
_____ _____.

33 These chemicals _____ _____ _____ bees and people.

34 Our little friends _____ _____ _____.

35 Let's not _____ _____ _____!

17 벌이 수분을 돕는 방법

18 수분은 무엇인가?

19 그것은 씨를 만들기 위해 한 꽃에서 다른 꽃으로 꽃가루가 옮겨지는 것이에요.

20 꽃가루는 무엇인가?

21 그것은 꽃에 의해 생산되는 아주 작은 노란색 가루예요.

22 벌은 왜 없어지고 있을까?

23 그 이유 중 하나는 기후 변화이다.

24 지구 온난화는 극도로 덥고 추운 날씨를 가져왔다.

25 벌은 이런 환경에서 살아남을 수 없다.

26 다른 이유는 농부들이 농작물에 사용하는 해로운 화학 물질이다.

27 이 화학 물질은 해로운 곤충뿐만 아니라 벌과 같은 이로운 곤충도 죽인다.

28 그러면 우리는 우리의 작고 노란 친구들을 돕기 위해 무엇을 할 수 있을까?

29 첫째, 우리는 더 많은 꽃과 나무를 심을 수 있다.

30 이것은 벌에게 살기 좋은 환경을 제공할 것이다.

31 또한 나무는 지구 온난화를 늦추는 데 도움이 된다.

32 둘째, 농작물에 해로운 화학 물질의 사용을 멈춰야만 한다.

33 이 화학 물질은 벌과 사람의 건강에 좋지 않다.

34 우리의 작은 친구들이 우리의 도움을 필요로 한다.

35 그들을 실망시키지 말자!

● 우리말을 참고하여 본문을 영작하시오.

1 사라지는 벌들
➡ _____

2 꿀벌들은 모두 어디로 갔을까?
➡ _____

3 요즘 꿀벌을 보는 것은 정말 어렵다.
➡ _____

4 벌들이 사라지고 있다!
➡ _____

5 벌 개체 수의 약 3분의 1 정도가 매년 죽는다.
➡ _____

6 이것은 벌들에게 나쁜 소식이지만, 사람들에게는 훨씬 더 나쁜 소식이다.
➡ _____

7 벌은 인간에게 매우 도움이 된다.
➡ _____

8 첫째, 벌은 우리에게 꿀을 준다.
➡ _____

9 꿀은 정말 굉장한 음식이다.
➡ _____

10 그것은 건강에 좋고 맛이 좋다.
➡ _____

11 꿀은 거의 영원히 상하지 않을 수 있다.
➡ _____

12 실제로 고대 이집트 때의 꿀은 오늘날에도 먹을 수 있다!
➡ _____

13 둘째, 벌은 사과와 딸기 같은 많은 농작물을 생산하는 데 도움이 된다.
➡ _____

14 이 농작물들은 스스로 생산될 수 없다.
➡ _____

15 그들은 벌의 도움이 필요하다.
➡ _____

16 벌은 수분 과정에서 도움을 준다.
➡ _____

17 벌이 수분을 돕는 방법
➡ _____

18 수분은 무엇인가?
➡ _____

19 그것은 씨를 만들기 위해 한 꽃에서 다른 꽃으로 꽃가루가 옮겨지는 것이에요.
➡ _____

20 꽃가루는 무엇인가?
➡ _____

21 그것은 꽃에 의해 생산되는 아주 작은 노란색 가루예요.
➡ _____

22 벌은 왜 없어지고 있을까?
➡ _____

23 그 이유 중 하나는 기후 변화이다.
➡ _____

24 지구 온난화는 극도로 덥고 추운 날씨를 가져왔다.
➡ _____

25 벌은 이런 환경에서 살아남을 수 없다.
➡ _____

26 다른 이유는 농부들이 농작물에 사용하는 해로운 화학 물질이다.
➡ _____

27 이 화학 물질은 해로운 곤충뿐만 아니라 벌과 같은 이로운 곤충도 죽인다.
➡ _____

28 그러면 우리는 우리의 작고 노란 친구들을 돕기 위해 무엇을 할 수 있을까?
➡ _____

29 첫째, 우리는 더 많은 꽃과 나무를 심을 수 있다.
➡ _____

30 이것은 벌에게 살기 좋은 환경을 제공할 것이다.
➡ _____

31 또한 나무는 지구 온난화를 늦추는 데 도움이 된다.
➡ _____

32 둘째, 농작물에 해로운 화학 물질의 사용을 멈춰야만 한다.
➡ _____

33 이 화학 물질은 벌과 사람의 건강에 좋지 않다.
➡ _____

34 우리의 작은 친구들이 우리의 도움을 필요로 한다.
➡ _____

35 그들을 실망시키지 말자!
➡ _____

[01~04] 다음 글을 읽고 물음에 답하시오.

ⓐWhere have all the honey bees gone? It is really hard to see ⓑthem these days. The bees are disappearing! ⓒAbout a third of the bee population dies every year. This is bad news for bees, but it's ⓓeven worse news for people.

01 위 글의 밑줄 친 문장 ⓐ에 쓰인 현재완료 have gone과 용법이 같은 것을 고르시오.

① How long have you lived in Busan?
② I have lost the book.
③ How many times have you seen it?
④ Has she finished her homework yet?
⑤ They have known each other for 5 years.

02 위 글의 밑줄 친 ⓑthem이 가리키는 것을 본문에서 찾아 쓰시오.

➡ _____

03 위 글의 밑줄 친 문장 ⓒ와 같은 뜻이 되도록 다음 문장의 한 단어를 고치시오.

About a third of the number of the bees increases every year.

➡ _____

04 위 글의 밑줄 친 ⓓeven과 바꿔 쓸 수 없는 말을 고르시오.

① still   ② very   ③ far
④ much   ⑤ a lot

[05~07] 다음 글을 읽고 물음에 답하시오.

Bees are very helpful to humans. First, bees give us honey. Honey is a truly wonderful food. It is good ___ⓐ___ our health and tastes great. Honey can last almost forever. In fact, honey ___ⓑ___ ancient Egypt can be eaten today! Second, bees help produce many crops such as apples and strawberries. These crops cannot be produced by themselves. They need the help of bees. Bees help in the process of pollination.

05 위 글의 빈칸 ⓐ와 ⓑ에 들어갈 전치사가 바르게 짝지어진 것은?

	ⓐ	ⓑ		ⓐ	ⓑ
①	for	in	②	at	by
③	in	from	④	at	in
⑤	for	from			

06 위 글의 제목으로 알맞은 것을 고르시오.

① The Reasons Bees Are Disappearing
② How Bees Help Pollination
③ What Bees Do for Humans
④ Honey Can Last Almost Forever
⑤ How to Save the Bees

07 According to the passage, which is NOT true?

① Bees are very harmful to humans.
② Honey is a truly excellent food.
③ Honey tastes great.
④ Honey can last a very long time.
⑤ Thanks to bees, many crops such as apples and strawberries can be produced.

[08~09] 다음 글을 읽고 물음에 답하시오.

Why are bees disappearing? ①One of the reasons is climate change. ②Global warming has brought extremely hot and cold weather. ③Countries around the world are trying to slow down global warming. ④Bees cannot survive in these conditions. ⑤Another reason is the harmful chemicals farmers use on crops. ⓐThese chemicals kill not only bad insects, but also good insects, like bees.

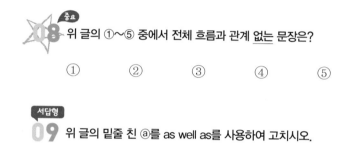

08 위 글의 ①~⑤ 중에서 전체 흐름과 관계 없는 문장은?

①   ②   ③   ④   ⑤

서답형

09 위 글의 밑줄 친 ⓐ를 as well as를 사용하여 고치시오.

➡ _____

_____

[10~12] 다음 글을 읽고 물음에 답하시오.

Then what can we do to help our little yellow friends? First, we can plant more flowers and trees. (A)이것은 벌에게 살기 좋은 환경을 제공할 것이다.   ⓐ , trees help slow down global warming. Second, the use of harmful chemicals on crops must be stopped. These chemicals are unhealthy for bees and people. Our little friends need our help. Let's not let them down!

10 위 글의 빈칸 ⓐ에 들어가기에 어울리지 <u>않는</u> 말을 고르시오.

① In addition   ② Moreover

③ Also   ④ On the other hand

⑤ Besides

서답형

11 위 글의 밑줄 친 (A)의 우리말에 맞게 한 단어를 보충하여, 주어진 어휘를 알맞게 배열하시오.

provide / to live / will / a good environment / this / bees / for

➡ _____

_____

서답형

12 다음 문장에서 위 글의 내용과 <u>다른</u> 부분을 찾아서 고치시오.

We can plant more flowers and trees to help our little yellow friends because trees help speed up global warming.

➡ _____

[13~15] 다음 글을 읽고 물음에 답하시오.

Where have all the honey bees gone? ⓐIt is really hard to see them these days. ⓑThe bees are disappeared! About a third of the bee population dies every year. ⓒThis is bad news for bees, but it's even worse news for people.

13 위 글의 밑줄 친 ⓐIt과 문법적 쓰임이 같은 것을 <u>모두</u> 고르시오.

① It's impossible to get there in time.

② She found it cheerful to have her meals in her room.

③ It is time for you to go to bed.

④ It is certain that we shall succeed.

⑤ Look! It's going up that tree.

서답형

14 위 글의 밑줄 친 ⓑ에서 어법상 <u>틀린</u> 부분을 찾아 고치시오.

➡ _____

서답형

15 위 글의 밑줄 친 ⓒThis가 가리키는 것을 본문에서 찾아 쓰시오.

➡ _____

_____

[16~18] 다음 글을 읽고 물음에 답하시오.

Bees are very helpful to humans. First, bees give us honey. Honey is a truly wonderful food. It is good for our health and tastes great. Honey can last almost forever. _____ⓐ_____, honey from ancient Egypt can be eaten today! Second, bees help produce many crops such as apples and strawberries. These crops cannot be produced by themselves. They need the help of bees. Bees help in the process of pollination.

How bees help pollination

• **What is pollination?**

It is moving pollen from one flower to another to make seeds.

• **What is pollen?**

It is a ⓑfine yellow powder produced by flowers.

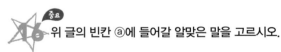

중요

16 위 글의 빈칸 ⓐ에 들어갈 알맞은 말을 고르시오.

① In contrast   ② In fact
③ Nonetheless   ④ However
⑤ Alternatively

17 위 글의 밑줄 친 ⓑfine과 같은 의미로 쓰인 것을 고르시오.

① 'How are you?' 'Fine, thanks.'
② Don't worry. Your speech was fine.
③ She paid over $100 in fine.
④ How can we protect ourselves from fine dust?
⑤ I hope it stays fine for the picnic.

서답형

18 Can many crops such as apples and strawberries be produced by themselves? If not, how can they be produced? Fill in the blanks (A)~(D) with suitable words.

> (A)_____, they (B)_____. They need the help of (C)_____. Bees help in the process of (D)_____.

[19~20] 다음 글을 읽고 물음에 답하시오.

Why are bees disappearing? One of the reasons is climate change. Global warming has brought extremely hot and cold weather. Bees cannot survive in these conditions. Another reason is the harmful chemicals farmers use on crops. ⓐThese chemicals kill not bad insects, but good insects, like bees.

서답형

19 위 글의 밑줄 친 ⓐ에서 흐름상 어색한 부분을 찾아 고치시오.

➡ _____

_____

서답형

20 Can bees survive in extremely hot and cold weather? Answer in English in a full sentence. (3 words)

➡ _____

[21~23] 다음 글을 읽고 물음에 답하시오.

Then what can we do to help our little yellow friends? (①) First, we can plant more flowers and trees. (②) Also, trees help slow down global warming. (③) Second, the use of harmful chemicals on crops must be stopped. (④) These chemicals are unhealthy for bees and people. (⑤) Our little friends need our help. Let's not let them down!

21 위 글의 흐름으로 보아, 주어진 문장이 들어가기에 가장 적절한 곳은?

> This will provide a good environment for bees to live in..

①   ②   ③   ④   ⑤

22 위 글의 주제로 알맞은 것을 고르시오.

① We should plant more flowers and trees to save bees.
② Why are bees disappearing?
③ What can we do to save bees?
④ Farmers must stop using the harmful chemicals on crops.
⑤ What do bees do for humans?

23 Which question CANNOT be answered after reading the passage?

① What will provide a good environment for bees to live in?
② Is it possible for trees to help slow down global warming?
③ How can it be possible to grow crops without using the harmful chemicals on them?
④ Why do we have to stop the use of harmful chemicals on crops?
⑤ Do bees need our help?

[24~27] 다음 글을 읽고 물음에 답하시오.

Bees are very helpful to humans. ①First, bees give us honey. ②Honey is a truly wonderful food. ③It is good for our health and tastes great. ④Honey can't last almost forever. ⑤In fact, honey from ancient Egypt can be eaten today! Second, bees help produce many crops such as apples and strawberries. ⓐThese crops cannot be produced by themselves. They need the help of bees. ⓑ벌은 '수분' 과정에서 도움을 준다.

How bees help pollination

• **What is pollination?**
It is ⓒmoving pollen from one flower to another to make seeds.
• **What is pollen?**
It is a fine yellow powder produced by flowers.

24 위 글의 밑줄 친 ①~⑤에서 흐름상 어색한 부분이 있는 문장을 찾아 고치시오.

➡ _____ 번, _____

25 위 글의 밑줄 친 ⓐThese crops가 가리키는 것을 본문에서 찾아 쓰시오.

➡ _____

26 위 글의 밑줄 친 ⓑ의 우리말에 맞게 주어진 어휘를 이용하여 7 단어로 영작하시오.

> in, process

➡ _____

27 위 글의 밑줄 친 ⓒmoving과 문법적 쓰임이 같은 것을 모두 고르시오.

① The process of moving pollen is simple.
② When bees fly from one flower to another, they are moving pollen.
③ The bees can't enjoy the nectar without moving pollen.
④ Moving pollen is very important to make seeds.
⑤ Many bees moving pollen help flowers make seeds.

[01~03] 다음 글을 읽고 물음에 답하시오.

　　Bees are very helpful to humans. First, bees give us honey. Honey is a truly wonderful food. It is good for our health and (A)[tastes / taste] great. Honey can last almost forever. In fact, ⓐhoney from ancient Egypt can be eaten today! Second, bees help (B)[produce / producing] many crops such as apples and strawberries. These crops cannot be produced by themselves. They need the help of bees. Bees help in the process of pollination.

How bees help pollination

• What is pollination?

It is moving pollen from one flower to another to make seeds.

• What is pollen?

It is a fine yellow powder (C)[producing / produced] by flowers.

01 위 글의 괄호 (A)~(C)에서 어법상 알맞은 낱말을 골라 쓰시오.

➡ (A)_____ (B)_____ (C)_____

02 위 글의 밑줄 친 ⓐ를 능동태로 고치시오.

➡ _____

03 Why are bees very helpful to humans? Fill in the blanks (A) and (B) with suitable words.

Because bees give us (A)_____ and help (B)_____ many crops such as apples and strawberries.

[04~06] 다음 글을 읽고 물음에 답하시오.

　　Why are bees disappearing? ⓐOne of the reasons are climate change. Global warming has brought extremely hot and cold weather. Bees cannot survive in ⓑthese conditions. Another reason is the harmful chemicals farmers use on crops. These chemicals kill not only bad insects, but also good insects, like bees.

04 위 글의 밑줄 친 ⓐ에서 어법상 틀린 부분을 찾아 고치시오.

➡ _____

05 위 글의 밑줄 친 ⓑ가 가리키는 것을 본문에서 찾아 쓰시오.

➡ _____

06 위 글을 읽고 벌들이 사라지고 있는 이유 두 가지를 우리말로 쓰시오.

➡ (1) _____
　 (2) _____

[07~09] 다음 글을 읽고 물음에 답하시오.

　　Then what can we do to help our little yellow friends? First, we can plant more flowers and trees. This will provide a good environment for bees to live in. Also, trees help slow down global warming. Second, ⓐ 농작물에 해로운 화학 물질의 사용을 멈춰야만 한다. These chemicals are unhealthy for bees and people. Our little friends need our help. ⓑ Let's not let down them!

07 위 글의 밑줄 친 ⓐ의 우리말에 맞게 주어진 어휘를 이용하여 10 단어로 영작하시오.

> of, on, must, stop

➡ _____

_____

08 위 글의 밑줄 친 ⓑ에서 어법상 틀린 부분을 찾아 고치시오.

➡ _____

09 What can we do to help bees? Fill in the blanks (A) and (B) with suitable words.

> We can (A)_____ more flowers and trees to provide a good environment for bees to live in and we must stop the use of (B)_____ _____ on crops.

[10~12] 다음 글을 읽고 물음에 답하시오.

Bees are very helpful to humans. First, bees give us honey. Honey is a truly wonderful food. It is good for our health and tastes great. (A)Honey can last almost forever. In fact, honey from ancient Egypt can be eaten today! Second, bees help produce many crops such as apples and strawberries. These crops cannot be produced by themselves. They need the help of bees. Bees help in the process of _____ⓐ_____.

10 주어진 영영풀이를 참고하여 빈칸 ⓐ에 철자 p로 시작하는 단어를 쓰시오.

> the transfer of pollen from a male part of a plant to a female part of a plant

➡ _____

11 위 글에서 (A)처럼 말한 이유를 우리말로 쓰시오.

➡ _____

_____

12 본문의 내용과 일치하도록 다음 빈칸 (A)에 알맞은 단어를 쓰시오.

> Many crops such as apples and strawberries cannot be produced by themselves (A)_____ the help of bees.

13 다음 글을 읽고 주어진 글의 빈칸 (A)~(C)에 알맞은 단어를 넣어, 꽃들이 벌의 수분 작용을 통해 씨앗을 만들게 되는 과정을 완성하시오. (본문의 단어를 사용하시오.)

> **How bees help pollination**
> • **What is pollination?**
> It is moving pollen from one flower to another to make seeds.
> • **What is pollen?**
> It is a fine yellow powder produced by flowers.

> Flowers produce a fine yellow powder called (A)_____, which bees move from one flower to another while they visit flowers. Such (B)_____ of bees enables flowers to make (C)_____.

구석구석

After You Read B

Problem

About a third of the bee population dies every year.
뒤에 단수 명사(population)가 나오므로 단수 취급한다.

Causes

1. Global warming has brought climate change.
bring-brought-brought

2. Farmers use the harmful chemicals on crops.
use A on B: B에 A를 사용하다

Solution

1. Plant more flowers and trees to provide a good environment for bees.
to부정사의 부사적 용법(목적)

2. Stop using harmful chemicals on crops.
stop+~ing: ~을 그만두다

구문해설 • population: 인구 • a third: 3분의 1 • global warming: 지구 온난화 • chemical: 화학 물질[제품] • crops: 농작물 • environment: 환경

문제점

벌 개체 수의 약 3분의 1 정도가 매년 죽는다.

원인

1. 지구 온난화가 기후 변화를 가져왔다.

2. 농부들이 농작물에 해로운 화학 물질을 사용한다.

해결책

1. 벌들에게 좋은 환경을 제공하기 위해 더 많은 꽃과 나무를 심어라.

2. 농작물에 해로운 화학 물질의 사용을 멈춰라.

Language Use - In Context

Facts about Cambodia

• Around half of Cambodia's population is under the age of 15.
부분을 나타내는 말은 뒤에 오는 명사의 수에 따라 그 수가 결정된다.

• Two-thirds of the country is covered with forest.
부분을 나타내는 말(Two-thirds of) 뒤에 단수 명사(the country)가 나왔으므로 단수 동사 is

• 40 percent of the people spend most of their money on food.
spend+(노력·시간+돈 등)+on 명사(in 동명사): ~하는 데 (노력·시간+돈) 등을 쓰다

구문해설 • around: 약, 대략 • population: 인구 • forest: 숲, 산림

캄보디아에 관한 사실

• 캄보디아 인구의 약 절반이 15세 이하이다.

• 이 나라의 3분의 2는 숲으로 덮여 있다.

• 사람들의 40 퍼센트는 그들 돈의 대부분을 음식에 쓴다.

Word Power

• Thank you for all your help.
감사 표현으로 'Thank you for ~.'를 쓰는 경우 for 뒤에 감사의 이유를 적는다. help는 여기서 명사로 '도움'의 의미로 사용되었다.

• A dictionary is very helpful for studying language.
help(명사)+ful: 형용사

• I didn't mean to cause you any harm.
mean to 동사원형: ~할 셈이다   cause는 4형식으로 사용되었다.

• Strong sunlight is very harmful to the skin.
harm(명사)+ful: 형용사

구문해설 • helpful: 도움이 되는 • be harmful to 명사: ~에 해롭다

• 당신의 모든 도움에 감사드립니다.

• 사전은 언어 공부에 매우 도움이 된다.

• 당신에게 해를 끼치려고 한 것은 아니었습니다.

• 강한 햇빛은 피부에 매우 해롭다.

01 다음 문장에서 쓰임이 자연스럽지 <u>않은</u> 것을 찾아 고치시오.

ⓐ Not only you but also Jamie like Korean pop songs.

ⓑ Many families break up because a lack of money.

ⓒ My mobile phone is extremely use.

➡ _____

_____

02 다음 밑줄 친 부분의 의미로 알맞지 <u>않은</u> 것은?

① I will <u>advise</u> you to stop changing jobs. (충고하다)

② If you don't need money, you can <u>donate</u> your old things. (기부하다)

③ Scientists found out that a <u>chemical</u> called dopamine is responsible. (화학의)

④ In <u>ancient</u> Greece, men and women wore different clothing. (고대의)

⑤ Let me explain our terms and <u>conditions</u> of business. (조건)

03 다음 빈칸에 알맞은 말을 고르시오.

Managers worry about employees leaving for other companies, but _____ they are more likely to stay.

① in fact
② therefore
③ nevertheless
④ probably
⑤ especially

04 다음 빈칸에 공통으로 들어갈 말을 쓰시오.

• I have already promised that I'd _____ part in that event.

• The government needs to _____ action to boost the economy.

[05~06] 다음 대화를 읽고 물음에 답하시오.

B: Jane, what's the matter?
G: My brother broke his leg.
B: Oh, I'm sorry to hear that.
G: I'm (A)_____ about him.
B: Don't worry. He'll be okay.

05 빈칸 (A)를 대화에 나온 단어를 이용하여 채우시오.

➡ _____

06 위 대화를 읽고 답할 수 있는 질문이 <u>모두</u> 몇 개인지 고르시오.

• When did Jane's brother break his leg?

• How does the boy feel about the news of Jane's brother?

• When will be Jane's brother okay?

• Which leg did Jane's brother break?

• What happened to Jane's brother?

① 1개   ② 2개   ③ 3개   ④ 4개   ⑤ 5개

[07~09] 다음 대화를 읽고 물음에 답하시오.

G: Are you ready ⓐ[to / for] our soccer game today, Sam?

B: Kathy, didn't you see the news?

G: No, I didn't. What did it say?

B: The yellow dust is terrible today.

G: Oh, no. Yellow dust can ⓑ[cause / reduce] many health problems.

B: Yeah, 나는 우리의 건강이 걱정돼.

G: (A)_____

B: You're right. I'll text the other team members right now.

G: Great idea.

07 위 대화의 괄호 ⓐ와 ⓑ에서 적절한 것을 골라 쓰시오.

➡ ⓐ _____, ⓑ _____

08 빈칸 (A)에 알맞은 말을 고르시오.

① We need to stretch our body before game.

② Let's play soccer right now.

③ We can play another day.

④ We need to look it up on the Internet.

⑤ We can play another soccer game.

09 밑줄 친 우리말과 일치하도록 주어진 단어를 이용하여 문장을 만드시오.

➡ _____

(worried)

[10~12] 다음 대화를 읽고 물음에 답하시오.

G: Jinsu, did you know ⓐ[how / that] polar bears are (A)_____ danger?

B: Yes. I read about it (B)_____ an article. It's because of global warming.

G: Right. 그들의 서식지가 녹아 없어지고 있고 그들의 먹이는 사라지고 있어. (melt, disappear)

B: We should do something about it.

G: Do you know how to slow down global warming?

B: Well, we can start by saving energy.

G: Right. We need to turn ⓑ[on / off] the lights when we leave the room.

B: That's a good idea.

10 빈칸 (A)와 (B)에 공통으로 들어갈 말을 쓰시오.

➡ _____

11 위 대화의 괄호 ⓐ와 ⓑ에서 적절한 것을 골라 쓰시오.

➡ ⓐ _____, ⓑ _____

12 밑줄 친 우리말과 일치하도록 주어진 단어를 이용하여 문장을 만드시오.

➡ _____

_____

Grammar

13 다음 중 어법상 옳은 문장을 모두 고르시오.

① One of the fastest growing sports in China are basketball.

② 30 percent of the students speak Chinese.

③ There is a number of languages spoken in India.

④ Take pictures anywhere! It can be use in water.

⑤ A lot of birds can be watched in this area.

14 다음을 수동태 문장으로 바꿔 쓸 때 빈칸에 알맞은 말을 쓰시오.

> Students should hand in the report before Aug. 15.
> → The report _____
>   by students before Aug. 15.

15 다음 빈칸에 들어갈 말이 나머지와 <u>다른</u> 하나는?

① The rest of them _____ teenagers.
② Some of the woodland _____ polluted.
③ About 70 percent of the students _____ from China.
④ Most of the girls _____ very kind and pretty.
⑤ A number of the documents _____ in French or German.

16 다음 빈칸에 알맞은 것은?

> Full of adventures! This book _____ by many teens in the future.

① loves
② is loved
③ will love
④ will have loved
⑤ will be loved

17 다음 @~ⓖ 중 어법상 옳은 것을 <u>모두</u> 고르시오.

> @ 20 percent of the students skip breakfast.
> ⓑ The colored part of your eyeball are called iris.
> ⓒ Half of the teenagers in the U.S. have their own bedrooms.
> ⓓ It cannot be completed in an ordinary way.

> ⓔ This work must be do before tonight.
> ⓕ The hero will be remembered forever.
> ⓖ How many jobs are going to be creating?

➡ _____

18 다음 중 어법상 적절한 문장은?

① One of the reasons are climate change.
② Half of my life have gone.
③ Most of the machines isn't ready to use yet.
④ Some of her family members are angry.
⑤ More than two thirds of people lives under $1 a day.

Reading

[19~20] 다음 글을 읽고 물음에 답하시오.

> Where have all the honey bees gone? It is really hard to see them these days. The bees are disappearing! @About a third of the bee population die every year. This is bad news for bees, but ⓑit's even worse news for people.

19 위 글의 밑줄 친 @에서 어법상 <u>틀린</u> 부분을 찾아 고치시오.

➡ _____

20 다음 빈칸에 알맞은 단어를 넣어 위 글의 밑줄 친 ⓑit이 가리키는 내용을 완성하시오. (본문의 단어를 변형하여 쓰시오.)

> Every year, about one-third of remaining bees _____ .

[21~23] 다음 글을 읽고 물음에 답하시오.

Bees are very helpful to humans. First, bees give us honey. Honey is a truly wonderful food. ⓐ그것은 건강에 좋고 맛이 좋다. Honey can last almost forever. In fact, honey from ancient Egypt can be eaten today! Second, bees help produce many crops such as apples and strawberries. These crops cannot be produced by themselves. They need the help of bees. Bees help in the process of pollination.

How bees help pollination

• What is pollination?
It is moving pollen from one flower to another to make seeds.

• What is pollen?
It is a fine yellow powder produced by flowers.

21 위 글의 밑줄 친 ⓐ의 우리말에 맞게 주어진 어휘를 알맞게 배열하시오.

> good / our health / it / tastes / for / great / and / is / .

➡ _____

22 다음 중 벌과 식물의 관계에 대한 이해가 옳지 <u>않은</u> 사람을 고르시오.

① 영호: Bees and plants help each other.
② 나리: That's right. They have a kind of symbiotic relationship*.
③ 명수: I don't think so. Bees only get honey from plants without any reward.
④ 주희: I can't agree with you. They help produce many crops.
⑤ 민식: Absolutely! Plants can make seeds thanks to the pollination of bees.

*symbiotic relationship: 공생관계

23 위 글의 주제로 알맞은 것을 고르시오.

① Honey is a truly wonderful food.
② What food is good for our health?
③ Bees help produce many crops.
④ What is pollination?
⑤ Bees are very helpful to humans.

[24~26] 다음 환경 보호에 관한 설문 결과를 참조하여 물음에 답하시오.

<설문지>

Survey on Saving the Environment

Q1 Do you turn off the lights when you leave a room? Y N

Q2 Do you take a shower in less than 5 minutes? Y N

Q3 Do you turn off the water when you brush your teeth? Y N

Q4 Do you recycle plastic? Y N

Q5 Do you use both sides of a sheet of paper? Y N

<설문결과>

	Q1	Q2	Q3	Q4	Q5
Yes / No	9 / 1	4 / 6	5 / 5	3 / 7	1 / 9

How Green My Friends Are

I surveyed 10 classmates today. The survey was about ⓐ_____. Most of them turn off the lights when they leave rooms. ⓑ_____ of them take a shower in less than 5 minutes. Half of them turn off the water when they brush their teeth. ⓒ_____ of them recycle plastic. Only 10 percent of them use both sides of a sheet of paper. I think my friends are not so ⓓgreen. They should think about the environment more.

24 위 글의 빈칸 ⓐ에 'How green are they?'를 알맞은 형태로 쓰시오.

➡ _____

25 Fill in the blanks ⓑ and ⓒ with suitable words.

➡ ⓑ _____ , ⓒ _____

26 위 글의 밑줄 친 ⓓgreen과 같은 뜻의 단어를 고르시오.

① economical　　② eco-friendly
③ considerate　　④ reusable
⑤ sensible

[27~29] 다음 글을 읽고 물음에 답하시오.

Then what can we do to help our little yellow friends? First, we can plant more flowers and trees. This will provide a good environment for bees ⓐto live in. Also, trees help slow down global warming. Second, the use of harmful chemicals on crops must be stopped. These chemicals are unhealthy for bees and people. Our little friends need our help. Let's not ⓑlet them down!

27 아래 〈보기〉에서 위 글의 밑줄 친 ⓐto live와 to부정사의 용법이 같은 것의 개수를 고르시오.

┌─── 보기 ├───
① There is no one to do it.
② To use your time well is important.
③ He worked hard only to fail.
④ I have nothing to drink.
⑤ He hopes to go swimming.
└──────────────

① 1개　② 2개　③ 3개　④ 4개　⑤ 5개

28 위 글의 밑줄 친 ⓑlet them down을 두 단어로 바꿔 쓰시오.

➡ _____

29 According to the passage, which is NOT true?

① We can plant more flowers and trees to help bees.
② Planting more flowers and trees will provide a good environment for bees to live in.
③ Planting trees helps slow down global warming.
④ We must stop to use the harmful chemicals on crops.
⑤ These chemicals are unhealthy not only for bees but also for people.

[30~31] 다음 글을 읽고 물음에 답하시오.

Problem
About a third of the bee population dies every year.
Causes
1. Global warming has brought climate change.
2. Farmers use the harmful chemicals on crops.
　　ⓐ
1. Plant more flowers and trees to provide a good environment for bees.
2. Stop using harmful chemicals on crops.

30 위 글의 빈칸 ⓐ에 들어갈 알맞은 단어를 쓰시오.

➡ _____

31 Which question CANNOT be answered after reading the passage?

① Why are bees disappearing?
② What has brought climate change?
③ How many harmful chemicals farmers use on crops?
④ To provide a good environment for bees, what do we need to do?
⑤ Is it OK if we continue using harmful chemicals on crops?

✎ 출제율 90%

01 다음 단어들의 관계가 <u>다른</u> 하나를 고르시오.

① carefully – carelessly
② disappear – appear
③ provide – supply
④ forever – temporarily
⑤ later – earlier

✎ 출제율 90%

02 그림을 참고하여 빈칸에 알맞은 단어를 쓰시오.

➡ He gave me about _____ _____
_____ the pear.

✎ 출제율 95%

03 다음 빈칸 (A)와 (B)에 들어갈 말로 알맞게 짝지어진 것은?

• I regret (A)_____ down the fans who were waiting for some good news.
• Why waste your precious time when you can (B)_____ up facts on smartphones easily and quickly?

    (A)   (B)   (A)   (B)
① letting – pick   ② letting – look
③ letting – take   ④ making – pick
⑤ making – look

✎ 출제율 95%

04 다음 우리말에 맞도록 빈칸에 알맞은 말을 쓰시오. (철자가 주어진 경우 주어진 철자로 시작할 것.)

(1) 충분한 수분작용이 없다면, 옥수수의 성장이 멈춰질 수 있다.
    ➡ Without sufficient p_____, the growth of the corn can be stopped.

(2) 나는 여행하는 데서 많은 즐거움을 얻는다.
    ➡ I get a lot of p_____ from traveling.

(3) 이 화학 물질을 사용하는 데 극도로 조심해야 할 필요가 있다.
    ➡ It is necessary to use e_____ caution with those chemicals.

(4) 현대의 생산 과정들은 복잡하고 비용이 많이 든다.
    ➡ Modern _____ _____ are complex and costly.

✎ 출제율 100%

05 빈칸 ⓐ~ⓔ 중에 들어갈 수 있는 말을 고르시오.

A: Can I ask you something?
B: ⓐ_____. What is it?
A: Do you know ⓑ_____ eat ⓒ_____?
B: Yes. You need ⓓ_____ ⓔ_____ fast food.

① what to   ② eating
③ Of course not   ④ less
⑤ health

[06~08] 다음 대화를 읽고 물음에 답하시오.

> A: (a)나는 아프리카의 배고픈 아이들이 걱정돼.
> B: Me, too. It's (A)_____.
> A: What can we do to help?
> B: We can donate money to them.

출제율 95%

06 빈칸 (A)에 들어갈 말로 적절한 것을 고르시오.

① popular   ② difficult
③ terrible   ④ strange
⑤ wonderful

출제율 90%

07 위 대화에서 다음 영영풀이에 해당하는 단어를 찾아 쓰시오.

> to give something to a person or an organization in order to help them

➡ _____

출제율 90%

08 밑줄 친 (a)의 우리말에 맞게 주어진 단어를 이용하여 영작하시오.

➡ _____
     (worried, in)

[09~12] 다음 대화를 읽고 물음에 답하시오.

> Minho: Linda, did you see the TV program, *The Sick Planet*?
> Linda: Yes, I did. (①) I'm worried about our planet.
> Minho: Me, too. (②) We should take action to ⓐ[save / share / spend] the Earth.
> Linda: You're right. Hey! Why don't we participate in Earth Hour?
> Minho: Earth Hour? What's that?
> Linda: It's a world movement for the ⓑ [economy / environment / industry].

> Minho: Sounds great! (③) 그것에 참여하는 방법을 아니?
> Linda: Sure. We (A)_____ our lights together for an hour. (④)
> Minho: That's so ⓒ[difficult / same / simple]! So, when do we do it?
> Linda: I'm not sure. (⑤)
> Minho: Let's look it up on the Internet.

출제율 100%

09 ①~⑤ 중 주어진 문장이 들어갈 곳은?

> It's different every year.

①   ②   ③   ④   ⑤

출제율 90%

10 빈칸 (A)에 들어갈 말로 적절한 것을 고르시오.

① pick up   ② put off
③ turn on   ④ turn down
⑤ turn off

출제율 100%

11 위 대화의 괄호 ⓐ~ⓒ에서 적절한 것을 골라 쓰시오.

➡ ⓐ_____ ⓑ_____ ⓒ_____

출제율 90%

12 밑줄 친 우리말과 일치하도록 주어진 단어를 이용하여 영작하시오.

➡ _____
     (how, take, know)

출제율 95%

13 다음 문장에서 어법상 틀린 부분을 찾아 바르게 고쳐 쓰시오.

> The greater part of the land are still barren.

➡ _____

14 출제율 90%

다음 빈칸에 알맞은 말이 순서대로 짝지어진 것은?

> • One quarter of grain grown in the states _____ up as bio-fuels.
> • Children should _____ from sun damage.

① end – protected
② end – protect
③ ends – be protected
④ ends – protecting
⑤ ending – have protected

15 출제율 95%

다음 중 수동태로 바꾼 문장 중 틀린 것은?

① You may water the plant later today.
   → The plant may be watered later today.
② Ted will allow his daughter to eat as much as she wants.
   → Ted's daughter is allowed to eat as much as she wants by him.
③ The students can decide the project by vote.
   → The project can be decided by vote by the students.
④ We should postpone the picnic to next week.
   → The picnic should be postponed to next week.
⑤ Tim has to pay the bill.
   → The bill has to be paid by Tim.

[16~17] 다음 글을 읽고 물음에 답하시오.

> Why are bees disappearing? One of the reasons is climate change. Global warming has brought extremely hot and cold weather. Bees cannot survive in these conditions. Another reason is the harmful chemicals farmers use on crops. These chemicals kill not only bad insects, but also good insects, like bees.

16 출제율 100%

위 글의 제목으로 알맞은 것을 고르시오.

① How to Save Bees
② What Brought Global Warming?
③ The Effect of the Harmful Chemicals
④ What Bees Do for Humans
⑤ The Reasons Bees Are Disappearing

17 출제율 95%

According to the passage, which is NOT true?

① One of the reasons bees are disappearing is climate change.
② Global warming has caused extremely hot and cold weather.
③ It is impossible for bees to survive in extremely hot and cold conditions.
④ Farmers use the harmless chemicals on crops.
⑤ The chemicals farmers use on crops kill not just bad insects, but good insects, like bees, as well.

[18~20] 다음 글을 읽고 물음에 답하시오.

> Bees are very helpful to humans. First, bees give us honey. Honey is a truly wonderful food. It is good for our health and tastes great. (①) Honey can ⓐlast almost forever. (②) In fact, honey from ancient Egypt can be eaten today! (③) Second, bees help produce many crops such as apples and strawberries. (④) They need the help of bees. (⑤) Bees help in the process of pollination.

18 출제율 100%

위 글의 ①~⑤ 중 흐름으로 보아, 주어진 문장이 들어가기에 가장 적절한 곳은?

> These crops cannot be produced by themselves.

①　②　③　④　⑤

19 위 글의 밑줄 친 ⓐlast와 같은 의미로 쓰인 것을 고르시오.

① He is the last man I want to see.
② It's a long time since I saw him last.
③ How long will this fine weather last?
④ She spent her last cent.
⑤ He who laughs last laughs best.

20 Why is it necessary for bees to help produce many crops? Fill in the blanks with suitable words.

> Because these crops cannot be produced _____ _____ .

[21~22] 다음 글을 읽고 물음에 답하시오.

World Water Day
• March 22
• Save water on this day.
• Nothing can survive without water.

GREEN UP DAY
• the first Saturday of May
• Pick up trash on this day.
• Trash hurts the environment.

PLASTIC BAG FREE DAY
• July 3
• Bring your own shopping bag on this day.
• A plastic bag doesn't break down easily.

21 본문의 내용과 일치하도록 다음 빈칸에 한 단어씩 알맞은 단어를 쓰시오.

> March 22 is World Water Day. People try to _____ _____ on this day.

22 On PLASTIC BAG FREE DAY, what should people do? Answer in English in a full sentence. (10 words)

➡ _____

_____

[23~25] 다음 글을 읽고 물음에 답하시오.

Then what can we do to help ①our little yellow friends? First, we can plant more ②flowers and trees. This will provide a good environment for ③bees (A)[to live / to live in]. Also, trees help (B)[promote / slow down] global warming. Second, the use of harmful chemicals on crops must (C)[stop / be stopped]. These chemicals are unhealthy for bees and people. ④Our little friends need our help. Let's not let ⑤them down!

23 위 글의 괄호 (A)~(C)에서 문맥이나 어법상 알맞은 낱말을 골라 쓰시오.

➡ (A)_____ (B)_____ (C)_____

24 밑줄 친 ①~⑤ 중에서 가리키는 대상이 나머지 넷과 다른 것은?

① ② ③ ④ ⑤

25 위 글의 내용과 일치하도록 다음 빈칸에 알맞은 단어를 본문에서 나오는 단어를 변형시켜 쓰시오.

> We must stop the use of harmful chemicals on crops because they are not _____ for bees and people.

서술형 실전문제

[01~02] 다음 대화에서 흐름상 또는 어법상 어색한 것을 찾아 바르게 고치시오.

01

> B: My neck hurts.
> G: Be careful to get text neck.
> B: Do you know how to prevent it?
> G: Yes. You need to stretch your next often.
> B: Okay, I will. Thanks.

➡ _____

02

> G: Jinsu, did you know that polar bears are in danger?
> B: Yes. I read about it in an article. It's because of global warming.
> G: Right. Their homes are melting away and their food is disappearing.
> B: We should do something about it.
> G: Do you know how to slowing down global warming?
> B: Well, we can start by saving energy.
> G: Right. We need to turn off the lights when we leave the room.
> B: That's a good idea.

➡ _____

03 밑줄 친 우리말을 about을 사용하여 4가지 문장으로 만드시오.

> A: 나는 사라지는 벌들이 걱정돼.
> B: Me, too. It's terrible.
> A: What can we do to help?
> B: We can plant more trees for them.

➡ (1) _____
   (2) _____
   (3) _____
   (4) _____

04 다음 문장을 수동태는 능동태로, 능동태는 수동태로 바꾸어 쓰시오.

(1) People must stop the use of harmful chemicals on crops.

➡ _____
_____

(2) We should allow students to use cell phones in class.

➡ _____
_____

(3) Who will clean the house from now on?

➡ _____
_____
_____

(4) I cannot answer that question right now.

➡ _____
_____

05 〈보기〉에 주어진 단어를 활용하여 빈칸을 알맞게 채우시오.

> ┤ 보기 ├
> be, have

(1) About half of the apples _____ rotten.
(2) Only a few of them _____ kept their conversion secret.
(3) Much of her life _____ devoted to education.
(4) The number of stars in the universe _____ incalculable.

06 다음 두 문장의 의미가 같도록 문장의 빈칸을 완성하시오.

(1) We must protect the individual rights at all times.
  = The individual rights _____ at all times.

(2) We should give up neither of them in a rush.

= Neither of them _____ in a rush.

(3) They can repair the watches at the shop.

= The watches _____ at the shop.

[07~09] 다음 글을 읽고 물음에 답하시오.

Bees are very (A)[harmful / helpful] to humans. First, bees give us honey. Honey is a truly wonderful food. It is good for our health and tastes (B)[great / greatly]. Honey can last almost forever. In fact, honey from ancient Egypt can be eaten today! Second, bees help produce many crops such as apples and strawberries. These crops cannot be produced by (C)[them / themselves]. They need the help of bees. Bees help in the process of pollination.

How bees help pollination

• **What is pollination?**

It is moving pollen from one flower to another to make seeds.

• **What is pollen?**

It is a fine yellow powder ⓐproduced by flowers.

07 위 글의 괄호 (A)~(C)에서 문맥이나 어법상 알맞은 낱말을 골라 쓰시오.

➡ (A)_____ (B)_____ (C)_____

08 위 글의 밑줄 친 ⓐ를 능동태로 고치시오.

➡ _____

09 본문의 내용과 일치하도록 다음 빈칸 (A)와 (B)에 알맞은 단어를 쓰시오.

Many crops need the help of (A)_____ because they cannot be produced alone. Bees help move (B)_____ from one flower to another.

[10~12] 다음 글을 읽고 물음에 답하시오.

Then what can we do to help our little yellow friends? First, we can plant more flowers and trees. ⓐThis will provide a good environment for bees to live in. Also, trees help slow down global warming. Second, the use of harmful chemicals on crops must be stopped. These chemicals are unhealthy for bees and people. Our little friends need ⓑour help. Let's not let them down!

10 위 글의 밑줄 친 ⓐThis가 가리키는 것을 동명사를 사용하여 쓰시오.

➡ _____

11 위 글의 밑줄 친 ⓑour help의 두 가지 종류를 본문에서 찾아 우리말로 쓰시오.

➡ (1) _____

_____

(2) _____

12 What's the benefit of planting more flowers and trees? Fill in the blanks (A) and (B) with suitable words.

By planting more flowers and trees, we will not only provide (A)_____ _____ _____ for bees to live in but also help slow down (B)_____ _____.

01 다음 주어진 표현과 〈조건〉을 보고 대화를 완성하시오.

조건

- 걱정을 표현하는 말을 사용할 것.
- should, help, worry를 이용할 것.

A: I've heard that the Amazon rainforest has been destroyed. _____ in the Amazon.

B: Yeah, The animals are losing their homes.

A: _____

B: _____ cutting down so many trees.

02 다음 포스터를 참고하여, 괄호 안에 주어진 표현을 배열하여 능동태의 문장을 쓰고 수동태의 문장으로 고쳐 쓰시오.

(the movie / we / watch / this Saturday / will)

(1) _____ (능동태)

(2) _____ (수동태)

03 다음 내용을 바탕으로 환경 보호에 관한 설문 결과를 쓰시오.

Survey on Saving the Environment

Q1 Do you turn off the lights when you leave a room? Y N

Q2 Do you take a shower in less than 5 minutes? Y N

Q3 Do you turn off the water when you brush your teeth? Y N

Q4 Do you recycle plastic? Y N

Q5 Do you use both sides of a sheet of paper? Y N

Yes / No	Q1	Q2	Q3	Q4	Q5
Yes	9	4	5	3	1
No	1	6	5	7	9

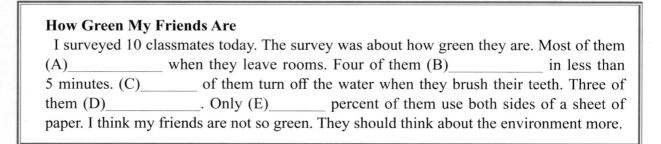

How Green My Friends Are

I surveyed 10 classmates today. The survey was about how green they are. Most of them (A)_____ when they leave rooms. Four of them (B)_____ in less than 5 minutes. (C)_____ of them turn off the water when they brush their teeth. Three of them (D)_____. Only (E)_____ percent of them use both sides of a sheet of paper. I think my friends are not so green. They should think about the environment more.

단원별 모의고사

01 다음 짝지어진 단어의 관계가 같도록 빈칸에 알맞은 말을 쓰시오.

> advise : advice = pollute : _____

02 빈칸 (A)와 (B)에 들어갈 말로 알맞은 것끼리 짝지어진 것을 고르시오.

> • In time, the natural waste (A)_____ down and changes into soil rich with nutrients.
> • The ice will (B)_____ away completely and flow into the river.

   (A)   (B)
① slows – melt
② slows – break
③ slows – go
④ breaks – melt
⑤ breaks – break

03 주어진 단어와 영영풀이가 잘못 연결된 것을 고르시오.

① adventure: an exciting experience in which dangerous or unusual things happen
② ancient: having existed for a very long time
③ deliver: to take goods, letters, etc to a particular place
④ fine: very wide or broad
⑤ pollen: a fine powder produced by flowers

04 다음 우리말에 맞도록 빈칸에 알맞은 말을 쓰시오. (철자가 주어진 경우 주어진 철자로 시작할 것.)

(1) 그 영향은 그의 생애 전체에 걸쳐 지속될 것이다.
➡ The effects will l_____ for the whole of his life.

(2) 너의 식단에서 지방의 양을 줄이도록 노력해라.
➡ Try to r_____ the amount of fat in your diet.

(3) Southwest Junior 고등학교는 아이들이 교복을 입는 것에 대해 부모님들에게 설문조사하는 중이다.
➡ Southwest Junior High is _____ parents about their children wearing uniforms.

(4) 이런 교통수단은 해로운 성분과 온실 가스를 배출하고, 이것은 대기 오염과 지구 온난화를 초래한다.
➡ These modes of t_____ emit h_____ elements and greenhouse gases, which lead to air _____ and _____ _____.

[05~06] 다음 대화를 읽고 물음에 답하시오.

A: (A)_____
B: I think it's terrible. I'm worried about (B)_____.
A: Do you know how to reduce (C)_____?
B: Yes. We need to use public transportation.

05 빈칸 (A)에 들어갈 말로 적절한 것은?

① What do you think of this picture?

② Can I ask you something?

③ Could you show me how to save the Earth?

④ Did you know this picture?

⑤ Are you ready to save the Earth?

06 그림을 참고하여 (B)와 (C)에 공통으로 들어갈 말을 두 단어로 쓰시오.

➡ _____

[07~08] 다음 대화를 읽고 물음에 답하시오.

B: Jane, what (A)_____?
G: My brother broke his leg.
B: Oh, I'm (B)_____.
G: (C)_____
B: Don't worry. He'll be okay.

07 빈칸 (A)와 (B)에 들어갈 말로 알맞은 것끼리 짝지어진 것을 고르시오.

(A)   (B)

① makes you happy – sorry to hear that

② makes you happy – glad to hear that

③ is the matter – sorry to hear that

④ is the matter – glad to hear that

⑤ is the matter – pleased to hear that

08 빈칸 (C)에 상대방에게 걱정을 표현하는 말을 이용하여 알맞게 채우시오.

➡ _____

[09~11] 다음 대화를 읽고 물음에 답하시오.

Minho: Linda, did you see the TV program, *The Sick Planet*?
Linda: Yes, I did. (a)나는 우리 지구가 걱정돼.
Minho: Me, too. We should take action to save the Earth.
Linda: You're right. Hey! Why don't we (A)_____ Earth Hour?
Minho: Earth Hour? What's that?
Linda: It's a world movement for the environment.
Minho: Sounds great! Do you know how to take part in it?
Linda: Sure. We turn off our lights together for an hour.
Minho: That's so simple! So, when do we do it?
Linda: I'm not sure. It's different every year.
Minho: Let's look it up on the Internet.

09 빈칸 (A)를 밑줄 친 부분과 같은 뜻이 되도록 2 단어로 채우시오.

➡ _____

10 밑줄 친 (a)의 우리말과 일치하도록 주어진 단어를 이용하여 영작하시오.

➡ _____ (worry, planet)

11 위 대화의 내용과 일치하는 것을 고르시오.

① Earth Hour를 하는 시간은 매년 정해져 있다.

② Linda와 민호는 Earth Hour를 알아보기 위해 TV program을 볼 것이다.

③ Earth Hour는 불을 1시간 동안 끔으로써 참여할 수 있다.

④ TV program인 *The Sick Planet*에서 지구 온난화에 대해 설명하고 있다.

⑤ Linda는 *The Sick Planet*을 보지 못했다.

[12~14] 다음 대화를 읽고 물음에 답하시오.

> G: Jinsu, did you know that polar bears are in danger?
>
> B: Yes. I read about it in an article. (①) 그건 지구 온난화 때문이야.
>
> G: Right. (②) Their homes are melting away and their food is disappearing. (③)
>
> B: We should do something about it. (④)
>
> G: (A) _____
>
> B: Well, we can start by saving energy.
>
> G: Right. (⑤)
>
> B: That's a good idea.

12 밑줄 친 ①~⑤ 중 주어진 문장이 들어갈 곳은?

> We need to turn off the lights when we leave the room.

① ② ③ ④ ⑤

13 빈칸 (A)에 들어갈 말로 적절한 것을 고르시오.

① Can you show me the polar bears?

② Do you know how to help the disappearing global warming?

③ Would you tell me how to donate food to them?

④ Do you know how to slow down global warming?

⑤ Would you tell me how to go to the polar area?

14 밑줄 친 우리말과 일치하도록 주어진 단어를 이용하여 영작하시오.

➡ _____ (of)

15 다음 중 어법상 어색한 것을 고르시오.

① 40 percent of the people spend most of their money on food.

② The rest of the papers is on the table.

③ The greater part of my books are in my room.

④ Only part of the men are equipped according to law.

⑤ Two-thirds of the increase has occurred in rural areas.

16 다음 밑줄 친 부분 중 어법상 어색한 것은?

① Do as you would be done by.

② Summer is coming! Your skin must be protected from the sun.

③ It should be finished by 2010, they said.

④ Enough water can't be had by any of us here.

⑤ The copper pipes may not be used to carry the gas.

17 다음 문장에서 어법상 어색한 것을 바르게 고치시오.

(1) This cheese should be sell by May 31st.

_____ ➡ _____

(2) This letter must deliver by tomorrow.

_____ ➡ _____

(3) A member can be become by anybody if he wants.

_____

_____ ➡

(4) I don't think half of those invited was present.

_____ ➡ _____

(5) Only a little of your help were needed.

_____ ➡ _____

18 다음 중 어법상 바르지 <u>않은</u> 것을 <u>모두</u> 고르시오.

① Half of the people have pets.
② Start your day with "Morning Soup." It can be cooked in 3 minutes.
③ About a quarter of the population of the country live in Seoul.
④ This medicine should be keep out of the reach of children.
⑤ These crops cannot be produced by themselves.

[19~21] 다음 글을 읽고 물음에 답하시오.

Bees are very helpful to humans. First, bees give us honey. Honey is a truly wonderful food. It is good for our health and tastes great. Honey can last almost forever. In fact, honey from ancient Egypt can be eaten today! Second, bees help produce many crops such as apples and strawberries. These crops cannot be produced by themselves. They need the help of bees. Bees help in the process of pollination.

How bees help pollination
• **What is pollination?**
It is moving pollen from one flower to another ⓐ<u>to make</u> seeds.
• **What is pollen?**
It is a fine yellow powder ⓑ<u>produced by flowers</u>.

19 위 글의 벌과 식물의 관계에 어울리지 <u>않는</u> 말을 고르시오.

① win-win
② cooperative
③ conflicting
④ coexistent
⑤ mutually beneficial

20 밑줄 친 ⓑ 앞에 생략된 말을 쓰시오.

➡ _____

21 위 글의 밑줄 친 ⓐ<u>to make</u>와 to부정사의 용법이 <u>다른</u> 것을 <u>모두</u> 고르시오.

① To make seeds, these crops need the help of bees.
② Bees continue to make seeds.
③ What do flowers need to make seeds?
④ These crops have no way to make seeds.
⑤ It is impossible to make seeds without pollination.

[22~24] 다음 글을 읽고 물음에 답하시오.

Then what can we do to help our little yellow friends? First, we can plant more flowers and trees. This will provide a good environment for bees to live in. Also, trees help slow ⓐ global warming. Second, the use of harmful chemicals ⓑ crops must be stopped. ⓒ<u>These chemicals</u> are unhealthy for bees and people. Our little friends need our help. ⓓ<u>그들을 실망시키지 말자!</u>

22 위 글의 빈칸 ⓐ와 ⓑ에 들어갈 말이 바르게 짝지어진 것은?

ⓐ	ⓑ		ⓐ	ⓑ
① down	– on		② to	– at
③ with	– to		④ down	– at
⑤ with	– on			

23 다음 빈칸에 알맞은 한 단어를 넣어 위 글의 밑줄 친 ⓒ<u>These chemicals</u>가 가리키는 것을 완성하시오.

➡ The harmful chemicals _____ on crops

24 위 글의 밑줄 친 ⓓ의 우리말에 맞게 5 단어로 영작하시오.

➡ _____

Lesson 3

Heal the World

의사소통 기능

- 원하는 행동 묻기
  A: What do you want me to do?
  B: Please put the clothes into the box.
- 당부하기
  A: Make sure you lock the doors.
  B: Okay, I will.

언어 형식

- 사역동사
  The project manager **had** us **meet** at 9 a.m.
- It ~ that 강조 구문
  It was a better tomorrow **that** we painted.

Words & Expressions

Key Words

- **amusement park** 놀이 공원
- **apply** [əplái] 통 지원하다
- **arrange** [əréindʒ] 통 배열하다
- **as** 접 ~할 때, ~하면서
- **background** [bǽkgraund] 명 배경
- **bake** [beik] 통 굽다
- **board** [bɔːrd] 명 칠판
- **clearly** [klíərli] 부 분명하게
- **decide** [disáid] 통 결심하다
- **deliver** [dilívər] 통 배달하다
- **divide** [diváid] 통 나누다
- **donation** [dounéiʃən] 명 기부, 기증
- **drawing** [drɔ́ːiŋ] 명 그림
- **elementary school** 초등학교
- **experience** [ikspíəriəns] 명 경험
- **friendly** [fréndli] 형 친절한
- **fur** [fəːr] 명 털
- **gym uniform** 체육복
- **land** [lænd] 통 내려앉다 명 땅, 육지
- **later** [léitər] 부 나중에, 후에
- **location** [loukéiʃən] 명 장소
- **manager** [mǽnidʒər] 명 운영자, 관리자
- **matter** [mǽtər] 통 문제되다, 중요하다
- **neat** [niːt] 형 깨끗한
- **neighborhood** [néidərhùd] 명 근처, 이웃
- **nursing home** 양로원

- **pack** [pæk] 통 짐을 꾸리다
- **paint** [peint] 명 물감 통 (그림물감으로) 그리다
- **plant** [plænt] 통 심다 명 식물
- **politely** [pəláitli] 부 예의 바르게
- **poster** [póustər] 명 벽보, 게시물
- **prepare** [pripɛ́ər] 통 준비하다
- **project** [prádʒekt] 명 과제
- **recycling bin** 재활용 쓰레기통
- **remove** [rimúːv] 통 없애다, 제거하다
- **reply** [riplái] 통 응답하다
- **rewarding** [riwɔ́ːrdiŋ] 형 보람 있는
- **select** [silékt] 통 선택하다, 선정하다
- **share** [ʃɛər] 통 나누다, 공유하다
- **shelf** [ʃelf] 명 책꽂이
- **site** [sait] 명 현장, 장소
- **soap** [soup] 명 비누
- **spot** [spat] 명 (특정한) 장소, 자리
- **suggest** [səgdʒést] 통 제안하다
- **the blind** 시각 장애인
- **the elderly** 나이 든 사람들
- **village** [vílidʒ] 명 마을
- **volunteer** [vàləntíər] 명 자원봉사 통 자원봉사하다
- **vote** [vout] 통 투표하다
- **wall painting** 벽화
- **water** [wɔ́ːtər] 통 물을 주다
- **wing** [wiŋ] 명 날개

Key Expressions

- **a light goes on in the head** 머릿속에 좋은 생각이 떠오르다
- **Anything else**? 그 이외에 다른 것 있나요?
- **be on time** 제시간에 도착하다
- **be proud of** ~ ~을 자랑스러워하다
- **get along with** ~ ~와 사이좋게 지내다
- **get on** 타다
- **get together** 모이다
- **get up** 일어나다
- **give a bath** 목욕시키다
- **give ~ a hand** ~에게 도움을 주다
- **How about** ~? ~는 어떤가요?

- **in front of** ~ ~ 앞에서
- **It's time to** ~. ~해야 할 시간이다.
- **keep ~ in mind** ~을 명심하다
- **line up** 줄서다
- **make sure** ~ 꼭 ~하다
- **pick up** 치우다, 줍다
- **so ~ that** ... 너무 ~해서 …하다
- **take a break** 휴식을 취하다
- **take a picture** 사진을 찍다
- **That's it**. 다됐어., 그게 다예요.
- **turn off** 끄다
- **Why don't we** ~? ~하는 것이 어떨까?

Word Power

※ 서로 비슷한 뜻을 가진 어휘

- □ **arrange** 배열하다 - **array** 배열하다
- □ **decide** 결심하다 - **determine** 결정하다
- □ **manager** 관리자 - **director** 책임자
- □ **neat** 깨끗한 - **tidy** 깔끔한

- □ **clearly** 분명하게 - **obviously** 명백하게
- □ **divide** 나누다 - **split** 쪼개다
- □ **matter** 중요하다 - **count** 중요하다
- □ **remove** 제거하다 - **eliminate** 제거하다

※ 서로 반대의 뜻을 가진 어휘

- □ **background** 배경 ↔ **foreground** 전경
- □ **friendly** 친절한 ↔ **hostile** 적대적인
- □ **later** 나중에, 후에 ↔ **earlier** 이전에
- □ **pack** 짐을 꾸리다 ↔ **unpack** 짐을 풀다

- □ **divide** 나누다 ↔ **combine** 결합하다
- □ **land** 착륙하다 ↔ **take off** 이륙하다
- □ **neat** 깨끗한 ↔ **dirty** 지저분한
- □ **politely** 예의 바르게 ↔ **impolitely** 무례하게

※ 동사 - 명사

- □ **apply** 지원하다 - **application** 지원서, 적용
- □ **decide** 결심하다 - **decision** 결정
- □ **divide** 나누다 - **division** 분할
- □ **prepare** 준비하다 - **preparation** 준비

- □ **arrange** 배열하다 - **arrangement** 배열, 준비
- □ **deliver** 배달하다 - **delivery** 배달
- □ **manage** 관리하다 - **management** 관리
- □ **select** 선택하다 - **selection** 선택

※ 형용사 - 명사

- □ **blind** 눈이 먼 - **the blind** 시각 장애인
- □ **experienced** 경험 많은 - **the experienced** 경험 많은 사람들

- □ **elderly** 나이 든 - **the elderly** 나이 든 사람들

English Dictionary

- □ **amusement park** 놀이 공원
  → a large park with many machines that you can ride on, such as roller coasters
  롤러코스터 같은 탈 수 있는 많은 기계가 있는 큰 공원

- □ **arrange** 정리하다
  → to put a group of things or people in a particular order or position
  한 무리의 물건이나 사람을 특정한 순서나 위치에 두다

- □ **background** 배경
  → the area that is behind the main thing that you are looking at
  당신이 보고 있는 주된 것 뒤에 있는 영역

- □ **bake** 굽다
  → to cook something using dry heat, in an oven
  오븐에서 건열을 사용해서 요리하다

- □ **deliver** 배달하다
  → to take something to a person or place
  무언가를 어떤 사람이나 장소로 가져가다

- □ **donation** 기부, 기증
  → something that you give to help a person or organization
  사람이나 기관을 돕기 위해 주는 어떤 것

- □ **drawing** 그림
  → a picture that you draw with a pencil, pen, etc.
  펜, 연필 등으로 그리는 그림

- □ **location** 장소
  → a particular place 특정한 장소

- □ **manager** 관리자
  → someone whose job is to manage part or all of a company or other organization
  회사나 다른 조직의 일부나 전체를 관리하는 일을 하는 사람

- □ **matter** 중요하다
  → to be important 중요하다

- □ **pack** 짐을 꾸리다
  → to put things into cases, bags, etc. ready for a trip
  여행 준비로 상자나 가방에 짐을 넣다

- □ **remove** 제거하다
  → to move or take something away from a place
  어떤 것을 한 장소에서 옮기거나 치우다

- □ **volunteer** 자원봉사자
  → a person who does a job without being paid
  대가를 받지 않고 어떤 일을 하는 사람

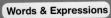

01 다음 밑줄 친 부분과 바꿔 쓸 수 있는 말을 고르시오.

> International travel can be a rich and <u>rewarding</u> adventure.

① expensive   ② satisfying
③ informative   ④ demanding
⑤ difficult

02 다음 빈칸에 들어갈 말을 고르시오.

> You're late again. It's important to be _____ time.

① at   ② by   ③ for   ④ on   ⑤ to

03 다음 〈보기〉에 있는 어휘를 이용하여 빈칸을 채울 수 <u>없는</u> 것을 고르시오. (형태 변화 가능)

> ┤ 보기 ├
> do   give   have   prepare

① Just make yourself at home while I _____ the baby a bath.
② You must _____ his advice in mind.
③ The most important thing is _____ our best.
④ Joe helped me _____ for the exam.
⑤ The children were _____ fun, chasing each other's shadows.

04 다음 밑줄 친 부분의 의미로 알맞지 <u>않은</u> 것은?

① You'd better <u>pack</u> your bags. We're leaving in an hour. (짐을 꾸리다)
② Soap and cold water will <u>remove</u> most food stains. (제거하다)
③ It doesn't <u>matter</u> what you wear, as long as you look neat and tidy. (문제, 어려움)
④ There was cat <u>fur</u> all over the chair. (털)
⑤ Even a small <u>donation</u> can make a big difference to one child's life. (기부)

05 다음 대화의 빈칸에 들어갈 말로 알맞은 것을 고르시오.

> A: I'm so tired.
> B: I _____ taking a rest.
> A: That's a good idea.

① suggest   ② share   ③ promise
④ explain   ⑤ expect

06 다음 빈칸 (A)~(C)에 알맞은 말로 짝지어진 것을 고르시오.

> • He (A)_____ together with some friends to plan a party for her.
> • Floor tiles can be difficult to clean. It is worth (B)_____ in mind when you choose a new floor.
> • (C)_____ sure to take this medicine after every meal.

(A)	(B)	(C)
① got	– keeping	– Take
② got	– keeping	– Make
③ got	– being	– Take
④ had	– being	– Make
⑤ had	– being	– Take

01 빈칸을 주어진 영영풀이에 해당하는 말을 이용하여 채우시오. (주어진 철자로 시작할 것.)

> to move or take something away from a place

> Illegally parked vehicles will be r_____ .

02 다음 빈칸에 알맞은 단어를 〈보기〉에서 골라 쓰시오. (단어는 한 번씩만 사용 가능)

> ┌ 보기 ┐
> along   on   together   up

(1) Get _____ early to be in time for the first train.
(2) They get _____ and study math on Wednesdays.
(3) We got _____ the train at Lime Street Station.
(4) I get _____ with my classmates.

03 두 문장의 의미가 같도록 문장을 완성할 때 빈칸에 들어갈 말을 쓰시오. (2 단어)

> It's time for self-introduction.
> ➡ It's time _____ yourself.

[04~05] 다음 빈칸에 공통으로 들어갈 말을 쓰시오.

04
· Why don't we pick _____ the trash?
· Cars lined _____ waiting to board the ship.

05
· Don't forget to water the _____ .
· We will _____ tomatoes and carrots in the garden.

06 다음 우리말에 맞도록 빈칸에 알맞은 말을 쓰시오. (철자가 주어진 경우 주어진 철자로 시작할 것)

(1) 비행기는 안전하게 착륙했다.
➡ The plane l_____ safely.
(2) 빗은 내가 머리를 단정하게 유지하는 것을 가능하게 한다.
➡ The comb enables me to keep my hair n_____ .
(3) Susan은 오후에 연세 드신 분들을 인터뷰할 것이다.
➡ Susan will interview _____ e_____ people in the afternoon.
(4) Descartes는 그 파리가 똑같은 지점에 두 번 정말로 앉았는지 아닌지 궁금했다.
➡ Descartes wondered if the fly ever landed on the same s_____ twice.

07 다음 우리말에 맞게 주어진 단어를 바르게 배열하시오.

(1) 그들은 스스로를 아주 자랑스러워해야 한다.
(must, themselves, they, so, of, proud, be)
➡ _____

(2) 이 상황이 아주 중요하다.
(situation, a, matters, this, lot)
➡ _____

(3) 내가 일찍 끝나면 도와줄게.
(I, I'll, finish, give, hand, early, a, if)
➡ _____

Conversation

1 원하는 행동 묻기

> A: What do you want me to do? 내가 무엇을 하길 원하니?
> B: Please put the clothes into the box. 옷을 상자 안에 넣어 줘.

- 'What do you want me to do?'는 상대방에게 도움을 주고자 할 때 그 사람이 구체적으로 필요로 하는 도움이 무엇인지 묻는 표현이다. 대답으로는 'I want you to ~.' 또는 Please로 시작하는 명령문을 사용해 말할 수 있다. 'What would you like to ~?'는 'What do you want to ~?'와 비슷한 표현이지만 더 부드럽게 말할 때 자주 쓰인다.

- 상대방이 원하는 행동을 물어볼 때 동사 'want, would like'는 '목적어+목적격보어(to부정사)'의 구조가 된다. 상대방이 누구에게 원하는지 그 대상을 목적어로 하고, 그가 해야 할 행동을 목적격보어로 써서 'What do you want 목적어+to부정사?', 'What would you like 목적어+to부정사?'의 구조가 되도록 한다.

- 상대방이 원하는 것을 물어보는 방법은 도움을 제안하는 표현으로도 나타낼 수 있다. 말하는 사람을 주어로 해서 상대에게 원하는 것을 물어볼 때는 'What can I do for you?', 'How may I help you?'가 될 수도 있다.

원하는 행동 묻기

- What would you like to ~?
- Do you want to ~?
- What do you want to ~?
- Would you like to ~?

도움을 제안하는 표현

- May/Can I help you? 도와 드릴까요?
- Would you like some help?
- Is there anything that I can help you?
- Do you need some help?
- What can I do for you?

핵심 Check

1. 다음 우리말과 일치하도록 빈칸에 알맞은 말을 쓰시오.

> A: What are you doing?
> B: I'm packing for my move tomorrow. Can you help me?
> A: Sure. _____ (내가 무엇을 하길 원하니?)
> B: Please put the clothes into the box.
> A: No problem.

2 당부하기

A: Make sure you lock the door. 반드시 문을 닫아라.
B: Okay, I will. 알았어요.

■ 'Make sure+주어+동사 ~.'는 상대방이 어떤 일을 잊지 않고 꼭 할 것을 당부할 때 사용할 수 있는 표현이다. 이에 대한 대답은 'Okay, I will.' 또는 'No problem.' 등으로 말할 수 있다. 'Make sure ~.'는 '~을 확실하게 하다.'의 뜻으로 명령문으로 나타내게 되면 '확실하게 해라, 반드시 ~해라.'의 의미로 상대에게 당부하는 표현이 된다. 'Be sure to ~.'도 마찬가지로 '반드시 ~해라.'의 의미가 된다.

■ 상대방에게 '~할 것을 잊지 말아라., ~할 것을 기억해라.'라고 당부할 때는 'Don't forget to+동사원형 ~.'으로 말할 수 있고 'Remember to 동사원형 ~.'으로 나타내기도 한다.

당부하기

- Make sure (that) ~ . 반드시 ~해라.
- Don't forget to ~. ~하는 것을 잊지 마라.
- Be sure to ~ . 반드시 ~해라.
- Please remember to ~. ~할 것을 기억해 주세요.

핵심 Check

2. 다음 우리말과 일치하도록 주어진 말을 이용해 빈칸에 알맞은 말을 쓰시오.

> A: It's time to go home.
> B: Yes. <u>문을 잠그는 거 명심해.</u> (make, lock)
> A: Okay, I will. Anything else?
> B: No, that's it. See you tomorrow.

➡ _____

3. 다음 주어진 문장을 적절하게 배열하시오.

> A: Hi, I'm Minsu. I'm here for the volunteer work.
> B: Thanks for coming, Minsu.
> A: What do you want me to do today?
> (A) Okay. Is there anything to keep in mind?
> (B) Please give the dog a bath.
> (C) Yes. Make sure you brush the fur first.
> (D) Okay, I will.

➡ _____

Listen and Speak 1 A

B: What are all these boxes ❶and books for?

G: I'm packing the books for the ❷donation center. ❸Can you give me a hand?

B: Sure. ❹What do you want me to do?

G: Please write ❺the address on the boxes.

B: No problem.

B: 이 박스와 책들은 다 무엇에 쓰려는 거니?

G: 기부 센터에 보내려고 책을 싸고 있어. 도와줄래?

B: 물론이야. 내가 무엇을 하길 원하니?

G: 박스에 주소를 좀 써 줘.

B: 그래.

❶ 접속사 and는 these boxes와 books를 연결하고 있다.

❷ donation: 기부, 기증

❸ 'give ~ a hand' 는 '~를 돕다'라는 관용적 표현으로, 이 표현을 이용해 'Can you give me a hand?'라고 하면, '나 좀 도와줄래?'의 의미로 상대방에게 도움을 요청할 때 사용하는 표현이다.

❹ 'What do you want me to do?'는 '너는 내가 무엇을 해 주기를 원하니?'라는 뜻으로 상대방이 원하는 행동이 무엇인지 물어보는 표현이다.

❺ address: 주소

Check(√) True or False

(1) The girl is packing the books. 　　　　　　　　　　　　　　　　T ☐ F ☐

(2) The girl wants the boy to help her. 　　　　　　　　　　　　　　T ☐ F ☐

Listen and Speak 2 A

B: Enjoy the concert, Mom.

W: Okay, ❶I will. Thanks. Your dinner is on the table.

B: All right. ❷Don't worry about me.

W: ❸Make sure you ❹feed the dog after you have dinner.

B: Okay. Mom, you should go now. Dad is waiting in the car.

B: 콘서트 재미있게 보세요, 엄마.

W: 그래. 고마워. 저녁은 식탁에 있어.

B: 알겠어요. 저는 걱정 마세요.

W: 저녁 먹은 후에 개 밥 주는 거 명심해라.

B: 알겠어요. 엄마, 이제 가셔야 해요. 아빠가 차에서 기다리고 계셔요.

❶ I will 다음에 enjoy the concert가 생략되어 있다.

❷ worry about: ~에 대해 걱정하다

❸ 'Make sure (that) 주어+동사 ~' 구문으로 상대방이 잊어버리지 않도록 중요한 일에 대해 강한 당부 또는 경고하는 의미를 나타낼 수 있다. '~을 확실히 하라, ~을 반드시 하라'의 뜻이다. 'Make sure (that) 주어+동사 ~' 대신에 'Make sure to+동사원형 ~', 'I think you should ~', 'Try to ~', 'Be sure to/that ~' 등을 통해서도 강한 당부, 충고, 경고의 의미를 나타낼 수 있다. '~을 반드시 하지 말 것'을 강하게 당부하거나 경고할 경우에는 'Make sure not to+동사원형' 또는 'Make sure (that) you don't ~'를 사용할 수 있다.

❹ feed: 먹이를 주다

Check(√) True or False

(3) Mom is going to go to the concert. 　　　　　　　　　　　　　　T ☐ F ☐

(4) Mom is planning to eat dinner with the boy. 　　　　　　　　　　T ☐ F ☐

Listen and Speak 1 B

B: What is this ❶mess?

G: I'm baking cookies.

B: Why are you baking so many cookies?

G: ❷They're for the people at the nursing home.

B: That's very nice of you.

G: ❸Can you give me a hand?

B: Sure. ❹What do you want me to do?

G: Please put the cookies in the gift boxes. Three cookies in each box.

B: Okay.

B: 이 엉망진창은 뭐니?
G: 쿠키를 굽고 있어.
B: 왜 이렇게 많은 쿠키를 굽고 있니?
G: 쿠키는 양로원에 계신 분들을 위한 거야.
B: 정말 착하구나.
G: 도와줄래?
B: 물론이야. 내가 무엇을 하길 원하니?
G: 선물 상자에 쿠키를 좀 넣어 줘. 상자 하나에 쿠키 3개씩.
B: 알겠어.

❶ mess: (지저분하고) 엉망인 상태
❷ 여기서 They는 many cookies를 받는 인칭대명사이다.
❸ 상대방에게 도움을 요청할 때 'Can you give me a hand?'로 말할 수 있다. 'Can you do me a favor?'로 바꿔 말할 수도 있다.
❹ 'What do you want to me to do?'는 '너는 내가 무엇을 하기를 원하니?'로 상대방이 원하는 것이 무엇인지 묻는 표현이다. 여기서 want는 5형식 동사로 'me'는 목적어 'to do'가 목적격보어로 사용되었다.

Check(√) True or False

(5) The boy will put three cookies in one box. T ☐ F ☐

(6) The girl is baking a few cookies. T ☐ F ☐

Real Life Talk Step 3

A: Hi, I'm Minsu. ❶I'm here for the volunteer work.

B: ❷Thanks for coming, Minsu.

A: ❸What do you want me to do today?

B: Please ❹give the dog a bath.

A: Okay. Is there anything ❺to keep in mind?

B: Yes. ❻Make sure you brush the fur first.

A: Okay, I will.

A: 안녕하세요. 저는 민수예요. 저는 봉사 활동을 하러 왔어요.
B: 와 주셔서 감사합니다.
A: 오늘 제가 무엇을 하길 원하세요?
B: 개를 목욕시켜 주세요.
A: 네. 명심해야 할 것이 있나요?
B: 네. 털을 먼저 빗길 것을 명심하세요.
A: 네. 그렇게 할게요.

❶ 'I'm here for 명사.'는 '~ 때문에 왔다. ~하러 왔다'라는 표현이며 'I'm here to 동사원형 ~.'으로 바꿔 쓸 수 있다. I'm here for the volunteer work. = I'm here to do volunteer work.
❷ thank (you) 뒤에 for를 쓰는 경우. for 뒤에 감사의 이유를 적는다.
❸ 상대방이 원하는 행동을 'What do you want me to do?(제가 무엇을 하기를 원하십니까?)'를 이용해서 물어볼 수 있다.
❹ give a bath: 목욕시키다
❺ to keep in mind가 앞의 anything을 수식하고 있다. keep in mind: 명심하다
❻ 상대방에게 당부의 말을 할 때는 '확실하게 하다'라는 의미의 make sure를 써서 'Make sure you+동사원형 ~'의 형태로 말한다. 비슷한 표현으로 'Don't forget to 동사원형 ~.'이 있다.

Check(√) True or False

(7) B wants Minsu to give the dog a bath. T ☐ F ☐

(8) Minsu should brush the fur after bathing the dog. T ☐ F ☐

Listen and Speak 1 C

A: What are you doing?

B: I'm ❶packing for my ❷move tomorrow. ❸Can you help me?

A: Sure. ❹What do you want me to do?

B: Please ❺move the chairs outside.

A: No problem.

❶ pack: 짐을 꾸리다
❷ move: 이사
❸ 상대방에게 도움을 요청할 때 'Can you help me?'로 말할 수 있다. 'Can you do me a favor?'나 'I was wondering if you could help me.'라고 바꿔 말할 수도 있다.
❹ 'What do you want me to do?'는 '너는 내가 무엇을 해 주기를 원하니?'라는 뜻으로 상대방이 원하는 행동이 무엇인지를 물어보는 표현이다.
❺ 여기서 move는 앞에 쓴 명사의 '이사'의 의미가 아니라 동사로 '옮기다'의 의미로 사용하였다. outside: 밖으로

Listen and Speak 2 B

B: Hello, class. Make groups of four people ❶and sit around the tables. Today ❷we're going to make bacon and egg sandwiches. ❸Keep in mind two rules for our class. First, ❹make sure you wash your hands before you start. Second, be careful ❺when you use a knife. All right, let's start.

❶ make와 sit은 접속사 and로 병렬로 연결되어 있다.
❷ 'be going to'는 '~할 것이다'의 의미로 가까운 미래의 계획을 말할 때 사용한다.
❸ keep in mind: 명심하다
❹ make sure ~: 꼭 ~해라, 확실하게 해라
❺ 여기서 when은 접속사로 '~할 때'의 의미로 사용되었다.

Listen and Speak 2 C

A: ❶It's time to go home.

B: Yes. ❷Make sure you lock the doors.

A: Okay, I will. Anything else?

B: No, that's it. See you tomorrow.

❶ It's time to 동사원형 ~: ~해야 할 시간이다
❷ 'Make sure (that) 주어 동사 ~'는 '꼭 ~해라, 확실하게 ~해라'라는 의미로 상대방에게 당부할 때 쓰는 표현이다. 'Be sure to 동사원형 ~.', 'Don't forget to 동사원형 ~.', 'Please remember to 동사원형 ~.' 등으로 바꿔 말할 수 있다.

Real Life Talk Watch a Video

Woman: Good morning. ❶What can I do for you?

Tony: Hi. ❷I'm here for the ❸volunteer work.

Woman: Oh, you ❹must be Tony.

Tony: That's right. ❺What do you want me to do today?

Woman: Please read this book for ❻the blind in the recording room.

Tony: No problem. Should I go in now?

Woman: Yes. Please go into Room 7.

Tony: Okay. Is there anything ❼to keep in mind?

Woman: Yes. ❽Make sure you read ❾slowly and clearly.

Tony: Okay. I'll ❿do my best.

❶ 'What can I do for you?'는 '무엇을 도와드릴까요?'의 의미로 상대방에게 도움을 제안할 때 사용하는 표현이다.
❷ 'I'm here for ~.'는 '나는 ~을 위해[~하러] 왔어요.'의 의미로 온 목적에 대해 말할 때 사용할 수 있다.
❸ volunteer: 자원봉사
❹ must는 '~임에 틀림없다'의 의미로 강한 추측을 나타낼 때 사용한다.
❺ 'What do you want me to do?'는 '제가 무엇을 하기 원하세요?'라는 뜻으로 상대방이 원하는 행동이 무엇인지를 물어보는 표현이다.
❻ 'the+형용사'는 복수 보통명사로 여기서 the blind는 blind people을 의미한다.
❼ to keep in mind는 앞의 명사 anything을 수식하고 있다. (to부정사의 형용사 용법) keep in mind: 명심하다
❽ make sure ~: 꼭 ~해라, 확실하게 ~해라
❾ slowly와 clearly는 앞의 동사인 read를 수식하고 있다.
❿ do one's best: 최선을 다하다

Real Life Talk Step 1

A: ❶What do you want to do?

B: I ❷want to ❸teach English to the children.

❶ 'What do you want to do?'는 '너는 무엇을 하기를 원하니?'로 상대방이 원하는 것이 무엇인지 묻는 표현이다.
❷ want는 to부정사를 목적어로 받는 동사이다.
❸ 'teach English to the children'을 4형식인 'teach the children English'로 바꿔 쓸 수 있다.

● 다음 우리말과 일치하도록 빈칸에 알맞은 말을 쓰시오.

Listen and Speak 1 A

B: _____ are all these boxes and books _____?

G: I'm _____ the books for the _____ center. Can you _____ _____ _____ hand?

B: Sure. What do you _____ me _____ do?

G: Please write the _____ _____ the boxes.

B: No problem.

해석

B: 이 박스와 책들은 다 무엇에 쓰려는 거니?
G: 기부 센터에 보내려고 책을 싸고 있어. 도와줄래?
B: 물론이야. 내가 무엇을 하길 원하니?
G: 박스에 주소를 좀 써 줘.
B: 그래.

Listen and Speak 1 B

B: What is _____ _____?

G: I'm _____ cookies.

B: _____ are you baking so _____ cookies?

G: _____ _____ the people at the nursing home.

B: That's very _____ _____ you.

G: _____ _____ _____ me a hand?

B: Sure. What _____ _____ _____ _____ to do?

G: Please _____ the cookies in the gift boxes. Three cookies in _____ box.

B: Okay.

B: 이 엉망진창은 뭐니?
G: 쿠키를 굽고 있어.
B: 왜 이렇게 많은 쿠키를 굽고 있니?
G: 쿠키는 양로원에 계신 분들을 위한 거야.
B: 정말 착하구나.
G: 도와줄래?
B: 물론이야. 내가 무엇을 하길 원하니?
G: 선물 상자에 쿠키를 좀 넣어 줘. 상자 하나에 쿠키 3개씩.
B: 알겠어.

Listen and Speak 1 C

1. **A:** What are you _____?

   B: I'm _____ _____ my move tomorrow. _____ _____ _____ me?

   A: Sure. _____ _____ _____ _____ _____ me to do?

   B: Please _____ _____ _____ _____ the box.

   A: No problem.

2. **A:** What are you doing?

   B: I'm _____ _____ my _____ tomorrow. _____ _____ _____ _____?

   A: Sure. What do you want me to do?

   B: Please _____ the chairs _____.

   A: No problem.

1. **A:** 너 뭐 하고 있니?
   B: 내일 이사를 위해 짐을 싸는 중이야. 도와줄래?
   A: 물론이지. 내가 무엇을 하길 원하니?
   B: 옷을 상자 안에 넣어 줘.
   A: 그래.

2. **A:** 너 뭐 하고 있니?
   B: 내일 이사를 위해 짐을 싸는 중이야. 도와줄래?
   A: 물론이지. 내가 무엇을 하길 원하니?
   B: 의자를 밖으로 옮겨 줘.
   A: 그래.

3. **A:** _____ _____ _____ _____?

   B: I'm _____ _____ my _____ tomorrow. _____ _____ _____ _____?

   A: Sure. _____ _____ _____ _____ _____ _____ _____?

   B: Please _____ _____ the trach.

   A: No problem.

> 3. **A:** 너 뭐 하고 있니?
> **B:** 내일 이사를 위해 짐을 싸는 중이야. 도와줄래?
> **A:** 물론이지. 내가 무엇을 하길 원하니?
> **B:** 쓰레기를 밖에 갖다 버려 줘.
> **A:** 그래.

Listen and Speak 2 A

B: _____ the concert, Mom.

W: Okay, I _____. Thanks. Your dinner _____ _____ the table.

B: All right. Don't _____ _____ me.

W: _____ _____ _____ _____ the dog _____ you have dinner.

B: Okay. Mom, you _____ go now. Dad is waiting in the car.

> **B:** 콘서트 재미있게 보세요, 엄마.
> **W:** 그래. 고마워. 저녁은 식탁에 있어.
> **B:** 알겠어요. 저는 걱정 마세요.
> **W:** 저녁 먹은 후에 개 밥 주는 거 명심해라.
> **B:** 알겠어요. 엄마, 이제 가셔야 해요. 아빠가 차에서 기다리고 계셔요.

Listen and Speak 2 B

B: Hello, class. _____ _____ _____ four people and _____ around the tables. Today we're going _____ _____ bacon and egg sandwiches. _____ _____ _____ two rules for our class. First, _____ _____ you wash your hands _____ _____ _____. _____, be careful _____ you use a knife. All right, _____ start.

> **B:** 안녕하세요, 여러분. 4명씩 모둠을 만들어 탁자에 둘러앉으세요. 오늘 우리는 베이컨 달걀 샌드위치를 만들 거예요. 우리 수업의 두 가지 규칙에 유의하세요. 첫째, 시작하기 전에 손을 씻는 것을 명심하세요. 둘째, 칼을 사용할 때 조심하세요. 좋아요, 시작해 봐요.

Listen and Speak 2 C

1. **A:** It's time _____ _____ home.

   B: Yes. _____ _____ you lock the doors.

   A: Okay, I will. _____ else?

   B: No, _____ it. See you tomorrow.

2. **A:** It's _____ _____ go home.

   B: Yes. _____ _____ _____ _____ the board.

   A: Okay, I will. _____ _____?

   B: No, that's it. See you tomorrow.

3. **A:** _____ _____ _____ _____ home.

   B: Yes. _____ _____ you _____ _____ _____.

   A: Okay, I _____. Anything else?

   B: No, that's it. See you tomorrow.

> 1. **A:** 집에 갈 시간이야.
> **B:** 응. 문 잠그는 거 명심해.
> **A:** 알겠어, 그렇게 할게. 또 다른 건?
> **B:** 없어, 그게 전부야. 내일 보자.
>
> 2. **A:** 이제 집에 갈 시간이야.
> **B:** 응. 칠판 닦는 거 명심해.
> **A:** 알겠어, 그렇게 할게. 또 다른 건?
> **B:** 없어, 그게 전부야. 내일 보자.
>
> 3. **A:** 이제 집에 갈 시간이야.
> **B:** 응. 식물에 물 주는 거 명심해.
> **A:** 알겠어, 그렇게 할게. 또 다른 건?
> **B:** 없어, 그게 전부야. 내일 보자.

해석

Real Life Talk Watch a Video

Woman: Good morning. _____ _____ _____ _____ for you?

Tony: Hi. I'm _____ _____ the volunteer work.

Woman: Oh, you _____ _____ Tony.

Tony: That's right. _____ _____ _____ _____ _____ _____ today?

Woman: Please _____ this book _____ _____ _____ in the recording room.

Tony: No problem. Should I go in now?

Woman: Yes. Please _____ _____ Room 7.

Tony: Okay. Is there _____ _____ _____ _____ mind?

Woman: Yes. _____ _____ _____ read _____ _____ _____.

Tony: Okay. I'll _____ _____ _____.

Woman: 안녕하세요. 무엇을 도와드릴까요?

Tony: 안녕하세요. 저는 봉사 활동을 하러 왔어요.

Woman: 오, Tony군요.

Tony: 맞아요. 오늘 제가 무엇을 하길 원하세요?

Woman: 녹음실에서 시각 장애인들을 위해 이 책을 읽어 주세요.

Tony: 알겠어요. 지금 들어가야 하나요?

Woman: 네. 7번 방으로 들어가 주세요.

Tony: 네. 명심해야 할 것이 있나요?

Woman: 네. 천천히 그리고 명확하게 읽어야 하는 것을 명심하세요.

Tony: 네. 최선을 다할게요.

Real Life Talk Step 3

1. **A:** Hi, I'm Minsu. _____ _____ _____ the volunteer work.

   B: Thanks _____ coming, Minsu.

   A: What _____ _____ _____ _____ _____ _____ today?

   B: Please _____ the dog _____ _____.

   A: Okay. _____ _____ _____ to keep in mind?

   B: Yes. _____ _____ you brush the fur first.

   A: Okay, I will

2. **A:** Hi, I'm Tony. _____ _____ _____ _____ _____ _____.

   B: _____ _____ coming, Tony.

   A: _____ _____ _____ _____ _____ _____ _____ today?

   B: Please record a book _____ _____ _____.

   A: Okay. _____ _____ _____ _____ _____ _____ ?

   B: Yes. Make _____ you read slowly and clearly.

   A: Okay, I will.

1. A: 안녕하세요. 저는 민수예요. 저는 봉사 활동을 하러 왔어요.
   B: 민수 군, 와 주셔서 감사합니다.
   A: 오늘 제가 무엇을 하길 원하세요?
   B: 개를 목욕시켜 주세요.
   A: 네. 명심해야 할 것이 있나요?
   B: 네. 털을 먼저 빗길 것을 명심하세요.
   A: 네. 그렇게 할게요.

2. A: 안녕하세요. 저는 Tony예요. 저는 봉사 활동을 하러 왔어요.
   B: Tony 군, 와 주셔서 감사합니다.
   A: 오늘 제가 무엇을 하길 원하세요?
   B: 시각 장애인들을 위해 책을 녹음해 주세요.
   A: 네. 유념해야 할 것이 있나요?
   B: 네. 천천히 그리고 명확하게 읽어야 하는 것을 명심하세요.
   A: 네. 그렇게 할게요.

[01~02] 다음 대화를 읽고 물음에 답하시오.

> B: What are all these boxes and books for?
> G: I'm packing the books for the donation center. Can you give me a hand?
> B: Sure. What do you want (A)_____?
> G: (B)_____
> B: No problem.

01 빈칸 (A)에 알맞은 말을 고르시오.

① doing　　　　② me doing　　　　③ to do
④ me to do　　　⑤ me to have done

02 빈칸 (B)에 알맞은 말을 고르시오.

① Let's write the address on the boxes.
② I don't want to write the address on the boxes.
③ Did you write the address on the boxes?
④ Why don't we write the address on the boxes?
⑤ Please write the address on the boxes.

03 다음 대화의 빈칸에 들어갈 말을 〈보기〉에서 골라 순서대로 바르게 배열하시오.

> B: What is this mess?
> G: _____
> B: _____
> G: _____
> B: _____
> G: _____
> B: Sure. What do you want me to do?
> G: Please put the cookies in the gift boxes. Three cookies in each box.
> B: Okay.

┤ 보기 ├
(A) They're for the people at the nursing home.
(B) That's very nice of you.
(C) I'm baking cookies.
(D) Can you give me a hand?
(E) Why are you baking so many cookies?

➡ _____

다음 대화의 빈칸에 들어갈 말로 알맞은 것을 고르시오.

> A: What are you doing?
> B: I'm packing for my move tomorrow. Can you help me?
> A: Sure. _____
> B: Please move the chairs outside.
> A: No problem.

① What would you like me to do this year?
② What do you want me to do?
③ What do you want to do?
④ What did you move?
⑤ Why didn't you pack your books?

[02~04] 다음 대화를 읽고 물음에 답하시오.

> B: Enjoy the concert, Mom. (①)
> W: Okay, I will. Thanks. (②) Your dinner is on the table.
> B: All right. Don't worry about me. (③)
> W: Make (A)_____ you feed the dog after you have dinner. (④)
> B: Okay. Mom, you should go now. (⑤)

02 위 대화의 ①~⑤ 중 주어진 문장이 들어갈 알맞은 곳은?

> Dad is waiting in the car.

①   ②   ③   ④   ⑤

03 빈칸 (A)에 알맞은 말을 고르시오.

① such   ② just   ③ right
④ sure   ⑤ true

04 위 대화를 읽고 답할 수 없는 질문을 고르시오.

① What should the boy do after having dinner?
② What does the boy worry about?
③ Where is the boy's dinner?
④ Where is the boy's dad?
⑤ Where is the boy's mom going to go?

[05~07] 다음 대화를 읽고 물음에 답하시오.

> B: What are all these boxes and books for? (①)
> G: I'm (A)_____ the books for the donation center. (②)
> B: Sure. (③) What do you want me to do?
> G: (④) Please write the address on the boxes. (⑤)
> B: No problem.

05 위 대화의 ①~⑤ 중 주어진 문장이 들어갈 알맞은 곳은?

> Can you give me a hand?

①   ②   ③   ④   ⑤

06 빈칸 (A)에 알맞은 말을 고르시오.

① packing   ② picking
③ putting   ④ spending
⑤ getting

위 대화를 읽고 답할 수 <u>없는</u> 질문을 고르시오.

① Is the boy going to help the girl?

② What is the girl doing now?

③ How many books is the girl going to send to the donation center?

④ What are the books for?

⑤ What will the boy do after conversation?

08 다음 대화의 빈칸에 들어갈 말로 알맞은 것을 고르시오.

> A: Hi! I'm here for the volunteer work.
> B: Thanks for coming.
> A: What do you want me to do today?
> B: Please deliver meals to the elderly.
> A: Okay. Is there anything to keep in mind?
> B: Yes. _____
> A: Okay, I will.

① Make sure you greet them politely.

② Remember to make home-made meals.

③ Be sure to take two tablets with water before meals.

④ Don't forget not to eat between meals.

⑤ You'd better donate them to the elderly.

09 다음 중 짝지어진 대화가 <u>어색한</u> 것은?

① A: Your computer is always on. It uses a lot of electricity.
   B: I'm sorry. I didn't know that.
   A: Make sure you turn it off when you're not using it.

② A: You didn't water the plant. Make sure you water it regularly.
   B: Okay. I will.

③ A: I forgot to close the window. It's all wet.
   B: Be sure to close the window next time.

④ A: Did you say the movie starts at 7:00?
   B: Yeah, make sure you go to the movie theater after 7:30.

⑤ A: It's really cold today.
   B: Make sure you wear your warm coat.

[10~11] 다음 대화를 읽고 물음에 답하시오.

> B: (①) Hello, class. (②) Make groups of four people and sit around the tables. (③) Today we're going to make bacon and egg sandwiches. (④) First, make sure you wash your hands before you start. (⑤) Second, be careful when you use a knife. All right, let's start.

10 위 대화의 ①~⑤ 중 주어진 문장이 들어갈 알맞은 곳은?

> Keep in mind two rules for our class.

①   ②   ③   ④   ⑤

11 위 대화를 읽고 답할 수 <u>없는</u> 질문을 고르시오.

① What are they going to make?

② What class is it?

③ How many hours does it take to make bacon and egg sandwiches?

④ How many rules are there to keep in mind during the class?

⑤ How many people do make a group?

[01~03] 다음 대화를 읽고 물음에 답하시오.

Woman: Good morning. What can I do for you?

Tony: Hi. I'm here for the volunteer work.

Woman: Oh, you must be Tony.

Tony: That's right. 오늘 제가 무엇을 하길 원하세요?

Woman: (A)Please read this book for blind in the recording room.

Tony: No problem. Should I go in now?

Woman: Yes. Please go into Room 7.

Tony: Okay. Is there anything to keep ⓐ[at / in / for] mind?

Woman: Yes. Make sure you read slowly and clearly.

Tony: Okay. I'll ⓑ[do / keep / make] my best.

01 위 대화의 괄호 ⓐ와 ⓑ에서 적절한 것을 골라 쓰시오.

➡ ⓐ _____ ⓑ _____

02 밑줄 친 우리말과 일치하도록 주어진 단어를 이용해 문장을 만드시오.

➡ _____

(want, do)

03 밑줄 친 (A)에서 어색한 부분을 찾아 고쳐 쓰시오.

➡ _____

04 다음 대화의 빈칸 (A)와 (B)에 알맞은 말을 쓰시오.

B: What is this mess?

G: I'm baking cookies.

B: Why are you baking so many cookies?

G: They're for the people at the nursing home.

B: That's very nice of you.

G: Can you (A)_____ me a hand?

B: Sure. What do you (B)_____ me to do?

G: Please put the cookies in the gift boxes. Three cookies in each box.

B: Okay.

➡ (A) _____ (B) _____

05 다음 대화의 괄호 (A)와 (B)에서 적절한 것을 골라 쓰시오.

A: It's time (A)[to go / to going / going] home.

B: Yes. Make sure you (A)[lock / locking / to lock] the doors.

A: Okay, I will. Anything else?

B: No, that's it. See you tomorrow.

➡ (A) _____ (B) _____

06 다음 대화의 밑줄 친 문장과 같은 의미가 되도록 주어진 단어를 이용해 문장을 만드시오.

A: What are you doing?

B: I'm packing for my move tomorrow. Can you help me?

A: Sure. What do you want me to do?

B: Please take out the trash.

A: No problem.

➡ _____ (like)

Grammar

1 사역동사 have/make/let 5형식 문장

> • The project manager **had** us **meet** at 9 a.m. 프로젝트 책임자는 우리를 오전 9시에 만나게 했다.
> • We **had** the car **serviced.** 우리는 차를 점검 받았다.

■ 사역동사
- 의미: 목적어가 ~하게 하다[시키다]/두다
- 종류: make, have, let 등
- 형태: '주어+have/make/let+목적어+목적격보어(동사원형)'

■ 사역동사는 '사역동사+목적어+목적격보어'의 형태로 주어가 아니라 대상(목적어)이 행동을 하게 만들거나 하도록 허용한다는 의미를 가지는 동사를 말하며, have, make, let이 있다.
- Laughter can **make** us **feel** better. 웃음이 우리의 기분을 나아지게 할 수 있다.
- Don't **let** her **upset** you. 그녀 때문에 속 썩이지 마.

■ 목적격보어로 목적어와의 관계가 능동일 경우 동사원형이 오며 '~(목적어)가 …하게(목적격보어)하다'의 뜻을 갖는다. 수동일 경우 '~(목적어)가 …(목적격보어)을 당하게[되게] 하다'의 뜻으로 make, have 는 목적격보어로 과거분사를 쓰고, let은 'be p.p.' 형태를 쓴다.
- I **had** him **wash** my car. 〈능동〉 나는 그에게 내 차를 닦게 했다. (그가 차를 닦는 것으로 능동)
- I **had** my car **washed**. 〈수동〉 나는 내 차가 세차되도록 했다. (차가 세차되는 것으로 수동)

■ 'help'와 'get'의 쓰임
   ※ help는 목적격보어로 동사원형이나 to부정사가 오며 뜻의 차이는 없다.
- I **helped** Alisha **do** her science homework. 나는 Alisha가 과학 숙제를 하는 것을 도와주었다.
  = I **helped** Alisha **to do** her science homework.
   ※ get이 '~하게 하다'라는 사역동사의 뜻으로 쓰일 때 목적격보어로 to부정사를 쓴다.
- Mom **got** me **to eat** vegetables. 〈능동〉 엄마는 내가 야채를 먹도록 하셨다.
- I **got** my car **washed**. 〈수동〉 나는 내 차가 세차되도록 했다.

핵심 Check

1. 다음 괄호 안에서 알맞은 말을 고르시오.
   (1) Please let me (know / to know) your preferred date.
   (2) It makes me (feeling / feel) at home.

2 It is[was] ~ that 강조 구문

- **It was** a better tomorrow **that** we painted. 우리가 그린 것은 바로 더 나은 내일이었다.
- **It is** the book **that** everybody is talking about. 모든 사람이 말하고 있는 것은 바로 그 책이다.

■ It ~ that 강조 구문
  - 의미: ···한 것은 바로 ~이다[이었다]
  - 형태: It is/was ~ that ...

■ 'It ~ that 강조 구문'은 'It is/was ~ that ...'의 형태로, 강조하고자 하는 부분을 It is/was와 that 사이에 넣고, 나머지 부분을 that 뒤에 써서 주어, 목적어, 부사(구/절) 등을 강조한다.

  - I suggested this idea at the club meeting.
    → **It** was I **that** suggested this idea at the club meeting. (주어 강조)
    → **It** was this idea **that** I suggested at the club meeting. (목적어인 명사 강조)
    → **It** was at the club meeting **that** I suggested this idea. (부사구 강조)

■ 'It ~ that ...' 강조 구문에서 강조하는 대상이 주어일 경우, that을 관계대명사 who(사람일 경우) 또는 which(사물이나 동물일 경우)로 바꿔 쓸 수 있다.

  - I met her at the airport yesterday. 나는 그녀를 공항에서 어제 만났다.
    → **It was** I **that[who]** met her at the airport yesterday.
    → **It was** her **that[who/whom]** I met at the airport yesterday.

■ 'It ~ that ...' 강조 구문에서 강조하는 대상이 부사(구/절)일 경우 that 다음에 완전한 절이 나오지만 그 외의 경우에는 불완전한 절이 나오는 것에 유의한다.

  - **It is** a new computer **that[which]** I want to buy. 내가 사고 싶은 것은 바로 새 컴퓨터이다. (that 다음에 buy의 목적어가 없는 불완전한 절)
  - **It was** at the party **that** I met Susan. 내가 Susan을 만난 것은 바로 그 파티에서였다. (that 다음에 완전한 절)

핵심 Check

2. 다음 괄호 안에서 알맞은 말을 고르시오.
  (1) It is my watch (that / what) I am looking for.
  (2) (It / That) was at the park that I met her by chance.
  (3) It is her (whom / which) I love.

01 다음 빈칸에 들어갈 말로 알맞은 것은?

> My mom had me _____ her food.

① taste   ② tasted   ③ to taste

④ tasting   ⑤ to tasting

02 다음 각 문장의 빈칸에 공통으로 들어갈 말로 알맞은 것은?

> • It was a big tree _____ he painted on the wall yesterday.
> • It was in 1969 _____ Apollo 11 landed on the moon.

① which   ② when   ③ who

④ that   ⑤ what

03 다음 중 어법상 바르지 않은 것은?

① It was on the day that we had dinner together.

② It was Dan who broke the vase.

③ It is Lucy whom he loves.

④ It was in the park that we played basketball yesterday.

⑤ It was Jim which I met again.

04 다음 우리말에 맞게 주어진 어휘를 바르게 배열하시오.

(1) Brown 씨는 그의 아들이 파티에 가게 허락했다.

     (Mr. Brown, the party, his son, go, let, to)

     ➡ _____

(2) 프로젝트 책임자는 우리를 오전 9시에 만나게 했다.

     (the project manager, us, had, meet, 9 a.m., at)

     ➡ _____

(3) 그들은 내게 그 이야기 전체를 반복하게 만들었다.

     (me, they, story, repeat, whole, made, the)

     ➡ _____

(4) 그녀는 내가 이 숙제를 끝낼 수 있도록 도와주었다.

     (this assignment, she, me, complete, helped, to)

     ➡ _____

01 다음 중 어법상 어색한 것은?

① He let me finishing playing the piano.
② Mom let me watch TV after I finished my homework.
③ The heavy traffic made me worry about being late.
④ She had her computer repaired.
⑤ Ms. White has us be on time for every class.

02 다음 중 어법상 옳은 것은?

① It was he which went to the station to see her off.
② It was the book which I bought last Saturday.
③ That was last Friday that I found the golden rings.
④ It was at the restaurant which I met Anna.
⑤ It was yesterday what I looked for the key.

서답형
03 다음 중 밑줄 친 부분의 쓰임이 〈보기〉와 같은 것을 모두 고르시오.

┌─ 보기 ├─
Mom <u>made</u> me bake some bread.

ⓐ She <u>made</u> the waiter bring some water.
ⓑ He <u>made</u> me a model airplane.
ⓒ He <u>made</u> toward the door.
ⓓ The springshower <u>makes</u> the grass grow.
ⓔ It <u>makes</u> no difference.

➡ _____

[04~05] 다음 우리말을 알맞게 영작한 것을 고르시오. (04–1개, 05–2개)

04
선생님은 우리가 읽은 것에 관해 뭔가를 그리게 하셨다.

① The teacher had us drew something about what we had read.
② The teacher had us to draw something about that we had read.
③ The teacher had us drawing something about what we had read.
④ The teacher had us draw something about what we had read.
⑤ The teacher had us draw something about that we had read.

05
우리가 그린 것은 바로 더 나은 내일이었다.

① It was a better tomorrow what we painted.
② It was a better tomorrow which we painted.
③ It was a better tomorrow where we painted.
④ It was a better tomorrow when we painted.
⑤ It was a better tomorrow that we painted.

 06 다음 문장의 빈칸에 들어갈 말로 가장 적절한 것은?

He made me _____ the work.

① finished   ② finishing   ③ finish
④ to finish   ⑤ to finishing

07 다음 〈보기〉의 밑줄 친 that과 쓰임이 같은 것은?

> 보기
>
> It was flowers that my club members planted in the garden on April 5th.

① He couldn't walk that fast.

② That's not the computer I bought last week.

③ It was the cookies that Amy made for me yesterday.

④ It is certain that he will come.

⑤ Give me that chair, not this one.

08 다음 문장의 빈칸 (A), (B), (C)에 들어갈 말로 가장 적절한 것은?

> • Don't let him (A)_____ your evening.
> • I had the paper (B)_____ for the meeting.
> • They got their children (C)_____ outside.

	(A)	(B)	(C)
①	spoiling	copied	to play
②	spoiling	copy	playing
③	spoil	to copy	play
④	spoil	copied	to play
⑤	spoil	copy	play

09 다음 중 It ~ that 쓰임이 나머지 넷과 다른 하나는?

① It was the vase that Jake broke at home yesterday.

② It is important that students develop an awareness of how the Internet can be used.

③ It was in the restaurant that I met Sam yesterday.

④ It was her wallet that she lost after playing badminton at the park.

⑤ It was yesterday that she made me bake some cake.

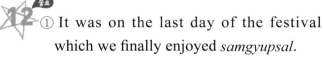 **10** 다음 문장의 빈칸 (A), (B)에 들어갈 말로 가장 적절한 것은?

> Some teachers at school (A)_____ us advice. Ms. Green makes us (B)_____ quiet in class. Mr. Johns has us (C)_____ up trash on the ground.

	(A)	(B)	(C)
①	give	be	pick
②	give	to be	picked
③	gives	be	picking
④	gives	to be	picked
⑤	giving	are	pick

[11~12] 다음 중 어법상 올바른 문장은?

11 ① Let her goes home right now.

② My mom had me cleaned my room.

③ The movie make me think about my own choices.

④ The teacher got us draw something strange.

⑤ The maid helped the princess to dress for the party.

12 ① It was on the last day of the festival which we finally enjoyed *samgyupsal*.

② It was last Saturday which the girl first saw the fireworks.

③ It was the hen that laid two eggs on the roof last week.

④ It was when Jake told me something which I realized my mistake.

⑤ It is in the city which my best friend met the girl.

서답형

13 다음 문장에서 어법상 어색한 부분을 바르게 고치시오.

(1) Carrie had her room paint white.

    _____ ➡ _____

(2) She let her daughter to play computer games.

    _____ ➡ _____

(3) Leslie helped him escaping from the pressures of living up to others' expectations.

    _____ ➡ _____

(4) It was last week which John borrowed a novel from the library.

    _____ ➡ _____

(5) It was his smartphone what Bob dropped in the toilet this morning.

    _____ ➡ _____

(6) It was in this school which I studied when I was young.

    _____ ➡ _____

서답형

14 다음 괄호 안에서 알맞은 것을 고르시오.

(1) His kindness made her (feel / to feel) good and (smile / to smile) at him.

(2) Clare got her computer (fix / fixed) at the store.

(3) I asked her (remain / to remain) seated.

(4) It was yesterday (which / that) they planted trees.

(5) It was Tom (who / which) broke it.

중요

15 다음 문장의 빈칸에 알맞지 <u>않은</u> 말은?

The woman _____ me clean the windows.

① made   ② helped   ③ let
④ had   ⑤ got

16 주어진 문장을 'my favorite movie character'를 강조하는 문장으로 바르게 고친 것은?

I started to paint my favorite movie character.

① It was my favorite movie character where I started to paint.
② It was my favorite movie character what I started to paint.
③ It was my favorite movie character how I started to paint.
④ It is my favorite movie character what I started to paint.
⑤ It was my favorite movie character that I started to paint.

중요

17 다음 빈칸에 알맞은 말을 고르시오.

He always _____ all of his appointments.

① gets her arrange
② gets her arranged
③ makes her arrange
④ makes her arranged
⑤ helps her arranged

18 다음 빈칸에 알맞은 말을 고르시오.

The team was _____ increase the competition level.

① made   ② making
③ to making   ④ made to
⑤ to made

01 다음 문장에서 어법상 어색한 것을 바르게 고쳐 다시 쓰시오.

(1) The project manager let us painted anything we wanted.

➡ _____

_____

(2) She wasn't happy with our work and made us to start over.

➡ _____

_____

(3) They immediately had the meeting cancel.

➡ _____

(4) When you cut them into pieces, let them marinated.

➡ _____

_____

(5) You in this country helped us becoming free.

➡ _____

(6) It was Susan which I had a date with at the park last Saturday.

➡ _____

_____

(7) It was the train which Kimberly lost her wallet.

➡ _____

_____

(8) It was last Friday where Mina flew a drone at the school.

➡ _____

_____

02 다음 두 문장을 주어진 〈조건〉에 맞춰 〈보기〉와 같이 한 문장으로 완성하시오.

┌── 보기 ──┐
- My sister said her homework was difficult.
- So, my mom ordered me to help her.
→ My mom made me help my sister.
└──────────┘

(1) 동사 let을 이용하여 8 단어로 쓸 것.

┌──────────────────────────────┐
- I asked him to play the piano with me.
- So he allowed me to play the piano with him.
└──────────────────────────────┘

➡ _____

(2) 동사 have와 fix를 이용하여 5 단어로 쓸 것.

┌──────────────────────────────┐
- Her computer was out of order.
- She called the repair shop and asked them to repair it.
└──────────────────────────────┘

➡ _____

03 다음 그림을 보고 각 질문에 'It ~ that' 강조 구문을 사용하여 답하시오.

(1) Who found a deer behind a tree?

➡ _____

(2) What did Mina find behind a tree?

➡ _____

(3) Where did Mina find a deer?

➡ _____

04 주어진 단어를 이용하여 〈보기〉와 같이 문장을 바꿔 쓰시오.

┌─── 보기 ───
│ Ms. Brown tells us to be quiet in class.
│ (have)
│ → Ms. Brown has us be quiet in class.
└─────────

(1) I told my sister to bring my gym uniform. (have)

➡ _____

(2) Ashley asked me to fix dinner. (get)

➡ _____

(3) He ordered me to wash his car. (make)

➡ _____

(4) The doctor allowed her to return to work. (let)

➡ _____

05 다음 문장을 주어진 단어를 강조하는 문장으로 고쳐 쓰시오.

┌─────────────────────────┐
│ I bought this nice jacket at the store last │
│ Sunday. │
└─────────────────────────┘

(1) I

➡ _____
_____

(2) bought

➡ _____

(3) this nice jacket

➡ _____
_____

(4) at the store

➡ _____
_____

(5) last Sunday

➡ _____
_____

06 다음 그림을 보고 주어진 어휘를 이용하여 빈칸에 알맞은 말을 쓰시오.

┌─────────────────────────┐
│ My son feels ill. I'd better have him │
│ _____ to the hospital. (take) │
└─────────────────────────┘

07 다음 우리말과 일치하도록 괄호 안에 주어진 어휘를 이용하여 영작하시오.

(1) Peter는 가끔 그의 개가 그의 침대에서 자게 내버려 둔다. (sometimes, let, on his bed)

➡ _____

(2) 우리 아빠는 내가 많은 책을 읽도록 시키신다. (my dad, make, lots of)

➡ _____

(3) 당신은 이 그림을 제가 어디다 걸기를 원하세요? (want, hang, this picture)

➡ _____

(4) John이 지난주에 한 도서관에서 빌린 것은 바로 그 소설이었다. (it, the novel, a library, borrow)

➡ _____
_____

(5) 내가 그녀를 처음으로 만난 것은 바로 2014년이었다. (it, for the first time)

➡ _____
_____

Reading

Paint a Better Tomorrow

Hi. My name is Homin. This is me in front of the wall painting. The
~ 앞에

wings are so pretty, aren't they? Many people like to take pictures in
= the wings

front of wall paintings. They make old neighborhoods bright and new.
= Wall paintings   목적어   brightly and newly (×)

Last month, I visited a village with wall paintings in Yeosu. As I
~이 있는

was taking a picture, a light went on in my head. I thought, "I'm in
머릿속에 좋은 생각이 떠올랐다.

the school art club. Why don't we do wall paintings like these?" I
= How[What] about doing ~?   ~와 같은(전치사)

suggested this idea at the next club meeting, and the members loved it.
this idea(Homin's idea)

We found a teen volunteer project on the Internet. The project was
인터넷에서

to do a wall painting in our neighborhood. We applied for it, and two
명사적 용법의 to부정사(보어)   the project

weeks later, our club was selected!
수동태

The day of the project finally came. The project manager had us meet
= at last = in the end: 마침내   have+사람+원형부정사

at the painting site at 9 a.m. The wall was in very poor condition. There
be in poor[bad] condition: 상태가 나쁘다   유도부사

were strange writings and drawings on some parts.
was(×)   주어

Other parts had old posters on them. We removed the posters first and

painted over the writings and drawings with white paint.
~으로(도구)

wing 날개
neighborhood 근처, 이웃
village 마을
teen 십 대의; 십 대
select 선택하다, 선정하다
manager 운영자, 관리자
site 현장, 장소
remove 없애다, 제거하다
spot (특정한) 장소, 자리
background (경치, 그림, 무대의) 배경

확인문제

- 다음 문장이 본문의 내용과 일치하면 T, 일치하지 <u>않으면</u> F를 쓰시오.

1 Wall paintings make old neighborhoods bright and new. ☐

2 As Homin was painting a picture, a light went on in his head. ☐

3 Homin suggested his idea at the next club meeting, and the members loved it. ☐

4 Homin and the school art club members found a teen volunteer project on the
   Internet. ☐

5 Homin and the school art club members met at the painting site at 9 a.m. ☐

6 Homin and the school art club members removed the writings and drawings first
   and painted over the posters with white paint. ☐

The manager let us paint anything we wanted. We decided to paint
something cute because the wall was near an elementary school. We
divided into three groups and began painting. I was in the group with
Minsu and Jiwon. I chose my spot and started to paint my favorite
movie character. Minsu painted some flowers and Jiwon did some
background drawings.

Our club painted for about five hours. After we finished, we got
together and shared the day's experiences. Minsu was very proud of
his flower painting. He said, "My flower is so real that a bee landed
on it." I said, "Drawing on a wall was much harder than drawing on
paper."

We all agreed that our wall painting wasn't perfect. But it didn't
matter. We made our neighborhood a little brighter and happier. We
were proud of ourselves. We didn't just paint pictures on a wall that
day. It was a better tomorrow that we painted.

decide to ~하기로 결정하다
cute 귀여운
elementary 초등의
character 등장인물, 캐릭터
background 배경
get together 모이다
land 내려앉다
matter 중요하다, 문제되다
perfect 완벽한
be proud of ~을 자랑스럽게 여기다

📎 **확인문제**

● 다음 문장이 본문의 내용과 일치하면 T, 일치하지 <u>않으면</u> F를 쓰시오.

1 Homin and the school art club members decided to paint something cute because the wall was near an elementary school. ☐

2 They divided into four groups and began painting. ☐

3 Minsu painted some flowers and Jiwon did some background drawings. ☐

4 Drawing on paper was much harder than drawing on a wall. ☐

5 Homin and the school art club members all agreed that their wall painting wasn't perfect. ☐

6 Homin and the school art club members just painted pictures on a wall that day. ☐

● 우리말을 참고하여 빈칸에 알맞은 말을 쓰시오.

1 **Paint a** _____ _____

2 Hi. _____ _____ _____ Homin.

3 _____ _____ _____ in front of the wall painting.

4 The wings are so pretty, _____ _____?

5 Many people like to _____ _____ in front of wall paintings.

6 They make _____ _____ bright and new.

7 Last month, I visited a village _____ _____ _____ in Yeosu.

8 As I was taking a picture, _____ _____ _____ _____ _____ _____.

9 I thought, "_____ _____ the school art club.

10 _____ _____ _____ do wall paintings like these?"

11 I _____ _____ _____ at the next club meeting, and the members loved it.

12 We found a teen volunteer project _____ _____ _____.

13 The project was _____ _____ _____ _____ in our neighborhood.

14 We _____ _____ it, and two weeks later, our club _____ _____!

15 The day of the project _____ _____.

16 The project manager _____ _____ _____ at the painting site at 9 a.m.

17 The wall _____ _____ _____ _____ _____.

1	더 나은 내일을 그려라
2	안녕. 내 이름은 호민이야.
3	벽화 앞에 있는 사람이 나야.
4	날개가 예뻐. 그렇지 않니?
5	많은 사람들이 벽화 앞에서 사진 찍는 것을 좋아해.
6	벽화는 오래된 마을을 밝고 새롭게 만들어.
7	지난달에 나는 여수에 있는 벽화 마을을 방문했어.
8	내가 사진을 찍을 때 머릿속에 좋은 생각이 떠올랐어.
9	나는 생각했어. "나는 학교 미술 동아리에 있잖아.
10	우리가 이것처럼 벽화를 그리면 어떨까?"
11	나는 이 아이디어를 다음 동아리 모임에서 제안했고, 동아리 부원들은 그것을 아주 좋아했어.
12	우리는 인터넷에서 청소년 봉사 프로젝트를 찾았어.
13	그 프로젝트는 우리 마을에 벽화를 그리는 것이었어.
14	우리는 거기에 지원했고, 2주 후에 우리 동아리가 선택되었어!
15	마침내 프로젝트 날이 되었어.
16	프로젝트 책임자는 우리를 오전 9시에 그림 그리는 곳에서 만나게 했어.
17	벽은 상태가 별로 좋지 않았어.

18 There were _____ _____ _____ _____ on some parts.

19 _____ _____ had old posters on them.

20 We removed the posters first and painted over the writings and drawings _____ _____ _____ .

21 The manager _____ _____ _____ anything we wanted.

22 We decided to paint _____ _____ because the wall was near an elementary school.

23 We _____ _____ three groups and began painting.

24 I _____ _____ _____ _____ with Minsu and Jiwon.

25 I _____ _____ _____ and started to paint my favorite movie character.

26 Minsu painted some flowers and Jiwon _____ some _____ _____ .

27 Our club painted _____ _____ five hours.

28 After we finished, we _____ _____ and _____ the day's experiences.

29 Minsu _____ _____ _____ _____ his flower painting.

30 He said, "My flower is _____ real _____ a bee landed on it."

31 I said, "Drawing on a wall was _____ _____ than drawing on paper."

32 We all agreed that our wall painting _____ _____ .

33 But it didn't _____ .

34 We made our neighborhood _____ _____ _____ _____ _____ .

35 We were proud of _____ .

36 We _____ _____ _____ pictures on a wall that day.

37 It was _____ _____ _____ that we painted.

18 몇 군데에는 이상한 낙서와 그림이 있었어.

19 다른 부분에는 오래된 포스터들이 붙어 있었어.

20 우리는 먼저 포스터들을 제거하고 낙서와 그림을 흰 페인트로 덧칠했어.

21 책임자는 우리가 원하는 어떤 것이든 그리게 했어.

22 우리는 그 벽이 초등학교 근처에 있어서 귀여운 뭔가를 그리기로 했어.

23 우리는 세 그룹으로 나뉘어 그리기 시작했어.

24 나는 민수와 지원이와 같은 그룹이었어.

25 나는 내 구역을 정해서 가장 좋아하는 영화 캐릭터를 그리기 시작했어.

26 민수는 몇 송이의 꽃을 그렸고 지원이는 배경 그림을 그렸어.

27 우리 동아리는 약 다섯 시간 동안 그림을 그렸어.

28 끝난 후에 우리는 모여서 그날의 경험을 함께 이야기했어.

29 민수는 자신이 그린 꽃 그림을 정말 자랑스러워했어.

30 그는 "내 꽃이 정말 진짜 같아서 벌이 꽃에 앉았어."라고 말했어.

31 나는 "벽에 그리는 것이 종이에 그리는 것보다 훨씬 힘들었어."라고 말했어.

32 우리 모두는 우리 벽화가 완벽하지는 않다는 것에 동의했어.

33 하지만 그것은 중요하지 않았어.

34 우리는 동네를 조금 더 밝고 행복하게 만들었어.

35 우리는 우리 자신이 자랑스러웠어.

36 우리는 그날 벽에 그림만 그린 게 아니었어.

37 우리가 그린 것은 바로 더 나은 내일이었어.

● 우리말을 참고하여 본문을 영작하시오.

1 더 나은 내일을 그려라
➡ _____

2 안녕. 내 이름은 호민이야.
➡ _____

3 벽화 앞에 있는 사람이 나야.
➡ _____

4 날개가 예뻐, 그렇지 않니?
➡ _____

5 많은 사람들이 벽화 앞에서 사진 찍는 것을 좋아해.
➡ _____

6 벽화는 오래된 마을을 밝고 새롭게 만들어.
➡ _____

7 지난달에 나는 여수에 있는 벽화 마을을 방문했어.
➡ _____

8 내가 사진을 찍을 때 머릿속에 좋은 생각이 떠올랐어.
➡ _____

9 나는 생각했어. "나는 학교 미술 동아리에 있잖아.
➡ _____

10 우리가 이것처럼 벽화를 그리면 어떨까?"
➡ _____

11 나는 이 아이디어를 다음 동아리 모임에서 제안했고, 동아리 부원들은 그것을 아주 좋아했어.
➡ _____

12 우리는 인터넷에서 청소년 봉사 프로젝트를 찾았어.
➡ _____

13 그 프로젝트는 우리 마을에 벽화를 그리는 것이었어.
➡ _____

14 우리는 거기에 지원했고, 2주 후에 우리 동아리가 선택되었어!
➡ _____

15 마침내 프로젝트 날이 되었어.
➡ _____

16 프로젝트 책임자는 우리를 오전 9시에 그림 그리는 곳에서 만나게 했어.
➡ _____

17 벽은 상태가 별로 좋지 않았어.
➡ _____

18 몇 군데에는 이상한 낙서와 그림이 있었어.
➡ _____

19 다른 부분에는 오래된 포스터들이 붙어 있었어.
➡ _____

20 우리는 먼저 포스터들을 제거하고 낙서와 그림을 흰 페인트로 덧칠했어.
➡ _____

21 책임자는 우리가 원하는 어떤 것이든 그리게 했어.
➡ _____

22 우리는 그 벽이 초등학교 근처에 있어서 귀여운 뭔가를 그리기로 했어.
➡ _____

23 우리는 세 그룹으로 나뉘어 그리기 시작했어.
➡ _____

24 나는 민수와 지원이와 같은 그룹이었어.
➡ _____

25 나는 내 구역을 정해서 가장 좋아하는 영화 캐릭터를 그리기 시작했어.
➡ _____

26 민수는 몇 송이의 꽃을 그렸고 지원이는 배경 그림을 그렸어.
➡ _____

27 우리 동아리는 약 다섯 시간 동안 그림을 그렸어.
➡ _____

28 끝난 후에 우리는 모여서 그날의 경험을 함께 이야기했어.
➡ _____

29 민수는 자신이 그린 꽃 그림을 정말 자랑스러워했어.
➡ _____

30 그는 "내 꽃이 정말 진짜 같아서 벌이 꽃에 앉았어."라고 말했어.
➡ _____

31 나는 "벽에 그리는 것이 종이에 그리는 것보다 훨씬 힘들었어."라고 말했어.
➡ _____

32 우리 모두는 우리 벽화가 완벽하지는 않다는 것에 동의했어.
➡ _____

33 하지만 그것은 중요하지 않았어.
➡ _____

34 우리는 동네를 조금 더 밝고 행복하게 만들었어.
➡ _____

35 우리는 우리 자신이 자랑스러웠어.
➡ _____

36 우리는 그날 벽에 그림만 그린 게 아니었어.
➡ _____

37 우리가 그린 것은 바로 더 나은 내일이었어.
➡ _____

[01~04] 다음 글을 읽고 물음에 답하시오.

Hi. My name is Homin. This is me in front of the wall painting. ⓐThe wings are so pretty, isn't it? Many people like to take pictures in front of wall paintings. They make old neighborhoods bright and new.

(①) Last month, I visited a village with wall paintings in Yeosu. (②) I thought, "I'm in the school art club. (③) Why don't we do wall paintings like these?" (④) I suggested ⓑthis idea at the next club meeting, and the members loved it. (⑤)

We found a teen volunteer project on the Internet. The project was to do a wall painting in our neighborhood. We applied for it, and two weeks later, our club was selected!

서답형

01 위 글의 밑줄 친 ⓐ에서 어법상 틀린 부분을 찾아 고치시오.

➡ _____

02 위 글의 흐름으로 보아, 주어진 문장이 들어가기에 가장 적절한 곳은?

> As I was taking a picture, a light went on in my head.

①   ②   ③   ④   ⑤

서답형

03 위 글의 밑줄 친 ⓑthis idea가 가리키는 것을 본문에서 찾아 쓰시오.

➡ _____

04 According to the passage, which is NOT true?

① Wall paintings make old neighborhoods bright and new.
② Last month, Homin visited a village with wall paintings in Yeosu.
③ While Homin was taking a picture, a bright idea occurred to him.
④ The school art club members loved Homin's idea.
⑤ Homin's art club was selected for a teen volunteer project two weeks after he visited Yeosu.

[05~07] 다음 글을 읽고 물음에 답하시오.

The day of the project (A)finally came. The project manager had us meet at the painting site at 9 a.m. (B)벽은 상태가 별로 좋지 않았어. There were strange writings and drawings on some parts. Other parts had old posters on them. We ___ⓐ___ the posters first and painted over the writings and drawings with white paint.

05 위 글의 빈칸 ⓐ에 들어갈 알맞은 말을 고르시오.

① protected   ② removed   ③ prevented
④ maintained   ⑤ destroyed

06 위 글의 밑줄 친 (A)finally와 바꿔 쓸 수 있는 말을 모두 고르시오.

① above all   ② at last   ③ at least
④ most of all   ⑤ in the end

서답형

07 위 글의 밑줄 친 (B)의 우리말에 맞게 주어진 어휘를 이용하여 7 단어로 영작하시오.

> in, poor

➡ _____

[08~10] 다음 글을 읽고 물음에 답하시오.

Last month, I visited a village with wall paintings in Yeosu. As I was taking a picture, a light went on in my head. I thought, "I'm in the school art club. Why don't we do wall paintings like (A)these?" I suggested this idea at the next club meeting, and the members loved it.

We found a teen volunteer project ⓐ_____ the Internet. The project was to do a wall painting in our neighborhood. We applied ⓑ_____ it, and two weeks later, our club was selected!

08 위 글의 빈칸 ⓐ와 ⓑ에 들어갈 전치사가 바르게 짝지어진 것은?

ⓐ	ⓑ		ⓐ	ⓑ
① to – for			② on – with	
③ on – for			④ from – on	
⑤ to – with				

서답형

09 본문의 내용과 일치하도록 다음 빈칸 (A)와 (B)에 알맞은 단어를 쓰시오.

> Homin came up with an idea while he was (A)_____ _____ _____ at a village with wall paintings in Yeosu, and suggested to the art club members that they should do (B)_____ _____ like those.

서답형

10 위 글의 밑줄 친 (A)these가 가리키는 것을 10자에서 15자 사이의 우리말로 쓰시오.

➡ _____

[11~12] 다음 글을 읽고 물음에 답하시오.

Our club painted for about five hours. After we finished, we got together and shared the day's experiences. Minsu was very proud of his flower painting. He said, "My flower is so real that a bee landed on it." I said, "Drawing on a wall was much harder than drawing on paper."

We all agreed that our wall painting wasn't perfect. But it didn't ⓐmatter. We made our neighborhood a little brighter and happier. We were proud of ourselves. We didn't just paint pictures on a wall that day. It was a better tomorrow that we painted.

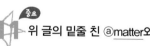

11 위 글의 밑줄 친 ⓐmatter와 같은 의미로 쓰인 것을 고르시오.

① It's a private matter.
② Give me the printed matter.
③ Does it really matter who did it?
④ It's a matter of life and death.
⑤ All matter is solid, liquid, or gas.

12 위 글의 제목으로 알맞은 것을 고르시오.

① Look! I Painted This Incredible Flower!
② Which Is Harder, Drawing on a Wall or Drawing on Paper?
③ Our Wall Painting Wasn't Perfect. So What?
④ We Painted Pictures on a Wall
⑤ What Did We Paint? A Better Tomorrow!

[13~14] 다음 글을 읽고 물음에 답하시오.

Our club painted ①during about five hours. After we finished, we got together and shared the day's experiences. Minsu was very proud of his flower painting. He said, "My flower is so real ②as to a bee landed on it." I said, "Drawing on a wall was much harder than drawing on paper."

We all agreed that our wall painting wasn't perfect. But ⓐit didn't matter. We made our neighborhood ③very brighter and happier. We were proud of ④us. We didn't just paint pictures on a wall that day. It was a better tomorrow ⑤what we painted.

13 위 글의 밑줄 친 ⓐ와 바꿔 쓸 수 <u>없는</u> 문장을 고르시오.

① it wasn't important
② it didn't count
③ it wasn't significant
④ it made a difference
⑤ it wasn't of importance

서답형
14 위 글의 밑줄 친 ①~⑤ 중 어법상 <u>틀린</u> 번호를 찾아 <u>모두</u> 고치시오.

➡ _____

_____

[15~17] 다음 글을 읽고 물음에 답하시오.

The day of the project finally came. The project manager had us meet at the painting site at 9 a.m. The wall was in very ⓐpoor condition. There were strange writings and drawings on some parts. Other parts had old posters on them. We removed the posters first and painted over the writings and drawings with white paint.

The manager let us paint anything we wanted. ⓑWe decided to paint something cute so the wall was near an elementary school. We divided into three groups and began painting. I was in the group with Minsu and Jiwon. I chose my spot and started to paint my favorite movie character. Minsu painted some flowers and Jiwon did some background drawings.

<I: Homin>

서답형
15 위 글의 밑줄 친 ⓐpoor와 바꿔 쓸 수 있는 단어를 쓰시오.

➡ _____

서답형
16 위 글의 밑줄 친 ⓑ에서 흐름상 <u>어색한</u> 부분을 찾아 고치시오.

➡ _____

중요
17 Which question CANNOT be answered after reading the passage?

① When did they meet at the painting site?
② Was it possible for them to start doing a wall painting right away?
③ Were there any rules to follow about what to paint?
④ When they decided their subject matter, did they consider where the painting site was?
⑤ What was Homin's favorite movie character?

[18~20] 다음 글을 읽고 물음에 답하시오.

Last month, I visited a village with wall paintings in Yeosu. As I was taking a picture, a light went on in my head. I thought, "I'm in the school art club. Why don't we do wall paintings like these?" I suggested this idea at the next club meeting, and the members loved it.

We found a teen volunteer project on the Internet. The project was (A)to do a wall painting in our neighborhood. We applied for it, and two weeks later, our club ⓐ !

<I: Homin>

서답형

18 위 글의 빈칸 ⓐ에 select를 알맞은 형태로 쓰시오.

➡ _____

19 위 글의 밑줄 친 (A)to do와 to부정사의 용법이 같은 것을 모두 고르시오.

① I think it valuable to do a wall painting.
② Are there any volunteers to do a wall painting?
③ What do we need to do a wall painting?
④ I chose my spot to do a wall painting.
⑤ My hobby is to do a wall painting.

20 위 글의 제목으로 알맞은 것은?

① How about Doing Wall Paintings like These?
② The Hot Places with Wall Paintings
③ Taking Pictures before Wall Paintings
④ Why Don't We Volunteer Together?
⑤ Valuable Teen Volunteer Projects

[21~23] 다음 글을 읽고 물음에 답하시오.

The day of the project finally came. (A) The project manager had us to meet at the painting site at 9 a.m. The wall was in very poor condition. There were strange writings and drawings on ⓐ parts. ⓑ parts had old posters on them. We removed the posters first and painted over the writings and drawings with white paint.

(B)The manager let us to paint anything we wanted. We decided to paint something cute because the wall was near an elementary school. We divided into three groups and began painting. I was in the group with Minsu and Jiwon. I chose my spot and started to paint my favorite movie character. Minsu painted some flowers and Jiwon did some background drawings.

21 위 글의 빈칸 ⓐ와 ⓑ에 들어갈 알맞은 말을 고르시오.

① each – Another   ② some – Others
③ a few – The other ④ each – Most
⑤ some – Other

서답형

22 위 글의 밑줄 친 (A)와 (B)에서 어법상 틀린 부분을 찾아 고치시오.

➡ (A) _____
   (B) _____

23 위 글의 주제로 알맞은 것을 고르시오.

① the explanation about the poor condition of the wall
② the strange writings and drawings on the wall
③ the process for doing a wall painting
④ the subject matter suitable for a wall painting
⑤ how to divide groups effectively

[01~03] 다음 글을 읽고 물음에 답하시오.

Hi. My name is Homin. (A)[It is / This is] me in front of the wall painting. The wings are (B)[so / such] pretty, ⓐ_____ _____? Many people like to take pictures in front of wall paintings. ⓑThey make old neighborhoods (C)[bright and new / brightly and newly].

01 위 글의 빈칸 ⓐ에 들어갈 알맞은 부가의문문을 쓰시오.

➡ _____

02 위 글의 괄호 (A)~(C)에서 어법상 알맞은 낱말을 골라 쓰시오.

➡ (A)_____ (B)_____ (C)_____

03 위 글의 밑줄 친 ⓑThey가 가리키는 것을 본문에서 찾아 쓰시오.

➡ _____

[04~06] 다음 글을 읽고 물음에 답하시오.

Last month, I visited a village with wall paintings in Yeosu. As I was taking a picture, ⓐ머릿속에 좋은 생각이 떠올랐어. I thought, "I'm in the school art club. Why don't we do wall paintings like these?" I suggested this idea at the next club meeting, and the members loved ⓑit.

We found a teen volunteer project on the Internet. The project was to do a wall painting in our neighborhood. We applied for ⓒit, and two weeks later, our club was selected!

<I: Homin>

04 밑줄 친 ⓐ의 우리말에 맞게 주어진 어휘를 이용하여 7 단어로 영작하시오.

light, went

➡ _____

05 밑줄 친 ⓑit, ⓒit이 가리키는 것을 각각 본문에서 찾아 다음 빈칸에 쓰시오.

ⓑit: this ___(A)___
ⓒit: the ___(B)___ to do a wall painting in our neighborhood

➡ (A)_____ (B)_____

06 As a volunteer work, why did Homin suggest doing wall paintings of all things? Fill in the blanks with suitable words.

He did so because he was in the _____ _____ _____.

[07~09] 다음 글을 읽고 물음에 답하시오.

The day of the project finally came. The project manager had us meet at the painting site at 9 a.m. ⓐThe wall was in very poor condition. There were strange writings and drawings on some parts. Other parts had old posters on them. We removed the posters first and painted over the writings and drawings with white paint.

The manager let us paint ⓑanything we wanted. We decided to paint something cute because the wall was near an elementary school. We divided into three groups and began painting. I was in the group with Minsu and Jiwon. I chose my spot and started to paint my favorite movie character. Minsu painted some flowers and Jiwon did some background drawings. <I: Homin>

07 위 글의 밑줄 친 ⓐ의 구체적인 내용을 우리말로 쓰시오.

➡ _____

_____

08 위 글의 밑줄 친 ⓑanything과 바꿔 쓸 수 있는 단어를 쓰시오.

➡ _____

09 위 글에서 호민이와 친구들이 벽화 작업을 한 과정을 우리말로 쓰시오.

➡ (1) _____

(2) _____

(3) _____

(4) _____

(5) _____

[10~11] 다음 글을 읽고 물음에 답하시오.

Our club painted for about five hours. After we finished, we got together and shared the day's experiences. Minsu was very proud of his flower painting. He said, "ⓐMy flower is so real that a bee landed on it." I said, "Drawing on a wall was much harder than drawing on paper."

We all agreed that our wall painting wasn't perfect. But it didn't matter. We made our neighborhood a little brighter and happier. We were proud of ourselves. We didn't just paint pictures on a wall that day. ⓑIt was a better tomorrow that we painted.

10 (1) 위 글의 밑줄 친 ⓐ와 같은 뜻이 되도록 다음 빈칸에 알맞은 단어를 쓰시오. (2) 위 글의 밑줄 친 강조 구문 ⓑ를 강조되지 않은 보통의 문장으로 고치시오.

➡ (1) My flower is real _____ for a bee to land on.

(2) _____

11 본문의 내용과 일치하도록 다음 빈칸 (A)와 (B)에 알맞은 단어를 쓰시오.

Though all the club members agreed that their wall painting was (A)_____, it didn't matter. They took (B)_____ in themselves because they made their neighborhood a little brighter and happier.

[12~13] 다음 글을 읽고 물음에 답하시오.

Our club painted for about five hours. After we finished, we got together and ⓐ_____ the day's experiences. Minsu was very proud of his flower painting. He said, "My flower is so real that a bee landed on it." I said, "ⓑDrawing on a wall was much harder than drawing on paper."

We all agreed that our wall painting wasn't perfect. But it didn't matter. We made our neighborhood a little brighter and happier. We were proud of ourselves. We didn't just paint pictures on a wall that day. It was a better tomorrow that we painted.

12 다음과 같은 뜻이 되도록 위 글의 빈칸 ⓐ에 들어갈 알맞은 한 단어를 쓰시오.

had the day's experiences in common

➡ _____

13 밑줄 친 ⓑ를 다음과 같이 바꿔 쓸 때 빈칸에 들어갈 알맞은 단어를 쓰시오.

➡ (1) Drawing on paper was not _____ hard _____ drawing on a wall.

(2) Drawing on paper was much _____ hard than drawing on a wall.

After You Read B

Project: Paint a Better Tomorrow
DATE: April 15
MEETING TIME: 9 a.m.
Do you like painting? Do you want to make your neighborhood brighter?
= to paint   목적격보어로 쓰인 형용사(비교급)
Right now, the wall is in very poor condition.
상태
You need to remove the old posters and paint over the strange writings with

white paint. You can paint anything you want!
= whatever
email: volunteer@1365.go.kr

구문해설 • neighborhood: 근처, 이웃 • right now: 지금은, 지금 당장 • remove: 없애다, 제거하다
• be in poor[bad] condition: 보존 상태가 나쁘다, 건강이 좋지 않다

프로젝트: 더 나은 내일을 그려라
날짜: 4월 15일
만나는 시간: 오전 9시
당신은 그림 그리기를 좋아하십니까? 당신의 동네를 더 밝게 만들기를 원합니까? 지금, 벽은 상태가 별로 좋지 않습니다. 당신은 먼저 오래된 포스터들을 제거하고 이상한 낙서를 흰 페인트로 덧칠할 필요가 있습니다. 당신은 원하는 어떤 것이든 그릴 수 있습니다!
이메일: volunteer@1365.go.kr

Word Power

Sally got up early and prepared for school. She said goodbye to her mom. Her
(잠자리에서) 일어났다   ~을 준비했다
mom said, "Try to get along with your friends and have fun." Sally replied,
try to 동사원형: ~하려고 노력하다   ~와 잘 지내다   즐거운 시간을 보내다
"Okay, I will," and got on the school bus.
(탈것에) 타다

Sally는 일찍 일어나서 학교에 갈 준비를 했다. 그녀는 엄마에게 작별인사를 했다. 엄마는 "친구들과 잘 지내고 즐거운 시간을 보내라."라고 말했다. Sally는 "그럴게요."라고 대답하고 스쿨 버스를 탔다.

Think and Write

Volunteer Work Diary
I volunteered at Dream Library. I read English books to children.
= I read children English books.
I tried to read like a voice actor. The volunteer manager had me arrange the
전치사   사역동사 have+목적어+원형부정사   목적격보어(동사원형)
books on the shelves. The books were so heavy that I had to take a break every
너무 ~해서 …하다

30 minutes. After I finished, the shelves looked very neat. I felt very proud. It
every+기수+복수 명사   look+형용사 보어   feel+형용사 보어
was a fun and rewarding experience.

구문해설 • voice actor: 성우 • take a break: 쉬다 • rewarding: 득이 되는, 할 보람이 있는, (~할 만한)
가치가 있는

봉사 활동 일기

나는 Dream 도서관에서 자원봉사를 했다. 나는 아이들에게 영어책을 읽어 줬다. 나는 성우처럼 읽으려고 노력했다. 자원봉사 책임자는 내게 책을 책장에 정리하라고 했다. 책이 너무 무거워서 나는 30분마다 쉬어야 했다. 끝난 후에는 책장이 아주 깔끔해 보였다. 나는 매우 자랑스러움을 느꼈다. 재미있고 보람된 경험이었다.

Words & Expressions

01 다음 빈칸에 들어갈 알맞은 말을 고르시오.

> I was going to _____ breakfast so that my mom could rest in the morning.

① decide ② realize ③ ready
④ apply ⑤ prepare

02 다음 밑줄 친 부분의 의미가 다른 하나를 고르시오.

① He called me as I was writing a science report.
② As I got home, my little brother was crying.
③ You have to show your ticket as you go in.
④ As the elevator was broken, we had to walk up the stairs.
⑤ I saw Peter as I was getting off the bus.

03 밑줄 친 부분과 바꿔 쓸 수 있는 말을 주어진 철자로 시작하여 쓰시오.

> His clothes were always tidy and clean.

➡ n_____

04 다음 빈칸에 공통으로 들어갈 말을 쓰시오.

> • Let's _____ a ten-minute break.
> • Do you want me to _____ a picture of you?

Conversation

[05~06] 다음 대화를 읽고 물음에 답하시오.

> B: What are all these boxes and books for? (①)
> G: I'm packing the books for the donation center. (②) (A)Can you give me a hand? (③)
> B: Sure. (④)
> G: (⑤) Please write the address on the boxes.
> B: No problem.

05 ①~⑤ 중 주어진 문장이 들어갈 곳은?

> What do you want me to do?

① ② ③ ④ ⑤

06 밑줄 친 (A)와 바꿔 쓸 수 있는 말을 고르시오.

① What can I do for you?
② Let me help you.
③ Can you do me a favor?
④ May I help you?
⑤ Can I give you a hand?

07 빈칸 ⓐ~ⓔ에 들어가지 않는 말을 고르시오. (대·소문자 무시)

> B: ⓐ_____ the concert, Mom.
> W: Okay, I ⓑ_____. Thanks. Your dinner is on the table.
> B: All right. ⓒ_____ about me.
> W: ⓓ_____ sure you feed the dog after you ⓔ_____ dinner.
> B: Okay. Mom, you should go now. Dad is waiting in the car.

① make ② have ③ will
④ enjoy ⑤ worry

08 주어진 문장 이후에 올 대화의 순서를 바르게 배열한 것을 고르시오.

> What are you doing?

> (A) Please tape the boxes.
> (B) I'm packing for my move tomorrow. Can you help me?
> (C) Sure. What do you want me to do?
> (D) No problem.

① (B) – (A) – (C) – (D)
② (B) – (C) – (A) – (D)
③ (C) – (A) – (B) – (D)
④ (C) – (B) – (A) – (D)
⑤ (C) – (D) – (B) – (A)

[09~12] 다음 대화를 읽고 물음에 답하시오.

Woman: Good morning. What can I do for you?
Tony: Hi. I'm here for the volunteer work. (①)
Woman: Oh, you (A)must be Tony. (②)
Tony: That's right. What do you want me to do today?
Woman: Please read this book for the blind in the recording room. (③)
Tony: No problem. (④)
Woman: Yes. Please go into Room 7.
Tony: Okay. (⑤) Is there anything to keep in mind?
Woman: Yes. Make sure you read slowly and clearly.
Tony: Okay. I'll do my best.

09 ①~⑤ 중 주어진 문장이 들어갈 곳은?

> Should I go in now?

①　　②　　③　　④　　⑤

10 위 대화에서 다음 영영풀이에 해당하는 단어를 찾아 쓰시오.

> someone who dose something without expecting any reward

➡ _____

11 밑줄 친 (A)must와 같은 의미로 쓰인 것을 고르시오.

① Sam must be nearly 90 years old now.
② You must not download the movie.
③ I must do my homework first.
④ You must not eat junk food.
⑤ You must study English every day.

12 위 대화를 읽고 답할 수 없는 질문을 고르시오.

① What will Tony keep in mind when he's reading the book?
② Has ever Tony volunteered?
③ Which room is Tony going to go into for recording?
④ For whom is Tony going to record the book?
⑤ What are Tony going to do for the blind?

Grammar

13 주어진 단어를 어법에 맞게 빈칸에 쓰시오.

(1) The police officer had him _____ the rule. (follow)
(2) Mr. Park makes us _____ many questions in class. (ask)
(3) The band let their photos _____ by the audience. (take)
(4) If you really hurry, you can have it _____ quite soon. (write)

14 다음 밑줄 친 부분과 바꿔 쓸 수 있는 것은?

> It was the amusement park <u>that</u> everyone voted for.

① what   ② when   ③ who
④ where   ⑤ which

15 다음 문장을 각각의 주어진 단어를 강조하는 문장으로 고쳐 쓰시오.

> I played hide and seek with my friends in the park yesterday.

(1) I
➡ _____
_____

(2) played
➡ _____
_____

(3) hide and seek
➡ _____
_____

(4) with my friends
➡ _____
_____

(5) in the park
➡ _____
_____

(6) yesterday
➡ _____
_____

16 다음 중 어법상 바르지 <u>않은</u> 것은?

① I had my computer mend.
② Daniel made his brother turn off the TV.
③ Please don't let them be hurt.
④ It was no easy matter getting him to change his mind.
⑤ I let my dog sleep on my bed.

17 다음 중 어법상 올바른 문장을 고르시오.

① My sister always helps me cleans the garden.
② Ms. Parker made them watering the plants.
③ She had her daughter's name called through the speaker.
④ I remember hearing him came in.
⑤ He advised her not smoke.

18 밑줄 친 말을 강조할 때, 빈칸에 알맞은 말을 쓰시오.

> Suji found <u>her dog</u> in the park.
> ➡ _____ _____ her dog _____
> Suji found in the park.

19 다음 괄호 안에서 어법상 알맞은 것을 고르시오.

(1) My grandpa made me (open / to open) the window.
(2) The teacher let us (read / reading) the book.
(3) It will make the request (take / be taken) seriously.

(4) It was in the park (which / that) Suji found her dog.

(5) It was potato pizza (which / what) we finally selected.

(6) It is every year (what / that) they plan to plant trees.

20 괄호 안에 주어진 어휘를 활용하여 글자 수에 맞게 다음 우리말을 영작하시오.

(1) Brown 선생님은 학생들이 체육관에서 줄을 서게 했다. (Mr. Brown, the gym, make, line up, the, 10 단어)

➡ _____

(2) 어제 창문을 깬 것은 바로 새였다. (the window, a bird, break, that, 9 단어)

➡ _____

Reading

[21~23] 다음 글을 읽고 물음에 답하시오.

Last month, I visited a village with wall paintings in Yeosu. As I was taking a picture, ⓐa light went on in my head. I thought, "I'm in the school art club. Why don't we do wall paintings like these?" I suggested this idea at the next club meeting, and the members loved it.

We found a teen volunteer project on the Internet. The project was to do a wall painting in our neighborhood. We applied for it, and two weeks later, our club was selected!

<I: Homin>

21 위 글의 밑줄 친 ⓐ와 바꿔 쓸 수 있는 말로 옳지 <u>않은</u> 것을 고르시오.

① a good idea occurred to me
② I hit upon a good idea
③ I was lost in a daydream
④ a good idea flashed on me
⑤ I came up with a good idea

22 위 글에서 알 수 있는 호민이의 성격으로 알맞은 것을 <u>두 개</u> 고르시오.

① active   ② passive
③ selfish   ④ considerate
⑤ arrogant

23 본문의 내용과 일치하도록 다음 빈칸에 알맞은 단어를 쓰시오.

> Homin and the school art club members decided to join a _____ _____ because they wanted to do wall paintings.

[24~26] 다음 글을 읽고 물음에 답하시오.

The day of the project finally came. (①) The project manager had us meet at the painting site at 9 a.m. (②) There were strange writings and drawings on some parts. (③) Other parts had old posters on them. (④) We removed the posters first and painted over the writings and drawings with white paint. (⑤)

The manager let us paint anything we wanted. We decided to paint something cute because the wall was near an elementary school. We divided into three groups and began painting. I was in the group with Minsu and Jiwon. I chose my spot and started to paint my favorite movie character. Minsu painted some flowers and Jiwon did some background drawings.

<I: Homin>

24 위 글의 흐름으로 보아, 주어진 문장이 들어가기에 가장 적절한 곳은?

> The wall was in very poor condition.

①   ②   ③   ④   ⑤

25 위 글의 제목으로 가장 알맞은 것을 고르시오.

① D-day for the Project Finally Has Come!
② The Poor Condition of the Wall
③ Let's Remove the Posters First
④ Wow! We Can Paint Anything We Want!
⑤ I'll Paint My Favorite Movie Character

26 According to the passage, which is NOT true?

① Homin and his friends met at the painting site at 9 a.m.
② Some parts of the wall had strange writings and drawings on them.
③ After painting over the writings and drawings with white paint, they removed the posters.
④ They decided to paint something cute because there was an elementary school near the painting site.
⑤ It was Minsu who painted some flowers.

[27~30] 다음 글을 읽고 물음에 답하시오.

Our club painted for about five hours. After we finished, we got together and shared the day's experiences. Minsu was very proud of his flower painting. He said, "My flower is so real that a bee landed on ⓐit." I said,

"ⓑDrawing on a wall was much harder than drawing on paper."

We all agreed that our wall painting wasn't perfect. But ⓒit didn't matter. ⓓ우리는 동네를 조금 더 밝고 행복하게 만들었어. We were proud of ourselves. We didn't just paint pictures on a wall that day. It was a better tomorrow that we painted.

27 위 글의 밑줄 친 ⓐit, ⓒit이 가리키는 것을 각각 본문에서 찾아 쓰시오.

➡ ⓐ _____ , ⓒ _____

28 아래 〈보기〉에서 위 글의 밑줄 친 ⓑDrawing과 문법적 쓰임이 같은 것의 개수를 고르시오.

> ┌── 보기 ──┐
> ① Do you know the man drawing on a wall?
> ② It was no use drawing on a wall.
> ③ His hobby was drawing on a wall.
> ④ I saw them drawing on a wall.
> ⑤ He was drawing on a wall.

① 1개   ② 2개   ③ 3개   ④ 4개   ⑤ 5개

29 위 글의 밑줄 친 ⓓ의 우리말에 맞게 주어진 어휘를 이용하여 9 단어로 영작하시오.

> little, bright, our neighborhood

➡ _____

30 How long did it take for the club members to do the wall painting? Answer in English in a full sentence.

➡ _____

01 빈칸에 들어갈 말이 나머지와 <u>다른</u> 하나를 고르시오.

① The boys _____ up and go to the bathroom.

② Please _____ off the light so that I can sleep.

③ Where can I _____ on the subway?

④ Many relatives can _____ together in the living room.

⑤ It is great that we _____ along with our friends.

02 두 문장이 같은 의미가 되도록 빈칸을 채우시오.

The computer is too expensive for me to buy.
= The computer is _____ expensive _____ I can't buy it.

[03~04] 다음 빈칸에 들어갈 알맞은 말을 고르시오.

03

I _____ to four universities and was accepted by all of them.

① divided   ② replied   ③ applied
④ suggested   ⑤ mattered

04

It was as if a light _____ on in their heads.

① had   ② went   ③ made
④ hit   ⑤ stroke

[05~06] 다음 대화를 읽고 물음에 답하시오.

A: What are you doing?
B: (①) Can you help me?
A: Sure. (②) What do you want me to do? (③)
B: (④) (A)Please put the clothes into the box.
A: No problem. (⑤)

05 ①~⑤ 중 주어진 문장이 들어갈 곳은?

I'm packing for my move tomorrow.

①   ②   ③   ④   ⑤

06 밑줄 친 (A) 대신 쓸 수 있는 말을 <u>모두</u> 고르시오.

① I'm looking for putting the clothes into the box.

② I want to put the clothes into the box.

③ I'd like you to put the clothes into the box.

④ I hope to put the clothes into the box.

⑤ I want you to put the clothes into the box.

[07~08] 다음 글을 읽고 물음에 답하시오.

B: Hello, class. (A)_____ groups of four people and sit around the tables. Today we're going to (B)_____ bacon and egg sandwiches. <u>우리 수업의 두 가지 규칙에 유의하세요.</u> First, (C)_____ sure you wash your hands before you start. Second, be careful when you use a knife. All right, let's start.

07 빈칸 (A)~(C)에 공통으로 들어갈 말을 쓰시오. (대·소문자 무시)

➡ _____

08 밑줄 친 우리말과 일치하도록 주어진 단어를 이용해 문장을 만드시오. (mind, for) (8 words)

➡ _____

[09~12] 다음 대화를 읽고 물음에 답하시오.

A: Hi, I'm Minsu. (①)
B: Thanks (A)_____ coming, Minsu. (②)
A: What do you want me to do today?
B: Please (B)_____ the dog a bath. (③)
A: Okay. (④) Is there anything to keep in mind?
B: Yes. (⑤) Make sure you brush the fur first.
A: Okay, I will.

출제율 95%

09 ①~⑤ 중 주어진 문장이 들어갈 곳은?

| I'm here for the volunteer work. |

①   ②   ③   ④   ⑤

출제율 95%

10 빈칸 (A)에 알맞은 말을 고르시오

① for   ② with   ③ in   ④ to   ⑤ of

출제율 90%

11 빈칸 (B)에 알맞은 말을 쓰시오.

➡ _____

출제율 100%

12 A와 B 두 사람의 관계를 고르시오.

① teacher – student
② boss – employee
③ waiter – guest
④ volunteer – volunteer manager
⑤ client – staff

출제율 95%

13 다음 중 어법상 <u>어색한</u> 것은?

① She helped me to organize the party.
② The dentist made me open my mouth.
③ The manager let Minho use her phone.
④ The doctor had the pain reduce.
⑤ Ms. Kim has us get along with our friends.

출제율 100%

14 다음 중 어법상 올바른 문장을 <u>모두</u> 고르시오. (정답 2개)

① My friend let me riding his bike.
② Cloe had the trash on the ground pick up.
③ My father got me to bring him the newspaper.
④ Mom makes me to water the plants.
⑤ It was yesterday that Emily saw me at the mall.
⑥ It was the toilet that Bob dropped his smartphone this morning.
⑦ It was a drone who Mina flew at the park last Friday.

출제율 90%

15 밑줄 친 부분을 강조하는 문장으로 고쳐 쓰시오.

(1) <u>What he said</u> worried me.

➡ _____

(2) I played soccer <u>with my friends</u> after school.

➡ _____

(3) <u>My club members</u> planted flowers in the garden on April 5th.

➡ _____
_____

[16~18] 다음 글을 읽고 물음에 답하시오.

Last month, I visited a village with wall paintings in Yeosu. As I was taking a picture, a light went on in my head. I thought, "I'm in the school art club. Why don't we do wall paintings ⓐlike these?" I suggested this idea at the next club meeting, and the members loved it.

We found a teen volunteer project on the Internet. The project was to do a wall painting in our neighborhood. We applied for it, and two weeks later, our club was selected!   <I: Homin>

16 출제율 95%

위 글의 밑줄 친 ⓐlike와 같은 의미로 쓰인 것을 고르시오.

① Which dress do you like best?

② They acted in like manner.

③ I have never seen the like before.

④ How did you like the book?

⑤ You have to do it like this.

17 출제율 100%

위 글의 주제로 알맞은 것을 고르시오.

① to introduce a village with wall paintings in Yeosu

② to do wall paintings as a volunteer work

③ how to take pictures in front of wall paintings well

④ the difficulty of having a good idea

⑤ the importance of the cooperative work

18 출제율 90%

본문의 내용과 일치하도록 다음 빈칸 (A)와 (B)에 알맞은 단어를 쓰시오.

After the school art club members accepted Homin's (A)_____, they did a search on the Internet and applied for a (B)_____ _____ _____ to do a wall painting in their neighborhood. Two weeks later, their club was selected.

[19~21] 다음 글을 읽고 물음에 답하시오.

The day of the project finally came. The project manager had us meet at the painting site at 9 a.m. The wall was ⓐ very poor condition. There were strange writings and drawings on some parts. Other parts had old posters on them. We removed the posters first and painted over the writings and drawings with white paint.

The manager let us paint anything we wanted. We decided to paint something cute because the wall was near an elementary school. We divided ⓑ three groups and began painting. I was in the group with Minsu and Jiwon. I chose my spot and started to paint my favorite movie ⓒcharacter. Minsu painted some flowers and Jiwon did some background drawings.

<I: Homin>

19 출제율 95%

위 글의 빈칸 ⓐ와 ⓑ에 들어갈 전치사가 바르게 짝지어진 것은?

ⓐ	ⓑ		ⓐ	ⓑ
① at – by			② in – by	
③ in – into			④ at – for	
⑤ on – into				

20 출제율 90%

위 글의 밑줄 친 ⓒcharacter와 같은 의미로 쓰인 것을 고르시오.

① He is a man of good character.

② She has a face without any character.

③ What does this Chinese character mean?

④ She performed the leading character.

⑤ What is the character of the Americans?

✍ 출제율 95%

21 다음 중 위 글에 대한 이해가 옳지 <u>않은</u> 사람을 고르시오.

① 현경: At 9 a.m., Homin met his friends at the painting site where they would do the project.

② 정수: Yes. They removed the old posters first before they painted over the writings and drawings with white paint.

③ 단비: Besides, the manager had them paint something cute because the wall was near an elementary school.

④ 창훈: There were three groups and Homin was in the group with Minsu and Jiwon.

⑤ 명식: Exactly, and it was Jiwon who painted some background drawings.

[22~24] 다음 글을 읽고 물음에 답하시오.

Our club painted for about five hours. After we finished, we got together and shared the day's experiences. Minsu was very proud of his flower painting. He said, "My flower is so real that a bee landed on it." I said, "Drawing on a wall was much harder than drawing on paper."

We all agreed that our wall painting wasn't perfect. (①) We made our neighborhood a little brighter and happier. (②) We were proud of ourselves. (③) We didn't just paint pictures on a wall that day. (④) It was a better tomorrow that we painted. (⑤)　　　　〈I: Homin〉

✍ 출제율 90%

22 위 글의 흐름으로 보아, 주어진 문장이 들어가기에 가장 적절한 곳은?

> But it didn't matter.

①　　②　　③　　④　　⑤

✍ 출제율 100%

23 마지막 부분에서 동아리 부원들이 느꼈을 심경으로 알맞은 것을 <u>두 개</u> 고르시오.

① disappointment　② satisfaction
③ depression　④ shame
⑤ self-esteem

✍ 출제율 95%

24 According to the passage, which is NOT true?

① After finishing the project, they got together and shared the day's experiences.

② To Homin, drawing on paper was much harder than drawing on a wall.

③ Homin's club members all agreed that their wall painting wasn't perfect.

④ Thanks to Homin's club members, their neighborhood became a little brighter and happier.

⑤ Homin's club members took pride in themselves.

[25~26] 다음 글을 읽고 물음에 답하시오.

Volunteer Work Diary
Name: Minsu Kim
Date: Friday, May 3rd
I volunteered at Dream Library. I read English books to children. I tried to read like a voice actor. The volunteer manager had me arrange the books on the shelves. The books were so heavy that I had to take a break every 30 (A)[minute / minutes]. After I finished, the shelves looked very (B)[neat / neatly]. I felt very proud. It was a fun and (C)[rewarding / rewarded] experience.

✍ 출제율 100%

25 위 글의 괄호 (A)~(C)에서 어법상 알맞은 낱말을 골라 쓰시오.

➡ (A)_____ (B)_____ (C)_____

✍ 출제율 95%

26 위 글을 읽고 김민수의 봉사 활동에 대해 알 수 <u>없는</u> 것을 고르시오.

① When did he volunteer?
② Where did he volunteer?
③ What did he do?
④ How long did he volunteer?
⑤ How did he feel?

01 대화의 흐름상 빈칸에 들어갈 말을 주어진 단어를 이용해 쓰시오. (2개)

> B: What are all these boxes and books for?
>
> G: I'm packing the books for the donation center. Can you give me a hand?
>
> B: Sure. _____
>
> G: Please write the address on the boxes.
>
> B: No problem.

➡ _____ (want, me)

➡ _____ (like, me)

[02~03] 다음 대화를 읽고 물음에 답하시오.

> Woman: Good morning. What can I do for you?
>
> Tony: Hi. I'm here for the volunteer work.
>
> Woman: Oh, you must be Tony.
>
> Tony: That's right. What do you want me to do today?
>
> Woman: Please read this book for the blind in the recording room.
>
> Tony: No problem. Should I go in now?
>
> Woman: Yes. Please go into Room 7.
>
> Tony: Okay. (A)Is there anything to keeping in mind?
>
> Woman: Yes. (B)Make sure you read slowly and clearly.
>
> Tony: Okay. I'll do my best.

02 밑줄 친 (A)에서 어법상 어색한 것을 찾아 바르게 고치시오.

➡ _____

03 밑줄 친 (B)와 바꿔 쓸 수 있는 문장을 주어진 조건에 맞춰 쓰시오.

➡ _____ (Be)

➡ _____ (forget)

➡ _____
(remember)

04 다음 우리말을 괄호 안에 주어진 어휘를 이용하여 영작하시오.

(1) 그는 우리가 그의 작품을 사진 찍도록 허용했다. (let, pictures, artwork)

➡ _____

(2) 내가 지금 그리고 있는 것은 흰색 곰이다. (that, a, draw)

➡ _____

(3) 카메라를 청소하려면 돈이 얼마나 들죠? (it, have, would, cost, clean, how)

➡ _____
_____

05 어법상 어색한 것을 고쳐 문장을 다시 쓰시오.

(1) My mom made me to prepare dinner.

➡ _____

(2) My boss let the work done by tomorrow.

➡ _____

(3) Linda had her wallet steal on her way home.

➡ _____

(4) It was the restaurant that I saw Juliet calling her friend.

➡ _____
_____

(5) It is because they have no jobs which they cannot afford to buy them.

➡ _____
_____

[06~08] 다음 글을 읽고 물음에 답하시오.

Last month, I visited a village with wall paintings in Yeosu. As I was taking a picture, a light went on in my head. I thought, "I'm in the school art club. Why don't we do wall paintings like these?" I suggested this idea at the next club meeting, and the members loved it.

We found a teen volunteer project on the Internet. The project was to do a wall painting in our neighborhood. We ___ⓐ___ for it, and two weeks later, our club was selected! <I: Homin>

06 주어진 영영풀이를 참고하여 빈칸 ⓐ에 철자 a로 시작하는 단어를 시제에 맞게 쓰시오.

> to write a letter or fill in a form in order to ask formally for something

➡ _____

07 호민이가 자신의 아이디어를 동아리 모임에서 제안하는 내용을 (1) 동명사, (2) 부가의문문을 사용하여 쓰시오.

➡ (1) _____ doing wall paintings like these?

  (2) Let's do wall paintings like these, _____?

08 Where did Homin and the school art club members find a teen volunteer project? Answer in English in a full sentence. (6 words)

➡ _____

[09~11] 다음 글을 읽고 물음에 답하시오.

The day of the project finally came. The project manager had us meet at the painting site at 9 a.m. The wall was in very (A)[good / poor] condition. There were strange writings and drawings on some parts. Other parts had old posters on ⓐthem. We removed the posters first and painted over the writings and drawings with white paint.

The manager let us paint anything we wanted. We decided (B)[to paint / painting] something cute because the wall was (C)[near / nearly] an elementary school. We divided into three groups and began painting. I was in the group with Minsu and Jiwon. I chose my spot and started to paint my favorite movie character. Minsu painted some flowers and Jiwon did some background drawings.

09 위 글의 괄호 (A)~(C)에서 문맥이나 어법상 알맞은 낱말을 골라 쓰시오.

➡ (A)_____ (B)_____ (C)_____

10 위 글의 밑줄 친 ⓐthem이 가리키는 것을 본문에서 찾아 쓰시오.

➡ _____

11 What did they have to do before they actually started to do a wall painting at the painting site? Answer in English in a full sentence.

➡ _____

_____

01 다음 그림을 보고 당부하는 말을 주어진 단어를 이용하여 빈칸에 쓰시오.

> A: It looks like it will rain in a minute.
> B: Yeah. I think so, too.
> A: I have to go to take class in half an hour.
> B: _____ with you. (take, sure, that)

02 다음 그림을 보고, 'It ~ that ...' 강조 구문을 활용하여 자유롭게 영작하시오.

(1) _____
(2) _____
(3) _____
(4) _____

03 다음 내용을 바탕으로 봉사 활동 일기를 쓰시오.

> Date: Friday, May 3rd
>
> Place: Dream Library
>
> What I did:
>
> • I read English books to children.
>
> • I arranged the books on the shelves.
>
> How I felt: I felt very proud.

> **Volunteer Work Diary**
>
> Name: Minsu Kim
> Date: (A)_____
>   I volunteered at (B)_____ . I read (C)_____ to children. I tried to read like a voice actor. The volunteer manager had me (D)_____ on the shelves. The books were so heavy that I had to take a break every 30 minutes. After I finished, the shelves looked very neat. I felt (E)_____ . It was a fun and rewarding experience.

단원별 모의고사

01 다음 짝지어진 단어의 관계가 같도록 빈칸에 알맞은 말을 쓰시오.

> neat : tidy = location : s_____

02 빈칸 (A)와 (B)에 들어갈 말로 알맞은 것끼리 짝지어진 것을 고르시오.

> • Please line (A)_____ and take your turn.
> • She must be very proud (B)_____ herself.
> • The bus came right (C)_____ time.

   (A) (B) (C)
① up – of – on
② up – in – on
③ on – of – at
④ for – in – at
⑤ for – of – on

03 〈보기〉에 있는 어휘를 이용하여 빈칸을 채울 수 없는 것을 고르시오. (형태 변화 가능) (한 단어는 한 번만 사용)

> ┤ 보기 ├
> plant   reply   select   share

① We _____ four applicants for interview.
② They helped me _____ trees.
③ Her mother _____ that she should go and see the doctor.
④ 'Did you see Simon today?' 'Of course,' Nathalie _____ with a smile.
⑤ Will you _____ fries with me?

04 주어진 영영풀이에 해당하는 말을 이용하여 빈칸을 채우시오.

> the area that is behind the main thing that you are looking at

> It's important to understand other people, people from different _____s.

05 〈보기〉에서 빈칸 (A)와 (B)에 알맞은 말을 골라 쓰시오

> ┤ 보기 ├
> at for in out to with

A: What are you doing?
B: I'm packing for my move tomorrow. Can you help me?
A: Sure. What do you want me (A)_____ do?
B: Please take (B)_____ the trash.
A: No problem.

06 밑줄 친 부분에서 흐름상 또는 어법상 어색한 것을 바르게 고치시오.

> B: Hello, class. <u>Make groups of four people and to sit around the tables.</u> Today we're going to make bacon and egg sandwiches. Keep in mind two rules for our class. <u>First, make sure you wash your hands after you start.</u> Second, be careful when you use a knife. All right, let's start.

➡ _____

[07~09] 다음 대화를 읽고 물음에 답하시오.

B: What is this mess? (①)
G: I'm baking ⓐcookies. (②)
B: Why are you baking so ⓑmany?
G: ⓒThey're for the people at the nursing home. (③)
B: ⓓThat's very nice of you. (④)
G: Can you give me a hand?
B: Sure. (⑤)
G: Please put ⓔthem in the gift boxes. Three cookies in each box.
B: Okay.

07 ①~⑤ 중 주어진 문장이 들어갈 곳은?

What do you want me to do?

①   ②   ③   ④   ⑤

08 다음 ⓐ~ⓔ 중 가리키는 대상이 다른 하나를 고르시오.

① ⓐ   ② ⓑ   ③ ⓒ   ④ ⓓ   ⑤ ⓔ

09 위 대화를 읽고 답할 수 없는 질문을 고르시오.

① Is the boy going to help the girl?
② Why is the girl baking so many cookies?
③ How many cookies will the boy put in each box?
④ How many cookies has the girl baked?
⑤ What is the girl doing now?

10 밑줄 친 우리말과 일치하도록 주어진 어구를 이용하여 영작하시오.

A: It's time to go home.
B: Yes. 불을 끄는 거 명심해. (turn, make, the lights)
A: Okay, I will. Anything else?
B: No, that's it. See you tomorrow.

➡ _____

[11~13] 다음 대화를 읽고 물음에 답하시오.

Woman: Good morning. What can I do for you?
Tony: Hi. I'm here (A)_____ the volunteer work.
Woman: Oh, you must be Tony.
Tony: That's right. What do you want me to do today?
Woman: Please read this book for the blind in the recording room.
Tony: No problem. Should I go in now?
Woman: Yes. Please go into Room 7.
Tony: Okay. (a)명심해야 할 것이 있나요?
Woman: Yes. Make sure you read (B)_____.
Tony: Okay. I'll do my best.

11 빈칸 (A)에 알맞은 전치사를 쓰시오.

➡ _____

12 빈칸 (B)에 알맞은 말을 고르시오.

① slowly and clearly
② slow and steady
③ fast and early
④ hard and late
⑤ high and quick

13 밑줄 친 (a)의 우리말과 일치하도록 주어진 단어를 이용하여 영작하시오.

➡ _____
(anything, keep)

14 빈칸을 채워 주어진 문장과 같은 의미의 문장을 쓰시오.

Ms. Smith had us hand in the report on time.
= Ms. Smith had the report _____ _____ by us.

15 다음 문장의 밑줄 친 부분을 강조하는 문장을 쓰시오.

(1) <u>We</u> found a teen volunteer project on the Internet.

➡ _____

_____

(2) We decided to paint <u>something cute</u> because the wall was near an elementary school.

➡ _____

_____

(3) Our club was selected <u>two weeks later</u>.

➡ _____

_____

(4) Mike built a tree house <u>near the park</u>.

➡ _____

_____

16 다음 중 밑줄 친 부분의 쓰임이 <u>다른</u> 하나는?

① Climbing so high <u>made</u> me feel dizzy.

② They <u>made</u> him bulid a windmill at the top of the mountain.

③ Sandra <u>made</u> her daughter a nice dress.

④ The teacher <u>made</u> Minsu paint some flowers on the wall.

⑤ My mom <u>made</u> me get up at 7 every morning.

17 다음 중 어법상 <u>어색한</u> 것을 <u>모두</u> 고르시오.

① Suji made him find her dog.

② Mr. White had his bags check when he passed the gate.

③ She had me help the old lady getting on the bus.

④ It was on the roof that the hen laid two eggs last week.

⑤ It was in 2010 that Tom met Sarah in New York.

⑥ It was saw that Emily me at the mall yesterday.

⑦ It was carefully that he rescued the injured.

[18~20] 다음 글을 읽고 물음에 답하시오.

Last month, I visited a village with wall paintings in Yeosu. ⓐ<u>As</u> I was taking a picture, a light went on in my head. I thought, "I'm in the school art club. Why don't we do wall paintings like these?" I suggested this idea at the next club meeting, and the members loved it.

ⓑ<u>We founded a teen volunteer project on the Internet.</u> The project was to do a wall painting in our neighborhood. We applied for it, and two weeks later, our club was selected!

<I: Homin>

18 위 글의 밑줄 친 ⓐ<u>As</u>와 문법적 쓰임이 같은 것을 고르시오.

① This is twice <u>as</u> large as that.

② Do in Rome <u>as</u> the Romans do.

③ <u>As</u> he is honest, he is trusted by everyone.

④ He came up <u>as</u> I was speaking.

⑤ He regarded me <u>as</u> a fool.

19 위 글의 밑줄 친 ⓑ에서 흐름상 <u>어색한</u> 부분을 찾아 고치시오.

➡ _____

20 위 글을 읽고 답할 수 <u>없는</u> 질문을 고르시오.

① Where did Homin visit last month?

② How many pictures did Homin take there?

③ What school club is Homin in?

④ Did Homin's club members accept his suggestion?

⑤ What project did Homin and his club members apply for?

[21~23] 다음 글을 읽고 물음에 답하시오.

Our club painted for about five hours. After we finished, we got together and shared the day's experiences. Minsu was very proud of his flower painting. He said, "My flower is so real that a bee landed on it." I said, "ⓐ벽에 그리는 것이 종이에 그리는 것보다 훨씬 힘들었어."

We all agreed that our wall painting wasn't perfect. But it didn't matter. We made our neighborhood a little brighter and happier. We were proud of ourselves. ⓑWe didn't just paint pictures on a wall that day. It was a better tomorrow that we painted.

21 위 글의 밑줄 친 ⓐ의 우리말에 맞게 한 단어를 보충하여, 주어진 어휘를 알맞게 배열하시오.

> harder / on paper / drawing / on a wall / than / was / drawing

➡ _____

_____

22 위 글의 밑줄 친 ⓑ를 다음과 같이 바꿔 쓸 때 빈칸에 들어갈 알맞은 말을 세 단어로 쓰시오.

➡ What we painted on a wall that day was rather _____ _____ _____, not just pictures.

23 위 글의 주제로 알맞은 것을 고르시오.

① sharing the experience of laborious wall painting

② the difficulty of drawing on a wall

③ self-esteem gained by rewarding volunteer work

④ carrying out a mission imperfectly

⑤ trying to make our neighborhood more convenient

[24~25] 다음 글을 읽고 물음에 답하시오.

Project: Paint a Better Tomorrow
DATE: April 15
MEETING TIME: 9 a.m.
  Do you like painting? Do you want to make your neighborhood brighter? Right now, the wall is in very poor condition. You need to remove the old posters and paint over the strange writings with white paint. You can paint anything you want!
email: volunteer@1365.go.kr

24 위 글의 종류로 알맞은 것을 고르시오.

① article   ② essay

③ summary   ④ review

⑤ advertisement

25 다음 문장에서 위 글의 내용과 <u>다른</u> 부분을 찾아서 고치시오.

> If you are interested in this project, you can apply for it by sending a text message.

➡ _____

Lesson 4

Open a Book, Open Your Mind

 의사소통 기능

- 의견 묻기
  A: How do you feel about single food diet?
  B: I think it's easy but unhealthy.
- 동의하기
  A: I think reading books on a smartphone is
     good. We can read anytime.
  B: I'm with you on that.

 언어 형식

- the+비교급 ~, the+비교급 …
  The more Stanley dug, **the stronger** he became.
- 접속사 since
  It couldn't be real gold **since** it was too light.

Words & Expressions

Key Words

- **acting** [ǽktiŋ] 명 (연극, 영화에서의) 연기
- **actually** [ǽktʃuəli] 부 실제로
- **adventure** [ədvéntʃər] 명 모험
- **assign** [əsáin] 동 (사람을) 배치하다
- **awake** [əwéik] 형 잠들지 않은, 깨어 있는
- **beat** [bi:t] 동 (심장이) 고동치다, 때리다
- **bone** [boun] 명 뼈
- **bottom** [bátəm] 명 맨 아래, 바닥
- **brain** [brein] 명 머리, 지능
- **brush** [brʌʃ] 동 털다
- **caffeine** [kæfí:n] 명 카페인
- **carefully** [kɛ́ərfəli] 부 조심스럽게
- **character** [kǽriktər] 명 품성, 인격
- **convenience** [kənví:njəns] 명 편리, 편의
- **convenient** [kənví:njənt] 형 편리한
- **cruel** [krú:əl] 형 잔혹한, 잔인한
- **detective** [ditéktiv] 명 형사, 탐정
- **dig** [dig] 동 (구멍 등을) 파다
- **dirt** [də:rt] 명 흙
- **driverless** [dráivərlis] 형 운전사가 없는
- **helpful** [hélpfəl] 형 유용한, 도움이 되는
- **hole** [houl] 명 구덩이, 구멍
- **letter** [létər] 명 문자, 편지

- **light** [lait] 형 가벼운
- **marry** [mǽri] 동 결혼하다
- **muscle** [mʌ́sl] 명 근육
- **object** [ábdʒikt] 명 물건
- **popular** [pápjulər] 형 인기 있는
- **raise** [reiz] 동 키우다, 기르다
- **return** [ritə́:rn] 동 돌려주다, 반품하다
- **scary** [skɛ́əri] 형 무서운
- **scene** [si:n] 명 장면
- **shiny** [ʃáini] 형 빛나는, 반짝거리는
- **skip** [skip] 동 (일을) 거르다, 빼먹다
- **sleepy** [slí:pi] 형 졸리는
- **sneakers** [sní:kərz] 명 운동화
- **spend** [spend] 동 쓰다
- **steal** [sti:l] 동 훔치다
- **suddenly** [sʌ́dnli] 부 갑자기
- **summary** [sʌ́məri] 명 요약, 개요
- **tube** [tju:b] 명 통, 관
- **unfortunately** [ənfɔ́rtʃənətli] 부 불행히도
- **wide** [waid] 형 폭넓은, 폭이 ~인
- **yell** [jel] 동 고함치다

Key Expressions

- **a pair of** 한 쌍의
- **at the bottom of** ~의 바닥에서
- **be full of** ~로 가득 차다
- **belong to** ~의 것이다, ~ 소유이다
- **brush off** 털다
- **build character** 덕성을 기르다, 인성을 키우다
- **day off** 휴일, 쉬는 날
- **end up** 결국 ~이 되다
- **fall in love with** ~와 사랑에 빠지다
- **I'm with you on that.** 그 점에 대해서는 동의해.

- **in fact** 사실
- **look like** ~처럼 보이다
- **look up** 찾아보다
- **not ~ at all** 전혀 ~가 아닌
- **pick up** ~을 집다
- **put down** 내려놓다
- **stand for** ~을 의미하다
- **stay awake** 깨어 있다
- **That is why** ~ 그것이 ~한 이유이다
- **try one's best** 최선을 다하다

Word Power

※ 서로 비슷한 뜻을 가진 어휘
- [ ] **actually** 실제로 – **really** 사실은
- [ ] **carefully** 조심스럽게 – **thoughtfully** 신중하게
- [ ] **dangerous** 위험한 – **risky** 위험한

- [ ] **assign** 배치하다 – **allocate** 배치하다
- [ ] **cruel** 잔혹한 – **brutal** 잔혹한
- [ ] **focus** 집중하다 – **concentrate** 집중하다

※ 서로 반대의 뜻을 가진 어휘
- [ ] **awake** 잠들지 않은 ↔ **asleep** 잠든
- [ ] **carefully** 조심스럽게 ↔ **carelessly** 부주의하게
- [ ] **leave** 떠나다 ↔ **arrive** 도착하다
- [ ] **marry** 결혼하다 ↔ **divorce** 이혼하다
- [ ] **useful** 유용한 ↔ **useless** 쓸모없는

- [ ] **bottom** 맨 아래 ↔ **top** 꼭대기
- [ ] **convenient** 편리한 ↔ **inconvenient** 불편한
- [ ] **light** 가벼운 ↔ **heavy** 무거운
- [ ] **unfortunately** 불행히도 ↔ **fortunately** 다행히도

※ 동사 – 명사
- [ ] **assign** (사람을) 배치하다 – **assignment** 배치
- [ ] **inform** 알려주다 – **information** 정보

- [ ] **detect** 탐지하다 – **detective** 형사
- [ ] **marry** 결혼하다 – **marriage** 결혼

※ 명사 – 형용사
- [ ] **adventure** 모험 – **adventurous** 모험적인
- [ ] **convenience** 편리, 편의 – **convenient** 편리한
- [ ] **information** 정보 – **informative** 유익한, 정보를 주는
- [ ] **thirst** 갈증 – **thirsty** 목마른

- [ ] **character** 품성, 인격 – **characteristic** 특유의
- [ ] **danger** 위험 – **dangerous** 위험한
- [ ] **reason** 이유 – **reasonable** 합리적인

English Dictionary

- [ ] **assign** (사람을) 배치하다
  → to send someone to a particular group or place as part of a job
  누군가를 일의 일부로 특정 집단이나 장소로 보내다

- [ ] **awake** 잠들지 않은, 깨어 있는
  → not sleeping
  잠자고 있지 않은

- [ ] **bottom** 맨 아래, 바닥
  → the lowest part of something
  무언가의 가장 낮은 부분

- [ ] **brush** 털다
  → to remove something with a brush or with your hand
  손이나 솔로 무언가를 제거하다

- [ ] **day off** 휴일, 쉬는 날
  → a day when you do not go to work, school, etc.
  출근 또는 출석하지 않는 날

- [ ] **dig** (구멍 등을) 파다
  → to move soil, sand, snow, etc., in order to create a hole
  구멍을 만들기 위하여 흙, 모래, 눈 등을 이동시키다

- [ ] **hole** 구덩이, 구멍
  → an empty space in something solid
  무언가 단단한 것에 비어 있는 공간

- [ ] **muscle** 근육
  → a body tissue that can contract and produce movement
  동작을 만들어 내고 수축할 수 있는 신체 조직

- [ ] **object** 물건
  → a thing that you can see and touch but is not alive
  볼 수 있고 만질 수 있지만 살아 있지 않은 것

- [ ] **shiny** 빛나는, 반짝거리는
  → smooth and bright   매끄럽고 반짝이는

- [ ] **skip** (일을) 거르다, 빼먹다
  → to pass over or not do something
  지나치거나 어떤 일을 하지 않다

- [ ] **tube** 통, 관
  → a long and empty object that is usually round, like a pipe
  파이프처럼 보통 둥근, 길고 속이 비어 있는 물건

- [ ] **wide** 폭이 ~인
  → measured from side to side
  옆에서 옆으로 측정된

01 다음 빈칸에 들어갈 말로 적절한 것을 고르시오.

> The new teacher was _____ to the science laboratory.

① promoted
② appeared
③ made
④ encouraged
⑤ assigned

02 다음 밑줄 친 부분의 의미로 알맞지 않은 것은?

① In fact, Kobe was too busy to spend time looking out the window. (사실은, 실제로는)
② The money belongs to him. (~의 소유이다)
③ Many people have to look up the meaning of this word in the dictionary. (위를 보다)
④ I could not put the book down, so I read it in one sitting. (내려놓다)
⑤ The mud at the bottom of rivers and lakes also provides food and shelter. (~의 바닥에서)

03 다음 영영풀이가 나타내는 말을 고르시오.

> an empty space in something solid

① pole
② bone
③ hole
④ wound
⑤ hall

[04~05] 다음 밑줄 친 부분과 의미가 가장 가까운 것을 고르시오.

04

> When you hit the drum, you feel good.

① fall
② catch
③ keep
④ beat
⑤ reach

05

> A: What do the letters "U.S.A" mean?
> B: It means United States of America.

① calls for
② gets on
③ takes in
④ stands for
⑤ runs into

06 다음 빈칸에 들어갈 말이 나머지와 다른 하나를 고르시오. (대·소문자 구분 안 함)

① He bought _____ sneakers.
② All he needed was _____ glasses.
③ There was _____ scissors on the table.
④ _____ clothes were piled high on the chair.
⑤ _____ gloves is a nice present.

07 다음 빈칸 (A)~(C)에 알맞은 말로 짝지어진 것을 고르시오.

> • I (A)_____ in love with him because of his kind nature.
> • Reading good books helps to (B)_____ good character.
> • I am so tired that it is difficult for me to (C)_____ awake.

	(A)	(B)	(C)
①	fell	build	try
②	fell	build	stay
③	fell	catch	stay
④	began	catch	try
⑤	began	catch	stay

[01~02] 다음 빈칸에 공통으로 들어갈 말을 쓰시오.

01
- She bent down to pick _____ her glove.
- Can you look _____ the opening times on the website?
- Online shopping is the reason I end _____ spending all my money.

02
- I've known Joanna _____ she was born.
- _____ nobody cared, they didn't know about his hobby.

03 다음 괄호 안의 단어를 문맥에 맞게 고쳐 쓰시오.

_____(fortunate), I won't be able to attend the meeting.

04 다음 우리말에 맞게 주어진 단어를 바르게 배열하시오.

그들에게 우주 정착지를 설계하라는 과제가 맡겨졌다. (assigned, a, were, to, they, settlement, design, Space)

➡ _____

05 다음 빈칸에 알맞은 단어를 〈보기〉에서 골라 쓰시오.

┌─ 보기 ─┐
convenient detective driverless wide

(1) It should be _____ enough to allow plenty of space for food preparation.
(2) Google says the _____ cars are safer than those with human drivers.
(3) The family thought it was more _____ to eat in the kitchen.
(4) She hired a private _____ in an attempt to find her daughter.

06 다음 우리말에 맞도록 빈칸에 알맞은 말을 쓰시오. (철자가 주어진 경우, 주어진 철자로 시작할 것)

(1) 장발장은 결국 감옥에 들어가게 되었다.
➡ Jean Valjean e_____ _____ in prison.
(2) 그는 나의 어깨를 때렸다.
➡ He h_____ _____ _____ the shoulder.
(3) 이 소스는 준비하고 요리하는 데 25분이 걸린다.
➡ This sauce _____ 25 minutes _____ prepare and cook.
(4) 우리가 높이 올라갈수록 점점 더 추워진다.
➡ _____ _____ we go up, _____ _____ it becomes.
(5) 그게 바로 내가 배가 심하게 아팠던 이유였어.
➡ That _____ _____ I had such a bad pain in my belly.

Conversation

① 의견 묻기

> A: How do you feel about single food diet?
> 너는 한 가지 음식만 먹는 다이어트에 대하여 어떻게 생각하니?
>
> B: I think it's easy but unhealthy. 그것은 쉽지만 건강에 좋지 않다고 생각해.

■ 주어진 주제에 관하여 상대방의 의견을 물어볼 때는 'How do you feel about ~?(~에 관해 어떻게 생각하니?)', 'What do you think about ~?(~에 대하여 어떻게 생각하니?)', 'What's your opinion on[about] ~?(~에 대한 의견이 무엇이니?)'와 같은 표현을 사용하여 의견을 물어볼 수 있으며, 'I think ~.'의 표현을 사용해 자신의 의견을 말할 수 있다. 'How do you like ~?'는 '~가 마음에 드니?'의 의미로 상대방이 만족하는지 등의 의견을 물어보는 표현이다.

■ 경험한 일을 바탕으로 하여 상대방의 의견이나 감정을 물을 때는 'Do you find it ~?(너는 ~가 …하다고 생각하니?)'를 사용할 수 있다. 주로 가목적어 it을 사용하여 'find it+형용사+to부정사'의 형태가 되고 목적격보어로 쓰이는 다양한 형용사 다음에 진목적어인 to부정사가 따라온다.

■ 상대방의 의견을 물어보는 표현으로 'Do you think it is easy/hard to ~?(너는 ~하는 것이 쉽다고/어렵다고 생각하니?)'를 사용할 수 있고, 'Would you find it easy/hard to ~ if you had the chance to ~?(만약 네가 ~할 기회가 있다면 너는 ~하는 것이 쉽다고/어렵다고 생각하니?)'와 같이 물어볼 수 있다.

상대방의 의견 묻기

- How do you feel about ~? (~에 대하여 어떻게 생각하니?)
- What do you think about ~? (~에 대하여 어떻게 생각하니?)
- What's your opinion on[about] ~? (~에 대한 의견이 무엇이니?)
- How do you like ~? (~가 마음에 드니?)
- Can you give me your thoughts on ~? (~에 대한 네 생각을 알려줄래?)
- Do you have any opinions on[about] ~? (~에 대한 의견이 있니?)

핵심 Check

1. 다음 대화의 빈칸에 주어진 의미에 해당하는 적절한 말을 쓰시오. (주어진 단어를 이용할 것)

> B: Hi, Amy. Welcome to Korea.
>
> G: Long time no see, Minho. How have you been?
>
> B: Great. How did you come here from the airport?
>
> G: I came here by subway.
>
> B: _____? (feel)
>
> (한국 지하철에 대해서 어떻게 생각하니?)
>
> G: I think it's very clean.

2 동의하기

A: I think reading books on a smartphone is good. We can read anytime.
나는 스마트폰으로 책을 읽는 것이 좋다고 생각해. 우리는 언제든지 읽을 수 있어.

B: I'm with you on that. 나는 그 점에 대해 너에게 동의해.

- 상대방의 말이나 의견에 동의할 때는 'I agree (with you).(나는 동의한다.)', 'I'm with you on that.(나는 그 점에 대해서 너에게 동의한다.)', 'You can say that again.(맞아.)' 등으로 말한다. 또한 상대방의 의견에 동의하지 않을 때는 'I don't agree.' 또는 'I don't think so.' 등으로 표현할 수 있고, 반대하는 의견을 제기할 때는 'I am against+명사.(나는 ~에 반대한다.)'로 표현할 수 있다.

- 상대방의 말이나 의견에 전적으로 동의할 때, 다음과 같은 표현을 쓸 수 있다.
  • You're telling me. / That's precisely my point. 내 말이 바로 그 말이야.
  • You can say that again. / I'm in favor of that. 너의 의견에 동의해.

- 상대방의 말에 동의할 때는 '나도 그래.'의 의미로 'Me, too.' 또는 'So + 동사 + 주어.'의 형태를 쓸 수 있다. 이때 사용하는 동사는 be동사, do, does, did를 포함하는 조동사이다. 부정문에 이어지는 경우에는 so 대신 neither를 사용하여 'Neither+동사+주어.'라고 하거나 'Me neither.'라고 할 수 있다.

동의하기

• I couldn't agree with you more. (전적으로 동감이다.)
• No doubt about it. (그렇고말고.)
• You have a point there. (그것은 일리가 있어요.)

• That's exactly how I feel. (내 생각도 바로 그거야.)
• You are absolutely right. (당신이 전적으로 옳습니다.)
• You read my mind. (텔레파시가 통했나 보구나.)

반대하기

• I don't agree with you. (나는 동의하지 않아.)
• I am against+명사. (나는 ~에 반대한다.)

• I don't think so. (나는 그렇게 생각하지 않아.)

핵심 Check

2. 다음 밑줄 친 말을 대신해서 쓰기에 적절하지 <u>않은</u> 것은?

> B: Did you enjoy the movie?
> G: Yes, I liked it a lot.
> B: What did you like most about it?
> G: The acting was so great.
> B: <u>I'm with you on that.</u>

① I agree with you.　② You can say that again.　③ You're telling me.
④ You read my mind.　⑤ I'm against that.

Listen and Speak 1 A

B: Hi, Amy. Welcome to Korea.

G: ❶Long time no see, Minho. ❷How have you been?

B: ❸Great. How did you come here from the airport?

G: I came here ❹by subway.

B: ❺How do you feel about the subway in Korea?

G: ❻I think it's very clean.

B: 안녕, Amy. 한국에 온 걸 환영해.
G: 오랜만이야, 민호야. 어떻게 지냈니?
B: 잘 지냈어. 공항에서 여기에 어떻게 왔니?
G: 여기까지 지하철을 타고 왔어.
B: 한국 지하철에 관해 어떻게 생각하니?
G: 매우 깨끗하다고 생각해.

❶ Long time no see.: 오랜만이야.
❷ 안부를 묻는 표현에는 'How are you?' 이외에도 'How have you been?', 'What's up?' 'What's going on?'과 같은 다양한 표현들이 있다.
❸ 'How have you been?'에 대한 응답을 할 때 'I've been'은 생략되기도 한다.
❹ by+교통수단: 교통수단을 이용해, 교통수단으로
❺ 'How do you feel about ~?'은 '~에 관해 어떻게 생각하니?'라는 뜻으로 상대방의 의견을 묻는 표현이다. about이 전치사이므로 뒤에 동사가 오려면 '-ing' 형태의 동명사를 써야 한다. 비슷한 표현으로 'What do you think of[about] ~?', 'What's your opinion about ~?', 'What do you say to ~?' 등이 있다. (= What do you think of[about] the subway in Korea? = What's your opinion about the subway in Korea? = What do you say to the subway in Korea?)
❻ think와 it's 사이에는 접속사 that이 생략되어 있다. 여기서 it은 앞 문장의 the subway in Korea(한국 지하철)를 받는 인칭대명사이다.

Check(√) True or False

(1) The boy and the girl are at the airport.   T ☐ F ☐

(2) The girl thinks that the subway in Korea is dirty.   T ☐ F ☐

Listen and Speak 2 A

B: Did you enjoy the movie?

G: Yes, I ❶liked it ❷a lot.

B: ❸What did you like most about it?

G: The acting was so great.

B: ❹I'm with you on that.

B: 영화 재미있었니?
G: 응, 아주 좋았어.
B: 무엇이 가장 좋았니?
G: 연기가 아주 멋졌어.
B: 나도 그 점에 동의해.

❶ 'Did you ~?'로 질문했으므로, 과거시제인 liked로 대답하고 있다.
❷ a lot: 많이
❸ 'What did you like most about it?'은 의문사 what(무엇)을 사용해 무엇이 가장 좋았는지를 묻고 있다.
❹ 'I'm with you on that.'은 '나는 그 점에 동의해.'라는 뜻으로 상대방의 의견에 동의할 때 사용할 수 있는 표현이다.

Check(√) True or False

(3) The girl enjoyed the movie.   T ☐ F ☐

(4) The boy and the girl liked the acting most about the movie.   T ☐ F ☐

Listen and Speak 1 B

G: Brian, did you hear the news?

B: ❶What news?

G: We can use smartphones ❷during classes from next week.

B: Yes, I heard that.

G: ❸How do you feel about it?

B: ❹I think it will be very useful. I can ❺look up words ❻I don't know.

G: Yeah. We can also find information on the Internet.

B: Right. It will be very ❼helpful.

G: Brian, 너 그 소식 들었니?
B: 어떤 소식?
G: 우리는 다음 주부터 수업 중에 스마트폰을 사용할 수 있어.
B: 응. 그 소식을 들었어.
G: 넌 그것에 관해 어떻게 생각하니?
B: 매우 유용할 거라고 생각해. 모르는 단어들을 찾아볼 수 있잖아.
G: 그래. 우리는 또한 인터넷으로 정보를 찾을 수도 있어.
B: 맞아. 매우 도움이 될 거야.

❶ What은 의문형용사로 뒤에 명사가 오며, '어떤 ~' 또는 '무슨 ~'으로 해석한다.
❷ during은 '~ 동안에'의 의미로, 전치사이기 때문에 뒤에 명사가 온다.
❸ 'How do you feel about ~?'은 '~에 관해 어떻게 생각하세요?'라는 뜻으로 상대방의 의견을 물을 때 사용하는 표현이다. about 뒤에는 명사(구)나 동명사(구)를 넣어 말한다.
❹ 의견을 묻는 질문에 'I think ~.'의 표현을 사용해 자신의 의견을 말할 수 있다.
❺ look up: (사전·참고 자료·컴퓨터 등에서 정보를) 찾아보다
❻ words와 I don't know 사이에 목적격 관계대명사 which나 that이 생략되어 있다.
❼ helpful: 도움이 되는

Check(√) True or False

(5) The girl and the boy can look up words by using smartphones during classes.　　T ☐ F ☐

(6) The girl doesn't agree with the boy's idea that using smarphones during classes is very useful.　T ☐ F ☐

Listen and Speak 2 C

A: ❶How do you feel about reading books on a smartphone?

B: I think it's good. We can read anytime.

A: ❷I'm with you on that. / I don't agree. It's not good for our eyes.

A: 스마트폰으로 책 읽는 것에 대해 어떻게 생각하니?
B: 좋다고 생각해. 언제든지 읽을 수 있잖아.
A: 동의해. / 동의하지 않아. 그것은 우리의 눈에 나빠.

❶ 'How do you feel about ~?'은 '~에 관해 어떻게 생각하니?'라는 뜻으로 상대방의 의견을 물을 때 사용하는 표현이다. about 뒤에는 명사(구)나 동명사(구)를 넣어 말한다. 비슷한 표현으로 'What do you think about ~?', 'What's your opinion on ~?', 'Can you give me your thoughts on ~?', 'Do you have any opinions on[about] ~?' 등이 있다.
❷ 'I'm with you on that.'은 '나는 그 말에 동의해.'라는 뜻으로 상대방의 의견에 동의할 때 사용할 수 있는 표현이다. 동의하지 않을 때는 'I don't agree.' 또는 'I don't think so.' 등으로 표현할 수 있다.

Check(√) True or False

(7) B thinks that reading books on a smartphone is good for our eyes.　　T ☐ F ☐

(8) By using smartphones, people can read books anytime.　　T ☐ F ☐

Listen and Speak 1 C

> A: ❶Can I ask you a difficult question?
> B: Sure. ❷I'll try my best.
> A: ❸How do you feel about the ❹driverless car?
> B: ❺I think it's ❻convenient but dangerous.

❶ 어떤 내용을 요청할 때에는 'Can I ~?(내가 ~해도 되나요?)'를 사용할 수 있다. 여기서 ask는 4형식 구조로 간접목적어(you)와 직접목적어(a difficult question)를 취하고 있다.

❷ try one's best: 최선을 다하다

❸ '~에 대해 어떻게 생각하니?'라고 상대방의 의견을 묻는 표현으로는 'How do you feel about ~?', 'What do you think about ~?', 'What's your opinion on ~?', 'Can you give me your thoughts on ~?', 'Do you have any opinions on[about] ~?' 등이 있다.

❹ driverless: 운전사가 없는

❺ 'I think that ~.'은 의견을 말할 때 사용하는 표현으로 'In my opinion, ~' 과 같은 의미이다.

❻ convenient: 편리한

Listen and Speak 2 B

> B: Hey, Jessica. Why ❶are you always drinking energy drinks?
> G: Because ❷they ❸help me ❹stay awake.
> B: ❺I'm with you on that, but they have too much caffeine.
> G: Well, they help me ❻focus on my studies.
> B: ❼Did you know that too much caffeine can hurt your bones?
> G: Oh, I didn't know that.
> B: ❽I think you should drink energy drinks less often.
> G: Maybe you're right. Thanks, Tom.

❶ 부사(구) always, all the time 등과 현재진행형(be+동사ing)을 사용해 습관 적인 행동을 표현할 수 있다.

❷ they는 앞 문장의 energy drinks를 의미한다.

❸ 동사 help는 뒤에 목적어와 목적격보어가 나와서 '(목적어)가 ~하는 것을 돕다'의 의미를 나타낸다. 이때 목적격보어로는 동사원형과 to부정사 모두 올 수 있다.

❹ stay는 자동사로 뒤에 형용사가 오며 '~인 채로 있다'의 의미를 가진다. awake: 잠들지 않은, 깨어 있는

❺ 상대방의 말이나 의견에 동의할 때, 'I'm with you on that.(나는 그 말에 동 의해.)'을 사용할 수 있다.

❻ focus on: ~에 집중하다

❼ 'Did[Do] you know that ~?'는 '너는 ~을 알고 있었니?'의 의미로 상대 방에게 무언가에 대해 알고 있는지 물어보는 표현이다. 'Have you heard about ~?'으로도 물어볼 수 있다.

❽ 'I think you should+동사원형 ~.'은 '내 생각에 너는 ~해야 해.'의 의미 로 상대방에게 충고할 때 쓰는 표현이다. 그 외에 'You'd better ~.', 'Why don't you ~?', 'What[How] about ~?', 'I advise you to ~.' 등을 쓸 수 있다.

Real Life Talk Watch a Video

> Tony: What are all these boxes, Suji?
> Suji: ❶They're items I ordered online.
> Tony: You like shopping on the Internet, don't you?
> Suji: Yes, I do. ❷How do you feel about online shopping, Tony?
> Tony: ❸I don't like it at all.
> Suji: Why?
> Tony: ❹It's very difficult to know what an item actually looks like.
> Suji: ❺I'm with you on that.
> Tony: It's also difficult ❻to return an item if you don't like it.
> Suji: ❼You're right, but I think ❽it's very convenient.
> Tony: Well, ❾convenience ❿isn't everything.

❶ items와 I ordered online 사이에 목적격 관계대명사 which나 that이 생략 되어 있다.

❷ 'How do you feel about ~?'은 '~에 관해 어떻게 생각하세요?'라는 뜻으 로 상대방의 의견을 물을 때 사용하는 표현이다. about 뒤에는 명사(구)나 동명사(구)를 넣어 말한다.

❸ not ~ at all: 전혀 ~가 아닌

❹ 문장 맨앞의 It은 가주어이며, 'to know what an item actually looks like' 는 진주어이다. know의 목적어로 '의문사+주어+동사'의 간접의문문이 사 용되었다.

❺ 'I'm with you on that.'은 '나는 그 말에 동의해.'라는 뜻으로 상대방의 의 견에 동의할 때 사용할 수 있는 표현이다. 동의하지 않을 때는 'I don't agree.' 또는 'I don't think so.' 등으로 표현할 수 있다.

❻ to return은 진주어로 to부정사의 명사적 용법으로 사용되었다. return: 돌 려주다, 반품하다. if는 '만약 ~라면'의 의미로 조건의 부사절을 이끄는 접 속사이다.

❼ 'You're right.'은 상대방의 의견에 동의할 때 사용하는 표현이다.

❽ think와 it's very convenient 사이에 접속사 that이 생략되어 있다. 인칭 대명사 it은 online shopping 또는 shopping on the Internet을 받는다. convenient: 편리한

❾ convenience: 편리, 편의

❿ not과 전체를 나타내는 말(always, all, every 등)이 함께 쓰이면 '항상[모 두] ~인 것은 아니다'란 의미로 일부를 부정한다.

● 다음 우리말과 일치하도록 빈칸에 알맞은 말을 쓰시오.

Listen and Speak 1 A

B: Hi, Amy. Welcome _____ Korea.

G: _____ time _____ see, Minho. _____ have you _____?

B: Great. _____ did you come _____ _____ the airport?

G: I came here _____ subway.

B: _____ do you feel _____ the subway in Korea?

G: I think it's very _____.

해석

B: 안녕, Amy. 한국에 온 걸 환영해.
G: 오랜만이야, 민호야. 어떻게 지냈니?
B: 잘 지냈어. 공항에서 여기에 어떻게 왔니?
G: 여기까지 지하철을 타고 왔어.
B: 한국 지하철에 관해 어떻게 생각하니?
G: 매우 깨끗하다고 생각해.

Listen and Speak 1 B

G: Brian, _____ did you _____ the news?

B: _____ news?

G: We _____ use smartphones _____ classes _____ next week.

B: Yes, I _____ that.

G: _____ do you feel about it?

B: I think it will be very _____. I can _____ _____ _____ _____ _____ _____.

G: Yeah. We can also _____ information on the Internet.

B: Right. It will be very _____.

G: Brian, 너 그 소식 들었니?
B: 어떤 소식?
G: 우리는 다음 주부터 수업 중에 스마트폰을 사용할 수 있어.
B: 응, 그 소식을 들었어.
G: 넌 그것에 관해 어떻게 생각하니?
B: 매우 유용할 거라고 생각해. 모르는 단어들을 찾아볼 수 있잖아.
G: 그래. 우리는 또한 인터넷으로 정보를 찾을 수도 있어.
B: 맞아. 매우 도움이 될 거야.

Listen and Speak 1 C

1. A: _____ _____ _____ you a difficult question?

   B: Sure. I'll try my _____.

   A: _____ do you _____ about the _____ food diet?

   B: I think it's easy but _____.

2. A: Can I _____ you a _____ question?

   B: Sure. I'll _____ my best.

   A: _____ _____ _____ _____ about the AI robot?

   B: I think it's _____ _____ scary.

3. A: _____ _____ _____ a difficult question?

   B: Sure. I'll _____ _____ _____.

   A: _____ _____ _____ _____ animal testing?

   B: I think it's _____ _____ _____.

1. A: 어려운 질문을 해도 될까?
   B: 물론이지. 최선을 다할게.
   A: 싱글 푸드 다이어트에 대해 어떻게 생각하니?
   B: 쉽지만 건강에 해롭다고 생각해.

2. A: 어려운 질문을 해도 될까?
   B: 물론이지. 최선을 다할게.
   A: AI 로봇에 대해 어떻게 생각하니?
   B: 도움이 되지만 무섭다고 생각해.

3. A: 어려운 질문을 해도 될까?
   B: 물론이지. 최선을 다할게.
   A: 동물 실험에 대해 어떻게 생각하니?
   B: 도움이 되지만 잔인하다고 생각해.

Listen and Speak 2 A

B: _____ _____ _____ the movie?

G: Yes, I liked it _____ lot.

B: _____ _____ _____ _____ most about it?

G: The acting _____ so great.

B: I'm _____ _____ _____ that.

Listen and Speak 2 B

B: Hey, Jessica. _____ are you _____ _____ energy drinks?

G: Because they _____ _____ _____ awake.

B: _____ _____ _____ that, but they have _____ much caffeine.

G: Well, they _____ _____ _____ _____ _____ my studies.

B: Did you _____ _____ _____ _____ _____ can hurt your bones?

G: Oh, I didn't know that.

B: I think you _____ _____ energy drinks _____ often.

G: Maybe you're right. Thanks, Tom.

Listen and Speak 2 C

1. **A:** _____ _____ _____ _____ _____ _____ books on a smartphone?

   B: I think it's good. We can read _____.

   A: I'm _____ _____ _____ _____ . / I don't agree. It's _____ _____ our eyes.

2. **A:** _____ _____ _____ _____ _____ skipping breakfast?

   B: I think it's good. We can sleep _____.

   A: _____ _____ _____ _____ _____ . / I don't agree. Our brain may not work well.

3. **A:** _____ _____ _____ _____ _____ eating fast food?

   B: I think it's bad. Fast food has a lot of fat.

   A: _____ _____ _____ _____ _____ . / _____ _____ _____ . We can save time.

해석

B: 그 영화 재미있었니?
G: 응, 아주 좋았어.
B: 무엇이 가장 좋았니?
G: 연기가 아주 멋졌어.
B: 나도 그 점에 동의해.

B: 얘, Jessica. 너는 왜 늘 에너지 음료를 마시니?
G: 에너지 음료가 깨어 있는 데 도움이 되기 때문이야.
B: 그 점에는 동의하지만, 에너지 음료에는 카페인이 너무 많아.
G: 음, 공부에 집중하는 데 도움이 돼.
B: 너무 많은 카페인은 뼈를 다치게 할 수 있다는 것을 알고 있었니?
G: 아, 그건 몰랐어.
B: 내 생각에 넌 에너지 음료를 덜 자주 마셔야 해.
G: 네 말이 맞는 거 같아. 고마워, Tom.

1. **A:** 스마트폰으로 책 읽는 것에 대해 어떻게 생각하니?
   B: 좋다고 생각해. 언제든지 읽을 수 있잖아.
   A: 동의해. / 동의하지 않아. 그것은 우리의 눈에 나빠.

2. **A:** 아침을 건너뛰는 것을 어떻게 생각하니?
   B: 좋다고 생각해. 우리는 잠을 더 잘 수 있어.
   A: 동의해. / 나는 동의하지 않아. 우리의 뇌가 잘 작동하지 않을 수 있어.

3. **A:** 패스트 푸드를 먹는 것에 대해 어떻게 생각하니?
   B: 나쁘다고 생각해. 패스트 푸드는 많은 지방을 가지고 있어.
   A: 동의해. / 나는 동의하지 않아. 우리는 시간을 절약할 수 있어.

Real Life Talk Watch a Video

Tony: _____ are all these boxes, Suji?

Suji: _____ _____ _____ _____ online.

Tony: You like shopping on the Internet, don't you?

Suji: Yes, I do. _____ _____ _____ _____ _____ online shopping, Tony?

Tony: I don't like it _____ _____.

Suji: Why?

Tony: It's very _____ _____ _____ an item actually looks _____.

Suji: I'm with you on that.

Tony: It's also _____ _____ _____ an item if you don't like it.

Suji: You're right, but I think it's very _____.

Tony: Well, _____ isn't everything.

Real Life Talk Step 2

1. **A:** How do you _____ _____ _____ on the Internet?

   B: I like it a lot.

   A: _____ _____ _____ _____ the reason?

   B: I can _____ _____ I want.

   A: _____ _____ _____ on that.

2. **A:** _____ _____ _____ _____ _____ _____ _____ pets?

   B: I don't like it.

   A: Can you tell me the reason?

   B: It's a lot of _____ _____ _____ _____ _____ them.

   A: I _____ _____. They're so cute and _____ _____ _____.

Check up Dialogue Champion

A: _____ _____ _____ _____ _____ _____ _____ smartphones in class?

B: I think smartphones are _____ in class. We can _____ _____ information on them.

A: I'm _____ _____ _____ _____.

해석

Tony: 이 상자들은 전부 뭐니, 수지야?
수지: 내가 온라인으로 주문한 물건들이야.
Tony: 너 인터넷으로 쇼핑하는 걸 좋아하는구나, 그렇지 않니?
수지: 응, 그래. 넌 온라인 쇼핑에 관해 어떻게 생각하니, Tony?
Tony: 난 전혀 좋아하지 않아.
수지: 왜?
Tony: 물건이 실제로 어떻게 생겼는지 알기가 매우 어렵거든.
수지: 그 점에는 동의해.
Tony: 만약 물건이 마음에 들지 않으면 물건을 돌려보내는 것도 어려워.
수지: 네 말이 맞지만, 온라인 쇼핑은 매우 편리하다고 생각해.
Tony: 음, 편리함이 전부는 아니야.

1. A: 인터넷에서 쇼핑하는 것을 어떻게 생각해?
   B: 나는 아주 좋아해.
   A: 이유를 말해 줄 수 있니?
   B: 내가 원할 때마다 쇼핑할 수 있어.
   A: 나도 동의해.

2. A: 애완동물을 기르는 것을 어떻게 생각해?
   B: 나는 좋아하지 않아.
   A: 이유를 말해 줄 수 있니?
   B: 애완동물을 돌보기 위해 할 일이 많아.
   A: 나는 동의하지 않아. 그들은 아주 귀엽고, 우리를 기쁘게 해줘.

A: 수업 시간에 스마트폰을 사용하는 것에 대해 어떻게 생각해?
B: 수업 시간에 스마트폰은 유용하다고 생각해. 우리는 스마트폰으로 정보를 찾을 수 있어.
A: 나는 그 점에 동의해.

Conversation 시험대비 기본평가

01 다음 대화의 밑줄 친 부분과 바꿔 쓸 수 없는 것은?

> A: How do you feel about shopping on the Internet?
> B: I like it a lot.
> A: Can you tell me the reason?
> B: I can shop whenever I want.
> A: I'm with you on that.

① I couldn't agree with you more.

② That's exactly how I feel.

③ I don't think so.

④ You are absolutely right.

⑤ No doubt about it.

02 다음 빈칸에 알맞은 말을 고르시오.

> G: Brian, did you hear the news?
> B: What news?
> G: We can use smartphones during classes from next week.
> B: Yes, I heard that.
> G: _____
> B: I think it will be very useful. I can look up words I don't know.

① Have you heard about it?   ② How do you feel about it?

③ Why do you think so?   ④ What do you mean?

⑤ What do you know about it?

03 대화가 자연스럽게 연결되도록 (A)~(D)를 순서대로 가장 적절하게 배열한 것은?

> (A) I think it's helpful but cruel.
> (B) How do you feel about animal testing?
> (C) Can I ask you a difficult question?
> (D) Sure. I'll try my best.

① (B)–(A)–(C)–(D)   ② (B)–(C)–(A)–(D)

③ (C)–(A)–(B)–(D)   ④ (C)–(B)–(A)–(D)

⑤ (C)–(D)–(B)–(A)

[01~02] 다음 대화를 읽고 물음에 답하시오.

> B: Hi, Amy. Welcome to Korea. (①)
> G: Long time no see, Minho. (②)
> B: Great. (③) How did you come here from the airport?
> G: I came here by subway. (④)
> B: How do you feel about the subway in Korea? (⑤)
> G: I think it's very clean.

01 위 대화의 ①~⑤ 중 주어진 문장이 들어갈 알맞은 곳은?

> How have you been?

①　　②　　③　　④　　⑤

02 위 대화의 내용과 일치하지 <u>않거나</u> 알 수 <u>없는</u> 것은?

① Amy thinks that the subway in Korea is very clean.
② Amy came here from the airport by subway.
③ Minho and Amy haven't seen each other for a long time.
④ Amy has never been to Korea before.
⑤ Minho has been great.

[03~04] 다음 대화를 읽고 물음에 답하시오.

> B: Hey, Jessica. Why are you always drinking energy drinks?
> G: _____
> B: I'm with you on that, but they have too much caffeine.
> G: Well, they help me focus on my studies.
> B: Did you know that too much caffeine can

> hurt your bones?
> G: Oh, I didn't know that.
> B: I think you should drink energy drinks less often.
> G: Maybe you're right. Thanks, Tom.

03 위 대화의 빈칸에 들어갈 말로 알맞은 것을 고르시오.

① Because I like to drink herb tea.
② Because I haven't slept well lately.
③ I don't like to drink energy drinks.
④ I'm always drinking water these days.
⑤ Because they help me stay awake.

04 위 대화의 내용과 일치하지 <u>않는</u> 것은?

① Tom은 너무 많은 카페인이 뼈를 다치게 한다는 것을 알고 있다.
② Tom은 카페인이 집중하는 데 도움이 된다는 것에 동의하고 있다.
③ Jessica는 에너지 음료를 늘 마신다.
④ Jessica는 대화 후에 에너지 음료를 덜 마실지도 모른다.
⑤ Tom은 Jessica에게 에너지 음료를 덜 자주 마시라고 충고하고 있다.

[05~06] 다음 대화를 읽고 물음에 답하시오.

> G: Brian, did you hear the news?
> B: What news?
> G: _____
> B: _____
> G: _____
> B: _____
> G: Yeah. We can also find information on the Internet.
> B: ⓐ_____ It will be very helpful.

05 위 대화의 빈칸에 들어갈 말을 〈보기〉에서 골라 순서대로 바르게 배열한 것은?

┌─ 보기 ─┐
(A) How do you feel about it?
(B) We can use smartphones during classes from next week.
(C) Yes, I heard that.
(D) I think it will be very useful. I can look up words I don't know.
└────┘

① (B) – (A) – (C) – (D)
② (B) – (C) – (A) – (D)
③ (C) – (A) – (B) – (D)
④ (C) – (B) – (A) – (D)
⑤ (C) – (D) – (B) – (A)

06 빈칸 ⓐ에 알맞은 말이 〈보기〉에서 모두 몇 개인지 고르시오.

┌─ 보기 ─┐
• I'm with you on that.
• You have a point there.
• I couldn't agree with you more.
• That's exactly how I feel.
• No doubt about it.
• You are absolutely right.
└────┘

① 2개   ② 3개   ③ 4개   ④ 5개   ⑤ 6개

[07~08] 다음 대화를 읽고 물음에 답하시오.

A: (A)_____ do you feel about using smarphones in class?
B: I don't like it.
A: Can you tell me the reason?
B: Many students will play games on the smartphones.
A: (B)_____ It can be very helpful to search for information on the smartphones.

07 위 대화의 빈칸 (A)에 알맞은 말을 고르시오.

① How   ② Why   ③ What
④ Which   ⑤ How about

08 위 대화의 빈칸 (B)에 알맞은 말을 모두 고르시오.

① I couldn't agree with you more.
② I don't think so.
③ I totally disagree.
④ No doubt about it.
⑤ I'm not sure about that.

09 다음 중 짝지어진 대화가 어색한 것을 모두 고르시오.

① A: The movie is interesting. Don't you think so?
   B: I don't think so. In my opinion, the story is good.
② A: I think that the new teacher is very kind.
   B: I think so, too. She also teaches very well.
③ A: I think science is an interesting subject. How do you feel about science?
   B: I think so, too.
④ A: How do you feel about online shopping?
   B: In my opinion, it saves time.
⑤ A: How do you feel about the school lunch?
   B: I don't think so. I think the food is delicious.

[01~02] 다음 대화를 읽고 물음에 답하시오.

G: Brian, did you hear the news?
B: What news?
G: We can use smartphones during classes from next week.
B: Yes, I heard that.
G: (A)넌 그것에 관해 어떻게 생각하니?
B: I think it will be very useful. I can look (B)_____ words I don't know.
G: Yeah. We can also find information on the Internet.
B: Right. It will be very helpful.

01 밑줄 친 (A)를 주어진 단어를 이용하여 영작하시오.

➡ _____ (how)

02 빈칸 (B)에 알맞은 말을 쓰시오.

➡ _____

[03~05] 다음 대화를 읽고 물음에 답하시오.

Tony: What are all these boxes, Suji?
Suji: (A)_____ (ordered, items, they, online, I, are)
Tony: You like shopping on the Internet, don't you?
Suji: Yes, I do. How do you feel about online shopping, Tony?
Tony: I don't like it at all.
Suji: Why?
Tony: It's very difficult to know what an item actually looks like.
Suji: I'm ⓐ_____ you ⓑ_____ that.

Tony: It's also difficult to return an item if you don't like it.
Suji: You're right, but I think it's very (B)_____.
Tony: Well, convenience isn't everything.

03 빈칸 (A)를 괄호 안에 주어진 단어를 알맞게 배열하여 채우시오.

➡ _____

04 상대방의 의견에 동의하는 말을 할 때 빈칸 ⓐ와 ⓑ에 알맞은 말을 쓰시오.

➡ ⓐ _____ ⓑ _____

05 빈칸 (B)에 들어갈 말을 대화에 나오는 단어를 이용하여 알맞은 형태로 바꿔 쓰시오.

➡ _____

[06~07] 다음 대화를 읽고 물음에 답하시오.

A: (A)패스트 푸드를 먹는 것에 대해 어떻게 생각하니?
B: I think it's bad. Fast food has a lot of fat.
A: (B)_____ We can save time.

06 밑줄 친 (A)를 주어진 단어를 이용하여 영작하시오.

➡ _____
   (feel, eat)

07 대화의 흐름상 빈칸 (B)에 들어갈 말을 주어진 단어를 이용해서 쓰시오.

➡ _____ (agree)

Grammar

1 'the 비교급 ~ the 비교급…'

> • **The more** Stanley dug, **the stronger** he became.
> Stanley는 많이 파면 팔수록, 더 힘이 세졌다.
>
> • **The more** I want to get something done, **the less** I call it work.
> 나는 뭔가가 이루어지기를 원하면 원할수록 그것을 더 일이라고 생각하지 않는다.

■ the 비교급(+주어+동사) ~, the 비교급+주어+동사 …

 • 형태: The+비교급(+주어+동사) ~, the+비교급(+주어+동사) …

 • 의미: ~하면 할수록 더 …하다

■ 'the 비교급(+주어+동사) ~, the 비교급(+주어+동사) …' 구문은 정도가 점점 더해지거나 덜해지는 것을 표현할 때 사용한다.

 • **The sooner, the better**. 빠르면 빠를수록 더 좋다.

■ 최상급이 아닌 비교급임에도 the를 쓰는 것에 주의해야 하며, be동사나 반복되는 어구는 종종 생략된다. 'the 비교급(+주어+동사) ~, the 비교급+주어+동사 …'에서 앞에 나오는 'the'는 관계부사이며, 뒤에 나오는 'the'는 지시부사이다.

 • **The higher** we climb, **the colder** it will become. 우리가 높이 오르면 오를수록, 더 추워질 것이다.

 • Paradoxically, **the less** she ate, **the fatter** she got. 역설적이게도 그녀는 적게 먹을수록 더 살이 쪘다.

■ 'the 비교급+주어+동사 ~, the 비교급+주어+동사 …' 구문은 'As+주어+동사+비교급 ~, 주어+동사+비교급 …'으로 바꿔 쓸 수 있다.

 • **The more** you chase money, **the harder** it is to catch it.
 = As you chase money more, it is harder to catch it. 돈은 더 좇을수록 손에 쥐기 힘들어진다.

 cf. '비교급 and 비교급'은 '점점 더 ~하다'의 뜻이다.

 • It's getting **harder and harder** to find parking close to the office.
 사무실 근처에 주차할 데 찾기가 갈수록 힘들어요.

핵심 Check

1. 다음 괄호 안에서 알맞은 말을 고르시오.

 (1) The (long / longer) he stayed there, the less he liked the people.

 (2) The more you have, the (more / most) you want.

2 접속사 since

- It couldn't be real gold **since** it was too light. 그것은 너무 가벼웠기 때문에 진짜 금일 리가 없었다.
- It's years **since** we last met. 우리가 마지막으로 만난 후로 오래 되었다.

- since는 이유를 나타내는 접속사로 쓰여, '~이기 때문에'의 뜻으로 이유를 나타내는 부사절을 이끌며 because, as로 바꿔 쓸 수 있다.
  - **Since** we live in the computer era, you should get used to personal computers.
    = **Because**[**As**] we live in the computer era, you should get used to personal computers.
    우리는 컴퓨터 시대에 살고 있으니까 PC를 익혀야 한다.

- since의 그 밖의 쓰임

  (1) 시간의 접속사: '~한 이후로'의 뜻으로, 시간의 부사절을 이끄는 since와 함께 쓰는 주절은 현재완료나 과거완료 시제로 쓴다.
  - It's been three years to the day **since** we met. 우리가 만난 지 정확히 3년이다.
  - He has been collecting stamps **since** he was eight. 그는 8살 때부터 우표를 모아 오고 있다.

  (2) 전치사: '~ 이후(from then till now)'의 뜻으로, 'since+명사(구)'나 'ever since+명사(구)'의 형태로 쓰인다.
  - You've grown **since** the last time I saw you! 지난번 봤을 때보다 많이 컸구나!
  - The rain has been continuous **since** this morning. 비가 오늘 아침부터 계속 내리고 있다.

  (3) 부사: '그 이후로'의 뜻이며, 주로 완료형 동사나 'ever since'의 형태로 쓰인다.
  - He left home two weeks ago and we haven't heard from him **since**.
    그는 2주 전에 집을 떠났는데 그 이후로 우리는 그에게서 소식을 못 들었다.
  - I have not seen him **since**. 그 후로 나는 그를 만나지 못했다..

핵심 Check

2. 다음 괄호 안에서 알맞은 말을 고르시오.

(1) We canceled the picnic (since / though) it rained a lot.

(2) He has changed a lot (unless / since) the accident.

(3) (Because / Before) he was so happy, he was smiling broadly.

Grammar 시험대비 기본평가

01 다음 빈칸에 들어갈 말로 알맞은 것은?

> The _____ you give, the more you get back.

① few   ② many   ③ little

④ more   ⑤ most

02 다음 문장의 빈칸에 공통으로 들어갈 말로 알맞은 것은? (대·소문자 무시)

> • _____ she was tired, she took some rest.
> • Many diets fail _____ they are boring.

① Unless   ② If   ③ Since

④ That   ⑤ Though

03 다음 중 어법상 바르지 <u>않은</u> 것은?

① The older we grow, the weaker we become.

② The long the nails get, the more strange they become.

③ The more you practice, the better you do.

④ She hasn't seen Laura since her schooldays.

⑤ We thought that, since we were in the area, we'd stop by and see them.

04 다음 우리말에 맞게 주어진 어휘를 바르게 배열하시오.

(1) Stanley는 많이 파면 팔수록, 더 힘이 세졌다.

   (Stanley, he, became, dug, stronger, more, the, the)

   ➡ _____

(2) 나는 그에 대해 더 많이 들을수록, 그에 대한 동정심이 더 많아졌다.

   (I, I, felt, heard, him, him, sympathetic, more, more, the, the, for, about)

   ➡ _____

(3) 그는 아팠기 때문에 학교에 갈 수 없었다. (부사절로 시작할 것)

   (he, he, school, go, was, couldn't, sick, since, to)

   ➡ _____

 다음 중 어법상 <u>어색한</u> 것은?

① The more you exercise, the healthier you become.

② The much sugar in the orange juice, the short the shelf life.

③ The longer, the better.

④ The more you study, the more you get to know all the scientific stuff.

⑤ The warmer it gets, the less clothes you need.

02 다음 중 어법상 옳은 것은?

① Jane was bored since she waited so long.

② He didn't go to school though it was a holiday.

③ Such changes have not been seen because the invention of the printing press.

④ Unless Tom was tired, he stopped working.

⑤ I was bitten by a dog once and I've been afraid of them ever before.

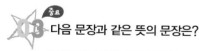 다음 문장과 같은 뜻의 문장은?

As he gets older, he becomes wiser.

① Because he gets old, he becomes wise.

② He got the old, so he became the wise.

③ The old he gets, the wise he becomes.

④ The older he gets, the wiser he becomes.

⑤ The oldest he gets, the wisest he becomes.

 다음 밑줄 친 부분과 바꿔 쓸 수 있는 것은?

It couldn't be real gold <u>since</u> it was too light.

① whether　② that　③ if

④ unless　⑤ because

[05~06] 다음 우리말을 알맞게 영작한 것을 <u>모두</u> 고르시오.

05

너는 공부를 열심히 하면 할수록, 더 영리해질 것이다.

① Harder you study, smarter you will become.

② The hardest you study, the smartest you will become.

③ The harder you study, the smarter you will become.

④ Because you study harder, you will become the smarter.

⑤ As you study harder, you will become smarter.

06

피곤했기 때문에 나는 일찍 집에 갔다.

① Unless I felt very tired, I went home early.

② If I felt very tired, I went home early.

③ Since I felt very tired, I went home early.

④ When I felt very tired, I went home early.

⑤ Because I felt very tired, I went home early.

07 다음 우리말과 일치하는 문장을 쓸 때, 빈칸에 알맞은 말은?

> 음식이 매울수록 그녀는 더 좋아한다.
> = _____ the food is, the more she likes it.

① Spice ② Spicer ③ Spicest
④ The spicier ⑤ The spiciest

08 다음 〈보기〉의 밑줄 친 since와 쓰임이 같은 것은?

> ┤ 보기 ├
> Since I was busy, I couldn't help my friend.

① We've lived here since 1994.
② I have permission to get married since I am old enough.
③ She has moved house six times since she came here.
④ It's a long time since her death.
⑤ I have not seen him since.

09 다음 문장의 빈칸 (A), (B)에 들어갈 말로 가장 적절한 것은?

> (A)_____ the race, (B)_____ the warm-up.

	(A)	(B)
①	The shorter	the longer
②	The shorter	longer
③	The short	the long
④	Shorter	the longer
⑤	Shorter	longer

10 다음 문장의 빈칸에 알맞은 말을 모두 고르시오.

> I couldn't sleep _____ the bed was so uncomfortable.

① since ② that ③ what
④ because ⑤ where

11 다음 문장과 비슷한 뜻이 되도록 비교급을 사용하여 바꿔 쓰시오.

(1) As it is colder, the hole becomes larger and deeper.

➡ _____

(2) If you have stronger will, you will learn more.

➡ _____

12 다음 중 since의 쓰임이 나머지와 다른 하나는?

① Many improvements have been made since this century began.
② I can get away from the office since we're not very busy just now.
③ We have both changed since we parted.
④ He has worked since he left school.
⑤ He has learned a lot since he came here.

13 다음 문장을 어법에 맞게 고쳐 쓰시오.

(1) This book is better of the two.

➡ _____

(2) Harder he tried to get out, deeper he went.

➡ _____

(3) Little people spend, slow the economy growth becomes.

➡ _____
_____

[14~15] 다음 중 어법상 올바른 문장은?

14
① The older she got, the pretty she got.
② The less I tell you, the more safe you'll be.
③ The lower a country's GNP is, the happier the country's people are.
④ Smaller portion of the two will be paid to him.
⑤ It was getting dark and dark, and we hurried to the shore.

15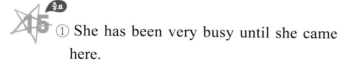
① She has been very busy until she came here.
② We lost because of we played badly.
③ I was forced to take a taxi while the last bus had left.
④ The train was delayed though a tree had fallen across the line.
⑤ Life was harder then because neither of us had a job.

16 다음 문장에서 어법상 어색한 부분을 바르게 고치시오.

(1) Though I had no time to text you yesterday, I could not reply.
＿＿＿＿＿＿ ➡ ＿＿＿＿＿＿

(2) She didn't come to the meeting if she was busy last weekend.
＿＿＿＿＿＿ ➡ ＿＿＿＿＿＿

(3) He took his jacket off because the heat.
＿＿＿＿＿＿ ➡ ＿＿＿＿＿＿

17 다음 괄호 안에서 알맞은 것을 고르시오.

(1) (The more / The much) stress I get, (the more / the much) nervous I become.
(2) (The closer / Close) I got to her, (the happier / happy) I became.
(3) (Bigger / The bigger) the eyes, (better / the better) the eyesight.
(4) (Although / Because) I was so tired, I couldn't concentrate.
(5) He resigned (since / because of) bad health.

18 다음 빈칸에 들어갈 수 <u>없는</u> 것은?

> The harder I practice, ＿＿＿＿＿ I become.

① the more merry
② the better
③ the more interested
④ the happier
⑤ the more excited

19 다음 주어진 문장과 의미가 같은 것을 <u>모두</u> 고르시오.

> He gave up his job in advertising because he couldn't stand the pace.

① He gave up his job in advertising if he couldn't stand the pace.
② He gave up his job in advertising since he couldn't stand the pace.
③ He gave up his job in advertising although he couldn't stand the pace.
④ He gave up his job in advertising whether he couldn't stand the pace.
⑤ He gave up his job in advertising as he couldn't stand the pace.

01 다음 두 문장을 〈보기〉와 같이 한 문장으로 완성하시오.

> ┌─ 보기 ─┐
> • You laugh much.
> • You become happy.
> → The more you laugh, the happier you become.

(1) • You are young.
   • It is easy to learn.
   ➡ _____

(2) • The picture is large.
   • It will take long for people to download.
   ➡ _____
   _____

02 다음 문장에서 어법상 어색한 것을 바르게 고쳐 다시 쓰시오.

(1) The old he grew, the poor his memory became.
   ➡ _____
   _____

(2) I think the hard I work, the much I move up in the world.
   ➡ _____
   _____

(3) Ann is taller and more beautiful of the two sisters.
   ➡ _____
   _____

(4) This dictionary is a lot better of the two.
   ➡ _____

(5) The plan failed because lack of money.
   ➡ _____

(6) The accident happened because of nobody paid attention to the warning signs.
   ➡ _____
   _____

(7) They've been best friends before they were children.
   ➡ _____

(8) She had only spoken to him once though the party.
   ➡ _____

03 다음 그림을 보고 주어진 어휘를 이용하여 빈칸에 알맞은 말을 쓰시오.

(1) _____ it gets, _____ she becomes. (hot, exhausted)

(2) _____ she wants to drink something cold, _____ she feels. (much, thirsty)

04 다음 두 문장을 since를 이용해 한 문장으로 쓰시오.

(1) • I was hungry.

　　• I had a whole pizza.

　　(since로 시작하는 부사절이 주절의 앞에 위치할 것)

　　➡ _____

(2) • I didn't enjoy the book.

　　• I couldn't identify with any of the main characters.

　　(since로 시작하는 부사절이 주절의 뒤에 위치할 것)

　　➡ _____

　　_____

05 다음 문장과 비슷한 뜻이 되도록 비교급을 사용하여 바꿔 쓰시오.

(1) If you read many books, you will know many things.

　　➡ _____

(2) If you start early, you arrive there soon.

　　➡ _____

(3) As you win more arguments, you'll have fewer friends.

　　➡ _____

(4) As one's mind is healthier, one's body will be healthier.

　　➡ _____

　　_____

06 괄호 안에 주어진 어휘를 이용하여 빈칸에 알맞은 말을 쓰시오.

(1) The more you practice, _____. (you, do, good)

(2) The hotter you feel, _____ _____. (you, drink, much, water)

(3) The fewer hours they work, _____ _____. (they, have, little, holiday time)

07 다음 우리말과 일치하도록 괄호 안에 주어진 어휘를 이용하여 영작하시오.

(1) 우리는 나이가 들면 들수록, 더 현명해진다. (grow, become, old, wise)

　　➡ _____

(2) 너는 높이 올라가면 올라갈수록, 더 멀리 본다. (climb, see, high, far)

　　➡ _____

(3) 너는 덜 쓰면 덜 쓸수록, 더 많이 절약한다. (save, spend, much, little)

　　➡ _____

(4) 나는 돈이 없어서 먹을 것을 하나도 살 수 없었다. (buy, anything, since, no money)

　　➡ _____

　　_____

(5) 그녀는 대학을 떠난 이후로 많은 책을 써 왔다. (has written, since, left college)

　　➡ _____

　　_____

Reading

HOLES

"Dig harder, Stanley! The harder you dig, the faster you'll finish!"
_{The+비교급(+주어+동사) ~, the+비교급(+주어+동사): ~할수록, (점점) 더 …하다}

yelled Mr. Sir. Stanley Yelnats couldn't dig any harder since every
_{any: 부정문에서 '전혀, 조금도'의 뜻으로 형용사나 부사의 의미를 강조   since: 이유나 원인을 나타내는 절을 이끄는 접속사   every: 모든, 단수 명사와 함께 쓰임.}

single muscle hurt. He was thirsty and hungry. He wanted to go home.

Unfortunately, Stanley's home for the next 18 months would be right
_{과거 시제에서 will의 과거형으로 would를 쓴다.}

here, at Camp Green Lake.
_{here와 at Camp Green Lake는 동격으로 콤마(,)로 연결}

   Camp Green Lake was a terrible name. It wasn't green and there was

no lake. Camp Green Lake was hot and full of sand. In fact, it wasn't
_{실제로는, 사실은}

even a camp. It was a place for bad boys. Then what was a good boy
_{예상 밖의 놀라운 일을 나타내는 말, ~조차도}

like Stanley doing here? He was sent to the camp for stealing a pair of
_{쌍을 이루는 물건의 수량을 표현할 때 사용}

sneakers.

   Stanley didn't really steal a pair of sneakers. He was just in the wrong

place at the wrong time. One day, he was walking home from school.
_{One day: 미래의 어느 시기나 과거의 특정한 날을 가리킨다.   과거진행형: ~하는 중이었다}

Suddenly, a pair of old sneakers fell from the sky. The sneakers hit him
_{'갑자기'라는 뜻의 부사로 문장 전체를 수식   fall from the sky: 하늘에서 떨어지다}

on the head.
_{hit+사람+on+the+신체 부위: ~의 …을 때리다}

   He started running with the sneakers to tell his father what happened.
_{to부정사의 부사적 용법(목적)   간접의문문(의문사 주어+동사)}

A few minutes later, the police stopped Stanley and asked him why
_{시간+later: ~ 시간이 지난 후에   ~를 멈추게 했다}

he was running. Unfortunately for Stanley, the sneakers belonged to
_{asked의 직접목적어로 쓰인 간접의문문}

a famous baseball player, Clyde Livingstone. That was why Stanley

ended up at Camp Green Lake.
_{end up+특정 장소나 상황: 결국 (어떤 처지)에 처하게 되다}

hole 구덩이, 구멍
dig (구멍 등을) 파다
muscle 근육
unfortunately 불행히도
belong to ~의 소유이다[것이다]
end up 결국 ~이 되다

📎 **확인문제**

● 다음 문장이 본문의 내용과 일치하면 T, 일치하지 <u>않으면</u> F를 쓰시오.

1 Because every single muscle hurt, Stanley Yelnats couldn't dig any harder. ☐

2 Stanley's home for the next two years would be at Camp Green Lake. ☐

3 Camp Green Lake wasn't green and there was no lake. ☐

4 Stanley started to run with the sneakers to tell his father what happened. ☐

5 The sneakers belonged to a famous basketball player, Clyde Livingstone. ☐

Stanley was assigned to Group D in the camp. There were six other
be assigned to: ~에 배치되다. 능동태: assign+목적어+to. ~(목적어)를 …에 배치하다
boys in Stanley's group. They all had cool names like X-Ray, Zigzag
Stanley를 포함하면 총 7명의 소년이 있었다.
and Zero. Each boy had to dig one hole every day. It had to be about
~해야 했다(의무)   각 소년이 매일 파야 하는 구덩이
150cm deep and 150cm wide. Mr. Sir said, "You are digging to build
깊이와 너비가 150센티미터 정도가 되어야 함을 의미   to부정사의 부사적 용법(목적)
character."

The more Stanley dug, the stronger he became. It took less time to
It+takes+시간+to부정사구: ~하는 데 (…의) 시간이 걸리다
finish his hole each day. In his second week, as Stanley was finishing
~하는 동안에(접속사)
his hole, he saw something shiny in the dirt. Stanley's heart beat
-thing으로 끝나는 부정대명사를 수식하는 형용사는 뒤에 위치
faster. He heard that anyone who found something interesting would
heard의 목적어를 이끄는 접속사 주격 관계대명사   -thing으로 끝나는 부정대명사를 수식하는 형용사는 뒤에 위치
be given the day off. He carefully picked up the shiny object and
brushed off the dirt. It was a small gold tube. But it couldn't be real
the small gold tube. couldn't: ~일 리가 없었다(강한 부정적인 추측)
gold since it was too light. There were two letters, *KB*, at the bottom
since: 원인이나 이유를 나타내는 절을 이끄는 접속사
of the tube. What did KB stand for? Stanley's heart beat even faster.
= represent = symbolize: ~을 상징하다   '훨씬, 더욱'(비교급을 강조)

assign (사람을) 배치하다
wide 폭이 ~인
character 품성, 인격
shiny 빛나는, 반짝거리는
dirt 흙
beat (심장이) 고동치다, 때리다
day off 휴일, 쉬는 날
object 물건
brush off 털다, 털어 내다
tube 통, 관
bottom 맨 아래, 바닥
stand for ~을 의미하다

확인문제

● 다음 문장이 본문의 내용과 일치하면 T, 일치하지 <u>않으면</u> F를 쓰시오.

1 There were seven boys in Stanley's group including Stanley. ☐
2 The hole each boy had to dig every day had to be about 150cm deep and 150cm
  wide. ☐
3 It took more time for Stanley to finish his hole each day. ☐
4 In his second week, Stanley saw something shiny in the dirt. ☐
5 The shiny object was a small tube which was made of real gold. ☐

● 우리말을 참고하여 빈칸에 알맞은 말을 쓰시오.

HOLES

1 "Dig _____, Stanley!

2 The _____ you dig, _____ _____ you'll finish!" yelled Mr. Sir.

3 Stanley Yelnats couldn't dig _____ _____ since every single muscle hurt.

4 He was _____ and _____.

5 He wanted to _____ _____.

6 Unfortunately, Stanley's home for the next **18** months _____ _____ right here, at Camp Green Lake.

7 Camp Green Lake was a _____ name.

8 It wasn't green and there was _____ _____.

9 Camp Green Lake was hot and _____ _____ _____.

10 _____ _____, it wasn't _____ a camp.

11 It was _____ _____ _____ _____ _____.

12 Then what was a good boy _____ Stanley doing here?

13 He was sent to the camp _____ _____ a pair of sneakers.

14 Stanley _____ _____ _____ a pair of sneakers.

15 He was just _____ _____ _____ _____ at the wrong time.

16 One day, he was walking home _____ _____.

17 Suddenly, a pair of old sneakers _____ _____ the sky.

18 The sneakers _____ _____ _____ _____ _____.

구덩이

1 "더 열심히 파, Stanley!

2 네가 열심히 파면 팔수록, 너는 더 빨리 끝낼 거야!" Sir 씨가 소리를 질렀다.

3 Stanley Yelnats는 모든 근육 하나하나가 아팠기 때문에 더 열심히 팔 수가 없었다.

4 그는 목이 마르고 배가 고팠다.

5 그는 집에 가고 싶었다.

6 불행히도, 앞으로 **18**개월 동안 Stanley의 집은 바로 여기 Green Lake 캠프가 될 것이었다.

7 Green Lake 캠프는 형편없는 이름이었다.

8 그곳은 초록색도 아니었고 호수도 없었다.

9 Green Lake 캠프는 뜨거웠고 온통 모래였다.

10 사실 그곳은 캠프조차 아니었다.

11 그곳은 나쁜 소년들을 위한 곳이었다.

12 그렇다면 Stanley 같이 착한 소년이 여기서 무엇을 하고 있었을까?

13 그는 운동화 한 켤레를 훔쳤다는 이유로 캠프에 보내졌다.

14 Stanley가 정말로 운동화 한 켤레를 훔친 것은 아니었다.

15 그는 그저 잘못된 시간에 잘못된 장소에 있었다.

16 어느 날, 그는 학교에서 집으로 걸어가고 있었다.

17 갑자기, 낡은 운동화 한 켤레가 하늘에서 떨어졌다.

18 그 운동화는 그의 머리에 맞았다.

19 He started running with the sneakers to tell his father _____ _____.

20 A few minutes later, the police _____ Stanley and asked him _____ _____ _____.

21 Unfortunately _____ Stanley, the sneakers _____ a famous baseball player, Clyde Livingstone.

22 _____ _____ _____ Stanley ended up at Camp Green Lake.

23 Stanley _____ _____ _____ Group D in the camp.

24 There were _____ _____ _____ in Stanley's group.

25 They all had _____ names _____ X-Ray, Zigzag and Zero.

26 Each boy had to dig _____ _____ _____ _____.

27 It had to be _____ 150cm _____ and 150cm _____.

28 Mr. Sir said, "You are digging _____ _____ _____."

29 _____ _____ Stanley dug, _____ _____ he became.

30 _____ _____ less time _____ _____ his hole each day.

31 In his second week, as Stanley was finishing his hole, he saw _____ _____ in the dirt.

32 Stanley's heart _____ _____.

33 He heard that _____ _____ found something interesting would _____ _____ _____ _____ _____.

34 He carefully picked up the shiny object and _____ the dirt.

35 It was a _____ _____ _____.

36 But it _____ _____ real gold _____ it was too light.

37 There were two letters, *KB*, _____ _____ _____ the tube.

38 What did KB _____ _____?

39 Stanley's heart beat _____ faster.

---

19 그는 그의 아버지에게 무슨 일이 일어났는지 말하기 위해 운동화를 가지고 달리기 시작했다.

20 몇 분 후에, 경찰이 Stanley를 멈춰 세웠고 그가 왜 달리고 있었는지를 그에게 물었다.

21 Stanley에게는 불행히도, 그 운동화는 유명한 야구 선수인 Clyde Livingstone의 것이었다.

22 그것이 Stanley가 Green Lake 캠프에 오게 된 이유였다.

23 Stanley는 캠프에서 D 그룹에 배치되었다.

24 Stanley의 그룹에는 6명의 다른 소년들이 있었다.

25 그들은 모두 X-Ray, Zigzag, Zero와 같은 멋진 이름을 가지고 있었다.

26 각 소년은 매일 구덩이를 하나를 파야 했다.

27 그것은 150cm 정도 깊이와 150cm 정도 너비여야 했다.

28 Sir 씨는 "너희들은 인격을 수양하기 위해 구덩이를 파고 있는 것이야."라고 말했다.

29 Stanley는 많이 파면 팔수록, 더 힘이 세졌다.

30 하루하루 구덩이를 끝내는 데 시간이 덜 걸렸다.

31 그가 온 지 두 번째 주, Stanley가 자기 구덩이를 끝내 가고 있었을 때, 그는 흙 속에서 빛나는 뭔가를 봤다.

32 Stanley의 심장은 더 빨리 뛰었다.

33 그는 흥미로운 뭔가를 발견한 사람은 그 날을 쉬게 된다고 들었다.

34 그는 조심스럽게 그 빛나는 물체를 집어 흙을 털어 냈다.

35 그것은 작은 금색 통이었다.

36 그러나 그것은 너무 가벼웠기 때문에 진짜 금일 리가 없었다.

37 그 통의 바닥에는 KB라는 두 글자가 있었다.

38 KB는 무엇을 의미할까?

39 Stanley의 심장은 훨씬 더 빨리 뛰었다.

• 우리말을 참고하여 본문을 영작하시오.

HOLES

1 "더 열심히 파, Stanley!

➡ _____

2 네가 열심히 파면 팔수록, 너는 더 빨리 끝낼 거야!" Sir 씨가 소리를 질렀다.

➡ _____

3 Stanley Yelnats는 모든 근육 하나하나가 아팠기 때문에 더 열심히 팔 수가 없었다.

➡ _____

4 그는 목이 마르고 배가 고팠다.

➡ _____

5 그는 집에 가고 싶었다.

➡ _____

6 불행히도, 앞으로 18개월 동안 Stanley의 집은 바로 여기 Green Lake 캠프가 될 것이었다.

➡ _____

7 Green Lake 캠프는 형편없는 이름이었다.

➡ _____

8 그곳은 초록색도 아니었고 호수도 없었다.

➡ _____

9 Green Lake 캠프는 뜨거웠고 온통 모래였다.

➡ _____

10 사실 그곳은 캠프조차 아니었다.

➡ _____

11 그곳은 나쁜 소년들을 위한 곳이었다.

➡ _____

12 그렇다면 Stanley 같이 착한 소년이 여기서 무엇을 하고 있었을까?

➡ _____

13 그는 운동화 한 켤레를 훔쳤다는 이유로 캠프에 보내졌다.

➡ _____

14 Stanley가 정말로 운동화 한 켤레를 훔친 것은 아니었다.

➡ _____

15 그는 그저 잘못된 시간에 잘못된 장소에 있었다.

➡ _____

16 어느 날, 그는 학교에서 집으로 걸어가고 있었다.

➡ _____

17 갑자기, 낡은 운동화 한 켤레가 하늘에서 떨어졌다.

➡ _____

18 그 운동화는 그의 머리에 맞았다.

➡ _____

19 그는 그의 아버지에게 무슨 일이 일어났는지 말하기 위해 운동화를 가지고 달리기 시작했다.
➡ _____

20 몇 분 후에, 경찰이 Stanley를 멈춰 세웠고 그가 왜 달리고 있었는지를 그에게 물었다.
➡ _____

21 Stanley에게는 불행히도, 그 운동화는 유명한 야구 선수인 Clyde Livingstone의 것이었다.
➡ _____

22 그것이 Stanley가 Green Lake 캠프에 오게 된 이유였다.
➡ _____

23 Stanley는 캠프에서 D 그룹에 배치되었다.
➡ _____

24 Stanley의 그룹에는 6명의 다른 소년들이 있었다.
➡ _____

25 그들은 모두 X-Ray, Zigzag, Zero와 같은 멋진 이름을 가지고 있었다.
➡ _____

26 각 소년은 매일 구덩이 하나를 파야 했다.
➡ _____

27 그것은 150cm 정도 깊이와 150cm 정도 너비여야 했다.
➡ _____

28 Sir 씨는 "너희들은 인격을 수양하기 위해 구덩이를 파고 있는 것이야."라고 말했다.
➡ _____

29 Stanley는 많이 파면 팔수록, 더 힘이 세졌다.
➡ _____

30 하루하루 구덩이를 끝내는 데 시간이 덜 걸렸다.
➡ _____

31 그가 온 지 두 번째 주, Stanley가 자기 구덩이를 끝내 가고 있었을 때, 그는 흙 속에서 빛나는 뭔가를 봤다.
➡ _____

32 Stanley의 심장은 더 빨리 뛰었다.
➡ _____

33 그는 흥미로운 뭔가를 발견한 사람은 그 날을 쉬게 된다고 들었다.
➡ _____

34 그는 조심스럽게 그 빛나는 물체를 집어 흙을 털어 냈다.
➡ _____

35 그것은 작은 금색 통이었다.
➡ _____

36 그러나 그것은 너무 가벼웠기 때문에 진짜 금일 리가 없었다.
➡ _____

37 그 통의 바닥에는 KB라는 두 글자가 있었다.
➡ _____

38 KB는 무엇을 의미할까?
➡ _____

39 Stanley의 심장은 훨씬 더 빨리 뛰었다.
➡ _____

[01~03] 다음 글을 읽고 물음에 답하시오.

"Dig harder, Stanley! The harder you dig, the faster you'll finish!" yelled Mr. Sir. Stanley Yelnats couldn't dig any harder (A) since every single muscle hurt. He was thirsty and hungry. He wanted to go home. Unfortunately, Stanley's home for the next 18 months would be right here, at Camp Green Lake.

Camp Green Lake was a terrible name. It wasn't green and there was no lake. Camp Green Lake was hot and full of sand. In fact, it wasn't even a camp. It was a place ⓐ_____ bad boys. Then what was a good boy like Stanley doing here? He was sent to the camp ⓑ_____ stealing a pair of sneakers.

서답형

01 위 글의 빈칸 ⓐ와 ⓑ에 공통으로 들어갈 알맞은 전치사를 쓰시오.

➡ _____

02 위 글의 밑줄 친 (A)since와 문법적 쓰임이 같은 것을 고르시오.

① It is two years since I left school.
② She's been off work since Tuesday.
③ He hasn't phoned since he went to Berlin.
④ Since we live in the computer era, you should get used to personal computers.
⑤ He left home two weeks ago and we haven't heard from him since.

03 According to the passage, which is NOT true?

① Mr. Sir yelled at Stanley.
② Stanley was unable to dig any harder.

③ Camp Green Lake was named after its color.
④ Camp Green Lake was filled with sand.
⑤ Camp Green Lake wasn't even a camp.

[04~06] 다음 글을 읽고 물음에 답하시오.

ⓐStanley는 많이 파면 팔수록, 더 힘이 세져 갔다. ⓑIt took less time finishing his hole each day. In his second week, as Stanley was finishing his hole, he saw something shiny in the dirt. Stanley's heart beat faster. He heard that anyone who found something interesting would be given the day off. He carefully picked up the shiny object and brushed off the dirt. It was a small gold tube. But it couldn't be real gold since it was too light. There were two letters, *KB*, at the bottom of the tube. What did KB stand for? Stanley's heart beat ⓒeven faster.

서답형

04 위 글의 밑줄 친 ⓐ의 우리말에 맞게 주어진 어휘를 이용하여 8 단어로 영작하시오.

the, became

➡ _____

서답형

05 위 글의 밑줄 친 ⓑ에서 어법상 틀린 부분을 찾아 고치시오.

➡ _____

06 위 글의 밑줄 친 ⓒeven과 바꿔 쓸 수 없는 말을 고르시오.

① much ② still ③ far
④ very ⑤ a lot

[07~09] 다음 글을 읽고 물음에 답하시오.

Stanley didn't really steal a pair of sneakers. He was just in the wrong place at the wrong time. One day, he was walking home from school. ⓐSuddenly, a pair of old sneakers fell from the sky. The sneakers hit him on the head.

He started running with the sneakers to tell his father what happened. A few minutes later, the police stopped Stanley and asked him why he was running. Unfortunately for Stanley, the sneakers belonged to a famous baseball player, Clyde Livingstone. That was why Stanley ended up at Camp Green Lake.

07 위 글에서 Stanley가 느꼈을 심경으로 가장 알맞은 것을 고르시오.

① ashamed ② unfair ③ excited
④ pleased ⑤ bored

08 위 글의 밑줄 친 ⓐSuddenly와 바꿔 쓸 수 없는 말을 고르시오.

① All at once ② Abruptly
③ All of a sudden ④ Urgently
⑤ Unexpectedly

09 위 글을 읽고 알 수 없는 것을 고르시오.

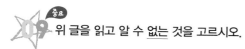

① Did Stanley really steal a pair of sneakers?
② What was Stanley doing when a pair of sneakers fell from the sky?
③ What did the sneakers hit when they fell from the sky?
④ Why did a pair of sneakers fall from the sky?
⑤ When did the police stop Stanley?

[10~12] 다음 글을 읽고 물음에 답하시오.

ⓐThe more Stanley dug, the stronger he became. It took less time to finish his hole each day. In his second week, as Stanley was finishing his hole, he saw ①something shiny in the dirt. Stanley's heart beat faster. He heard that anyone who found something interesting would be given the day off. He carefully picked up ②the shiny object and brushed off the dirt. It was a small gold tube. But ③it couldn't be real gold since ④it was too light. There were two letters, *KB*, at the bottom of the tube. What did ⑤KB stand for? Stanley's heart beat even faster.

10 밑줄 친 ①~⑤ 중에서 가리키는 대상이 나머지 넷과 다른 것은?

① ② ③ ④ ⑤

서답형
11 위 글의 밑줄 친 ⓐ를 As를 사용하여 아래와 같이 바꿨을 때, 문법적으로 어색한 부분을 찾아 고치시오.

As Stanley dug the more, he became the stronger.

➡ _____

서답형
12 Why did Stanley's heart beat faster? Answer in English beginning with "Because".

➡ _____
_____

[13~15] 다음 글을 읽고 물음에 답하시오.

Stanley was assigned to Group D in the camp. There were six other boys in Stanley's group. They all had cool names like X-Ray, Zigzag and Zero. Each boy had to dig one hole every day. It had to be about 150cm deep and 150cm wide. Mr. Sir said, "You are digging @to build character."

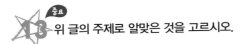 위 글의 주제로 알맞은 것을 고르시오.

① the number of the members of Group D to which Stanley was assigned
② the cool names of the boys in Group D to which Stanley was assigned
③ the size of the hole that each boy had to dig every day
④ the duty the members of Group D had to do every day
⑤ the reason Mr. Sir said that the boys were digging the hole to build character

14 아래 〈보기〉에서 위 글의 밑줄 친 @to build와 to부정사의 용법이 다른 것의 개수를 고르시오.

┌─ 보기 ├─
① I expect him to build it.
② How many people do you need to build it?
③ Who was the first man to build it?
④ Is it easy to build it?
⑤ I have no money to build it.
└─────────────

① 1개   ② 2개   ③ 3개   ④ 4개   ⑤ 5개

서답형
15 What was the size of the hole the boys had to dig every day? Fill in the blanks (A) and (B) with suitable words.

┌─────────────────────────┐
│ The (A)_____ of the hole was about 150 centimeters and its (B)_____ was also about 150 centimeters. │
└─────────────────────────┘

[16~18] 다음 글을 읽고 물음에 답하시오.

Stanley didn't really steal a pair of sneakers. He was just in the wrong place at the wrong time. One day, he was walking home from school. Suddenly, a pair of old sneakers fell from the sky. The sneakers hit him on the head.
He started running with the sneakers @to tell his father what happened. A few minutes later, the police stopped Stanley and asked him why he was running. Unfortunately for Stanley, the sneakers belonged to a famous baseball player, Clyde Livingstone. That was why Stanley ended up at Camp Green Lake.

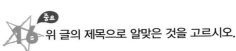 위 글의 제목으로 알맞은 것을 고르시오.

① Sneakers from the Sky? Unbelievable!
② Unjustly Accused Stanley
③ Wow, I Got the Free Sneakers!
④ Why Was Stanley in the Wrong Place?
⑤ Clyde Livingstone Lost His Sneakers

17 위 글의 밑줄 친 @to tell과 to부정사의 용법이 같은 것을 모두 고르시오.

① He was happy to tell his father the news.
② It's time to tell his father the news.
③ It was too late to tell his father the news.
④ He tried to tell his father the news.
⑤ He had no courage to tell his father the news.

서답형
18 Whose were the sneakers which fell from the sky? Answer in English in a full sentence. (4 words)

➡ _____

[19~22] 다음 글을 읽고 물음에 답하시오.

"Dig harder, Stanley! (A)네가 열심히 파면 팔수록, 너는 더 빨리 끝낼 거야!" yelled Mr. Sir. Stanley Yelnats couldn't dig any harder since every single muscle hurt. He was thirsty and hungry. He wanted to go home. Unfortunately, Stanley's home for the next 18 months would be right here, at Camp Green Lake.

Camp Green Lake was a terrible name. It wasn't green and there was no lake. Camp Green Lake was hot and full of sand. ⓐ_____, it wasn't even a camp. It was a place for bad boys. Then what was a good boy like Stanley doing here? He ___ⓑ___ to the camp for stealing a pair of sneakers.

19 위 글의 빈칸 ⓐ에 들어갈 알맞은 말을 고르시오.

① Therefore
② In fact
③ By contrast
④ However
⑤ Similarly

서답형
20 위 글의 빈칸 ⓑ에 send를 알맞은 형태로 쓰시오.

➡ _____

서답형
21 위 글의 밑줄 친 (A)의 우리말에 맞게 주어진 어휘를 알맞게 배열하시오.

you'll / harder / finish / the / dig / faster / you / the / ,

➡ _____

서답형
22 Why couldn't Stanley dig any harder? Answer in English in a full sentence using "since".

➡ _____

[23~25] 다음 글을 읽고 물음에 답하시오.

Stanley was ___ⓐ___ to Group D in the camp. There were six other boys in Stanley's group. They all had cool names like X-Ray, Zigzag and Zero. Each boy had to dig one hole every day. It had to be about ⓑ150cm deep and 150cm wide. Mr. Sir said, "You are digging to build ⓒcharacter."

서답형
23 주어진 영영풀이를 참고하여 빈칸 ⓐ에 철자 a로 시작하는 단어를 알맞은 형태로 쓰시오.

to send someone to a particular place, group, or person, usually in order to work at that place or for that person

➡ _____

서답형
24 위 글의 밑줄 친 ⓑ를 영어로 읽는 법을 쓰시오.

➡ _____

중요
25 위 글의 밑줄 친 ⓒcharacter와 같은 의미로 쓰인 것을 고르시오.

① He was a man of character.
② Who is the major character in the book?
③ I like the character of the country.
④ Your password can only start with an alphabetic character or number.
⑤ This area has the character of desert areas.

[01~02] 다음 글을 읽고 물음에 답하시오.

The more Stanley dug, the stronger he became. It took (A)[less / more] time to finish his hole each day. In his second week, as Stanley was finishing his hole, he saw something shiny in the dirt. Stanley's heart beat faster. He heard that anyone who found something interesting would ⓐ the day off. He carefully picked up the shiny object and brushed off the dirt. It was a small gold tube. But it couldn't be real gold (B)[if / since] it was too light. There were two letters, *KB*, at the bottom of the tube. What did KB stand (C)[by / for]? Stanley's heart beat even faster.

01 위 글의 빈칸 ⓐ에 give를 알맞은 형태로 쓰시오.

➡ _____

02 위 글의 괄호 (A)~(C)에서 문맥이나 어법상 알맞은 낱말을 골라 쓰시오.

➡ (A)_____ (B)_____ (C)_____

[03~05] 다음 글을 읽고 물음에 답하시오.

Stanley didn't really steal a pair of sneakers. ⓐHe was just in the right place at the right time. One day, he was walking home from school. Suddenly, a pair of old sneakers fell from the sky. The sneakers hit him on the head.

He started running with the sneakers to tell his father what happened. A few minutes later, the police stopped Stanley and asked him why he was running. Unfortunately for

Stanley, the sneakers belonged to a famous baseball player, Clyde Livingstone. ⓑ그것이 Stanley가 Green Lake 캠프에 오게 된 이유였다.

03 위 글의 밑줄 친 ⓐ에서 흐름상 어색한 부분을 찾아 고치시오. (두 군데)

➡ _____

04 위 글의 밑줄 친 ⓑ의 우리말에 맞게 주어진 어휘를 이용하여 10 단어로 영작하시오.

why, ended up

➡ _____

_____

05 Why did Stanley start running with the sneakers? Fill in the blanks with suitable words.

He started running with them in order that he _____ _____ his father what happened.

[06~07] 다음 글을 읽고 물음에 답하시오.

Stanley was assigned to Group D in the camp. There were six other boys in Stanley's group. They all had cool names like X-Ray, Zigzag and Zero. Each boy had to dig one hole every day. ⓐ그것은 150cm 정도 깊이와 150cm 정도 너비여야 했다. Mr. Sir said, "You are digging to build character."

06 다음 문장에서 위 글의 내용과 다른 부분을 찾아서 고치시오.

> There were six boys including Stanley in Group D.

➡ _____

07 위 글의 밑줄 친 ⓐ의 우리말에 맞게 주어진 어휘를 알맞게 배열하시오.

> deep / about / it / 150cm / to / 150cm / and / had / be / wide

➡ _____

[08~09] 다음 글을 읽고 물음에 답하시오.

> The more Stanley dug, the stronger he became. ⓐIt took less time to finish his hole each day. In his second week, as Stanley was finishing his hole, he saw something shiny in the dirt. Stanley's heart beat faster. He heard that anyone who found something interesting would be given the day off. He carefully picked up the shiny object and brushed off the dirt. It was a small gold tube. But it couldn't be real gold since it was too light. There were two letters, *KB*, at the bottom of the tube. What did KB ⓑstand for? Stanley's heart beat even faster.

08 밑줄 친 ⓐ를 다음과 같이 바꿔 쓸 때 빈칸에 들어갈 알맞은 단어를 쓰시오.

➡ Stanley spent less time _____ his hole each day.

09 위 글의 밑줄 친 ⓑstand for와 바꿔 쓸 수 있는 단어를 쓰시오.

➡ _____

[10~12] 다음 글을 읽고 물음에 답하시오.

> "Dig harder, Stanley! ⓐThe harder you dig, the faster you'll finish!" yelled Mr. Sir. Stanley Yelnats couldn't dig any harder since every single muscle hurt. He was thirsty and hungry. He wanted to go home. Unfortunately, Stanley's home for the next 18 months would be right here, at Camp Green Lake.
>
> Camp Green Lake was a terrible name. It wasn't green and there was no lake. Camp Green Lake was hot and full of sand. In fact, it wasn't even a camp. It was a place for bad boys. Then what was a good boy ⓑlike Stanley doing here? He was sent to the camp for stealing a pair of sneakers.

10 위 글의 밑줄 친 ⓐ를 As로 시작하여 고치시오.

➡ _____

11 위 글의 밑줄 친 ⓑ와 바꿔 쓸 수 있는 말을 쓰시오.

➡ _____

12 다음 빈칸 (A)~(C)에 알맞은 단어를 넣어 Camp Green Lake에 대한 소개를 완성하시오.

> Camp Green Lake was not (A)_____ _____ but a place for bad boys. Unlike its name, it wasn't (B)_____ and there was no lake. In fact, it was hot and filled with (C)_____.

해석

After You Read B

Monday, August 5th

Unfortunately, the camp isn't green and there is no lake. I'm in Group D. My
→ Fortunately

group members have cool names like X-Ray, Zigzag and Zero. We have to dig
= such as   = must

one hole about 150cm deep and 150cm wide. The good news is this: anyone
명사: depth   명사: width   뒤에 나오는 내용을 가리킨다.

who finds something interesting can get the day off. I hope I can be the one.
= whoever   −thing으로 끝나는 대명사를 수식하는 형용사는 대명사 뒤에 위치   the one 뒤에 'who can get the day off'가 생략됨.

구문해설 •unfortunately: 불행히도 •dig: (구멍 등을) 파다 •hole: 구덩이, 구멍 •wide: 폭이 ~인

8월 5일, 월요일

불행히도, 캠프는 초록색도 아니고 호수도 없다. 나는 D 그룹에 있다. 나의 그룹 멤버들은 X-Ray, Zigzag, Zero와 같은 멋진 이름들을 가지고 있다. 우리는 150cm 정도 깊이와 150cm 정도 너비의 구덩이 하나를 파야 한다. 좋은 소식은 다음과 같다. 흥미로운 뭔가를 발견한 사람은 그 날을 쉴 수 있다. 내가 그 사람이기를 바란다.

Word Power

• She bought a pair of shoes for 15 dollars.
  쌍으로 이루어진 것, 2개의 비슷한 것이 하나의 물건을 이룰 때 'a pair of+복수명사'의 형태로 쓴다.

• I found a pair of glasses under the chair.
  안경 한 개(2개의 비슷한 것이 하나의 물건을 이루는 것)

• He packed three pairs of jeans in his bag.
  three가 있으므로 pair에 명사의 복수형 어미 s가 들어간다.

구문해설 •pack: (짐을) 싸다

• 그녀는 구두 한 켤레를 15 달러에 샀다.
• 나는 의자 아래에서 안경 한 개를 찾았다.
• 그는 가방에 청바지 세 벌을 쌌다.

Think and Write

Kate Barlow was a teacher in Green Lake. She was very popular.

Many rich men in the town wanted to marry her. But Kate fell in love with
           형용사구   명사적 용법의 to부정사

Sam, a poor man. The rich men tried to hurt Sam.
    동격   명사적 용법의 to부정사

Later, Sam was found dead. Kate became sad and left the town.
                      보어로 쓰인 형용사

구문해설 •fall in love with: ~와 사랑에 빠지다

Kate Barlow는 그린 레이크 마을의 교사였다. 그녀는 매우 인기가 있었다. 마을의 많은 부유한 남자들이 그녀와 결혼하고 싶어했다. 그러나 Kate는 가난한 남자인 Sam과 사랑에 빠졌다. 부유한 남자들은 Sam을 다치게 하려고 했다. 나중에 Sam은 죽은 채로 발견되었다. Kate는 슬퍼서 마을을 떠났다.

01 다음 짝지어진 단어의 관계가 같도록 빈칸에 알맞은 말을 쓰시오.

> asleep : awake = _____ : top

[02~03] 다음 빈칸에 알맞은 단어를 고르시오.

02

> The _____ of a man is known from his conversations.

① education ② community ③ taste
④ character ⑤ production

03

> You can _____ the next chapter if you have covered the topic in class.

① count ② skip ③ publish
④ include ⑤ figure

04 다음 우리말에 맞도록 빈칸에 알맞은 말을 쓰시오.

(1) 그것이 자외선 차단제를 사용하는 것이 중요한 이유이다.
➡ That is _____ it is important to use sunscreen.

(2) 그 케이크는 자동차처럼 보이게 장식되어 있었다.
➡ The cake was decorated to _____ _____ a car.

(3) 나는 이 단어를 사전에서 찾아보았는데 실려 있지 않았다.
➡ I've tried to _____ _____ this word in the dictionary, but haven't been able to find it.

[05~06] 다음 대화를 읽고 물음에 답하시오.

> B: Hi, Amy. Welcome (A)_____ Korea.
> G: Long time no see, Minho. ⓐ_____ have you been?
> B: Great. How did you come here (B)_____ the airport?
> G: I came here (C)_____ subway.
> B: ⓑ_____ do you feel (D)_____ the subway in Korea?
> G: I think it's very clean.

05 빈칸 (A)~(D)에 들어가지 <u>않는</u> 말을 고르시오.

① from ② for ③ to
④ about ⑤ by

06 빈칸 ⓐ와 ⓑ에 공통으로 들어갈 말을 쓰시오.

➡ _____

[07~08] 다음 대화를 읽고 물음에 답하시오.

> G: Brian, did you hear the news?
> B: What news?
> G: We can use smartphones (A)[during / while / after / when] classes from next week.
> B: Yes, I heard that.
> G: How do you feel about it?
> B: I think it will be very (B)[different / useless / useful / careful]. (C)_____(look, don't, I, know, words, I, up, can)
> G: Yeah. We can also find information on the Internet.
> B: Right. It will be very helpful.

07 위 대화의 괄호 (A)와 (B)에서 적절한 것을 골라 쓰시오.

➡ (A) _____ (B) _____

08 빈칸 (C)를 괄호 안에 주어진 단어를 알맞게 배열하여 채우시오.

➡ _____

[09~12] 다음 대화를 읽고 물음에 답하시오.

> Tony: What are all these boxes, Suji?
> Suji: They're items I ordered online. (①)
> Tony: You like shopping on the Internet, don't you? (②)
> Suji: Yes, I do. (③)
> Tony: I don't like it at all.
> Suji: Why?
> Tony: It's very difficult to know what an item actually looks like. (④)
> Suji: 그 점에는 동의해.
> Tony: It's also difficult to (A)_____ an item if you don't like it. (⑤)
> Suji: You're right, but I think it's very convenient.
> Tony: Well, convenience isn't everything.

09 ①~⑤ 중 주어진 문장이 들어갈 곳은?

> How do you feel about online shopping, Tony?

①   ②   ③   ④   ⑤

10 빈칸 (A)에 알맞은 말을 고르시오.

① borrow   ② result   ③ save
④ lend   ⑤ return

11 밑줄 친 우리말과 일치하도록 주어진 단어를 사용해 영작하시오. (on)

➡ _____

12 위 대화의 내용과 일치하지 <u>않는</u> 것을 <u>모두</u> 고르시오.

① Tony doesn't like shopping on the Internet.
② Suji doesn't agree with the idea that Tony has about online shopping.
③ Suji ordered items online.
④ Tony thinks that online shopping has many benefits.
⑤ Suji likes online shopping.

Grammar

13 다음 중 어법상 알맞은 것은?

① The more angrier Judy got, the more loudly she yelled.
② The high the expectation, the great the disappointment.
③ The more I got to know her, the more I liked her.
④ More technology develops, more people seem to miss traditional forms of communication.
⑤ The more you exercise, the healthier get.

14 주어진 단어의 형태가 바르게 짝지어진 것은?

> _____ you are to someone, _____ you need to be. (close, respectful)

① Close – respectful
② Closer – more respectful
③ The close – more respectful
④ The closer – the much respectful
⑤ The closer – the more respectful

15 다음 밑줄 친 부분과 바꿔 쓸 수 있는 것을 <u>모두</u> 고르면?

> <u>Because</u> I got up late, I had to run to school.

① Since ② That ③ What
④ As ⑤ While

16 다음 그림을 보고 주어진 어휘를 이용하여 빈칸에 알맞은 말을 쓰시오.

(1) _____ he works, _____ he becomes. (much, tired)

(2) _____ he tries to be awake, _____ he feels. (much, sleepy)

17 다음 중 빈칸에 들어갈 가장 적절한 말은?

> Tim fell asleep during English class since _____.

① he stayed up the night before
② he felt awakening
③ it made him awake
④ it was very interesting
⑤ it was too bright to sleep

18 우리말과 일치하도록 괄호 안에 주어진 어휘를 이용하여 빈칸에 알맞게 쓰시오.

(1) 과일이 신선하면 할수록, 그것은 더 맛이 좋다.

➡ _____, the better it tastes. (the fruit, fresh)

(2) 햇빛이 매우 강했기 때문에 그녀는 모자를 써야 했다.

➡ _____, she had to wear her hat. (the sunlight, strong)

19 다음 괄호 안에서 어법상 알맞은 것을 고르시오.

(1) (The nearer / nearer) the inn, (the longer / longer) the road.

(2) The Earth keeps getting (the warmer and the warmer / warmer and warmer) every year.

(3) My throat is sore (because / because of) a very bad cold.

(4) I couldn't call my friend (since / while) I didn't have my phone.

(5) (As / Before) it was raining, we couldn't go out.

Reading

[20~22] 다음 글을 읽고 물음에 답하시오.

"Dig harder, Stanley! The harder you dig, the faster you'll finish!" yelled Mr. Sir. Stanley Yelnats couldn't dig any harder since every single muscle hurt. He was thirsty and hungry. He wanted to go home. Unfortunately, Stanley's home for the next 18 months would be right here, at Camp Green Lake.

①Camp Green Lake was a terrible name. ② It wasn't green and there was no lake. Camp Green Lake was hot and full of sand. ⓐIn fact, ③it wasn't even ④a camp. It was a place for bad boys. ⓑ그렇다면 Stanley 같이 착한 소년이 여기서 무엇을 하고 있었을까? He was sent to ⑤the camp for stealing a pair of sneakers.

20 밑줄 친 ①~⑤ 중에서 가리키는 대상이 나머지 넷과 <u>다른</u> 것은?

①   ②   ③   ④   ⑤

21 위 글의 밑줄 친 ⓐIn fact와 바꿔 쓸 수 <u>없는</u> 말을 고르시오. (2개)

① Actually   ② Thus
③ Reasonably   ④ To tell the truth
⑤ As a matter of fact

22 위 글의 밑줄 친 ⓑ의 우리말에 맞게 주어진 어휘를 이용하여 10 단어로 영작하시오.

> good, like

➡ _____

[23~25] 다음 글을 읽고 물음에 답하시오.

Stanley didn't really steal a pair of sneakers. (①) He was just in the wrong place at the wrong time. (②) One day, he was walking home from school. (③) Suddenly, a pair of old sneakers fell from the sky. (④)

He started running with the sneakers to tell his father ___ⓐ___ happened. (⑤) A few minutes later, the police stopped Stanley and asked him why he was running. ⓑUnderfortunately for Stanley, the sneakers were belonged to a famous baseball player, Clyde Livingstone. That was why Stanley ended up at Camp Green Lake.

23 위 글의 빈칸 ⓐ에 들어갈 알맞은 말을 고르시오.

① which   ② when
③ that   ④ where
⑤ what

24 위 글의 흐름으로 보아, ①~⑤ 중 다음 주어진 문장이 들어가기에 가장 적절한 곳은?

> The sneakers hit him on the head.

①   ②   ③   ④   ⑤

25 위 글의 밑줄 친 ⓑ에서 어법상 틀린 부분을 찾아 고치시오.

➡ _____

[26~27] 다음 글을 읽고 물음에 답하시오.

Stanley was assigned to Group D in the camp. There were six other boys in Stanley's group. They all had ⓐ<u>cool</u> names like X-Ray, Zigzag and Zero. Each boy had to dig one hole every day. It had to be about 150cm deep and 150cm wide. Mr. Sir said, "You are digging to build character."

26 위 글의 밑줄 친 ⓐ<u>cool</u>과 같은 의미로 쓰인 것을 고르시오.

① She tried to remain <u>cool</u> and calm.
② It's a <u>cool</u> movie.
③ Let's sit in the shade and keep <u>cool</u>.
④ The rain will <u>cool</u> the air.
⑤ He felt sorry to receive a <u>cool</u> response from the public.

27 According to the passage, which is NOT true?

① Stanley belonged to Group D in the camp.
② There were seven boys in Stanley's group including Stanley.
③ The names of the other boys in Stanley's group were cool.
④ The boys cooperated to dig a hole every day.
⑤ The depth of the hole was the same as its width.

[28~30] 다음 글을 읽고 물음에 답하시오.

Stanley didn't really steal a pair of sneakers. He was just in the wrong place at the wrong time.

One day, he was walking (A)[home / to home] from school. Suddenly, a pair of old sneakers fell from the sky. The sneakers hit him on (B)[his / the] head.

He started running with the sneakers to tell his father what happened. A few minutes later, the police stopped Stanley and asked him why he was running. Unfortunately ⓐ_____ Stanley, the sneakers belonged ⓑ_____ a famous baseball player, Clyde Livingstone. That was (C)[because / why] Stanley ended up at Camp Green Lake.

28 위 글의 빈칸 ⓐ와 ⓑ에 들어갈 전치사가 바르게 짝지어진 것은?

	ⓐ	ⓑ		ⓐ	ⓑ
①	for	to	②	on	at
③	to	on	④	for	at
⑤	on	to			

29 위 글의 괄호 (A)~(C)에서 문맥이나 어법상 알맞은 낱말을 골라 쓰시오.

➡ (A)_____ (B)_____ (C)_____

30 According to the passage, which is NOT true?

① Stanley wasn't a thief who stole a pair of sneakers.
② A pair of awesome sneakers fell from the sky.
③ Stanley started to run with the sneakers so as to tell his father what happened.
④ The police stopped Stanley and asked him the reason for which he was running.
⑤ Clyde Livingstone was a famous baseball player.

출제율 95%

01 빈칸 (A)와 (B)에 들어갈 말로 알맞은 것끼리 짝지어진 것을 고르시오.

> • It wasn't her fault, but she was (A) _____ her best to help.
> • It's good to (B)_____ on developing something that'll be more profitable.

	(A)	(B)
①	trying	share
②	making	share
③	trying	focus
④	making	focus
⑤	trying	attend

출제율 100%

02 다음 빈칸에 들어갈 말을 〈보기〉에서 찾아 쓰시오. (단어는 한 번씩만 사용, 형태 변화 가능.)

> ┤ 보기 ├
> brush dig order raise

(1) Remember to specify your size when _____ clothes.

(2) She said that the world is too dangerous to _____ children.

(3) Mud _____ off easily when it is dry.

(4) The worker uses a machine to _____ the hole.

[03~04] 빈칸에 공통으로 들어갈 말을 쓰시오. (주어진 철자로 시작할 것.)

출제율 90%

03
> • He couldn't e_____ open the door.
> • The female blue whale is e_____ bigger than the male.

출제율 90%

04
> • I've earned my own living s_____ I was seven.
> • Washing without soap would be best, s_____ all soaps can pollute lakes and streams.

출제율 95%

05 다음 빈칸 (A)와 (B)에 들어갈 말로 알맞게 짝지어진 것은?

> A: How do you feel about shopping on the Internet?
> B: (A)_____
> A: Can you tell me the (B)_____?
> B: I can shop whenever I want.
> A: I'm with you on that.

	(A)	(B)
①	I like it a lot.	reason
②	I like it a lot.	purpose
③	I like it a lot.	way
④	I don't like it.	opinion
⑤	I don't like it.	reason

출제율 95%

06 다음 대화의 괄호 (A)~(C)에서 적절한 것을 골라 쓰시오.

> A: How do you feel about (A)[eating / to eat] fast food?
> B: I think it's (B)[bad / good]. Fast food has a lot of fat.
> A: I don't agree. We can (C)[save / spend] time.

B: Hey, Jessica. Why are you always ⓐto drink energy drinks?

G: Because they help me ⓑstaying awake.

B: (A)_____, but they have too ⓒmany caffeine.

G: Well, they help me focus ⓓin my studies.

B: Did you know that too ⓒmany caffeine ⓔcan hurt your bones?

G: Oh, I didn't know that.

B: I think you should drink energy drinks less often.

G: Maybe you're right. Thanks, Tom.

✎ 출제율 95%

07 빈칸 (A)에 알맞은 말이 〈보기〉에서 모두 몇 개인지 고르시오.

┌─ 보기 ┐
- I couldn't agree with you more.
- Absolutely not.
- You're absolutely right.
- I'm not sure about that.
- No doubt about it.
└─────────┘

① 1개 ② 2개 ③ 3개 ④ 4개 ⑤ 5개

✎ 출제율 95%

08 ⓐ~ⓔ 중 흐름상 또는 어법상 옳은 것을 고르시오.

① ⓐ ② ⓑ ③ ⓒ ④ ⓓ ⑤ ⓔ

✎ 출제율 90%

09 위 대화에서 다음 영영풀이에 해당하는 단어를 찾아 쓰시오.

┌───────────────────────┐
│   not sleeping   │
└───────────────────────┘

➡ _____

Tony: What are all these boxes, Suji?

Suji: They're items I ordered online. (①)

Tony: You like shopping on the Internet, don't you?

Suji: Yes, I do. (②) 넌 온라인 쇼핑에 관해 어떻게 생각하니, Tony?

Tony: I don't like ⓐit at all.

Suji: Why? (③)

Tony: ⓑIt's very difficult to know what an item actually looks like.

Suji: I'm with you on that. (④)

Tony: ⓒIt's also difficult to return an item if you don't like ⓓit.

Suji: You're right, but I think ⓔit's very convenient.

Tony: Well. (⑤)

✎ 출제율 100%

10 ①~⑤ 중 주어진 문장이 들어갈 곳은?

┌───────────────────────────────┐
│   Convenience isn't everything.   │
└───────────────────────────────┘

①   ②   ③   ④   ⑤

✎ 출제율 90%

11 밑줄 친 우리말과 일치하도록 주어진 단어를 이용해 영작하시오.

➡ _____

(feel, about, online)

✎ 출제율 95%

12 밑줄 친 ⓐ~ⓔ 중 가리키는 것이 같은 것끼리 모은 것을 고르시오.

① ⓐ, ⓑ   ② ⓐ, ⓒ
③ ⓐ, ⓓ   ④ ⓐ, ⓔ
⑤ ⓐ, ⓓ, ⓔ

출제율 95%

13 다음 중 어법상 올바른 것은?

① The more you chew bread, the sweet it tastes.

② I think the more he has, the more he wants.

③ Since the mother began to clean it, the lamp was very dirty.

④ He bought two pair of sneakers and a cap at the store.

⑤ Though he had a headache, Jack went to see the doctor.

출제율 100%

14 다음 중 어법상 올바른 문장을 <u>모두</u> 고르시오. (정답 2개)

① The hard you study, the good you will do.

② This is because hotter it is, more energy it has.

③ The more we recycle, the less garbage ends up in landfills.

④ While he was sleepy, Mr. Smith went to bed early.

⑤ The game will be canceled since the weather is bad.

⑥ Because of he was sick, he couldn't go to school.

⑦ Ann drank two glass of waters since she was thirsty.

출제율 85%

15 괄호 안에 주어진 어휘를 활용하여 글자 수에 맞게 다음 우리말을 영작하시오.

(1) 그 의자가 좋으면 좋을수록, 너는 더 편하게 느낀다. (good, comfortable, the chair, feel, 10 단어)

➡ _____

(2) Tom은 피곤했기 때문에 일하는 것을 멈췄다. (since, tired, stop, work, 7 단어)

➡ _____

[16~18] 다음 글을 읽고 물음에 답하시오.

Stanley ___ⓐ___ to Group D in the camp. There were six other boys in Stanley's group. They all had cool names like X-Ray, Zigzag and Zero. ⓑ각 소년은 매일 구덩이 하나를 파야 했다. It had to be ⓒabout 150cm deep and 150cm wide. Mr. Sir said, "You are digging to build character."

출제율 90%

16 위 글의 빈칸 ⓐ에 assign을 알맞은 형태로 쓰시오.

➡ _____

출제율 95%

17 위 글의 밑줄 친 ⓑ의 우리말에 맞게 주어진 어휘를 이용하여 9 단어로 영작하시오.

each, one, every

➡ _____

출제율 90%

18 위 글의 밑줄 친 ⓒabout과 바꿔 쓸 수 있는 말을 <u>모두</u> 고르시오.

① accurately   ② roughly

③ around   ④ exactly

⑤ approximately

[19~20] 다음 글을 읽고 물음에 답하시오.

Kate Barlow was a teacher in Green Lake. She was very popular. ⓐMany rich men in the town wanted to marry with her. But Kate fell in love with Sam, a poor man. The rich men tried to hurt Sam. Later, Sam was found dead. Kate became sad and left the town.

After 20 years, Kate returned to Green Lake with a lot of treasure. But Green Lake became a desert. She hid all her treasure somewhere in Green Lake. Many people wanted to find the treasure.

19 위 글의 밑줄 친 ⓐ에서 어법상 틀린 부분을 찾아 고치시오.

➡ _____

20 위 글을 읽고 알 수 없는 것을 고르시오.

① Where did Kate Barlow teach?
② Why was Kate Barlow very popular?
③ With whom did Kate fall in love?
④ What did the rich men try to do?
⑤ Where did Kate hide all her treasure?

[21~23] 다음 글을 읽고 물음에 답하시오.

"Dig harder, Stanley! The harder you dig, the faster you'll finish!" yelled Mr. Sir. Stanley Yelnats couldn't dig any harder since every single muscle hurt. He was thirsty and hungry. He wanted to go home. Unfortunately, Stanley's home for the next 18 months would be (A)right here, at Camp Green Lake.

Camp Green Lake was a terrible name. (①) It wasn't green and there was no lake. (②) Camp Green Lake was hot and full of sand. (③) In fact, it wasn't even a camp. (④) Then what was a good boy like Stanley doing here? (⑤) He was sent to the camp for stealing ⓐ_____ sneakers.

21 위 글의 빈칸 ⓐ에 들어갈 알맞은 말을 쓰시오.

➡ _____

22 위 글의 밑줄 친 (A)right와 같은 의미로 쓰인 것을 고르시오.

① Turn right at the end of the street.
② I don't feel quite right today.
③ What gives you the right to do that?
④ Take the first street on the right.
⑤ Lee was standing right behind her.

23 위 글의 흐름으로 보아, 주어진 문장이 들어가기에 가장 적절한 곳은?

> It was a place for bad boys.

①   ②   ③   ④   ⑤

[24~25] 다음 글을 읽고 물음에 답하시오.

Monday, August 5th
Unfortunately, the camp isn't green and there is no lake. I'm in Group D. My group members have cool names like X-Ray, Zigzag and Zero. We have to dig one hole about 150cm deep and 150cm wide. The good news is this: anyone who finds something interesting can get the ⓐ_____. I hope I can be the one.

24 주어진 영영풀이를 참고하여 빈칸 ⓐ에 철자 d로 시작하는 단어를 쓰시오.

> a day when you do not go to work, even though it is usually a working day

➡ _____

25 위 글의 종류로 알맞은 것을 고르시오.

① e-mail   ② essay
③ diary   ④ review
⑤ article

01 다음 대화에서 흐름상 어색한 것을 찾아 바르게 고치시오.

> B: Hey, Jessica. ①Why are you always drinking energy drinks?
> G: ②Because they help me stay awake.
> B: I'm with you on that, but they have too much caffeine.
> G: Well, they help me focus on my studies.
> B: Did you know that too much caffeine can hurt your bones?
> G: Oh, ③I didn't know that.
> B: ④I think you should drink energy drinks more often.
> G: ⑤Maybe you're right. Thanks, Tom.

➡ _____

02 다음 대화의 밑줄 친 부분 중 흐름상 어색한 것을 찾아 바르게 고치시오.

> A: How do you feel about reading books on a smartphone?
> B: I think it's good. We can read anytime.
> A: I'm with you on that. It's not good for our eyes.

➡ _____

03 밑줄 친 문장과 바꿔 쓸 수 있는 문장을 주어진 단어를 써서 바꿔 쓰시오.

> B: Hey, Jessica. Why are you always drinking energy drinks?
> G: Because they help me stay awake.

> B: I'm with you on that, but they have too much caffeine.
> G: Well, they help me focus on my studies.

➡ _____

(couldn't, more)

04 어법상 어색한 것을 찾아 바르게 고쳐 문장을 다시 쓰시오.

(1) I think older she grows, smarter she becomes.

➡ _____

(2) Ann drank a lot of water though she was thirsty.

➡ _____

(3) He closed the window because of the wind was blowing outside.

➡ _____

(4) Venus is hot though it is near the sun.

➡ _____

05 다음 문장을 접속사가 없는 문장으로 바꿔 쓰시오.

(1) As you dig harder, you'll finish faster.

➡ _____

(2) As we go up higher, it becomes colder.

➡ _____

"Dig harder, Stanley! The harder you dig, the faster you'll finish!" yelled Mr. Sir. ⓐStanley Yelnats couldn't dig any harder though every single muscle hurt. He was thirsty and hungry. He wanted to go home. Unfortunately, Stanley's home for the next ⓑ18 months would be right here, at Camp Green Lake.

Camp Green Lake was a terrible name. It wasn't green and there was no lake. Camp Green Lake was hot and full of sand. In fact, it wasn't even a camp. It was a place for bad boys. Then what was a good boy like Stanley doing here? He was sent to the camp for stealing a pair of sneakers.

06 위 글의 밑줄 친 ⓐ에서 흐름상 어색한 부분을 찾아 고치시오.

➡ _____

07 위 글의 밑줄 친 ⓑ를 다음과 같이 바꿔 쓸 때 빈칸에 들어갈 알맞은 말을 두 단어로 쓰시오.

➡ one and _____ _____ years 또는 one
year and _____ _____

08 Why was Stanley Yelnats sent to Camp Green Lake? Fill in the blank with a suitable word.

> He was sent there on the grounds that
> he _____ a pair of sneakers.
>
> *on the grounds that: …라는 이유로

Stanley didn't really steal a pair of sneakers. He was just in the wrong place at the wrong time. One day, he was walking home from school. Suddenly, a pair of old sneakers fell from the sky. The sneakers hit him on the head.

He started running with the sneakers to tell his father what happened. ⓐA few minutes later, the police stopped Stanley and asked him why was he running. Unfortunately for Stanley, the sneakers belonged to a famous baseball player, Clyde Livingstone. ⓑThat was why Stanley ended up at Camp Green Lake.

09 위 글의 밑줄 친 ⓐ에서 어법상 틀린 부분을 찾아 고치시오.

➡ _____

10 위 글의 밑줄 친 ⓑ를 다음과 같이 바꿔 쓸 때 빈칸에 들어갈 알맞은 단어를 쓰시오.

➡ For that _____, Stanley ended up at Camp Green Lake.

11 위 글의 내용을 다음과 같이 정리하고자 한다. 빈칸 (A)와 (B)에 들어갈 알맞은 단어를 본문에서 찾아 쓰시오.

> One day, a pair of old sneakers fell from the sky and hit Stanley (A)_____
> _____ _____. He ran with the sneakers just to tell his father what happened, but he (B)_____ _____
> at Camp Green Lake because of the sneakers.

01 친구와 한국 음식 중 가장 맛있는 음식에 대한 의견을 말하고 있다. 다음 주어진 표현과 〈조건〉을 보고 대화를 완성하시오.

> ┌─ 조건 ────────────────────────────────────┐
> - 동의하기나 반대 의견 말하기에 관한 표현을 반드시 사용할 것.
> - 완벽한 문장으로 답할 것.
> └──┘

> **A:** I think Kimchi is the best Korean food. How _____ (about, feel)
> **B:** _____ (on, with)
> **A:** Can you tell me why?
> **B:** _____ (delicious, healthy)

02 다음 그림을 보고, since를 활용하여 자유롭게 영작하시오.

(1) _____

(2) _____

03 다음 내용을 바탕으로 Stanley의 관점에서 경험한 내용을 쓴 글을 완성하시오.

> 1. A pair of sneakers fell from the sky. Stanley picked them up and started running home.
> 2. The police stopped Stanley. He was sent to Camp Green Lake.
> 3. Stanley met six other boys in Group D. Each boy had to dig one hole every day.
> 4. Stanley found a shiny gold tube in the dirt. He saw two letters at the bottom of it.

> On my way home, I was hit by (A)_____. I picked them up and started
> (B)_____. The police stopped me and I was sent to (C)_____.
> At the camp, I met six other boys in Group D. I had to dig (D)_____. One
> day, I found a shiny gold tube with two letters (E)_____ of it.

단원별 모의고사

01 빈칸을 주어진 영영풀이에 해당하는 말을 이용하여 채우시오.

> to send someone to a particular group or place as part of a job

> If an individual is _____ to a position out of his or her abilities, success will be harder to expect.

02 두 단어의 관계가 나머지와 다른 하나를 고르시오.

① dangerous – risky
② useful – useless
③ cruel – brutal
④ focus – concentrate
⑤ assign – allocate

03 빈칸 (A)와 (B)에 들어갈 말로 알맞은 것끼리 짝지어진 것을 고르시오.

> • My suitcase was full (A)_____ books.
> • The crown stands (B)_____ royal dignity.

	(A)	(B)		(A)	(B)
①	of	– for	②	of	– on
③	with	– for	④	with	– on
⑤	with	– in			

04 다음 우리말에 맞도록 빈칸에 알맞은 말을 쓰시오.

(1) 한 시간 후에, 혈당 수치를 측정하기 위해서 피 검사를 할 것이다.
➡ One _____ _____, you'll have a blood test to measure your blood sugar level.

(2) 커피는 그가 자지 않고 깨어 있도록 도와줄 것 이다.
➡ The coffee will help him _____ _____.

(3) 저 사진은 전혀 그녀처럼 보이지 않는다.
➡ That photograph doesn't look _____ her _____ _____.

05 주어진 문장 다음에 이어질 대화의 순서를 바르게 배열한 것을 고르시오.

> How do you feel about shopping on the Internet?

> (A) I can shop whenever I want.
> (B) Can you tell me the reason?
> (C) I like it a lot.
> (D) I'm with you on that.

① (B) – (A) – (C) – (D)
② (B) – (C) – (A) – (D)
③ (C) – (A) – (B) – (D)
④ (C) – (B) – (A) – (D)
⑤ (C) – (D) – (B) – (A)

[06~07] 다음 대화를 읽고 물음에 답하시오.

A: 수업 시간에 스마트폰을 사용하는 것에 대해 어떻게 생각해?
B: I think smartphones are useful in class. (A) _____ (can, them, on, for, we, search, information)
A: I'm with you on that.

06 빈칸 (A)를 괄호 안에 주어진 단어를 알맞게 배열하여 채우시오.

➡ _____

07 밑줄 친 우리말과 일치하도록 주어진 단어를 이용해 문장을 만드시오.

➡ _____

_____

(feel, use, in, about)

[08~10] 다음 대화를 읽고 물음에 답하시오.

B: Hey, Jessica. (A)[What / Why / How] are you always drinking energy drinks?

G: Because they help me stay awake.

B: ⓐ_____ (caffeine, with, they, you, much, on, I'm, have, too, that, but)

G: Well, ⓑ공부에 집중하는 데 도움이 돼.

B: Did you know (B)[what / that] too much caffeine can hurt your bones?

G: Oh, I didn't know that.

B: I think you should drink energy drinks less often.

G: Maybe you're right. Thanks, Tom.

08 빈칸 ⓐ를 괄호 안에 주어진 단어를 알맞게 배열하여 채우시오.

➡ _____

_____

09 위 대화의 괄호 (A), (B)에서 적절한 것을 고르시오.

➡ (A) _____ (B) _____

10 밑줄 친 ⓑ의 우리말과 일치하도록 주어진 단어를 이용해 영작하시오.

➡ _____ (they, focus, 7 단어)

[11~12] 다음 대화를 읽고 물음에 답하시오.

B: Hi, Amy. Welcome to Korea. (①)

G: Long time no see, Minho. (②) How have you been? (③)

B: Great. (④)

G: I came here by subway. (⑤)

B: (A)How do you feel about the subway in Korea?

G: I think it's very clean.

11 ①~⑤ 중 주어진 문장이 들어갈 곳은?

How did you come here from the airport?

①   ②   ③   ④   ⑤

12 밑줄 친 문장 (A)와 바꿔 쓸 수 있는 문장을 주어진 단어를 이용해 쓰시오.

➡ _____

(about, what)

➡ _____

(opinion)

13 빈칸을 채워 주어진 문장과 같은 의미의 문장을 쓰시오.

(1) As you fear something more, it will appear to be bigger.

= The more _____

_____ .

(2) As the top of a tower is higher, it commands a finer view.

= The higher _____

_____ .

14 다음 우리말을 주어진 어휘를 이용하여 영작하시오.

(1) 화가 날수록 카멜레온의 색깔은 더 밝아진다.
(the chameleon, its color, become, angry, bright)

➡ _____

_____

(2) 더 열심히 공부할수록 너는 더 좋은 성적을 얻을 수 있을 거야. (grades, study, get, good, hard)

➡ _____

_____

(3) 그 운동화 때문에 그는 Camp Green Lake로 보내졌다. (because, sneakers, send)

➡ _____

_____

(4) 지난여름 이후 모든 것이 매우 많이 달라졌다.
(everything, have, change, since, so)

➡ _____

_____

15 다음 문장의 빈칸에 들어갈 수 <u>없는</u> 말을 고르시오.

The _____, the better.

① shorter ② longer ③ richer
④ less ⑤ sweater

16 다음 중 어법상 어색한 것을 <u>모두</u> 고르시오.

① The drier the air is, the more water you need.
② The early they start, the soon they will arrive.
③ The more you study, the more you learn.
④ We didn't go on a picnic because of it rained a lot.

⑤ Stanley Yelnats couldn't dig any harder since every single muscle hurt.
⑥ Mina went home early though she felt very tired.
⑦ Since everything can be done by robots, life is more convenient.

[17~18] 다음 글을 읽고 물음에 답하시오.

"Dig harder, Stanley! The harder you dig, the faster you'll finish!" yelled Mr. Sir. Stanley Yelnats couldn't dig any harder since every single muscle hurt. He was thirsty and hungry. He wanted to go home. Unfortunately, Stanley's home for the next 18 months would be right here, at Camp Green Lake.

Camp Green Lake was a ⓐ_____ name. It wasn't green and there was no lake. Camp Green Lake was hot and full of sand. In fact, it wasn't even a camp. It was a place for bad boys. Then what was a good boy ⓑlike Stanley doing here? He was sent to the camp for stealing a pair of sneakers.

17 위 글의 빈칸 ⓐ에 들어갈 알맞은 말을 고르시오.

① cool ② terrific
③ reasonable ④ awesome
⑤ terrible

18 위 글의 밑줄 친 ⓑlike와 같은 의미로 쓰인 것을 고르시오.

① She's wearing a dress <u>like</u> mine.
② Which bag do you <u>like</u> best?
③ Wild flowers <u>like</u> primroses are becoming rare.
④ He ran <u>like</u> the wind.
⑤ She acts <u>like</u> she owns the place.

단원별 모의고사

[19~20] 다음 글을 읽고 물음에 답하시오.

Stanley didn't really steal a pair of sneakers. He was just in the wrong place at the wrong time. One day, he was walking home from school. Suddenly, a pair of old sneakers fell from the sky. ⓐ그 운동화는 그의 머리에 맞았다. ⓑHe started running with the sneakers to tell his father what was happened. A few minutes later, the police stopped Stanley and asked him why he was running. Unfortunately for Stanley, the sneakers belonged to a famous baseball player, Clyde Livingstone. That was why Stanley ended up at Camp Green Lake.

19 위 글의 밑줄 친 ⓐ의 우리말에 맞게 주어진 어휘를 이용하여 7단어로 영작하시오.

> hit, on

➡ _____

20 위 글의 밑줄 친 ⓑ에서 어법상 틀린 부분을 찾아 고치시오.

➡ _____

[21~22] 다음 글을 읽고 물음에 답하시오.

The more Stanley dug, the stronger he became. (①) It took less time to finish his hole each day. (②) Stanley's heart beat faster. (③) He heard that anyone who found something interesting would be given the day off. (④) He carefully picked up the shiny object and brushed off the dirt. (⑤) It was a small gold tube. But it couldn't be real gold since it was too light. There were two letters, *KB*, at the bottom of the tube. What did KB stand for? Stanley's heart beat even faster.

21 위 글의 흐름으로 보아, 주어진 문장이 들어가기에 가장 적절한 곳은?

> In his second week, as Stanley was finishing his hole, he saw something shiny in the dirt.

①   ②   ③   ④   ⑤

22 According to the passage, which is NOT true?

① As Stanley dug more, he became stronger.
② Stanley spent less time finishing his hole each day.
③ Anyone who found something interesting would be given the day off.
④ What Stanley found was a small gold tube.
⑤ There were two letters, *KB*, at the top of the tube.

[23~24] 다음 글을 읽고 물음에 답하시오.

Stanley was assigned to Group D in the camp. There were six other boys in Stanley's group. They all had cool names like X-Ray, Zigzag and Zero. Each boy had to dig one hole every day. ⓐIt had to be about 150cm deep and 150cm wide. Mr. Sir said, "ⓑYou are digging to build character."

23 위 글의 밑줄 친 ⓐIt이 가리키는 것을 본문에서 찾아 쓰시오.

➡ _____

24 위 글의 밑줄 친 ⓑ를 다음과 같이 바꿔 쓸 때 빈칸에 들어갈 알맞은 말을 쓰시오.

➡ (1) You are digging _____ build character. (2) You are digging _____ you _____ build character.

INSIGHT
on the textbook
교과서 파헤치기

※ 다음 영어를 우리말로 쓰시오.

01	instead		22	improve
02	lose		23	as
03	base		24	string
04	triangle		25	again
05	by		26	pretty
06	call		27	role
07	stuck		28	creatively
08	challenge		29	suggest
09	mess		30	upset
10	same		31	wrap
11	point		32	bad cold
12	close		33	still
13	stick		34	marathon
14	competition		35	such as
15	relationship		36	by itself
16	teamwork		37	in a hurry
17	later		38	get well
18	detail		39	in the end
19	score		40	divide up
20	divide		41	in detail
21	each		42	right away
			43	spend A on B

※ 다음 우리말을 영어로 쓰시오.

01 꽤, 매우

02 끈, 줄

03 역할

04 바쁜

05 전화하다, 부르다

06 마라톤

07 같은

08 (정도, 차이) ~의 차(이)로, ~만큼

09 엉망인 상태

10 과제, 도전

11 (경기 등에서) 점수

12 움직일 수 없는

13 세부, 상세

14 여전히

15 창의적으로

16 제안하다

17 나누다

18 각각의; 각각

19 개량하다, 향상시키다

20 (경기 등에서) 득점

21 대신에

22 ~로서

23 후에

24 (사물의) 맨 아래 부분

25 관계

26 막상막하의, 우열을 가리기 힘든

27 막대기처럼 기다랗고 가는 것

28 (시합에서) 지다

29 팀워크, 협동 작업

30 독감

31 삼각형

32 속상한, 기분이 상한

33 감다, 싸다

34 (경연) 대회, 시합, 경쟁

35 병이 나아지다

36 즉각, 곧바로

37 ~와 같은

38 마침내

39 홀로, 저절로

40 상세하게

41 서둘러, 급히

42 A를 B에 쓰다

43 분담하다, 분배하다

※ 다음 영영풀이에 알맞은 단어를 <보기>에서 골라 쓴 후, 우리말 뜻을 쓰시오.

1 _____ : fairly or more than a little: _____

2 _____ : to telephone someone: _____

3 _____ : to make better: _____

4 _____ : a state of confusion and disorderliness: _____

5 _____ : a running race that is about 26 miles (42 kilometers) long: _____

6 _____ : the lowest part or surface of something: _____

7 _____ : the activity of working well together as a team: _____

8 _____ : to separate people or things into smaller groups or parts: _____

9 _____ : to not win a game, argument, election, war, etc.: _____

10 _____ : the way in which people feel and behave towards each other: _____

11 _____ : impossible or unable to move from a particular position: _____

12 _____ : a minor point or aspect of something, as opposed to the central ones:
_____

13 _____ : finishing or being played, fought, etc. with both sides almost equal:
_____

14 _____ : the actions and activities assigned to or required or expected of a person
or group: _____

15 _____ : an event in which people compete with each other to find out who is the
best at something: _____

16 _____ : something that needs a lot of skill, energy, and determination to deal
with or achieve: _____

보기			
challenge	competition	base	teamwork
lose	call	pretty	mess
close	role	divide	marathon
stuck	detail	relationship	improve

※ 다음 우리말과 일치하도록 빈칸에 알맞은 말을 쓰시오.

Listen and Speak 1 A

B: Amy, _____ _____ you _____?

G: I've _____ great. _____ _____ you, Mike?

B: _____ so good. I _____ a _____ _____.

G: Oh, no! _____ _____ soon.

B: Thanks.

B: Amy, 어떻게 지냈니?
G: 잘 지냈어. 너는 어때, Mike?
B: 별로야. 독감에 걸렸어.
G: 어, 저런! 빨리 나아.
B: 고마워.

Listen and Speak 1 B

G: Hi, Jinsu! _____ in the _____ _____ again!

B: Yeah! _____ to see you, Sora. _____ _____ _____ been?

G: _____ _____ great. How _____ you?

B: _____ _____ busy. I have a piano _____ next week.

G: Oh! I _____ know you _____ the piano.

B: Really? _____ _____ the piano _____ 5 years.

G: You _____ be _____ _____ it. Good _____ your _____!

B: Thanks.

G: 안녕, 진수야! 우리 또 같은 반이구나!
B: 응! 만나서 반가워, 소라야. 어떻게 지냈니?
G: 잘 지냈어. 너는 어때?
B: 난 좀 바빴어. 다음 주에 피아노 경연이 있어.
G: 오! 네가 피아노를 치는지 몰랐어.
B: 정말? 난 피아노를 5년간 쳤어.
G: 넌 분명 피아노를 잘 치겠구나. 경연에서 행운을 빌어!
B: 고마워.

Listen and Speak 1 C

1. **A:** Mina, _____ have _____ _____?

   B: I've _____ good. How is _____?

   A: Pretty good. My _____ _____ _____ nice.

2. **A:** How _____ _____ _____?

   B: I've _____ good. How _____ _____ _____?

   A: _____ so. I _____ a _____.

3. **A:** _____ _____ _____ been?

   B: _____ _____ good. _____ is everything?

   A: _____ good. My new _____ are exciting.

4. **A:** _____ _____ _____?

   B: _____ _____ good. How is _____?

   A: So so. I _____ _____ _____ homework.

1. **A:** 미나야, 어떻게 지냈니?
   B: 잘 지냈어. 어떻게 지냈니?
   A: 잘 지냈어. 나의 새로운 반 친구가 좋아.
2. **A:** 어떻게 지냈니?
   B: 잘 지냈어. 어떻게 지냈니?
   A: 그저 그래. 감기에 걸렸어.
3. **A:** 어떻게 지냈니?
   B: 잘 지냈어. 어떻게 지냈니?
   A: 좋아. 내 새로운 수업이 재미있어.
4. **A:** 어떻게 지냈니?
   B: 잘 지냈어. 어떻게 지냈니?
   A: 그저 그래. 숙제가 너무 많아.

Listen and Speak 2 A

B: Susan, you look _____. Do you _____ _____ _____ news?

G: Our team _____ an A on the science project.

B: That's great!

G: Our team _____ _____ _____ _____.

B: _____ happy _____ _____ that.

B: Susan, 신나 보이네. 좋은 소식이 있니?

G: 우리 팀이 과학 프로젝트에서 A를 받았어.

B: 잘됐다!

G: 우리 팀은 팀워크가 최고였어.

B: 그 말을 들으니 기뻐.

Listen and Speak 2 B

G: Andy, _____ _____ the basketball game go?

B: Our team _____.

G: Oh, I'm _____ _____ _____ that.

B: It's okay. It was a _____ game.

G: What _____ the _____?

B: It was 80 _____ 79. We _____ _____ _____ _____.

G: That was really _____!

B: Yeah. We _____ really well _____ a team.

G: _____ wonderful! I want _____ _____ your next game.

G: Andy, 농구 경기는 어땠니?

B: 우리 팀이 졌어.

G: 오, 그 말을 들으니 안타까워.

B: 괜찮아. 정말 좋은 경기였어.

G: 점수는 어떻게 되었니?

B: 80 대 79였어. 우린 1점 차이로 졌어.

G: 정말 막상막하였네!

B: 응. 우린 하나의 팀으로 경기를 정말 잘했어.

G: 정말 멋지다! 너희 다음번 경기를 보고 싶어.

Listen and Speak 2 C

1. **A:** Bob, you look _____.

   B: I came _____ _____ _____ the _____.

   A: I'm _____ _____ _____ that.

2. **A:** Ann, you _____ _____.

   B: I _____ _____ _____ _____ my friend.

   A: I'm _____ _____ _____ _____.

3. **A:** Tom, you _____ _____.

   B: I _____ the school _____ _____.

   A: I'm _____ _____ _____ that.

4. **A:** Bomi, you look _____.

   B: I _____ my dog.

   A: I'm _____ _____ _____ that.

1. **A:** Bob, 너 행복해 보인다.
   B: 마라톤에서 1등으로 들어왔어.
   A: 그 말을 들으니 기뻐.
2. **A:** Ann, 너 속상해 보인다.
   B: 나는 내 친구와 싸웠어.
   A: 그 말을 들으니 안타까워.
3. **A:** Tom, 너 행복해 보인다.
   B: 나는 학교 춤 경연대회에서 이겼어.
   A: 그 말을 들으니 기뻐.
4. **A:** Bomi, 너 속상해 보인다.
   B: 난 개를 잃어버렸어.
   A: 그 말을 들으니 안타까워.

5. **A:** Jim, you _____ _____.

   B: I _____ a new _____.

   A: I'm _____ _____ _____ that.

6. **A:** Jane, you look _____.

   B: I _____ my _____.

   A: I'm _____ to _____ that.

Real Life Talk Step 1

Minho: Linda! Is that you? _____ _____ no _____.

Linda: Minho! It's _____ a long time.

Minho: _____ _____ you _____?

Linda: I've _____ good. How _____ you?

Minho: I've _____ really busy _____ school. _____ your new school?

Linda: It's wonderful. I've _____ new friends.

Minho: That's great! _____ _____ _____ _____ that.

Linda: Thanks. Oh! I _____ _____ go to my _____ _____ now.

Minho: You still _____ my _____, right?

Linda: Yeah. I'll _____ you _____. _____ a good day!

Minho: You, _____. Bye!

Real Life Talk Step 2

1. **A:** _____ _____ _____ _____?

   B: I've _____ great.

   A: _____ was your _____?

   B: Wonderful. I _____ a ski camp.

   A: That's great. I'm happy _____ _____.

2. **A:** How _____ _____ _____?

   B: _____ so _____.

   A: _____ come?

   B: I _____ my dog.

   A: Oh, no! _____ _____ to hear that.

---

5. A: Jim, 너 행복해 보인다.
   B: 새 자전거를 샀어.
   A: 그 말을 들으니 기뻐.
6. A: Jane, 너 속상해 보인다.
   B: 나의 새로운 스마트폰을 떨어뜨렸어.
   A: 그 말을 들으니 안타까워.

민호: Linda! 너구나? 오랜만이야.
Linda: 민호야! 오랜만이야.
민호: 어떻게 지냈니?
Linda: 잘 지냈어. 너는 어때?
민호: 난 학교에서 정말 바빴어. 새 학교는 어때?
Linda: 정말 좋아. 새 친구들을 많이 사귀었어.
민호: 잘됐다! 그 말을 들으니 기뻐.
Linda: 고마워. 오! 난 지금 바이올린 수업에 가야 해.
민호: 아직 내 번호 가지고 있지, 그렇지?
Linda: 응. 내가 나중에 전화할게. 좋은 하루 보내!
민호: 너도. 안녕!

1. A: 어떻게 지냈니?
   B: 잘 지냈어.
   A: 방학은 어땠어?
   B: 좋았어. 난 스키 캠프에 들어갔어.
   A: 잘됐네. 그 말을 들으니 기뻐.
2. A: 어떻게 지냈니?
   B: 좋지 않아.
   A: 왜?
   B: 난 개를 잃어버렸어.
   A: 어, 저런! 그 말을 들으니 안타까워.

※ 다음 우리말에 맞도록 대화를 영어로 쓰시오.

Listen and Speak 1 A

B: _____

G: _____

B: _____

G: _____

B: _____

B: Amy, 어떻게 지냈니?
G: 잘 지냈어. 너는 어때, Mike?
B: 별로야. 독감에 걸렸어.
G: 어, 저런! 빨리 나아.
B: 고마워.

Listen and Speak 1 B

G: _____

B: _____

G: _____

B: _____

G: _____

B: _____

G: _____

B: _____

G: 안녕, 진수야! 우리 또 같은 반이구나!
B: 응! 만나서 반가워, 소라야. 어떻게 지냈니?
G: 잘 지냈어. 너는 어때?
B: 난 좀 바빴어. 다음 주에 피아노 경연이 있어.
G: 오! 네가 피아노를 치는지 몰랐어.
B: 정말? 난 피아노를 5년간 쳤어.
G: 넌 분명 피아노를 잘 치겠구나. 경연에서 행운을 빌어!
B: 고마워.

Listen and Speak 1 C

1. A: _____

   B: _____

   A: _____

2. A: _____

   B: _____

   A: _____

3. A: _____

   B: _____

   A: _____

4. A: _____

   B: _____

   A: _____

1. A: 미나야, 어떻게 지냈니?
   B: 잘 지냈어. 어떻게 지냈니?
   A: 잘 지냈어. 나의 새로운 반 친구가 좋아.
2. A: 어떻게 지냈니?
   B: 잘 지냈어. 어떻게 지냈니?
   A: 그저 그래. 감기에 걸렸어.
3. A: 어떻게 지냈니?
   B: 잘 지냈어. 어떻게 지냈니?
   A: 좋아. 내 새로운 수업이 재미있어.
4. A: 어떻게 지냈니?
   B: 잘 지냈어. 어떻게 지냈니?
   A: 그저 그래. 숙제가 너무 많아.

Listen and Speak 2 A

B: _____

G: _____

B: _____

G: _____

B: _____

B: Susan, 신나 보이네. 좋은 소식이 있니?
G: 우리 팀이 과학 프로젝트에서 A를 받았어.
B: 잘됐다!
G: 우리 팀은 팀워크가 최고였어.
B: 그 말을 들으니 기뻐.

Listen and Speak 2 B

G: _____

B: _____

G: _____

B: _____

G: _____

B: _____

G: _____

B: _____

G: _____

G: Andy, 농구 경기는 어땠니?
B: 우리 팀이 졌어.
G: 오, 그 말을 들으니 안타까워.
B: 괜찮아. 정말 좋은 경기였어.
G: 점수는 어떻게 되었니?
B: 80 대 79였어. 우린 1점 차이로 졌어.
G: 정말 막상막하였네!
B: 응. 우린 하나의 팀으로 경기를 정말 잘했어.
G: 정말 멋지다! 너희 다음번 경기를 보고 싶어.

Listen and Speak 2 C

1. A: _____

   B: _____

   A: _____

2. A: _____

   B: _____

   A: _____

3. A: _____

   B: _____

   A: _____

4. A: _____

   B: _____

   A: _____

1. A: Bob, 너 행복해 보인다.
   B: 마라톤에서 1등으로 들어왔어.
   A: 그 말을 들으니 기뻐.
2. A: Ann, 너 속상해 보인다.
   B: 나는 내 친구와 싸웠어.
   A: 그 말을 들으니 안타까워.
3. A: Tom, 너 행복해 보인다.
   B: 나는 학교 춤 경연대회에서 이겼어.
   A: 그 말을 들으니 기뻐.
4. A: Bomi, 너 속상해 보인다.
   B: 난 개를 잃어버렸어.
   A: 그 말을 들으니 안타까워.

5. A: _____
   B: _____
   A: _____

6. A: _____
   B: _____
   A: _____

5. A: Jim, 너 행복해 보인다.
   B: 새 자전거를 샀어.
   A: 그 말을 들으니 기뻐.
6. A: Jane, 너 속상해 보인다.
   B: 나의 새로운 스마트폰을 떨어뜨렸어.
   A: 그 말을 들으니 안타까워.

Real Life Talk Step 1

Minho: _____
Linda: _____
Minho: _____
Linda: _____
Minho: _____
Linda: _____
Minho: _____
Linda: _____
Minho: _____
Linda: _____
Minho: _____

민호: Linda! 너구나? 오랜만이야.
Linda: 민호야! 오랜만이야.
민호: 어떻게 지냈니?
Linda: 잘 지냈어. 너는 어때?
민호: 난 학교에서 정말 바빴어. 새 학교는 어때?
Linda: 정말 좋아. 새 친구들을 많이 사귀었어.
민호: 잘됐다! 그 말을 들으니 기뻐.
Linda: 고마워. 오! 난 지금 바이올린 수업에 가야 해.
민호: 아직 내 번호 가지고 있지, 그렇지?
Linda: 응. 내가 나중에 전화할게. 좋은 하루 보내!
민호: 너도. 안녕!

Real Life Talk Step 2

1. A: _____
   B: _____
   A: _____
   B: _____
   A: _____

2. A: _____
   B: _____
   A: _____
   B: _____
   A: _____

1. A: 어떻게 지냈니?
   B: 잘 지냈어.
   A: 방학은 어땠어?
   B: 좋았어. 난 스키 캠프에 들어갔어.
   A: 잘됐네. 그 말을 들으니 기뻐.
2. A: 어떻게 지냈니?
   B: 좋지 않아.
   A: 왜?
   B: 난 개를 잃어버렸어.
   A: 어, 저런! 그 말을 들으니 안타까워.

※ 다음 우리말과 일치하도록 빈칸에 알맞은 것을 골라 쓰시오.

1 _____ the _____ _____!
A. Challenge   B. Try   C. Marshmallow

2 You _____ : 20 _____ of spaghetti, 1 marshmallow, 1 meter of _____, 1 meter of _____
A. need   B. string   C. sticks   D. tape

3 Rules: _____ _____ _____ four people.
A. has   B. team   C. each

4 You _____ _____ _____ the tallest tower in your _____.
A. class   B. to   C. have   D. build

5 The marshmallow _____ _____ _____ _____.
A. on   B. be   C. top   D. must

6 The tower must _____ _____ _____.
A. itself   B. by   C. stand

7 The _____ _____ is 15 _____.
A. limit   B. time   C. minutes

8 This activity is _____ for: _____ Relationships, _____ Problems, Thinking _____
A. Solving   B. good   C. Creatively   D. Building

9 _____ did you do the _____ _____?
A. challenge   B. how   C. marshmallow

10 _____ _____ does the marshmallow _____ _____ _____.
A. differently   B. challenge   C. team   D. every

11 _____ look _____ some _____.
A. examples   B. let's   C. at

12 _____ _____ do you like _____?
A. one   B. best   C. which

13 TEAM A: _____ before you _____.
A. act   B. think

14 We had _____ _____ _____.
A. ideas   B. many   C. good

15 We talked about _____ idea _____ _____.
A. detail   B. each   C. in

16 It was not easy _____ _____ _____ _____ the best idea.
A. choose   B. for   C. to   D. us

17 _____ the teacher _____, "Five minutes _____."
A. left   B. suddenly   C. said

18 _____ _____ _____, we taped the _____ of spaghetti together.
A. sticks   B. hurry   C. in   D. a

19 Then, we _____ the _____ _____ them.
A. around   B. wrapped   C. string

---

1 마시멜로 과제를 해보세요!

2 여러분은 필요해요: 스파게티 면 20개, 마시멜로 1개, 테이프 1미터, 끈 1미터

3 규칙: 각 팀은 4명입니다.

4 반에서 가장 높은 탑을 만들어야 합니다.

5 마시멜로는 꼭대기에 있어야 합니다.

6 탑은 스스로 서 있어야 합니다.

7 제한 시간은 15분입니다.

8 이 활동은 여기에 좋아요: 관계를 맺는 것, 문제를 해결하는 것, 창의적으로 생각하는 것

9 마시멜로 과제를 어떻게 했나요?

10 모든 팀은 마시멜로 과제를 다르게 해요.

11 몇몇 예들을 살펴봐요.

12 어떤 예가 가장 마음에 드나요?

13 A팀: 행동하기 전에 생각해라.

14 우리에겐 좋은 아이디어가 많았어요.

15 우리는 각 아이디어에 대해 자세히 이야기했어요.

16 우리는 가장 좋은 아이디어를 고르는 것이 쉽지 않았어요.

17 갑자기 선생님께서 "5분 남았어요."라고 말씀하셨어요.

18 서둘러서 우리는 스파게티 면들을 테이프로 붙였어요.

19 그리고 나서 끈으로 스파게티 면 둘레를 둘렀어요.

20 The _____ got _____ to the tape and it was a big _____.
A. mess   B. string   C. stuck

21 _____ one second _____, I _____ the marshmallow on _____!
A. top   B. put   C. with   D. left

22 TEAM B: _____ _____ _____.
A. it   B. do   C. just

23 We didn't _____ much _____ _____ _____.
A. planning   B. time   C. spend   D. on

24 _____ the members started _____ the tower _____ _____.
A. right   B. all   C. away   D. building

25 _____ first tower _____ _____ a tent.
A. like   B. looked   C. our

26 It wasn't _____ _____.
A. tall   B. very

27 We _____ _____.
A. again   B. tried

28 The next tower was _____ but it couldn't _____ _____ _____.
A. tall   B. stand   C. itself   D. by

29 _____ many _____, it was _____ for us to _____ a beautiful and tall tower.
A. build   B. tries   C. possible   D. after

30 It _____ _____ the _____ Tower of Pisa.
A. like   B. Leaning   C. looked

31 We _____ made _____ we _____!
A. wanted   B. what   C. finally

32 TEAM C: We're _____ _____.
A. team   B. one

33 We didn't _____ _____ _____ the best idea.
A. choose   B. to   C. try

34 _____, we took a good idea and _____ _____ it.
A. on   B. instead   C. improved

35 One student said we _____ a _____ _____.
A. base   B. needed   C. strong

36 _____ student _____ a triangle _____ for the _____.
A. shape   B. suggested   C. base   D. another

37 We all agreed and _____ _____ the _____ such as time checker and tape _____.
A. up   B. cutter   C. divided   D. roles

38 We _____ together _____ a _____.
A. as   B. worked   C. team

39 _____ the _____, we _____ our tall tower!
A. end   B. built   C. in

---

20 끈이 테이프에 붙었고 엉망진창이었어요.

21 1초를 남기고 제가 마시멜로를 꼭대기에 꽂았어요.

22 B팀: 그냥 해라.

23 우리는 계획하는 데 많은 시간을 보내지 않았어요.

24 모든 팀원들이 바로 탑을 만들기 시작했어요.

25 우리의 첫 번째 탑은 텐트 같았어요.

26 그건 그다지 높지 않았어요.

27 우리는 다시 시도했어요.

28 다음 탑은 높았지만 스스로 서 있지 못했어요.

29 많은 시도 후에 우리는 아름답고 높은 탑을 만들 수 있었어요.

30 그것은 피사의 사탑 같았어요.

31 우리는 결국 우리가 원하는 것을 만들었어요!

32 C팀: 우리는 한 팀이다.

33 우리는 가장 좋은 아이디어를 고르려고 하지 않았어요.

34 대신에 우리는 좋은 아이디어를 골라 발전시켰어요.

35 한 친구가 우리에겐 튼튼한 기반이 필요하다고 말했어요.

36 또 다른 친구는 기반으로 삼각형 모양을 제안했어요.

37 우리 모두는 동의했고 시간 점검하는 사람과 테이프 자르는 사람과 같이 역할을 나눴어요.

38 우리는 하나의 팀으로 함께했어요.

39 마침내 우리는 높은 탑을 만들었어요!

※ 다음 우리말과 일치하도록 빈칸에 알맞은 말을 쓰시오.

1 _____ the _____ _____!

2 _____ _____: 20 _____ of spaghetti, 1 marshmallow, 1 meter of tape, 1 meter of _____

3 Rules: _____ _____ _____ four people.

4 You _____ _____ _____ the _____ _____ in your class.

5 The marshmallow _____ _____ _____ _____ _____.

6 The tower _____ _____ _____ _____.

7 The _____ _____ is 15 _____.

8 This activity _____ _____ _____: _____ Relationships, _____ Problems, Thinking _____

9 _____ did you do the marshmallow _____?

10 _____ _____ _____ the marshmallow challenge _____.

11 Let's _____ _____ some _____.

12 _____ _____ do you _____ _____?

13 TEAM A: _____ before you _____.

14 We had _____ _____ _____.

15 We talked about _____ idea _____.

16 _____ was not easy _____ _____ _____ the best idea.

17 Suddenly the teacher said, "_____ _____ _____."

18 _____ _____ _____, we _____ the sticks of spaghetti _____.

19 Then, we _____ _____ _____ _____ them.

---

1 마시멜로 과제를 해보세요!

2 여러분은 필요해요: 스파게티 면 20개, 마시멜로 1개, 테이프 1미터, 끈 1미터

3 규칙: 각 팀은 4명입니다.

4 반에서 가장 높은 탑을 만들어야 합니다.

5 마시멜로는 꼭대기에 있어야 합니다.

6 탑은 스스로 서 있어야 합니다.

7 제한 시간은 15분입니다.

8 이 활동은 여기에 좋아요: 관계를 맺는 것, 문제를 해결하는 것, 창의적으로 생각하는 것

9 마시멜로 과제를 어떻게 했나요?

10 모든 팀은 마시멜로 과제를 다르게 해요.

11 몇몇 예들을 살펴봐요.

12 어떤 예가 가장 마음에 드나요?

13 A팀: 행동하기 전에 생각해라.

14 우리에겐 좋은 아이디어가 많았어요.

15 우리는 각 아이디어에 대해 자세히 이야기했어요.

16 우리는 가장 좋은 아이디어를 고르는 것이 쉽지 않았어요.

17 갑자기 선생님께서 "5분 남았어요."라고 말씀하셨어요.

18 서둘러서 우리는 스파게티 면들을 테이프로 붙였어요.

19 그리고 나서 끈으로 스파게티 면 둘레를 둘렀어요.

20 The string _____ _____ _____ the tape and it was a big _____.

21 _____ _____ _____ _____, I put the marshmallow on top!

22 TEAM B: _____ _____ _____.

23 We didn't _____ _____ _____ on _____.

24 All the members started building the tower _____ _____.

25 Our first tower _____ _____ a tent.

26 It wasn't _____ _____.

27 We _____ _____.

28 The next tower was tall but it _____ _____ _____ _____.

29 _____ _____ _____, it was possible _____ _____ _____ a beautiful and tall tower.

30 It looked like the _____ _____ _____ _____.

31 We _____ made _____ _____ _____!

32 TEAM C: We're _____ _____.

33 We _____ _____ _____ _____ the best idea.

34 _____, we took a good idea and _____ _____ it.

35 One student said we needed _____ _____ _____.

36 _____ student _____ a triangle shape _____ _____ _____.

37 We all agreed and _____ _____ the roles _____ _____ time checker and tape cutter.

38 We worked together _____ _____ _____.

39 _____ _____ _____, we _____ our tall tower!

20 끈이 테이프에 붙었고 엉망진창이었어요.

21 1초를 남기고 제가 마시멜로를 꼭대기에 꽂았어요.

22 B팀: 그냥 해라.

23 우리는 계획하는 데 많은 시간을 보내지 않았어요.

24 모든 팀원들이 바로 탑을 만들기 시작했어요.

25 우리의 첫 번째 탑은 텐트 같았어요.

26 그건 그다지 높지 않았어요.

27 우리는 다시 시도했어요.

28 다음 탑은 높았지만 스스로 서 있지 못했어요.

29 많은 시도 후에 우리는 아름답고 높은 탑을 만들 수 있었어요.

30 그것은 피사의 사탑 같았어요.

31 우리는 결국 우리가 원하는 것을 만들었어요!

32 C팀: 우리는 한 팀이다.

33 우리는 가장 좋은 아이디어를 고르려고 하지 않았어요.

34 대신에 우리는 좋은 아이디어를 골라 발전시켰어요.

35 한 친구가 우리에겐 튼튼한 기반이 필요하다고 말했어요.

36 또 다른 친구는 기반으로 삼각형 모양을 제안했어요.

37 우리 모두는 동의했고 시간 점검하는 사람과 테이프 자르는 사람과 같이 역할을 나눴어요.

38 우리는 하나의 팀으로 함께했어요.

39 마침내 우리는 높은 탑을 만들었어요!

※ 다음 문장을 우리말로 쓰시오.

1 Try the Marshmallow Challenge!
➡ _____

2 You need: 20 sticks of spaghetti, 1 marshmallow, 1 meter of tape, 1 meter of string
➡ _____

3 Rules: Each team has four people.
➡ _____

4 You have to build the tallest tower in your class.
➡ _____

5 The marshmallow must be on top.
➡ _____

6 The tower must stand by itself.
➡ _____

7 The time limit is 15 minutes.
➡ _____

8 This activity is good for: Building Relationships, Solving Problems, Thinking Creatively
➡ _____

9 How did you do the marshmallow challenge?
➡ _____

10 Every team does the marshmallow challenge differently.
➡ _____

11 Let's look at some examples.
➡ _____

12 Which one do you like best?
➡ _____

13 TEAM A: Think before you act.
➡ _____

14 We had many good ideas.
➡ _____

15 We talked about each idea in detail.
➡ _____

16 It was not easy for us to choose the best idea.
➡ _____

17 Suddenly the teacher said, "Five minutes left."
➡ _____

18 In a hurry, we taped the sticks of spaghetti together.
➡ _____

19 Then, we wrapped the string around them.
➡ _____

20 The string got stuck to the tape and it was a big mess.

➡ _____

21 With one second left, I put the marshmallow on top!

➡ _____

22 TEAM B: Just do it.

➡ _____

23 We didn't spend much time on planning.

➡ _____

24 All the members started building the tower right away.

➡ _____

25 Our first tower looked like a tent.

➡ _____

26 It wasn't very tall.

➡ _____

27 We tried again.

➡ _____

28 The next tower was tall but it couldn't stand by itself.

➡ _____

29 After many tries, it was possible for us to build a beautiful and tall tower.

➡ _____

30 It looked like the Leaning Tower of Pisa.

➡ _____

31 We finally made what we wanted!

➡ _____

32 TEAM C: We're one team.

➡ _____

33 We didn't try to choose the best idea.

➡ _____

34 Instead, we took a good idea and improved on it.

➡ _____

35 One student said we needed a strong base.

➡ _____

36 Another student suggested a triangle shape for the base.

➡ _____

37 We all agreed and divided up the roles such as time checker and tape cutter.

➡ _____

38 We worked together as a team.

➡ _____

39 In the end, we built our tall tower!

➡ _____

※ 다음 괄호 안의 단어들을 우리말에 맞도록 바르게 배열하시오.

1 (the / Try / Challenge! / Marshmallow)

➡ _____

2 (need: / you // sticks / 20 / spaghetti, / of / marshmallow, / 1 / meter / 1 / tape, / of / meter / 1 / string / of)

➡ _____

_____

3 (rules: / team / each / four / has / people.)

➡ _____

4 (have / you / to / the / build / tower / tallest / your / in / class.)

➡ _____

5 (marshmallow / the / be / must / top. / on)

➡ _____

6 (tower / the / stand / must / itself. / by)

➡ _____

7 (time / the / is / limit / minutes. / 15)

➡ _____

8 (activity / this / good / is / for: / Relationships, / Building / Problems, / Solving / Creatively / Thinking)

➡ _____

_____

9 (did / how / do / you / marshmallow / the / challenge?)

➡ _____

10 (team / every / the / does / challenge / marshmallow / differently.)

➡ _____

11 (look / let's / some / at / examples.)

➡ _____

12 (one / which / like / do / best? / you)

➡ _____

13 (A: / TEAM // before / think / act. / you)

➡ _____

1 마시멜로 과제를 해보세요!

2 여러분은 필요해요: 스파게티 면 20개, 마시멜로 1개, 테이프 1미터, 끈 1미터

3 규칙: 각 팀은 4명입니다.

4 반에서 가장 높은 탑을 만들어야 합니다.

5 마시멜로는 꼭대기에 있어야 합니다.

6 탑은 스스로 서 있어야 합니다.

7 제한 시간은 15분입니다.

8 이 활동은 여기에 좋아요: 관계를 맺는 것, 문제를 해결하는 것, 창의적으로 생각하는 것

9 마시멜로 과제를 어떻게 했나요?

10 모든 팀은 마시멜로 과제를 다르게 해요.

11 몇몇 예들을 살펴봐요.

12 어떤 예가 가장 마음에 드나요?

13 A팀: 행동하기 전에 생각해라.

14 (had / we / good / ideas. / many)

➡ _____

15 (talked / we / each / about / in / idea / detail.)

➡ _____

16 (was / it / easy / not / us / for / choose / to / best / the / idea.)

➡ _____

17 (the / suddenly / said, / teacher / minutes / left." / "five)

➡ _____

18 (a / in / hurry, / taped / we / sticks / the / spaghetti / of / together.)

➡ _____

19 (we / then, / the / wrapped / around / them. / string)

➡ _____

20 (string / the / stuck / got / the / to / tape / and / was / it / a / mess. / big)

➡ _____

21 (one / with / left, / second / put / I / marshmallow / the / top! / on)

➡ _____

22 (B: / TEAM / do / it. / just)

➡ _____

23 (didn't / we / much / spend / on / planning. / time)

➡ _____

24 (the / all / members / buildinig / started / tower / the / away. / right)

➡ _____

25 (first / our / looked / tower / a / like / tent.)

➡ _____

26 (wasn't / it / tall. / very)

➡ _____

14 우리에겐 좋은 아이디어가 많았
어요.

15 우리는 각 아이디어에 대해 자
세히 이야기했어요.

16 우리는 가장 좋은 아이디어를
고르는 것이 쉽지 않았어요.

17 갑자기 선생님께서 "5분 남았
어요."라고 말씀하셨어요.

18 서둘러서 우리는 스파게티 면들
을 테이프로 붙였어요.

19 그리고 나서 끈으로 스파게티
면 둘레를 둘렀어요.

20 끈이 테이프에 붙었고 엉망진창
이었어요.

21 1초를 남기고 제가 마시멜로를
꼭대기에 꽂았어요.

22 B팀: 그냥 해라.

23 우리는 계획하는 데 많은 시간
을 보내지 않았어요.

24 모든 팀원들이 바로 탑을 만들
기 시작했어요.

25 우리의 첫 번째 탑은 텐트 같았
어요.

26 그건 그다지 높지 않았어요.

27 (tried / again. / we)

➡ _____

28 (next / the / was / tower / but / tall / couldn't / it / by / itself. / stand)

➡ _____

29 (many / after / tries, / was / it / for / possible / to / us / a / build / beautiful / tall / and / tower.)

➡ _____

_____

30 (looked / it / the / like / Tower / Leaning / Pisa. / of)

➡ _____

31 (finally / we / what / made / wanted! / we)

➡ _____

32 (C: / TEAM / one / we're / team.)

➡ _____

33 (didn't / we / to / try / the / choose / idea. / best)

➡ _____

34 (we / instead, / took / good / a / idea / and / on / improved / it.)

➡ _____

35 (student / one / we / said / a / needed / base. / strong)

➡ _____

36 (student / another / a / suggested / shape / triangle / the / for / base.)

➡ _____

37 (all / we / agreed / and / up / divided / roles / the / as / such / checker / time / and / cutter. / tape)

➡ _____

_____

38 (worked / we / as / together / team. / a)

➡ _____

39 (the / in / end, / built / we / tall / tower! / our)

➡ _____

27 우리는 다시 시도했어요.

28 다음 탑은 높았지만 스스로 서 있지 못했어요.

29 많은 시도 후에 우리는 아름답 고 높은 탑을 만들 수 있었어요.

30 그것은 피사의 사탑 같았어요.

31 우리는 결국 우리가 원하는 것 을 만들었어요!

32 C팀: 우리는 한 팀이다.

33 우리는 가장 좋은 아이디어를 고르려고 하지 않았어요.

34 대신에 우리는 좋은 아이디어를 골라 발전시켰어요.

35 한 친구가 우리에겐 튼튼한 기 반이 필요하다고 말했어요.

36 또 다른 친구는 기반으로 삼각 형 모양을 제안했어요.

37 우리 모두는 동의했고 시간 점 검하는 사람과 테이프 자르는 사람과 같이 역할을 나눴어요.

38 우리는 하나의 팀으로 함께했어요.

39 마침내 우리는 높은 탑을 만들 었어요!

※ 다음 우리말을 영어로 쓰시오.

1 마시멜로 과제를 해보세요!
➡ _____

2 여러분은 필요해요: 스파게티 면 20개, 마시멜로 1개, 테이프 1미터, 끈 1미터
➡ _____

3 규칙: 각 팀은 4명입니다.
➡ _____

4 반에서 가장 높은 탑을 만들어야 합니다.
➡ _____

5 마시멜로는 꼭대기에 있어야 합니다.
➡ _____

6 탑은 스스로 서 있어야 합니다.
➡ _____

7 제한 시간은 15분입니다.
➡ _____

8 이 활동은 여기에 좋아요: 관계를 맺는 것, 문제를 해결하는 것, 창의적으로 생각하는 것
➡ _____

9 마시멜로 과제를 어떻게 했나요?
➡ _____

10 모든 팀은 마시멜로 과제를 다르게 해요.
➡ _____

11 몇몇 예들을 살펴봐요.
➡ _____

12 어떤 예가 가장 마음에 드나요?
➡ _____

13 A팀: 행동하기 전에 생각해라.
➡ _____

14 우리에겐 좋은 아이디어가 많았어요.
➡ _____

15 우리는 각 아이디어에 대해 자세히 이야기했어요.
➡ _____

16 우리는 가장 좋은 아이디어를 고르는 것이 쉽지 않았어요.
➡ _____

17 갑자기 선생님께서 "5분 남았어요."라고 말씀하셨어요.
➡ _____

18 서둘러서 우리는 스파게티 면들을 테이프로 붙였어요.
➡ _____

19 그리고 나서 끈으로 스파게티 면 둘레를 둘렀어요.
➡ _____

20 끈이 테이프에 붙었고 엉망진창이었어요.
➡ _____

21 1초를 남기고 제가 마시멜로를 꼭대기에 꽂았어요.
➡ _____

22 B팀: 그냥 해라.
➡ _____

23 우리는 계획하는 데 많은 시간을 보내지 않았어요.
➡ _____

24 모든 팀원들이 바로 탑을 만들기 시작했어요.
➡ _____

25 우리의 첫 번째 탑은 텐트 같았어요.
➡ _____

26 그건 그다지 높지 않았어요.
➡ _____

27 우리는 다시 시도했어요.
➡ _____

28 다음 탑은 높았지만 스스로 서 있지 못했어요.
➡ _____

29 많은 시도 후에 우리는 아름답고 높은 탑을 만들 수 있었어요.
➡ _____

30 그것은 피사의 사탑 같았어요.
➡ _____

31 우리는 결국 우리가 원하는 것을 만들었어요!
➡ _____

32 C팀: 우리는 한 팀이다.
➡ _____

33 우리는 가장 좋은 아이디어를 고르려고 하지 않았어요.
➡ _____

34 대신에 우리는 좋은 아이디어를 골라 발전시켰어요.
➡ _____

35 한 친구가 우리에겐 튼튼한 기반이 필요하다고 말했어요.
➡ _____

36 또 다른 친구는 기반으로 삼각형 모양을 제안했어요.
➡ _____

37 우리 모두는 동의했고 시간 점검하는 사람과 테이프 자르는 사람과 같이 역할을 나눴어요.
➡ _____

38 우리는 하나의 팀으로 함께했어요.
➡ _____

39 마침내 우리는 높은 탑을 만들었어요!
➡ _____

구석구석 지문 Test

※ 다음 우리말과 일치하도록 빈칸에 알맞은 말을 쓰시오.

Think and Write Step 2

1. My _____ Group _____

2. My best group project was _____ a video _____ _____
   _____ _____.

3. The name of our group _____ 'The Stars' and we _____
   _____ _____.

4. First, we _____ a _____ _____.

5. _____, we _____ _____ the _____.

6. I _____ _____ _____ of reporter.

7. _____ was _____ _____ _____ _____ _____ the
   meeting time.

8. But our video _____ _____ _____ _____ great!

9. I learned _____ many _____ are _____ _____ one.

Think and Write Step 2

1. My _____ _____ _____

2. My best group project was _____ a _____ _____ about
   Paris.

3. _____ _____ _____ _____ _____ _____ was 'The Travelers'
   and we _____ _____ _____ _____.

4. First, we _____ Paris _____.

5. Then, we _____ _____ _____ _____ _____ _____.

6. I _____ _____ _____ _____ _____ a map of Paris.

7. _____ was difficult _____ _____
   _____.

8. But _____ _____ _____ _____ _____ _____ helped me.

9. I learned that _____ _____ _____ _____ _____ _____.

Project Culture Step 2

1. In Korea, _____ is natural _____ _____ _____ _____
   someone's _____.

2. But in _____ _____, _____ someone their age _____
   _____.

3. So _____ _____ when you _____.

1. 나의 최고의 모둠 과제
2. 나의 최고의 모둠 과제는 우리 학교를 소개하는 비디오 만들기였다.
3. 우리 모둠의 이름은 'The Stars'였고 4명의 모둠원이 있었다.
4. 먼저 우리는 함께 대화문을 썼다.
5. 다음으로 우리는 역할을 나누었다.
6. 나는 리포터의 역할을 맡았다.
7. 우리는 만나는 시간을 정하는 것이 어려웠다.
8. 하지만 우리 비디오는 훌륭하게 만들어졌다!
9. 나는 여러 사람이 한 사람보다 낫다는 것을 배웠다.

1. 나의 최고의 모둠 과제
2. 나의 최고의 모둠 과제는 파리에 대한 여행 안내 책자를 만드는 것이었다.
3. 우리 모둠의 이름은 'The Travelers'였고, 여섯 명의 모둠원이 있었다.
4. 먼저, 우리는 함께 파리를 조사했다.
5. 다음으로 우리는 역할을 나누었다.
6. 나는 파리의 지도를 그리는 역할을 맡았다.
7. 나는 지도를 그리는 것이 어려웠다.
8. 하지만 모둠원 중의 한 명이 나를 도와주었다.
9. 나는 협동 작업이 더 좋은 결과를 만든다는 것을 배웠다.

1. 한국에서는 누군가의 나이를 묻는 것은 자연스러운 것이다.
2. 그러나 서양의 국가들에서는, 누군가에게 그들의 나이를 묻는 것은 무례하다.
3. 그러므로 여행할 때 조심하라.

※ 다음 우리말을 영어로 쓰시오.

Think and Write Step 2

1. 나의 최고의 모둠 과제
➡ _____

2. 나의 최고의 모둠 과제는 우리 학교를 소개하는 비디오 만들기였다.
➡ _____

3. 우리 모둠의 이름은 'The Stars'였고 4명의 모둠원이 있었다.
➡ _____

4. 먼저 우리는 함께 대화문을 썼다.
➡ _____

5. 다음으로 우리는 역할을 나누었다.
➡ _____

6. 나는 리포터의 역할을 맡았다.
➡ _____

7. 우리는 만나는 시간을 정하는 것이 어려웠다.
➡ _____

8. 하지만 우리 비디오는 훌륭하게 만들어졌다!
➡ _____

9. 나는 여러 사람이 한 사람보다 낫다는 것을 배웠다.
➡ _____

Think and Write Step 2

1. 나의 최고의 모둠 과제
➡ _____

2. 나의 최고의 모둠 과제는 파리에 대한 여행 안내 책자를 만드는 것이었다.
➡ _____

3. 우리 모둠의 이름은 'The Travelers'였고, 여섯 명의 모둠원이 있었다.
➡ _____

4. 먼저, 우리는 함께 파리를 조사했다.
➡ _____

5. 다음으로 우리는 역할을 나누었다.
➡ _____

6. 나는 파리의 지도를 그리는 역할을 맡았다.
➡ _____

7. 나는 지도를 그리는 것이 어려웠다.
➡ _____

8. 하지만 모둠원 중의 한 명이 나를 도와주었다.
➡ _____

9. 나는 협동 작업이 더 좋은 결과를 만든다는 것을 배웠다.
➡ _____

Project Culture Step 2

1. 한국에서는 누군가의 나이를 묻는 것은 자연스러운 것이다.
➡ _____

2. 그러나 서양의 국가들에서는, 누군가에게 그들의 나이를 묻는 것은 무례하다.
➡ _____

3. 그러므로 여행할 때 조심하라.
➡ _____

※ 다음 영어를 우리말로 쓰시오.

01 almost _____

02 harm _____

03 ancient _____

04 condition _____

05 powder _____

06 reduce _____

07 survive _____

08 crop _____

09 recycle _____

10 donate _____

11 extreme _____

12 around _____

13 extremely _____

14 adventure _____

15 forever _____

16 harmful _____

17 survey _____

18 insect _____

19 produce _____

20 last _____

21 opinion _____

22 disappear _____

23 pollution _____

24 climate _____

25 pencil holder _____

26 deliver _____

27 pollen _____

28 environment _____

29 pollination _____

30 carefully _____

31 seed _____

32 chemical _____

33 provide _____

34 pleasure _____

35 a quarter of _____

36 break down _____

37 by oneself _____

38 less than _____

39 slow down _____

40 take part in _____

41 A such as B _____

42 let ~ down _____

43 a sheet of paper _____

※ 다음 우리말을 영어로 쓰시오.

01	화학 물질	
02	지속하다	
03	약 ~, 대략	
04	의견	
05	생산하다	
06	꽃가루	
07	고대의	
08	제공하다	
09	곡식	
10	사라지다	
11	환경	
12	재활용하다	
13	수분작용, 꽃가루 옮기기	
14	거의	
15	기후	
16	줄이다	
17	씨앗	
18	배달하다	
19	즐거움	
20	양치질하다	
21	설문조사; 설문조사를 하다	

22	기부하다	
23	가루	
24	극심한	
25	모험	
26	미세한, 섬세한	
27	영원히	
28	전 세계적인	
29	해로움, 피해	
30	오염	
31	살아남다	
32	극심하게	
33	해로운	
34	곤충	
35	사실	
36	버리다	
37	분해되다	
38	~보다 적은, ~ 이하	
39	뽑다, 집다	
40	B와 같은 A	
41	혼자서	
42	샤워하다	
43	종이 한 장	

※ 다음 영영풀이에 알맞은 단어를 <보기>에서 골라 쓴 후, 우리말 뜻을 쓰시오.

1 _____ : very thin or narrow: _____

2 _____ : a fine powder produced by flowers: _____

3 _____ : to become impossible to see: _____

4 _____ : to continue to live or exist: _____

5 _____ : having existed for a very long time: _____

6 _____ : a small creature such as a fly or ant, that has six legs: _____

7 _____ : a black and yellow flying insect that makes honey: _____

8 _____ : a plant such as wheat, rice, or fruit that is grown by farmers: _____

9 _____ : to take goods, letters, etc. to a particular place: _____

10 _____ : to make something less or smaller in size, quantity, price, etc.: _____

11 _____ : the process of making air, water, soil, etc. dirty; the state of being dirty:
_____

12 _____ : the small hard part produced by a plant, from which a new plant can
grow: _____

13 _____ : to give something to a person or an organization in order to help them:
_____

14 _____ : an exciting experience in which dangerous or unusual things happen:
_____

15 _____ : to treat things that have already been used so that they can be used again:
_____

16 _____ : an investigation of the opinions, behaviour, etc. of a particular group of
people, which is usually done by asking them questions: _____

보기			
recycle	reduce	survive	insect
donate	deliver	fine	crop
ancient	pollen	disappear	bee
survey	pollution	seed	adventure

※ 다음 우리말과 일치하도록 빈칸에 알맞은 말을 쓰시오.

Listen and Speak 1 A

B: Jane, _____ the _____?

G: My brother _____ his leg.

B: Oh, _____ _____ _____ _____ that.

G: I'm _____ _____ him.

B: _____ worry. He'll be okay.

B: Jane, 무슨 일 있니?
G: 내 남동생이 다리가 부러졌어.
B: 오, 그 말을 들으니 안타까워.
G: 동생이 걱정돼.
B: 걱정하지 마. 동생은 괜찮을 거야.

Listen and Speak 1 B

G: Are you _____ _____ our soccer game today, Sam?

B: Kathy, _____ you _____ the news?

G: No, I _____. What _____ it _____?

B: The yellow dust is _____ today.

G: Oh, no. _____ _____ can cause many _____ problems.

B: Yeah, _____ _____ _____ our health.

G: We can play _____ day.

B: You're right. I'll _____ _____ _____ team members _____ _____.

G: Great idea.

G: 오늘 축구 경기를 할 준비가 됐니, Sam?
B: Kathy, 뉴스 못 봤니?
G: 응, 못 봤어. 뉴스에서 뭐라고 했니?
B: 오늘 황사가 정말 심각하대.
G: 오, 안 돼. 황사는 많은 건강상의 문제를 일으킬 수 있어.
B: 응, 나는 우리의 건강이 걱정돼.
G: 우리 다른 날 경기를 할 수도 있잖아.
B: 맞아. 내가 당장 다른 팀원들에게 문자를 보낼게.
G: 좋은 생각이야.

Listen and Speak 1 C

1. A: _____ _____ about _____ _____.

   B: Me, too. It's _____.

   A: _____ can we do _____ _____?

   B: We can use _____ plastic.

2. A: I'm _____ _____ _____ bees.

   B: Me, too. It's _____.

   A: _____ _____ we do to help?

   B: We can _____ _____ trees for them.

3. A: _____ _____ _____ hungry children in Africa.

   B: Me, _____. It's _____.

   A: _____ _____ _____ _____ to help?

   B: We can _____ money _____ them.

1. A: 나는 지구 온난화가 걱정돼.
   B: 나도. 그건 끔찍해.
   A: 우리가 돕기 위해 무엇을 할 수 있을까?
   B: 우리가 플라스틱을 덜 사용할 수 있어.

2. A: 나는 사라지는 벌들이 걱정돼.
   B: 나도. 그건 끔찍해.
   A: 우리가 돕기 위해 무엇을 할 수 있을까?
   B: 우리가 더 많은 나무들을 심을 수 있어.

3. A: 나는 아프리카의 배고픈 아이들이 걱정돼.
   B: 나도. 그건 끔찍해.
   A: 우리가 돕기 위해 무엇을 할 수 있을까?
   B: 우리가 그들에게 돈을 기부할 수 있어.

Listen and Speak 2 A

B: My neck _____.

G: Be _____ _____ _____ get text neck.

B: _____ _____ _____ _____ _____ it?

G: Yes. You _____ _____ _____ your neck often.

B: Okay, I will. Thanks.

B: 목이 아파.
G: '텍스트넥'이 되지 않도록 조심해.
B: 너는 그걸 막는 방법을 아니?
G: 응. 너는 목을 자주 스트레칭해야 해.
B: 응, 그럴게, 고마워.

Listen and Speak 2 B

G: Jinsu, did you _____ _____ polar bears are _____ _____?

B: Yes. I read about it in an _____. _____ _____ _____ global warming.

G: Right. Their homes _____ _____ _____ and their food is _____.

B: We should do _____ _____ it.

G: Do you know _____ _____ _____ _____ _____ _____ _____?

B: Well, we can start _____ _____ energy.

G: Right. We _____ _____ _____ _____ the lights _____ we _____ the room.

B: That's a good idea.

G: 진수야, 너는 북극곰이 위험에 처해 있다는 걸 알고 있었니?
B: 응. 기사에서 그것에 관해 읽었어. 그건 지구 온난화 때문이야.
G: 맞아. 그들의 서식지가 녹아 없어지고 있고 그들의 먹이는 사라지고 있어.
B: 우리는 그것과 관련해 뭔가를 해야 해.
G: 너는 지구 온난화를 늦추는 방법을 아니?
B: 음, 우리는 에너지를 절약하는 것부터 시작할 수 있어.
G: 맞아. 우리는 방을 나올 때 불을 꺼야 해.
B: 좋은 생각이야.

Listen and Speak 2 C 1

A: _____ I _____ you _____?

B: Of _____. What is it?

A: _____ _____ _____ _____ to do a team project well?

B: Yes. You need _____ listen _____ to _____ _____.

A: 뭐 좀 물어봐도 되니?
B: 물론이지. 뭔데?
A: 어떻게 조별과제를 잘하는지 아니?
B: 응. 너는 다른 사람들의 의견을 주의 깊게 들을 필요가 있어.

Listen and Speak 2 C 2

A: Can I _____ you _____?

B: Of _____. What is it?

A: Do you _____ _____ _____ _____ water?

B: Yes. You _____ _____ _____ _____ the water _____ you _____ _____ _____.

A: 뭐 좀 물어봐도 되니?
B: 물론이지. 뭔데?
A: 물을 절약하는 방법을 아니?
B: 응. 양치질을 할 때 물을 끌 필요가 있어.

Listen and Speak 2 C 3

A: Can I _____ you something?

B: Of course. What is it?

A: Do ytou know _____ _____ _____ _____?

B: Yes. You _____ _____ _____ _____ fast food.

A: 뭐 좀 물어봐도 되니?
B: 물론이지. 뭔데?
A: 너는 건강하게 먹는 방법을 아니?
B: 응. 패스트 푸드를 덜 먹을 필요가 있어.

Real Life Talk Step 1

Minho: Linda, _____ _____ _____ the TV program, *The Sick Planet*?

Linda: Yes, I _____. _____ _____ _____ our planet.

Minho: Me, too. We _____ _____ _____ _____ _____ the Earth.

Linda: You're _____. Hey! Why _____ _____ _____ _____ _____ Earth Hour?

Minho: Earth Hour? What's that?

Linda: It's a world _____ for the _____.

Minho: Sounds great! _____ _____ _____ _____ _____ _____ _____ it?

Linda: Sure. We turn _____ our lights _____ _____ an hour.

Minho: That's so _____! So, _____ do we do it?

Linda: I'm not sure. It's _____ _____ _____.

Minho: Let's _____ _____ _____ on the Internet.

민호: Linda, '병든 행성'이라는 TV 프로그램 봤니?
Linda: 응, 봤어. 나는 우리 지구가 걱정돼.
민호: 나도. 우리는 지구를 구하기 위해 조치를 취해야 해.
Linda: 맞아. 얘! 우리 'Earth Hour'에 참여하는 게 어때?
민호: 'Earth Hour'? 그게 뭐니?
Linda: 그건 환경을 위한 세계적인 운동이야.
민호: 좋을 거 같아! 그것에 참여하는 방법을 아니?
Linda: 물론이야. 한 시간 동안 전등들을 함께 끄는 거야.
민호: 정말 간단하네! 그러면 언제 그것을 하는 거니?
Linda: 잘 모르겠어. 그건 매년 달라.
민호: 인터넷에서 찾아보자.

Real Life Talk Step 2

A: _____ _____ _____ _____ of this picture?

B: I think it's _____. _____ _____ _____ air pollution.

A: _____ _____ _____ _____ air pollution?

B: Yes. We _____ _____ use _____ _____.

A: 이 그림에 대해 어떻게 생각하니?
B: 끔찍하다고 생각해. 나는 공기 오염이 걱정돼.
A: 공기 오염을 줄이는 방법을 아니?
B: 응. 우리는 대중교통을 이용할 필요가 있어.

※ 다음 우리말에 맞도록 대화를 영어로 쓰시오.

Listen and Speak 1 A

B: _____

G: _____

B: _____

G: _____

B: _____

B: Jane, 무슨 일 있니?
G: 내 남동생이 다리가 부러졌어.
B: 오, 그 말을 들으니 안타까워.
G: 동생이 걱정돼.
B: 걱정하지 마. 동생은 괜찮을 거야.

Listen and Speak 1 B

G: _____

B: _____

G: _____

B: _____

G: _____

B: _____

G: _____

B: _____

G: _____

G: 오늘 축구 경기를 할 준비가 됐니, Sam?
B: Kathy, 뉴스 못 봤니?
G: 응, 못 봤어. 뉴스에서 뭐라고 했니?
B: 오늘 황사가 정말 심각하대.
G: 오, 안 돼. 황사는 많은 건강상의 문제를 일으킬 수 있어.
B: 응, 나는 우리의 건강이 걱정돼.
G: 우리 다른 날 경기를 할 수도 있잖아.
B: 맞아. 내가 당장 다른 팀원들에게 문자를 보낼게.
G: 좋은 생각이야.

Listen and Speak 1 C

1. A: _____

   B: _____

   A: _____

   B: _____

2. A: _____

   B: _____

   A: _____

   B: _____

3. A: _____

   B: _____

   A: _____

   B: _____

1. A: 나는 지구 온난화가 걱정돼.
   B: 나도. 그건 끔찍해.
   A: 우리가 돕기 위해 무엇을 할 수 있을까?
   B: 우리가 플라스틱을 덜 사용할 수 있어.

2. A: 나는 사라지는 벌들이 걱정돼.
   B: 나도. 그건 끔찍해.
   A: 우리가 돕기 위해 무엇을 할 수 있을까?
   B: 우리가 더 많은 나무들을 심을 수 있어.

3. A: 나는 아프리카의 배고픈 아이들이 걱정돼.
   B: 나도. 그건 끔찍해.
   A: 우리가 돕기 위해 무엇을 할 수 있을까?
   B: 우리가 그들에게 돈을 기부할 수 있어.

Listen and Speak 2 A

B: _____

G: _____

B: _____

G: _____

B: _____

B: 목이 아파.
G: '텍스트넥'이 되지 않도록 조심해.
B: 너는 그걸 막는 방법을 아니?
G: 응. 너는 목을 자주 스트레칭해야 해.
B: 응, 그럴게, 고마워.

Listen and Speak 2 B

G: _____

B: _____

G: _____

B: _____

G: _____

B: _____

G: _____

B: _____

G: 진수야, 너는 북극곰이 위험에 처해 있다는 걸 알고 있었니?
B: 응. 기사에서 그것에 관해 읽었어. 그건 지구 온난화 때문이야.
G: 맞아. 그들의 서식지가 녹아 없어지고 있고 그들의 먹이는 사라지고 있어.
B: 우리는 그것과 관련해 뭔가를 해야 해.
G: 너는 지구 온난화를 늦추는 방법을 아니?
B: 음, 우리는 에너지를 절약하는 것부터 시작할 수 있어.
G: 맞아. 우리는 방을 나올 때 불을 꺼야 해.
B: 좋은 생각이야.

Listen and Speak 2 C 1

A: _____

B: _____

A: _____

B: _____

A: 뭐 좀 물어봐도 되니?
B: 물론이지. 뭔데?
A: 어떻게 조별과제를 잘하는지 아니?
B: 응. 너는 다른 사람들의 의견을 주의 깊게 들을 필요가 있어.

Listen and Speak 2 C 2

A: _____

B: _____

A: _____

B: _____

A: 뭐 좀 물어봐도 되니?
B: 물론이지. 뭔데?
A: 물을 절약하는 방법을 아니?
B: 응. 양치질을 할 때 물을 끌 필요가 있어.

Listen and Speak 2 C 3

A: _____

B: _____

A: _____

B: _____

A: 뭐 좀 물어봐도 되니?
B: 물론이지. 뭔데?
A: 너는 건강하게 먹는 방법을 아니?
B: 응. 패스트 푸드를 덜 먹을 필요가 있어.

Real Life Talk Step 1

Minho: _____

Linda: _____

Minho: _____

Linda: _____

Minho: _____

Linda: _____

Minho: _____

Linda: _____

Minho: _____

Linda: _____

Minho: _____

민호: Linda, '병든 행성'이라는 TV 프로그램 봤니?
Linda: 응, 봤어. 나는 우리 지구가 걱정돼.
민호: 나도. 우리는 지구를 구하기 위해 조치를 취해야 해.
Linda: 맞아. 얘! 우리 'Earth Hour'에 참여하는 게 어때?
민호: 'Earth Hour'? 그게 뭐니?
Linda: 그건 환경을 위한 세계적인 운동이야.
민호: 좋을 거 같아! 그것에 참여하는 방법을 아니?
Linda: 물론이야. 한 시간 동안 전등들을 함께 끄는 거야.
민호: 정말 간단하네! 그러면 언제 그것을 하는 거니?
Linda: 잘 모르겠어. 그건 매년 달라.
민호: 인터넷에서 찾아보자.

Real Life Talk Step 2

A: _____

B: _____

A: _____

B: _____

A: 이 그림에 대해 어떻게 생각하니?
B: 끔찍하다고 생각해. 나는 공기 오염이 걱정돼.
A: 공기 오염을 줄이는 방법을 아니?
B: 응. 우리는 대중교통을 이용할 필요가 있어.

※ 다음 우리말과 일치하도록 빈칸에 알맞은 것을 골라 쓰시오.

1 _____ _____

    A. Bees   B. Disappearing

2 Where _____ _____ the honey bees _____ ?

    A. gone   B. have   C. all

3 _____ is really hard _____ _____ them _____ days.

    A. these   B. see   C. it   D. to

4 The _____ are _____ !

    A. disappearing   B. bees

5 _____ a _____ of the bee _____ dies _____ year.

    A. every   B. third   C. population   D. about

6 This is _____ _____ for bees, but it's _____ _____ news for people.

    A. worse   B. bad   C. news   D. even

7 Bees are very _____ _____ _____ .

    A. to   B. helpful   C. humans

8 First, bees _____ _____ _____ .

    A. us   B. give   C. honey

9 Honey is a _____ _____ _____ .

    A. food   B. wonderful   C. truly

10 It is _____ _____ our _____ and _____ great.

    A. tastes   B. good   C. health   D. for

11 Honey can _____ _____ _____ .

    A. forever   B. last   C. almost

12 In _____ , honey from _____ Egypt can _____ _____ today!

    A. fact   B. eaten   C. ancient   D. be

13 Second, bees help _____ many _____ _____ apples and strawberries.

    A. such   B. crops   C. as   D. produce

14 These crops cannot _____ _____ _____ _____ .

    A. by   B. be   C. themselves   D. produced

15 They _____ the _____ of _____ .

    A. help   B. need   C. bees

16 Bees help _____ _____ _____ _____ pollination.

    A. of   B. the   C. in   D. process

1 사라지는 벌들

2 꿀벌들은 모두 어디로 갔을까?

3 요즘 꿀벌을 보는 것은 정말 어렵다.

4 벌들이 사라지고 있다!

5 벌 개체 수의 약 3분의 1 정도가 매년 죽는다.

6 이것은 벌들에게 나쁜 소식이지만, 사람들에게는 훨씬 더 나쁜 소식이다.

7 벌은 인간에게 매우 도움이 된다.

8 첫째, 벌은 우리에게 꿀을 준다.

9 꿀은 정말 굉장한 음식이다.

10 그것은 건강에 좋고 맛이 좋다.

11 꿀은 거의 영원히 상하지 않을 수 있다.

12 실제로 고대 이집트 때의 꿀은 오늘날에도 먹을 수 있다!

13 둘째, 벌은 사과와 딸기 같은 많은 농작물을 생산하는 데 도움이 된다.

14 이 농작물들은 스스로 생산될 수 없다.

15 그들은 벌의 도움이 필요하다.

16 벌은 수분 과정에서 도움을 준다.

17 _____ bees _____ _____
A. help   B. how   C. pollination

18 _____ is _____?
A. pollination   B. what

19 It is _____ _____ from one flower to _____ to make _____.
A. pollen   B. seeds   C. moving   D. another

20 _____ is _____?
A. pollen   B. what

21 It is a _____ yellow _____ _____ by flowers.
A. produced   B. fine   C. powder

22 _____ are _____ _____?
A. disappearing B. bees   C. why

23 One of the _____ is _____ _____.
A. change   B. reasons   C. climate

24 _____ _____ has brought _____ hot and cold _____.
A. warming   B. weather   C. extremely   D. global

25 Bees _____ _____ in these _____.
A. conditions   B. survive   C. cannot

26 _____ _____ is the _____ chemicals farmers use on _____.
A. harmful   B. reason   C. crops   D. another

27 These chemicals kill _____ _____ bad insects, _____ also good _____, like bees.
A. but   B. only   C. insects   D. not

28 Then _____ can we do _____ _____ our _____ yellow friends?
A. little   B. help   C. what   D. to

29 First, we can _____ more _____ and _____.
A. flowers   B. plant   C. trees

30 This will _____ a good environment _____ bees to _____.
A. in   B. provide   C. live   D. for

31 Also, trees _____ _____ _____ global warming.
A. slow   B. help   C. down

32 Second, the _____ of _____ chemicals on _____ must be _____.
A. stopped   B. harmful   C. crops   D. use

33 These _____ are _____ _____ bees and people.
A. unhealthy   B. for   C. chemicals

34 Our _____ friends _____ our _____.
A. help   B. little   C. need

35 Let's not _____ _____ _____!
A. them   B. let   C. down

17 벌이 수분을 돕는 방법

18 수분은 무엇인가?

19 그것은 씨를 만들기 위해 한 꽃에서 다른 꽃으로 꽃가루가 옮겨지는 것이에요.

20 꽃가루는 무엇인가?

21 그것은 꽃에 의해 생산되는 아주 작은 노란색 가루예요.

22 벌은 왜 없어지고 있을까?

23 그 이유 중 하나는 기후 변화이다.

24 지구 온난화는 극도로 덥고 추운 날씨를 가져왔다.

25 벌은 이런 환경에서 살아남을 수 없다.

26 다른 이유는 농부들이 농작물에 사용하는 해로운 화학 물질이다.

27 이 화학 물질은 해로운 곤충뿐만 아니라 벌과 같은 이로운 곤충도 죽인다.

28 그러면 우리는 우리의 작고 노란 친구들을 돕기 위해 무엇을 할 수 있을까?

29 첫째, 우리는 더 많은 꽃과 나무를 심을 수 있다.

30 이것은 벌에게 살기 좋은 환경을 제공할 것이다.

31 또한 나무는 지구 온난화를 늦추는 데 도움이 된다.

32 둘째, 농작물에 해로운 화학 물질의 사용을 멈춰야만 한다.

33 이 화학 물질은 벌과 사람의 건강에 좋지 않다.

34 우리의 작은 친구들이 우리의 도움을 필요로 한다.

35 그들을 실망시키지 말자!

Step2

※ 다음 우리말과 일치하도록 빈칸에 알맞은 말을 쓰시오.

1 _____ Bees

2 Where _____ all the honey bees _____?

3 _____ is really hard _____ _____ them _____ _____.

4 The bees are _____!

5 About _____ _____ of the bee population dies _____ _____.

6 This is _____ _____ for bees, but it's _____ _____ _____ for people.

7 Bees are very _____ _____ _____.

8 _____, bees _____ _____ _____ _____.

9 Honey is a _____ _____ food.

10 It _____ _____ _____ _____ our health and _____ great.

11 Honey can _____ _____ _____.

12 _____ _____, honey from ancient Egypt _____ _____ _____ today!

13 _____, bees _____ _____ many crops _____ _____ apples and strawberries.

14 These crops cannot _____ _____ _____ _____.

15 They _____ _____ _____ of bees.

16 Bees help _____ _____ _____ _____ _____.

1 사라지는 벌들

2 꿀벌들은 모두 어디로 갔을까?

3 요즘 꿀벌을 보는 것은 정말 어렵다.

4 벌들이 사라지고 있다!

5 벌 개체 수의 약 3분의 1 정도가 매년 죽는다.

6 이것은 벌들에게 나쁜 소식이지만, 사람들에게는 훨씬 더 나쁜 소식이다.

7 벌은 인간에게 매우 도움이 된다.

8 첫째, 벌은 우리에게 꿀을 준다.

9 꿀은 정말 굉장한 음식이다.

10 그것은 건강에 좋고 맛이 좋다.

11 꿀은 거의 영원히 상하지 않을 수 있다.

12 실제로 고대 이집트 때의 꿀은 오늘날에도 먹을 수 있다!

13 둘째, 벌은 사과와 딸기 같은 많은 농작물을 생산하는 데 도움이 된다.

14 이 농작물들은 스스로 생산될 수 없다.

15 그들은 벌의 도움이 필요하다.

16 벌은 수분 과정에서 도움을 준다.

17 _____ bees help _____

18 _____ is _____?

19 It is _____ _____ _____ one flower _____ another _____ _____ _____.

20 What is _____?

21 It is a _____ _____ _____ _____ _____ flowers.

22 _____ are bees _____?

23 _____ _____ the _____ is _____ _____.

24 _____ _____ has brought _____ hot and cold weather.

25 Bees _____ _____ in these _____.

26 _____ _____ is the _____ _____ _____ use on crops.

27 These chemicals kill _____ _____ bad insects, _____ _____ good insects, _____ bees.

28 Then _____ can we do _____ _____ our little yellow friends?

29 First, we can plant _____ _____ _____ _____.

30 This will _____ a good environment _____ bees _____ _____ _____.

31 Also, trees help _____ _____ _____ _____.

32 Second, the use of harmful chemicals on crops _____ _____ _____.

33 These chemicals _____ _____ _____ bees and people.

34 Our _____ friends _____ _____ _____.

35 _____ not _____ _____ _____!

17	벌이 수분을 돕는 방법
18	수분은 무엇인가?
19	그것은 씨를 만들기 위해 한 꽃에서 다른 꽃으로 꽃가루가 옮겨지는 것이에요.
20	꽃가루는 무엇인가?
21	그것은 꽃에 의해 생산되는 아주 작은 노란색 가루예요.
22	벌은 왜 없어지고 있을까?
23	그 이유 중 하나는 기후 변화이다.
24	지구 온난화는 극도로 덥고 추운 날씨를 가져왔다.
25	벌은 이런 환경에서 살아남을 수 없다.
26	다른 이유는 농부들이 농작물에 사용하는 해로운 화학 물질이다.
27	이 화학 물질은 해로운 곤충뿐만 아니라 벌과 같은 이로운 곤충도 죽인다.
28	그러면 우리는 우리의 작고 노란 친구들을 돕기 위해 무엇을 할 수 있을까?
29	첫째, 우리는 더 많은 꽃과 나무를 심을 수 있다.
30	이것은 벌에게 살기 좋은 환경을 제공할 것이다.
31	또한 나무는 지구 온난화를 늦추는 데 도움이 된다.
32	둘째, 농작물에 해로운 화학 물질의 사용을 멈춰야만 한다.
33	이 화학 물질은 벌과 사람의 건강에 좋지 않다.
34	우리의 작은 친구들이 우리의 도움을 필요로 한다.
35	그들을 실망시키지 말자!

※ 다음 문장을 우리말로 쓰시오.

1 Disappearing Bees

➡ _____

2 Where have all the honey bees gone?

➡ _____

3 It is really hard to see them these days.

➡ _____

4 The bees are disappearing!

➡ _____

5 About a third of the bee population dies every year.

➡ _____

6 This is bad news for bees, but it's even worse news for people.

➡ _____

7 Bees are very helpful to humans.

➡ _____

8 First, bees give us honey.

➡ _____

9 Honey is a truly wonderful food.

➡ _____

10 It is good for our health and tastes great.

➡ _____

11 Honey can last almost forever.

➡ _____

12 In fact, honey from ancient Egypt can be eaten today!

➡ _____

13 Second, bees help produce many crops such as apples and strawberries.

➡ _____

14 These crops cannot be produced by themselves.

➡ _____

15 They need the help of bees.

➡ _____

16 Bees help in the process of pollination.

➡ _____

17 How bees help pollination
➡ _____

18 What is pollination?
➡ _____

19 It is moving pollen from one flower to another to make seeds.
➡ _____

20 What is pollen?
➡ _____

21 It is a fine yellow powder produced by flower
➡ _____

22 Why are bees disappearing?
➡ _____

23 One of the reasons is climate change.
➡ _____

24 Global warming has brought extremely hot and cold weather.
➡ _____

25 Bees cannot survive in these conditions.
➡ _____

26 Another reason is the harmful chemicals farmers use on crops.
➡ _____

27 These chemicals kill not only bad insects, but also good insects, like bees.
➡ _____

28 Then what can we do to help our little yellow friends?
➡ _____

29 First, we can plant more flowers and trees.
➡ _____

30 This will provide a good environment for bees to live in.
➡ _____

31 Also, trees help slow down global warming.
➡ _____

32 Second, the use of harmful chemicals on crops must be stopped.
➡ _____

33 These chemicals are unhealthy for bees and people.
➡ _____

34 Our little friends need our help.
➡ _____

35 Let's not let them down!
➡ _____

※ 다음 괄호 안의 단어들을 우리말에 맞도록 바르게 배열하시오.

1 (Bees / Disappearing)

➡ _____

2 (have / where / the / all / bees / honey / gone?)

➡ _____

3 (is / it / hard / really / see / to / these / them / days.)

➡ _____

4 (bees / the / disappearing! / are)

➡ _____

5 (a / about / of / third / the / population / bee / every / dies / year.)

➡ _____

6 (is / this / news / bad / bees, / for / it's / but / worse / even / news / people. / for)

➡ _____

7 (are / bees / helpful / very / humans. / to)

➡ _____

8 (bees / first, / us / honey. / give)

➡ _____

9 (is / honey / truly / a / food. / wonderful)

➡ _____

10 (is / it / for / good / health / our / tastes / great. / and)

➡ _____

11 (can / honey / almost / forever. / last)

➡ _____

1 사라지는 벌들

2 꿀벌들은 모두 어디로 갔을까?

3 요즘 꿀벌을 보는 것은 정말 어렵다.

4 벌들이 사라지고 있다!

5 벌 개체 수의 약 3분의 1 정도가 매년 죽는다.

6 이것은 벌들에게 나쁜 소식이지만, 사람들에게는 훨씬 더 나쁜 소식이다.

7 벌은 인간에게 매우 도움이 된다.

8 첫째, 벌은 우리에게 꿀을 준다.

9 꿀은 정말 굉장한 음식이다.

10 그것은 건강에 좋고 맛이 좋다.

11 꿀은 거의 영원히 상하지 않을 수 있다.

12 (fact, / in / from / honey / Egypt / ancient / be / can / today! / eaten)

➡ _____

13 (bees / second, / produce / help / crops / many / as / such / strawberries. / and / apples)

➡ _____

14 (crops / these / be / cannot / by / produced / themselves.)

➡ _____

15 (need / they / help / of / the / bees.)

➡ _____

16 (help / bees / the / in / process / pollination. / of)

➡ _____

17 (bees / how / pollination / help)

➡ _____

18 (is / what / pollination?)

➡ _____

19 (is / it / pollen / moving / one / from / flower / another / to / make / seeds. / to)

➡ _____

20 (is / what / pollen?)

➡ _____

21 (is / it / fine / a / powder / yellow / by / flowers. / produced)

➡ _____

22 (are / why / disappearing? / bees)

➡ _____

23 (of / one / reasons / the / climate / change. / is)

➡ _____

12 실제로 고대 이집트 때의 꿀은 오늘날에도 먹을 수 있다!

13 둘째, 벌은 사과와 딸기 같은 많은 농작물을 생산하는 데 도움이 된다.

14 이 농작물들은 스스로 생산될 수 없다.

15 그들은 벌의 도움이 필요하다.

16 벌은 수분 과정에서 도움을 준다.

17 벌이 수분을 돕는 방법

18 수분은 무엇인가?

19 그것은 씨를 만들기 위해 한 꽃에서 다른 꽃으로 꽃가루가 옮겨지는 것이에요.

20 꽃가루는 무엇인가?

21 그것은 꽃에 의해 생산되는 아주 작은 노란색 가루예요.

22 벌은 왜 없어지고 있을까?

23 그 이유 중 하나는 기후 변화이다.

24 (warming / global / brought / has / hot / extremely / cold / and / weather.)

➡ _____

25 (cannot / bees / in / survive / conditions. / these)

➡ _____

26 (reason / another / the / is / chemicals / harmful / use / farmers / crops. / on)

➡ _____

27 (chemicals / these / not / kill / only / insects, / bad / also / good / but / insects, / bees. / like)

➡ _____

28 (what / then / we / can / to / do / help / little / our / friends? / yellow)

➡ _____

29 (we / first, / plant / can / flowers / more / trees. / and)

➡ _____

30 (will / this / a / provide / environment / good / bees / for / in. / live / to)

➡ _____

31 (trees / also, / slow / help / global / down / warming.)

➡ _____

32 (the / second, / of / use / chemicals / harmful / crops / on / be / must / stopped.)

➡ _____

33 (chemicals / these / unhealthy / are / bees / and / for / people.)

➡ _____

34 (little / our / need / friends / help. / our)

➡ _____

35 (not / let's / them / let / down!)

➡ _____

24 지구 온난화는 극도로 덥고 추운 날씨를 가져왔다.

25 벌은 이런 환경에서 살아남을 수 없다.

26 다른 이유는 농부들이 농작물에 사용하는 해로운 화학 물질이다.

27 이 화학 물질은 해로운 곤충뿐만 아니라 벌과 같은 이로운 곤충도 죽인다.

28 그러면 우리는 우리의 작고 노란 친구들을 돕기 위해 무엇을 할 수 있을까?

29 첫째. 우리는 더 많은 꽃과 나무를 심을 수 있다.

30 이것은 벌에게 살기 좋은 환경을 제공할 것이다.

31 또한 나무는 지구 온난화를 늦추는 데 도움이 된다.

32 둘째. 농작물에 해로운 화학 물질의 사용을 멈춰야만 한다.

33 이 화학 물질은 벌과 사람의 건강에 좋지 않다.

34 우리의 작은 친구들이 우리의 도움을 필요로 한다.

35 그들을 실망시키지 말자!

※ **다음 우리말을 영어로 쓰시오.**

1 사라지는 벌들

➡ _____

2 꿀벌들은 모두 어디로 갔을까?

➡ _____

3 요즘 꿀벌을 보는 것은 정말 어렵다.

➡ _____

4 벌들이 사라지고 있다!

➡ _____

5 벌 개체 수의 약 3분의 1 정도가 매년 죽는다.

➡ _____

6 이것은 벌들에게 나쁜 소식이지만, 사람들에게는 훨씬 더 나쁜 소식이다.

➡ _____

7 벌은 인간에게 매우 도움이 된다.

➡ _____

8 첫째, 벌은 우리에게 꿀을 준다.

➡ _____

9 꿀은 정말 굉장한 음식이다.

➡ _____

10 그것은 건강에 좋고 맛이 좋다.

➡ _____

11 꿀은 거의 영원히 상하지 않을 수 있다.

➡ _____

12 실제로 고대 이집트 때의 꿀은 오늘날에도 먹을 수 있다!

➡ _____

13 둘째, 벌은 사과와 딸기 같은 많은 농작물을 생산하는 데 도움이 된다.

➡ _____

14 이 농작물들은 스스로 생산될 수 없다.

➡ _____

15 그들은 벌의 도움이 필요하다.

➡ _____

16 벌은 수분 과정에서 도움을 준다.

➡ _____

17 벌이 수분을 돕는 방법

➡ _____

18 수분은 무엇인가?

➡ _____

19 그것은 씨를 만들기 위해 한 꽃에서 다른 꽃으로 꽃가루가 옮겨지는 것이에요.

➡ _____

20 꽃가루는 무엇인가?

➡ _____

21 그것은 꽃에 의해 생산되는 아주 작은 노란색 가루예요.

➡ _____

22 벌은 왜 없어지고 있을까?

➡ _____

23 그 이유 중 하나는 기후 변화이다.

➡ _____

24 지구 온난화는 극도로 덥고 추운 날씨를 가져왔다.

➡ _____

25 벌은 이런 환경에서 살아남을 수 없다.

➡ _____

26 다른 이유는 농부들이 농작물에 사용하는 해로운 화학 물질이다.

➡ _____

27 이 화학 물질은 해로운 곤충뿐만 아니라 벌과 같은 이로운 곤충도 죽인다.

➡ _____

28 그러면 우리는 우리의 작고 노란 친구들을 돕기 위해 무엇을 할 수 있을까?

➡ _____

29 첫째, 우리는 더 많은 꽃과 나무를 심을 수 있다.

➡ _____

30 이것은 벌에게 살기 좋은 환경을 제공할 것이다.

➡ _____

31 또한 나무는 지구 온난화를 늦추는 데 도움이 된다.

➡ _____

32 둘째, 농작물에 해로운 화학 물질의 사용을 멈춰야만 한다.

➡ _____

33 이 화학 물질은 벌과 사람의 건강에 좋지 않다.

➡ _____

34 우리의 작은 친구들이 우리의 도움을 필요로 한다.

➡ _____

35 그들을 실망시키지 말자!

➡ _____

※ 다음 우리말과 일치하도록 빈칸에 알맞은 말을 쓰시오.

After You Read B

1. _____

2. About _____ _____ of the _____ _____ _____ every year.

3. _____

4. 1. _____ _____ has _____ climate change.

5. 2. Farmers _____ the _____ chemicals _____ _____.

6. _____

7. 1. _____ more flowers and trees _____ _____ a good _____ _____ _____.

8. 2. _____ _____ _____ _____ on crops.

1. 문제점
2. 벌 개체 수의 약 3분의 1 정도가 매년 죽는다.
3. 원인
4. 1. 지구 온난화가 기후 변화를 가져왔다.
5. 2. 농부들이 농작물에 해로운 화학 물질을 사용한다.
6. 해결책
7. 1. 벌들에게 좋은 환경을 제공하기 위해 더 많은 꽃과 나무를 심어라.
8. 2. 농작물에 해로운 화학 물질의 사용을 멈춰라.

Language Use - In Context

1. _____ _____ Cambodia

2. _____ _____ _____ Cambodia's population _____ the _____ _____ 15.

3. _____ of the country _____ _____ _____ forest.

4. 40 percent of the people _____ _____ _____ their money _____ _____.

1. 캄보디아에 관한 사실
2. 캄보디아 인구의 약 절반이 15세 이하이다.
3. 이 나라의 3분의 2는 숲으로 덮여 있다.
4. 사람들의 40 퍼센트는 그들 돈의 대부분을 음식에 쓴다.

Word Power

1. _____ _____ _____ all your _____.

2. A dictionary is very _____ _____ _____ language.

3. I didn't _____ _____ you any _____.

4. Strong sunlight _____ very _____ the _____.

1. 당신의 모든 도움에 감사드립니다.
2. 사전은 언어 공부에 매우 도움이 된다.
3. 당신에게 해를 끼치려고 한 것은 아니었습니다.
4. 강한 햇빛은 피부에 매우 해롭다.

※ 다음 우리말을 영어로 쓰시오.

After You Read B

1. 문제점
   ➡ _____

2. 벌 개체 수의 약 3분의 1 정도가 매년 죽는다
   ➡ _____

3. 원인
   ➡ _____

4. 1. 지구 온난화가 기후 변화를 가져왔다.
   ➡ _____

5. 2. 농부들이 농작물에 해로운 화학 물질을 사용한다.
   ➡ _____

6. 해결책
   ➡ _____

7. 1. 벌들에게 좋은 환경을 제공하기 위해 더 많은 꽃과 나무를 심어라.
   ➡ _____

8. 2. 농작물에 해로운 화학 물질의 사용을 멈춰라.
   ➡ _____

Language Use - In Context

1. 캄보디아에 관한 사실
   ➡ _____

2. 캄보디아 인구의 약 절반이 15세 이하이다.
   ➡ _____

3. 이 나라의 3분의 2는 숲으로 덮여 있다.
   ➡ _____

4. 사람들의 40 퍼센트는 그들 돈의 대부분을 음식에 쓴다.
   ➡ _____

Word Power

1. 당신의 모든 도움에 감사드립니다.
   ➡ _____

2. 사전은 언어 공부에 매우 도움이 된다.
   ➡ _____

3. 당신에게 해를 끼치려고 한 것은 아니었습니다.
   ➡ _____

4. 강한 햇빛은 피부에 매우 해롭다.
   ➡ _____

※ 다음 영어를 우리말로 쓰시오.

01	later	22	arrange
02	location	23	remove
03	vote	24	divide
04	wall painting	25	clearly
05	background	26	matter
06	bake	27	neat
07	rewarding	28	politely
08	neighborhood	29	donation
09	spot	30	manager
10	prepare	31	plant
11	nursing home	32	reply
12	select	33	suggest
13	deliver	34	volunteer
14	site	35	pick up
15	experience	36	get along with ~
16	friendly	37	be proud of ~
17	shelf	38	get together
18	fur	39	keep ~ in mind
19	pack	40	take a break
20	apply	41	make sure ~
21	recycling bin	42	be on time
		43	give ~ a hand

※ 다음 우리말을 영어로 쓰시오.

01 배경

02 운영자, 관리자

03 짐을 꾸리다

04 물감

05 기부, 기증

06 문제되다, 중요하다

07 깨끗한

08 현장, 장소

09 보람 있는

10 놀이 공원

11 경험

12 지원하다

13 분명하게

14 재활용 쓰레기통

15 배열하다

16 투표하다

17 선택하다, 선정하다

18 (특정한) 장소, 자리

19 벽화

20 양로원

21 예의 바르게

22 책꽂이

23 배달하다

24 근처, 이웃

25 준비하다

26 없애다, 제거하다

27 나누다

28 제안하다

29 자원봉사; 자원봉사하다

30 마을

31 응답하다

32 날개

33 나누다, 공유하다

34 칠판

35 치우다, 줍다

36 ~을 자랑스러워하다

37 줄서다

38 목욕시키다

39 휴식을 취하다

40 모이다

41 제 시간에 도착하다

42 ~와 사이좋게 지내다

43 ~에게 도움을 주다

※ 다음 영영풀이에 알맞은 단어를 <보기>에서 골라 쓴 후, 우리말 뜻을 쓰시오.

1 _____ : to be important: _____

2 _____ : a particular place: _____

3 _____ : to put a seed, flower, or plant in the ground: _____

4 _____ : to take something to a person or place: _____

5 _____ : to put things into cases, bags, etc. ready for a trip: _____

6 _____ : to move or take something away from a place: _____

7 _____ : a picture that you draw with a pencil, pen, etc.: _____

8 _____ : a person who does a job without being paid: _____

9 _____ : to cook something using dry heat, in an oven: _____

10 _____ : something that you give to help a person or organization: _____

11 _____ : to separate or make something separate into parts: _____

12 _____ : to put a group of things or people in a particular order or position:
_____

13 _____ : the area that is behind the main thing that you are looking at: _____

14 _____ : to choose someone or something from a group of people or things:
_____

15 _____ : a large park with many machines that you can ride on, such as roller
coasters: _____

16 _____ : someone whose job is to manage part or all of a company or other
organization: _____

보기			
manager	arrange	divide	location
pack	bake	donation	select
amusement park	volunteer	background	matter
deliver	remove	drawing	plant

※ 다음 우리말과 일치하도록 빈칸에 알맞은 말을 쓰시오.

Listen and Speak 1 A

B: _____ are all these boxes and books _____?

G: I'm _____ the books for the _____ center. Can you _____ _____ _____ hand?

B: Sure. What do you _____ me _____ do?

G: Please _____ the _____ _____ the boxes.

B: No _____.

Listen and Speak 1 B

B: What is _____ _____?

G: I'm _____ cookies.

B: _____ are you _____ so _____ cookies?

G: _____ _____ the people at the _____ _____.

B: That's very _____ _____ you.

G: _____ _____ me a _____?

B: Sure. What _____ _____ _____ _____ to do?

G: Please _____ the cookies in the _____ _____. Three cookies in _____ box.

B: Okay.

Listen and Speak 1 C

1. A: What are you _____?

   B: I'm _____ _____ my _____ tomorrow. _____ _____ _____ me?

   A: Sure. _____ _____ _____ _____ me _____ _____?

   B: Please _____ _____ _____ _____ the box.

   A: No problem.

2. A: What _____ you _____?

   B: I'm _____ _____ my _____ tomorrow. _____ _____ _____?

   A: Sure. What do you _____ _____ _____ _____?

   B: Please _____ the chairs _____.

   A: No problem.

B: 이 박스와 책들은 다 무엇에 쓰려는 거니?

G: 기부 센터에 보내려고 책을 싸고 있어. 도와줄래?

B: 물론이야. 내가 무엇을 하길 원하니?

G: 박스에 주소를 좀 써 줘.

B: 그래.

B: 이 엉망진창은 뭐니?

G: 쿠키를 굽고 있어.

B: 왜 이렇게 많은 쿠키를 굽고 있니?

G: 쿠키는 양로원에 계신 분들을 위한 거야.

B: 정말 착하구나.

G: 도와줄래?

B: 물론이야. 내가 무엇을 하길 원하니?

G: 선물 상자에 쿠키를 좀 넣어 줘. 상자 하나에 쿠키 3개씩.

B: 알겠어.

1. A: 너 뭐 하고 있니?
   B: 내일 이사를 위해 짐을 싸는 중이야. 도와줄래?
   A: 물론이지. 내가 무엇을 하길 원하니?
   B: 옷을 상자 안에 넣어 줘.
   A: 그래.

2. A: 너 뭐 하고 있니?
   B: 내일 이사를 위해 짐을 싸는 중이야. 도와줄래?
   A: 물론이지. 내가 무엇을 하길 원하니?
   B: 의자를 밖으로 옮겨 줘.
   A: 그래.

3. **A:** _____ _____ _____ _____?

   B: I'm _____ _____ my _____ tomorrow. _____ _____ _____ _____?

   A: Sure. _____ _____ _____ _____ _____ _____ _____?

   B: Please _____ _____ the trach.

   A: No problem.

Listen and Speak 2 A

B: _____ the concert, Mom.

W: Okay, I _____. Thanks. Your dinner _____ _____ the table.

B: All right. _____ _____ _____ me.

W: _____ _____ _____ _____ the dog _____ you have dinner.

B: Okay. Mom, you _____ go now. Dad is waiting in the car.

Listen and Speak 2 B

B: Hello, class. _____ _____ _____ four people and _____ around the tables. Today we're going _____ _____ bacon and egg sandwiches. _____ _____ _____ two rules for our class. First, _____ _____ you wash your hands _____ _____ _____. _____, be careful _____ you use a knife. All right, _____ start.

Listen and Speak 2 C

1. **A:** It's time _____ _____ home.

   B: Yes. _____ _____ you _____ the doors.

   A: Okay, I will. _____ else?

   B: No, _____ it. See you tomorrow.

2. **A:** It's _____ _____ go home.

   B: Yes. _____ _____ _____ _____ the board.

   A: Okay, I will. _____ _____?

   B: No, that's it. See you tomorrow.

3. **A:** _____ _____ _____ _____ home.

   B: Yes. _____ _____ you _____ _____ _____.

   A: Okay, I _____. Anything _____?

   B: No, that's it. See you tomorrow.

---

3. **A:** 너 뭐 하고 있니?
   B: 내일 이사를 위해 짐을 싸는 중이야. 도와줄래?
   A: 물론이지. 내가 무엇을 하길 원하니?
   B: 쓰레기를 밖에 갖다 버려 줘.
   A: 그래.

B: 콘서트 재미있게 보세요, 엄마.
W: 그래, 고마워. 저녁은 식탁에 있어.
B: 알겠어요. 저는 걱정 마세요.
W: 저녁 먹은 후에 개 밥 주는 거 명심해라.
B: 알겠어요. 엄마, 이제 가셔야 해요. 아빠가 차에서 기다리고 계셔요.

B: 안녕하세요, 여러분. 4명씩 모둠을 만들어 탁자에 둘러앉으세요. 오늘 우리는 베이컨 달걀 샌드위치를 만들 거예요. 우리 수업의 두 가지 규칙에 유의하세요. 첫째, 시작하기 전에 손을 씻는 것을 명심하세요. 둘째, 칼을 사용할 때 조심하세요. 좋아요, 시작해 봐요.

1. **A:** 집에 갈 시간이야.
   B: 응. 문 잠그는 거 명심해.
   A: 알겠어, 그렇게 할게. 또 다른 건?
   B: 없어, 그게 전부야. 내일 보자.

2. **A:** 이제 집에 갈 시간이야.
   B: 응. 칠판 닦는 거 명심해.
   A: 알겠어, 그렇게 할게. 또 다른 건?
   B: 없어, 그게 전부야. 내일 보자.

3. **A:** 이제 집에 갈 시간이야.
   B: 응. 식물에 물 주는 거 명심해.
   A: 알겠어, 그렇게 할게. 또 다른 건?
   B: 없어, 그게 전부야. 내일 보자.

Real Life Talk Watch a Video

Woman: Good morning. _____ _____ _____ _____ for you?

Tony: Hi. I'm _____ _____ the _____ _____.

Woman: Oh, you _____ _____ Tony.

Tony: That's right. _____ _____ _____ _____ _____ _____ today?

Woman: Please _____ this book _____ _____ _____ in the _____ _____.

Tony: No problem. _____ I _____ in now?

Woman: Yes. Please _____ Room 7.

Tony: Okay. Is there _____ _____ _____ mind?

Woman: Yes. _____ _____ _____ read _____ _____ _____.

Tony: Okay. I'll _____ _____ _____.

Real Life Talk Step 3

1. A: Hi, I'm Minsu. _____ _____ _____ the volunteer work.

   B: Thanks _____ _____, Minsu.

   A: What _____ _____ _____ _____ today?

   B: Please _____ the dog _____ _____.

   A: Okay. _____ _____ _____ to _____ _____ _____?

   B: Yes. _____ _____ you _____ the _____ first.

   A: Okay, I will.

2. A: Hi, I'm Tony. _____ _____ _____ _____.

   B: _____ _____ coming, Tony.

   A: _____ _____ _____ _____ _____ today?

   B: Please record a book _____ _____ _____.

   A: Okay. _____ _____ _____ _____ _____ ?

   B: Yes. Make _____ you read _____ and _____.

   A: Okay, I will.

Woman: 안녕하세요. 무엇을 도와드릴까요?

Tony: 안녕하세요. 저는 봉사 활동을 하러 왔어요.

Woman: 오, Tony군요.

Tony: 맞아요. 오늘 제가 무엇을 하길 원하세요?

Woman: 녹음실에서 시각 장애인들을 위해 이 책을 읽어 주세요.

Tony: 알겠어요. 지금 들어가야 하나요?

Woman: 네. 7번 방으로 들어가 주세요.

Tony: 네. 명심해야 할 것이 있나요?

Woman: 네. 천천히 그리고 명확하게 읽어야 하는 것을 명심하세요.

Tony: 네. 최선을 다할게요.

1. A: 안녕하세요. 저는 민수예요. 저는 봉사 활동을 하러 왔어요.
   B: 민수 군, 와 주셔서 감사합니다.
   A: 오늘 제가 무엇을 하길 원하세요?
   B: 개를 목욕시켜 주세요.
   A: 네. 명심해야 할 것이 있나요?
   B: 네. 털을 먼저 빗길 것을 명심하세요.
   A: 네. 그렇게 할게요.

2. A: 안녕하세요. 저는 Tony예요. 저는 봉사 활동을 하러 왔어요.
   B: Tony 군, 와 주셔서 감사합니다.
   A: 오늘 제가 무엇을 하길 원하세요?
   B: 시각 장애인들을 위해 책을 녹음해 주세요.
   A: 네. 유념해야 할 것이 있나요?
   B: 네. 천천히 그리고 명확하게 읽어야 하는 것을 명심하세요.
   A: 네. 그렇게 할게요.

※ 다음 우리말에 맞도록 대화를 영어로 쓰시오.

Listen and Speak 1 A

B: _____

G: _____

B: _____

G: _____

B: _____

B: 이 박스와 책들은 다 무엇에 쓰려는 거니?
G: 기부 센터에 보내려고 책을 싸고 있어. 도와줄래?
B: 물론이야. 내가 무엇을 하길 원하니?
G: 박스에 주소를 좀 써 줘.
B: 그래.

Listen and Speak 1 B

B: _____

G: _____

B: _____

G: _____

B: _____

G: _____

B: _____

G: _____

B: _____

B: 이 엉망진창은 뭐니?
G: 쿠키를 굽고 있어.
B: 왜 이렇게 많은 쿠키를 굽고 있니?
G: 쿠키는 양로원에 계신 분들을 위한 거야.
B: 정말 착하구나.
G: 도와줄래?
B: 물론이야. 내가 무엇을 하길 원하니?
G: 선물 상자에 쿠키를 좀 넣어 줘. 상자 하나에 쿠키 3개씩.
B: 알겠어.

Listen and Speak 1 C

1. A: _____

   B: _____

   A: _____

   B: _____

   A: _____

2. A: _____

   B: _____

   A: _____

   B: _____

   A: _____

1. A: 너 뭐 하고 있니?
   B: 내일 이사를 위해 짐을 싸는 중이야. 도와줄래?
   A: 물론이지. 내가 무엇을 하길 원하니?
   B: 옷을 상자 안에 넣어 줘.
   A: 그래.

2. A: 너 뭐 하고 있니?
   B: 내일 이사를 위해 짐을 싸는 중이야. 도와줄래?
   A: 물론이지. 내가 무엇을 하길 원하니?
   B: 의자를 밖으로 옮겨 줘.
   A: 그래.

3. A: _____

   B: _____

   A: _____

   B: _____

   A: _____

Listen and Speak 2 A

B: _____

W: _____

B: _____

W: _____

B: _____

Listen and Speak 2 B

B: _____

   _____

   _____

   _____

Listen and Speak 2 C

1. A: _____

   B: _____

   A: _____

   B: _____

2. A: _____

   B: _____

   A: _____

   B: _____

3. A: _____

   B: _____

   A: _____

   B: _____

---

3. A: 너 뭐 하고 있니?
   B: 내일 이사를 위해 짐을 싸는 중이야. 도와줄래?
   A: 물론이지. 내가 무엇을 하길 원하니?
   B: 쓰레기를 밖에 갖다 버려 줘.
   A: 그래.

B: 콘서트 재미있게 보세요, 엄마.
W: 그래. 고마워. 저녁은 식탁에 있어.
B: 알겠어요. 저는 걱정 마세요.
W: 저녁 먹은 후에 개 밥 주는 거 명심해라.
B: 알겠어요. 엄마, 이제 가셔야 해요. 아빠가 차에서 기다리고 계셔요.

B: 안녕하세요, 여러분. 4명씩 모둠을 만들어 탁자에 둘러앉으세요. 오늘 우리는 베이컨 달걀 샌드위치를 만들 거예요. 우리 수업의 두 가지 규칙에 유의하세요. 첫째, 시작하기 전에 손을 씻는 것을 명심하세요. 둘째, 칼을 사용할 때 조심하세요. 좋아요, 시작해 봐요.

1. A: 집에 갈 시간이야.
   B: 응. 문 잠그는 거 명심해.
   A: 알겠어, 그렇게 할게. 또 다른 건?
   B: 없어, 그게 전부야. 내일 보자.

2. A: 이제 집에 갈 시간이야.
   B: 응. 칠판 닦는 거 명심해.
   A: 알겠어, 그렇게 할게. 또 다른 건?
   B: 없어, 그게 전부야. 내일 보자.

3. A: 이제 집에 갈 시간이야.
   B: 응. 식물에 물 주는 거 명심해.
   A: 알겠어, 그렇게 할게. 또 다른 건?
   B: 없어, 그게 전부야. 내일 보자.

Real Life Talk Watch a Video

Woman: _____

Tony: _____

Woman: _____

Tony: _____

Woman: _____

Tony: _____

Woman: _____

Tony: _____

Woman: _____

Tony: _____

Woman: 안녕하세요. 무엇을 도와드릴까요?

Tony: 안녕하세요. 저는 봉사 활동을 하러 왔어요.

Woman: 오, Tony군요.

Tony: 맞아요. 오늘 제가 무엇을 하길 원하세요?

Woman: 녹음실에서 시각 장애인들을 위해 이 책을 읽어 주세요.

Tony: 알겠어요. 지금 들어가야 하나요?

Woman: 네. 7번 방으로 들어가 주세요.

Tony: 네. 명심해야 할 것이 있나요?

Woman: 네. 천천히 그리고 명확하게 읽어야 하는 것을 명심하세요.

Tony: 네. 최선을 다할게요.

Real Life Talk Step 3

1. A: _____

   B: _____

   A: _____

   B: _____

   A: _____

   B: _____

   A: _____

2. A: _____

   B: _____

   A: _____

   B: _____

   A: _____

   B: _____

   A: _____

1. A: 안녕하세요. 저는 민수예요. 저는 봉사 활동을 하러 왔어요.
   B: 민수 군, 와 주셔서 감사합니다.
   A: 오늘 제가 무엇을 하길 원하세요?
   B: 개를 목욕시켜 주세요.
   A: 네. 명심해야 할 것이 있나요?
   B: 네. 털을 먼저 빗길 것을 명심하세요.
   A: 네. 그렇게 할게요.

2. A: 안녕하세요. 저는 Tony예요. 저는 봉사 활동을 하러 왔어요.
   B: Tony 군, 와 주셔서 감사합니다.
   A: 오늘 제가 무엇을 하길 원하세요?
   B: 시각 장애인들을 위해 책을 녹음해 주세요.
   A: 네. 유념해야 할 것이 있나요?
   B: 네. 천천히 그리고 명확하게 읽어야 하는 것을 명심하세요.
   A: 네. 그렇게 할게요.

※ 다음 우리말과 일치하도록 빈칸에 알맞은 것을 골라 쓰시오.

1 _____ a _____ _____
A. Tomorrow   B. Paint   C. Better

2 Hi. _____ _____ _____ Homin.
A. is   B. name   C. my

3 _____ is me in _____ of the _____ painting.
A. front   B. wall   C. this

4 The wings are _____ pretty, _____ _____?
A. they   B. so   C. aren't

5 Many people like to _____ pictures in _____ of wall _____.
A. paintings   B. take   C. front

6 They make _____ _____ _____ and new.
A. bright   B. neighborhoods   C. old

7 _____ month, I visited a _____ _____ wall paintings in Yeosu.
A. with   B. last   C. village

8 As I was taking a picture, a _____ _____ _____ in my _____.
A. head   B. went   C. light   D. on

9 I _____, "I'm _____ the school _____ club.
A. in   B. art   C. thought

10 _____ _____ _____ do wall paintings _____ these?"
A. we   B. why   C. like   D. don't

11 I _____ this _____ at the next club _____, and the members loved it.
A. meeting   B. suggested   C. idea

12 We _____ a _____ _____ project _____ the Internet.
A. teen   B. found   C. on   D. volunteer

13 The project was _____ do a _____ _____ in our _____.
A. to   B. neighborhood   C. painting   D. wall

14 We _____ _____ it, and two weeks _____, our club was _____!
A. for   B. selected   C. applied   D. later

15 The _____ of the project _____ _____.
A. came   B. day   C. finally

16 The project manager _____ _____ _____ at the painting _____ at 9 a.m.
A. site   B. meet   C. had   D. us

17 The wall was _____ very _____ _____.
A. poor   B. condition   C. in

1 더 나은 내일을 그려라

2 안녕. 내 이름은 호민이야.

3 벽화 앞에 있는 사람이 나야.

4 날개가 예뻐, 그렇지 않니?

5 많은 사람들이 벽화 앞에서 사진 찍는 것을 좋아해.

6 벽화는 오래된 마을을 밝고 새롭게 만들어.

7 지난달에 나는 여수에 있는 벽화 마을을 방문했어.

8 내가 사진을 찍을 때 머릿속에 좋은 생각이 떠올랐어.

9 나는 생각했어. "나는 학교 미술 동아리에 있잖아.

10 우리가 이것처럼 벽화를 그리면 어떨까?

11 나는 이 아이디어를 다음 동아리 모임에서 제안했고, 동아리 부원들은 그것을 아주 좋아했어.

12 우리는 인터넷에서 청소년 봉사 프로젝트를 찾았어.

13 그 프로젝트는 우리 마을에 벽화를 그리는 것이었어.

14 우리는 거기에 지원했고, 2주 후에 우리 동아리가 선택되었어!

15 마침내 프로젝트 날이 되었어.

16 프로젝트 책임자는 우리를 오전 9시에 그림 그리는 곳에서 만나게 했어.

17 벽은 상태가 별로 좋지 않았어.

18 There were _____ _____ and _____ on some _____.
    A. writings   B. parts   C. strange   D. drawings

19 _____ _____ had old posters _____ them.
    A. on   B. parts   C. other

20 We _____ the posters first and painted _____ the writings and drawings _____ white _____.
    A. with   B. removed   C. paint   D. over

21 The manager _____ _____ _____ anything we wanted.
    A. us   B. let   C. paint

22 We _____ to paint _____ _____ because the wall was _____ an elementary school.
    A. cute   B. near   C. something   D. decided

23 We _____ _____ three groups and _____ painting.
    A. into   B. divided   C. began

24 I _____ _____ the _____ _____ Minsu and Jiwon.
    A. with   B. in   C. group   D. was

25 I _____ my _____ and started to _____ my favorite movie _____.
    A. character   B. chose   C. paint   D. spot

26 Minsu _____ some flowers and Jiwon _____ some _____.
    A. background   B. did   C. drawings   D. painted

27 Our club painted _____ _____ five _____.
    A. hours   B. for   C. about

28 _____ we _____, we got _____ and _____ the day's experiences.
    A. shared   B. together   C. finished   D. after

29 Minsu _____ _____ _____ _____ his flower painting.
    A. of   B. was   C. proud   D. very

30 He said, "My flower is _____ real _____ a bee _____ it."
    A. landed   B. so   C. that   D. on

31 I said, "Drawing on a wall was _____ _____ _____ _____ on paper."
    A. than   B. drawing   C. harder   D. much

32 We all _____ that our wall painting _____ _____.
    A. perfect   B. agreed   C. wasn't

33 _____ it _____ _____.
    A. matter   B. but   C. didn't

34 We made our neighborhood _____ _____ _____ and _____.
    A. brighter   B. a   C. happier   D. little

35 We were _____ _____ _____.
    A. of   B. proud   C. ourselves

36 We _____ _____ _____ pictures _____ a wall that day.
    A. just   B. didn't   C. paint   D. on

37 It was _____ _____ _____ that we _____.
    A. better   B. tomorrow   C. a   D. painted

---

18 몇 군데에는 이상한 낙서와 그림이 있었어.

19 다른 부분에는 오래된 포스터들이 붙어 있었어.

20 우리는 먼저 포스터들을 제거하고 낙서와 그림을 흰 페인트로 덧칠했어.

21 책임자는 우리가 원하는 어떤 것이든 그리게 했어.

22 우리는 그 벽이 초등학교 근처에 있어서 귀여운 뭔가를 그리기로 했어.

23 우리는 세 그룹으로 나뉘어 그리기 시작했어.

24 나는 민수와 지원이와 같은 그룹이었어.

25 나는 내 구역을 정해서 가장 좋아하는 영화 캐릭터를 그리기 시작했어.

26 민수는 몇 송이의 꽃을 그렸고 지원이는 배경 그림을 그렸어.

27 우리 동아리는 약 다섯 시간 동안 그림을 그렸어.

28 끝난 후에 우리는 모여서 그날의 경험을 함께 이야기했어.

29 민수는 자신이 그린 꽃 그림을 정말 자랑스러워했어.

30 그는 "내 꽃이 정말 진짜 같아서 벌이 꽃에 앉았어."라고 말했어.

31 나는 "벽에 그리는 것이 종이에 그리는 것보다 훨씬 힘들었어." 라고 말했어.

32 우리 모두는 우리 벽화가 완벽하지는 않다는 것에 동의했어.

33 하지만 그것은 중요하지 않았어.

34 우리는 동네를 조금 더 밝고 행복하게 만들었어.

35 우리는 우리 자신이 자랑스러웠어.

36 우리는 그날 벽에 그림만 그린 게 아니었어.

37 우리가 그린 것은 바로 더 나은 내일이었어.

Step2

※ 다음 우리말과 일치하도록 빈칸에 알맞은 말을 쓰시오.

1 Paint a _____ _____

2 Hi. _____ _____ _____ Homin.

3 _____ _____ _____ in _____ of the wall painting.

4 The wings are so pretty, _____ _____?

5 Many people like to _____ _____ in front of _____ _____.

6 They make _____ _____ _____ and new.

7 _____ _____, I visited a village _____ _____ in Yeosu.

8 _____ I was taking a picture, _____ _____ _____ _____ _____ _____ _____.

9 I _____, "_____ _____ the school art club.

10 _____ _____ _____ do wall paintings _____ these?"

11 I _____ _____ _____ at the next club meeting, and the members loved it.

12 We _____ a teen volunteer project _____ _____ _____.

13 The project was _____ _____ in our neighborhood.

14 We _____ _____ it, and two weeks _____, our club _____ _____!

15 The day of the project _____ _____.

16 The project manager _____ _____ _____ at the _____ _____ at 9 a.m.

17 The wall _____ _____ _____ _____ _____.

1 더 나은 내일을 그려라

2 안녕. 내 이름은 호민이야.

3 벽화 앞에 있는 사람이 나야.

4 날개가 예뻐, 그렇지 않니?

5 많은 사람들이 벽화 앞에서 사진 찍는 것을 좋아해.

6 벽화는 오래된 마을을 밝고 새롭게 만들어.

7 지난달에 나는 여수에 있는 벽화 마을을 방문했어.

8 내가 사진을 찍을 때 머릿속에 좋은 생각이 떠올랐어.

9 나는 생각했어. "나는 학교 미술 동아리에 있잖아.

10 우리가 이것처럼 벽화를 그리면 어떨까?

11 나는 이 아이디어를 다음 동아리 모임에서 제안했고, 동아리 부원들은 그것을 아주 좋아했어.

12 우리는 인터넷에서 청소년 봉사 프로젝트를 찾았어.

13 그 프로젝트는 우리 마을에 벽화를 그리는 것이었어.

14 우리는 거기에 지원했고, 2주 후에 우리 동아리가 선택되었어!

15 마침내 프로젝트 날이 되었어.

16 프로젝트 책임자는 우리를 오전 9시에 그림 그리는 곳에서 만나게 했어.

17 벽은 상태가 별로 좋지 않았어.

18 There were _____ _____ _____ _____ on some parts.

19 _____ _____ had old posters on them.

20 We removed the posters first and _____ _____ the writings and drawings _____ _____ _____.

21 The manager _____ _____ _____ anything we wanted.

22 We _____ _____ paint _____ _____ because the wall was near an elementary school.

23 We _____ _____ three groups and began painting.

24 I _____ _____ _____ _____ with Minsu and Jiwon.

25 I _____ _____ _____ and started to paint my favorite _____ _____.

26 Minsu _____ some flowers and Jiwon _____ some _____ _____.

27 Our club painted _____ _____ five hours.

28 After we _____, we _____ _____ and _____ the day's _____.

29 Minsu _____ _____ _____ _____ his flower painting.

30 He said, "My flower is _____ real _____ a bee _____ it."

31 I said, "_____ on a wall was _____ _____ _____ drawing on paper."

32 We all agreed that our wall painting _____ _____.

33 But it didn't _____.

34 We made our neighborhood _____ _____ _____ _____.

35 We _____ _____ _____ _____.

36 We _____ _____ _____ pictures on a wall that day.

37 It was _____ _____ _____ that we painted.

18 몇 군데에는 이상한 낙서와 그림이 있었어.

19 다른 부분에는 오래된 포스터들이 붙어 있었어.

20 우리는 먼저 포스터들을 제거하고 낙서와 그림을 흰 페인트로 덧칠했어.

21 책임자는 우리가 원하는 어떤 것이든 그리게 했어.

22 우리는 그 벽이 초등학교 근처에 있어서 귀여운 뭔가를 그리기로 했어.

23 우리는 세 그룹으로 나뉘어 그리기 시작했어.

24 나는 민수와 지원이와 같은 그룹이었어.

25 나는 내 구역을 정해서 가장 좋아하는 영화 캐릭터를 그리기 시작했어.

26 민수는 몇 송이의 꽃을 그렸고 지원이는 배경 그림을 그렸어.

27 우리 동아리는 약 다섯 시간 동안 그림을 그렸어.

28 끝난 후에 우리는 모여서 그날의 경험을 함께 이야기했어.

29 민수는 자신이 그린 꽃 그림을 정말 자랑스러워했어.

30 그는 "내 꽃이 정말 진짜 같아서 벌이 꽃에 앉았어."라고 말했어.

31 나는 "벽에 그리는 것이 종이에 그리는 것보다 훨씬 힘들었어."라고 말했어.

32 우리 모두는 우리 벽화가 완벽하지는 않다는 것에 동의했어.

33 하지만 그것은 중요하지 않았어.

34 우리는 동네를 조금 더 밝고 행복하게 만들었어.

35 우리는 우리 자신이 자랑스러웠어.

36 우리는 그날 벽에 그림만 그린 게 아니었어.

37 우리가 그린 것은 바로 더 나은 내일이었어.

※ 다음 문장을 우리말로 쓰시오.

1 Paint a Better Tomorrow

➡ _____

2 Hi. My name is Homin.

➡ _____

3 This is me in front of the wall painting.

➡ _____

4 The wings are so pretty, aren't they?

➡ _____

5 Many people like to take pictures in front of wall paintings.

➡ _____

6 They make old neighborhoods bright and new.

➡ _____

7 Last month, I visited a village with wall paintings in Yeosu.

➡ _____

8 As I was taking a picture, a light went on in my head.

➡ _____

9 I thought, "I'm in the school art club.

➡ _____

10 Why don't we do wall paintings like these?"

➡ _____

11 I suggested this idea at the next club meeting, and the members loved it.

➡ _____

12 We found a teen volunteer project on the Internet.

➡ _____

13 The project was to do a wall painting in our neighborhood.

➡ _____

14 We applied for it, and two weeks later, our club was selected!

➡ _____

15 The day of the project finally came.

➡ _____

16 The project manager had us meet at the painting site at 9 a.m.

➡ _____

17 The wall was in very poor condition.

➡ _____

18 There were strange writings and drawings on some parts.
➡ _____

19 Other parts had old posters on them.
➡ _____

20 We removed the posters first and painted over the writings and drawings with white paint.
➡ _____

21 The manager let us paint anything we wanted.
➡ _____

22 We decided to paint something cute because the wall was near an elementary school.
➡ _____

23 We divided into three groups and began painting.
➡ _____

24 I was in the group with Minsu and Jiwon.
➡ _____

25 I chose my spot and started to paint my favorite movie character.
➡ _____

26 Minsu painted some flowers and Jiwon did some background drawings.
➡ _____

27 Our club painted for about five hours.
➡ _____

28 After we finished, we got together and shared the day's experiences.
➡ _____

29 Minsu was very proud of his flower painting.
➡ _____

30 He said, "My flower is so real that a bee landed on it."
➡ _____

31 I said, "Drawing on a wall was much harder than drawing on paper."
➡ _____

32 We all agreed that our wall painting wasn't perfect.
➡ _____

33 But it didn't matter.
➡ _____

34 We made our neighborhood a little brighter and happier.
➡ _____

35 We were proud of ourselves.
➡ _____

36 We didn't just paint pictures on a wall that day.
➡ _____

37 It was a better tomorrow that we painted.
➡ _____

※ 다음 괄호 안의 단어들을 우리말에 맞도록 바르게 배열하시오.

1 (a / Paint / Tomorrow / Better)
➡ _____

2 (hi. // name / my / Homin. / is)
➡ _____

3 (is / this / in / me / of / front / wall / the / painting.)
➡ _____

4 (wings / the / so / are / pretty, / they? / aren't)
➡ _____

5 (people / many / to / like / pictures / take / front / in / wall / of / paintings.)
➡ _____

6 (make / they / neighborhoods / old / new. / and / bright)
➡ _____

7 (month, / last / visited / I / village / a / wall / with / paintings / Yeosu. / in)
➡ _____

8 (I / as / taking / was / picture, / a / light / a / in / went / on / head. / my)
➡ _____

9 (thought, / I / in / "I'm / the / art / school / club.)
➡ _____

10 (don't / why / do / we / paintings / wall / these?" / like)
➡ _____

11 (suggested / I / idea / this / the / at / next / meeting, / club / and / members / the / it. / loved)
➡ _____

12 (found / we / teen / a / volunteer / on / project / Internet. / the)
➡ _____

13 (project / the / to / was / do / painting / wall / a / our / in / neighborhood.)
➡ _____

1 더 나은 내일을 그려라

2 안녕. 내 이름은 호민이야.

3 벽화 앞에 있는 사람이 나야.

4 날개가 예뻐, 그렇지 않니?

5 많은 사람들이 벽화 앞에서 사진 찍는 것을 좋아해.

6 벽화는 오래된 마을을 밝고 새롭게 만들어.

7 지난달에 나는 여수에 있는 벽화 마을을 방문했어.

8 내가 사진을 찍을 때 머릿속에 좋은 생각이 떠올랐어.

9 나는 생각했어. "나는 학교 미술 동아리에 있잖아.

10 우리가 이것처럼 벽화를 그리면 어떨까?

11 나는 이 아이디어를 다음 동아리 모임에서 제안했고, 동아리 부원들은 그것을 아주 좋아했어.

12 우리는 인터넷에서 청소년 봉사 프로젝트를 찾았어.

13 그 프로젝트는 우리 마을에 벽화를 그리는 것이었어.

14 (applied / we / it, / for / two / and / later, / weeks / club / our / selected! / was)

➡ _____

15 (day / the / of / project / the / came. / finally)

➡ _____

16 (project / the / had / manager / us / at / meet / the / site / painting / 9 / a.m. / at)

➡ _____

17 (wall / the / in / was / very / condition. / poor)

➡ _____

18 (were / there / writings / strange / and / on / drawings / parts. / some)

➡ _____

19 (parts / other / old / had / on / posters / them.)

➡ _____

20 (removed / we / posters / the / and / first / over / painted / writings / the / and / drawings / white / with / paint.)

➡ _____

➡ _____

21 (manager / the / us / let / anything / paint / wanted. / we)

➡ _____

22 (decided / we / paint / to / cute / something / the / because / wall / near / was / elementary / school. / an)

➡ _____

➡ _____

23 (divided / we / three / into / and / groups / painting. / began)

➡ _____

24 (was / I / the / in / group / with / Jiwon. / and / Minsu)

➡ _____

25 (chose / I / spot / my / and / to / started / my / paint / movie / favorite / character.)

➡ _____

14 우리는 거기에 지원했고, 2주 후에 우리 동아리가 선택되었어!

15 마침내 프로젝트 날이 되었어.

16 프로젝트 책임자는 우리를 오전 9시에 그림 그리는 곳에서 만나게 했어.

17 벽은 상태가 별로 좋지 않았어.

18 몇 군데에는 이상한 낙서와 그림이 있었어.

19 다른 부분에는 오래된 포스터들이 붙어 있었어.

20 우리는 먼저 포스터들을 제거하고 낙서와 그림을 흰 페인트로 덧칠했어.

21 책임자는 우리가 원하는 어떤 것이든 그리게 했어.

22 우리는 그 벽이 초등학교 근처에 있어서 귀여운 뭔가를 그리기로 했어.

23 우리는 세 그룹으로 나뉘어 그리기 시작했어.

24 나는 민수와 지원이와 같은 그룹이었어.

25 나는 내 구역을 정해서 가장 좋아하는 영화 캐릭터를 그리기 시작했어.

26 (painted / Minsu / flowers / some / and / did / Jiwon / background / some / drawings.)

➡ _____

27 (club / our / painted / about / for / hours. / five)

➡ _____

28 (we / after / finished, / got / we / together / shared / and / the / experiences. / day's)

➡ _____

29 (was / Minsu / proud / very / his / of / painting. / flower)

➡ _____

30 (said, / he / flower / "my / so / is / real / a / that / bee / on / it." / landed)

➡ _____

31 (said, / I / on / "drawing / wall / a / was / harder / much / drawing / than / paper." / on)

➡ _____

32 (all / we / that / agreed / our / painting / wall / perfect. / wasn't)

➡ _____

33 (it / but / matter. / didn't)

➡ _____

34 (made / we / neighborhood / our / little / a / happier. / and / brighter)

➡ _____

35 (were / we / of / proud / ourselves.)

➡ _____

36 (didn't / we / paint / just / on / pictures / wall / a / day. / that)

➡ _____

37 (was / it / better / a / that / tomorrow / painted. / we)

➡ _____

26 민수는 몇 송이의 꽃을 그렸고 지원이는 배경 그림을 그렸어.

27 우리 동아리는 약 다섯 시간 동안 그림을 그렸어.

28 끝난 후에 우리는 모여서 그날의 경험을 함께 이야기했어.

29 민수는 자신이 그린 꽃 그림을 정말 자랑스러워했어.

30 그는 "내 꽃이 정말 진짜 같아서 벌이 꽃에 앉았어."라고 말했어.

31 나는 "벽에 그리는 것이 종이에 그리는 것보다 훨씬 힘들었어." 라고 말했어.

32 우리 모두는 우리 벽화가 완벽하지는 않다는 것에 동의했어.

33 하지만 그것은 중요하지 않았어.

34 우리는 동네를 조금 더 밝고 행복하게 만들었어.

35 우리는 우리 자신이 자랑스러웠어.

36 우리는 그날 벽에 그림만 그린 게 아니었어.

37 우리가 그린 것은 바로 더 나은 내일이었어.

※ 다음 우리말을 영어로 쓰시오.

1 더 나은 내일을 그려라

➡ _____

2 안녕. 내 이름은 호민이야.

➡ _____

3 벽화 앞에 있는 사람이 나야.

➡ _____

4 날개가 예뻐, 그렇지 않니?

➡ _____

5 많은 사람들이 벽화 앞에서 사진 찍는 것을 좋아해.

➡ _____

6 벽화는 오래된 마을을 밝고 새롭게 만들어.

➡ _____

7 지난달에 나는 여수에 있는 벽화 마을을 방문했어.

➡ _____

8 내가 사진을 찍을 때 머릿속에 좋은 생각이 떠올랐어.

➡ _____

9 나는 생각했어. "나는 학교 미술 동아리에 있잖아.

➡ _____

10 우리가 이것처럼 벽화를 그리면 어떨까?"

➡ _____

11 나는 이 아이디어를 다음 동아리 모임에서 제안했고, 동아리 부원들은 그것을 아주 좋아했어.

➡ _____

12 우리는 인터넷에서 청소년 봉사 프로젝트를 찾았어.

➡ _____

13 그 프로젝트는 우리 마을에 벽화를 그리는 것이었어.

➡ _____

14 우리는 거기에 지원했고, 2주 후에 우리 동아리가 선택되었어!

➡ _____

15 마침내 프로젝트 날이 되었어.

➡ _____

16 프로젝트 책임자는 우리를 오전 9시에 그림 그리는 곳에서 만나게 했어.

➡ _____

17 벽은 상태가 별로 좋지 않았어.

➡ _____

18 몇 군데에는 이상한 낙서와 그림이 있었어.
➡ _____

19 다른 부분에는 오래된 포스터들이 붙어 있었어.
➡ _____

20 우리는 먼저 포스터들을 제거하고 낙서와 그림을 흰 페인트로 덧칠했어.
➡ _____

21 책임자는 우리가 원하는 어떤 것이든 그리게 했어.
➡ _____

22 우리는 그 벽이 초등학교 근처에 있어서 귀여운 뭔가를 그리기로 했어.
➡ _____

23 우리는 세 그룹으로 나뉘어 그리기 시작했어.
➡ _____

24 나는 민수와 지원이와 같은 그룹이었어.
➡ _____

25 나는 내 구역을 정해서 가장 좋아하는 영화 캐릭터를 그리기 시작했어.
➡ _____

26 민수는 몇 송이의 꽃을 그렸고 지원이는 배경 그림을 그렸어.
➡ _____

27 우리 동아리는 약 다섯 시간 동안 그림을 그렸어.
➡ _____

28 끝난 후에 우리는 모여서 그날의 경험을 함께 이야기했어.
➡ _____

29 민수는 자신이 그린 꽃 그림을 정말 자랑스러워했어.
➡ _____

30 그는 "내 꽃이 정말 진짜 같아서 벌이 꽃에 앉았어."라고 말했어.
➡ _____

31 나는 "벽에 그리는 것이 종이에 그리는 것보다 훨씬 힘들었어."라고 말했어.
➡ _____

32 우리 모두는 우리 벽화가 완벽하지는 않다는 것에 동의했어.
➡ _____

33 하지만 그것은 중요하지 않았어.
➡ _____

34 우리는 동네를 조금 더 밝고 행복하게 만들었어.
➡ _____

35 우리는 우리 자신이 자랑스러웠어.
➡ _____

36 우리는 그날 벽에 그림만 그린 게 아니었어.
➡ _____

37 우리가 그린 것은 바로 더 나은 내일이었어.
➡ _____

※ 다음 우리말과 일치하도록 빈칸에 알맞은 말을 쓰시오.

After You Read B

1. Project: _____ a _____ _____

2. _____ : _____ 15

3. _____ _____ : 9 a.m.

4. Do you _____ _____?

5. Do you want to _____ _____ _____ _____?

6. _____ _____, the wall is in very _____ _____.

7. You _____ _____ _____ the old posters and _____ _____ the strange writings _____ _____ _____.

8. You can paint _____ _____ _____!

9. _____: volunteer@1365.go.kr

1. 프로젝트: 더 나은 내일을 그려라
2. 날짜: 4월 15일
3. 만나는 시간: 오전 9시
4. 당신은 그림 그리기를 좋아하십니까?
5. 당신의 동네를 더 밝게 만들기를 원합니까?
6. 지금, 벽은 상태가 별로 좋지 않습니다.
7. 당신은 먼저 오래된 포스터들을 제거하고 이상한 낙서를 흰 페인트로 덧칠할 필요가 있습니다.
8. 당신은 원하는 어떤 것이든 그릴 수 있습니다!
9. 이메일: volunteer@1365.go.kr

Word Power

1. Sally _____ _____ early and _____ _____ school.

2. She _____ _____ _____ her mom.

3. Her mom said, "_____ _____ _____ _____ _____ your friends and _____ _____."

4. Sally _____, "Okay, I will," and _____ _____ the school bus.

1. Sally는 일찍 일어나서 학교 갈 준비를 했다.
2. 그녀는 엄마에게 작별인사를 했다.
3. 엄마는 "친구들과 잘 지내고 즐거운 시간을 보내라."라고 말했다.
4. Sally는 "그럴게요."라고 대답하고 스쿨 버스를 탔다.

Think and Write

1. _____ _____ Diary

2. I _____ at Dream _____.

3. I _____ English books _____ _____.

4. I _____ _____ read _____ a _____ _____.

5. The _____ manager _____ me _____ the books _____ _____ _____.

6. The books were _____ heavy _____ I had to _____ _____ _____ _____ 30 _____.

7. _____ I _____, the shelves _____ very _____.

8. I _____ very _____.

9. It was a fun and _____ _____.

1. 봉사 활동 일기
2. 나는 Dream 도서관에서 자원봉사를 했다.
3. 나는 아이들에게 영어책을 읽어 줬다.
4. 나는 성우처럼 읽으려고 노력했다.
5. 자원봉사 책임자는 내게 책을 책장에 정리하라고 했다.
6. 책이 너무 무거워서 나는 30분마다 쉬어야 했다.
7. 끝난 후에는 책장이 아주 깔끔해 보였다.
8. 나는 매우 자랑스러움을 느꼈다.
9. 재미있고 보람된 경험이었다.

※ 다음 우리말을 영어로 쓰시오.

After You Read B

1. 프로젝트: 더 나은 내일을 그려라
   ➡
2. 날짜: 4월 15일
   ➡
3. 만나는 시간: 오전 9시
   ➡
4. 당신은 그림 그리기를 좋아하십니까?
   ➡
5. 당신의 동네를 더 밝게 만들기를 원합니까?
   ➡
6. 지금, 벽은 상태가 별로 좋지 않습니다.
   ➡
7. 당신은 먼저 오래된 포스터들을 제거하고 이상한 낙서를 흰 페인트로 덧칠할 필요가 있습니다.
   ➡
8. 당신은 원하는 어떤 것이든 그릴 수 있습니다!
   ➡
9. 이메일: volunteer@1365.go.kr
   ➡

Word Power

1. Sally는 일찍 일어나서 학교 갈 준비를 했다.
   ➡
2. 그녀는 엄마에게 작별인사를 했다.
   ➡
3. 엄마는 "친구들과 잘 지내고 즐거운 시간을 보내라."라고 말했다.
   ➡
4. Sally는 "그럴게요."라고 대답하고 스쿨 버스를 탔다.
   ➡

Think and Write

1. 봉사 활동 일기
   ➡
2. 나는 Dream 도서관에서 자원봉사를 했다.
   ➡
3. 나는 아이들에게 영어책을 읽어 줬다.
   ➡
4. 나는 성우처럼 읽으려고 노력했다.
   ➡
5. 자원봉사 책임자는 내게 책을 책장에 정리하라고 했다.
   ➡
6. 책이 너무 무거워서 나는 30분마다 쉬어야 했다.
   ➡
7. 끝난 후에는 책장이 아주 깔끔해 보였다.
   ➡
8. 나는 매우 자랑스러움을 느꼈다.
   ➡
9. 재미있고 보람된 경험이었다.
   ➡

※ 다음 영어를 우리말로 쓰시오.

01	shiny	
02	dirt	
03	adventure	
04	brain	
05	dig	
06	beat	
07	brush	
08	wide	
09	assign	
10	convenient	
11	cruel	
12	bone	
13	acting	
14	detective	
15	skip	
16	driverless	
17	helpful	
18	convenience	
19	steal	
20	hole	
21	light	

22	marry	
23	summary	
24	muscle	
25	awake	
26	raise	
27	return	
28	scene	
29	character	
30	bottom	
31	unfortunately	
32	carefully	
33	suddenly	
34	object	
35	put down	
36	be full of	
37	stand for	
38	pick up	
39	end up	
40	at the bottom of	
41	look up	
42	belong to	
43	fall in love with	

※ 다음 우리말을 영어로 쓰시오.

01	훔치다	
02	(구멍 등을) 파다	
03	모험	
04	근육	
05	품성, 인격	
06	흙	
07	머리, 지능	
08	갑자기	
09	털다	
10	(사람을) 배치하다	
11	구덩이, 구멍	
12	요약, 개요	
13	조심스럽게	
14	뼈	
15	장면	
16	폭넓은, 폭이 ~인	
17	빛나는, 반짝거리는	
18	졸리는	
19	편리, 편의	
20	실제로	
21	형사, 탐정	

22	(일을) 거르다, 빼먹다	
23	고함치다	
24	가벼운	
25	잠들지 않은, 깨어 있는	
26	(심장이) 고동치다, 때리다	
27	불행히도	
28	키우다, 기르다	
29	맨 아래, 바닥	
30	편리한	
31	돌려주다, 반품하다	
32	잔혹한, 잔인한	
33	(연극, 영화에서의) 연기	
34	인기 있는	
35	~와 사랑에 빠지다	
36	사실	
37	~을 의미하다	
38	휴일, 쉬는 날	
39	내려놓다	
40	결국 ~이 되다	
41	깨어 있다	
42	~의 바닥에서	
43	찾아보다	

※ 다음 영영풀이에 알맞은 단어를 <보기>에서 골라 쓴 후, 우리말 뜻을 쓰시오.

1 _____ : not sleeping: _____

2 _____ : measured from side to side: _____

3 _____ : the lowest part of something: _____

4 _____ : smooth and bright: _____

5 _____ : an empty space in something solid: _____

6 _____ : to pass over or not do something: _____

7 _____ : a day when you do not go to work, school, etc.: _____

8 _____ : a thing that you can see and touch but is not alive: _____

9 _____ : to remove something with a brush or with your hand: _____

10 _____ : to move soil, sand, snow, etc., in order to create a hole: _____

11 _____ : a body tissue that can contract and produce movement: _____

12 _____ : a long and empty object that is usually round, like a pipe: _____

13 _____ : the activity or profession of performing in plays, movies, etc.:

_____

14 _____ : to send someone to a particular group or place as part of a job:

_____

15 _____ : to take something that does not belong to you in a way that is wrong or

illegal: _____

16 _____ : to shout loudly, for example because you are angry, excited, frightened,

or in pain: _____

보기			
yell	steal	muscle	acting
awake	hole	shiny	object
brush	dig	assign	tube
day off	bottom	wide	skip

※ 다음 우리말과 일치하도록 빈칸에 알맞은 말을 쓰시오.

Listen and Speak 1 A

B: Hi, Amy. _____ _____ Korea.

G: _____ time _____ see, Minho. _____ have you _____?

B: Great. _____ did you come _____ _____ the airport?

G: I came here _____ _____.

B: _____ do you _____ _____ the subway in Korea?

G: I think it's very _____.

Listen and Speak 1 B

G: Brian, _____ did you _____ the news?

B: _____ news?

G: We _____ use smartphones _____ _____ _____ next week.

B: Yes, I _____ that.

G: _____ do you _____ about it?

B: I think it will be very _____. I can _____ _____ _____

_____ _____ _____.

G: Yeah. We _____ _____ _____ information on the Internet.

B: Right. It will be very _____.

Listen and Speak 1 C

1. A: _____ _____ _____ you a difficult question?

   B: Sure. I'll _____ my _____.

   A: _____ do you _____ about the _____ food diet?

   B: I think it's _____ but _____.

2. A: Can I _____ you a _____ question?

   B: Sure. I'll _____ my best.

   A: _____ _____ _____ _____ about the AI robot?

   B: I think it's _____ _____ _____.

3. A: _____ _____ _____ _____ a difficult question?

   B: Sure. I'll _____ _____ _____.

   A: _____ _____ _____ _____ _____ animal testing?

   B: I think it's _____ _____ _____.

Listen and Speak 2 A

B: _____ _____ _____ the movie?

G: Yes, I liked it _____ _____.

B: _____ _____ _____ _____ _____ about it?

G: The _____ _____ so great.

B: I'm _____ _____ _____ that.

B: 그 영화 재미있었니?
G: 응, 아주 좋았어.
B: 무엇이 가장 좋았니?
G: 연기가 아주 멋졌어.
B: 나도 그 점에 동의해.

Listen and Speak 2 B

B: Hey, Jessica. _____ are you _____ _____ energy drinks?

G: Because they _____ _____ _____ _____.

B: _____ _____ _____ _____ that, but they have _____ _____ _____.

G: Well, they _____ _____ _____ _____ my studies.

B: Did you _____ _____ _____ _____ _____ _____ can hurt your bones?

G: Oh, I didn't know that.

B: I think you _____ _____ energy drinks _____ _____.

G: _____ you're right. Thanks, Tom.

B: 얘, Jessica. 너는 왜 늘 에너지 음료를 마시니?
G: 에너지 음료가 깨어 있는 데 도움이 되기 때문이야.
B: 그 점에는 동의하지만, 에너지 음료에는 카페인이 너무 많아.
G: 음, 공부에 집중하는 데 도움이 돼.
B: 너무 많은 카페인은 뼈를 다치게 할 수 있다는 것을 알고 있었니?
G: 아, 그건 몰랐어.
B: 내 생각에 넌 에너지 음료를 덜 자주 마셔야 해.
G: 네 말이 맞는 거 같아. 고마워, Tom.

Listen and Speak 2 C

1. **A:** _____ _____ _____ _____ _____ _____ books on a smartphone?

   B: I think it's good. We can read _____.

   A: I'm _____ _____ _____ _____. / I don't agree. It's _____ _____ _____ our eyes.

2. **A:** _____ _____ _____ _____ _____ _____ breakfast?

   B: I think it's good. We can sleep _____.

   A: _____ _____ _____ _____ _____ _____. / I don't agree. Our brain _____ _____ _____ well.

3. **A:** _____ _____ _____ _____ _____ _____ fast food?

   B: I think it's bad. Fast food has _____ _____ _____ _____.

   A: _____ _____ _____ _____ _____. / _____ _____ _____. We _____ _____ time.

1. **A:** 스마트폰으로 책 읽는 것에 대해 어떻게 생각하니?
   B: 좋다고 생각해. 언제든지 읽을 수 있잖아.
   A: 동의해. / 동의하지 않아. 그것은 우리의 눈에 나빠.

2. **A:** 아침을 건너뛰는 것을 어떻게 생각하니?
   B: 좋다고 생각해. 우리는 잠을 더 잘 수 있어.
   A: 동의해. / 나는 동의하지 않아. 우리의 뇌가 잘 작동하지 않을 수 있어.

3. **A:** 패스트 푸드를 먹는 것에 대해 어떻게 생각하니?
   B: 나쁘다고 생각해. 패스트 푸드는 많은 지방을 가지고 있어.
   A: 동의해. / 나는 동의하지 않아. 우리는 시간을 절약할 수 있어.

Real Life Talk Watch a Video

Tony: _____ are all these boxes, Suji?

Suji: _____ _____ _____ _____ online.

Tony: You like shopping on the Internet, _____ _____?

Suji: Yes, I do. _____ _____ _____ _____ _____ online

shopping, Tony?

Tony: I don't like it _____ _____.

Suji: Why?

Tony: It's very _____ _____ _____ _____ an item _____

_____ _____.

Suji: I'm _____ _____ _____ that.

Tony: It's also _____ _____ _____ an item if you don't like it.

Suji: You're _____, but I think it's very _____.

Tony: Well, _____ isn't _____.

Real Life Talk Step 2

1. **A:** How do you _____ _____ _____ on the Internet?

   B: I like it _____ _____.

   A: _____ _____ _____ _____ the reason?

   B: I can _____ _____ I want.

   A: _____ _____ _____ on that.

2. **A:** _____ _____ _____ _____ _____ _____ _____ pets?

   B: I don't like it.

   A: Can you _____ _____ the _____?

   B: It's a lot of _____ _____ _____ _____ _____ them.

   A: I _____ _____. They're so _____ and _____ _____

   _____.

Check up Dialogue Champion

A: _____ _____ _____ _____ _____ _____ smartphones

_____ _____?

B: I think smartphones are _____ in class. We can _____ _____

_____ on them.

A: I'm _____ _____ _____ _____.

Tony: 이 상자들은 전부 뭐니, 수지야?
수지: 내가 온라인으로 주문한 물건들이
야.
Tony: 너 인터넷으로 쇼핑하는 걸 좋아
하는구나, 그렇지 않니?
수지: 응, 그래. 넌 온라인 쇼핑에 관해
어떻게 생각하니, Tony?
Tony: 난 전혀 좋아하지 않아.
수지: 왜?
Tony: 물건이 실제로 어떻게 생겼는지
알기가 매우 어렵거든.
수지: 그 점에는 동의해.
Tony: 만약 물건이 마음에 들지 않으면
물건을 돌려보내는 것도 어려워.
수지: 네 말이 맞지만, 온라인 쇼핑은 매
우 편리하다고 생각해.
Tony: 음, 편리함이 전부는 아니야.

1. A: 인터넷에서 쇼핑하는 것을 어떻
게 생각해?
B: 나는 아주 좋아해.
A: 이유를 말해 줄 수 있니?
B: 내가 원할 때마다 쇼핑할 수 있
어.
A: 나도 동의해.

2. A: 애완동물을 기르는 것을 어떻게
생각해?
B: 나는 좋아하지 않아.
A: 이유를 말해 줄 수 있니?
B: 애완동물을 돌보기 위해 할 일이
많아.
A: 나는 동의하지 않아. 그들은 아주
귀엽고, 우리를 기쁘게 해줘.

A: 수업 시간에 스마트폰을 사용하는 것
에 대해 어떻게 생각해?
B: 수업 시간에 스마트폰은 유용하다고
생각해. 우리는 스마트폰으로 정보를
찾을 수 있어.
A: 나는 그 점에 동의해.

※ 다음 우리말에 맞도록 대화를 영어로 쓰시오.

Listen and Speak 1 A

B: _____

G: _____

B: _____

G: _____

B: _____

G: _____

B: 안녕, Amy. 한국에 온 걸 환영해.
G: 오랜만이야, 민호야. 어떻게 지냈니?
B: 잘 지냈어. 공항에서 여기에 어떻게 왔니?
G: 여기까지 지하철을 타고 왔어.
B: 한국 지하철에 관해 어떻게 생각하니?
G: 매우 깨끗하다고 생각해.

Listen and Speak 1 B

G: _____

B: _____

G: _____

B: _____

G: _____

B: _____

G: _____

B: _____

G: Brian, 너 그 소식 들었니?
B: 어떤 소식?
G: 우리는 다음 주부터 수업 중에 스마트폰을 사용할 수 있어.
B: 응, 그 소식을 들었어.
G: 넌 그것에 관해 어떻게 생각하니?
B: 매우 유용할 거라고 생각해. 모르는 단어들을 찾아볼 수 있잖아.
G: 그래. 우리는 또한 인터넷으로 정보를 찾을 수도 있어.
B: 맞아. 매우 도움이 될 거야.

Listen and Speak 1 C

1. A: _____

   B: _____

   A: _____

   B: _____

2. A: _____

   B: _____

   A: _____

   B: _____

3. A: _____

   B: _____

   A: _____

   B: _____

1. A: 어려운 질문을 해도 될까?
   B: 물론이지. 최선을 다할게.
   A: 싱글 푸드 다이어트에 대해 어떻게 생각하니?
   B: 쉽지만 건강에 해롭다고 생각해.

2. A: 어려운 질문을 해도 될까?
   B: 물론이지. 최선을 다할게.
   A: AI 로봇에 대해 어떻게 생각하니?
   B: 도움이 되지만 무섭다고 생각해.

3. A: 어려운 질문을 해도 될까?
   B: 물론이지. 최선을 다할게.
   A: 동물 실험에 대해 어떻게 생각하니?
   B: 도움이 되지만 잔인하다고 생각해.

Listen and Speak 2 A

B: _____

G: _____

B: _____

G: _____

B: _____

B: 그 영화 재미있었니?
G: 응, 아주 좋았어.
B: 무엇이 가장 좋았니?
G: 연기가 아주 멋졌어.
B: 나도 그 점에 동의해.

Listen and Speak 2 B

B: _____

G: _____

B: _____

G: _____

B: _____

G: _____

B: _____

G: _____

B: 얘, Jessica. 너는 왜 늘 에너지 음료를 마시니?
G: 에너지 음료가 깨어 있는 데 도움이 되기 때문이야.
B: 그 점에는 동의하지만, 에너지 음료에는 카페인이 너무 많아.
G: 음, 공부에 집중하는 데 도움이 돼.
B: 너무 많은 카페인은 뼈를 다치게 할 수 있다는 것을 알고 있었니?
G: 아, 그건 몰랐어.
B: 내 생각에 넌 에너지 음료를 덜 자주 마셔야 해.
G: 네 말이 맞는 거 같아. 고마워, Tom.

Listen and Speak 2 C

1. A: _____

   B: _____

   A: _____

2. A: _____

   B: _____

   A: _____

3. A: _____

   B: _____

   A: _____

1. A: 스마트폰으로 책 읽는 것에 대해 어떻게 생각하니?
   B: 좋다고 생각해. 언제든지 읽을 수 있잖아.
   A: 동의해. / 동의하지 않아. 그것은 우리의 눈에 나빠.

2. A: 아침을 건너뛰는 것을 어떻게 생각하니?
   B: 좋다고 생각해. 우리는 잠을 더 잘 수 있어.
   A: 동의해. / 나는 동의하지 않아. 우리의 뇌가 잘 작동하지 않을 수 있어.

3. A: 패스트 푸드를 먹는 것에 대해 어떻게 생각하니?
   B: 나쁘다고 생각해. 패스트 푸드는 많은 지방을 가지고 있어.
   A: 동의해. / 나는 동의하지 않아. 우리는 시간을 절약할 수 있어.

Real Life Talk Watch a Video

Tony: _____

Suji: _____

Tony: _____

Suji: _____

Tony: _____

Suji: _____

Tony: _____

Suji: _____

Tony: _____

Suji: _____

Tony: _____

Real Life Talk Step 2

1. A: _____

   B: _____

   A: _____

   B: _____

   A: _____

2. A: _____

   B: _____

   A: _____

   B: _____

   A: _____

Check up Dialogue Champion

A: _____

B: _____

_____

A: _____

Tony: 이 상자들은 전부 뭐니, 수지야?
수지: 내가 온라인으로 주문한 물건들이야.
Tony: 너 인터넷으로 쇼핑하는 걸 좋아하는구나, 그렇지 않니?
수지: 응, 그래. 넌 온라인 쇼핑에 관해 어떻게 생각하니, Tony?
Tony: 난 전혀 좋아하지 않아.
수지: 왜?
Tony: 물건이 실제로 어떻게 생겼는지 알기가 매우 어렵거든.
수지: 그 점에는 동의해.
Tony: 만약 물건이 마음에 들지 않으면 물건을 돌려보내는 것도 어려워.
수지: 네 말이 맞지만, 온라인 쇼핑은 매우 편리하다고 생각해.
Tony: 음, 편리함이 전부는 아니야.

1. A: 인터넷에서 쇼핑하는 것을 어떻게 생각해?
   B: 나는 아주 좋아해.
   A: 이유를 말해 줄 수 있니?
   B: 내가 원할 때마다 쇼핑할 수 있어.
   A: 나도 동의해.

2. A: 애완동물을 기르는 것을 어떻게 생각해?
   B: 나는 좋아하지 않아.
   A: 이유를 말해 줄 수 있니?
   B: 애완동물을 돌보기 위해 할 일이 많아.
   A: 나는 동의하지 않아. 그들은 아주 귀엽고, 우리를 기쁘게 해줘.

A: 수업 시간에 스마트폰을 사용하는 것에 대해 어떻게 생각해?
B: 수업 시간에 스마트폰은 유용하다고 생각해. 우리는 스마트폰으로 정보를 찾을 수 있어.
A: 나는 그 점에 동의해.

※ 다음 우리말과 일치하도록 빈칸에 알맞은 것을 골라 쓰시오.

HOLES

1 "________ ________, Stanley!"
A. harder B. dig

2 The ________ you dig, ________ ________ you'll finish!" ________ Mr. Sir.
A. yelled B. the C. harder D. faster

3 Stanley Yelnats couldn't dig any ________ ________ every single ________ ________.
A. muscle B. harder C. hurt D. since

4 He was ________ and ________.
A. hungry B. thirsty

5 He wanted ________ ________ ________.
A. home B. go C. to

6 Unfortunately, Stanley's home ________ the next 18 months ________ ________ right here, ________ Camp Green Lake.
A. be B. for C. at D. would

7 Camp Green Lake was ________ ________ ________.
A. terrible B. name C. a

8 It wasn't green and ________ ________ ________ ________.
A. no B. there C. lake D. was

9 Camp Green Lake was ________ and ________ ________ ________.
A. full B. hot C. sand D. of

10 ________ ________, it wasn't ________ a camp.
A. fact B. even C. in

11 It was a ________ ________ ________ boys.
A. for B. place C. bad

12 Then ________ was a good boy ________ Stanley ________ here?
A. like B. what C. doing

13 He was ________ to the camp for ________ a ________ ________ sneakers.
A. stealing B. sent C. of D. pair

14 Stanley ________ ________ ________ a pair of sneakers.
A. really B. didn't C. steal

15 He was just ________ the wrong ________ ________ the ________ time.
A. at B. place C. in D. wrong

16 One day, he was ________ ________ ________ ________.
A. home B. walking C. school D. from

17 ________, a ________ of old sneakers ________ ________ the sky.
A. fell B. suddenly C. from D. pair

18 The sneakers ________ ________ ________ the ________.
A. on B. hit C. head D. him

구덩이

1 "더 열심히 파, Stanley!

2 네가 열심히 파면 팔수록, 너는 더 빨리 끝낼 거야!" Sir 씨가 소리를 질렀다.

3 Stanley Yelnats는 모든 근육 하나하나가 아팠기 때문에 더 열심히 팔 수가 없었다.

4 그는 목이 마르고 배가 고팠다.

5 그는 집에 가고 싶었다.

6 불행히도, 앞으로 18개월 동안 Stanley의 집은 바로 여기 Green Lake 캠프가 될 것이었다.

7 Green Lake 캠프는 형편없는 이름이었다.

8 그곳은 초록색도 아니었고 호수도 없었다.

9 Green Lake 캠프는 뜨거웠고 온통 모래였다.

10 사실 그곳은 캠프조차 아니었다.

11 그곳은 나쁜 소년들을 위한 곳이었다.

12 그렇다면 Stanley 같이 착한 소년이 여기서 무엇을 하고 있었을까?

13 그는 운동화 한 켤레를 훔쳤다는 이유로 캠프에 보내졌다.

14 Stanley가 정말로 운동화 한 켤레를 훔친 것은 아니었다.

15 그는 그저 잘못된 시간에 잘못된 장소에 있었다.

16 어느 날, 그는 학교에서 집으로 걸어가고 있었다.

17 갑자기, 낡은 운동화 한 켤레가 하늘에서 떨어졌다.

18 그 운동화는 그의 머리에 맞았다.

19 He started running _____ the sneakers to _____ his father _____ _____.
   A. happened   B. what   C. tell   D. with

20 A _____ minutes later, the police _____ Stanley and asked him _____ he was _____.
   A. stopped   B. why   C. running   D. few

21 Unfortunately _____ Stanley, the sneakers _____ _____ a _____ baseball player, Clyde Livingstone.
   A. belonged   B. famous   C. for   D. to

22 That was _____ Stanley _____ _____ _____ Camp Green Lake.
   A. up   B. why   C. at   D. ended

23 Stanley _____ _____ _____ Group D in the camp.
   A. was   B. to   C. assigned

24 _____ were _____ _____ _____ in Stanley's group.
   A. other   B. there   C. boys   D. six

25 They all _____ _____ _____ _____ X-Ray, Zigzag and Zero.
   A. cool   B. had   C. like   D. names

26 _____ boy _____ to _____ one _____ every day.
   A. dig   B. each   C. hole   D. had

27 It had _____ be _____ 150cm _____ and 150cm _____.
   A. deep   B. about   C. wide   D. to

28 Mr. Sir said, "You are _____ _____ _____ _____ _____."
   A. build   B. digging   C. to   D. character

29 The _____ Stanley _____, the _____ he _____.
   A. stronger   B. more   C. became   D. dug

30 It _____ time to _____ his hole _____ day.
   A. less   B. each   C. took   D. finish

31 In his second week, as Stanley was _____ his hole, he saw _____ _____ in the _____.
   A. dirt   B. shiny   C. finishing   D. something

32 Stanley's _____ _____ _____.
   A. faster   B. heart   C. beat

33 He heard that anyone who found _____ _____ would be _____ the day _____.
   A. given   B. intersting   C. off   D. something

34 He carefully _____ _____ the shiny object and _____ _____ the dirt.
   A. off   B. picked   C. brushed   D. up

35 It was a _____ _____ _____.
   A. tube   B. gold   C. small

36 But it _____ real gold _____ it was too _____.
   A. be   B. light   C. since   D. couldn't

37 _____ were two _____, *KB*, at the _____ of the _____.
   A. letters   B. tube   C. there   D. bottom

38 What _____ KB _____ _____?
   A. stand   B. did   C. for

39 Stanley's heart _____ _____ _____.
   A. even   B. beat   C. faster

---

19 그는 그의 아버지에게 무슨 일이 일어났는지 말하기 위해 운동화를 가지고 달리기 시작했다.

20 몇 분 후에, 경찰이 Stanley를 멈춰 세웠고 그가 왜 달리고 있었는지를 그에게 물었다.

21 Stanley에게는 불행히도, 그 운동화는 유명한 야구 선수인 Clyde Livingstone의 것이었다.

22 그것이 Stanley가 Green Lake 캠프에 오게 된 이유였다.

23 Stanley는 캠프에서 D 그룹에 배치되었다.

24 Stanley의 그룹에는 6명의 다른 소년들이 있었다.

25 그들은 모두 X-Ray, Zigzag, Zero와 같은 멋진 이름을 가지고 있었다.

26 각 소년은 매일 구덩이를 하나를 파야 했다.

27 그것은 150cm 정도 깊이와 150cm 정도 너비여야 했다.

28 Sir 씨는 "너희들은 인격을 수양하기 위해 구덩이를 파고 있는 것이야."라고 말했다.

29 Stanley는 많이 파면 팔수록, 더 힘이 세졌다.

30 하루하루 구덩이를 끝내는 데 시간이 덜 걸렸다.

31 그가 온 지 두 번째 주, Stanley가 자기 구덩이를 끝내 가고 있었을 때, 그는 흙 속에서 빛나는 뭔가를 봤다.

32 Stanley의 심장은 더 빨리 뛰었다.

33 그는 흥미로운 뭔가를 발견한 사람은 그 날을 쉬게 된다고 들었다.

34 그는 조심스럽게 그 빛나는 물체를 집어 흙을 털어 냈다.

35 그것은 작은 금색 통이었다.

36 그러나 그것은 너무 가벼웠기 때문에 진짜 금일 리가 없었다.

37 그 통의 바닥에는 KB라는 두 글자가 있었다.

38 KB는 무엇을 의미할까?

39 Stanley의 심장은 훨씬 더 빨리 뛰었다.

※ 다음 우리말과 일치하도록 빈칸에 알맞은 말을 쓰시오.

HOLES

1 " _____ _____, Stanley!

2 _____ _____ you dig, _____ _____ you'll finish!" _____ Mr. Sir.

3 Stanley Yelnats couldn't dig _____ _____ _____ every single muscle _____.

4 He was _____ and _____.

5 He wanted to _____ _____.

6 _____, Stanley's home _____ the next 18 months _____ _____ right here, at Camp Green Lake.

7 Camp Green Lake was _____ _____ _____.

8 It wasn't green and _____ was _____ _____.

9 Camp Green Lake was _____ and _____ _____ _____.

10 _____ _____, it wasn't _____ a camp.

11 It was _____ _____ _____ _____ _____ _____.

12 Then what was a good boy _____ Stanley _____ here?

13 He _____ _____ to the camp _____ _____ a pair of sneakers.

14 Stanley _____ _____ _____ a pair of sneakers.

15 He was just _____ _____ _____ _____ _____ at the _____ _____.

16 One day, he was _____ _____ _____.

17 Suddenly, _____ _____ old sneakers _____ _____ the sky.

18 The sneakers _____ _____ _____ _____.

구덩이

1 "더 열심히 파, Stanley!

2 네가 열심히 파면 팔수록, 너는 더 빨리 끝낼 거야!" Sir 씨가 소리를 질렀다.

3 Stanley Yelnats는 모든 근육 하나하나가 아팠기 때문에 더 열심히 팔 수가 없었다.

4 그는 목이 마르고 배가 고팠다.

5 그는 집에 가고 싶었다.

6 불행히도, 앞으로 18개월 동안 Stanley의 집은 바로 여기 Green Lake 캠프가 될 것이었다.

7 Green Lake 캠프는 형편없는 이름이었다.

8 그곳은 초록색도 아니었고 호수도 없었다.

9 Green Lake 캠프는 뜨거웠고 온통 모래였다.

10 사실 그곳은 캠프조차 아니었다.

11 그곳은 나쁜 소년들을 위한 곳이었다.

12 그렇다면 Stanley 같이 착한 소년이 여기서 무엇을 하고 있었을까?

13 그는 운동화 한 켤레를 훔쳤다는 이유로 캠프에 보내졌다.

14 Stanley가 정말로 운동화 한 켤레를 훔친 것은 아니었다.

15 그는 그저 잘못된 시간에 잘못된 장소에 있었다.

16 어느 날, 그는 학교에서 집으로 걸어가고 있었다.

17 갑자기, 낡은 운동화 한 켤레가 하늘에서 떨어졌다.

18 그 운동화는 그의 머리에 맞았다.

19 He started running _____ the sneakers to tell his father _____ _____.

20 _____ _____ _____ later, the police _____ Stanley and asked him _____ _____ _____ _____.

21 Unfortunately _____ Stanley, the sneakers _____ _____ a famous baseball player, Clyde Livingstone.

22 _____ _____ _____ Stanley _____ _____ at Camp Green Lake.

23 Stanley _____ _____ Group D in the camp.

24 There were _____ _____ _____ in Stanley's group.

25 They all had _____ names _____ X-Ray, Zigzag and Zero.

26 Each boy had to dig _____ _____ _____ _____.

27 It had to be _____ 150cm _____ and 150cm _____.

28 Mr. Sir said, "You are digging _____ _____."

29 _____ _____ Stanley dug, _____ _____ he became.

30 _____ _____ less time _____ _____ his hole _____ _____.

31 In his second week, as Stanley was finishing his hole, he saw _____ _____ _____ _____ _____.

32 Stanley's heart _____ _____.

33 He heard that _____ _____ found something interesting would _____ _____ _____ _____ _____.

34 He carefully _____ _____ the shiny object and _____ _____ the dirt.

35 It was a _____ _____ _____.

36 But it _____ _____ real gold _____ it was too light.

37 There were two _____, *KB*, _____ _____ the tube.

38 What did KB _____ _____?

39 Stanley's heart _____ _____ _____.

19 그는 그의 아버지에게 무슨 일이 일어났는지 말하기 위해 운동화를 가지고 달리기 시작했다.

20 몇 분 후에, 경찰이 Stanley를 멈춰 세웠고 그가 왜 달리고 있었는지를 그에게 물었다.

21 Stanley에게는 불행히도, 그 운동화는 유명한 야구 선수인 Clyde Livingstone의 것이었다.

22 그것이 Stanley가 Green Lake 캠프에 오게 된 이유였다.

23 Stanley는 캠프에서 D 그룹에 배치되었다.

24 Stanley의 그룹에는 6명의 다른 소년들이 있었다.

25 그들은 모두 X-Ray, Zigzag, Zero와 같은 멋진 이름을 가지고 있었다.

26 각 소년은 매일 구덩이 하나를 파야 했다.

27 그것은 150cm 정도 깊이와 150cm 정도 너비여야 했다.

28 Sir 씨는 "너희들은 인격을 수양하기 위해 구덩이를 파고 있는 것이야."라고 말했다.

29 Stanley는 많이 파면 팔수록, 더 힘이 세졌다.

30 하루하루 구덩이를 끝내는 데 시간이 덜 걸렸다.

31 그가 온 지 두 번째 주, Stanley가 자기 구덩이를 끝내 가고 있었을 때, 그는 흙 속에서 빛나는 뭔가를 봤다.

32 Stanley의 심장은 더 빨리 뛰었다.

33 그는 흥미로운 뭔가를 발견한 사람은 그 날을 쉬게 된다고 들었다.

34 그는 조심스럽게 그 빛나는 물체를 집어 흙을 털어 냈다.

35 그것은 작은 금색 통이었다.

36 그러나 그것은 너무 가벼웠기 때문에 진짜 금일 리가 없었다.

37 그 통의 바닥에는 KB라는 두 글자가 있었다.

38 KB는 무엇을 의미할까?

39 Stanley의 심장은 훨씬 더 빨리 뛰었다.

Step3

※ 다음 문장을 우리말로 쓰시오.

HOLES

1 "Dig harder, Stanley!
➡ _____

2 The harder you dig, the faster you'll finish!" yelled Mr. Sir.
➡ _____

3 Stanley Yelnats couldn't dig any harder since every single muscle hurt.
➡ _____

4 He was thirsty and hungry.
➡ _____

5 He wanted to go home.
➡ _____

6 Unfortunately, Stanley's home for the next 18 months would be right here, at Camp Green Lake.
➡ _____

7 Camp Green Lake was a terrible name.
➡ _____

8 It wasn't green and there was no lake.
➡ _____

9 Camp Green Lake was hot and full of sand.
➡ _____

10 In fact, it wasn't even a camp.
➡ _____

11 It was a place for bad boys.
➡ _____

12 Then what was a good boy like Stanley doing here?
➡ _____

13 He was sent to the camp for stealing a pair of sneakers.
➡ _____

14 Stanley didn't really steal a pair of sneakers.
➡ _____

15 He was just in the wrong place at the wrong time.
➡ _____

16 One day, he was walking home from school.
➡ _____

17 Suddenly, a pair of old sneakers fell from the sky.
➡ _____

18 The sneakers hit him on the head.
➡ _____

19 He started running with the sneakers to tell his father what happened.
➡ _____

20 A few minutes later, the police stopped Stanley and asked him why he was running.
➡ _____

21 Unfortunately for Stanley, the sneakers belonged to a famous baseball player, Clyde Livingstone.
➡ _____

22 That was why Stanley ended up at Camp Green Lake.
➡ _____

23 Stanley was assigned to Group D in the camp.
➡ _____

24 There were six other boys in Stanley's group.
➡ _____

25 They all had cool names like X-Ray, Zigzag and Zero.
➡ _____

26 Each boy had to dig one hole every day.
➡ _____

27 It had to be about 150cm deep and 150cm wide.
➡ _____

28 Mr. Sir said, "You are digging to build character."
➡ _____

29 The more Stanley dug, the stronger he became.
➡ _____

30 It took less time to finish his hole each day.
➡ _____

31 In his second week, as Stanley was finishing his hole, he saw something shiny in the dirt.
➡ _____

32 Stanley's heart beat faster.
➡ _____

33 He heard that anyone who found something interesting would be given the day off.
➡ _____

34 He carefully picked up the shiny object and brushed off the dirt.
➡ _____

35 It was a small gold tube.
➡ _____

36 But it couldn't be real gold since it was too light.
➡ _____

37 There were two letters, *KB*, at the bottom of the tube.
➡ _____

38 What did KB stand for?
➡ _____

39 Stanley's heart beat even faster.
➡ _____

※ 다음 괄호 안의 단어들을 우리말에 맞도록 바르게 배열하시오.

HOLES

1 (harder, / "dig / Stanley!)

➡ _____

2 (harder / the / dig, / you / faster / the / finish!" / you'll / Mr. / yelled / Sir.)

➡ _____

3 (Yelnats / Stanley / dig / couldn't / harder / any / every / since / single / hurt. / muscle)

➡ _____

4 (was / he / hungry. / and / thirsty)

➡ _____

5 (wanted / he / go / to / home.)

➡ _____

6 (Stanley's / unfortunately, / home / for / next / the / months / 18 / be / would / here, / right / Camp / at / Lake. / Green)

➡ _____

7 (Green / Camp / was / Lake / a / name. / terrible)

➡ _____

8 (wasn't / it / and / green / was / there / lake. / no)

➡ _____

9 (Green / Camp / Lake / hot / was / full / and / sand. / of)

➡ _____

10 (fact, / in / wasn't / it / a / even / camp.)

➡ _____

11 (was / it / place / a / bad / for / boys.)

➡ _____

12 (what / then / was / good / a / like / boy / doing / Stanley / here?)

➡ _____

13 (was / he / to / sent / camp / the / stealing / for / pair / of / sneakers. / a)

➡ _____

구덩이

1 "더 열심히 파, Stanley!

2 네가 열심히 파면 팔수록, 너는 더 빨리 끝낼 거야!" Sir 씨가 소리를 질렀다.

3 Stanley Yelnats는 모든 근육 하나하나가 아팠기 때문에 더 열심히 팔 수가 없었다.

4 그는 목이 마르고 배가 고팠다.

5 그는 집에 가고 싶었다.

6 불행히도, 앞으로 18개월 동안 Stanley의 집은 바로 여기 Green Lake 캠프가 될 것이었다.

7 Green Lake 캠프는 형편없는 이름이었다.

8 그곳은 초록색도 아니었고 호수도 없었다.

9 Green Lake 캠프는 뜨거웠고 온통 모래였다.

10 사실 그곳은 캠프조차 아니었다.

11 그곳은 나쁜 소년들을 위한 곳이었다.

12 그렇다면 Stanley 같이 착한 소년이 여기서 무엇을 하고 있었을까?

13 그는 운동화 한 켤레를 훔쳤다는 이유로 캠프에 보내졌다.

14 (didn't / Stanley / steal / really / pair / a / sneakers. / of)

➡ _____

15 (was / he / in / just / the / place / wrong / the / at / time. / wrong)

➡ _____

16 (day, / one / he / was / walking / from / home / school.)

➡ _____

17 (a / suddenly, / of / pair / sneakers / old / from / fell / sky. / the)

➡ _____

18 (sneakers / the / him / hit / the / on / head.)

➡ _____

19 (started / he / with / running / sneakers / the / tell / to / father / his / happened. / what)

➡ _____

20 (few / a / later, / minutes / police / the / Stanley / stopped / asked / and / why / him / he / running. / was)

➡ _____

➡ _____

21 (for / unfortunately / Stanley, / sneakers / the / belonged / a / to / baseball / famous / player. / Livingstone. / Clyde)

➡ _____

➡ _____

22 (was / that / Stanley / why / up / ended / Camp / at / Lake. / Green)

➡ _____

23 (was / Stanley / assigned / Group / to / in / D / camp. / the)

➡ _____

24 (were / there / other / six / in / boys / group. / Stanley's)

➡ _____

25 (all / they / cool / had / like / names / Zigzag / X-Ray / Zero. / and)

➡ _____

---

14 Stanley가 정말로 운동화 한 켤레를 훔친 것은 아니었다.

15 그는 그저 잘못된 시간에 잘못된 장소에 있었다.

16 어느 날, 그는 학교에서 집으로 걸어가고 있었다.

17 갑자기, 낡은 운동화 한 켤레가 하늘에서 떨어졌다.

18 그 운동화는 그의 머리에 맞았다.

19 그는 그의 아버지에게 무슨 일이 일어났는지 말하기 위해 운동화를 가지고 달리기 시작했다.

20 몇 분 후에, 경찰이 Stanley를 멈춰 세웠고 그가 왜 달리고 있었는지를 그에게 물었다.

21 Stanley에게는 불행히도, 그 운동화는 유명한 야구 선수인 Clyde Livingstone의 것이었다.

22 그것이 Stanley가 Green Lake 캠프에 오게 된 이유였다.

23 Stanley는 캠프에서 D 그룹에 배치되었다.

24 Stanley의 그룹에는 6명의 다른 소년들이 있었다.

25 그들은 모두 X-Ray, Zigzag, Zero와 같은 멋진 이름을 가지고 있었다.

26 (boy / each / to / had / one / dig / every / hole / day.)

➡ _____

27 (had / it / be / to / 150cm / about / and / deep / wide. / 150cm)

➡ _____

28 (Sir / Mr. / said, / are / "you / digging / build / to / character.")

➡ _____

29 (more / the / dug, / Stanely / stronger / the / became. / he)

➡ _____

30 (took / it / time / less / finish / to / hole / his / day. / each)

➡ _____

31 (his / in / week, / second / Stanley / as / finishing / was / hole, / his / saw / he / shiny / something / in / dirt. / the)

➡ _____

_____

32 (heart / Stanley's / faster. / beat)

➡ _____

33 (heard / he / anyone / that / found / who / interesting / something / be / would / the / given / off. / day)

➡ _____

_____

34 (carefully / he / up / picked / shiny / the / and / object / off / brushed / dirt. / the)

➡ _____

_____

35 (was / it / a / gold / small / tube.)

➡ _____

36 (it / but / be / couldn't / gold / real / it / since / too / was / light.)

➡ _____

37 (were / there / letters, / two / at / *KB*, / the / of / bottom / tube. / the)

➡ _____

38 (did / what / stand / KB / for?)

➡ _____

39 (heart / Stanley's / beat / faster. / even)

➡ _____

---

26 각 소년은 매일 구덩이를 하나를 파야 했다.

27 그것은 150cm 정도 깊이와 150cm 정도 너비여야 했다.

28 Sir 씨는 "너희들은 인격을 수양 하기 위해 구덩이를 파고 있는 것이야."라고 말했다.

29 Stanley는 많이 파면 팔수록, 더 힘이 세졌다.

30 하루하루 구덩이를 끝내는 데 시간이 덜 걸렸다.

31 그가 온 지 두 번째 주, Stanley 가 자기 구덩이를 끝내 가고 있 었을 때, 그는 흙 속에서 빛나는 뭔가를 봤다.

32 Stanley의 심장은 더 빨리 뛰었다.

33 그는 흥미로운 뭔가를 발견한 사람은 그 날을 쉬게 된다고 들 었다.

34 그는 조심스럽게 그 빛나는 물 체를 집어 흙을 털어 냈다.

35 그것은 작은 금색 통이었다.

36 그러나 그것은 너무 가벼웠기 때문에 진짜 금일 리가 없었다.

37 그 통의 바닥에는 KB라는 두 글 자가 있었다.

38 KB는 무엇을 의미할까?

39 Stanley의 심장은 훨씬 더 빨리 뛰었다.

※ 다음 우리말을 영어로 쓰시오.

HOLES

1 "더 열심히 파, Stanley!

➡ _____

2 네가 열심히 파면 팔수록, 너는 더 빨리 끝낼 거야!" Sir 씨가 소리를 질렀다.

➡ _____

3 Stanley Yelnats는 모든 근육 하나하나가 아팠기 때문에 더 열심히 팔 수가 없었다.

➡ _____

4 그는 목이 마르고 배가 고팠다.

➡ _____

5 그는 집에 가고 싶었다.

➡ _____

6 불행히도, 앞으로 18개월 동안 Stanley의 집은 바로 여기 Green Lake 캠프가 될 것이었다.

➡ _____

7 Green Lake 캠프는 형편없는 이름이었다.

➡ _____

8 그곳은 초록색도 아니었고 호수도 없었다.

➡ _____

9 Green Lake 캠프는 뜨거웠고 온통 모래였다.

➡ _____

10 사실 그곳은 캠프조차 아니었다.

➡ _____

11 그곳은 나쁜 소년들을 위한 곳이었다.

➡ _____

12 그렇다면 Stanley 같이 착한 소년이 여기서 무엇을 하고 있었을까?

➡ _____

13 그는 운동화 한 켤레를 훔쳤다는 이유로 캠프에 보내졌다.

➡ _____

14 Stanley가 정말로 운동화 한 켤레를 훔친 것은 아니었다.

➡ _____

15 그는 그저 잘못된 시간에 잘못된 장소에 있었다.

➡ _____

16 어느 날, 그는 학교에서 집으로 걸어가고 있었다.

➡ _____

17 갑자기, 낡은 운동화 한 켤레가 하늘에서 떨어졌다.

➡ _____

18 그 운동화는 그의 머리에 맞았다.

➡ _____

19 그는 그의 아버지에게 무슨 일이 일어났는지 말하기 위해 운동화를 가지고 달리기 시작했다.
➡ _____

20 몇 분 후에, 경찰이 Stanley를 멈춰 세웠고 그가 왜 달리고 있었는지를 그에게 물었다.
➡ _____

21 Stanley에게는 불행히도, 그 운동화는 유명한 야구 선수인 Clyde Livingstone의 것이었다.
➡ _____

22 그것이 Stanley가 Green Lake 캠프에 오게 된 이유였다.
➡ _____

23 Stanley는 캠프에서 D 그룹에 배치되었다.
➡ _____

24 Stanley의 그룹에는 6명의 다른 소년들이 있었다.
➡ _____

25 그들은 모두 X-Ray, Zigzag, Zero와 같은 멋진 이름을 가지고 있었다.
➡ _____

26 각 소년은 매일 구덩이를 하나 파야 했다.
➡ _____

27 그것은 150cm 정도 깊이와 150cm 정도 너비여야 했다.
➡ _____

28 Sir 씨는 "너희들은 인격을 수양하기 위해 구덩이를 파고 있는 것이야."라고 말했다.
➡ _____

29 Stanley는 많이 파면 팔수록, 더 힘이 세졌다.
➡ _____

30 하루하루 구덩이를 끝내는 데 시간이 덜 걸렸다.
➡ _____

31 그가 온 지 두 번째 주, Stanley가 자기 구덩이를 끝내 가고 있었을 때, 그는 흙 속에서 빛나는 뭔가를 봤다.
➡ _____

32 Stanley의 심장은 더 빨리 뛰었다.
➡ _____

33 그는 흥미로운 뭔가를 발견한 사람은 그 날을 쉬게 된다고 들었다.
➡ _____

34 그는 조심스럽게 그 빛나는 물체를 집어 흙을 털어 냈다.
➡ _____

35 그것은 작은 금색 통이었다.
➡ _____

36 그러나 그것은 너무 가벼웠기 때문에 진짜 금일 리가 없었다.
➡ _____

37 그 통의 바닥에는 KB라는 두 글자가 있었다.
➡ _____

38 KB는 무엇을 의미할까?
➡ _____

39 Stanley의 심장은 훨씬 더 빨리 뛰었다.
➡ _____

※ 다음 우리말과 일치하도록 빈칸에 알맞은 말을 쓰시오.

After You Read B

1. Monday, _____ _____

2. _____, the camp isn't green and _____ _____ _____
   _____.

3. I'm _____ Group D. My group members _____
   _____ _____ X-Ray, Zigzag and Zero.

4. We _____ _____ _____ one hole _____ 150cm _____
   and 150cm _____.

5. The good news is this: _____ _____ finds _____ _____
   can _____ _____ _____ _____.

6. I _____ I _____ _____ the one.

1. 8월 5일, 월요일
2. 불행히도, 캠프는 초록색도 아니고 호수도 없다.
3. 나는 D 그룹에 있다. 나의 그룹 멤버들은 X-Ray, Zigzag, Zero와 같은 멋진 이름들을 가지고 있다.
4. 우리는 150cm 정도 깊이와 150cm 정도 너비의 구덩이 하나를 파야 한다.
5. 좋은 소식은 다음과 같다: 흥미로운 뭔가를 발견한 사람은 그 날을 쉴 수 있다.
6. 내가 그 사람이기를 바란다.

Word Power

1. She _____ _____ _____ _____ _____ _____ _____ 15
   dollars.

2 I _____ _____ _____ _____ _____ under the chair.

3 He _____ _____ _____ _____ _____ in his bag.

1. 그녀는 구두 한 켤레를 15달러에 샀다.
2 나는 의자 아래에서 안경 한 개를 찾았다.
3 그는 가방에 청바지 세 벌을 샀다.

Think and Write

1. Kate Barlow _____ _____ _____ Green Lake.

2. She _____ _____ _____.

3. _____ _____ _____ in the town wanted _____ _____
   _____.

4. But Kate _____ _____ _____ _____ _____ Sam, a _____
   _____.

5. The rich men _____ _____ _____ Sam.

6. _____, Sam was _____ _____. Kate _____ _____ and
   _____ the town.

1. Kate Barlow는 그린 레이크 마을의 교사였다.
2. 그녀는 매우 인기가 있었다.
3. 마을의 많은 부유한 남자들이 그녀와 결혼하고 싶어했다.
4. 그러나 Kate는 가난한 남자인 Sam과 사랑에 빠졌다.
5. 부유한 남자들은 Sam을 다치게 하려고 했다.
6. 나중에 Sam은 죽은 채로 발견되었다. Kate는 슬퍼서 마을을 떠났다.

※ 다음 우리말을 영어로 쓰시오.

After You Read B

1. 8월 5일, 월요일

   ➡ _____

2. 불행히도, 캠프는 초록색도 아니고 호수도 없다.

   ➡ _____

3. 나는 D 그룹에 있다. 나의 그룹 멤버들은 X-Ray, Zigzag, Zero와 같은 멋진 이름들을 가지고 있다.

   ➡ _____

4. 우리는 150cm 정도 깊이와 150cm 정도 너비의 구덩이 하나를 파야 한다.

   ➡ _____

5. 좋은 소식은 다음과 같다: 흥미로운 뭔가를 발견한 사람은 그 날을 쉴 수 있다.

   ➡ _____

6. 내가 그 사람이기를 바란다.

   ➡ _____

Word Power

1. 그녀는 구두 한 켤레를 15달러에 샀다.

   ➡ _____

2. 나는 의자 아래에서 안경 한 개를 찾았다.

   ➡ _____

3. 그는 가방에 청바지 세 벌을 쌌다.

   ➡ _____

Think and Write

1. Kate Barlow는 그린 레이크 마을의 교사였다.

   ➡ _____

2. 그녀는 매우 인기가 있었다.

   ➡ _____

3. 마을의 많은 부유한 남자들이 그녀와 결혼하고 싶어했다.

   ➡ _____

4. 그러나 Kate는 가난한 남자인 Sam과 사랑에 빠졌다.

   ➡ _____

5. 부유한 남자들은 Sam을 다치게 하려고 했다.

   ➡ _____

6. 나중에 Sam은 죽은 채로 발견되었다. Kate는 슬퍼서 마을을 떠났다.

   ➡ _____

MEMO

MEMO

I Can't, but We Can

시험대비 실력평가 p.08

01 ② 02 ⑤ 03 ①, ⑤ 04 ① 05 ③

01 point: (경기 등에서) 점수 / 우리는 1점 차로 졌다. ①, ③, ⑤: point: 요점 ④ point at: ~을 가리키다 ① 그는 강연의 요점을 적어 두었다. ② David은 수학 점수가 가장 높다. ③ 나는 그의 연설의 요점을 이해할 수 없었다. ④ 여자는 컴퓨터 화면을 가리키고 있다. ⑤ 요점은 간단합니다: 너무 많이 걱정하지 마라.

02 ① 그것들 또한 창의적으로 생각하도록 도와줄 수 있다. ② 각각의 발표에 단지 한 시간씩만 허락되었다. ③ 십대들은 새로운 과제를 직면하고 팀워크, 통솔력, 계획을 포함한 기술들을 배울 것이다. ④ 이 서핑 대회는 개들을 위한 것이었다. ⑤ pretty: 꽤, 매우 / 어제까지는 꽤 따뜻했다.

03 in the end: 마침내 (= finally = at last) / 결국 그 사랑 이야기는 해피 엔딩이 아닐 것이다.

04 ① stuck: 움직일 수 없는 / 늦어서 미안해. 교통체증에 갇혀 꼼짝 못했어. ② upset: 속상한, 기분이 상한 / 나는 내 여동생 때문에 매우 속상하다. ③ same: 같은 / 결국 아이들은 부모와 같은 방식으로 음식을 먹는다. ④ instead: 대신에 / 커피 대신에 차를 마실 게요. ⑤ busy: 바쁜 / Rachel은 자기가 너무 바빠서 올 수 없을 것이다라고 말했다.

05 (A) have a fight with ~: ~와 싸우다 / Jamie는 오늘 아침에 화가 나 보였어. 아마 엄마랑 싸웠을 거야. (B) spend A on B: A를 B에 쓰다 / 그들은 너무 많은 시간을 컴퓨터 게임에 낭비한다.

서술형 시험대비 p.09

01 ⓑ lately → late
02 (p)retty
03 competition
04 in
05 (b)ase
06 (1) try (2) spend (3) have (4) see
07 (1) (p)retty busy (2) (s)uggest
08 (1) I scored two goals right away and my team won the game by one goal.
(2) They are still talking.

01 lately: 최근에 late: 늦은; 늦게 ⓐ 이른 아침이다. ⓑ 나는 항상 늦게 일어난다. ⓒ 파티를 취소하기에는 너무 늦다.

02 pretty: 꽤, 매우(= fairly, very) / 우리는 꽤 자주 영화관에 갔다.

03 compete: 경쟁하다 competition: (경연) 대회, 시합, 경쟁 / 나는 이곳에 공정한 경쟁이 있다고 들었다.

04 in a hurry: 서둘러, 급히 / 만약 일들을 급히 한다면 실수를 할 것이다. in detail: 상세하게 / 그녀는 학교에 대한 미래 계획에 대해 상세하게 말했다.

05 base: (사물의) 맨 아래 부분 / 물건의 가장 낮은 부분이나 표면

06 (1) try to 동사원형: ~하려고 애쓰다 / 항상 최선을 다하려고 노력해라. (2) spend A on B: A를 B에 쓰다 / 얼마나 많은 시간을 숙제하는 데 쓰니? (3) have a fight with ~: ~와 싸우다 / 내가 동생이랑 싸우면, 엄마는 항상 동생 편을 든다. (4) Long time no see.: 오랜만이야.

07 (1) pretty: 꽤, 매우 busy: 바쁜 (2) suggest: 제안하다

08 (1) score: (경기 등에서) 득점 right away: 즉각, 곧바로 by: (정도·차이) ~의 차(이)로, ~만큼 (2) still: 여전히

교과서
Conversation

핵심 Check p.10~11

1 How have you been? 2 (B) → (C) → (A) → (D)
3 I'm sorry to hear that.

교과서 대화문 익히기

Check(√) True or False p.12~13

1 F 2 T 3 F 4 T 5 T 6 T 7 F 8 T

교과서 확인학습 p.15~17

Listen and Speak 1 A

how, been / been, about / Not, have / Get

Listen and Speak 1 B

We're / It's good, How have you / I've been / I've been pretty, competition / didn't, played / I've played / must, at, luck in

Listen and Speak 1 C

1. how, you been / been, everything / are
2. have you been / is everything / So, have
3. How have you / I've been, How, Pretty
4. How have you been / I've been, everything / have

Listen and Speak 2 A

excited, have any good / got / had the best / I'm, to hear

Listen and Speak 2 B

how did / lost / sorry to hear / great / was, score / to, lost by / close / played / That's

Listen and Speak 2 C

1. happy / in first in / happy to hear
2. upset / had a fight with / sorry to hear that
3. look happy / won / happy to hear
4. upset / lost / sorry to hear
5. look happy / bought / happy to hear
6. upset / dropped / sorry, hear

Real Life Talk Step 1

Long time / been / How, been / been, about / been, at, How's / made many / I'm happy / have to / have, number / call, Have / too

Real Life Talk Step 2

1. How have you been / How, vacation / joined / to hear that
2. have you been / Not / How / lost / I'm sorry

시험대비 기본평가

p.18

01 ④   02 ③   03 ①, ④

01 'I've been great.'으로 응답하는 것으로 보아 안부를 묻는 'how have you been?(어떻게 지냈니?)'이 어울린다.

02 주어진 문장은 '어떻게 지냈니?'의 의미로 안부를 묻는 표현이므로, (C)에서 잘 지냈다고 대답하며, (A)에서 방학은 어떻게 보냈는지 질문을 하자 (B)에서 스키 캠프에 들어갔다고 대답한다. (D)에서 상대방의 좋은 소식에 대해 'I'm happy to hear that.'으로 기쁨을 표현한다.

03 핸드폰을 떨어뜨린 상대방에 유감을 표현하는 말을 할 수 있다. 유감을 표현하는 말에는 'I'm sorry to hear that.(그 말을 들으니 유감이야.)', 'What a pity!(정말 안됐구나!)', 'That's a pity.(안됐다.)', 'That's too bad.(정말 안됐다.)' 등이 있다.

시험대비 실력평가

p.19~20

01 ④   02 ③   03 happy   04 ④
05 ①   06 ②   07 ②
08 (A) good (B) have played   09 ④   10 ⑤
11 ④

01 상대방이 한 말에 대하여 기쁨을 표현할 때 'I'm happy[glad] to hear that.'이라고 말할 수 있다. 'I had a fight with my friend.'는 친구와 싸움을 했다는 내용이므로 유감을 표현하는 'I'm sorry to hear that.'이 어울린다.

02 최근에 많이 못 만났다고 어떻게 지내는지 안부를 묻는 표현에 유감을 표하는 대답을 하는 것은 어색하다.

03 상대방이 한 말에 대하여 기쁨을 표현할 때 'I'm happy to hear that.(그 말을 들으니 기뻐.)'이라고 말할 수 있다.

04 주어진 문장은 점수가 80 대 79점이었다고 말하는 것이므로 점수를 물어보는 질문인 'What was the score?'에 대답하는 자리에 들어가는 것이 적절하다.

05 go: (일의 진행이 어떻게) 되다

06 ① Andy 팀은 이겼는가? (아니오.) ② 언제 농구 경기가 있었나? ③ Andy가 참여한 경기의 점수는 몇 점인가?(80 대 79) ④ Andy의 농구 팀은 몇 점 차이로 졌는가? (1점 차이) ⑤ Andy는 농구팀을 어떻게 생각하고 있는가? (한 팀으로서 잘 경기했다.)

07 주어진 문장은 안부를 묻는 말이므로, 'I've been great.(잘 지냈어.)'와 어울린다.

08 (A) 같은 반이 되어서 좋아하는 소라에게 진수가 'Yeah!'라고 말했으므로, 너를 보게 되어 좋다는 말이 어울린다. (B) 현재까지 계속되는 행위이므로 현재완료가 적절하다.

09 ④ 진수의 피아노 대회는 다음 주이다.

10 안부를 묻는 말에, (C) 좋다고 대답하며, 상대방의 안부도 이어서 물어본다. (D) 민호는 바빴다고 대답하며, Linda의 새 학교는 어떤지 질문하자 (B) 좋다고 말하며 새로운 친구들을 많이 사귀었다고 말한다. (A) 잘됐다고 얘기하며 기쁨을 표현한다.

11 상대방의 안부를 물을 때에는 'How is everything?', 'How have you been (doing)', 'How's it going?', 'How are you doing?', 'What have you been up to?' 등의 표현을 사용할 수 있다.

서술형 시험대비

p.21

01 how
02 (B) to   (C) by
03 ⓐ lost   ⓑ close

04 (A) How   (B) How
05 Long time no see.
06 I'm happy to hear that.
07 (A) been   (B) was

01 특정한 경험이 어땠는지를 'How did ~ go?'로 물어볼 수 있다.
go: (일의 진행이 어떻게) 되다

02 (B) '(점수가) A 대 B'의 뜻으로 말할 때 대조, 대비의 의미를 가진 전치사 to를 사용하여 'A to B'라고 표현한다. (C) by: (정도·차이) ~의 차(이)로, ~만큼

03 ⓐ G가 'I'm sorry to hear that.'으로 상대방에게 유감을 표현하고 있으므로, B가 경기에서 진 것을 추론할 수 있다. lose: 지다 (lose-lost-lost) ⓑ 점수가 80 대 79이며 1점 차이인 것으로 보아 막상막하인 것을 알 수 있다. close: 막상막하의

04 How have you been?: 어떻게 지냈니? 'How come?'은 '왜?'의 의미로, 이유를 물을 때 사용하는 표현이다.

05 'Long time no see.'는 '오랜만이야.'의 의미로 'It's been a long time.과 바꿔 쓸 수 있다.

06 'I'm happy to hear that.'은 '그 말을 들으니 기뻐.'의 의미로, 상대방의 좋은 소식을 듣고 기쁨을 표현하는 말이다.

07 (A) 안부를 물어보는 'How have you been?(어떻게 지냈니?)'에 대해 'It's been great.(잘 지냈어.)'으로 대답할 수 있다. (B) 'I joined a ski camp.'라고 대답한 것으로 보아, 과거의 경험에 대해서 묻는 'How was ~?(~가 어땠니?)' 표현을 사용했음을 알 수 있다.

교과서
Grammar

핵심 Check   p.22~23

1 (1) to   (2) for   (3) of
2 (1) what   (2) what   (3) What

시험대비 기본평가   p.24

01 ④   02 ③   03 ③
04 (1) to talk   (2) It   (3) for   (4) of   (5) What   (6) what

01 it을 가주어로 하고 to부정사를 진주어로 하는 ④번이 적절하다.

02 tell의 직접목적어와 think의 목적어 역할을 할 수 있는 것으로 선행사를 포함하는 관계대명사 what이 나와야 한다.

---

03 to부정사의 의미상의 주어가 일반적인 사람일 경우는 보통 생략한다.

04 (1) 진주어로 to부정사가 적절하다. (2) 가주어로는 This가 아니라 It을 쓴다. (3) to부정사의 의미상의 주어는 to부정사 바로 앞에 'for+대명사의 목적격'으로 나타낸다. (4) 문장에 쓰인 형용사가 nice, kind, smart, wise 등과 같이 사람의 성향, 성격을 나타내는 말일 때는 'of+대명사의 목적격'으로 쓴다. (5) want의 목적어와 is의 보어 역할을 할 수 있는 what이 적절하다. (6) put off와 do의 목적어 역할을 할 수 있는 what이 적절하다.

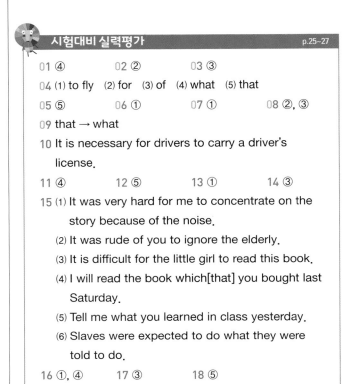

시험대비 실력평가   p.25~27

01 ④   02 ②   03 ③
04 (1) to fly   (2) for   (3) of   (4) what   (5) that
05 ⑤   06 ①   07 ①   08 ②, ③
09 that → what
10 It is necessary for drivers to carry a driver's license.
11 ④   12 ⑤   13 ①   14 ③
15 (1) It was very hard for me to concentrate on the story because of the noise.
(2) It was rude of you to ignore the elderly.
(3) It is difficult for the little girl to read this book.
(4) I will read the book which[that] you bought last Saturday.
(5) Tell me what you learned in class yesterday.
(6) Slaves were expected to do what they were told to do.
16 ①, ④   17 ③   18 ⑤

01 ① It's so kind of you to help me. ② It isn't easy to teach music to little children. ③ It's good to hear your voice on the phone again. ⑤ It's necessary to know when to draw the line.

02 believe와 see의 목적어 역할을 할 수 있도록 that을 what으로 고쳐야 한다. hand in: ~을 제출하다

03 전치사 to와 say의 목적어 역할을 할 수 있는 것은 what이다. 가주어로 It이 나와 있고 진주어로 to부정사가 나와 있으므로 빈칸에는 to부정사의 의미상의 주어가 나와야 한다. 사람의 성향이나 성격을 나타내는 형용사가 아니므로 for가 적절하다.

04 (1) 진주어로 to부정사가 적절하다. (2) to부정사의 의미상의 주어는 to부정사 바로 앞에 'for+명사의 목적격'으로 나타낸다. (3) 문장에 쓰인 형용사가 사람의 성향이나 성격을 나타내는 말일 때는 'for+대명사의 목적격'이 아니라 'of+대명사의 목적격'으로 쓴다. (4) buy의 목적어가 없으므로 what이 이끄는 절이

have의 목적어가 되도록 해야 한다. (5) 선행사로 all이 있으므로 관계대명사 that이 적절하다. all을 없애고, what만 써도 어법상 바른 문장이다.

05 Tell의 직접목적어와 heard의 목적어 역할을 할 수 있는 what이 적절하다.

06 to부정사의 의미상의 주어는 to부정사 바로 앞에 'for+명사의 목적격'의 형태로 쓴다.

07 ② It is very important for us to study foreign languages. ③ It was silly of me to believe what he said. ④ It was careless of her to open the door for the stranger. ⑤ It is difficult for us to swim in this river.

08 what이 관계대명사인지 의문대명사인지 구분하는 문제로 보통 의문대명사 what은 '무엇이 ~인(한)지'로, 관계대명사 what은 '~하는 것'으로 해석한다. ① 의문대명사 ② 관계대명사 ③ 관계대명사 ④ 의문대명사 ⑤ 의문대명사

09 what is called: 소위, 이른바

10 'It ~ for ... to부정사' 구문을 이용하여 쓴다.

11 the things which[that]의 역할을 하는 what을 이용하여 나타내도록 한다.

12 가주어로 It을 쓰고 to부정사의 의미상의 주어로 사람의 성향이나 성격을 나타내는 형용사가 아니므로 for를 쓴다.

13 ①번은 선행사가 있으므로 which나 that이 들어가야 하고 나머지는 선행사가 없으므로 what이 적절하다. go over: ~을 복습하다

14 to부정사의 의미상의 주어는 to부정사 바로 앞에 'for+명사의 목적격'으로 나타내지만 문장에 쓰인 형용사가 nice, kind, smart, wise 등과 같이 사람의 성향이나 성격을 나타내는 말일 때는 'for+대명사의 목적격'이 아니라 'of+대명사의 목적격'으로 쓴다.

15 (1) 의미상의 주어로 for me를 쓴다. (2) 문장에 쓰인 형용사가 사람의 성향, 성격을 나타내는 말이므로 'for+대명사의 목적격'이 아니라 'of+대명사의 목적격'으로 쓴다. (3) 의미상의 주어로 'for+명사의 목적격'이 나왔으므로 진주어로 to부정사를 쓴다. (4) the book이 선행사로 나왔으므로 what이 아니라 which나 that을 써야 한다. (5) which를 Tell과 learned의 목적어 역할을 할 수 있는 what으로 고쳐야 한다. (6) that을 두 개의 do의 목적어 역할을 할 수 있는 what으로 고쳐야 한다. concentrate: 집중하다, slave: 노예

16 ① of her로 의미상의 주어가 나와 있으므로 to부정사가 적절하다. ④ do와 suggest의 목적어 역할을 해야 하므로 that을 what으로 고쳐야 한다.

17 for kids로 의미상의 주어가 있으므로 진주어로 to부정사를 써야 하고 가주어로 it을 쓴 ③번이 적절하다.

18 선행사가 없고 tell의 직접목적어와 was의 주어 역할을 해야 하므로 관계대명사 what이 적절하다.

01 (1) for him to   (2) of her to
02 (1) I believe what happened 100 years ago was wrong.
  (2) What matters most is inner beauty and self confidence.
  (3) It is very nice of you to adopt the abandoned dog.
  (4) It is really wonderful for him to jog early in the morning.
  (5) Is it possible for you to meet me today at three?
03 (1) what you want to drink
  (2) what I want
04 (1) of you to send
  (2) for a child to swim
05 (1) This is different from what I expected.
  (2) Bob couldn't accept what Theresa offered.
  (3) What was said by Tina was surprising.
  (4) What is important is present, not past.
06 (1) of me → for me
  (2) for you → of you
  (3) for them to not → of them not to
  (4) what → that[which]
  (5) That → What
  (6) that → what
07 (1) careful of her to avoid the argument
  (2) dangerous for children to walk home alone
08 (1) It is lucky for you to have a relative living in Seoul.
  (2) Is it safe to walk the streets alone at night?
  (3) It was not easy for the police to calm down the angry crowd.
  (4) Do you remember what we talked about yesterday?
  (5) We had to choose from what remained.

01 '가주어(It) ~ for[of] ...(의미상의 주어) 진주어(to부정사)' 구문을 이용한다.

02 (1)~(2) 선행사를 포함하는 관계대명사 what을 이용하여 배열한다. what이 선행사를 포함하므로 문장에서 두 가지의 역할을 함에 유의한다. (3)~(5) '가주어(it) ~ for(of) …(의미상의 주어) 진주어(to부정사)' 구문을 이용한다.

03 선행사를 포함하는 관계대명사 what을 이용한다.

04 '가주어(It) ~ for[of] ...(의미상의 주어) 진주어(to부정사)' 구문을 이용한다.

05 the thing(s) which[that]의 역할을 하는 what을 이용하여

하나의 문장으로 쓴다.

06 (1) to부정사의 의미상의 주어는 to부정사 앞에 'for+대명사의 목적격'으로 나타낸다. (2) 문장에 쓰인 형용사가 사람의 성향, 성격을 나타내는 말일 때는 의미상의 주어로 'of+대명사의 목적격'으로 쓴다. (3) 의미상의 주어로 'of+대명사의 목적격'이 적절하고, to부정사의 부정은 to부정사 앞에 not이나 never를 써서 'not[never]+to부정사'로 나타낸다. (4) the book이라는 선행사가 있으므로 what을 that[which]으로 고쳐 쓴다. (5) That을 do의 목적어와 is의 주어 역할을 할 수 있는 What으로 고쳐야 한다. (6) 선행사가 없으므로 that을 what으로 고쳐야 한다.

07 가주어(It) ~ for[of] ...(의미상의 주어) 진주어(to부정사)' 구문을 이용한다. 사람의 성격을 나타내는 형용사의 경우 의미상의 주어로 'of+목적격'을 쓴다.

08 (1)~(3) '가주어(it) ~ for(of) …(의미상의 주어) 진주어(to부정사)' 구문을 이용한다. to부정사의 의미상의 주어를 'for+명사의 목적격'으로 나타낸다. (4) remember의 목적어와 about의 목적어 역할을 할 수 있는 what을 이용한다. (5) from의 목적어와 remained의 주어 역할을 할 수 있는 what을 이용한다.
relative: 친척

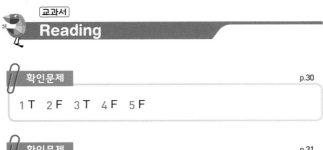

Reading

확인문제 p.30

1 T 2 F 3 T 4 F 5 F

확인문제 p.31

1 T 2 F 3 T 4 F 5 T 6 F

교과서 확인학습 A p.32~33

01 Marshmallow Challenge
02 You need, sticks
03 Each team has
04 have to build
05 must be on top
06 by itself
07 time limit
08 is good for: Building, Creatively
09 How
10 Every team does, differently
11 look at
12 Which one

13 Think, act
14 many good ideas
15 in detail
16 for us to choose
17 Five minutes left
18 In a hurry
19 wrapped the string
20 got stuck to
21 With one second left
22 Just do it
23 spend much time
24 right away
25 looked like
26 very tall
27 tried again
28 stand by itself
29 After many tries
30 Leaning Tower of Pisa
31 what we wanted
32 one team
33 didn't try to choose
34 improved on
35 a strong base
36 for the base
37 such as
38 as a team
39 In the end

교과서 확인학습 B p.34~35

1 Try the Marshmallow Challenge!
2 You need: 20 sticks of spaghetti, 1 marshmallow, 1 meter of tape, 1 meter of string
3 Rules: Each team has four people.
4 You have to build the tallest tower in your class.
5 The marshmallow must be on top.
6 The tower must stand by itself.
7 The time limit is 15 minutes.
8 This activity is good for: Building Relationships, Solving Problems, Thinking Creatively
9 How did you do the marshmallow challenge?
10 Every team does the marshmallow challenge differently.
11 Let's look at some examples.
12 Which one do you like best?
13 TEAM A: Think before you act.
14 We had many good ideas.

15 We talked about each idea in detail.

16 It was not easy for us to choose the best idea.

17 Suddenly the teacher said, "Five minutes left."

18 In a hurry, we taped the sticks of spaghetti together.

19 Then, we wrapped the string around them.

20 The string got stuck to the tape and it was a big mess.

21 With one second left, I put the marshmallow on top!

22 TEAM B: Just do it.

23 We didn't spend much time on planning.

24 All the members started building the tower right away.

25 Our first tower looked like a tent.

26 It wasn't very tall.

27 We tried again.

28 The next tower was tall but it couldn't stand by itself.

29 After many tries, it was possible for us to build a beautiful and tall tower.

30 It looked like the Leaning Tower of Pisa.

31 We finally made what we wanted!

32 TEAM C: We're one team.

33 We didn't try to choose the best idea.

34 Instead, we took a good idea and improved on it.

35 One student said we needed a strong base.

36 Another student suggested a triangle shape for the base.

37 We all agreed and divided up the roles such as time checker and tape cutter.

38 We worked together as a team.

39 In the end, we built our tall tower!

시험대비 실력평가
p.36~39

01 by itself 02 ③ 03 any place → top

04 ④ 05 ③

06 We finally made what we wanted! 또는 Finally we made what we wanted!

07 ④ 08 ① 09 ④ 10 ⑤

11 전반부에 어울리는 속담: ⑤번, 후반부에 어울리는 속담: ②번

12 have[get, take, throw] a look at

13 example 14 ⑤ 15 ④

16 (A) build relationships (B) solve problems
   (C) think creatively 17 ②

18 ② 19 ④

20 (A) a good idea (B) the best idea

21 (A) looked like (B) by itself (C) for us

22 ⓐ first ⓑ next[second] ⓒ final[last]

23 (A) Leaning Tower of Pisa (B) what they wanted

01 by itself: 홀로[혼자], 도움을 받지 않고 1. 사람에 의해 직접적으로 통제되지 않은 채로, 2. 근처에 아무 것도 없는 채로; 홀로

02 '핀'은 마시멜로 과제에 필요한 준비물에 속하지 않는다.

03 마시멜로는 탑의 '꼭대기'에 있어야 한다.

04 마시멜로 과제를 하는 가장 좋은 방법이 무엇인지는 대답할 수 없다. ① Four. ② We have to build the tallest tower in our class. ③ On top of the tower. ⑤ It is good for building relationships, solving problems, and thinking creatively.

05 ⓐ와 ③: ~와 비슷한(전치사), look like: ~처럼 보이다, ① 비슷한(형용사), ② ~하는 대로[~처럼](접속사), ④ 좋아하다(동사), ⑤ (예를 들어) ~와 같은(전치사)

06 'what'을 보충하면 된다.

07 Team B가 탑을 만드는 데 얼마 걸렸는지는 대답할 수 없다. ① No. ② It looked like a tent. ③ No, it wasn't very tall. ⑤ It looked like the Leaning Tower of Pisa.

08 ⓐ stick to: ~에 달라[들러]붙다, stick-stuck-stuck, ⓑ with: [부대상황을 나타내는 구를 이끌어] ~하여, ~한 채로, ~하면서, (명사·대명사+전치사가 달린 구·부사·형용사·분사 등의 보충적 요소를 거느림)

09 주어진 문장의 them에 주목한다. ④번 앞 문장의 'the sticks of spaghetti'를 받고 있으므로 ④번이 적절하다.

10 '1초를 남기고 내가 마시멜로를 꼭대기에 꽂았다'고 했으므로, Team A는 시간 내에 탑을 만들 수 있었다. in time: 시간에 맞춰[늦지 않게]

11 이 글의 전반부는 각 아이디어에 대해 자세히 이야기하면서 가장 좋은 아이디어를 고르려다가 시간이 5분만 남게 된 상황이므로, 어울리는 속담으로는 ⑤번이 적절하고, 후반부는 급히 완성하느라고 서두르면서 엉망진창으로 간신히 완성하는 내용이므로, 어울리는 속담으로는 ②번이 적절하다. ② 급히 서두르면 일을 망친다(서둘러서 엉성하게 하여 시간을 번다 해도 제대로 고치지 않으면 안 되므로 그만큼 시간을 낭비한다는 뜻). ⑤ 사공이 많으면 배가 산으로 올라간다(어떤 일에 관여하는 사람이 너무 많으면 일을 망친다는 뜻). ① 어려울 때 친구가 진정한 친구이다. ③ 유유상종(같은 유형의 사람들은 서로 함께 모이는 경향이 있다는 뜻). ④ 손 안에 든 새 한 마리가 숲 속에 있는 두 마리보다 낫다.

12 look at = have[get, take, throw] a look at

13 some examples 중 하나를 가리킨다.

14 '모든 팀은 마시멜로 과제를 다르게 해요. 몇몇 예들을 살펴봐

7

요.'라고 했으므로, 본문 뒤에는 '마시멜로 과제를 다르게 하는 몇몇 예들'이 나올 것이라고 하는 것이 적절하다.

15 탑은 스스로 서 있어야 한다.

16 마시멜로 과제는 '관계를 맺는 것', '문제를 해결하는 것', '창의적으로 생각하는 것'에 도움이 된다.

17 앞의 내용과 다른 두 번째 대안을 소개하고 있으므로 Instead가 가장 적절하다. ① 그러므로, ③ 비슷하게, 유사하게, 마찬가지로, ⑤ 즉, 다시 말해

18 (A)와 ①, ⑤: 명사적 용법, ②, ③, ④: 부사적 용법

19 이 글은 '역할을 나눠 하나의 팀으로 함께 해서 마침내 높은 탑을 만들었다'는 내용의 글이므로, 주제로는 ④번 '성공하는 팀은 역할 분담과 협동을 필요로 한다.'가 적절하다. ② 십인십색(十人十色), 사람마다 제각각이다. ③ 튼튼한 기반이 없으면 모든 것이 사상누각이다.

20 Team C의 멤버들은 '가장 좋은 아이디어'를 고르는 대신에 '좋은 아이디어'를 골라 발전시켰다.

21 (A) look+형용사, look like+명사, (B) '스스로' 서 있지 못했다고 해야 하므로 'by itself'가 적절하다. by itself: 홀로[혼자], 도움을 받지 않고, of itself: 자연히, 저절로, (C) to부정사의 의미상의 주어를 써야 하므로 'for us'가 적절하다. 앞에 사람의 성질을 나타내는 형용사가 있을 때는 의미상의 주어를 'of+목적격'으로 씀.

22 ⓐ Team B의 '첫 번째' 탑, ⓑ Team B의 '다음[두 번째]' 탑, ⓒ Team B의 '마지막' 탑을 가리킨다.

23 Team B의 마지막 탑은 '피사의 사탑' 같았다. 멤버들이 많은 실수를 저질렀지만, 그들은 계속 시도했고, 많은 시도 후에 결국 '그들이 원하는 것'을 만들었다.

서술형 시험대비 p.40~41

01 difficulty[a hard time/trouble/a problem]
02 the sticks of spaghetti
03 With one second left
04 choosing
05 do it 또는 try it
06 It couldn't stand by itself.
07 that → what
08 Team C didn't try to choose the best idea. Instead, they took a good idea and improved on it.
09 (A) a triangle shape (B) the roles (C) as a team
10 occurred to
11 After we taped the sticks of spaghetti together, 또는 After taping the sticks of spaghetti together,
12 time
13 on a triangle shape for the base
14 1단계: 가장 좋은 아이디어를 고르는 대신에 좋은 아이디어를

골라 발전시켰다.
2단계: 한 친구가 튼튼한 기반이 필요하다고 말했고 다른 친구는 기반으로 삼각형 모양을 제안했다
3단계: 모두 제안에 동의했고 시간 점검하는 사람과 테이프 자르는 사람과 같이 역할을 나눴다.
4단계: 하나의 팀으로 함께해서 마침내 높은 탑을 만들었다.

01 have difficulty[a hard time/trouble/a problem] ~ing: ~하는 데 고생하다
02 '스파게티 면들'을 가리킨다.
03 with: [부대상황을 나타내는 구를 이끌어] ~하여, ~한 채로, ~하면서, (명사·대명사+전치사가 달린 구·부사·형용사·분사 등의 보충적 요소를 거느림)
04 Team A는 실제로 탑을 만드는 것보다 가장 좋은 아이디어를 고르는 것에 더 많은 시간을 보냈다. spend+시간+~ing: ~하는 데 (시간을) 보내다
05 Team B는 계획하는 데 많은 시간을 보내지 않고 바로 탑을 만들기 시작했고 많은 시도 후에 결국 그들이 원하는 것을 만들었기 때문에, Team B의 특징을 묘사하기에 알맞은 문장으로는 '그냥 해라.'가 적절하다.
06 그것은 스스로 서 있지 못했다.
07 선행사가 없기 때문에 that을 선행사를 포함한 관계대명사 what으로 고치는 것이 적절하다.
08 Team C의 멤버들은 가장 좋은 아이디어를 고르려고 하지 않고, 대신에 좋은 아이디어를 골라 발전시켰다.
09 Team C의 멤버들 모두 기반으로 '삼각형 모양'에 동의했고, '역할'을 나눠, '하나의 팀으로' 함께해서 마침내 높은 탑을 만들었다.
10 occur to: ~에게 떠오르다
11 After+주어+동사, 또는 After ~ing로 고치는 것이 적절하다.
12 Team A의 멤버들은 그들의 제한 시간을 현명하게 사용하지 못했다. 그들은 하마터면 제한시간을 초과할 뻔 했지만, 그럭저럭 시간에 맞춰 과제를 수행했다. come[go] near ~ing: 거의[하마터면] …할 뻔하다, manage to: 그럭저럭 ~하다
13 우리 모두는 '기반으로 삼각형 모양'에 동의했다.
14 본문의 내용을 순서대로 쓰는 것이 적절하다.

영역별 핵심문제 p.43~47

01 ①   02 at   03 have
04 (1) Wrap (2) lose (3) call (4) go   05 ④
06 how have you been?   07 ②
08 I'm happy to hear that.   09 ③   10 ②
11 It's been a long time.   12 ②   13 ④

14 What I expected to see there was

15 ④ 16 (1) What I bought (2) his daughter

what is really valuable (3) get what they want

17 ② 18 ⓒ, ⓔ, ⑨

19 (1) That is what I wanted to say.

(2) I was hardly aware of what I was doing.

(3) We must remember what we learned in class.

(4) It is a pleasure to work with you again.

(5) It is important for us to help people in need.

(6) It is impolite of you to ignore his invitation.

20 ② 21 ⑤ 22 ② 23 ①

24 could, were able to 25 ③ 26 ⑤

27 (A) Instead (B) Another (C) divided

28 ① 29 ③ 30 to make

01 early: 이른 early: 일찍 ①번은 부사로, 이외의 보기들은 형용사로 사용되었다. ① 그들은 파티에 일찍 도착했다. ② 그들은 이른 저녁을 먹고 있다. ③ 이른 아침은 하루 중 가장 좋은 시간[때]이다. ④ 학교 가기에는 꽤 이른 시간이다. ⑤ 우리는 이른 아침식사를 했다.

02 be busy at (동)명사: ~으로 바쁘다 / 펌프질[펌프로 물 푸기]하느라고 바쁘니? be good at (동)명사: ~을 잘하다, ~에 능숙하다 / 나는 운동을 별로 잘하지 못한다.

03 have a cold: 감기에 걸리다 / 난 감기에 걸려서 냄새를 못 맡는다. have a fight with ~: ~와 싸우다 / 난 너와 싸우고 싶지 않다.

04 (1) wrap: 감다, 싸다 / 그것이 파손되지 않도록 잘 포장해라. (2) lose: (시합·선거에서) 지다 / 나는 그가 선거에서 지지 않기를 바란다. (3) call: 전화하다 / 몇 시에 Tony가 전화했니? (4) go: (일의 진행이 어떻게) 되다 / 프랑스어 시험이 어떻게 되었니?

05 get well: 병이 나아지다

06 상대방에게 그동안 어떻게 지냈는지 안부를 물을 때 'How have you been?(어떻게 지냈니?)'이라고 말한다.

07 'Do you have any good news?(무슨 좋은 소식이 있니?)'라고 말하고 있으므로 excited(신난, 흥분한)하게 보이는 것이 어울린다.

08 'I'm happy to hear that.'은 '그 말을 들으니 기쁘구나.'의 의미로 상대방이 한 말에 대하여 기쁨을 표현할 때 사용한다.

09 빈칸에는 개를 잃어버렸다는 상대방에게 유감을 표현하는 말이 어울린다. 유감을 표현하는 말에는 'I'm sorry to hear that.(그 말을 들으니 유감이야.)', 'What a pity!(정말 안됐구나!)', 'That's a pity.(안됐다.)', 'That's too bad.(정말 안됐다.)' 등이 있다.

10 주어진 문장은 새로운 학교생활이 어떤지 물어보고 있으므로 'It's wonderful. I've made many new friends.(좋아. 새로

운 친구들을 많이 사귀었어.)'라는 대답과 잘 어울리므로 ②가 적절하다.

11 한동안 보지 못했던 상대방에게 반가움을 나타내는 표현으로 'Long time no see.(오랜만이야.)'와 'It's been a long time.' 등이 있다.

12 ⓑ는 hear, 나머지 빈칸에는 have가 들어간다. ⓐ How have you been?: 어떻게 지냈니? ⓑ I'm happy to hear that.: 그 말을 들으니 기뻐. ⓒ have to 동사원형: ~해야 한다 ⓓ have: 가지다 ⓔ Have a good day!: 좋은 하루를 보내!

13 to부정사의 의미상의 주어는 to부정사 바로 앞에 'for+대명사의 목적격'으로 나타내지만 문장에 쓰인 형용사가 nice, kind, smart, wise 등과 같이 사람의 성향, 성격을 나타내는 말일 때는 'for+대명사의 목적격'이 아니라 'of+대명사의 목적격'으로 쓴다.

14 선행사를 포함하는 관계대명사 what을 이용하여 '~하는 것'을 나타낸다.

15 의미상의 주어 앞에 전치사 for가 있으므로 빈칸에는 사람의 성격을 나타내는 형용사 silly는 알맞지 않다.

16 선행사를 포함한 관계대명사 what(= the thing(s) which[that])을 이용한다.

17 ②에는 사람의 성격이나 성질을 나타내는 형용사(foolish)가 왔으므로 의미상의 주어로 'of+대명사의 목적격'이 적절하다. 나머지는 모두 'for+대명사의 목적격'이 적절하다.

18 ⓐ that → what ⓑ make → makes ⓓ of your teeth → for your teeth ⓕ being → to be

19 (1)~(3) 선행사를 포함한 관계대명사 what을 이용한다. (4) 'It ~ to부정사' 구문을 이용한다. (5)~(6) '가주어(It) ~ for[of] …(의미상의 주어) 진주어(to부정사)' 구문을 이용한다. to부정사의 의미상의 주어를 'for+대명사의 목적격'으로 나타내지만, 문장에 쓰인 형용사가 사람의 성향, 성격을 나타내는 말일 때는 'of+대명사의 목적격'을 쓴다.

20 Love is what helps mend a broken heart. 선행사가 없으므로 that을 선행사를 포함하는 관계대명사 what으로 바꾸는 것이 적절하다.

21 이 글은 과제를 수행할 가장 좋은 아이디어를 고르려다가 시간이 5분만 남게 되어, 서두르면서 간신히 완성하는 내용이므로, Team A의 특징을 묘사하기에 알맞은 문장으로는 '행동하기 전에 생각해라.'가 적절하다.

22 ① come up with: ~을 생각해 내다, ② briefly: 간단히, in detail = minutely: 상세하게, ⑤ get[become]+p.p.: 동작 수동태(be동사 대신 get[become]을 써서, 상태의 변화나 동작의 의미를 강조하는 수동태)

23 Team A가 얼마나 많은 좋은 아이디어를 가졌는지는 대답할 수 없다. ② No. ③ Because the teacher said, "Five minutes left." ④ They wrapped the string around the

sticks of spaghetti. ⑤ It got stuck to the tape.

24 could나 were able to로 바꾸는 것이 적절하다. we were capable of building a beautiful and tall tower도 같은 뜻이다.

25 스스로 서 있지 못한 탑은 두 번째 탑이다.

26 ⓐ improve on: ~보다 나은 결과[실적]를 내다, ⓑ for: [용도·적응] ~의[으로], ~에 적합한

27 (A) 가장 좋은 아이디어를 고르는 '대신에' 좋은 아이디어를 골라 발전시켰다고 해야 하므로 Instead가 적절하다. in addition: 게다가, (B) 세 명 이상 중에서 '또 다른 친구'라고 해야 하므로 Another가 적절하다. the other: (둘 중의) 다른 하나, (C) 역할을 '나눴'고 해야 하므로 divided가 적절하다. divide up: 분배하다, 나눠 갖다, decide on: (여러 가지 가능성 가운데) ~으로 결정하다

28 ⓒ와 ① [역할·자격·기능·성질 따위를 나타내어] ~으로(서)(전치사), acknowledge: 인정하다, ② [이유·원인] ~이므로, ~ 때문에(접속사), ③ [보통 as ... as ~로 형용사·부사 앞에서] ~와 같은 정도로, 마찬가지로(as ... as ~에서, 앞의 as는 지시부사, 뒤의 as는 접속사), ④ [때] ~할 때(접속사), ⑤ [비례] ~함에 따라, ~할수록(접속사)

29 네 명의 멤버가 역할을 나눠서 훌륭한 비디오를 만들었기 때문에 '백지장도 맞들면 낫다(여러 사람이 한 사람보다 낫다는 뜻)'라고 하는 것이 적절하다. ① 제때의 바늘 한번이 아홉 바느질을 던다.(호미로 막을 데 가래로 막는다.) ② 쇠뿔도 단김에 빼라.(기회를 놓치지 말라는 뜻.) ④ 유유상종(같은 유형의 사람들은 서로 함께 모이는 경향이 있다는 뜻.) ⑤ 늦더라도 하지 않는 것보다 낫다.

30 동명사 보어 making을 'to make'와 바꿔 쓸 수 있다.

단원별 예상문제
p.48~51

01 ⑤   02 ③
03 (1) relationship (2) score (3) role   04 ⑤
05 ②   06 ①, ②, ③   07 ③, ⑤
08 ⓐ for ⓑ at   09 ④   10 lose
11 I'm sorry to hear that.   12 ③   13 ③
14 ④   15 what   16 ②, ④
17 The string got stuck to the tape and it was a big
    mess.
18 enough time → one second   19 ④
20 ②   21 (A) tried (B) trial
22 ④   23 ①   24 ①, ②, ⑤   25 ②, ④

01 hardly: 거의 ~ 아니다 ① 그는 머리를 천천히 흔들었다. ② 그 책은 오래되었기 때문에 주의 깊게 다뤄져야 한다. ③ 그 게임의 표를 사는 것이 가능하니? ④ 버스는 5분 일찍 왔다. ⑤ 나는 너를 거의 이해할 수 없었다.

02 mess: 엉망인 상태

03 (1) relationship: 관계 / 그 둘의 관계가 크게 달라졌습니다. (2) score: (경기 등에서) 득점 / 최종 점수는 Southampton팀은 2점, Leeds United팀은 9점이었다. (3) role: 역할 play a role: 역할을 하다 / 그것은 최근 토론에서 중요한 역할을 했다.

04 divide up: 분담하다, 분배하다 / 할 일이 많기 때문에, 우리는 일을 분담하는 것이 좋겠다.

05 G가 'Oh! I didn't know you played the piano.(나는 네가 피아노를 치는 것을 몰랐어.)'라고 말했으므로, B가 피아노 치는 것에 대해 먼저 이야기해야 한다.

06 'I've been great.(잘 지내고 있어.)'이라고 대답하므로 안부를 묻는 말이 어울린다. 상대방에게 그동안 어떻게 지냈는지 안부를 물을 때 'How have you been?'이라고 말한다. 'How's everything?', 'What have you been up to?'로 바꾸어 쓸 수 있다.

07 ①, ②, ④는 pretty가 부사로 '꽤, 매우'의 의미로 사용되었다. ③, ⑤는 형용사로 '예쁜'의 의미로 사용되었다. ① 나는 그가 그렇다고 말할 것을 꽤 확신한다. ② 나는 시험장에 들어갈 때 꽤 긴장했다. ③ 우리는 예쁜, 나무로 줄지어진 길을 걸었다. ④ 나는 그 시험이 꽤 쉬웠다고 생각했다. ⑤ 아주 오래 전에, 그녀는 예뻤음에 틀림없다.

08 ⓐ 현재완료와 'for+숫자+시간 단위(~ 동안)'를 같이 써서 '계속' 용법으로 쓸 수 있다. while은 접속사로 뒤에 절이 오지만 during은 전치사로서 다음에 명사 혹은 명사구가 온다. ⓑ be good at (동)명사: ~을 잘하다, ~에 능숙하다

09 A가 'How come?(왜)'이라고 묻자 개를 잃어버렸다고 말하는 것으로 보아 B는 잘 지내고 있지 않으므로 'Not so good.'이 어울린다. 개를 잃어버린 B에게 A가 할 수 있는 말은 유감을 표현하는 'I'm sorry to hear that.(그 말을 들으니 유감이야.)'이 어울린다.

10 lose(–lost–lost): (시합·농쟁 등에서) 지다 / 경기, 논쟁, 선거, 전쟁 등에서 이기지 못하다

11 상대방에게 좋지 않은 일이 있을 경우, 'I'm sorry to hear that.(그 말을 들으니 유감이야.)'을 사용하여 유감을 나타낼 수 있다.

12 대화에서 close는 '막상막하의, 우열을 가리기 힘든'의 의미로 사용했다. ① 닫다, (눈을) 감다 ② 가까이 ④ 친밀한 ⑤ 가까이, 바짝 ③ 막상막하의, 우열을 가리기 힘든 / 경기는 처음부터 끝까지 막상막하였다.

13 첫 번째 문장에서는 선행사가 없으므로 선행사를 포함하는 관계대명사 what이 적절하다. 두 번째 문장에서는 to부정사의 의미상의 주어를 to부정사 바로 앞에 'for+대명사의 목적격'으로 나타낸다.

14 ① It is boring for me to fish in the lake. ② It's great to hear that you received the award. ③ It's fun to do different things. ⑤ It was exciting for him to ride a boat.

15 관계대명사 what은 선행사를 포함하는 관계대명사로 the thing which[that]를 나타낸다.

16 ⓐ와 ②, ④: 가주어, ① 가목적어, ③, ⑤: 비인칭 주어

17 get stuck to: ~에 붙다

18 '1초'를 남기고 마시멜로를 꼭대기에 꽂았다고 했다.

19 ① spend+시간+on[in] ~ing: ~하는 데 시간을 보내다, ② start는 목적어로 to부정사와 동명사를 둘 다 쓸 수 있다. ③ by itself: 홀로[혼자], 도움을 받지 않고, ④ at least: 적어도, at last: 결국, ⑤ what은 선행사를 포함한 관계대명사로 the thing which로 바꿔 쓸 수 있다.

20 이 글은 '계획하는 데 많은 시간을 보내지 않고 바로 탑을 만들기 시작한 다음, 많은 시도 후에 결국 원하는 것을 만들었다'는 내용의 글이므로, 어울리는 속담으로는 ②번 '모로 가도 서울만 가면 된다.'가 적절하다.

21 여러분이 여러 번 시도한 것은 멋진 일이었어요. 나는 여러분들이 시행착오로부터 많은 것을 배웠다고 확신해요. 여러분들은 결국 아름답고 높은 탑을 만들었어요. 잘했어요! trial: try의 파생형 명사형, trial and error: 시행착오

22 이 글은 역할을 나눠 하나의 팀으로 함께하며 마침내 높은 탑을 만드는 내용이므로, Team C의 특징을 묘사하기에 알맞은 문장으로는 '우리는 한 팀이다.'가 적절하다.

23 Team C가 왜 가장 좋은 아이디어를 고르는 대신 좋은 아이디어를 골라 발전시켰는지는 대답할 수 없다. ② They agreed on a triangle shape for the base. ③ No, they divided up the roles. ④ Yes. ⑤ Yes.

24 글쓴이가 지도를 그리는 것을 어려워할 때, 한 모둠원이 도와줬다고 했기 때문에, '협동 작업'이 더 좋은 결과를 만든다고 하는 것이 적절하다. ① cooperation: 협력, 합동, 협동, ② teamwork: 협동 작업, ⑤ collaboration: 공동 작업, 협동, ③ competition: 경쟁, ④ responsibility: 책임

25 (A)와 ①, ③, ⑤: 동명사, ②, ④: 현재분사

서술형 실전문제   p.52~53

01 Pretty bad. → Pretty good.

02 I'm glad to hear that. / I'm pleased to hear that.

03 How have you been? / What have you been up to? / How have you been doing?

04 (1) I cannot remember what happened last night.

(2) Mina liked what I cooked for her yesterday.

(3) Tell me what you want me to do.

05 (1) for them   (2) for her   (3) of him   (4) of you

06 (1) to live in Korea   (2) was wise of Matthew to stay

(3) what he was doing

07 a good idea

08 We worked together as a team.

09 (A) a good idea   (B) divided up

10 left

11 5 minutes

12 1단계: 좋은 아이디어에 대해 자세히 이야기했다.

2단계: 서둘러서 스파게티 면들을 테이프로 붙였다.

3단계: 끈으로 스파게티 면 둘레를 둘렀다.

4단계: (1초를 남기고 글쓴이가) 마시멜로를 꼭대기에 꽂았다.

01 새로운 수업이 재미있다는 말로 보아 'Pretty bad.(꽤 안 좋아.)'는 어울리지 않는다.

02 상대방이 한 말에 대하여 기쁨을 표현할 때 'I'm happy/glad/pleased to hear that.(그 말을 들으니 기뻐.)'을 쓸 수 있다.

03 'I've been great.(잘 지냈어.)'라고 대답하는 것으로 보아 빈칸에는 상대방의 안부를 묻는 말이 들어가야 어울린다. 상대방에게 그동안 어떻게 지냈는지 안부를 물을 때 'How have you been?', 'What have you been up to?', 'How have you been doing?' 등으로 말할 수 있다.

04 what은 선행사를 포함한 관계대명사로 '~하는 것'으로 해석하며, the thing(s) which[that]를 나타낸다.

05 to부정사의 의미상의 주어는 to부정사 바로 앞에 'for+대명사의 목적격'으로 나타낸다. 이때 문장에 쓰인 형용사가 nice, kind, smart, wise 등과 같이 사람의 성향, 성격을 나타내는 말일 때는 'of+대명사의 목적격'으로 쓴다.

06 (1) 'It ~ to부정사' 구문을 이용하고 전치사 in의 목적어로 Korea를 쓴다. (2) '가주어(It) ~ of ...(의미상의 주어) 진주어(to부정사)' 구문을 이용한다. (3) what = the thing(s) which[that]

07 '좋은 아이디어'를 가리킨다.

08 as: ~로, ~로서(전치사)

09 여러분들은 '좋은 아이디어'를 골라 발전시켰어요. 또한, 나는 여러분들이 역할을 '나눠' 모두가 역할을 가졌던 것이 인상 깊었어요. 여러분들의 높은 탑은 튼튼해 보였어요.

10 5분이 '남았다'고 해야 하므로 left가 적절하다. 'We have five minutes left.'에서 'We have'를 생략한 것이다.

11 처음에 가장 좋은 아이디어를 고르는 데 너무 많은 시간을 써서, '5분' 이내에 그들의 과제를 완성해야 했기 때문이다.

12 본문의 내용을 순서대로 쓰는 것이 적절하다.

|모범답안|

01 (e)xcited / I won first place in the singing contest. / I'm happy/glad/pleased to hear that.

02 (1) It was not easy for him to ride a horse.
 (2) It's necessary for us to make a wise decision.
 (3) It was careless of him to leave her alone.
 (4) It is difficult for her to learn Greek.

03 (A) making a video   (B) The Stars   (C) wrote a dialogue   (D) the roles   (E) reporter   (F) the meeting time   (G) many heads

01 win first place: 1등을 하다, contest: 대회, 상대방이 한 말에 대하여 기쁨을 표현할 때 'I'm glad[happy, pleased] to hear that.'이라고 말할 수 있다.

단원별 모의고사   p.55~58

01 (1) (b)ase   (2) early   02 ④   03 ①
04 challenge   05 I've been pretty busy.   06 ④
07 (u)pset   08 I had a fight with my friend.
09 I'm sorry to hear that. / That's too bad. / What a pity!
10 close   11 (A) What   (B) as   12 ⑤
13 ③   14 ②   15 ③
16 (1) That → What   (2) which → what
 (3) what → that[which], 또는 the thing what→what
 (4) of → for   (5) for → of
17 ①
18 (1) for you to listen carefully to what your teacher tells you
 (2) of him to deliver those heavy boxes to my house
19 mess   20 (A) ideas   (B) in a hurry
21 ③
22 it was possible for us to build a beautiful and tall tower
23 1단계: 계획하는 데 많은 시간을 보내지 않고, 모든 팀원들이 바로 탑을 만들기 시작했다.
 2단계: 첫 번째 탑은 텐트 같았고, 그다지 높지 않았다.
 3단계: 다음 탑은 높았지만 스스로 서 있지 못했다.
 4단계: 많은 시도 후에 아름답고 높은 탑을 만들 수 있었다.
24 improved   25 ①, ④   26 ③

01 (1) 주어진 단어들은 동의어 관계이다. pretty: 꽤, 매우 quite: 매우 bottom: 바닥, 아래 base: (사물의) 맨 아래 부분 (2) 형용사와 부사의 관계이다. happy: 행복한 happily: 행복하게

early: 이른 early: 일찍 / early는 형용사와 부사의 형태가 같다.

02 ① 며칠 후에 진호가 나에게 편지 한 통을 주었다. ② 나는 너무 기분이 상해서 못 먹겠다. ③ 너의 전화번호를 말해 주겠니? ④ close: 막상막하의, 우열을 가리기 힘든 / 그것은 두 팀 사이의 막상막하인 경기였다. ⑤ 그는 100표가 못 되는 표 차이로 졌다.

03 (A) be busy at (동)명사: ~으로 바쁘다 / 그는 일로 바빴다. (B) such as: ~와 같은 / 그는 라디오 같은 것을 분해하는 것을 좋아했다.

04 challenge: 과제, 도전 / 어떤 것을 해결하거나 달성하기 위해 많은 기술, 에너지, 결정들이 필요한 것 / 3일 동안 자전거를 타는 것은 큰 도전이었다.

05 pretty: 꽤, 매우 busy: 바쁜

06 위의 대화에서 must는 '~임에 틀림없다'의 의미로 사용되었다. ④ 이외의 보기들은 '~해야 한다'의 의미로 사용하였다. ① 이 상자는 조심스럽게 옮겨져야 한다. ② 너는 빨간 불에서 멈춰야 한다. ③ 너는 잔디 위를 걸어서는 안 된다. ④ 그녀가 노래 부르는 걸 보니 매우 행복함에 틀림이 없다. ⑤ 나는 숙제를 먼저 해야 한다.

07 친구와 싸웠고 B는 이에 대해 유감을 표현하고 있으므로 upset이 어울린다. upset: 속상한, 기분이 상한

08 have a fight with ~: ~와 싸우다

09 농구 경기에 진 B에게 유감을 표현하는 말을 할 수 있다. 유감을 표현하는 말에는 'I'm sorry to hear that.(그 말을 들으니 유감이야.)', 'What a pity!(정말 안됐구나!)', 'That's too bad.(정말 안됐다.)' 등이 있다.

10 close: 막상막하의, 우열을 가리기 힘든 / 양쪽이 거의 같게 끝마치거나 경기하거나 다투는

11 (A) What was the score?: 점수는 어땠니? score: (경기 등에서) 점수, 득점 (B) as: ~로서

12 ⓔ는 made ⓐ~ⓓ에는 been이 들어간다. 상대방에게 그동안 어떻게 지냈는지 안부를 물을 때 'How have you been?'이라고 말하고, 'I've been good.'으로 대답할 수 있다.

13 ① Linda는 얼마나 많은 새 친구를 새로운 학교에서 사귀었나? ② 얼마나 오랫동안 Linda는 바이올린 수업을 들었는가? ③ Linda는 Minho의 전화번호를 가지고 있는가? (Yes.) ④ 대화 후에 그들은 언제 만날 것인가? ⑤ 얼마나 오랫동안 그들은 보지 못했는가?

14 to부정사의 의미상의 주어로 문장에 쓰인 형용사가 사람의 성향, 성격을 나타내는 말일 때는 'of+대명사의 목적격'으로 쓴다.

15 첫 번째 빈칸에는 선행사가 없으므로 what이 적절하고, 두 번째 빈칸에는 선행사가 있으므로 that이 적절하다.

16 (1) That을 did의 목적어와 was의 주어 역할을 할 수 있는 What으로 고친다. (2) which를 decide와 do의 목적어 역

할을 할 수 있는 what으로 고친다. (3) what = the thing that[which] (4) to부정사의 의미상 주어는 'for+목적격'의 형태로 쓴다. (5) 의미상의 주어로 문장에 쓰인 형용사가 사람의 성향, 성격을 나타내는 말일 때는 'of+대명사의 목적격'으로 쓴다.

17 <보기>와 ①의 what은 선행사를 포함하는 관계대명사이고, 나머지는 모두 의문대명사이다.

18 '가주어(It) 진주어(to부정사)' 구문을 이용하고 to부정사의 의미상의 주어로 to부정사 바로 앞에 'for+대명사의 목적격'으로 나타낸다. 이때 문장에 쓰인 형용사가 사람의 성향, 성격을 나타내는 말일 때는 'of+대명사의 목적격'으로 쓴다.

19 mess: 엉망인 상태

20 여러분들은 많은 좋은 '아이디어'를 가졌어요! 여러분들은 '서둘러서' 탑을 만들었지만, 모두가 열심히 일했어요. 멋진 작업이었어요!

21 right away = at once = right now = immediately = in no time: 금방, 바로, 즉시, ③ exactly: 정확히, 꼭, 틀림없이

22 'it: 가주어, for us: 의미상의 주어, to build ~: 진주어' 구문으로 쓰는 것이 적절하다.

23 본문의 내용을 순서대로 쓰는 것이 적절하다.

24 took과 병렬구문을 이루도록 과거시제로 쓴다.

25 in the end: 마침내(= finally, at last, in the long run), ① 미리, ④ 무엇보다도, 특히

26 ③ Team C의 멤버들은 기반으로 '삼각형' 모양에 동의했다. square: 정사각형

Go Green

01 ②   02 ③   03 ⑤   04 ③
05 ③   06 ③   07 (c)rop

01 ②를 제외한 명사들은 '-ful'을 붙여서 harmful, useful, careful, helpful로 형용사로 만들 수 있다. condition: 상태, 조건 conditional: 조건적인

02 주어진 문장에서 fine은 '미세한, 섬세한'의 의미로 사용되었다. / 그것들이 미세한 세부사항들과 희미한 것들을 볼 수 있게 해준다. ① 맑은, 비가 안 오는 / 내일 날이 맑으면 우리는 외출할 것이다. ② 질 높은, 좋은 / 많은 사람들은 베토벤의 5번 교향곡이 좋은 작품이라고 생각한다. ③ 미세한, 섬세한 / 전문가조차 미세한 점들을 찾아내지 못했다. ④ (제안 · 결정 등이) 괜찮은[좋은] / 만약 당신이 치킨 대신에 치즈를 사용하기를 원한다면, 그것도 좋다. ⑤ 질 높은, 좋은 / 그것은 좋은 음식과 와인 덕분에 선발되었다.

03 disappointed: 실망한 let ~ down: ~을 실망시키다 / 희생자 가족들은 사법제도가 그들을 실망시킨 것을 느낀다.

04 (A) in danger: 위기에 처하여 / 그의 행동은 아이의 생명을 위기에 처하게 했다. (B) look something up: (사전, 컴퓨터 등에서 정보를) 검색하다, 찾아보다 / 나는 "loquacious"가 무슨 뜻인지 몰라서 사전에서 찾아봐야만 했다.

05 by oneself: 혼자서 / 준비를 도와주시겠어요? 나 혼자 그것을 못 하겠어요. by+동명사: ~함으로써 / 소년은 거짓말을 함으로써 아버지를 속이려고 했다.

06 not only A but also B: A뿐만 아니라 B도 / 그녀는 음악뿐만 아니라 미술에도 싫증을 느낀다.

07 crop: 곡식 / 농부에 의해서 재배되는 밀, 쌀, 과일 같은 식물

01 (l)asted
02 harmful
03 down
04 away
05 (1) such as   (2) (w)orried about   (3) less than
   (4) take part in, stressful   (5) (g)one
   (6) (c)arefully (b)ecause of
06 (1) turn   (2) picked   (3) participate   (4) take

01 last: 지속하다 / 더운 날씨가 6월에 계속되었다.

02 harm: 해로움, 피해 harmful: 해로운 / 의사들은 흡연의 해로운 피해에 대해 경고해 왔다.

03 slow down: 속도를 늦추다 / 말을 하는 것은 먹는 속도를 줄이는 데 도움을 줄 수 있다. let ~ down: ~을 실망시키다 / 나는 그녀를 신뢰하고 그녀는 나를 실망시키지 않을 것이다.

04 melt away: 차츰 사라지다 / 나는 갑자기 그에게 미안함을 느꼈고 나의 분노는 차츰 사라졌다. throw away: 버리다 / 유리병, 깡통, 그리고 신문을 버리지 마세요.

05 (1) A such as B: B와 같은 A (2) be worried about: ~에 대하여 걱정하다 (3) less than: ~보다 적은, ~ 이하 (4) take part in: ~에 참가하다 stressful: 스트레스가 많은 (5) have gone: 사라지고 없다 (6) carefully: 조심스럽게 because of: ~ 때문에

06 (1) turn off: [등불·라디오·텔레비전을] 끄다 / 불 끄는 것을 잊지 마. (2) pick up: 뽑다, 집다 / 그는 편지를 집어들고 읽었다. (3) participate in: ~에 참가하다 / 그 반의 모든 사람들은 이들 토론에 적극적으로 참여할 것이 기대된다. (4) take action: [~하기 위한] 조치를 취하다, 행동을 취하다 / 우리가 행동을 취하기 전에 일이 어떻게 돌아가는지 지켜볼 수 있는 시간이 더 필요하다.

교과서
Conversation

1 I'm worried about global warming.
2 (B) → (C) → (A) → (D)
3 Do you know how to do a team project well?

교과서 대화문 익히기

1 T   2 F   3 F   4 T   5 F   6 T   7 T   8 T

Listen and Speak 1 A

what's / broke / I'm sorry / worried / Don't

Listen and Speak 1 B

ready for / didn't / Yellow dust, health / I'm worried about / another / text the other, right

Listen and Speak 1 C

1. I'm worried / terrible / What / less

2. worried about disappearing / terrible / What can / plant more

3. I'm worried about / What can we do / donate, to

Listen and Speak 2 A

hurts / careful not to / Do you know how to / to stretch

Listen and Speak 2 B

know that / It's because of / are melting away, disappearing / something about / how to slow down global warming / by saving / need to turn off / when, leave

Listen and Speak 2 C 1

Can / Do you know how / to, carefully, opinions

Listen and Speak 2 C 2

know how to save / need to turn off / when, your

Listen and Speak 2 C 3

ask / how to eat / to eat less

Real Life Talk Step 1

did you see / did, I'm worried about / should take action to / don't we participate in / movement / Do you know how to take part in / off, together for / simple, when / different / look it up

Real Life Talk Step 2

What do you think / terrible, I'm worried about / Do you know how to reduce / need to, public transportation

01 ②   02 ④   03 ②

01 방법을 물어볼 때는 'Do you know how to ~?' 또는 'Could you tell me how to ~?', 'Would you tell me how to ~?', 'Would you explain to me how to ~?' 등을 사용할 수 있다.

02 ④ why to save → how to save

03 그림에 대한 상대방의 생각을 물어보고 (B) 끔찍하다고 대답하며, 공기 오염에 대해 걱정이 된다고 말한다. (A) 공기 오염을 줄이기 위한 방법을 물어보자 (C) 대중교통을 이용할 필요가 있다고 대답한다.

01 ①	02 ⑤	03 ③	04 ③
05 ①	06 ④	07 ②	08 ②
09 (D) → (A) → (E) → (B) → (C)			10 ③

01 주어진 문장은 '뉴스에서 뭐라고 했니?'의 의미로 여기서 it은 the news를 의미한다. 뉴스의 내용인 황사에 대한 설명이 대답으로 나오고 있으므로 ①번이 적절하다.

02 'I'm worried about ~.'은 걱정을 나타내는 표현으로 전치사 about 뒤에는 명사나 대명사, 동명사를 써서 '나는 ~에 대해 걱정한다.'라는 의미를 나타낸다.

03 전화를 하지 않고 문자를 보낼 것이다. text: (휴대전화로) 문자를 보내다

04 'Do you know how to 동사원형 ~?'은 '~하는 방법을 아니?'라는 의미로 상대방에게 방법을 물을 때 사용하는 표현이다.

05 주어진 문장에서 It은 북극곰이 위험에 처해 있는 것을 가리키므로 ①번이 어울린다.

06 how to 동사원형: ~하는 방법, slow down: [속도·진행]을 늦추다

07 ① 왜 북극곰이 위험에 처해 있는가? (지구 온난화 때문에) ② 물을 절약하기 위해 그들은 무엇을 할 것인가? ③ 진수는 지구 온난화를 늦추는 방법을 아는가? (네) ④ 진수는 북극곰이 위험에 처해 있다는 사실을 어떻게 알게 되었는가? (기사를 읽고) ⑤ 지구 온난화는 북극곰에게 어떤 영향을 미쳤는가? (집과 먹이가 사라지게 하였다.)

08 대회에 참가하는 방법을 물어보는 말에 그렇게 하라는 대답은 어색하고 참가하는 방법에 대한 설명이 답으로 나와야 한다.

09 민호가 지구를 지키기 위해 행동을 취해야 한다고 말한다. (D) 맞다며, 지구를 지키기 위한 방법으로 Earth Hour에 참가하는 것을 권유한다. (A) Earth Hour가 무엇인지 질문하자 (E) 환경에 대한 세계적 운동이라고 대답한다. (B) 좋다고 대답하며 Earth Hour에 참여하는 방법을 아는지 묻자 (C) 한 시간 동안 불을 끄는 것이라고 대답한다.

10 플라스틱을 적게 써서 도울 수 있는 문제는 지구 온난화(global warming)이다. 걱정 표현은 scared, worried, nervous 등의 형용사를 이용하여 말할 수 있다. 또한 걱정이 되는 것이 두려움이나 무서움을 포함하고 있을 때는 scared, frightened, terrified 등을 써서 말할 수도 있다.

01 disappearing
02 (A) to get   (B) to prevent   (C) to stretch
03 (A) of   (B) by
04 Do you know how to slow down global warming?
05 (A) What   (B) how
06 I'm worried about air pollution.

01 appear: 나타나다 disappear: 사라지다 / 벌들이 사라지는 것에 대해 걱정하고, 사라지는 벌들에 대해서 할 수 있는 것이 더 많은 나무를 심는 것이므로 disappearing이 어울린다.

02 (A) 'Be careful not to 동사원형 ~.'은 '~하지 않도록 주의해라.'라는 의미로 상대방이 잊어버리지 않도록 중요한 일에 대해 강한 당부 또는 경고하는 의미를 나타낼 수 있다. (B) 'Do you know how to 동사원형 ~?'은 '~하는 방법을 아니?'라는 의미로 상대방에게 방법을 물을 때 사용하는 표현이다. (C) 상대방에게 어떤 것을 하라고 조언할 경우에는 'You need to 동사원형 ~.'으로 말할 수 있다.

03 (A) 'It's because of ~.'를 이용해 앞에 말한 북극곰이 위험에 처한 이유에 대해 말하고 있다. because of: ~ 때문에 (B) by 동명사: ~함으로써

04 'Do you know how to ~?'는 '너는 ~하는 방법을 아니?'의 의미로 상대방에게 방법을 물을 때 사용할 수 있다. slow down: [속도·진행]을 늦추다 global warming: 지구 온난화

05 (A) 무언가에 대하여 상대방의 의견을 물을 때 'What do you think of ~?(~에 대해 어떻게 생각하니?)'를 사용할 수 있다. (B) 'Do you know how to 동사원형 ~?'은 '~하는 방법을 아니?'라는 의미로 상대방에게 방법을 물을 때 사용하는 표현이다.

06 be worried about: ~에 대해 걱정하다 pollution: 오염

Grammar
교과서

1 (1) is   (2) know   (3) is
2 (1) must be protected   (2) should be done

01 ④   02 ⑤   03 ③
04 (1) must be purchased
    (2) should not be allowed
    (3) Can the disease be cured

01 부분을 나타내는 말은 뒤에 오는 명사의 수에 따라 그 수가 결정되는데, Some of 다음에 her family members라고 복수 명사가 나오므로 ④번이 적절하다.

02 조동사가 있는 문장의 수동태는 '조동사+be+과거분사'의 형태로 나타낸다.

03 부분을 나타내는 말은 뒤에 오는 명사의 수에 따라 그 수가 결정되는데, One third of 다음에 all votes라고 복수 명사가 나오므로 were가 적절하다.

04 (1) 조동사가 있는 문장의 수동태는 '조동사+be+과거분사'의 형태로 나타낸다. (2) 조동사가 있는 문장의 수동태의 부정문은 '조동사+not+be+과거분사'의 형태로 나타낸다. (3) 조동사가 있는 문장의 수동태의 의문문은 '조동사+주어+be+과거분사 ~?'의 형태로 나타낸다.

01 ②   02 ①   03 ⑤
04 (1) dies   (2) is   (3) know   (4) tries   (5) will be
    (6) cannot be   (7) appear   (8) resembles
05 More than three-quarters of these women were in their 20s.
06 (1) were   (2) can be heard   (3) should be climbed
07 ③   08 ④   09 ②
10 People have to be licensed to work in most states.
11 ④   12 ⑤   13 ①   14 ③
15 ①, ④
16 (1) Two-thirds of the country is covered with forest.
    (2) Much of the country is covered by forest.
    (3) About a quarter of the callers are female.
    (4) This homework must be finished by tomorrow.
    (5) The change will occur in April next year.
    (6) The word can be found in the dictionary.

01 ① Part of that apple is rotten. ③ Twelve percent of all Internet sites use pop-up ads. ④ About one third of the milk was spilled. ⑤ Most of the earth's surface is water. gum: 잇몸

02 Many weather effects have to be specially created. 조동사가 있는 문장의 수동태는 '조동사+be+과거분사'의 형태로 나타낸다. agricultural products: 농산물

03 조동사가 있는 문장의 수동태는 '조동사+be+과거분사'의 형태로 나타낸다.

04 (1)~(2) 부분을 나타내는 말은 뒤에 오는 명사의 수에 따라 수가 결정된다. (3) 'A few of+복수 명사'가 주어일 경우 복수

동사가 나온다. (4) one of+복수 명사+단수 동사 (5)~(6) 조동사가 있는 문장의 수동태는 '조동사+be+과거분사'의 형태로 나타내며, 부정문은 '조동사+not+be+과거분사'의 형태로 쓴다. (7) appear는 자동사이므로 수동태로 쓰이지 않는다. (8) resemble은 타동사이지만 상태를 나타내는 말로 수동태로 쓰이지 않는다.

05 부분을 나타내는 말은 뒤에 오는 명사의 수에 따라 그 수가 결정되는데, three-quarters of 다음에 these women이라고 복수 명사가 나오므로 be동사를 were로 써야 한다.

06 (1) 부분을 나타내는 말은 뒤에 오는 명사의 수에 따라 그 수가 결정되는데, The rest of 다음에 his days라고 복수 명사가 나오므로 were가 적절하다. (2), (3) 조동사가 있는 문장의 수동태는 '조동사+be+과거분사'의 형태로 나타낸다.

07 첫 번째 빈칸에는 부분을 나타내는 말은 뒤에 오는 명사의 수에 따라 그 수가 결정되는데, half of 다음에 Cambodia's population이라고 단수 명사가 나오므로 is가 적절하다. 두 번째 빈칸에는 조동사가 있는 문장의 수동태의 부정문은 '조동사+not+be+과거분사'의 형태로 나타낸다.

08 조동사가 있는 문장의 수동태는 '조동사+be+과거분사'의 형태로 나타낸다.

09 부분을 나타내는 말은 뒤에 오는 명사의 수에 따라 그 수가 결정되는데, Most of 다음에 the buildings라고 복수 명사가 나오므로 need가 적절하다. need+동명사 = need to be+과거분사: ~을 필요로 하다

10 조동사가 있는 문장의 수동태는 '조동사+be+과거분사'의 형태로 나타낸다.

11 'one of+복수 명사'가 주어일 경우 핵심이 되는 주어가 one이므로 동사는 단수로 쓴다.

12 능동태를 수동태로 바꿀 때, 목적어를 주어로 쓰고, 주어는 'by+목적격'으로 쓰며(일반인의 경우 보통 생략함), 동사는 조동사가 있는 경우 '조동사+be+과거분사'의 형태로 쓴다.

13 부분을 나타내는 말이 있는 어구가 주어로 쓰일 때 뒤에 단수 명사가 나오면 단수 동사를 쓰고, 복수 명사가 나오면 복수 동사를 쓴다. ①번은 단수 명사 the money가 나왔으므로 was가 들어가야 하고 나머지는 모두 복수 명사이므로 were가 적절하다.

14 'few of+복수 명사' 주어는 복수 동사로 받는다. Last night으로 시제가 과거로 표시되어야 함에 주의한다.

15 ① My e-mail address will remain unchanged. remain은 자동사로 수동태로 쓰지 않는다. ④ Three fifths of 다음에 the money가 단수 명사이므로 are를 is로 고쳐야 한다.

16 (1) 부분을 나타내는 말의 뒤에 단수 명사가 나왔으므로 단수 동사 is를 쓴다. (2) 'much of+단수 명사' 주어는 단수 동사로 받는다. (3) 부분을 나타내는 말의 뒤에 복수 명사가 나왔으므로 복수 동사 are를 쓴다. (4) This homework가 주어이므로 수동태로 써야 하고, 조동사가 있는 문장의 수동태는 '조동사+be+과거

분사'의 형태로 쓴다. (5) occur는 자동사이므로 수동태로 쓰이지 않는다. (6) 조동사가 있는 문장의 수동태는 '조동사+be+과거분사'의 형태로 쓴다.

01 (1) The report should be handed in by all participants by May 18.
(2) The event may be held at a school or in a park by them.
(3) A lot of vegetables and fruits must be eaten by us.
(4) My pet dog has to be walked by me after supper.

02 (1) Life may be compared to a voyage.
(2) When is it going to be put on the market?
(3) Here are some of the main characters.
(4) The number of Internet users is really growing.

03 (1) of the water was spilled
(2) must be kept

04 (1) is[was] wasted   (2) has begun

05 (1) A quarter of the money was spent on books.
(2) A number of fish were flopping on the deck.
(3) A little of her personal touch was needed to him.
(4) The field might be destroyed because of the cold.
(5) Cultural change can happen for three different reasons.
(6) The fact has to be treated as a top secret.

06 (1) was spent   (2) will be sent

07 (1) The greater part of the students have gone home.
(2) Most of them sit behind a desk all day.
(3) About half of the food they eat is used to keep them warm.
(4) Disease should be treated at the very beginning.
(5) His silence can be read as agreement.

08 (1) About two thirds of the potato pizza Emily bought was eaten by Hannah.
(2) Some of the story books Tom has can be read by Bob.

01 능동태를 수동태로 바꿀 때, 능동태의 목적어를 수동태의 주어로 쓰고, 주어는 'by+목적격'으로 문장의 뒤에 쓰며(보통 일반인의 경우 생략함.), 동사는 조동사가 있는 경우 '조동사+be+과거분사'의 형태로 쓴다.

02 (1) be동사를 추가하여 '조동사+be+과거분사'의 형태로 쓴다.

(2) 'be going to'의 to를 추가하여 쓴다. (3) main characters 가 주어로 복수이므로 are를 추가한다. (4) 'the number of' 다음에 복수 명사가 와도 단수 동사로 받는다. is를 추가한다.

03 (1) 물이 엎질러진 것이므로 수동태를 이용하고 the water가 단수이므로 was로 써야 한다. (2) 비밀로 간직되어야 하는 것이므로 수동태를 이용하고 '조동사+be+과거분사'의 형태로 쓴다.

04 부분을 나타내는 말 뒤에 오는 명사가 단수이면 단수 동사를 쓰고 복수이면 복수 동사를 쓴다.

05 (1) 부분을 나타내는 말의 뒤에 단수 명사가 나왔으므로 단수 동사 was를 쓴다. (2) 'a number of' 다음에는 복수 명사가 나오며 복수 동사로 받는다. (3) '(a) little of' 다음에는 단수 명사가 나오며 단수 동사로 받는다. (4) The field가 주어이므로 수동태로 써야 하고, 조동사가 있는 문장의 수동태는 '조동사+be+과거분사'의 형태로 쓴다. (5) happen은 자동사이므로 수동태로 쓰이지 않는다. (6) has to가 있으므로 'has to be treated'의 형태로 써야 한다.

06 (1) 부분을 나타내는 말(The rest of)의 뒤에 단수 명사(his life)가 나왔으므로 단수 동사 was를 이용하여 수동태로 쓴다. (2) Catalogs가 주어이므로 수동태로 써야 하고, 조동사 will이 있으므로 'will+be+과거분사'의 형태로 쓴다.

07 (1)~(3) 부분을 나타내는 말 뒤에 오는 명사가 단수이면 단수 동사를 쓰고 복수이면 복수 동사를 쓴다. (4), (5) 조동사가 있는 문장의 수동태는 '조동사+be+과거분사'의 형태로 쓴다. (4)번에서 very는 명사 앞에서 그 명사를 강조한다.

08 부분을 나타내는 말은 뒤에 오는 명사의 수에 따라 그 수가 결정되며 조동사가 있는 문장의 수동태는 '조동사+be+과거분사'의 형태로 나타낸다.

교과서
Reading

확인문제   p.84

1 T   2 F   3 T   4 F   5 T   6 F

확인문제   p.85

1 T   2 F   3 T   4 F   5 T   6 F

교과서 확인학습 A   p.86~87

01 Disappearing   02 have, gone
03 It, to see   04 disappearing   05 a third

06 bad news, even worse news
07 helpful to   08 First
09 truly wonderful   10 is good for
11 last almost forever
12 can be eaten
13 Second, help produce, such as
14 be produced by themselves
15 need the help   16 in the process of
17 pollination   18 What
19 moving pollen, to make seeds
20 pollen
21 fine yellow powder produced
22 disappearing
23 reasons, climate change
24 Global warming   25 cannot survive
26 Another reason
27 not only, but also   28 what, to help
29 more flowers and trees
30 provide, for   31 slow down
32 must be stopped
33 are unhealthy for
34 need our help
35 let them down

교과서 확인학습 B   p.88~89

1 Disappearing Bees
2 Where have all the honey bees gone?
3 It is really hard to see them these days.
4 The bees are disappearing!
5 About a third of the bee population dies every year.
6 This is bad news for bees, but it's even worse news for people.
7 Bees are very helpful to humans.
8 First, bees give us honey.
9 Honey is a truly wonderful food.
10 It is good for our health and tastes great.
11 Honey can last almost forever.
12 In fact, honey from ancient Egypt can be eaten today!
13 Second, bees help produce many crops such as apples and strawberries.
14 These crops cannot be produced by themselves.
15 They need the help of bees.
16 Bees help in the process of pollination.
17 How bees help pollination

18 What is pollination?

19 It is moving pollen from one flower to another to make seeds.

20 What is pollen?

21 It is a fine yellow powder produced by flowers.

22 Why are bees disappearing?

23 One of the reasons is climate change.

24 Global warming has brought extremely hot and cold weather.

25 Bees cannot survive in these conditions.

26 Another reason is the harmful chemicals farmers use on crops.

27 These chemicals kill not only bad insects, but also good insects, like bees.

28 Then what can we do to help our little yellow friends?

29 First, we can plant more flowers and trees.

30 This will provide a good environment for bees to live in.

31 Also, trees help slow down global warming.

32 Second, the use of harmful chemicals on crops must be stopped.

33 These chemicals are unhealthy for bees and people.

34 Our little friends need our help.

35 Let's not let them down!

시험대비 실력평가
p.90~93

01 ②   02 the honey bees

03 increases → decreases   04 ②

05 ⑤   06 ③   07 ①   08 ③

09 These chemicals kill good insects, like bees, as well as bad insects.   10 ④

11 This will provide a good environment for bees to live in.

12 speed up → slow down   13 ①, ④

14 disappeared → disappearing

15 About a third of the bee population dies every year.   16 ②   17 ④

18 (A) No (B) can't (C) bees (D) pollination

19 not bad insects, but good insects → not only bad insects, but also good insects

20 No, they can't.   21 ②   22 ③

23 ③   24 ④번, can't → can

25 many crops such as apples and strawberries

26 Bees help in the process of pollination.

27 ①, ③, ④

01 ⓐ의 have gone과 ②: 결과 용법, ①, ⑤: 계속 용법, ③ 경험 용법, ④ 완료 용법

02 '꿀벌'을 가리킨다.

03 약 3분의 1 정도가 '죽는다'는 것은 약 3분의 1이 '감소한다'는 것이기 때문에, decreases로 고치는 것이 적절하다. increase: 증가하다

04 ② very는 형용사나 부사의 원급을 강조하는 말이고, 나머지는 다 비교급을 강조하는 말이다.

05 ⓐ be good for: ~에 좋다, be good at: ~을 잘하다, ⓑ from: (출처·기원) ~ 출신의[에서 온]

06 위 글은 '벌이 인간에게 매우 도움이 된다.'는 내용의 글이므로, 제목으로는 ③번 '벌이 인간을 위해 해주는 것'이 적절하다.

07 ① 벌은 인간에게 매우 '도움이 된다.' harmful: 해로운

08 ④번의 these conditions는 ②번에서 언급하고 있는 상황을 가리키며, 그 사이의 '전 세계 국가들은 지구 온난화를 늦추려고 노력하고 있다'는 ③번 문장은 전체 글의 흐름에서 벗어난다.

09 not only A but also B = B as well as A: A뿐만 아니라 B도

10 앞에 나오는 내용에 추가하는 내용이 뒤에 이어지므로 'Also'와 같이 추가를 나타내는 연결사가 적절하다. ④ 다른 한편으로는, 반면에, 나머지는 다 '게다가', '더욱이'라는 뜻이다.

11 'in'을 보충하면 된다.

12 나무는 지구 온난화를 '늦춘다'고 하는 것이 적절하다. speed up: 속도를 더 내다[높이다]

13 ⓐ와 ①, ④: 가주어, ② 가목적어, ③ 비인칭 주어, to go는 time을 수식하는 형용사적 용법, ⑤ 그것(앞에 이미 언급되었거나 현재 이야기되고 있는 사물·동물을 가리킴)

14 disappear는 수동태로 쓸 수 없으므로, disappearing으로 고치는 것이 적절하다.

15 앞 문장의 내용을 가리킨다.

16 앞의 내용을 추가해서 설명하고 있으므로 In fact가 가장 적절하다(방금 한 말에 대해 자세한 내용을 덧붙일 때 씀). in fact: 사실(은), ① 그에 반해서, ③ 그렇기는 하지만, ⑤ 그 대신에, 그렇지 않으면(둘째 대안을 소개할 때 씀)

17 ⓑ와 ④: 아주 작은, ① 건강한, ② 괜찮은, 만족할 만한, ③ 벌금(명사), ⑤ 맑은, 비가 안 오는

18 사과와 딸기와 같은 많은 농작물들은 스스로 생산될 수 '없다'. 그들은 '벌'의 도움이 필요하다. 벌은 '수분' 과정에서 도움을 준다.

19 '이 화학 물질은 해로운 곤충뿐만 아니라 이로운 곤충도 죽인다'고 하는 것이 적절하다.

20 벌들은 극단적으로 덥고 추운 날씨에서 살아남을 수 없다.

21 주어진 문장의 This에 주목한다. ②번 앞 문장의 내용을 받고 있으므로 ②번이 적절하다.

22 이 글은 '벌들을 돕기 위해 우리가 할 수 있는 일들'에 관한 글이므로, 주제로는 ③번 '벌들을 구하기 위해 우리가 무엇을 할 수 있을까?'가 적절하다.

23 '해로운 화학 물질을 사용하지 않고 농작물을 기르는 것이 어떻게 가능할지'는 대답할 수 없다. ① Planting more flowers and trees. ② Yes. ④ Because they are unhealthy for bees and people. ⑤ Yes.

24 꿀이 정말 굉장한 음식이라는 내용이므로, 문맥상 ⑤번의 can을 can't로 고치는 것보다 ④번의 can't를 can으로 고치는 것이 적절하다.

25 '사과와 딸기와 같은 많은 농작물들'을 가리킨다.

26 in the process of: ~의 과정에서

27 ⓒ와 ①, ③, ④: 동명사 ②, ⑤: 현재분사 nectar: (꽃의) 꿀

10 pollination: 식물 수분 (작용), 식물의 수술에서 암술로 꽃가루를 옮기는 것

11 뒤에 이어지는 문장의 내용을 쓰면 된다.

12 사과와 딸기와 같은 많은 농작물들은 벌의 도움 '없이' 스스로 생산될 수 없다.

13 꽃들은 '꽃가루'라고 불리는 아주 작은 노란색 가루를 만들고, 벌들이 꽃을 방문할 때 그것을 한 꽃에서 다른 꽃으로 옮긴다. 벌들의 이런 '수분 과정' 덕분에 꽃들은 '씨앗'을 만들게 된다.

서술형 시험대비 p.94~95

01 (A) tastes (B) produce (C) produced
02 we can eat honey from ancient Egypt today
03 (A) honey (B) (to) produce   04 are → is
05 extremely hot and cold weather
06 (1) 기후 변화 때문이다.
   (2) 농부들이 농작물에 사용하는 해로운 화학 물질 때문이다.
07 the use of harmful chemicals on crops must be stopped
08 let down them → let them down
09 (A) plant (B) harmful chemicals
10 pollination
11 실제로, 고대 이집트 때의 꿀을 오늘날에도 먹을 수 있기 때문이다.
12 (A) without
13 (A) pollen (B) pollination (C) seeds

01 (A) 주어가 It이므로 tastes가 적절하다. (B) help 다음에 원형부정사나 to부정사를 써야 하므로 produce가 적절하다. (C) 꽃에 의해 '생산되는' 아주 작은 노란색 가루라고 해야 하므로 produced가 적절하다.
02 수동태의 끝에 생략된 by us를 주어 we로 바꿔서 능동태로 고치는 것이 적절하다.
03 벌이 우리에게 '꿀'을 주고 사과와 딸기와 같은 많은 농작물을 '생산하는 데' 도움이 되기 때문이다.
04 주어가 One이기 때문에, is로 고치는 것이 적절하다.
05 '극단적으로 덥고 추운 날씨'를 가리킨다.
06 (1) climate change, (2) the harmful chemicals farmers use on crops 때문이다.
07 the use of A on B: B에 A를 사용하는 것
08 인칭대명사 목적어를 부사 앞에 쓰는 것이 적절하다. let ~ down: ~를 실망시키다
09 벌들이 살기에 좋은 환경을 제공하기 위해 더 많은 꽃과 나무를 '심을 수 있고' 농작물에 '해로운 화학 물질'의 사용을 멈춰야만

영역별 핵심문제 p.97~101

01 ⓐ like → likes ⓑ because → because of
   ⓒ use → useful   02 ③   03 ①
04 take   05 worried   06 ②
07 ⓐ for ⓑ cause   08 ③
09 I'm worried about our health.   10 in
11 ⓐ that ⓑ off
12 Their homes are melting away and their food is disappearing.
13 ②, ⑤   14 should be handed in
15 ②   16 ⑤   17 ⓐ, ⓒ, ⓓ, ⓕ
18 ④   19 die → dies 20 disappear
21 It is good for our health and tastes great.
22 ③   23 ⑤   24 how green they are
25 ⓑ Four ⓒ Three   26 ②   27 ②
28 disappoint them   29 ④
30 Solutions 31 ③

01 ⓐ not only A but also B'는 'A뿐만이 아니라 B도' 라는 뜻을 지닌다. 이 표현을 쓸 때 이 구문의 성격상 A와 B의 문장 성분은 동일하여야 하며, 이 구문이 주어로 올 때는 동사를 B에 일치시켜 사용한다. ⓑ a lack of money는 명사구이므로 접속사인 because 대신에 because of를 사용해야 한다. ⓒ extremely: 극심하게 / 부사 extremely는 형용사 useful을 수식하고 있다.
02 ③ chemical: 화학 물질 / 과학자들은 도파민이라고 하는 화학 물질이 원인이라는 것을 발견했다. ① 나는 너에게 직장 바꾸는 것을 멈추라고 충고할 것이다. ② 당신이 돈이 필요 없다면 당신의 오래된 물건들을 기부할 수 있다. ④ 고대의 그리스에서, 남자와 여자는 다른 옷을 입었다. ⑤ 사업에 대한 용어와 조건을 설명하겠습니다.
03 in fact: 사실. 매니저들은 직원들이 다른 회사로 갈 것을 걱정하지만, 사실은 직원들은 머무르고 싶어 한다.
04 take part in: ~에 참가하다 / 그 행사에 참가하겠다고 이미 약속했습니다. take action: [~하기 위한] 조치를 취하다, 행동을 취하다 / 정부는 경기 활성화를 위한 조치를 취해야 한다.

05 be worried about: ~에 대하여 걱정하다

06 언제 Jane의 남동생이 다리가 부러졌는가? Jane의 남동생의 소식에 남자아이는 어떻게 느끼는가?(안타까움) 언제 Jane의 남동생이 괜찮아질까? Jane의 남동생은 어느 쪽 다리가 부러졌는가? Jane의 남동생에게 무슨 일이 일어났는가?(다리가 부러졌다.)

07 ⓐ ready: 준비된 'be ready' 다음에는 'to 동사원형'이나 'for 명사'가 올 수 있는데 our soccer game은 명사이므로 for가 어울린다. ⓑ cause: 야기하다, 일으키다 reduce: 줄이다. 황사가 건강 문제를 야기하는 것이지 줄이는 것이 아니므로 cause가 어울린다.

08 황사가 건강을 해치므로 다음에 경기하자고 말하고 남자아이는 다음에 경기하자는 것을 다른 멤버들에게 문자로 알릴 것이다.

09 be worried about: ~에 대하여 걱정하다, health: 건강

10 (A) in danger: 위기에 처하여 (B) in an article: 어떤 기사에서

11 ⓐ 상대방에게 방법이 아니라 아는 내용을 확인하고 있으므로 that이 적절하다. 'Did you know that ~?'은 '너는 ~를 아니?'의 의미이다. that은 접속사로 뒤에 주어와 동사가 온다. ⓑ 에너지를 절약하기 위해서는 방을 떠날 때 불을 꺼야 한다. turn off: 끄다

12 melt away: 차츰 사라지다 disappear: 사라지다

13 ① One of the fastest growing sports in China is basketball. ③ There are a number of languages spoken in India. ④ Take pictures anywhere! It can be used in water.

14 조동사가 있는 수동태는 '조동사+be+과거분사'의 형태로 쓴다.

15 ②에는 부분을 나타내는 말(Some of)의 뒤에 단수 명사(the woodland)가 나왔으므로 단수 동사 is가 적절하다. 나머지는 모두 are가 적절하다.

16 This book이 주어이고 in the future가 있으므로 조동사 will이 있는 수동태로 'will be+과거분사'의 형태가 적절하다.

17 ⓑ are → is ⓔ do → done ⓖ creating → created. iris: 홍채(虹彩)

18 ① One of the reasons is climate change. ② Half of my life has gone. ③ Most of the machines aren't ready to use yet. ⑤ More than two thirds of people live under $1 a day.

19 부분이나 분수를 나타내는 말 뒤에 단수 명사가 오면 단수 취급해야 하므로, dies로 고치는 것이 적절하다.

20 remaining: 남아 있는

21 be good for: ~에 좋다

22 ③ 벌들이 수분 과정을 통해 많은 농작물을 생산하도록 돕기 때문에, '아무 보답 없이 식물로부터 꿀을 얻기만 한다'는 것은 옳지 않다.

23 이 글은 '벌들이 인간에게 매우 도움이 된다'는 내용의 글이므로, 주제로는 ⑤번이 적절하다.

24 간접의문문의 순서로 쓰는 것이 적절하다.

25 ⓑ 5분 이내에 샤워를 하는 사람은 '4명'이다. ⓒ 플라스틱을 재활용하는 사람은 '3명'이다.

26 ② green: 환경 보호의[친화적인], eco-friendly: 친환경적인, ① 경제적인, 실속 있는, ③ 사려 깊은, (남을) 배려하는, ④ 재사용할 수 있는, ⑤ 분별[양식] 있는, 합리적인

27 ⓐ와 ①, ④: 형용사적 용법, ②, ⑤: 명사적 용법, ③: 부사적 용법

28 let down = disappoint: 실망시키다

29 stop+to부정사: ~하기 위해 멈추다, stop+~ing: ~을 그만두다

30 '해결책'이 적절하다.

31 얼마나 많은 해로운 화학 물질을 농부들이 농작물에 사용하는지는 대답할 수 없다. ① Because global warming has brought climate change and farmers use the harmful chemicals on crops. ② Global warming has brought it. ④ We need to plant more flowers and trees. ⑤ No.

단원별 예상문제 p.102~105

01 ③ 02 a quarter of 03 ②
04 (1) (p)ollination (2) (p)leasure (3) (e)xtreme
(4) production processes
05 ④ 06 ③ 07 donate
08 I'm worried about hungry children in Africa.
09 ⑤ 10 ⑤
11 ⓐ save ⓑ environment ⓒ simple
12 Do you know how to take part in it?
13 are → is 14 ③ 15 ② 16 ⑤
17 ④ 18 ④ 19 ③ 20 by themselves 21 save water
22 They should bring their own shopping bag on this day.
23 (A) to live in (B) slow down (C) be stopped
24 ② 25 healthy

01 ③은 동의어 관계이지만 이외의 보기들은 반의어 관계이다. ① carefully: 조심스럽게 carelessly: 부주의하게 ② disappear: 사라지다 appear: 나타나다 ③ provide: 제공하다 supply: 제공하다 ④ forever: 영원히 temporarily: 일시적으로 ⑤ later: 나중에 earlier: 이전의

02 a quarter of ~: ~의 4분의 1

03 (A) let ~ down: ~을 실망시키다 / 좋은 소식을 기다리던 팬들을 실망시켜 죄송합니다. (B) look something up: (사전, 컴퓨터 등에서 정보를) 검색하다, 찾아보다 / 스마트폰에서 쉽

21

고 빠르게 정보를 검색할 수 있는데 왜 네 소중한 시간을 낭비하니?

04 (1) pollination: 수분작용, 꽃가루 옮기기 (2) pleasure: 즐거움 (3) extreme: 극심한 chemical: 화학물질 (4) production: 생산 process: 과정

05 ⓐ Of course / 물어봐도 되는지에 대한 질문에 긍정의 대답을 주고 무엇인지 묻고 있다. ⓑ how to / 'Do you know how to ~?'는 '너는 ~하는 방법을 아니?'의 의미로 상대방에게 방법을 물을 때 사용할 수 있다. ⓒ healthy / healthy: 건강한, 건강에 좋은 ⓓ to eat / need 다음에는 to 부정사를 목적어로 사용할 수 있다. ⓔ less / 건강하게 먹기 위해서는 패스트푸드를 덜 먹을 필요가 있다. less: 덜, 더 적은

06 아프리카의 배고픈 아이들에 대한 묘사는 형용사 'terrible(끔찍한)'이 어울린다.

07 donate 기부하다 / 돕기 위하여 사람이나 단체에 무엇인가를 주다

08 be worried about: ~에 대하여 걱정하다 hungry: 배고픈

09 Earth Hour에 참여하는 방법이 '불을 한 시간 동안 끄는 것'이라고 말하는 Linda의 말에, 민호는 언제 불을 끄느냐고 물었더니 확실하지 않고 매년 불을 끄는 시간이 다르다고 말한다.

10 turn off: [등불·라디오·텔레비전을] 끄다

11 ⓐ save: 구하다 / 지구에 대해서 걱정하고, 지구를 구하는 행동을 취해야 한다고 말하고 있다. ⓐ environment: 환경 ⓒ simple: 간단한 / Earth Hour에 참여하는 방법으로 불을 한 시간 동안 끄는 것은 간단하다.

12 'Do you know how to ~?'는 '너는 ~하는 방법을 아니?'의 의미로 상대방에게 방법을 물을 때 사용할 수 있다. take part in: ~에 참가하다

13 부분을 나타내는 말은 뒤에 오는 명사의 수에 따라 그 수가 결정되는데, part of 다음의 land가 단수 명사이므로 동사는 is가 적절하다.

14 첫 번째 문장에서는 부분을 나타내는 말(One quarter of)의 뒤에 단수 명사(grain)가 나왔으므로 단수 동사 ends가 적절하다. 두 번째 문장에서는 조동사가 있으므로 '조동사+be+과거분사'의 형태로 쓴다.

15 ② 조동사 will이 있으므로 'will be+과거분사'의 형태로 쓴다.

16 위 글은 '벌이 사라지고 있는 이유'에 관한 글이므로, 제목으로는 ⑤번 '벌이 사라지고 있는 이유들'이 적절하다.

17 농부들은 '해로운' 화학 물질들을 사용한다.

18 주어진 문장의 These crops에 주목한다. ④번 앞 문장의 many crops such as apples and strawberries를 받고 있으므로 ④번이 적절하다.

19 ⓐ와 ③: (일정 기간) 계속하다, 지속[존속]하다(동사), ① 결코 ~할 것 같지 않은(형용사), ② 전번에, 요전에(부사), ④ 최후에 남은(형용사), ⑤ 최후에, 마지막에(부사)

20 '스스로' 생산될 수 없기 때문이다. by oneself: 혼자, 도움을 받지 않고

21 3월 22일은 세계 물의 날이다. 사람들은 이 날 물을 '절약하려고' 노력한다.

22 그들은 자신의 쇼핑백을 가지고 와야 한다.

23 (A) 형용사적 용법의 to부정사가 수식하는 명사가 to부정사에 쓰인 전치사의 목적어에 해당하므로 to live in이 적절하다. (B) 나무는 지구 온난화를 '늦춘다'고 해야 하므로 slow down이 적절하다. promote: 촉진[고취]하다, (C) 해로운 화학 물질의 사용을 '멈춰야만' 한다고 해야 하므로 be stopped가 적절하다.

24 ②를 제외한 나머지는 다 '벌들'을 지칭한다.

25 농작물에 해로운 화학 물질을 사용하는 것이 벌과 사람의 건강에 '좋지' 않기 때문에 멈춰야만 한다.

서술형 실전문제
p.106~107

01 to get → not to get

02 how to slowing down → how to slow down

03 (1) I'm worried about disappearing bees.
   (2) I'm concerned about disappearing bees.
   (3) I'm nervous about disappearing bees.
   (4) I'm anxious about disappearing bees.

04 (1) The use of harmful chemicals on crops must be stopped (by people).
   (2) Students should be allowed to use cell phones in class (by us).
   (3) By whom will the house be cleaned from now on? / Who will the house be cleaned from now on by?
   (4) That question cannot be answered by me right now.

05 (1) are (2) have (3) was (4) is

06 (1) must be protected
   (2) should be given up
   (3) can be repaired

07 (A) helpful (B) great (C) themselves

08 (which/that) flowers produce

09 (A) bees (B) pollen

10 Planting more flowers and trees

11 (1) (벌에게 살기 좋은 환경을 제공하기 위해) 더 많은 꽃과 나무를 심는 것.
   (2) 농작물에 해로운 화학 물질의 사용을 멈추는 것.

12 (A) a good environment (B) global warming

01 'Be careful not to 동사원형 ~.'은 '~하지 않도록 주의해라'라는 의미로 상대방이 잊어버리지 않도록 중요한 일에 대해 강한 당부 또는 경고하는 의미를 나타낼 수 있다.

02 'Do you know how to 동사원형 ~?'은 '~하는 방법을 아니?'
란 의미로 상대방에게 방법을 물을 때 사용하는 표현이다.

03 걱정이 된다는 것을 나타내는 표현은 'I'm worried about ~.'
또는 'I'm concerned about ~.'라고 한다. 걱정이 되는 것은
불안하거나 문제가 있는 것을 나타낼 수 있으므로, 걱정을 나타
내는 nervous나 anxious를 이용해서 말할 수도 있다.

04 조동사가 있는 수동태는 '조동사+be+과거분사'의 형태로 쓴다.

05 (1) 부분을 나타내는 말 뒤에 오는 명사가 단수이면 단수 동사를
쓰고, 복수이면 복수 동사를 쓴다. (2) a few of+복수 명사+
복수 동사 (3) much of+단수 명사+단수 동사 (4) the number
of+복수 명사+단수 동사. incalculable: 헤아릴 수 없는, 무수
한

06 조동사가 있는 수동태는 '조동사+be+과거분사'의 형태로 쓴다.

07 (A) 뒤에 벌들이 인간에게 도움이 되는 내용이 나오므로
helpful이 적절하다. harmful: 해로운, (B) 감각동사 tastes
뒤에 형용사 보어를 써야 하므로 great가 적절하다. (C) '스스
로' 생산될 수 없다고 해야 하므로 themselves가 적절하다. by
oneself: 혼자, 도움을 받지 않고

08 (which/that is) produced by flowers를 능동태로 고치면 된
다.

09 많은 농작물들은 스스로 생산될 수 없기 때문에 '벌'의 도움을 필
요로 한다. 벌은 한 꽃에서 다른 꽃으로 '꽃가루'를 옮기는 것을 돕
는다.

10 '더 많은 꽃과 나무를 심는 것'을 가리킨다.

11 '더 많은 꽃과 나무를 심는 것'과 '농작물에 해로운 화학 물질의
사용을 멈추는 것'을 가리킨다.

12 더 많은 꽃과 나무를 심음으로써 벌에게 살기 '좋은 환경'을 제공
할 뿐만 아니라 '지구 온난화'를 늦추도록 도울 것이다.

창의사고력 서술형 문제
p.108

|모범답안|

01 I'm worried about animals / What should we do
to help them? / We should stop

02 (1) We will watch the movie this Saturday.
(2) The movie will be watched by us this Saturday.

03 (A) turn off the lights   (B) take a shower
(C) Half   (D) recycle plastic   (E) 10

01 be worried about: ~에 대하여 걱정하다 should: ~해야 한다

단원별 모의고사
p.109~112

01 pollution   02 ④   03 ④
04 (1) (l)ast (2) (r)educe (3) surveying
(4) (t)ransportation, (h)armful, pollution, global
warming
05 ①   06 air pollution   07 ③
08 I'm worried[concerned/anxious] about him.
09 participate in
10 I'm worried about our planet.
11 ③   12 ⑤   13 ④
14 It's because of global warming.
15 ②   16 ④
17 (1) sell → sold   (2) deliver → be delivered
(3) A member can be become by anybody → Anybody
can become a member
(4) was → were   (5) were → was
18 ③, ④   19 ③   20 which[that] is
21 ②, ④, ⑤   22 ①   23 used
24 Let's not let them down!

01 주어진 단어들은 동사와 명사의 관계이다. advise: 충고하다
advice: 충고 pollute: 오염시키다 pollution: 오염

02 (A) break down: 분해되다 / 머지않아 그 자연 쓰레기는 분해
되어 영양이 풍부한 흙으로 변한다. (B) melt away: 차츰 사라
지다 / 얼음은 완전히 녹아서 강으로 흘러 들어갈 것입니다.

03 ④ fine: 미세한, 섬세한 very thin or narrow 매우 가늘거나
좁은 ① adventure: 모험 / 위험하거나 특이한 일이 일어나는
흥미로운 경험 ② ancient: 고대의 / 긴 시간 동안 존재해 온 ③
deliver: 배달하다 / 상품, 편지 등을 어떤 특별한 장소로 가지고
가다 ⑤ pollen: 꽃가루 / 꽃에 의해서 생산된 미세한 가루

04 (1) last: 지속하다 (2) reduce: 줄이다 (3) survey: 설문조
사를 하다 (4) transportation: 교통 emit: (빛·열·냄새·소
리 따위를) 내다, 방출하다 harmful: 해로운 pollution: 오염
global warming: 지구 온난화

05 'I think it's terrible.(끔찍하다고 생각해)'이라고 대답하고 있
으므로, 빈칸에는 상대방의 의견을 묻는 질문이 어울린다. 그러므
로 빈칸에는 'What do you think of ~?(~에 대해 어떻게 생각
하니?)'를 사용한 ①이 적절하다.

06 air: 공기 pollution: 오염

07 (A) 남동생의 다리가 부러졌다는 대답에는 'what makes
you happy?(무엇이 너를 기쁘게 하니?)'보다 'what's the
matter?(무슨 일이야?)'가 더 어울린다. (B) 남동생의 다리가
부러졌다는 사실에 유감을 표현하는 'I'm sorry to hear that.'
이 적절하다.

08 be worried[concerned/anxious] about: ~에 대하여 걱정

하다

09 participate in: ~에 참가하다 take part in: ~에 참가하다

10 be worried about: ~에 대하여 걱정하다 planet: 행성

11 ① Earth Hour의 시간은 매년 다르다. ② Earth Hour를 알아보기 위해 인터넷을 찾아볼 것이다. ④ TV program인 *The Sick Planet*이 무슨 내용이었는지는 언급되어 있지 않다. ⑤ Linda는 The Sick Planet을 보았다.

12 주어진 문장이 ⑤번에 들어가 에너지를 절약하는 방법을 제안하고 남자아이가 그 방법이 좋은 생각이라고 말하는 것이 자연스럽다.

13 북극곰이 지구 온난화 때문에 집과 식량을 잃어가는 상황이라고 얘기하고 있으므로, 지구 온난화의 속도를 늦추는 방법에 대해서 묻는 것이 어울린다.

14 because of 명사: ~ 때문에 global warming: 지구 온난화

15 부분을 나타내는 말 뒤에 오는 명사가 단수이면 단수 동사를 쓰고 복수이면 복수 동사를 쓴다. rural: 시골의, 지방의

16 '상태'나 '소유'를 나타내는 타동사는 수동태로 쓰이지 않음에 주의한다.

17 (1) 조동사가 있는 수동태는 '조동사+be+과거분사'의 형태로 쓴다. (2) This letter가 주어이므로 'must be delivered'로 고치는 것이 적절하다. (3) become은 자동사이므로 수동태로 쓰이지 않는다. (4) 부분을 나타내는 말(half of) 뒤에 오는 those invited가 복수이므로 복수 동사 were를 써야 한다. (5) (a) little of+단수 명사+단수 동사

18 ③ About a quarter of the population of the country lives in Seoul. ④ This medicine should be kept out of the reach of children.

19 벌과 식물은 '상생 관계'이다. ③ conflicting: 서로 싸우는, 상충[상반]되는, ① 모두에게 유리한[모두가 득을 보는], ② 협력[협동]하는, ④ 공존하는, ⑤ 상호 이익이 되는

20 주격 관계대명사 'which/that+be동사'가 생략되어 있다.

21 ⓐ와 ①, ③: 부사적 용법, ②, ⑤: 명사적 용법, ④: 형용사적 용법

22 ⓐ slow down: ~을 늦추다, ⓑ the use of A on B: B에 A를 사용하는 것

23 농작물에 '사용된' 해로운 화학 물질을 가리킨다.

24 Let's not: ~하지 말자

Heal the World

| 01 ② | 02 ④ | 03 ② | 04 ③ |
| 05 ① | 06 ② | | |

01 rewarding: 보람 있는 satisfying: 만족시키는

02 be on time: 제시간에 도착하다 / 또 늦었구나. 시간 약속을 지키는 것은 중요한단다.

03 ① give, give a bath: 목욕시키다 / 내가 아기를 목욕시킬 동안 편안하게 있어. ② keep ~ in mind: ~을 명심하다 / 너는 그의 충고를 명심해야 한다. ③ doing, do one's best: 최선을 다하다 / 가장 중요한 것은 최선을 다하는 것이다. ④ prepare, prepare for ~: ~을 준비하다 / Joe는 내가 시험 준비하는 것을 도와주었다. ⑤ having, have fun: 즐거운 시간을 보내다 / 그 아이들은 서로의 그림자를 쫓으며 재미있게 놀고 있었다.

04 ① 너의 가방들을 꾸리는 게 좋겠다. 우리는 한 시간 뒤에 떠날 거야. ② 비누와 차가운 물은 대부분의 음식 얼룩을 제거할 것이다. ③ matter: 문제되다 / 깔끔하게 보인다면, 무엇을 입던 문제가 되지 않는다. ④ 의자에 온통 고양이 털이 있다. ⑤ 심지어 아무리 작은 기부라도 한 아이의 인생에 큰 차이를 만들 수 있다.

05 suggest: 제안하다 take a rest: 휴식하다

06 (A) get together: 모이다 / 그는 그녀를 위한 파티를 계획하기 위해 몇몇 친구들과 모였다. (B) keep in mind: 명심하다 / 바닥 타일은 청소하기 힘들 수 있다. 그것은 새로운 바닥을 고를 때 기억할 가치가 있다. (C) make sure ~: 꼭 ~하다, 확실하게 ~하다 / 매끼 식사 후에 이 약을 꼭 드세요.

01 (r)emoved

02 (1) up   (2) together   (3) on   (4) along

03 to introduce

04 up

05 plant

06 (1) (l)anded   (2) (n)eat   (3) the (e)lderly   (4) (s)pot

07 (1) They must be so proud of themselves.

   (2) This situation matters a lot.

   (3) I'll give a hand if I finish early.

01 remove: 제거하다 / 어떤 것을 한 장소에서 옮기거나 치우다 / 불법 주차 차량들은 치워진다.

02 (1) get up: (잠자리에서) 일어나다 / 첫 기차에 늦지 않게 일찍 일어나라. (2) get together: 모이다 / 그들은 수요일마다 모여서 수학을 공부한다. (3) get on: (탈것에) 타다 / 우리는 Lime Street역에서 기차를 탔다. (4) get along with ~: ~와 잘 지내다 / 나는 반 친구들과 잘 지낸다.

03 It's time to 동사원형 ~: ~해야 할 시간이다 (= It's time for (동)명사 ~.) / 자기 소개를 할 시간이다.

04 pick up: 치우다, 줍다 / 쓰레기를 줍는 게 어떨까? line up: 줄 서다 / 자동차들이 줄을 지어 배에 타려고 기다리고 있었다.

05 plant: 식물; 심다 / 식물에 물 주는 것을 잊지 말아라. 우리는 토마토와 당근을 정원에 심을 것이다.

06 (1) land: 착륙하다 (2) neat: 깨끗한 (3) the elderly (people): 나이 든 사람들 (4) spot: 장소, 지점

07 (1) be proud of ~: ~을 자랑스러워하다 (2) matter: 문제가 되다, 중요하다 (3) give ~ a hand ~에게 도움을 주다

교과서
Conversation

1 What do you want me to do?
2 Make sure you lock the door.
3 (B) → (A) → (C) → (D)

교과서 대화문 익히기

1 T   2 T   3 T   4 F   5 T   6 F   7 T   8 F

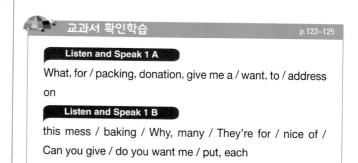

교과서 확인학습

Listen and Speak 1 A

What, for / packing, donation, give me a / want, to / address on

Listen and Speak 1 B

this mess / baking / Why, many / They're for / nice of / Can you give / do you want me / put, each

1. doing / packing for, Can you help / What do you want / put the clothes into

2. packing for, move, Can you help me / move, outside

3. What are you doing / packing for, move, Can you help me / What do you want me to do / take out

Listen and Speak 2 A

Enjoy / will, is on / worry about / Make sure you feed, after / should

Listen and Speak 2 B

Make groups of, sit, to make, Keep in mind, make sure, before you start, Second, when, let's

Listen and Speak 2 C

1. to go / Make sure / Anything / that's

2. time to / Make sure you clean / Anything else

3. It's time to go / Make sure, water the plants / will

Real Life Talk Watch a Video

What can I do / here for / must be / What do you want me to do / read, for the blind / go into / anything to keep in / Make sure you read, slowly and clearly / do my best

Real Life Talk Step 3

1. I'm here for / for / do you want me to do / give, a bath / Is there anything / Make sure

2. I'm here for the volunteer / Thanks for / What do you want me to do / for the blind / Is there anything to keep in mind /sure

---

시험대비 기본평가   p.126

01 ④   02 ⑤

03 (C) → (E) → (A) → (B) → (D)

01 'What do you want me to do?'는 '너는 내가 무엇을 해 주기를 원하니?'라는 뜻으로 상대방이 원하는 행동이 무엇인지를 물어보는 표현이다. me는 want의 목적어이고 to do는 목적격 보어이다.

02 빈칸에는 무엇을 해 주기를 원하는지 묻는 말에 대한 대답으로 어떠한 것을 해달라고 요청하는 말이 어울린다.

03 엉망진창이 된 상황을 보고 무슨 일인지 남자아이가 질문하자 (C) 쿠키를 굽고 있다고 대답한다. (E) 많은 쿠키를 굽는 이유를 물어보고 (A) 양로원에 계신 분들을 위한 것이라고 대답한다. (B) 착하다고 말하자 (D) 여자아이는 남자아이에게 도움을 요청한다. 남자아이는 승낙하고 무엇을 도울지 물어본다.

시험대비 실력평가   p.127~128

01 ②	02 ⑤	03 ④	04 ②
05 ②	06 ①	07 ③	08 ①
09 ④	10 ④	11 ③	

01 빈칸에는 도움을 요청하는 말에 상대방이 구체적으로 무엇을 원하는지 묻는 말인 'What do you want me to do?(제가 무엇을 하기를 원하십니까?)'가 어울린다.

02 주어진 문장은 아빠가 차에서 기다리고 있다는 말로, 남자아이가 엄마가 가셔야 한다고 말하는 내용과 연결되는 것이 적절하다.

03 상대방이 꼭 하기를 원하는 내용을 말하기 위해서 'make sure'를 사용한다. 'make sure'는 '꼭 ~해라, 확실하게 ~해라'의 의미를 가지고 있다.

04 ① 남자아이는 저녁 먹은 후에 무엇을 해야 하는가? (개 밥을 줘야 한다.) ② 남자아이는 무엇을 걱정하는가? ③ 남자아이의 저녁식사는 어디에 있는가? (식탁 위에) ④ 아빠는 어디에 있는가? (차 안에) ⑤ 엄마는 어디를 갈 것인가? (콘서트)

05 주어진 문장은 '도와줄래?'의 의미로 상대방에게 도움을 요청할 때 사용하는 표현이다. 'Sure.(물론이야.)'라고 요청에 대한 대답을 하는 것과 어울리므로 ②에 들어가야 적절하다.

06 'What are all these boxes and books for?(이 박스와 책들은 다 무엇에 쓰려는 거니?)'와 'Please write the address on the boxes.(박스에 주소를 좀 써 줘.)' 두 문장에서 책을 포장하고 있다는 것을 알 수 있다. pack: 짐을 꾸리다

07 ① 남자아이는 여자아이를 도울 것인가? (네) ② 여자아이는 지금 무엇을 하는 중인가? (책을 싸고 있다.) ③ 여자아이는 얼마나 많은 책들을 기부 센터에 보낼 것인가? ④ 책은 무엇에 쓰려는 것인가? (기부 센터에 보내기 위한 책들이다.) ⑤ 대화가 끝나고 남자아이는 무엇을 할 것인가? (박스에 주소를 쓸 것이다.)

08 노인들에게 식사를 배달하는데 'Is there anything to keep in mind?(유념해야 할 것이 있나요?)'라고 묻고 있다. greet: 인사하다 politely: 예의 바르게

09 영화 시작이 7시인데 반드시 7시 30분 이후에 가라고 당부하는 것은 어색하다.

10 keep in mind: 명심하다. 두 가지 규칙을 명심하라고 얘기하고 그 두 가지가 무엇인지 구체적으로 말하는 것이 적절하다.

11 ① 무엇을 만들 것인가? (베이컨 달걀 샌드위치) ② 무슨 수업인가? (요리 수업) ③ 베이컨 달걀 샌드위치를 만드는 데 몇 시간이 걸리는가? ④ 수업 시간에 얼마나 많은 유의해야 할 규칙이 있는가? (2 개) ⑤ 몇 명이 한 그룹을 만드는가? (4명)

서술형 시험대비   p.129

01 ⓐ in   ⓑ do

02 What do you want me to do today?

03 blind → the blind

04 (A) give　(B) want

05 (A) to go　(B) lock

06 What would you like me to do?

01 ⓐ keep in mind: 명심하다 ⓑ do one's best: 최선을 다하다

02 'What do you want me to do?'는 '제가 무엇을 하길 원하세요?'라는 뜻으로 상대방이 원하는 것이 무엇인지 물어보는 표현이다.

03 'the+형용사'는 복수 보통명사로 여기서 the blind는 blind people을 의미한다. 책을 시각 장애인들을 위해 읽어 주는 것이므로 the blind가 어울린다.

04 (A) 'give ~ a hand'는 '~를 돕다'라는 관용적 표현으로, 이 표현을 이용해 'Can you give me a hand?'라고 하면, '너 나 좀 도와줄래?'의 의미로 상대방에게 도움을 요청할 때 사용하는 표현이다. (B) 'What do you want to me to do?'는 '너는 내가 무엇을 하기를 원하니?'로 상대방이 원하는 것이 무엇인지 묻는 표현이다.

05 (A) It's time to 동사원형 ~: ~해야 할 시간이다 (B) 'Make sure (that) 주어+동사 ~' 구문으로 상대방이 잊어버리지 않도록 중요한 일에 대해 강한 당부 또는 경고하는 의미를 나타낼 수 있다. '~을 확실히 하라, ~을 반드시 하라'의 뜻이다.

06 'What do you want me to ~?'와 'What would you like me to ~?'는 '너는 내가 무엇을 하기를 원하니?'의 의미로 상대방이 원하는 행동을 물어볼 때 사용하는 표현이다.

[교과서]
Grammar

핵심 Check
p.130~131

1 (1) know　(2) feel

2 (1) that　(2) It　(3) whom

시험대비 기본평가
p.132

01 ①　　02 ④　　03 ⑤

04 (1) Mr. Brown let his son go to the party.

(2) The project manager had us meet at 9 a.m.

(3) They made me repeat the whole story.

(4) She helped me to complete this assignment.

01 사역동사 have 뒤의 목적보어 자리에는 원형부정사를 쓴다.

02 'It ~ that 강조 구문'은 'It is/was ~ that ...'의 형태로, 강조하고자 하는 부분을 It is/was와 that 사이에 넣고, 나머지 부분을 that 뒤에 써서 주어, 목적어, 부사(구/절) 등을 강조한다. 공통으로 that이 들어가는 것이 적절하다.

03 It was Jim who[that] I met again. 강조되는 어구가 사람일 때는 that 대신에 who[whom]를 쓸 수 있다.

04 (1) let+목적어+원형부정사(go) (2) have+목적어+원형부정사(meet) (3) make+목적어+원형부정사(repeat) (4) help+목적어+to부정사(원형부정사 / to complete) 등에 유의하여 영작한다.

시험대비 실력평가
p.133~135

01 ①　　02 ②　　03 ⓐ, ⓓ

04 ④　　05 ②, ⑤　　06 ③　　07 ③

08 ④　　09 ②　　10 ①　　11 ⑤

12 ③

13 (1) paint → painted　(2) to play → play

(3) escaping → escape[to escape]

(4) which → that　(5) what → that[which]

(6) which → that

14 (1) feel, smaile　(2) fixed　(3) to remain

(4) that　(5) who

15 ⑤　　16 ⑤　　17 ③　　18 ④

01 He let me finish playing the piano. 사역동사 let의 목적보어로 동사원형이 적절하다.

02 ① which → that[who] ③ That → It ④ which → that ⑤ what → that

03 <보기>와 ⓐ, ⓓ는 목적보어로 동사원형이 사용된 사역동사 make이다 ⓑ 4형식 동사(수여동사) ⓒ (어느 방향으로) 나아가다(자동사) ⓔ 3형식 동사

04 '사역동사 had+목적어+목적보어 draw'와 관계대명사 what을 이용한다.

05 'a better tomorrow'를 강조하는 것이므로 which나 that을 써야 한다.

06 made가 사역동사이므로 목적보어로 동사원형이 온다.

07 <보기>와 ③번은 강조구문의 that이다. ① 지시부사 ② 지시대명사 ④ 접속사 ⑤ 지시형용사

08 (A) 사역동사 let 뒤의 목적보어로 동사원형, (B) the paper가 복사되는 것이므로 수동의 의미를 갖는 과거분사, (C) get은 사역동사가 아니므로 목적보어로 to부정사를 받는다.

09 ②번은 'It: 가주어, that절: 진주어'이고 나머지는 모두 It ~

27

10 (A) 주어가 복수이므로 give, (B)에는 사역동사 make의 목적
보어로 원형부정사가 적절하다. (C)에는 사역동사 have의 목적
보어로 원형부정사가 적절하다.

11 ① goes → go ② cleaned → clean ③ make → makes
④ draw → to draw

12 ① which → that ② which → that ④ which → that
⑤ which → that

13 (1) 목적어와 목적격보어의 관계가 수동이므로 목적격보어로 과
거분사를 쓰는 것이 적절하다. (2) 목적어와 관계가 능동이므로
목적격보어로 동사원형이 적절하다. (3) help는 준사역동사로
목적격보어로 원형부정사나 to부정사를 받으므로 escaping을
escape나 to escape로 고쳐야 한다. (4) last week을 강조하
는 것으로 전치사가 없어서 last week을 선행사처럼 생각할 수
있지만 여기서는 last week이 부사구이므로 that이 적절하다.
(5) 강조하는 것이 his smartphone이므로 what을 that이나
which로 고치는 것이 적절하다. (6) in this school을 강조하
는 것으로 school을 선행사로 생각하면 안 된다. which를 that
으로 고친다.

14 (1) 사역동사는 목적격보어로 동사원형이 나온다. (2) get의 목
적격보어로 수동의 의미가 필요하므로 과거분사가 적절하다.
(3) ask는 목적격보어로 to부정사가 나온다. (4) 강조하는 것이
yesterday이므로 that이 적절하다. (5) 강조하는 것이 Tom이
므로 who가 적절하다.

15 get은 사역동사의 뜻으로 쓰일 때 목적어와 목적격보어의 관계
가 능동일 경우 목적격 보어로 to부정사를 쓴다.

16 'my favorite movie character'를 강조하는 것으로 'It was ~
that[which] ...'가 적절하다.

17 get은 사역동사의 뜻으로 쓰일 때 목적어와 목적격보어의 관계가
능동일 경우 목적격보어로 to부정사를 쓴다.

18 사역동사 make는 수동태에서 목적격보어가 to부정사로 바뀐다.

서술형 시험대비 　　　　　　　　　　　p.136~137

01 (1) The project manager let us paint anything we
wanted.
(2) She wasn't happy with our work and made us
start over.
(3) They immediately had the meeting cancelled.
(4) When you cut them into pieces, let them be
marinated.
(5) You in this country helped us (to) become free.
(6) It was Susan that(who/whom) I had a date with
at the park last Saturday.

(7) It was in the train that Kimberly lost her wallet.
(8) It was last Friday that Mina flew a drone at the
school.

02 (1) He let me play the piano with him.
(2) She had her computer fixed.

03 (1) It was Mina that[who] found a deer behind a
tree.
(2) It was a deer that[which] Mina found behind a
tree.
(3) It was behind a tree that Mina found a deer.

04 (1) I had my sister bring my gym uniform.
(2) Ashley got me to fix dinner.
(3) He made me wash his car.
(4) The doctor let her return to work.

05 (1) It was I that[who] bought this nice jacket at the
store last Sunday.
(2) I did buy this nice jacket at the store last Sunday.
(3) It was this nice jacket that[which] I bought at
the store last Sunday.
(4) It was at the store that I bought this nice jacket
last Sunday.
(5) It was last Sunday that I bought this nice jacket
at the store.

06 taken

07 (1) Peter sometimes lets his dog sleep on his bed.
(2) My dad makes me read lots of books.
(3) Where do you want me to hang this picture?
(4) It was the novel that[which] John borrowed from
a library last week.
(5) It was in 2014 that I met her for the first time.

01 (1) 사역동사 let 뒤에 원형부정사를 쓴다. (2) 사역동사 make
뒤에 원형부정사를 쓴다. (3) 회의가 취소되는 수동이므로 과거
분사로 바꾼다. (4) 목적어와의 관계가 수동일 경우 let은 목적
격보어로 'be p.p.' 형태를 쓴다. (5) help는 목적격보어로 동사
원형이나 to부정사가 나온다. (6) 강조하는 것이 'Susan'이므로
that이나 who 또는 whom을 쓰는 것이 적절하다. (7) which
다음에 완전한 절이 나오므로 the train을 강조하는 것으로 볼
수 없다. 'in the train'을 강조하는 것으로 that을 쓰는 것이 적
절하다. (8) 강조하는 것이 'last Friday'이므로 that을 쓰는 것
이 적절하다.

02 (1) 'allowed ~ to부정사'는 사역동사 let을 이용한다. (2) 목적
어와 목적격보어의 관계가 수동일 경우 사역동사의 목적격보어로
과거분사를 쓴다.

03 It was와 that 사이에 강조하고자 하는 부분을 넣고, that 대신에
사람이면 who, 사물이나 동물이면 which를 쓸 수도 있다.

04 (1), (3), (4) 사역동사 have, make, let의 목적격보어로 목적

어와의 관계가 능동일 경우 원형부정사를 쓴다. (2) get은 목적어와 목적격보어의 관계가 능동일 경우 목적격보어로 to부정사를 쓴다.

05 과거시제이므로 강조하고자 하는 부분을 It was와 that 사이에 넣고, 나머지 부분을 that 뒤에 쓴다. 이때 that 대신에 사람이면 who, 사물이면 which를 사용할 수 있다. 또한 'It is[was] ~ that ...' 구문은 동사를 강조할 수 없으므로 동사는 동사 앞에 do/does/did를 사용하여 강조한다.

06 사역동사의 목적격보어로 '아들이 병원으로 데려가지는' 수동의 의미가 필요하므로 과거분사가 적절하다.

07 (1), (2) '사역동사+목적어+원형부정사'에 유의한다. (3) want는 목적격보어로 to부정사가 나온다. (4), (5) 강조하고자 하는 부분을 It was와 that 사이에 넣고, 나머지 부분을 that 뒤에 쓴다. 이때 that 대신에 사물이면 which를 사용할 수 있다.

Reading 교과서

확인문제   p.138

1 T   2 F   3 T   4 T   5 T   6 F

확인문제   p.139

1 T   2 F   3 T   4 F   5 T   6 F

교과서 확인학습 A   p.140~141

01 Better Tomorrow
02 My name is
03 This is me
04 aren't they
05 take pictures
06 old neighborhoods
07 with wall paintings
08 a light went on in my head
09 I'm in
10 Why don't we
11 suggested this idea
12 on the Internet
13 to do a wall painting
14 applied for, was selected
15 finally came
16 had us meet
17 was in very poor condition

18 strange writings and drawings
19 Other parts   20 with white paint
21 let us paint
22 something cute
23 divided into
24 was in the group
25 chose my spot
26 did, background drawings
27 for about   28 got together, shared
29 was very proud of
30 so, that   31 much harder
32 wasn't perfect
33 matter
34 a little brighter and happier
35 ourselves   36 didn't just paint
37 a better tomorrow

교과서 확인학습 B   p.142~143

1 Paint a Better Tomorrow
2 Hi. My name is Homin.
3 This is me in front of the wall painting.
4 The wings are so pretty, aren't they?
5 Many people like to take pictures in front of wall paintings.
6 They make old neighborhoods bright and new.
7 Last month, I visited a village with wall paintings in Yeosu.
8 As I was taking a picture, a light went on in my head.
9 I thought, "I'm in the school art club.
10 Why don't we do wall paintings like these?"
11 I suggested this idea at the next club meeting, and the members loved it.
12 We found a teen volunteer project on the Internet.
13 The project was to do a wall painting in our neighborhood.
14 We applied for it, and two weeks later, our club was selected!
15 The day of the project finally came.
16 The project manager had us meet at the painting site at 9 a.m.
17 The wall was in very poor condition.
18 There were strange writings and drawings on some parts.
19 Other parts had old posters on them.
20 We removed the posters first and painted over

the writings and drawings with white paint.

21 The manager let us paint anything we wanted.

22 We decided to paint something cute because the wall was near an elementary school.

23 We divided into three groups and began painting.

24 I was in the group with Minsu and Jiwon.

25 I chose my spot and started to paint my favorite movie character.

26 Minsu painted some flowers and Jiwon did some background drawings.

27 Our club painted for about five hours.

28 After we finished, we got together and shared the day's experiences.

29 Minsu was very proud of his flower painting.

30 He said, "My flower is so real that a bee landed on it."

31 I said, "Drawing on a wall was much harder than drawing on paper."

32 We all agreed that our wall painting wasn't perfect.

33 But it didn't matter.

34 We made our neighborhood a little brighter and happier.

35 We were proud of ourselves.

36 We didn't just paint pictures on a wall that day.

37 It was a better tomorrow that we painted.

시험대비 실력평가
p.144~147

01 isn't it → aren't they　　　02 ②

03 Why don't we do wall paintings like these?

04 ⑤　　　　　05 ②　　　　06 ②, ⑤

07 The wall was in very poor condition.　　08 ③

09 (A) taking a picture　(B) wall paintings

10 여수에 있는 벽화 마을의 벽화들　　　　11 ③

12 ⑤　　　　　13 ④

14 ①번 → for, ②번 → that, ③번 → a little[또는 much/
　even/still/far/a lot], ④번 → ourselves, ⑤번 →
　that[which]

15 bad　　　16 so → because(as/since)　17 ⑤

18 was selected　　　　19 ①, ⑤　　　　20 ①

21 ⑤

22 (A) to meet → meet, 또는 had → got
　　(B) to paint → paint 또는 let → allowed　23 ③

01 주어가 The wing이 아니라 The wings이므로, aren't they
　로 고치는 것이 적절하다.

---

02 주어진 문장의 'a light went on in my head'에 주목한다. ②
　번 다음 문장의 내용을 가리키므로 ②번이 적절하다.

03 '우리가 이것처럼 벽화를 그리면 어떨까?'라는 생각을 가리킨다.

04 호민이의 학교 미술 동아리가 청소년 봉사 프로젝트에 선택된
　것은 '그 프로젝트에 지원한지' 2주 후(two weeks after it
　applied for the project)였다.

05 오래된 포스터들이 붙어 있던 것을 '제거했다'고 하는 것이 적절
　하다. ① 보호했다, ③ 막았다, 예방했다, ④ 유지했다, ⑤ 파괴
　했다

06 '마침내' 프로젝트 날이 왔다고 하는 것이 적절하다. finally =
　at last = in the end: 마침내, ①, ④: 무엇보다도, 특히, ③ 적
　어도[최소한]

07 be in poor[bad] condition: 보존 상태가 나쁘다, 건강이 좋지 않
　다

08 ⓐ on the Internet: 인터넷 상에서, ⓑ apply for: ~에 신청
　하다, ~에 지원하다

09 호민이는 여수에 있는 벽화 마을에서 '사진을 찍는' 동안 어떤 아
　이디어가 떠올라서, 미술 동아리 부원들에게 그것처럼 '벽화'를
　그리자고 제안했다.

10 'wall paintings at a village with wall paintings in
　Yeosu'를 가리킨다.

11 ⓐ와 ③: 중요하다, 문제가 되다(동사), ①, ④: 문제, 일, 사건,
　② (쓰인·인쇄된) 것, 우편물, ⑤ 물질

12 이 글은 '동아리 부원들이 벽화를 그린 후, 자신들이 그날 벽에 그
　린 것은 단지 그림만이 아니라 더 나은 내일을 그린 것이라며 스스
　로를 대견하게 생각하는' 내용의 글이므로, 제목으로는 ⑤번 '우리
　가 무엇을 그렸냐고? 더 나은 내일!'이 적절하다. ① incredible:
　믿을 수 없는, ③ So what?: 그래서 어쩌라는 거야?

13 matter = count = be important = be of importance =
　be significant: 중요하다, ④ make a difference: 변화를 가
　져오다, 중요하다

14 ① 'for+숫자', 'during+기간을 나타내는 명사', ② so ~ that
　...: 너무 ~해서 …하다, ③ very는 형용사나 부사의 원급을 강
　조하는 말이므로, 비교급을 강조하는 말로 고치는 것이 적절하
　다. 다만 'a little'은 '약간'이라는 뜻이고, 'much/even/still/
　far/a lot'은 '훨씬'이라는 뜻이다. ④ 주어와 목적어가 같으므로
　재귀대명사로 고치는 것이 적절하다. ⑤ painted의 목적어에
　해당하는 'a better tomorrow'를 강조하는 것이므로 that이나
　which로 고치는 것이 적절하다.

15 be in poor[bad] condition: 보존 상태가 나쁘다, 건강이 좋
　지 않다

16 '그 벽이 초등학교 근처에 있어서 귀여운 뭔가를 그리기로 했다'
　고 해야 하므로, 이유를 나타내는 접속사로 고치는 것이 적절하
　다.

17 호민이가 가장 좋아하는 영화 캐릭터가 무엇인지는 대답할 수

없다. ① They met at 9 a.m. ② No. right away: 곧바로, 즉시, ③ No. The manager let them paint anything they wanted. ④ Yes. They decided to paint something cute because the wall was near an elementary school. subject matter: 소재

18 동아리가 '선택된' 것이므로 수동태로 쓰는 것이 적절하다.

19 (A) 와 ①, ⑤: 명사적 용법, ②, ④ 형용사적 용법, ③: 부사적 용법

20 이 글은 '글쓴이가 여수에 있는 벽화 마을을 방문하고 나서 학교 미술 동아리 부원들에게 벽화를 그리자고 제안한 다음, 청소년 봉사 프로젝트에 지원해서 선택되는' 내용이므로, 제목으로는 ①번 '이것들처럼 벽화를 그리면 어떨까?'가 적절하다.

21 some ~, others(other+복수명사) ~: 어떤 것[사람]들은 ~, 다른 것[사람]들은 ~, ⓑ 뒤에 명사가 있으므로 Others가 아니라 Other를 쓰는 것이 적절하다. each+단수명사, another+단수명사, the other: 둘 중 다른 하나

22 (A) have+목적어+원형부정사 = get+목적어+to부정사, (B) let+목적어+원형부정사 = allow+목적어+to부정사

23 이 글은 '벽화 그리기 위한 프로젝트를 행하는 과정'을 설명하는 글이므로, 주제로는 ③번 '벽화를 그리기 위한 과정'이 적절하다. ④ subject matter: 소재, ⑤ effectively: 효과적으로

서술형 시험대비
p.148~149

01 aren't they
02 (A) This is   (B) so   (C) bright and new
03 wall paintings
04 a light went on in my head
05 (A) idea   (B) project
06 school art club
07 몇 군데에는 이상한 낙서와 그림이 있었고, 다른 부분에는 오래된 포스터들이 붙어 있었다.
08 whatever
09 (1) 먼저 포스터들을 제거했다.
   (2) 낙서와 그림을 흰 페인트로 덧칠했다.
   (3) 호민이는 자신의 구역을 정해서 가장 좋아하는 영화 캐릭터를 그리기 시작했다.
   (4) 민수는 몇 송이의 꽃을 그렸다.
   (5) 지원이는 배경 그림을 그렸다.
10 (1) enough   (2) We painted a better tomorrow.
11 (A) imperfect   (B) pride
12 shared
13 (1) as[so], as   (2) less

01 주어가 The wings이므로, aren't they가 적절하다.
02 (A) 가까이 있는 사람을 소개할 때 'This is'를 사용한다. (B)

'so+형용사[부사]', 'such+a+형용사+명사'이므로 so가 적절하다. (C) 목적격보어로 형용사를 써야 하므로 bright and new가 적절하다.

03 '벽화'를 가리킨다. 'Many people'이라고 하지 않도록 조심해야 한다.

04 a light went on in my head: 머릿속에 좋은 생각이 떠올랐다

05 ⓑ 이 '아이디어', ⓒ 우리 마을에 벽화를 그리는 '프로젝트'를 가리킨다.

06 호민이가 봉사활동으로 하필이면 벽화를 그리자고 제안한 이유는 그가 '학교 미술 동아리'에 있기 때문이었다. of all things: 하필이면

07 뒤에 이어지는 문장의 내용을 쓰는 것이 적절하다.

08 anything (that) = whatever: (~하는) 것은 무엇이든지

09 그들은 먼저 별로 좋지 않았던 벽의 상태를 정리하고, 벽화 작업을 했다.

10 (1) so ~ that... = enough to 동사원형, to부정사나 전치사의 목적어가 주어와 같으면 생략한다. (2) 강조되었던 목적어를 동사 뒤에 쓰는 것이 적절하다.

11 (A) wasn't perfect = was imperfect, (B) be proud of = take pride in

12 share ~ = have ~ in common

13 A 비교급 than B = B not as(so) ~ as A = B less 원급 than A

영역별 핵심문제
p.151~155

01 ⑤	02 ④	03 (n)eat	04 take
05 ④	06 ③	07 ⑤	08 ②
09 ④	10 volunteer	11 ①	12 ②

13 (1) follow   (2) ask   (3) be taken   (4) written
14 ⑤
15 (1) It was I that[who] played hide and seek with my friends in the park yesterday.
   (2) I did play hide and seek with my friends in the park yesterday.
   (3) It was hide and seek that[which] I played with my friends in the park yesterday.
   (4) It was with my friends that I played hide and seek in the park yesterday.
   (5) It was in the park that I played hide and seek with my friends yesterday.
   (6) It was yesterday that I played hide and seek with my friends in the park.
16 ①   17 ③
18 It was, that[which]
19 (1) open   (2) read   (3) be taken   (4) that
   (5) which   (6) that

31

20 (1) Mr. Brown made the students line up at the gym.

(2) It was a bird that broke the window yesterday.

21 ③　　　　**22** ①, ④　　　　**23** volunteer project

24 ②　　　　**25** ①　　　　**26** ③

27 ⓐ my flower　ⓒ our wall painting wasn't perfect

28 ②

29 We made our neighborhood a little brighter and happier.

30 It took for about five hours (for them to do it).

01 prepare: 준비하다 / 나는 엄마가 아침에 쉬실 수 있도록 아침을 준비하려고 했었다.

02 as: ~할 때, ~ 때문에 ① 내가 과학 보고서를 쓰고 있을 때, 그가 나에게 전화했다. ② 내가 집에 도착했을 때, 나의 남동생이 울고 있었다. ③ 너는 들어갈 때 표를 보여 줘야 한다. ④ 엘리베이터가 고장 났기 때문에, 우리는 계단으로 올라가야 했다. ⑤ 내가 버스에서 내릴 때 Peter를 봤다.

03 neat: 단정한, 말쑥한 / 그의 옷은 항상 단정하고 깨끗했다.

04 take a break: 휴식을 취하다 / 10분 휴식을 취하자. take a picture: 사진을 찍다 / 제가 사진 찍어 드릴까요?

05 주어진 문장은 상대방이 원하는 행동이 무엇인지 물어보는 표현으로, 도움을 요청한 G에게 B가 수락하고 이어서 '내가 무엇을 하길 원하니?'라고 묻자 G는 B에게 박스에 주소를 써 달라고 얘기한다.

06 ③은 상대방에게 도움을 제안하는 표현이고, 나머지 보기들은 상대방에게 도움을 요청하는 표현들이다.

07 ⓒ는 자신에 대해서 걱정하지 말라는 의미이므로, worry가 아니라 don't worry가 어울린다. ⓐ Enjoy ⓑ will ⓒ Don't worry ⓓ Make ⓔ have

08 무엇을 하고 있는지 묻자 (B) 이사를 위해 짐을 싸는 중이라 대답하며 상대방에게 도움을 요청한다. (C) 요청을 수락하며, 무엇을 도와줘야 하는지 묻자 (A) 테이프로 상자를 묶어달라고 얘기하고 (D) 알았다고 대답한다.

09 주어진 문장은 '지금 들어가야 하나요?'의 의미로 'Yes. Please go into Room 7.(네. 7번 방으로 들어가 주세요.)'에 대한 질문이 될 수 있으므로 ④에 들어가는 것이 적절하다.

10 volunteer: 자원봉사자 / 대가를 기대하지 않고 어떤 일을 하는 사람

11 대화의 must는 '~임에 틀림없다'의 의미로 사용되었다. ①은 '~임에 틀림없다'로 강한 추측을 나타낼 때 사용한다. 이외의 보기들은 의무를 나타내는 '~해야 한다'의 의미로 사용되었다.

12 ① Tony는 책을 읽을 때 무엇을 명심해야 하는가?(천천히 그리고 명확하게 읽어야 한다.) ② Tony는 봉사활동을 전에 한 경험이 있는가? ③ Tony는 녹음을 위해 몇 번 방으로 갈 것인가?(7번) ④ 누구를 위해 Tony는 책을 녹음할 것인가?(시각 장애인

들) ⑤ Tony는 시각 장애인들을 위해 무엇을 할 예정인가?(책을 읽을 것이다.)

13 사역동사의 목적격보어로 목적어와의 관계가 능동일 경우 동사원형이 나오며, 수동일 경우 make, have는 목적격보어로 과거분사를 쓰고, let은 'be p.p.' 형태를 쓴다.

14 'It is[was] ~ that ...' 강조 구문에서 that 대신에 강조하는 것이 사람이면 who, 사물이면 which를 쓸 수 있다.

15 강조하고자 하는 부분을 It is[was]와 that 사이에 넣고, 나머지 부분을 that 뒤에 쓴다. that 대신에 강조하는 것이 사람이면 who, 사물이면 which를 쓸 수 있다. 하지만 'It is[was] ~ that ...' 구문은 동사를 강조할 수는 없고 동사는 동사 앞에 do/does/did를 사용하여 강조한다.

16 사역동사의 목적어와 목적격보어의 관계가 능동일 경우 동사원형이 나오며, 수동의 관계에 있을 경우 목적격보어로 과거분사를 쓴다. let은 'be p.p.' 형태를 쓴다. get은 목적격보어로 to부정사를 쓴다.

17 ① My sister always helps me (to) clean the garden. ② Ms. Parker made them water the plants. ④ I remember hearing him come[coming] in. ⑤ He advised her not to smoke.

18 'It is[was] ~ that ...' 구문은 강조하고자 하는 부분을 It is[was]와 that 사이에 넣고, 나머지 부분을 that 뒤에 쓰며, 강조하는 것이 사물이나 동물이면 that 대신에 which를 쓸 수 있다.

19 (1)~(3) 사역동사의 목적격보어로 목적어와의 관계가 능동일 경우 동사원형이 나오며, 수동의 관계에 있을 경우 과거분사를 쓴다. (4)~(6) 'It is[was] ~ that …' 구문에서 that 대신에 강조하는 것이 사람이면 who, 사물이나 동물이면 which를 쓸 수 있다.

20 (1) 사역동사의 목적격보어로 원형부정사를 쓴다. (2) 강조하고자 하는 부분을 It is[was]와 that 사이에 넣고, 나머지 부분을 that 뒤에 쓴다.

21 ③ be lost in a daydream: '공상에 잠기다[빠지다]', ⓐ와 나머지는 다 '좋은 생각이 떠올랐다', a light went on in my head: 머릿속에 좋은 생각이 떠올랐다

22 호민이가 여수에 있는 벽화 마을을 방문하고 나서 학교 미술 동아리 부원들에게 벽화를 그리자고 제안한 다음, 청소년 봉사 프로젝트에 지원하는 것으로 보아, '적극적'이고 '사려 깊은' 성격이라고 하는 것이 적절하다. ① 활동적인, 적극적인, ② 소극적인, 수동적인, ③ 이기적인, ④ 사려 깊은, (남을) 배려하는, ⑤ 거만한

23 호민이와 학교 미술 동아리 부원들은 벽화를 그리기를 원했기 때문에 '봉사 프로젝트'에 참여하기로 결정했다.

24 ②번 다음 문장의 'strange writings and drawings'에 주목한다. 주어진 문장의 'very poor condition'의 구체적인 예에 해당하므로 ②번이 적절하다.

25 이 글은 '호민이와 친구들이 벽화 그리는 프로젝트를 위해 만나서 벽화를 그리는' 내용의 글이므로, 제목으로는 ①번 '마침내 프로젝트를 위한 D-day가 되었어!'가 적절하다. D-day: 작전 행동 개시일, 중요한 작전·변화가 예정된 날

26 그들은 먼저 포스터들을 제거하고 낙서와 그림을 흰 페인트로 덧칠했다.

27 ⓐ '내 꽃', ⓒ '우리의 벽화가 완벽하지는 않다'는 것을 가리킨다.

28 ⓐ와 ②, ③: 동명사, ①, ④, ⑤: 현재분사

29 형용사의 비교급 앞에 a little을 붙여서 목적격보어로 쓰는 것이 적절하다.

30 동아리 부원들이 벽화를 그리는 데 약 다섯 시간이 걸렸다.

단원별 예상문제
p.156~159

01 ②   02 so, that   03 ③   04 ②
05 ①   06 ③, ⑤   07 make
08 Keep in mind two rules for our class.
09 ①   10 ①   11 give   12 ④
13 ④   14 ③, ⑤
15 (1) It was what he said that worried me.
   (2) It was with my friends that I played soccer after school.
   (3) It was my club members that[who] planted flowers in the garden on April 5th.
16 ⑤   17 ②
18 (A) suggestion   (B) teen volunteer project
19 ③   20 ④   21 ③   22 ①
23 ②, ⑤   24 ②
25 (A) minutes   (B) neat   (C) rewarding   26 ④

01 ① get, get up: (잠자리에서) 일어나다 / 그 소년들은 일어나서 화장실에 간다. ② turn, turn off: 끄다 / 내가 잘 수 있도록 불을 꺼주세요. ③ get, get on: (탈것에) 타다 / 지하철 타는 데가 어디입니까? ④ get, get together: 모이다 / 많은 친척들이 거실에 모일 수 있다. ⑤ get, get along with ~: ~와 잘 지내다 / 우리가 친구들과 잘 어울리는 것은 좋다.

02 so ~ that ...: 너무 ~해서 …하다 / 그 컴퓨터는 너무 비싸서 나는 살 수 없다.

03 apply: 지원하다, 신청하다 / 나는 4개의 대학에 지원했고, 모든 대학에서 받아들여졌다.

04 a light went on in the head: 머릿속에 좋은 생각이 떠올랐다 / 그것은 마치 그들에게 좋은 생각이 떠오른 것 같았다.

05 주어진 문장은 '내일 이사를 위해 짐을 싸는 중이야.'로 무엇을 하고 있는 중인지 묻는 'What are you doing?'의 대답이다.

06 'What do you want me to ~?'로 상대방이 원하는 행동을 물어볼 때 동사 'want, would like'를 이용해 대답할 수 있다. ②는 '나는 옷을 상자 안에 넣고 싶다.'의 의미로 맞지 않는다.

07 (A), (B) make: 만들다 (C) make sure ~: 꼭 ~해라, 확실하게 ~해라

08 keep in mind: 명심하다 rule: 규칙

09 주어진 문장은 '저는 봉사 활동을 하러 왔어요.'의 의미로, 자신이 온 목적을 말할 때 사용하는 표현이다.

10 Thanks 뒤에 for를 쓰는 경우, for 뒤에 감사의 이유를 적는다.

11 give a bath: 목욕시키다

12 봉사를 하러 온 A와 봉사 내용과 주의 사항을 가르쳐 주고 있는 B를 볼 때, 자원봉사자와 자원봉사 관리자의 관계임을 알 수 있다.

13 통증이 무엇을 줄이는 것이 아니라 줄어드는 것으로 목적어와의 관계가 수동이므로 과거분사가 적절하다.

14 ① 사역동사 let의 목적보어로 원형부정사, ② 목적어와의 관계가 수동이므로 과거분사, ④ 사역동사 make의 목적보어로 원형부정사, ⑥ that 다음에 나오는 절이 완전하고 Bob이 화장실을 떨어뜨릴 수는 없으므로 in을 the toilet 앞에 넣어 장소를 강조하는 문장으로 만들어야 한다. ⑦ a drone을 강조하는 것이므로 that이나 which를 써야 한다.

15 강조하고자 하는 부분을 It is[was]와 that 사이에 넣고, 나머지 부분을 that 뒤에 쓴다.

16 ⓐ와 ⑤: ~와 (똑)같이, ~처럼(전치사), ①, ④: 좋아하다(동사), ② 비슷한(형용사), ③ 비슷한 것(명사)

17 이 글은 '호민이와 학교 미술 동아리 부원들이 자원봉사 활동으로 벽화를 그리기로 결정하는 것'에 관한 글이므로, 주제로는 ②번 '자원봉사 활동으로 벽화를 그리기'가 적절하다.

18 학교 미술 동아리 부원들이 호민이의 '제안'을 수락한 뒤, 그들은 인터넷을 검색해서 그들 마을에 벽화를 그리는 '청소년 봉사 프로젝트'에 지원했다. 2주 후에 그들의 동아리가 선택되었다.

19 ⓐ be in poor[bad] condition: 보존 상태가 나쁘다, 건강이 좋지 않다, ⓑ divide into: ~으로 나뉘다

20 ⓒ와 ④: (소설 등의) 등장인물, (연극의) 역(役), (만화의) 캐릭터, leading character: 주역, ① 인격, 품성, ② 특성, 특질, 특색, ③ 글자, 부호, ⑤ (개인·국민의) 성격, 성질, 기질

21 책임자는 그들이 원하는 어떤 것이든 그리게 했다.

22 주어진 문장의 it에 주목한다. ①번 앞 문장의 'our wall painting wasn't perfect'를 받고 있으므로 ①번이 적절하다.

23 ① 실망, ② 만족감, ③ 우울함, ④ 수치심, ⑤ 자부심

24 호민이에게는 '벽'에 그리는 것이 '종이'에 그리는 것보다 훨씬 힘들었다.

25 (A) every 30 minutes: 30분마다, every+기수+복수명사: (빈도를 나타내어) 매~[~마다], (B) 감각동사 look의 보어이므로 형용사 neat이 적절하다. (C) 경험이 '보람을 받는' 것이 아니라 '보람을 주는' 것이므로 rewarding이 적절하다. rewarding: 보람 있는, 보람을 주는

26 얼마나 오래 봉사를 했는지는 알 수 없다.

01 What do you want me to do? /
    What would you like me to do?

02 to keeping → to keep

03 Be sure to read slowly and clearly. /
    Don't forget to read slowly and clearly. /
    Please remember to read slowly and clearly.

04 (1) He let us take pictures of his artwork.
    (2) It is a white bear that I am drawing now.
    (3) How much would it cost to have the camera
        cleaned?

05 (1) My mom made me prepare dinner.
    (2) My boss let the work be done by tomorrow.
    (3) Linda had her wallet stolen on her way home.
    (4) It was at[in] the restaurant that I saw Juliet
        calling her friend.
    (5) It is because they have no jobs that they
        cannot afford to buy them.

06 applied

07 (1) How[What] about   (2) shall we

08 They found it on the Internet.

09 (A) poor   (B) to paint   (C) near

10 other parts

11 They had to remove the posters first and paint
    over the writings and drawings with white paint.

01 'What would you like me to ~?'와 'What do you want me to ~?'는 '너는 내가 무엇을 하기를 원하니?'의 의미로 상대방이 원하는 행동을 물어볼 때 사용하는 표현이다.

02 to keep in mind는 앞의 대명사 anything을 수식하고 있다. (to부정사의 형용사적 용법) keep in mind: 명심하다

03 상대방이 꼭 하기를 원하는 내용을 강조하기 위해서 make sure를 사용한다. make sure는 '꼭 ~해라, 확실하게 ~해라'의 의미를 가지고 있다. 상대방에게 '꼭 ~해라', '~할 것을 잊지 말아라, ~할 것을 기억해라'라고 당부할 때는 'Be sure to 동사원형', 'Don't forget to 동사원형 ~'이나 'Remember to 동사원형 ~'으로 나타내기도 한다.

04 (1) 사역동사 let의 목적격보어로 동사원형이 나와야 한다. (2) It is와 that 사이에 a white bear를 넣어 강조한다. (3) 카메라가 청소되는 것이므로 수동의 의미를 나타내는 과거분사를 이용한다. 가격을 나타내는 비인칭주어 it을 써야 함에 주의한다.

05 (1) 사역동사 make의 목적격보어로 동사원형이 나와야 한다. (2) 목적어와의 관계가 수동일 경우 let은 목적격보어로 'be p.p.' 형태를 쓴다. (3) 지갑을 도난당한 것이므로 수동의 의미를 나타내는 과거분사를 써야 한다. (4) that 다음에 나오는 절이 완전하므로 'the restaurant'을 'at[in] the restaurant'으로 고쳐야 한다. (5) which 다음에 나오는 절이 완전하므로 which를

that으로 고쳐 부사절을 강조하는 문장으로 만들어야 한다.

06 apply: 신청하다, 지원하다, 과거시제로 쓰는 것이 적절하다. <영영풀이: 공식적으로 어떤 것을 요청하기 위해 편지를 쓰거나 양식에 기입하다>

07 Why don't we 동사원형? = How[What] about ~ing? = Let's 동사원형, shall we?: ~하는 게 어때?

08 호민이와 학교 미술 동아리 부원들이 청소년 봉사 프로젝트를 '찾은 곳은 인터넷에서'였다.

09 (A) 벽은 상태가 별로 '좋지 않았다'고 해야 하므로 poor가 적절하다. be in poor[bad] condition: 보존 상태가 나쁘다, 건강이 좋지 않다 (B) decide는 목적어로 to부정사를 써야 하므로 to paint가 적절하다. (C) 벽이 초등학교 '근처에' 있다고 해야 하므로 near가 적절하다. near: 가까운; 가까이, nearly: 거의

10 '다른 부분들'을 가리킨다.

11 그들은 먼저 포스터들을 제거하고 낙서와 그림을 흰 페인트로 덧칠해야 했다.

|모범답안|

01 B: Make sure that you take an umbrella

02 (1) It is the magician that[who] shows magic to
       children.
    (2) It is a pigeon that[which] the magician holds in
       his hands.
    (3) It is John that[who] is surprised at the magic.
    (4) It is Sam that[who] points at the pigeon.

03 (A) Friday, May 3rd   (B) Dream Library
    (C) English books   (D) arrange the books
    (E) very proud

01 상대방에게 '꼭 ~해라. 반드시 ~해라.'라고 당부할 때는 'Make sure ~.'라고 한다. Make sure 뒤에는 '주어+동사'의 형태가 나온다.

02 강조하고자 하는 부분을 It is[was]와 that 사이에 넣고, 나머지 부분을 that 뒤에 쓴다.

01 (s)pot   02 ①   03 ③

04 background   05 (A) to   (B) out

06 to sit → sit, after → before

07 ⑤   08 ④   09 ④

10 Make sure you turn off the lights.   11 for

12 ①   13 Is there anything to keep in mind?

14 handed in on time

15 (1) It was we that[who] found a teen volunteer project

on the Internet.

　　(2) It was something cute that[which] we decided to
　　　 paint because the wall was near an elementary
　　　 school.

　　(3) It was two weeks later that our club was selected.

　　(4) It was near the park that Mike built a tree
　　　 house.

16 ③　　　　17 ②, ③, ⑥, ⑦　　　　18 ④

19 founded → found　　20 ②

21 Drawing on a wall was much harder than drawing
　　on paper

22 a better tomorrow　　23 ③　　24 ⑤

25 a text message → an email

---

01 주어진 단어들은 동의어 관계이다. neat: 깨끗한 tidy: 깔끔한
　　location: 장소 spot: 장소, 지점

02 (A) line up: 줄서다 / 줄을 서서 기다려 주세요. (B) be
　　proud of ~: ~을 자랑스러워하다 / 그녀는 틀림없이 자신이 아
　　주 자랑스러울 것이다. (C) on time: 제시간에 / 버스는 정확히
　　제시간에 왔다.

03 ① selected, select: 선택하다 / 우리는 인터뷰를 위해서 4명의
　　지원자를 선택했다. ② plant, plant: 심다 / 그들은 내가 나무를
　　심는 것을 도왔다. ③ suggested, suggest: 제안하다 / 그녀의
　　엄마는 그녀가 병원에 가기를 제안했다. ④ replied, reply: 응
　　답하다 / '오늘 Simon을 봤어?' '물론이지' Nathalie가 웃으며
　　대답했다. ⑤ share, share: 나누다, 공유하다 / 나와 튀김을 같
　　이 먹을래?

04 background: 배경 / 보고 있는 주된 것 뒤에 있는 영역 / 다른
　　배경 출신의 사람들을 이해하는 것은 중요하다.

05 (A) 'What do you want to me to do?'는 '너는 내가 무엇을
　　하기를 원하니?'로 상대방이 원하는 것이 무엇인지 묻는 표현이다.
　　여기서 want는 5형식 동사로 'me'는 목적어, 'to do'가 목적격보
　　어로 사용되었다. (B) take out: 가지고 나가다 trash: 쓰레기

06 접속사 and로 make와 sit이 병렬로 연결되어 있다. 그러므로
　　sit은 to sit이 아니라 sit이 적절하다. 요리를 시작하기 전에 손을
　　닦는 것이 문맥상 어울리므로 after를 before로 고쳐야 한다.

07 주어진 문장은 '제가 무엇을 하기를 원하십니까?'이므로 상대
　　방이 어떤 것을 도와주기를 원한다는 대답인 'Please put the
　　cookies in the gift boxes.(선물 상자에 쿠키를 좀 넣어 줘.)'
　　의 앞이 어울린다.

08 ⓓ는 양로원에 계신 분들을 위해 쿠키를 굽고 있는 것을 의미하
　　고 나머지는 모두 쿠키를 의미한다.

09 ① 소년은 소녀를 도울 것인가? (네) ② 왜 소녀는 그토록 많은
　　쿠키를 굽고 있는가? (양로원에 계신 분들에게 주기 위해서) ③
　　소년은 상자 하나에 몇 개의 쿠키를 넣을 것인가? (3개) ④ 얼
　　마나 많은 쿠키를 소녀는 구웠는가? ⑤ 소녀는 지금 무엇을 하
　　고 있는가? (쿠키를 굽고 있다.)

10 make sure ~: 꼭 ~해라, 확실하게 ~해라 turn off: 끄다

11 'I'm here for ~.'는 '나는 ~을 위해[~하러] 왔어요.'의 의미로
　　온 목적에 대해 말할 때 사용할 수 있다.

12 빈칸은 동사인 read를 수식하고 있으므로 부사가 어울리며, 시각
　　장애인들을 위한 책을 읽어 녹음하고 있으므로 내용상 'slowly
　　and clearly(천천히 그리고 명확하게)'가 어울린다.

13 to keep in mind는 anything을 수식하고 있다.(to부정사의
　　형용사적 용법) keep in mind: 명심하다

14 보고서(report)가 제출되는 것이므로 과거분사로 쓰는 것이 적
　　절하다.

15 강조하고자 하는 부분을 시제에 맞춰 It is[was]와 that 사이에
　　넣고, 나머지 부분을 that 뒤에 쓴다. 이때 that 대신에 사람이면
　　who, 사물이면 which를 쓸 수 있다.

16 ③번은 4형식으로 쓰였고 나머지는 모두 목적어와 목적격보어
　　가 있는 5형식이다.

17 ② '가방들이 검사를 당하는 것'이므로 수동의 의미를 나타내는
　　'have+목적어+과거분사'가 적절하다. ③ 사역동사 have의 목
　　적보어로 동사원형이 나오고, help는 동사원형이나 to부정사가
　　나온다. ⑥, ⑦ 'It ~ that ...' 강조 구문은 동사나 양태 부사를
　　강조하는 데 쓰이지 않는다.

18 ⓐ와 ④: ~할 때(접속사), ① [보통 as ~ as ...로 형용사·부사
　　앞에서] …와 같은 정도로, (as ~ as ...에서, 앞의 as가 지시부
　　사, 뒤의 as는 접속사), ② ~와 같이(접속사), ③ ~이므로, ~이
　　기 때문에(접속사), ⑤ ~이라고, ~처럼(전치사)

19 인터넷에서 청소년 봉사 프로젝트를 '찾았다'고 해야 하므로
　　found로 고치는 것이 적절하다. find-found-found: 찾다, 발
　　견하다, found-founded-founded: 설립하다

20 호민이가 그곳에서 몇 장의 사진을 찍었는지는 알 수 없다. ① A
　　village with wall paintings in Yeosu. ③ The school art
　　club. ④ Yes. ⑤ A teen volunteer project to do a wall
　　painting in their neighborhood.

21 much를 보충하면 된다.

22 우리가 그날 벽에 그린 것은 단지 그림이 아니라, 오히려 더 나
　　은 내일이었다. rather: 오히려, 'rather+a+형용사+명사' 또는
　　'a+rather +형용사+명사'의 순서로 쓴다.

23 이 글은 '동아리 부원들이 벽화를 그린 후, 자신들이 그날 벽에
　　그린 것은 단지 그림만이 아니라 더 나은 내일을 그린 것이라
　　며 스스로를 대견하게 생각하는' 내용의 글이므로, 주제로는 ③
　　번 '보람 있는 자원봉사 일에 의해 얻어진 자부심'이 적절하다.
　　self-esteem: 자부심, rewarding: 보람 있는, ① laborious:
　　(많은 시간과 노력을 요하는) 힘든, ④ carry out: 수행하다, ⑤
　　convenient: 편리한

24 위 글은 자원봉사자를 모집하는 '광고'이다. ① (신문·잡지의)
　　글, 기사, ② 수필, ③ 요약, 개요, ④ (책·연극·영화 등에 대
　　한) 논평[비평], 감상문

25 이 프로젝트에 관심이 있으면, '이메일'을 보내어 신청할 수 있
　　다.

Lesson 4

Open a Book, Open Your Mind

| 01 ⑤ | 02 ③ | 03 ③ | 04 ④ |
| 05 ④ | 06 ④ | 07 ② | |

01 assign: (사람을) 배치하다 / 새로운 선생님이 과학 실험실 로 배치되었다.

02 ① 사실, Kobe는 너무 바빠서 창밖을 보는 시간을 가지지 못했다. ② 그 돈은 그의 소유이다. ③ look up: (사전·참고 자료·컴퓨터 등에서 정 보를) 찾아보다 / 많은 사람들은 사전에서 이 단어의 의미를 찾아봐야 한다. ④ 난 그 책을 내려놓을 수가 없어서 앉은 자리에서 다 읽었다. ⑤ 강과 호수 의 바닥에 있는 진흙 역시 식량과 은신처를 제공한다.

03 hole: 구덩이, 구멍 / 무언가 단단한 것에 비어 있는 공간

04 beat: ~을 치다, 두드리다, (심장이) 고동치다

05 stand for: ~을 의미하다

06 쌍으로 이루어진 것, 2개의 비슷한 것이 하나의 물건을 이룰 때 'a pair of+복수 명사'의 형태로 쓴다. ① a pair of sneakers: 운동화 한 켤레 / 그는 운동화 한 켤레를 샀다. ② a pair of glasses: 안경 한 개 / 그가 필요한 것은 안 경 하나였다. ③ a pair of scissors: 가위 하나 / 식탁 위 에 가위 하나가 있었다. ④ The, 그 옷들은 의자 위에 높이 쌓여 있었다. ⑤ A pair of gloves: 장갑 한 켤레 / 한 켤레 의 장갑은 좋은 선물이다.

07 (A) fall in love with: ~와 사랑에 빠지다 / 나는 그의 착 한 성품 때문에 그와 사랑에 빠졌다. (B) build character: 덕성 을 기르다, 인성을 키우다 / 좋은 책을 읽는 것은 인격 형성에 도움 이 된다. (C) stay awake: 깨어 있다 / 나는 너무 피곤해서 깨어 있기가 어렵다.

01 up
02 since
03 Unfortunately
04 They were assigned to design a Space settlement.
05 (1) wide (2) driverless (3) convenient (4) detective
06 (1) (e)nded up (2) (h)it me on (3) takes, to
    (4) The higher, the colder (5) was why

01 pick up: ~을 집다 / 그녀는 장갑을 주우려고 몸을 굽혔다. look up: (사전·참고 자료·컴퓨터 등에서 정보를) 찾아보다 / 웹사이트에서 개장[개점] 시간을 찾아볼 수 있니? end up: 결국 ~이 되다, 결국 (어떤 처지)에 처하게 되다 / 온라인 쇼핑이야말로 내 돈을 다 써버리고 마는 이유야.

02 since: ~이기 때문에, ~한 이후로 / 나는 그녀가 태어난 이래로 Joanna를 안다. 아무도 신경 쓰지 않았기 때문에 그들은 그의 취미에 대해 몰랐다.

03 fortunate: 운 좋은 unfortunately: 불행히도 / 불행히도 저는 그 회의에 참석할 수 없을 거예요.

04 assign: 맡기다, 부과하다 be assigned to 동사원형: ~하도록 맡겨지다

05 (1) wide: 폭넓은, 폭이 ~인 / 그것은 음식 준비를 위해 충분한 공간이 허락되어져야 한다. (2) driverless: 운전자가 없는 / 구글은 운전자 없는 자동차가 사람이 운전하는 자동차보다 안전하다고 말하고 있다. (3) convenient: 편리한 / 그 가족은 부엌에서 먹기가 더 편하다고 생각했다. (4) detective: 형사 / 그녀는 딸을 찾기 위해서 사립 탐정을 고용했다.

06 (1) end up: 결국 ~이 되다, 결국 (어떤 처지)에 처하게 되다 (2) hit+사람+on the+신체 부위: ~의 …을 때리다 (3) It+takes+시간+to부정사: ~하는 데 (…의) 시간이 걸리다 (4) The+비교급(+주어+동사) ~, the+비교급(+주어+동사) …: ~할수록 (점점) 더 …하다 (5) That was why ~: 그것이 ~한 이유였다

1 How do you feel about the subway in Korea 2 ⑤

1 F 2 F 3 T 4 T 5 T 6 F 7 F 8 T

Listen and Speak 1 A

to / Long, no, How, been / How, here from / by / How, about / clean

Listen and Speak 1 B

did, hear / What / can, during, from / heard / How / useful, look up words I don't know / find / helpful

Listen and Speak 1 C

1. Can I ask / best / How, feel, single / unhealthy
2. ask, difficult / try / How do you feel / helpful but
3. Can I ask you / try my best / How do you feel about / helpful but cruel

Listen and Speak 2 A

Did you enjoy / a / What did you like / was / with you on

Listen and Speak 2 B

Why, always drinking / help me stay / I'm with you on, too / help me focus on / know that too much caffeine / should drink, less

Listen and Speak 2 C

1. How do you feel about reading / anytime / with you on that, not good for
2. How do you feel about / more / I'm with you on that
3. How do you feel about / I'm with you on that / I don't agree

Real Life Talk Watch a Video

What / They're items I ordered / How do you feel about / at all / difficult to know what, like / difficult to return / convenient / convenience

Real Life Talk Step 2

1. feel about shopping / Can you tell me / shop whenever / I'm with you
2. How do you feel about raising / work to take care of / don't agree, make us happy

Check up Dialogue Champion

How do you feel about using / useful, search for / with you on that

01 ③　　　02 ②　　　03 ⑤

01 'I'm with you on that.'은 '나는 그 말에 동의해.'라는 뜻으로 상대방의 의견에 동의할 때 사용할 수 있는 표현이다. 바꿔 쓸 수 있는 표현으로 'I couldn't agree with you more.', 'That's exactly how I feel.', 'No doubt about it.', 'You

---

are absolutely right.', 'You have a point there.' 등이 있다. 동의하지 않을 때는 'I don't agree.' 또는 'I don't think so.' 등으로 표현할 수 있다.

02 빈칸 이후에 수업 중에 스마트폰을 사용하는 것에 대한 소년의 생각이 나오고 있으므로 빈칸에는 이에 대한 상대방의 의견을 묻는 것이 적절하다. 'How do you feel about ~?'은 '~에 관해 어떻게 생각하세요?'라는 뜻으로 상대방의 의견을 물을 때 사용할 수 있다.

03 (C) 어려운 질문을 해도 되는지 질문하자 (D) 괜찮다고 대답 하면서, 최선을 다하겠다고 말한다. (B) 동물 실험에 대한 상대방의 의견을 묻자 (A) 도움이 되지만 잔인하다고 생각한다고 대답한다.

01 ②　　　02 ④　　　03 ⑤　　　04 ②
05 ②　　　06 ⑤　　　07 ①
08 ②, ③, ⑤　09 ①, ⑤

01 주어진 문장은 '어떻게 지냈니?'의 의미로 상대방의 안부를 물을 때 사용하는 표현이다. 안부를 묻는 질문에 민호가 'Great.(잘 지냈어.)'라고 대답하는 것이 어울리므로 ②가 적절하다.

02 Amy가 한국에 와 본 경험이 있는지 없는지는 위의 대화에서 알 수 없다. ① Amy는 한국의 지하철이 깨끗하다고 생각한다. ② Amy는 공항에서 여기에 지하철을 타고 왔다. ③ 민호와 Amy는 오랜 시간 동안 보지 못했다. ④ Amy는 한국에 전에 와 본 적이 없다. ⑤ 민호는 잘 지냈다.

03 상대방에게 왜 에너지 음료를 늘 마시는지 묻고 있으므로, 이유에 대해 설명하는 ⑤가 적절하다.

04 Tom은 에너지 음료가 깨어 있는 데 도움이 된다는 것에 동의하고 있지만 공부에 집중하는 데 도움이 된다는 Jessica의 말에는 동의하는 말은 하지 않았다.

05 소식을 들었는지 묻는 질문에 어떤 소식이냐고 묻고 (B) 다음 주부터 수업 중에 스마트폰을 사용할 수 있다고 이야기한다. (C) 그 소식을 들었다고 대답하자 (A) 그에 대한 의견을 묻는다. (D) B는 그것이 유용할 거라고 생각한다고 이야기하며 수업 시간에 모르는 단어들을 찾아볼 수 있다고 말한다.

06 'I'm with you on that.'은 '나는 그 말에 동의해.'라는 뜻으로 상대방의 의견에 동의할 때 사용할 수 있는 표현이다. 바꿔 쓸 수 있는 표현으로 'I couldn't agree with you more.', 'That's exactly how I feel.', 'No doubt about it.', 'You

are absolutely right.', 'You have a point there.' 등이 있다. 동의하지 않을 때는 'I don't agree.' 또는 'I don't think so.' 등으로 표현할 수 있다.

07 'How do you feel about ~?'은 '~에 관해 어떻게 생각하세요?'라는 뜻으로 상대방의 의견을 물을 때 사용하는 표현이다.

08 B는 학생들이 수업 시간에 게임을 할 수 있어서 수업 시간에 핸드폰을 이용하는 것에 반대를 하지만 A는 스마트폰으로 정보를 찾을 수 있다고 얘기하는 것으로 보아 둘은 반대되는 의견을 가지고 있다. 상대방의 의견에 동의하지 않을 때, 'I don't think so.', 'I totally disagree.', 'I'm not sure about that.' 등을 사용할 수 있다.

09 ① 영화가 재미있다고 말하며 그렇지 않은지 묻는 말에 대한 대답으로 재미있지 않다고 말하며 이야기가 좋았다고 대답하는 것은 어울리지 않는다. ⑤ 학교 점심에 대한 의견을 묻는 말에 '그렇게 생각하지 않아.'라고 동의하지 않는 말을 하는 것은 어색하다.

서술형 시험대비   p.183

01 How do you feel about it?
02 up
03 They are items I ordered online.
04 ⓐ with   ⓑ on
05 convenient
06 How do you feel about eating fast food?
07 I don't agree.

01 'How do you feel about ~?'은 '~에 관해 어떻게 생각하세요?'라는 뜻으로 상대방의 의견을 물을 때 사용하는 표현이다.

02 look up: (사전·참고 자료·컴퓨터 등에서 정보를) 찾아보다

03 items와 I ordered online 사이에 목적격 관계대명사 which나 that이 생략되어 있다. order: 주문하다

04 'I'm with you on that.'은 '나는 그 말에 동의해.'라는 뜻으로 상대방의 의견에 동의할 때 사용할 수 있는 표현이다.

05 Tony가 편리함이 전부가 아니라고 말한 것으로 보아, 수지는 온라인으로 쇼핑하는 것이 편리하다고 말한 것을 유추할 수 있다. convenience: 편리, 편의 convenient: 편리한

06 'How do you feel about ~?'은 '~에 관해 어떻게 생각하세요?'라는 뜻으로 상대방의 의견을 물을 때 사용하는 표현이다.

07 상대방의 의견에 동의하지 않을 때는 'I don't agree.', 'I don't think so.', 'I totally disagree.', 'Absolutely not.', 'I'm not sure about that.' 등으로 표현할 수 있다.

핵심 Check   p.184~185

1 (1) longer   (2) more
2 (1) since   (2) since   (3) Because

시험대비 기본평가   p.186

01 ④   02 ③   03 ②
04 (1) The more Stanley dug, the stronger he became.
   (2) The more I heard about him, the more sympathetic I felt for him.
   (3) Since he was sick, he couldn't go to school.

01 the 비교급+주어+동사 ~, the 비교급+주어+동사 …: ~할수록 …하다

02 첫 번째 빈칸에는 뒤에 나오는 주절에 대한 이유가 나오는 것이 적절하고, 두 번째 빈칸에는 앞에 나온 주절에 대한 이유가 나오는 것이 적절하다. 그러므로 이유를 나타내는 부사절을 이끄는 since가 적절하다.

03 ② The long → The longer / the 비교급+주어+동사 ~, the 비교급+주어+동사 …: ~할수록 …하다

04 (1), (2) 'the 비교급+주어+동사 ~, the 비교급+주어+동사 …'의 형태로 '~할수록 …하다'라는 뜻으로, 점점 더해지거나 덜해지는 것을 표현할 때 사용한다. (3) since는 이유를 나타내는 접속사로 쓰여, '~이기 때문에'의 뜻으로 이유를 나타내는 부사절을 이끈다.

시험대비 실력평가   p.187~189

01 ②   02 ①   03 ④   04 ⑤
05 ③, ⑤   06 ③, ⑤   07 ④   08 ②
09 ①   10 ①, ④
11 (1) The colder it is, the larger and deeper the hole becomes.
   (2) The stronger will you have, the more you will learn.
12 ②
13 (1) This book is the better of the two.
   (2) The harder he tried to get out, the deeper he went.
   (3) The less people spend, the slower the economy growth becomes.

14 ③ 15 ⑤

16 (1) Though → Since[Because/As]

 (2) if → since[because/as]

 (3) because → because of

17 (1) The more, the more (2) The closer, the happier

 (3) The bigger, the better (4) Because

 (5) because of 18 ①

19 ②, ⑤

01 the 비교급+주어+동사 ~, the 비교급+주어+동사 …: ~할수록 …하다 The more sugar in the orange juice, the shorter the shelf life.

02 ② though → since[because, as] ③ because → since ④ Unless → Since[Because, As] ⑤ before → since

03 'the 비교급+주어+동사 ~, the 비교급+주어+동사 …: ~할수록 …하다' 구문은 'As+주어+동사+비교급 ~, 주어+동사+비교급 …'으로 바꿔 쓸 수 있다.

04 이유를 나타내는 접속사로 쓰인 since는 because나 as로 바꿔 쓸 수 있다.

05 the 비교급+주어+동사 ~, the 비교급+주어+동사 … = As+주어+동사+비교급 ~, 주어+동사+비교급 …: ~할수록 …하다

06 '~이기 때문에'의 뜻으로 이유를 나타내는 부사절을 이끄는 since[because]를 쓰는 것이 적절하다.

07 the 비교급+주어+동사 ~, the 비교급+주어+동사 …: ~할수록 …하다

08 <보기>와 ②번은 '이유'의 접속사이다. ① 전치사 ③ '시간'의 접속사 ④ 전치사 ⑤ 부사

09 the 비교급+주어+동사 ~, the 비교급+주어+동사 …: ~할수록 …하다

10 빈칸에는 이유를 나타내는 접속사로 쓰인 since, because나 as가 적절하다.

11 (1) the 비교급+주어+동사 ~, the 비교급+주어+동사 … = As+주어+동사+비교급 ~, 주어+동사+비교급 …: ~할수록 …하다 (2) '더 강한 의지를 갖는다면, 더 많이 배울 것이다.'라는 의미이므로 비교급을 이용하여 바꿔 쓰면, '강한 의지를 가질수록 더 많이 배울 것이다.'라고 쓸 수 있다.

12 ②번은 '이유'의 접속사이고 나머지는 모두 '시간'의 접속사로 쓰였다.

13 (1) 비교급에는 the를 사용하지 않는 것이 원칙이지만 문장 속에 'of the two'와 같이 비교의 대상이 명확히 둘인 경우 'the+비교급'으로 쓴다. (2), (3) the 비교급+주어+동사 ~, the 비교급+주어+동사 …: ~할수록 …하다

14 ① pretty → prettier ② more safe → safer ④ Smaller → The smaller ⑤ dark and dark → darker and darker

15 ① until → since ② because of → because ③ while → since[because, as] ④ though → since[because, as]

16 (1) Though는 양보절을 이끄는 접속사이므로 Though를 Since[Because/As]로 고치는 것이 적절하다. (2) if는 조건절을 이끄는 접속사이므로 if를 since[because/as]로 고치는 것이 적절하다. (3) because of는 전치사처럼 절이 아닌 구가 나오고, because는 접속사로 다음에 절이 나와야 한다.

17 (1)~(3) the 비교급+주어+동사 ~, the 비교급+주어+동사 …: ~할수록 …하다 (4) 이유를 나타내는 부사절을 이끄는 접속사 Because가 적절하다. (5) 뒤에 명사구가 이어지므로 because of가 적절하다.

18 the merrier로 쓰는 것이 적절하다.

19 이유를 나타내는 접속사 because는 since나 as로 바꿔 쓸 수 있다.

서술형 시험대비

p.190~191

01 (1) The younger you are, the easier it is to learn.

 (2) The larger the picture is, the longer it will take for people to download.

02 (1) The older he grew, the poorer his memory became.

 (2) I think the harder I work, the more I move up in the world.

 (3) Ann is the taller and the more beautiful of the two sisters.

 (4) This dictionary is a lot the better of the two.

 (5) The plan failed because of lack of money.

 (6) The accident happened because[as, since] nobody paid attention to the warning signs.

 (7) They've been best friends since they were children.

 (8) She had only spoken to him once since the party.

03 (1) The hotter, the more exhausted

 (2) The more, the more thirsty

04 (1) Since I was hungry, I had a whole pizza.

 (2) I didn't enjoy the book since I couldn't identify with any of the main characters.

05 (1) The more books you read, the more things you will know.

 (2) The earlier you start, the sooner you arrive there.

(3) The more arguments you win, the fewer friends you'll have.

(4) The healthier one's mind is, the healthier one's body will be.

06 (1) the better you do

(2) the more water you drink

(3) the less holiday time they have

07 (1) The older we grow, the wiser we become.

(2) The higher you climb, the farther you see.

(3) The less you spend, the more you save.

(4) I couldn't buy anything to eat since I had no money.

(5) She has written many books since she left college.

01 the 비교급+주어+동사 ~, the 비교급+주어+동사 …: ~할수록 …하다

02 (1)~(2) the 비교급+주어+동사 ~, the 비교급+주어+동사 …: ~할수록 …하다 (3)~(4) 비교급에는 the를 사용하지 않는 것이 원칙이지만 문장 속에 'of the two'와 같이 비교의 대상이 명확히 둘인 경우 'the+비교급'으로 쓴다. (5) because+주어+동사, because of+명사(구) (6) 'because of' 다음에는 명사(구)가 나와야 하므로 since나 because를 쓰는 것이 적절하다. (7) 의미상 before가 아니라 since가 적절하다. 현재완료 시제임에 유의한다. (8) though는 접속사이므로 다음에 절이 나와야 한다. 현재완료 시제이므로 since가 적절하다.

03 the 비교급+주어+동사 ~, the 비교급+주어+동사 …: ~할수록 …하다

04 since는 '~이기 때문에'의 뜻으로 이유를 나타내는 부사절을 이끌므로 이유를 나타내는 절에 since를 넣어 연결한다.

05 (1) '많은 책을 읽으면, 많은 것을 알게 될 것이다.'를 비교급을 이용하여 '더 많은 책을 읽을수록 더 많은 것을 알게 될 것이다.'라고 쓸 수 있다. (2) '일찍 출발하면, 그곳에 빨리 도착할 것이다.'를 비교급을 이용하여 '더 일찍 출발할수록 더 빨리 도착할 것이다.'라고 쓸 수 있다. (3), (4) the 비교급+주어+동사 ~, the 비교급+주어+동사 … = As+주어+동사+비교급 ~, 주어+동사+비교급 …: ~할수록 …하다

06 the 비교급+주어+동사 ~, the 비교급+주어+동사 …: ~할수록 …하다

07 (1)~(3) the 비교급+주어+동사 ~, the 비교급+주어+동사 …: ~할수록 …하다 (4) since를 '~이기 때문에'의 뜻으로 이유를 나타내는 접속사로 이용한다. (5) since를 '~ 이후로'의 뜻으로 시간의 부사절을 이끄는 접속사로 이용한다.

Reading

 교과서

확인문제   p.192

1 T 2 F 3 T 4 T 5 F

확인문제   p.193

1 T 2 T 3 F 4 T 5 F

교과서 확인학습 A   p.194~195

01 harder

02 harder, the faster

03 any harder

04 thirsty, hungry

05 go home

06 would be

07 terrible

08 no lake

09 full of sand

10 In fact, even

11 a place for bad boys

12 like

13 for stealing

14 didn't really steal

15 in the wrong place

16 from school

17 fell from

18 hit him on the head

19 what happened

20 stopped, why he was running

21 for, belonged to

22 That was why

23 was assigned to

24 six other boys

25 cool, like

26 one hole every day

27 about, deep, wide

28 to build character

29 The more, the stronger

30 It took, to finish

31 something shiny

32 beat faster

33 anyone who, be given the day off

34 brushed off

35 small gold tube

36 couldn't be, since

37 at the bottom of

38 stand for

39 even

1 "Dig harder, Stanley!

2 The harder you dig, the faster you'll finish!" yelled Mr. Sir.

3 Stanley Yelnats couldn't dig any harder since every single muscle hurt.

4 He was thirsty and hungry.

5 He wanted to go home.

6 Unfortunately, Stanley's home for the next 18 months would be right here, at Camp Green Lake.

7 Camp Green Lake was a terrible name.

8 It wasn't green and there was no lake.

9 Camp Green Lake was hot and full of sand.

10 In fact, it wasn't even a camp.

11 It was a place for bad boys.

12 Then what was a good boy like Stanley doing here?

13 He was sent to the camp for stealing a pair of sneakers.

14 Stanley didn't really steal a pair of sneakers.

15 He was just in the wrong place at the wrong time.

16 One day, he was walking home from school.

17 Suddenly, a pair of old sneakers fell from the sky.

18 The sneakers hit him on the head.

19 He started running with the sneakers to tell his father what happened.

20 A few minutes later, the police stopped Stanley and asked him why he was running.

21 Unfortunately for Stanley, the sneakers belonged to a famous baseball player, Clyde Livingstone.

22 That was why Stanley ended up at Camp Green Lake.

23 Stanley was assigned to Group D in the camp.

24 There were six other boys in Stanley's group.

25 They all had cool names like X-Ray, Zigzag and Zero.

26 Each boy had to dig one hole every day.

27 It had to be about 150cm deep and 150cm wide.

28 Mr. Sir said, "You are digging to build character."

29 The more Stanley dug, the stronger he became.

30 It took less time to finish his hole each day.

31 In his second week, as Stanley was finishing his hole, he saw something shiny in the dirt.

32 Stanley's heart beat faster.

33 He heard that anyone who found something interesting would be given the day off.

34 He carefully picked up the shiny object and brushed off the dirt.

35 It was a small gold tube.

36 But it couldn't be real gold since it was too light.

37 There were two letters, *KB*, at the bottom of the tube.

38 What did KB stand for?

39 Stanley's heart beat even faster.

01 for   02 ④   03 ③

04 The more Stanley dug, the stronger he became.

05 finishing → to finish

06 ④   07 ②   08 ④   09 ④

10 ⑤

11 the more → more, the stronger → stronger

12 Because he heard that anyone who found something interesting would be given the day off.

13 ④   14 ④

15 (A) depth   (B) width   16 ②   17 ①, ③

18 They were Clyde Livingstone's.

19 ②   20 was sent

21 The harder you dig, the faster you'll finish!

22 He couldn't dig any harder since every single muscle hurt.

23 assigned

24 one hundred and fifty centimeters

25 ①

01 ⓐ for: ~을 위한, ⓑ for: ~라는 이유로

02 (A)와 ④: 이유나 원인을 나타내는 절을 이끄는 접속사, ①, ③ ~한 이후로(접속사), ② ~부터[이후](전치사), ⑤ 그(때) 이후로(부사)

03 'It wasn't green and there was no lake.'라고 되어 있다. be named after: ~을 따서 명명되다

04 The+비교급(+주어+동사) ~, the+비교급(+주어+동사): ~할수록, (점점) 더 …하다

05 It+takes+시간+to부정사구: ~하는 데 (…의) 시간이 걸리다

06 very는 형용사나 부사의 원급을 강조하는 말이고, 나머지는 다 비교급을 강조하는 말이다.

07 정말로 운동화 한 켤레를 훔친 것이 아니었는데 Green Lake 캠프에 오게 되었으므로, '부당한' 심경을 느꼈을 것이라고 하는 것이 적절하다. unfair: 부당한, 불공평한, ① 부끄러운, ③ 흥분한, ⑤ 지루한

08 suddenly = all at once = abruptly = all of a sudden = unexpectedly: 갑자기, ④ urgently: 급히

09 운동화 한 켤레가 왜 하늘에서 떨어졌는지는 알 수 없다. ① No. ② He was walking home from school. ③ The sneakers hit Stanley on the head. ⑤ A few minutes after he started running with the sneakers.

41

10 ⑤는 빛나는 '물체의 바닥에 쓰여 있는 글자'를 가리키고, 나머지는 다 '빛나는 물체'를 가리킨다.

11 As로 시작하면 the를 삭제한 비교급을 본래의 자리에 쓰는 것이 적절하다.

12 그는 흥미로운 뭔가를 발견한 사람은 그 날을 쉬게 된다고 들었기 때문이다.

13 이 글은 'Stanley의 그룹에 속한 소년들이 매일 구덩이 하나를 파야 했다'는 내용의 글이므로, 주제로는 ④번 'D 그룹의 소년들이 매일 해야 했던 의무'가 적절하다.

14 ⓐ와 ②: 부사적 용법, ①, ④: 명사적 용법, ③, ⑤: 형용사적 용법

15 구덩이의 '깊이'는 150cm 정도였고 '너비'도 150cm 정도였다. depth: 깊이, width: 폭, 너비

16 이 글은 'Stanley가 정말로 운동화 한 켤레를 훔친 것이 아니었는데 Green Lake 캠프에 오게 되었다'는 내용의 글이므로, 제목으로는 ②번 '억울하게 누명을 쓴 Stanley'가 적절하다. accuse: 고발[기소/비난]하다

17 ⓐ와 ①, ③: 부사적 용법, ②, ⑤: 형용사적 용법, ④: 명사적 용법

18 그 운동화는 Clyde Livingstone의 것이었다.

19 ② 앞의 내용을 추가해서 설명하고 있으므로 In fact가 가장 적절하다. ③ 그에 반해서, 그와 대조적으로, ⑤ 비슷하게, 마찬가지로

20 캠프에 '보내진' 것이므로 수동태로 쓰는 것이 적절하다.

21 The+비교급(+주어+동사) ~, the+비교급(+주어+동사): ~할수록, (점점) 더 …하다

22 Stanley는 모든 근육 하나하나가 아팠기 때문에 더 열심히 팔 수가 없었다.

23 어떤 사람을 특정한 장소에서 또는 그 사람을 위해 일하도록, 특정한 장소나 그룹 또는 사람에게 보내는 것 / 수동태로 써야 하므로 과거분사 형태로 쓰는 것이 적절하다. assign: (사람을) 배치하다

24 cm를 읽을 때 앞에 복수가 있으면 centimeters로 읽는 것이 적절하다.

25 ⓒ와 ①: 품성, 인격, ② (책·영화 등의) 등장인물, ③, ⑤: 특징, 특질, ④ 문자

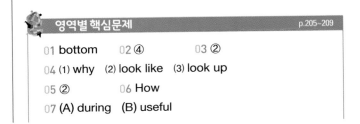

서술형 시험대비 p.202~203

01 be given

02 (A) less (B) since (C) for

03 right place → wrong place, right time → wrong time

04 That was why Stanley ended up at Camp Green Lake.

05 could[might] tell

06 six → seven

07 It had to be about 150cm deep and 150cm wide.

08 finishing

09 symbolize 또는 represent

10 As you dig harder, you'll finish faster!

11 such as

12 (A) a camp (B) green (C) sand

01 흥미로운 뭔가를 발견한 사람은 그 날을 '쉴 수 있게 되는 것'이므로, 수동태로 쓰는 것이 적절하다.

02 (A) Stanley는 많이 파면 팔수록, 더 힘이 세져 갔다고 했으므로, 하루하루 구덩이를 끝내는 데 시간이 '덜' 걸렸다고 하는 것이 적절하므로 less가 옳다. (B) 너무 가벼웠기 '때문에' 진짜 금일 리가 없었다고 해야 하므로, 원인이나 이유를 나타내는 부사절을 이끄는 접속사 since를 쓰는 것이 적절하다. (C) 'KB는 무엇을 의미할까'라고 해야 하므로 for가 옳다. stand by: (방관, 좌시하며) 가만히 있다, stand for: ~을 상징하다

03 Stanley는 학교에서 집으로 걸어가고 있다가 하늘에서 떨어진 낡은 운동화 한 켤레에 머리를 맞은 것 때문에 Green Lake 캠프에 오게 된 것이므로, 그는 그저 '잘못된 시간'에 '잘못된 장소'에 있었다고 하는 것이 적절하다.

04 That was why: 그것이 ~한 이유였다, end up+특정 장소나 상황: 결국 (어떤 처지)에 처하게 되다

05 그는 그의 아버지에게 무슨 일이 일어났는지 '말하기 위해' 운동화를 가지고 달리기 시작했다. '~하기 위해서'라는 뜻의 목적을 나타내는 부사적 용법의 to부정사는 'in order that 주어 can[may]'을 사용하여 복문으로 고치는 것이 가능하다.

06 D 그룹에는 Stanley를 포함하여 '7명'의 소년들이 있었다.

07 had to be: ~이어야 했다

08 spend+시간+~ing

09 stand for = symbolize = represent: ~을 상징하다

10 As로 시작하면 the를 삭제한 비교급을 본래의 자리에 쓰는 것이 적절하다.

11 like = such as: (예를 들어) ~ 같은

12 Green Lake 캠프는 '캠프'가 아니라 나쁜 소년들을 위한 곳이었다. 그것의 이름과는 달리 그곳은 '초록색'도 아니었고 호수도 없었다. 사실, 그곳은 뜨거웠고 온통 '모래'였다.

영역별 핵심문제 p.205~209

01 bottom   02 ④   03 ②

04 (1) why (2) look like (3) look up

05 ②   06 How

07 (A) during (B) useful

42 정답 및 해설

08 I can look up words I don't know.　　09 ③

10 ⑤　　　　11 I'm with you on that.　　12 ②, ④

13 ③　　　14 ⑤　　　15 ①, ④

16 (1) The more, the more tired

　　(2) The more, the more sleepy　　17 ①

18 (1) The fresher the fruit is

　　(2) Since[As/Because] the sunlight was very

　　　strong

19 (1) The nearer, the longer

　　(2) warmer and warmer

　　(3) because of　(4) since　(5) As

20 ④　　　　21 ②, ③

22 Then what was a good boy like Stanley doing

　　here?

23 ⑤　　　24 ④

25 were belonged → belonged　　　26 ②

27 ④　　　28 ①

29 (A) home　(B) the　(C) why

30 ②

01 (1) 주어진 단어들은 반의어 관계를 가지고 있다. asleep: 잠이
　　든 awake: 깨어 있는 bottom: 맨 아래 top: 꼭대기

02 character: 품성, 인격 / 어떤 사람의 인격은 그가 나누는 대화
　　를 통해 알 수 있다.

03 skip: (일을) 거르다, 빼먹다 / 수업 시간에 그 주제를 다루었으
　　면 다음 장은 건너뛰어도 된다.

04 (1) That is why ~: 그것이 ~한 이유이다 (2) look like: ~처
　　럼 보이다 (3) look up: (사전·참고 자료·컴퓨터 등에서 정보
　　를) 찾아보다

05 (A) to, Welcome to ~: ~에 온 것을 환영해 (B) from,
　　from: ~에서 부터 (C) by, by+교통수단: 교통수단을 이용해,
　　교통수단으로 (D) about, How do you feel about ~?: ~에
　　관해 어떻게 생각하니?

06 ⓐ 'How have you been?'은 '어떻게 지냈니?'의 의미로 상대
　　방의 안부를 묻는 표현이다. ⓑ 'How do you feel about ~?'
　　은 '~에 관해 어떻게 생각하니?'라는 뜻으로 상대방의 의견을 묻
　　는 표현이다.

07 (A) during은 '~ 동안에'의 의미로, 전치사이기 때문에 뒤에 명
　　사가 온다. (B) useful: 유용한

08 look up: (사전·참고 자료·컴퓨터 등에서 정보를) 찾아보다
　　words와 I don't know 사이에 목적격 관계대명사 which나
　　that이 생략되어 있다.

09 'How do you feel about ~?'은 '~에 관해 어떻게 생각하세
　　요?'라는 뜻으로 상대방의 의견을 물을 때 사용하는 표현이다. 여
　　기서는 온라인 쇼핑에 관한 상대방의 의견을 물어보고, Tony가

'전혀 좋아하지 않아.'라고 대답하는 것이 어울리므로 ③이 적절
하다.

10 return: 돌려주다, 반품하다

11 'I'm with you on that.'은 상대방의 의견에 동의할 때 사용할
　　수 있는 표현이다.

12 ① Tony는 인터넷으로 쇼핑하는 것을 좋아하지 않는다. ② 수
　　지는 Tony의 인터넷 쇼핑에 대한 생각에 동의하지 않는다. (동
　　의하고 있다.) ③ 수지는 온라인 쇼핑으로 물품을 주문했다. ④
　　Tony는 온라인 쇼핑이 많은 이점을 가지고 있다고 생각한다.
　　(물건이 실제로 어떻게 생겼는지 알기가 어렵고, 마음에 들지 않
　　으면 물건을 돌려보내는 것도 어렵다고 말하고 있다.) ⑤ 수지
　　는 온라인 쇼핑을 좋아한다.

13 ① The angrier Judy got, the more loudly she yelled.
　　② The higher the expectation, the greater the
　　disappointment. ④ The more technology develops,
　　the more people seem to miss traditional forms
　　of communication. ⑤ The more you exercise, the
　　healthier you get.

14 the 비교급+주어+동사 ~, the 비교급+주어+동사 …: ~할수록
　　…하다

15 '~이기 때문에'의 뜻으로 이유를 나타내는 부사절을 이끄는
　　since는 because나 as로 바꿔 쓸 수 있다.

16 the 비교급+주어+동사 ~, the 비교급+주어+동사 …: ~할수록
　　…하다

17 since로 이어지는 절이므로 적절한 이유를 나타내는 문장을 찾
　　는다.

18 (1) the 비교급+주어+동사 ~, the 비교급+주어+동사 …: ~할수
　　록 …하다 (2) 이유를 나타내는 접속사 since를 이용한다. 이때
　　since 대신에 as나 because를 쓸 수 있다.

19 (1) the 비교급+주어+동사 ~, the 비교급+주어+동사 …: ~할
　　수록 …하다 (2) '비교급 and 비교급'은 '점점 더 …하다'의 뜻
　　이다. (3) because+주어+동사, because of+명사(구) (4) 의
　　미상 '이유'를 나타내는 since가 적절하다. (5) as가 '이유'를 나
　　타내는 부사절을 이끌고 있는 문장이다.

20 ④는 '일반적인 캠프'를 가리키고, 나머지는 다 'Green Lake 캠
　　프'를 가리킨다.

21 in fact = actually = as a matter of fact = to tell the
　　truth: 사실, ② thus: 따라서 ③ reasonably: 합리적으로, 타
　　당[적정]하게

22 like: (예를 들어) ~ 같은

23 선행사를 포함하는 관계대명사 what을 쓰는 것이 적절하다.

24 주어진 문장의 The sneakers에 주목한다. ④번 앞 문장의 a
　　pair of old sneakers를 받고 있으므로 ④번이 적절하다.

25 belong은 자동사라서 수동태로 쓸 수 없으므로 were belonged를 belonged로 고치는 것이 적절하다.

26 ⓐ와 ②: 멋진, ① 차분한, 침착한, ③ 시원한, 서늘한, ④ ~을 서늘하게 하다, 식히다(동사), ⑤ 냉담한, 열의 없는

27 그룹의 소년들이 협동하여 구덩이를 판 것이 아니라, 각 소년이 매일 구덩이 하나를 파야 했다. cooperate: 협동하다

28 ⓐ Unfortunately for: ~에게 불행하게도, ⓑ belong to: ~의 소유이다(것이다)

29 (A) home이 부사로 쓰여 '~에, ~로'라는 뜻이므로, 전치사 없이 home으로 쓰는 것이 적절하다. (B) hit+사람+on+the+신체부위: ~의 …을 때리다, (C) That was why ~: 그것이 ~한 이유였다

30 '낡은' 운동화 한 켤레가 하늘에서 떨어졌다. awesome: 경탄할 만한, 어마어마한, 엄청난

단원별 예상문제
p.210~213

01 ③
02 (1) ordering (2) raise (3) brushes (4) dig
03 (e)ven 04 (s)ince 05 ①
06 (A) eating (B) bad (C) save 07 ③
08 ⑤ 09 awake 10 ⑤
11 How do you feel about online shopping
12 ④ 13 ② 14 ③, ⑤
15 (1) The better the chair is, the more comfortable you feel.
   (2) Since Tom was tired, he stopped working.
16 was assigned
17 Each boy had to dig one hole every day.
18 ②, ③, ⑤ 19 marry with → marry
20 ② 21 a pair of
22 ⑤ 23 ④ 24 day off 25 ③

01 (A) try one's best: 최선을 다하다 / 그것은 그녀의 잘못이 아니었지만, 그녀는 돕는 데 최선을 다했다. (B) focus on: ~에 집중하다 / 더 수익성 있는 상품 개발에 주력하는 편이 좋다.

02 (1) order: (물건, 음식을) 주문하다 / 의류를 주문할 때에는 잊지 말고 치수를 명시하세요. (2) raise: 키우다, 기르다 / 그녀는 아이를 양육하기에 참 위험한 세상이라고 말했다. (3) brush off: 털다, 털어 내다 / 진흙은 마르면 잘 털린다. (4) dig: (구멍 등을) 파다 / 인부가 기계로 구멍을 파고 있다.

03 even: ~조차도, (비교급 강조) 훨씬, 더욱 / 그는 문도 열 수 없었다. 암컷 흰긴수염고래는 수컷 흰긴수염고래보다 훨씬 더 크다.

04 since: ~이기 때문에, ~한 이후로 / 7살 이후로 나는 독립해서 살았다. 세제는 호수와 개울을 오염시킬 수 있기 때문에 가급적

사용하지 않는 것이 좋습니다.

05 (A) 원할 때 언제든지 쇼핑을 한다는 대답으로 보아 B는 온라인 쇼핑을 하는 것을 좋아한다. (B) reason: 이유

06 (A) 전치사 다음에는 명사나 동명사가 올 수 있다. (B) 패스트 푸드가 많은 지방을 가지고 있다고 말하고 있으므로, 패스트 푸드에 대해 안 좋다는 생각을 가지고 있다. (C) A는 B의 의견에 동의하지 않았으므로 패스트 푸드의 장점을 말하는 save(절약하다)가 spend(쓰다, 소비하다)보다 어울린다.

07 동의할 때 사용할 수 있는 표현이 적절하다. 'I couldn't agree with you more.', 'You are absolutely right.', 'No doubt about it.'

08 ⓐ drinking, 부사 always, all the time 등과 현재진행형(be+동사ing)을 사용해 습관적인 행동을 표현할 수 있다. ⓑ stay, help의 목적격 보어로는 동사원형과 to부정사 모두 올 수 있다. ⓒ much, caffeine은 셀 수 없는 명사로 much의 수식을 받을 수 있다. ⓓ on, focus on: ~에 집중하다

09 awake: 잠들지 않은, 깨어 있는 / 잠자고 있지 않은

10 주어진 문장은 '편리함이 전부는 아니야.'의 뜻으로 수지가 말하는 'I think it's very convenient.(온라인 쇼핑은 매우 편리하다고 생각해.)'에 대해 말할 수 있는 내용이다.

11 'How do you feel about ~?'은 '~에 관해 어떻게 생각하니?'라는 뜻으로 상대방의 의견을 물을 때 사용하는 표현이다.

12 ⓐ online shopping ⓑ 가주어 ⓒ 가주어 ⓓ an item ⓔ online shopping

13 ① The more you chew bread, the sweeter it tastes. ③ Since the lamp was very dirty, the mother began to clean it. ④ He bought two pairs of sneakers and a cap at the store. ⑤ Since[Because, As] he had a headache, Jack went to see the doctor.

14 ① The harder you study, the better you will do. ② This is because the hotter it is, the more energy it has. ④ As he was sleepy, Mr. Smith went to bed early. ⑥ Because he was sick, he couldn't go to school. ⑦ Ann drank two glasses of water since she was thirsty.

15 (1) the 비교급+주어+동사 ~, the 비교급+주어+동사 …: ~할수록 …하다 (2) since로 '이유'를 나타내는 부사절을 이끌도록 하고 stop은 동명사를 목적어로 받으므로 working으로 쓴다.

16 D 그룹에 '배치되었다'고 해야 하므로 수동태로 쓰는 것이 적절하다.

17 must의 과거 had to를 사용하는 것이 적절하다.

18 about = roughly = around = approximately: 대략, ①, ④: 정확히

19 marry는 타동사이므로, 전치사 없이 바로 목적어를 쓰는 것이

적절하다.

20 Kate Barlow가 왜 인기가 많았는지는 알 수 없다. ① In Green Lake. ③ With Sam. ④ They tried to hurt Sam. ⑤ Somewhere in Green Lake.

21 sneakers와 같이 짝을 이루는 명사를 셀 때는 'a pair of'를 사용하는 것이 적절하다.

22 (A)와 ⑤: 정확히, 바로(부사), ① 오른쪽으로(부사), ② (상태가) 좋은[정상인](형용사), ③ (법적, 도덕적) 권리[권한](명사), ④ 오른쪽(명사)

23 ④번 다음 문장의 Then에 주목한다. 주어진 문장의 내용에 대한 논리적인 결과를 나타내는 말이므로 ④번이 적절하다.

24 비록 근무일이지만 일하러 가지 않는 날, day off: (근무·일을) 쉬는 날

25 위 글은 '일기'이다. ② 수필, ④ (책•연극•영화 등에 대한) 논평[비평], 감상문, ⑤ (신문•잡지의) 글, 기사

서술형 실전문제   p.214~215

01 ④ more → less
02 I'm with you on that. → I don't agree.
03 I couldn't agree with you more
04 (1) I think the older she grows, the smarter she becomes.
   (2) Ann drank a lot of water since[as/because] she was thirsty.
   (3) He closed the window because the wind was blowing outside.
   (4) Venus is hot since[as/because] it is near the sun.
05 (1) The harder you dig, the faster you'll finish.
   (2) The higher we go up, the colder it becomes.
06 though → since[because, as]
07 a half, a half
08 stole
09 was he → he was
10 reason
11 (A) on the head   (B) ended up

01 너무 많은 카페인은 뼈를 다치게 할 수 있다는 것을 얘기하면서 상대방에게 에너지 음료를 더 자주 마셔야 한다고 말하는 것은 어색하므로 more를 less로 바꿔야 한다.

02 스마트폰으로 책을 읽는 것에 대해 A는 눈에 좋지 않다고 얘기하고 있으므로, 언제든지 책을 읽을 수 있다는 장점을 이야기하고 있는 B와는 반대의 의견을 가지고 있다. 그러므로 상대방의 의견에 반대하는 표현인 'I don't agree.'가 어울린다. be good

for: ~에 좋다

03 'I'm with you on that.'은 '나는 그 말에 동의해.'라는 뜻으로 상대방의 의견에 동의할 때 사용할 수 있는 표현이다. 바꿔쓸 수 있는 표현으로 'I couldn't agree with you more.', 'That's exactly how I feel.', 'No doubt about it.', 'You are absolutely right.', 'You have a point there.' 등이 있다.

04 (1) the 비교급+주어+동사 ~, the 비교급+주어+동사 …: ~할수록 …하다 (2), (4) 다음에 나오는 절이 '이유'를 나타내므로 though를 since[as/because]로 고쳐야 한다. (3) because+주어+동사, because of+명사(구)

05 the 비교급+주어+동사 ~, the 비교급+주어+동사 … = As+주어+동사+비교급 ~, 주어+동사+비교급 …: ~할수록 …하다

06 though를 이유나 원인을 나타내는 절을 이끄는 접속사 since[because, as]로 고치는 것이 적절하다.

07 eighteen months = one and a half years = one year and a half: 1년 반

08 그는 운동화 한 켤레를 훔쳤다는 이유로 Green Lake 캠프에 보내졌다.

09 asked의 직접목적어로 간접의문문을 써야 하므로, why he was running의 순서로 고치는 것이 적절하다.

10 That was (the reason) why는 For that reason으로 바꿔 쓰는 것이 적절하다. That was (the reason) why ~: '그것이 ~한 이유였다

11 어느 날, 낡은 운동화 한 켤레가 하늘에서 떨어져서 Stanley의 '머리에' 맞았다. 그는 단지 그의 아버지에게 무슨 일이 일어났는지 말하기 위해 운동화를 가지고 달렸지만 그 운동화 때문에 결국 Green Lake 캠프에 '오게 되었다.' end up: 결국 ~이 되다

창의사고력 서술형 문제   p.216

|모범답안|

01 do you feel about it? / I'm with you on that. / Because it's very delicious and healthy.
02 (1) They can't have lunch at the restaurant since it is closed.
   (2) They had to go back home since the cafe was closed.
03 (A) a pair of sneakers   (B) running home
   (C) Camp Green Lake   (D) one hole every day
   (E) at the bottom

01 How do you feel about ~?: ~에 관해 어떻게 생각하니?
02 '이유'를 나타내는 since를 이용하여 어법에 맞게 쓴다.

01 assigned　　02 ②　　　　03 ①
04 (1) hour later　(2) stay awake　(3) like, at all
05 ④
06 We can search for information on them.
07 How do you feel about using smartphones in class?
08 I'm with you on that, but they have too much caffeine.　　09 (A) Why　(B) that
10 they help me focus on my studies　　11 ④
12 What do you think about the subway in Korea? /
What's your opinion on the subway in Korea?
13 (1) you fear something, the bigger it will appear to be
(2) the top of a tower is, the finer view it commands
14 (1) The angrier the chameleon is, the brighter its color becomes.
(2) The harder you study, the better grades you can get.
(3) Because of the sneakers, he was sent to Camp Green Lake.
(4) Everything has changed so much since last summer.　　15 ⑤
16 ②, ④, ⑥　17 ⑤　　　18 ③
19 The sneakers hit him on the head.
20 was happened → happened　　21 ②
22 ⑤　　　23 One hole
24 (1) in order to　(2) in order that, may[can]

01 assign (사람을) 배치하다 / 누군가를 일의 일부로 특정 집단이나 장소로 보내다 / 어떤 사람이 자기 능력 밖의 자리에 배치된다면, 성공을 기대하기가 더 힘들 것이다.

02 ②는 반의어, 나머지 보기들은 동의어이다. ① dangerous: 위험한 risky: 위험한 ② useful: 유용한 useless: 쓸모없는 ③ cruel: 잔혹한 brutal: 잔혹한 ④ focus: 집중하다 concentrate: 집중하다 ⑤ assign: 배치하다 allocate: 할당하다, 배치하다

03 (A) be full of: ~로 가득 차다 / 내 가방에는 책이 가득 들어 있었다. (B) stand for: ~을 의미하다 / 왕관은 왕의 위엄을 의미한다[상징한다].

04 (1) 시간+later: ~ 시간이 지난 후에 (2) stay awake: 자지 않고 깨어 있다 (3) look like: ~처럼 보이다 not ~ at all: 전혀 ~ 않다

05 주어진 문장에서 'How do you feel about ~?(~에 대해 어떻게 생각하세요?)'는 의견을 묻는 표현으로, 인터넷 쇼핑하는 것을 어떻게 생각하는지 상대방의 의견을 묻고 있다. (C) 좋아한다고 대답하고 (B) 왜 좋아하는지 이유를 말해달라고 한다. (A) 원할 때마다 쇼핑을 할 수 있다고 대답하고 (D) 상대방도 이 의견에 동의한다.

06 search for: ~을 찾다

07 'How do you feel about ~?'은 '~에 관해 어떻게 생각하니?'라는 뜻으로 상대방의 의견을 물을 때 사용하는 표현이다.

08 'I'm with you on that.'은 '나는 그 말에 동의해.'라는 뜻으로 상대방의 의견에 동의할 때 사용할 수 있는 표현이다. 접속사 but이 두 문장을 연결하고 있다. caffeine: 카페인

09 (A) Jessica의 대답이 Because로 시작하는 것으로 볼 때, 이유에 관해서 질문하고 있다. (B) know의 목적어로 명사절이 나와야 한다. 이 명사절을 접속사 that이 연결하고 있다.

10 help는 뒤에 목적어와 목적격 보어가 와서 '(목적어)가 ~하는 것을 돕다'의 의미를 나타낸다. 이때 목적격 보어로는 동사원형과 to부정사 모두 올 수 있다. focus on: ~에 집중하다

11 주어진 문장은 공항에서 여기까지 어떻게 왔는지를 묻고 있으므로, 전철을 타고 왔다는 대답과 어울린다.

12 'How do you feel about ~?'은 '~에 관해 어떻게 생각하니?'라는 뜻으로 상대방의 의견을 물을 때 사용하는 표현이다. about 뒤에는 명사(구)나 동명사(구)를 넣어 말한다. 비슷한 표현으로 'What do you think about ~?', 'What's your opinion on ~?', 'Can you give me your thoughts on ~?', 'Do you have any opinions on/about ~?' 등이 있다.

13 'the 비교급, the 비교급' 구문은 'As+주어+동사+비교급 ~, 주어+동사+비교급 …'으로 바꿔 쓸 수 있다.

14 (1), (2) the 비교급+주어+동사 ~, the 비교급+주어+동사 …: ~할수록 …하다 (3) because of+명사(구) (4) since가 전치사로 'since+명사(구)'의 형태로 쓰여 '~ 이후'의 뜻을 갖는다.

15 the 비교급+주어+동사 ~, the 비교급+주어+동사 …: ~할수록 …하다 sweater는 명사이므로 적절하지 않다. sweeter로 쓰면 적절하다.

16 ② The earlier they start, the sooner they will arrive. ④ We didn't go on a picnic since[as/because] it rained a lot. ⑥ Mina went home early since[because, as] she felt very tired.

17 Green Lake 캠프는 초록색도 아니었고 호수도 없었고 뜨거웠고 온통 모래였다고 했으므로, Green Lake 캠프는 '끔찍한' 이름이었다고 하는 것이 적절하다. ① 멋진, ② 아주 좋은, 멋진, ③ 타당한, 합리적인, ④ 경탄할 만한

18 ⑥와 ③: (예를 들어) ~와 같은(전치사), ① ~와 비슷한(전치사), ② …을 좋아하다(동사), ④ ~처럼(전치사), ⑤ 마치 ~인 것처럼(접속사)

19 hit+사람+on+the+신체 부위: ~의 …을 때리다

20 happen은 자동사라서 수동태로 쓸 수 없으므로, happened로 고치는 것이 적절하다.

21 ②번 다음 문장의 내용에 주목한다. 주어진 문장의 결과로 심장이 더 빨리 뛰게 된 것이므로 ②번이 적절하다.

22 There were two letters, *KB*, at the 'bottom' of the tube.

23 '구덩이 하나'를 가리킨다.

24 '~하기 위해서'라는 뜻의 목적을 나타내는 부사적 용법의 to부정사는 'in order that 주어 can[may]'을 사용하여 복문으로 고치는 것이 가능하다. (1) 'so as to'도 가능하다. (2) 'so that ~ may[can]'도 가능하다.

교과서 파헤치기

Lesson 1

단어 TEST Step 1   p.02

01 대신에   02 (시합에서) 지다
03 (사물의) 맨 아래 부분   04 삼각형
05 (정도 · 차이) ~의 차(이)로, ~만큼   06 전화하다, 부르다
07 움직일 수 없는   08 과제, 도전   09 엉망인 상태
10 같은   11 (경기 등에서) 점수
12 막상막하의, 우열을 가리기 힘든
13 지팡이, 막대기, 막대기처럼 기다랗고 가는 것
14 (경연) 대회, 시합, 경쟁   15 관계
16 팀워크, 협동 작업 17 후에   18 세부, 상세
19 (경기 등에서) 득점 20 나누다   21 각각의; 각각
22 개량하다, 향상시키다   23 ~로서
24 끈, 줄   25 다시   26 꽤, 매우
27 역할   28 창의적으로   29 제안하다
30 속상한, 기분이 상한   31 감다, 싸다
32 독감   33 여전히   34 마라톤
35 ~와 같은   36 홀로, 저절로   37 서둘러, 급히
38 병이 나아지다   39 마침내   40 분담하다, 분배하다
41 상세하게   42 즉각, 곧바로   43 A를 B에 쓰다

단어 TEST Step 2   p.03

01 pretty   02 string   03 role
04 busy   05 call   06 marathon
07 same   08 by   09 mess
10 challenge   11 point   12 stuck
13 detail   14 still   15 creatively
16 suggest   17 divide   18 each
19 improve   20 score   21 instead
22 as   23 later   24 base
25 relationship 26 close   27 stick
28 lose   29 teamwork   30 bad cold
31 triangle   32 upset   33 wrap
34 competition   35 get well   36 right away
37 such as   38 in the end   39 by itself
40 in detail   41 in a hurry   42 spend A on B
43 divide up

단어 TEST Step 3   p.04

1 pretty, 꽤, 매우   2 call, 전화하다
3 improve, 개량하다, 향상시키다   4 mess, 엉망인 상태
5 marathon, 마라톤   6 base, (사물의) 맨 아래 부분
7 teamwork, 팀워크, 협동 작업   8 divide, 나누다
9 lose, (시합·싸움·선거 등에서) 지다   10 relationship, 관계
11 stuck, 움직일 수 없는   12 detail, 세부, 상세
13 close, 막상막하의, 우열을 가리기 힘든   14 role, 역할
15 competition, (경연) 대회, 시합, 경쟁
16 challenge, 과제, 도전

대화문 TEST Step 1   p.05~07

Listen and Speak 1 A

how have, been / been. How. about / Not. have, bad cold / Get well

Listen and Speak 1 B

We're, same class / It's good, How have you / I've been, about / I've been pretty, competition / didn't, played / I've played, for / must, good at, luck in, competition

Listen and Speak 1 C

1 how, you been / been, everything / new classmates are
2 have you been / been, is everything / So, have, bad cold
3 How have you / I've been, How / Pretty, classes
4 How have you been / I've been, everything / have lots of

Listen and Speak 2 A

excited, have any good / got / had the best teamwork / I'm, to hear

Listen and Speak 2 B

how did / lost / sorry to hear / great / was, score / to, lost by one point / close / played, as / That's, to watch

Listen and Speak 2 C

1 happy / in first in, marathon / happy to hear
2 look upset / had a fight with / sorry to hear that
3 look happy / won, dance contest / happy to hear
4 upset / lost / sorry to hear
5 look happy / bought, bike / happy to hear
6 upset / dropped, new smartphone / sorry, hear

Real Life Talk Step 1

Long time, see / been / How have, been / been, about / been, at, How's / made many / I'm happy to hear / have to, violin lesson / have, number / call, later, Have / too

대화문 TEST Step 2   p.08~10

Listen & Speak 1 A

B: Amy, how have you been?

G: I've been great. How about you, Mike?

B: Not so good. I have a bad cold.

G: Oh, no! Get well soon.

B: Thanks.

Listen & Speak 1 B

G: Hi, Jinsu! We're in the same class again!

B: Yeah! It's good to see you, Sora. How have you
   been?

G: I've been great. How about you?

B: I've been pretty busy. I have a piano competition
   next week.

G: Oh! I didn't know you played the piano.

B: Really? I've played the piano for 5 years.

G: You must be good at it. Good luck in your competition!

B: Thanks.

Listen and Speak 1 C

1 A: Mina, how have you been?

  B: I've been good. How is everything?

  A: Pretty good. My new classmates are nice.

2 A: How have you been?

  B: I've been good. How is everything?

  A: So so. I have a bad cold.

3 A: How have you been?

  B: I've been good. How is everything?

  A: Pretty good. My new classes are exciting.

4 A: How have you been?

  B: I've been good. How is everything?

  A: So so. I have lots of homework.

Listen and Speak 2 A

B: Susan, you look excited. Do you have any good
   news?

G: Our team got an A on the science project.

B: That's great!

G: Our team had the best teamwork.

B: I'm happy to hear that.

Listen and Speak 2 B

G: Andy, how did the basketball game go?

B: Our team lost.

G: Oh, I'm sorry to hear that.

B: It's okay. It was a great game.

G: What was the score?

B: It was 80 to 79. We lost by one point.

G: That was really close!

B: Yeah. We played really well as a team.

G: That's wonderful! I want to watch your next game.

Listen and Speak 2 C

1 A: Bob, you look happy.

  B: I came in first in the marathon.

  A: I'm happy to hear that.

2 A: Ann, you look upset.

  B: I had a fight with my friend.

  A: I'm sorry to hear that.

3 A: Tom, you look happy.

  B: I won the school dance contest.

  A: I'm happy to hear that.

4 A: Bomi, you look upset.

  B: I lost my dog.

  A: I'm sorry to hear that.

5 A: Jim, you look happy.

  B: I bought a new bike.

  A: I'm happy to hear that.

6 A: Jane, you look upset.

  B: I dropped my new smartphone.

  A: I'm sorry to hear that.

Real Life Talk Step 1

Minho: Linda! Is that you? Long time no see.

Linda: Minho! It's been a long time.

Minho: How have you been?

Linda: I've been good. How about you?

Minho: I've been really busy at school. How's your new
        school?

Linda: It's wonderful. I've made many new friends.

Minho: That's great! I'm happy to hear that.

Linda: Thanks. Oh! I have to go to my violin lesson
        now.

Minho: You still have my number, right?

Linda: Yeah. I'll call you later. Have a good day!

Minho: You, too. Bye!

Real Life Talk Step 2

1 A: How have you been?

  B: I've been great.

  A: How was your vacation?

  B: Wonderful. I joined a ski camp.

  A: That's great. I'm happy to hear that.

2 A: How have you been?

  B: Not so good.

  A: How come?

B: I lost my dog.

A: Oh, no! I'm sorry to hear that.

본문 TEST Step 1
p.11~12

01 Try, Marshmallow Challenge

02 need, sticks, tape, string

03 Each team has

04 have to build, class

05 must be on top   06 stand by itself

07 time limit, minutes

08 good, Building, Solving, Creatively

09 How, marshmallow challenge

10 Every team, challenge differently

11 Let's, at, examples

12 Which one, best   13 Think, act

14 many good ideas   15 each, in detail

16 for us to choose

17 Suddenly, said, left

18 In a hurry, sticks

19 wrapped, string around

20 string, stuck, mess

21 With, left, put, top   22 Just do it

23 spend, time on planning

24 All, building, right away

25 Our, looked like   26 very tall

27 tried again   28 tall, stand by itself

29 After, tries, possible, build

30 looked like, Leaning

31 finally, what, wanted   32 one team

33 try to choose   34 Instead, improved on

35 needed, strong base

36 Another, suggested, shap, base

37 divided up, roles, cutter

38 worked, as, team   39 In, end, built

본문 TEST Step 2
p.13~14

01 Try, Marshmallow Challenge

02 You need, sticks, string

03 Each team has

04 have to build, tallest tower

05 must be on top

06 must stand by itself

07 time limit, minutes

08 is good for, Building, Solving, Creatively

09 How, challenge

10 Every team does, differently

11 look at, examples

12 Which one, like best   13 Think, act

14 many good ideas   15 each, in detail

16 It, for us to choose

17 Five minutes left

18 In a hurry, taped, together

19 wrapped the string around

20 got stuck to, mess

21 With one second left

22 Just do it

23 spend much time, planning

24 right away   25 looked like   26 very tall

27 tried again   28 couldn't stand by itself

29 After many tries, for us to build

30 Leaning Tower of Pisa

31 finally, what we wanted   32 one team

33 didn't try to choose

34 Instead, improved on   35 a strong base

36 Another, suggested, for the base

37 divided up, such as

38 as a team   39 In the end, built

본문 TEST Step 3
p.15~16

1 마시멜로 과제를 해보세요!

2 여러분은 필요해요: 스파게티 면 20개, 마시멜로 1개, 테이프 1
미터, 끈 1미터

3 규칙: 각 팀은 4명입니다.

4 반에서 가장 높은 탑을 만들어야 합니다.

5 마시멜로는 꼭대기에 있어야 합니다.

6 탑은 스스로 서 있어야 합니다.

7 제한 시간은 15분입니다.

8 이 활동은 여기에 좋아요: 관계를 맺는 것, 문제를 해결하는 것,
창의적으로 생각하는 것

9 마시멜로 과제를 어떻게 했나요?

10 모든 팀은 마시멜로 과제를 다르게 해요.

11 몇몇 예들을 살펴봐요.

12 어떤 예가 가장 마음에 드나요?

13 A팀: 행동하기 전에 생각해라.

14 우리에겐 좋은 아이디어가 많았어요.

15 우리는 각 아이디어에 대해 자세히 이야기했어요.

16 우리는 가장 좋은 아이디어를 고르는 것이 쉽지 않았어요.

17 갑자기 선생님께서 "5분 남았어요."라고 말씀하셨어요.

18 서둘러서 우리는 스파게티 면들을 테이프로 붙였어요.

19 그리고 나서 끈으로 스파게티 면 둘레를 둘렀어요.

20 끈이 테이프에 붙었고 엉망진창이었어요.

21 1초를 남기고 제가 마시멜로를 꼭대기에 꽂았어요.

22 B팀: 그냥 해라.

23 우리는 계획하는 데 많은 시간을 보내지 않았어요.

24 모든 팀원들이 바로 탑을 만들기 시작했어요.

25 우리의 첫 번째 탑은 텐트 같았어요.

26 그건 그다지 높지 않았어요.

27 우리는 다시 시도했어요.

28 다음 탑은 높았지만 스스로 서 있지 못했어요.

29 많은 시도 후에 우리는 아름답고 높은 탑을 만들 수 있었어요.

30 그것은 피사의 사탑 같았어요.

31 우리는 결국 우리가 원하는 것을 만들었어요!

32 C팀: 우리는 한 팀이다.

33 우리는 가장 좋은 아이디어를 고르려고 하지 않았어요.

34 대신에 우리는 좋은 아이디어를 골라 발전시켰어요.

35 한 친구가 우리에겐 튼튼한 기반이 필요하다고 말했어요.

36 또 다른 친구는 기반으로 삼각형 모양을 제안했어요.

37 우리 모두는 동의했고 시간 점검하는 사람과 테이프 자르는 사람과 같이 역할을 나눴어요.

38 우리는 하나의 팀으로 함께했어요.

39 마침내 우리는 높은 탑을 만들었어요!

본문 TEST Step 4~Step 5   p.17~21

1 Try the Marshmallow Challenge!

2 You need: 20 sticks of spaghetti, 1 marshmallow, 1 meter of tape, 1 meter of string

3 Rules: Each team has four people.

4 You have to build the tallest tower in your class.

5 The marshmallow must be on top.

6 The tower must stand by itself.

7 The time limit is 15 minutes.

8 This activity is good for: Building Relationships, Solving Problems, Thinking Creatively

9 How did you do the marshmallow challenge?

10 Every team does the marshmallow challenge differently.

11 Let's look at some examples.

12 Which one do you like best?

13 TEAM A: Think before you act.

14 We had many good ideas.

15 We talked about each idea in detail.

16 It was not easy for us to choose the best idea.

17 Suddenly the teacher said, "Five minutes left."

18 In a hurry, we taped the sticks of spaghetti together.

19 Then, we wrapped the string around them.

20 The string got stuck to the tape and it was a big mess.

21 With one second left, I put the marshmallow on top!

22 TEAM B: Just do it.

23 We didn't spend much time on planning.

24 All the members started building the tower right away.

25 Our first tower looked like a tent.

26 It wasn't very tall.

27 We tried again.

28 The next tower was tall but it couldn't stand by itself.

29 After many tries, it was possible for us to build a beautiful and tall tower.

30 It looked like the Leaning Tower of Pisa.

31 We finally made what we wanted!

32 TEAM C: We're one team.

33 We didn't try to choose the best idea.

34 Instead, we took a good idea and improved on it.

35 One student said we needed a strong base.

36 Another student suggested a triangle shape for the base.

37 We all agreed and divided up the roles such as time checker and tape cutter.

38 We worked together as a team.

39 In the end, we built our tall tower!

구석구석지문 TEST Step 1   p.22

Think and Write Step 2

1. Best, Project

2. making, to introduce our school

3. was, had four members

4. wrote, dialogue together

5. Then, divided up, roles

6. took the role

7. It, difficult for us to set

8. turned out to be

9. that, heads, better than

Think and Write Step 2

1. Best Group Project

2. making, travel brochure

3. The name of our group, had six members

4. researched, together

5. divided up the roles

6. took the role of drawing

7. It, for me to draw a map

8. one of my team members

9. teamwork makes better results

Project Culture Step

1. it, for us to ask, age
2. western countries, asking, is rude
3. be careful, travel

구석구석지문 TEST Step 2 p.23

Think and Write Step 2

1. My Best Group Project
2. My best group project was making a video to introduce our school.
3. The name of our group was 'The Stars' and we had four members.
4. First, we wrote a dialogue together.
5. Then, we divided up the roles.
6. I took the role of reporter.
7. It was difficult for us to set the meeting time.
8. But our video turned out to be great!
9. I learned that many heads are better than one.

Think and Write Step 2

1. My Best Group Project
2. My best group project was making a travel brochure about Paris.
3. The name of our group was 'The Travelers' and we had six members.
4. First, we researched Paris together.
5. Then, we divided up the roles.
6. I took the role of drawing a map of Paris.
7. It was difficult for me to draw a map.
8. But one of my team members helped me.
9. I learned that teamwork makes better results.

Project Culture Step

1. In Korea, it is natural for us to ask someone's age.
2. But in western countries, asking someone their age is rude.
3. So be careful when you travel.

단어 TEST Step 1 p.24

01 거의	02 해로움, 피해	03 고대의
04 상태, 조건	05 가루	06 줄이다
07 살아남다	08 곡식	09 재활용하다
10 기부하다	11 극심한	12 약 ~, 대략
13 극심하게	14 모험	15 영원히
16 해로운	17 설문조사; 설문조사를 하다	
18 곤충	19 생산하다	20 지속하다
21 의견	22 사라지다	23 오염
24 기후	25 연필꽂이	26 배달하다
27 꽃가루	28 환경	
29 수분작용, 꽃가루 옮기기		30 조심스럽게
31 씨앗	32 화학 물질	33 제공하다
34 즐거움	35 ~의 4분의 1	36 분해되다
37 혼자서	38 ~보다 적은, ~ 이하	
39 속도를 늦추다	40 ~에 참가하다	41 B와 같은 A
42 ~을 실망시키다	43 종이 한 장	

단어 TEST Step 2 p.25

01 chemical	02 last	03 around
04 opinion	05 produce	06 pollen
07 ancient	08 provide	09 crop
10 disappear	11 environment	12 recycle
13 pollination	14 almost	15 climate
16 reduce	17 seed	18 deliver
19 pleasure	20 brush	21 survey
22 donate	23 powder	24 extreme
25 adventure	26 fine	27 forever
28 global	29 harm	30 pollution
31 survive	32 extremely	33 harmful
34 insect	35 in fact	36 throw away
37 break down	38 less than	39 pick up
40 A such as B	41 by oneself	42 take a shower
43 a sheet of paper		

단어 TEST Step 3 p.26

1 fine, 미세한, 섬세한 2 pollen, 꽃가루
3 disappear, 사라지다 4 survive, 살아남다
5 ancient, 고대의 6 insect, 곤충 7 bee, 벌
8 crop, 곡식 9 deliver, 배달하다 10 reduce, 줄이다
11 pollution, 오염 12 seed, 씨앗 13 donate, 기부하다

14 adventure, 모험　　15 recycle, 재활용하다

16 survey, 설문조사

Listen and Speak 1 A

what's, matter / broke / I'm sorry to hear / worried about / Don't

Listen and Speak 1 B

ready for / didn't, see / didn't, did, say / terrible / Yellow dust, health / I'm worried about / another / text the other, right now

Listen and Speak 1 C

1 I'm worried, global warming / terrible / What, to help / less

3 worried about disappearing / terrible / What can / plant more

3 I'm worried about / too, terrible / What can we do / donate, to

Listen and Speak 2 A

hurts / careful not to / Do you know how to prevent / need to stretch

Listen and Speak 2 B

know that, in danger / article, It's because of / are melting away, disappearing / something about / how to slow down global warming / by saving / need to turn off, when, leave

Listen and Speak 2 C 1

Can, ask, something / course / Do you know how / to, carefully, others' opinions

Listen and Speak 2 C 2

ask, something / course / know how to save / need to turn off, when brush your teeth

Listen and Speak 2 C 3

ask / how to eat healthy / need to eat less

Real Life Talk Step 1

did you see / did, I'm worried about / should take action to save / right, don't we participate in / movement, environment / Do you know how to take part in / off, together for / simple, when / different every year / look it up

Real Life Talk Step 2

What do you think / terrible, I'm worried about / Do you know how to reduce / need to, public transportation

Listen and Speak 1 A

B: Jane, what's the matter?

G: My brother broke his leg.

B: Oh, I'm sorry to hear that.

G: I'm worried about him.

B: Don't worry. He'll be okay.

Listen and Speak 1 B

G: Are you ready for our soccer game today, Sam?

B: Kathy, didn't you see the news?

G: No, I didn't. What did it say?

B: The yellow dust is terrible today.

G: Oh, no. Yellow dust can cause many health problems.

B: Yeah, I'm worried about our health.

G: We can play another day.

B: You're right. I'll text the other team members right now.

G: Great idea.

Listen and Speak 1 C

1 A: I'm worried about global warming.

　 B: Me, too. It's terrible.

　 A: What can we do to help?

　 B: We can use less plastic.

3 A: I'm worried about disappearing bees.

　 B: Me, too. It's terrible.

　 A: What can we do to help?

　 B: We can plant more trees for them.

3 A: I'm worried about hungry children in Africa.

　 B: Me, too. It's terrible.

　 A: What can we do to help?

　 B: We can donate money to them.

Listen and Speak 2 A

B: My neck hurts.

G: Be careful not to get text neck.

B: Do you know how to prevent it?

G: Yes. You need to stretch your neck often.

B: Okay, I will. Thanks.

Listen and Speak 2 B

G: Jinsu, did you know that polar bears are in danger?

B: Yes. I read about it in an article. It's because of global warming.

G: Right. Their homes are melting away and their food is disappearing.

B: We should do something about it.

G: Do you know how to slow down global warming?

B: Well, we can start by saving energy.

G: Right. We need to turn off the lights when we leave

the room.

B: That's a good idea.

A: Can I ask you something?

B: Of course. What is it?

A: Do you know how to do a team project well?

B: Yes. You need to listen carefully to others' opinions.

A: Can I ask you something?

B: Of course. What is it?

A: Do you know how to save water?

B: Yes. You need to turn off the water when you brush your teeth.

A: Can I ask you something?

B: Of course. What is it?

A: Do ytou know how to eat healthy?

B: Yes. You need to eat less fast food.

Minho: Linda, did you see the TV program, *The Sick Planet*?

Linda: Yes, I did. I'm worried about our planet.

Minho: Me, too. We should take action to save the Earth.

Linda: You're right. Hey! Why don't we participate in Earth Hour?

Minho: Earth Hour? What's that?

Linda: It's a world movement for the environment.

Minho: Sounds great! Do you know how to take part in it?

Linda: Sure. We turn off our lights together for an hour.

Minho: That's so simple! So, when do we do it?

Linda: I'm not sure. It's different every year.

Minho: Let's look it up on the Internet.

A: What do you think of this picture?

B: I think it's terrible. I'm worried about air pollution.

A: Do you know how to reduce air pollution?

B: Yes. We need to use public transportation.

01 Disappearing Bees

02 have all, gone

03 It, to see, these

04 bees, disappearing

05 About, third, population, every

06 bad news, even worse

07 helpful to humans   08 give us honey

09 truly wonderful food

10 good for, health, tastes

11 last almost forever

12 fact, ancient, be eaten

13 produce, crops such as

14 be produced by themselves

15 need, help, bees

16 in the process of

17 How, help pollination

18 What, pollination

19 moving pollen, another, seeds   20 What, pollen

21 fine, powder produced

22 Why, bees disappearing

23 reasons, climate change

24 Global warming, extremely, weather

25 cannot survive, conditions

26 Another reason, harmful, crops

27 not only, but, insects

28 what, to help, little

29 plant, flowers, trees

30 provide, for, live in

31 help slow down

32 use, harmful, crops, stopped

33 chemicals, unhealthy for

34 little, need, help   35 let them down

01 Disappearing   02 have, gone

03 It, to see, these days   04 disappearing

05 a third, every year

06 bad news, even worse news

07 helpful to humans

08 First, give us honey

09 truly wonderful

10 is good for, tastes

11 last almost forever

12 In fact, can be eaten

13 Second, help produce, such as

14 be produced by themselves

15 need the help   16 in the process of pollination

17 How, pollination

18 What, pollination

19 moving pollen from, to, to make seeds

20 pollen   21 fine yellow powder produced by

22 Why, disappearing

53

23 One of, reasons, climate change

24 Global warming, extremely

25 cannot survive, conditions

26 Another reason, harmful chemicals farmers

27 not only, but also, like   28 what, to help

29 more flowers and trees

30 provide, for, to live in

31 slow down global warming

32 must be stopped

33 are unhealthy for

34 little, need our help

35 Let's, let them down

28 그러면 우리는 우리의 작고 노란 친구들을 돕기 위해 무엇을 할 수 있을까?

29 첫째, 우리는 더 많은 꽃과 나무를 심을 수 있다.

30 이것은 벌에게 살기 좋은 환경을 제공할 것이다.

31 또한 나무는 지구 온난화를 늦추는 데 도움이 된다.

32 둘째, 농작물에 해로운 화학 물질의 사용을 멈춰야만 한다.

33 이 화학 물질은 벌과 사람의 건강에 좋지 않다.

34 우리의 작은 친구들이 우리의 도움을 필요로 한다.

35 그들을 실망시키지 말자!

1 사라지는 벌들

2 꿀벌들은 모두 어디로 갔을까?

3 요즘 꿀벌을 보는 것은 정말 어렵다.

4 벌들이 사라지고 있다!

5 벌 개체 수의 약 3분의 1 정도가 매년 죽는다.

6 이것은 벌들에게 나쁜 소식이지만, 사람들에게는 훨씬 더 나쁜 소식이다.

7 벌은 인간에게 매우 도움이 된다.

8 첫째, 벌은 우리에게 꿀을 준다.

9 꿀은 정말 굉장한 음식이다.

10 그것은 건강에 좋고 맛이 좋다.

11 꿀은 거의 영원히 상하지 않을 수 있다.

12 실제로 고대 이집트 때의 꿀은 오늘날에도 먹을 수 있다!

13 둘째, 벌은 사과와 딸기 같은 많은 농작물을 생산하는 데 도움이 된다.

14 이 농작물들은 스스로 생산될 수 없다.

15 그들은 벌의 도움이 필요하다.

16 벌은 수분 과정에서 도움을 준다.

17 벌이 수분을 돕는 방법

18 수분은 무엇인가?

19 그것은 씨를 만들기 위해 한 꽃에서 다른 꽃으로 꽃가루가 옮겨지는 것이에요.

20 꽃가루는 무엇인가?

21 그것은 꽃에 의해 생산되는 아주 작은 노란색 가루예요.

22 벌은 왜 없어지고 있을까?

23 그 이유 중 하나는 기후 변화이다.

24 지구 온난화는 극도로 덥고 추운 날씨를 가져왔다.

25 벌은 이런 환경에서 살아남을 수 없다.

26 다른 이유는 농부들이 농작물에 사용하는 해로운 화학 물질이다.

27 이 화학 물질은 해로운 곤충뿐만 아니라 벌과 같은 이로운 곤충도 죽인다.

1 Disappearing Bees

2 Where have all the honey bees gone?

3 It is really hard to see them these days.

4 The bees are disappearing!

5 About a third of the bee population dies every year.

6 This is bad news for bees, but it's even worse news for people.

7 Bees are very helpful to humans.

8 First, bees give us honey.

9 Honey is a truly wonderful food.

10 It is good for our health and tastes great.

11 Honey can last almost forever.

12 In fact, honey from ancient Egypt can be eaten today!

13 Second, bees help produce many crops such as apples and strawberries.

14 These crops cannot be produced by themselves.

15 They need the help of bees.

16 Bees help in the process of pollination.

17 How bees help pollination

18 What is pollination?

19 It is moving pollen from one flower to another to make seeds.

20 What is pollen?

21 It is a fine yellow powder produced by flowers.

22 Why are bees disappearing?

23 One of the reasons is climate change.

24 Global warming has brought extremely hot and cold weather.

25 Bees cannot survive in these conditions.

26 Another reason is the harmful chemicals farmers use on crops.

27 These chemicals kill not only bad insects, but also good insects, like bees.

28 Then what can we do to help our little yellow friends?

29 First, we can plant more flowers and trees.

30 This will provide a good environment for bees to live in.

31 Also, trees help slow down global warming.

32 Second, the use of harmful chemicals on crops must be stopped.

33 These chemicals are unhealthy for bees and people.

34 Our little friends need our help.

35 Let's not let them down!

After You Read B

1. Problem
2. a third, bee population dies
3. Causes
4. Global warming, brought
5. use, harmful, on crops
6. Solutions
7. Plant, to provide, environment for bees
8. Stop using harmful chemicals

Language Use - In Context

1. Facts about
2. Around half of, is under, age of
3. Two-third, is covered with
4. spend most of, on food

Word Power

1. Thank you for, help
2. helpful for studying
3. mean to cause, harm
4. is, harmful to, skin

After You Read B

1. Problem
2. About a third of the bee population dies every year.
3. Causes
4. 1. Global warming has brought climate change.
5. 2. Farmers use the harmful chemicals on crops.
6. Solutions
7. 1. Plant more flowers and trees to provide a good environment for bees.
8. 2. Stop using harmful chemicals on crops.

Language Use - In Context

1. Facts about Cambodia
2. Around half of Cambodia's population is under the age of 15.
3. Two-third of the country is covered with forest.
4. 40 percent of the people spend most of their money on food.

Word Power

1. Thank you for all your help.
2. A dictionary is very helpful for studying language.
3. I didn't mean to cause you any harm.
4. Strong sunlight is very harmful to the skin.

단어 TEST Step 1 · p.46

01 나중에, 후에	02 장소	03 투표하다
04 벽화	05 배경	06 굽다
07 보람 있는	08 근처, 이웃	09 (특정한) 장소, 자리
10 준비하다	11 양로원	12 선택하다, 선정하다
13 배달하다	14 현장, 장소	15 경험
16 친절한	17 책꽂이	18 털
19 짐을 꾸리다	20 지원하다	21 재활용 쓰레기통
22 배열하다	23 없애다, 제거하다	24 나누다
25 분명하게	26 문제되다, 중요하다	
27 깨끗한	28 예의 바르게	29 기부, 기증
30 운영자, 관리자	31 심다	32 응답하다
33 제안하다	34 자원봉사; 자원봉사하다	
35 치우다, 줍다	36 ~와 사이좋게 지내다	
37 ~을 자랑스러워하다		38 모이다
39 ~을 명심하다	40 휴식을 취하다	
41 꼭 ~하다	42 제시간에 도착하다	
43 ~에게 도움을 주다		

단어 TEST Step 2 · p.47

01 background	02 manager	03 pack
04 paint	05 donation	06 matter
07 neat	08 site	09 rewarding
10 amusement park		11 experience
12 apply	13 clearly	14 recycling bin
15 arrange	16 vote	17 select
18 spot	19 wall painting	20 nursing home
21 politely	22 shelf	23 deliver
24 neighborhood	25 prepare	26 remove
27 divide	28 suggest	29 volunteer
30 village	31 reply	32 wing
33 share	34 board	35 pick up
36 be proud of ~	37 line up	38 give a bath
39 take a break	40 get together	41 be on time
42 get along with ~		43 give ~ a hand

단어 TEST Step 3 · p.48

1 matter, 중요하다 2 location, 장소 3 plant, 심다
4 deliver, 배달하다 5 pack, 짐을 꾸리다
6 remove, 제거하다 7 drawing, 그림
8 volunteer, 자원봉사자 9 bake, 굽다
10 donation, 기부, 기증 11 divide, 나누다
12 arrange, 정리하다 13 background, 배경
14 select, 선택하다, 선정하다
15 amusement park, 놀이 공원 16 manager, 관리자

대화문 TEST Step 1 · p.49~51

Listen and Speak 1 A

What, for / packing, donation, give me a / want, to / write, address on / problem

Listen and Speak 1 B

this mess / baking / Why, baking, many / They're for, nursing home / nice of / Can you give, hand / do you want me / put, gift boxes, each

Listen and Speak 1 C

1 doing / packing for, move, Can you help / What do you want, to do / put the clothes into

2 are, doing / packing for, move, Can you help me / want me to do / move, outside

3 What are you doing / packing for, move, Can you help me / What do you want me to do / take out

Listen and Speak 2 A

Enjoy / will, is on / Don't worry about / Make sure you feed, after / should

Listen and Speak 2 B

Make groups of, sit, to make, Keep in mind, make sure, before you start, Second, when, let's

Listen and Speak 2 C

1 to go / Make sure, lock / Anything / that's

2 time to / Make sure you clean / Anything else

3 It's time to go / Make sure, water the plants / will, else

Real Life Talk Watch a Video

What can I do / here for, volunteer work / must be / What do you want me to do / read, for the blind, recording room / Should, go / go into / anything to keep in / Make sure you, slowly and clearly / do my best

Real Life Talk Step 3

1 I'm here for / for coming / do you want me to do / give, a bath / Is there anything, keep in mind / Make sure, brush, fur

2 I'm here for the volunteer / Thanks for / What do you want me to do / for the blind / Is there anything to keep in mind / sure, slowly, clearly

Listen and Speak 1 A

B: What are all these boxes and books for?

G: I'm packing the books for the donation center. Can you give me a hand?

B: Sure. What do you want me to do?

G: Please write the address on the boxes.

B: No problem.

Listen and Speak 1 B

B: What is this mess?

G: I'm baking cookies.

B: Why are you baking so many cookies?

G: They're for the people at the nursing home.

B: That's very nice of you.

G: Can you give me a hand?

B: Sure. What do you want me to do?

G: Please put the cookies in the gift boxes. Three cookies in each box.

B: Okay.

Listen and Speak 1 C

1 A: What are you doing?

B: I'm packing for my move tomorrow. Can you help me?

A: Sure. What do you want me to do?

B: Please put the clothes into the box.

A: No problem.

2 A: What are you doing?

B: I'm packing for my move tomorrow. Can you help me?

A: Sure. What do you want me to do?

B: Please move the chairs outside.

A: No problem.

3 A: What are you doing?

B: I'm packing for my move tomorrow. Can you help me?

A: Sure. What do you want me to do?

B: Please take out the trach.

A: No problem.

Listen and Speak 2 A

B: Enjoy the concert, Mom.

W: I will. Thanks. Your dinner is on the table.

B: All right. Don't worry about me.

W: Make sure you feed the dog after you have dinner.

B: Okay. Mom, you should go now. Dad is waiting in the car.

Listen and Speak 2 B

B: Hello, class. Make groups of four people and sit around the tables. Today we're going to make bacon and egg sandwiches. Keep in mind two rules for our class. First, make sure you wash your hands before you start. Second, be careful when you use a knife. All right, let's start.

Listen and Speak 2 C

1 A: It's time to go home.

B: Yes. Make sure you lock the doors.

A: Okay, I will. Anything else?

B: No, that's it. See you tomorrow.

2 A: It's time to go home.

B: Yes. Make sure you clean the board.

A: Okay, I will. Anything else?

B: No, that's it. See you tomorrow.

3 A: It's time to go home.

B: Yes. Make sure you water the plants.

A: Okay, I will. Anything else?

B: No, that's it. See you tomorrow.

Real Life Talk Watch a Video

Woman: Good morning. What can I do for you?

Tony: Hi. I'm here for the volunteer work.

Woman: Oh, you must be Tony.

Tony: That's right. What do you want me to do today?

Woman: Please read this book for the blind in the recording room.

Tony: No problem. Should I go in now?

Woman: Yes. Please go into Room 7.

Tony: Okay. Is there anything to keep in mind?

Woman: Yes. Make sure you read slowly and clearly.

Tony: Okay. I'll do my best.

Real Life Talk Step 3

1 A: Hi, I'm Minsu. I'm here for the volunteer work.

B: Thanks for coming, Minsu.

A: What do you want me to do today?

B: Please give the dog a bath.

A: Okay. Is there anything to keep in mind?

B: Yes. Make sure you brush the fur first.

A: Okay, I will.

2 A: Hi, I'm Tony. I'm here for the volunteer.

B: Thanks for coming, Tony.

A: What do you want me to do today?

B: Please record a book for the blind.

A: Okay. Is there anything to keep in mind?

B: Yes. Make sure you read slowly and clearly.

A: Okay, I will.

01 Paint, Better Tomorrow
02 My name is
03 This, front, wall
04 so, aren't they
05 take, front, paintings
06 old neighborhoods bright
07 Last, village with
08 light went on, head
09 thought, in, art
10 Why don't we, like
11 suggested, idea, meeting
12 found, teen volunteer, on
13 to, wall painting, neighborhood
14 applied for, later, selected
15 day, finally came
16 had us meet, site
17 in, poor condition
18 strange writings, drawings, parts
19 Other parts, on
20 removed, over, with, paint
21 let us paint
22 decided, something cute, near
23 divided into, began
24 was in, group with
25 chose, spot, paint, character
26 painted, did, background drawings
27 for about, hours
28 After, finished, together, shared
29 was very proud of
30 so, that, landed on
31 much harder than drawing
32 agreed, wasn't perfect
33 But, didn't matter
34 a little brighter, happier
35 proud of ourselves
36 didn't just paint, on
37 a better tomorrow, painted

13 to do a wall painting
14 applied for, later, was selected
15 finally came
16 had us meet, painting site
17 was in very poor condition
18 strange writings and drawings
19 Other parts
20 painted over, with white paint
21 let us paint
22 decided to, something cute
23 divided into
24 was in the group
25 chose my spot, movie character
26 painted, did, background drawings
27 for about
28 finished, got together, shared, experiences
29 was very proud of
30 so, that, landed on
31 Drawing, much harder than
32 wasn't perfect
33 matter
34 a little brighter and happier
35 were proud of ourselves
36 didn't just paint
37 a better tomorrow

1 더 나은 내일을 그려라
2 안녕. 내 이름은 호민이야.
3 벽화 앞에 있는 사람이 나야.
4 날개가 예뻐, 그렇지 않니?
5 많은 사람들이 벽화 앞에서 사진 찍는 것을 좋아해.
6 벽화는 오래된 마을을 밝고 새롭게 만들어.
7 지난달에 나는 여수에 있는 벽화 마을을 방문했어.
8 내가 사진을 찍을 때 머릿속에 좋은 생각이 떠올랐어.
9 나는 생각했어. "나는 학교 미술 동아리에 있잖아.
10 우리가 이것처럼 벽화를 그리면 어떨까?"
11 나는 이 아이디어를 다음 동아리 모임에서 제안했고, 동아리 부원들은 그것을 아주 좋아했어.
12 우리는 인터넷에서 청소년 봉사 프로젝트를 찾았어.
13 그 프로젝트는 우리 마을에 벽화를 그리는 것이었어.
14 우리는 거기에 지원했고, 2주 후에 우리 동아리가 선택되었어!
15 마침내 프로젝트 날이 되었어.
16 프로젝트 책임자는 우리를 오전 9시에 그림 그리는 곳에서 만나게 했어.
17 벽은 상태가 별로 좋지 않았어.
18 몇 군데에는 이상한 낙서와 그림이 있었어.
19 다른 부분에는 오래된 포스터들이 붙어 있었어.
20 우리는 먼저 포스터들을 제거하고 낙서와 그림을 흰 페인트로 덧칠했어.
21 책임자는 우리가 원하는 어떤 것이든 그리게 했어.

01 Better Tomorrow
02 My name is
03 This is me, front
04 aren't they
05 take pictures, wall paintings
06 old neighborhoods bright
07 Last month, with wall paintings
08 As, a light went on in my head
09 thought, I'm in
10 Why don't we, like
11 suggested this idea
12 found, on the Internet

22 우리는 그 벽이 초등학교 근처에 있어서 귀여운 뭔가를 그리기로 했어.

23 우리는 세 그룹으로 나뉘어 그리기 시작했어.

24 나는 민수와 지원이와 같은 그룹이었어.

25 나는 내 구역을 정해서 가장 좋아하는 영화 캐릭터를 그리기 시작했어.

26 민수는 몇 송이의 꽃을 그렸고 지원이는 배경 그림을 그렸어.

27 우리 동아리는 약 다섯 시간 동안 그림을 그렸어.

28 끝난 후에 우리는 모여서 그날의 경험을 함께 이야기했어.

29 민수는 자신이 그린 꽃 그림을 정말 자랑스러워했어.

30 그는 "내 꽃이 정말 진짜 같아서 벌이 꽃에 앉았어."라고 말했어.

31 나는 "벽에 그리는 것이 종이에 그리는 것보다 훨씬 힘들었어."라고 말했어.

32 우리 모두는 우리 벽화가 완벽하지는 않다는 것에 동의했어.

33 하지만 그것은 중요하지 않았어.

34 우리는 동네를 조금 더 밝고 행복하게 만들었어.

35 우리는 우리 자신이 자랑스러웠어.

36 우리는 그날 벽에 그림만 그린 게 아니었어.

37 우리가 그린 것은 바로 더 나은 내일이었어.

1 Paint a Better Tomorrow

2 Hi. My name is Homin.

3 This is me in front of the wall painting.

4 The wings are so pretty, aren't they?

5 Many people like to take pictures in front of wall paintings.

6 They make old neighborhoods bright and new.

7 Last month, I visited a village with wall paintings in Yeosu.

8 As I was taking a picture, a light went on in my head.

9 I thought, "I'm in the school art club.

10 Why don't we do wall paintings like these?"

11 I suggested this idea at the next club meeting, and the members loved it.

12 We found a teen volunteer project on the Internet.

13 The project was to do a wall painting in our neighborhood.

14 We applied for it, and two weeks later, our club was selected!

15 The day of the project finally came.

16 The project manager had us meet at the painting site at 9 a.m.

17 The wall was in very poor condition.

18 There were strange writings and drawings on some parts.

19 Other parts had old posters on them.

20 We removed the posters first and painted over the writings and drawings with white paint.

21 The manager let us paint anything we wanted.

22 We decided to paint something cute because the wall was near an elementary school.

23 We divided into three groups and began painting.

24 I was in the group with Minsu and Jiwon.

25 I chose my spot and started to paint my favorite movie character.

26 Minsu painted some flowers and Jiwon did some background drawings.

27 Our club painted for about five hours.

28 After we finished, we got together and shared the day's experiences.

29 Minsu was very proud of his flower painting.

30 He said, "My flower is so real that a bee landed on it."

31 I said, "Drawing on a wall was much harder than drawing on paper."

32 We all agreed that our wall painting wasn't perfect.

33 But it didn't matter.

34 We made our neighborhood a little brighter and happier.

35 We were proud of ourselves.

36 We didn't just paint pictures on a wall that day.

37 It was a better tomorrow that we painted.

After You Read B

1. Paint, Better Tomorrow

2. DATE, April

3. MEETING TIME

4. like painting

5. make your neighborhood brighter

6. Right now, poor condition

7. need to remove, paint over, with white paint

8. anything you want

9. email

Word Power

1. got up, prepared for

2. said goodbye to

3. Try to get along with, have fun

4. replied, got on

59

Think and Write

1. Volunteer Work
2. volunteered, Library
3. read, to children
4. tried to, like, voice actor
5. volunteer, had, arrange, on the shelves
6. so, that, take a break every, minutes
7. After, finished, looked, neat
8. felt, proud
9. rewarding experience

구석구석지문 TEST Step 2   p.67

After You Read B

1. Project: Paint a Better Tomorrow
2. DATE: April 15
3. MEETING TIME: 9 a.m.
4. Do you like painting?
5. Do you want to make your neighborhood brighter?
6. Right now, the wall is in very poor condition.
7. You need to remove the old posters and paint over the strange writings with white paint.
8. You can paint anything you want!
9. email: volunteer@1365.go.kr

Word Power

1. Sally got up early and prepared for school.
2. She said goodbye to her mom.
3. Her mom said, "Try to get along with your friends and have fun."
4. Sally replied, "Okay, I will," and got on the school bus.

Think and Write

1. Volunteer Work Diary
2. I volunteered at Dream Library.
3. I read English books to children.
4. I tried to read like a voice actor.
5. The volunteer manager had me arrange the books on the shelves.
6. The books were so heavy that I had to take a break every 30 minutes.
7. After I finished, the shelves looked very neat.
8. I felt very proud.
9. It was a fun and rewarding experience.

단어 TEST Step 1   p.68

01 빛나는, 반짝거리는
02 흙
03 모험
04 머리, 지능
05 (구멍 등을) 파다
06 (심장이) 고동치다, 때리다
07 털다
08 폭넓은, 폭이 ~인
09 (사람을) 배치하다
10 편리한
11 잔혹한, 잔인한
12 뼈
13 (연극, 영화에서의) 연기
14 형사, 탐정
15 (일을) 거르다, 빼먹다
16 운전사가 없는
17 유용한, 도움이 되는
18 편리, 편의
19 훔치다
20 구덩이, 구멍
21 가벼운
22 결혼하다
23 요약, 개요
24 근육
25 잠들지 않은, 깨어 있는
26 키우다, 기르다
27 돌려주다, 반품하다
28 장면
29 품성, 인격
30 맨 아래, 바닥
31 불행히도
32 조심스럽게
33 갑자기
34 물건
35 내려놓다
36 ~로 가득 차다
37 ~을 의미하다
38 ~을 집다
39 결국 ~이 되다
40 ~의 바닥에서
41 찾아보다
42 ~의 것이다, ~ 소유이다
43 ~와 사랑에 빠지다

단어 TEST Step 2   p.69

01 steal
02 dig
03 adventure
04 muscle
05 character
06 dirt
07 brain
08 suddenly
09 brush
10 assign
11 hole
12 summary
13 carefully
14 bone
15 scene
16 wide
17 shiny
18 sleepy
19 convenience
20 actually
21 detective
22 skip
23 yell
24 light
25 awake
26 beat
27 unfortunately
28 raise
29 bottom
30 convenient
31 return
32 cruel
33 acting
34 popular
35 fall in love with
36 in fact
37 stand for ~
38 day off
39 put down
40 end up
41 stay awake
42 at the bottom of
43 look up

1 awake, 잠들지 않은, 깨어 있는   2 wide, 폭이 ~인

3 bottom, 맨 아래, 바닥   4 shiny, 빛나는, 반짝거리는

5 hole, 구덩이, 구멍   6 skip, (일을) 거르다, 빼먹다

7 day off, 휴일, 쉬는 날   8 object, 물건

9 brush, 털다   10 dig, (구멍 등을) 파다   11 muscle, 근육

12 tube, 통, 관   13 acting, (연극, 영화에서의) 연기

14 assign, (사람을) 배치하다   15 steal, 훔치다

16 yell, 고함치다

Listen and Speak 1 A

Welcome to / Long, no, How, been / How, here from / by subway / How, feel about / clean

Listen and Speak 1 B

did, hear / What / can, during classes from / heard / How, feel / useful, look up words I don't know / can also find / helpful

Listen and Speak 1 C

1 Can I ask / try, best / How, feel, single / easy, unhealthy

2 ask, difficult / try / How do you feel / helpful but scary

3 Can I ask you / try my best / How do you feel about / helpful but cruel

Listen and Speak 2 A

Did you enjoy / a lot / What did you like most / acting was / with you on

Listen and Speak 2 B

Why, always drinking / help me stay awake / I'm with you on, too much caffeine / help me focus on / know that too much caffeine / should drink, less often / Maybe

Listen and Speak 2 C

1 How do you feel about reading / anytime / with you on that, not good for

2 How do you feel about skipping / more / I'm with you on that / may not work

3 How do you feel about eating / a lot of fat / I'm with you on that / I don't agree, can save

Real Life Talk Watch a Video

What / They're items I ordered / don't you / How do you feel about / at all / difficult to know what, actually looks like / with you on / difficult to return / right, convenient / convenience, everything

Real Life Talk Step 2

1 feel about shopping / a lot / Can you tell me / shop

whenever / I'm with you

2 How do you feel about raising / tell me, reason / work to take care of / don't agree, cute, make us happy

Check up Dialogue Champion

How do you feel about using, in class / useful, search for information / with you on that

Listen and Speak 1 A

B: Hi, Amy. Welcome to Korea.

G: Long time no see, Minho. How have you been?

B: Great. How did you come here from the airport?

G: I came here by subway.

B: How do you feel about the subway in Korea?

G: I think it's very clean.

Listen and Speak 1 B

G: Brian, did did you hear the news?

B: What news?

G: We can use smartphones during classes from next week.

B: Yes, I heard that.

G: How do you feel about it?

B: I think it will be very useful. I can look up words I don't know.

G: Yeah. We can also find information on the Internet.

B: Right. It will be very helpful.

Listen and Speak 1 C

1 A: Can I ask you a difficult question?

   B: Sure. I'll try my best.

   A: How do you feel about the single food diet?

   B: I think it's easy but unhealthy.

2 A: Can I ask you a difficult question?

   B: Sure. I'll try my best.

   A: How do you feel about the AI robot?

   B: I think it's helpful but scary.

3 A: Can I ask you a difficult question?

   B: Sure. I'll try my best.

   A: How do you feel about animal testing?

   B: I think it's helpful but cruel.

Listen and Speak 2 A

B: Did you enjoy the movie?

G: Yes, I liked it a lot.

B: What did you like most about it?

G: The acting was so great.

B: I'm with you on that.

B: Hey, Jessica. Why are you always drinking energy drinks?

G: Because they help me stay awake.

B: I'm with you on that, but they have too much caffeine.

G: Well, they help me focus on my studies.

B: Did you know that too much caffeine can hurt your bones?

G: Oh, I didn't know that.

B: I think you should drink energy drinks less often.

G: Maybe you're right. Thanks, Tom.

1 A: How do you feel about reading books on a smartphone?

   B: I think it's good. We can read anytime.

   A: I'm with you on that. / I don't agree. It's not good for our eyes.

2 A: How do you feel about skipping breakfast?

   B: I think it's good. We can sleep more.

   A: I'm with you on that. / I don't agree. Our brain may not work well.

3 A: How do you feel about eating fast food?

   B: I think it's bad. Fast food has a lot of fat.

   A: I'm with you on that. / I don't agree. We can save time.

Tony: What are all these boxes, Suji?

Suji: They're items I ordered online.

Tony: You like shopping on the Internet, don't you?

Suji: Yes, I do. How do you feel about online shopping, Tony?

Tony: I don't like it at all.

Suji: Why?

Tony: It's very difficult to know what an item actually looks like.

Suji: I'm with you on that.

Tony: It's also difficult to return an item if you don't like it.

Suji: You're right, but I think it's very convenient.

Tony: Well, convenience isn't everything.

1 A: How do you feel about shopping on the Internet?

   B: I like it a lot.

   A: Can you tell me the reason?

   B: I can shop whenever I want.

   A: I'm with you on that.

2 A: How do you feel about raising pets?

B: I don't like it.

A: Can you tell me the reason?

B: It's a lot of work to take care of them.

A: I don't agree. They're so cute and make us happy.

A: How do you feel about using smartphones in class?

B: I think smartphones are useful in class. We can search for information on them.

A: I'm with you on that.

01 Dig harder   02 harder, the faster, yelled

03 harder since, muscle hurt

04 thirsty, hungry

05 to go home   06 for, would be, at

07 a terrible name

08 there was no lake

09 hot, full of sand

10 In fact, even   11 place for bad

12 what, like, doing

13 sent, stealing, pair of

14 didn't really steal

15 in, place at, wrong

16 walking home from school

17 Suddenly, pair, fell from

18 hit him on, head

19 with, tell, what happened

20 few, stopped, why, running

21 for, belonged to, famous

22 why, ended up at

23 was assigned to

24 There, six other boys

25 had cool names like

26 Each, had, dig, hole

27 to, about, deep, wide

28 digging to build character

29 more, dug, stronger, became

30 took less, finish, each

31 finishing, something shiny, dirt

32 heart beat faster

33 something interesting, given, off

34 picked up, brushed off

35 small gold tube

36 couldn't be, since, light

37 There, letters, bottom, tube

38 did, stand for   39 beat even faster

01 Dig harder   02 The harder, the faster, yelled

03 any harder since, hurt

04 thirsty, hungry   05 go home

06 Unfortunately, for, would be

07 a terrible name

08 there, no lake   09 hot, full of sand

10 In fact, even   11 a place for bad boys

12 like, doing   13 was sent, for stealing

14 didn't really steal

15 in the wrong place, wrong time

16 walking home from school

17 a pair of, fell from

18 hit him on the head

19 with, what happened

20 A few minutes, stopped, why he was running

21 for, belonged to

22 That was why, ended up

23 was assigned to

24 six other boys   25 cool, like

26 one hole every day

27 about, deep, wide

28 to build character

29 The more, the stronger

30 It took, to finish, each day

31 something shiny in the dirt   32 beat faster

33 anyone who, be given the day off

34 picked up, brushed off

35 small gold tube

36 couldn't be, since

37 letters, at the bottom of

38 stand for   39 beat even faster

1 "더 열심히 파, Stanley!

2 네가 열심히 파면 팔수록, 너는 더 빨리 끝낼 거야!" Sir 씨가 소리를 질렀다.

3 Stanley Yelnats는 모든 근육 하나하나가 아팠기 때문에 더 열심히 팔 수가 없었다.

4 그는 목이 마르고 배가 고팠다.

5 그는 집에 가고 싶었다.

6 불행히도, 앞으로 18개월 동안 Stanley의 집은 바로 여기 Green Lake 캠프가 될 것이었다.

7 Green Lake 캠프는 형편없는 이름이었다.

8 그곳은 초록색도 아니었고 호수도 없었다.

9 Green Lake 캠프는 뜨거웠고 온통 모래였다.

10 사실 그곳은 캠프조차 아니었다.

11 그곳은 나쁜 소년들을 위한 곳이었다.

12 그렇다면 Stanley 같이 착한 소년이 여기서 무엇을 하고 있었을까?

13 그는 운동화 한 켤레를 훔쳤다는 이유로 캠프에 보내졌다.

14 Stanley가 정말로 운동화 한 켤레를 훔친 것은 아니었다.

15 그는 그저 잘못된 시간에 잘못된 장소에 있었다.

16 어느 날, 그는 학교에서 집으로 걸어가고 있었다.

17 갑자기, 낡은 운동화 한 켤레가 하늘에서 떨어졌다.

18 그 운동화는 그의 머리에 맞았다.

19 그는 그의 아버지에게 무슨 일이 일어났는지 말하기 위해 운동화를 가지고 달리기 시작했다.

20 몇 분 후에, 경찰이 Stanley를 멈춰 세웠고 그가 왜 달리고 있었는지를 그에게 물었다.

21 Stanley에게는 불행히도, 그 운동화는 유명한 야구 선수인 Clyde Livingstone의 것이었다.

22 그것이 Stanley가 Green Lake 캠프에 오게 된 이유였다.

23 Stanley는 캠프에서 D 그룹에 배치되었다.

24 Stanley의 그룹에는 6명의 다른 소년들이 있었다.

25 그들은 모두 X-Ray, Zigzag, Zero와 같은 멋진 이름을 가지고 있었다.

26 각 소년은 매일 구덩이 하나를 파야 했다.

27 그것은 150cm 정도 깊이와 150cm 정도 너비여야 했다.

28 Sir 씨는 "너희들은 인격을 수양하기 위해 구덩이를 파고 있는 것이야."라고 말했다.

29 Stanley는 많이 파면 팔수록, 더 힘이 세졌다.

30 하루하루 구덩이를 끝내는 데 시간이 덜 걸렸다.

31 그가 온 지 두 번째 주, Stanley가 자기 구덩이를 끝내 가고 있었을 때, 그는 흙 속에서 빛나는 뭔가를 봤다.

32 Stanley의 심장은 더 빨리 뛰었다.

33 그는 흥미로운 뭔가를 발견한 사람은 그 날을 쉬게 된다고 들었다.

34 그는 조심스럽게 그 빛나는 물체를 집어 흙을 털어 냈다.

35 그것은 작은 금색 통이었다.

36 그러나 그것은 너무 가벼웠기 때문에 진짜 금일 리가 없었다.

37 그 통의 바닥에는 KB라는 두 글자가 있었다.

38 KB는 무엇을 의미할까?

39 Stanley의 심장은 훨씬 더 빨리 뛰었다.

1 "Dig harder, Stanley!

2 The harder you dig, the faster you'll finish!" yelled Mr. Sir.

3 Stanley Yelnats couldn't dig any harder since every single muscle hurt.

4 He was thirsty and hungry.

5 He wanted to go home.

63

6 Unfortunately, Stanley's home for the next 18 months would be right here, at Camp Green Lake.

7 Camp Green Lake was a terrible name.

8 It wasn't green and there was no lake.

9 Camp Green Lake was hot and full of sand.

10 In fact, it wasn't even a camp.

11 It was a place for bad boys.

12 Then what was a good boy like Stanley doing here?

13 He was sent to the camp for stealing a pair of sneakers.

14 Stanley didn't really steal a pair of sneakers.

15 He was just in the wrong place at the wrong time.

16 One day, he was walking home from school.

17 Suddenly, a pair of old sneakers fell from the sky.

18 The sneakers hit him on the head.

19 He started running with the sneakers to tell his father what happened.

20 A few minutes later, the police stopped Stanley and asked him why he was running.

21 Unfortunately for Stanley, the sneakers belonged to a famous baseball player, Clyde Livingstone.

22 That was why Stanley ended up at Camp Green Lake.

23 Stanley was assigned to Group D in the camp.

24 There were six other boys in Stanley's group.

25 They all had cool names like X-Ray, Zigzag and Zero.

26 Each boy had to dig one hole every day.

27 It had to be about 150cm deep and 150cm wide.

28 Mr. Sir said, "You are digging to build character."

29 The more Stanley dug, the stronger he became.

30 It took less time to finish his hole each day.

31 In his second week, as Stanley was finishing his hole, he saw something shiny in the dirt.

32 Stanley's heart beat faster.

33 He heard that anyone who found something interesting would be given the day off.

34 He carefully picked up the shiny object and brushed off the dirt.

35 It was a small gold tube.

36 But it couldn't be real gold since it was too light.

37 There were two letters, *KB*, at the bottom of the tube.

38 What did KB stand for?

39 Stanley's heart beat even faster.

After You Read B

1. August 5th

---

2. Unfortunately, there is no lake

3. in, have cool names like

4. have to dig, about, deep, wide

5. anyone who, something interesting, get the day off

6. hope, can be

Word Power

1. bought a pair of shoes for

2. found a pair of glasses

3. packed three pairs of jeans

Think and Write

1. was a teacher in

2. was very popular

3. Many rich men, to marry her

4. fell in love with, poor man

5. tried to hurt

6. Later, found dead, became sad, left

After You Read B

1. Monday, August 5th

2. Unfortunately, the camp isn't green and there is no lake.

3. I'm in Group D. My group members have cool names like X-Ray, Zigzag and Zero.

4. We have to dig one hole about 150cm deep and 150cm wide.

5. The good news is this: anyone who finds something interesting can get the day off.

6. I hope I can be the one.

Word Power

1. She bought a pair of shoes for 15 dollars.

2. I found a pair of glasses under the chair.

3. He packed three pairs of jeans in his bag.

Think and Write

1. Kate Barlow was a teacher in Green Lake.

2. She was very popular.

3. Many rich men in the town wanted to marry her.

4. But Kate fell in love with Sam, a poor man.

5. The rich men tried to hurt Sam.

6. Later, Sam was found dead. Kate became sad and left the town.

◎ 선택형 문항의 답안은 컴퓨터용 수정 싸인펜을
  사용하여 OMR 답안지에 바르게 표기하시오.
◎ 서술형 문제는 답을 답안지에 반드시 검정
  볼펜으로 쓰시오.
◎ 총 30문항 100점 만점입니다. 문항별 배점
  은 각 문항에 표시되어 있습니다.

[인천 ○○중]

1. 다음 제시된 단어의 ⓐ : ⓑ 활용 관계가 다른 하나는?
(3점)

① quick
 - I took a ⓐ_____ shower.
 - The news spread ⓑ_____ through the
   town.
② careful
 - Be ⓐ_____ not to get hurt.
 - Drive ⓑ_____ on those icy roads.
③ easy
 - This machine is rather ⓐ_____ to use.
 - The water is so deep that we can't get there
   ⓑ_____.
④ sudden
 - It's a ⓐ_____ lightning in the clear sky.
 - ⓑ_____, it got cold and we had to return
   home.
⑤ different
 - Is there any ⓐ_____ between a stick and
   a string?
 - He looked at things a bit ⓑ_____.

[충북 ○○중]

2. 다음 중 단어의 영어 뜻이 올바르지 않은 것은? (3점)

① provide: to give something to somebody
② triangle: a shape with three straight sides
③ select: to choose something or someone
   from a group
④ stuck: difficult or impossible to move from
   a position
⑤ planet: a small hard object produced by a
   plant from which a new plant can grow

[울산 ○○중]

3. 다음 문장의 밑줄 친 부분이 어색한 것은? (2점)

① Thank you for all your <u>help</u>.
② I got up <u>late</u> this morning.
③ He took a <u>quickly</u> shower.
④ She solved the problem <u>easily</u>.
⑤ We could <u>hardly</u> understand the book.

[경북 ○○중]

4. 다음 중 우리말을 바르게 영작한 것을 고르면? (3점)

① 이것은 내가 기대했던 것과 다르다.
 → This is different that I expected.
② 나는 내가 사고 싶었던 것을 샀다.
 → I bought what I wanted to buy.
③ 그가 말하는 것은 사실이었다.
 → That he said was true.
④ 나는 내가 가장 좋아하는 것을 할 것이다.
 → I'll do which I like most.
⑤ 내가 해야 하는 것은 내 방을 청소하는 것이다.
 → The thing what I have to do is to clean
   my room.

Jenny: Hi, Taemin! We're in the same class again!

Taemin: Yeah! It's good to see you, Jenny. How have you been?

Jenny: (A)_____ How about you?

Taemin: I've been pretty busy. I have a piano competition next week.

Jenny: Oh! I didn't know you played the piano.

Taemin: Really? I've played the piano for 5 years.

Jenny: You must be good at it.
 (B)_____

Taemin: Thanks.

7. 위 대화의 빈칸 (B)에 들어갈 말로 알맞은 것은?
(3점)

① I'm happy to hear that.

② Good luck in your competition.

③ Everybody makes mistakes.

④ Don't worry. She will do well.

⑤ It's very nice of you to say so.

5. 위 대화의 빈칸 (A)에 들어갈 말로 적절하지 않은 것은?
(3점)

① So so.

② Pretty good.

③ Not so good.

④ It's been a long time.

⑤ I've been great.

6. 위 대화를 읽고 알 수 있는 것은?
(3점)

① Has Taemin ever won a prize in a piano contest?

② How does Taemin feel about the piano competition?

③ What is Jenny busy with these days?

④ How long has Taemin played the piano?

⑤ How long have they known each other?

8. 다음 (A)의 대화문을 (B)로 다시 썼을 때, 대화의 내용과 다른 것은?
(4점)

(A)

Yuna: Andy, how did the basketball game go?

Andy: Our team lost.

Yuna: Oh, I'm sorry to hear that.

Andy: It's okay. It was a great game.

Yuna: What was the score?

Andy: It was 80 to 79.

Yuna: That was really close!

Andy: Yeah. We played really well as a team.

Yuna: That's wonderful! I want to watch your next game.

↓

(B)

 Yuna met Andy yesterday. She asked about the ⓐresult of the basketball game. He said his team lost by ⓑtwo points. She felt sorry about the ⓒbad news. But he said it was ⓓokay because ⓔhis team played well.

① ⓐ   ② ⓑ   ③ ⓒ

④ ⓓ   ⑤ ⓔ

9. 다음 대화의 빈칸에 들어갈 수 없는 것은? (3점)

> B: Ann, you look excited. Do you have any news?
> G: _____
> B: I'm happy to hear that.

① I came in first in the marathon.

② I dropped my new smartphone.

③ I won the school dance contest.

④ My father bought me a new bike.

⑤ Our team got an A on the science project.

11. 위 글의 내용과 일치하지 않는 것은? (3점)

① 이 활동에는 1미터의 줄이 필요하다.

② 이 활동에는 8가지의 규칙이 있다.

③ 이 활동을 하는 데 제한 시간은 15분이다.

④ 이 활동은 문제를 해결하는 데 좋다.

⑤ 이 활동은 창의적으로 생각하는 데 좋다.

[10-11] 다음 글을 읽고 물음에 답하시오.

> You need:
> ⓐ20 stick of spaghetti, 1 marshmallow, 1 meter of tape, 1 meter of string
>
> Rules:
> ⓑEach team have four people.
> ⓒYou have to build the taller tower in your class.
> The marshmallow must be on top.
> ⓓThe tower must stand by itself.
> The time limit is 15 minutes.
>
> This activity is good for:
> - Building Relationships
> - Solving Problems
> - ⓔThinking Creativity

10. 위 글의 밑줄 친 ⓐ~ⓔ 중 어법상 올바른 것은? (4점)

① ⓐ 　　② ⓑ 　　③ ⓒ

④ ⓓ 　　⑤ ⓔ

12. 다음 글의 밑줄 친 부분 중 어법상 적절한 것을 고른 것은? (4점)

> We didn't spend much time on ⓐplanning. All the members started ⓑto build the tower right away. Our first tower looked like a tent. It wasn't very tall. We tried again. The next tower was tall but it couldn't stand ⓒby oneself. After ⓓmany tries, it was possible ⓔfor us build a beautiful and tall tower. It looked like the Leaning Tower of Pisa. We finally made ⓕwhat we wanted!

① ⓐ,ⓑ,ⓓ,ⓕ

② ⓐ,ⓒ,ⓓ,ⓔ

③ ⓐ,ⓓ,ⓔ,ⓕ

④ ⓑ,ⓒ,ⓓ,ⓕ

⑤ ⓑ,ⓒ,ⓔ,ⓕ

13. 다음은 지수가 쓴 영어 문장이다. 이 중 어법이 <u>어색한</u> 문장을 모두 묶은 것은? (3점)

> Ⓐ It was fun of us to ride a bicycle together.
> Ⓑ It is boring for he to watch the soccer game.
> Ⓒ It is not difficult for a baby to swim in the bathtub.
> Ⓓ It was kind for them to give me the information.
> Ⓔ It was careful of his not to talk too much about the news.

① Ⓐ, Ⓒ

② Ⓐ, Ⓑ

③ Ⓑ, Ⓒ, Ⓔ

④ Ⓑ, Ⓓ, Ⓔ

⑤ Ⓐ, Ⓑ, Ⓓ, Ⓔ

14. 다음 〈보기〉의 what과 문법적 쓰임이 <u>다른</u> 것은? (3점)

> **보기**
> <u>What</u> Minsoo said made me serious.

① Was that recipe <u>what</u> the chef suggested?

② He doesn't know <u>what</u> colors and shapes she likes.

③ <u>What</u> we usually do every Sunday morning is to cook mushroom soup.

④ I'm only interested in <u>what</u> I can do by myself.

⑤ Let me see <u>what</u> you bought for Mother's Day.

15. 다음 빈칸에 들어갈 말이 나머지와 <u>다른</u> 것은? (4점)

① It was wise _____ her to accept that offer.

② It is dangerous _____ you to go out alone.

③ It was kind _____ them to invite me to the party.

④ It was stupid _____ Clare to lend him money.

⑤ It is rude _____ him to be late for the meeting.

16. 다음 글의 빈칸에 들어갈 말로 가장 적절한 것은? (4점)

> My group project was making a video to introduce our school. The name of our group was "The Stars" and we had four members. First, we wrote a dialogue together. Then, we divided up the roles. I took the role of reporter. The rest of members did their own parts. It was a little difficult to set the meeting time. But our video turned out to be great! I learned that _____.

① life is full of ups and downs

② failure is a wonderful teacher

③ two heads are better than one

④ the early bird catches the worm

⑤ saying is one thing and doing another

TEAM A

We had many good ideas. We talked about each idea ⓐin detail. (가)It was not easy for us to choose the best idea. ⓑSuddenly the teacher said, "Five minutes left." ⓒIn a hurry, we taped the sticks of spaghetti together. Then we wrapped the string around them. The string ⓓgot stuck to the tape and it was a ⓔbig mess. With one second left, I put the marshmallow on top!

19. 위 글의 밑줄 친 (가)it와 용법이 다르게 쓰인 것은?

(3점)

① It was kind of you to do so.

② It was not very cold yesterday.

③ It is not difficult for him to swim in the sea.

④ It was hard for me to fix the computer.

⑤ It is important for them to work as a team.

17. 위 글의 밑줄 친 ⓐ~ⓔ의 의미가 올바르지 않은 것은?

(3점)

① ⓐ 자세히

② ⓑ 갑자기

③ ⓒ 서둘러

④ ⓓ 감았다

⑤ ⓔ 엉망진창

18. 위 글의 내용과 일치하는 것은?

(4점)

① 스파게티 면을 테이프로 붙였다.

② 시작하고 5분 만에 탑을 완성했다.

③ 떠오르는 모든 아이디어를 다 시도했다.

④ 스파게티 면 둘레를 끈으로 감지 않았다.

⑤ 마지막 순간에 마시멜로를 중간에 꽂았다.

20. 위 글을 읽고 답할 수 있는 질문은?

(4점)

① What was the best idea?

② What did the teacher say?

③ How did they make Team A?

④ How much did the marshmallow weigh?

⑤ How many sticks of spaghetti did Team A have?

[21-23] 다음 글을 읽고 물음에 답하시오.

Try the Marshmallow Challenge!

You need:
ⓐ20 sticks of spaghetti
1 marshmallow
1 meter of tape
ⓑ1 meter of string

Rules:
• Each team has four people.
• You have to build the tallest tower in your class.
• The marshmallow must be on top.
• The tower (가)must stand ⓒby itself.
• The time limit is 15 minutes.

This activity is good for:
ⓓBuilding Relationships
Solving Problems
ⓔThinking Creatively

21. 위 글의 밑줄 친 부분 (가)와 같은 의미로 쓰인 것은? (4점)

① He <u>must</u> love her very much.
② I <u>must</u> buy a ticket for the show.
③ Tom <u>must</u> be Jenny's younger brother.
④ There she is. She <u>must</u> be David's sister.
⑤ I heard something. Somebody <u>must</u> be at home.

22. 위 글의 밑줄 친 ⓐ~ⓔ 중 우리말 뜻으로 알맞지 <u>않은</u> 것은? (3점)

① 스파게티 20가닥   ② 1미터짜리 끈
③ 원래대로   ④ 관계 형성하기
⑤ 창의적으로 생각하기

23. 위 글을 읽고 알 수 <u>없는</u> 것은? (3점)

① 활동의 실제 사례
② 한 팀 당 사람 수
③ 활동의 도전 과제
④ 활동의 제한 시간
⑤ 활동에 필요한 재료

[24-26] 다음 글을 읽고 물음에 답하시오.

TEAM B
    We didn't ⓐspend much time on planning. All the members ⓑstarted to build the tower right away. Our first tower looked (가)_____ a tent. It wasn't very tall. We tried again. The next tower was tall but ⓒit couldn't stand by itself. After many tries, it was possible for us ⓓto build a beautiful and tall tower. It looked (가)_____ the Leaning Tower of Pisa. We finally made ⓔthat we wanted!

24. 위 글의 ⓐ~ⓔ 중 어법의 쓰임이 바르지 <u>않은</u> 것을 고르면? (3점)

① ⓐ   ② ⓑ   ③ ⓒ
④ ⓓ   ⑤ ⓔ

25. 위 글의 빈칸 (가)에 공통으로 들어갈 말을 쓰시오. (3점)

→ _____

26. 위 글을 읽고 답할 수 있는 질문의 개수는? (4점)

> ⓐ How was their first tower shape?
> ⓑ What does the final tower they made look like?
> ⓒ Did they spend much time on planning?
> ⓓ Was their first tower tall?
> ⓔ Who first started building the tower?

① 1개   ② 2개   ③ 3개

④ 4개   ⑤ 5개

28. 위 글을 통해 답을 할 수 있는 질문은? (3점)

① Whose idea was the best?

② How tall was their tower?

③ Who worked as a time checker?

④ What shape did they select for the base?

⑤ How long did they spend on their planning?

29. 위 글의 Team C의 활동 내용을 아래와 같이 요약할 때 빈칸 (A), (B)에 들어갈 내용으로 가장 적절한 것은? (4점)

> Instead of choosing the best way, Team C (A)_____ the good idea which was chosen. After (B)_____ ideas and dividing up the roles, the team finally made the tall tower.

	(A)	(B)
①	deleted	communicating
②	forgot	exchanging
③	required	dividing
④	suggested	giving up
⑤	developed	sharing

[27~30] 다음 글을 읽고 물음에 답하시오.

> TEAM C
>
> We didn't try ⓐto choose the best idea. Instead, we took a good idea and improved on it. One student said we needed a strong base. Another student suggested a triangle shape for the base. We all agreed and divided up the roles such as time checker and tape cutter. We worked together as a team. In the end, we built our tall tower!

27. 위 글의 밑줄 친 ⓐ와 같은 용법은? (3점)

① I need something cold to drink now.

② We should take action to save the Earth.

③ My group project was to make a video.

④ He was so excited to win the soccer game.

⑤ What can we do to help our little friends?

30. 위 글의 내용과 일치하는 것을 고르면? (4점)

① TEAM C는 각자의 역할을 나누었다.

② 결국에는 탑을 완성하지 못하고 말았다.

③ TEAM C는 동그란 모양의 받침을 선택했다.

④ 한 친구가 튼튼한 기초는 필요 없다고 했다.

⑤ TEAM C는 가장 훌륭한 아이디어를 선택했다.

◎ 선택형 문항의 답안은 컴퓨터용 수정 싸인펜을
  사용하여 OMR 답안지에 바르게 표기하시오.
◎ 서술형 문제는 답을 답안지에 반드시 검정
  볼펜으로 쓰시오.
◎ 총 30문항 100점 만점입니다. 문항별 배점
  은 각 문항에 표시되어 있습니다.

[경기 ○○중]

1. 다음 중 단어에 대한 설명으로 옳은 것은?   (3점)

① relationship: a very dirty or untidy condition

② detail: a long, thin piece of wood, metal, plastic, etc.

③ donation: something that you give to help a person or organization

④ population: a new or difficult task that tests somebody's ability and skill

⑤ pollination: a fine powder produced by flowers that is needed to make seeds

[경기 ○○중]

2. 다음 중 짝지어진 두 단어의 관계가 나머지와 <u>다르게</u> 의미상의 변화가 있는 것은?   (2점)

① hard - hardly

② easy - easily

③ quick - quickly

④ happy - happily

⑤ different - differently

[울산 ○○중]

3. 다음 중 어법상 옳은 것은?   (3점)

① It is rude for him to do such a thing.

② It is very impolite of him to say so to her.

③ It was kind of his to donate for the poor.

④ It is easy of his mom to make a cake.

⑤ It was dangerous of them to help those people.

[경북 ○○중]

4. 다음 대화의 밑줄 친 ⓐ～ⓔ 중 관계대명사 what은?   (3점)

A: ⓐWhat are you looking for?
B: I'm looking for a present for my mom.
A: Why don't you give her a jacket as a gift?
B: That's a good idea!
A: ⓑWhat color does she like?
B: She likes pink. ⓒWhat she buys is always pink.
A: ⓓWhat about this one? This is a 50 percent discount.
B: It looks good. ⓔWhat's the price?
A: It's 70 dollars.

① ⓐ   ② ⓑ   ③ ⓒ

④ ⓓ   ⑤ ⓔ

[인천 ○○중]

5. 다음 대화의 ⓐ～ⓔ 중 주어진 문장이 들어갈 알맞은 곳은?   (4점)

Do you have any good news?

A: Cathy, you looked excited. (A)
B: (B) Our team got an A on the social studies project.
A: That's wonderful! (C)
B: Our team had the best teamwork. (D)
A: (E) I'm pleased to hear that.

① (A)   ② (B)   ③ (C)

④ (D)   ⑤ (E)

6. 다음 중 우리말을 바르게 영작한 것을 고르면? (3점)

① 그가 말을 타는 것은 쉽지 않았다.

　→ That was not easy for him to ride a horse.

② 그 일을 포기하다니 그녀는 어리석었다.

　→ It was silly for her to give up the work.

③ 우리가 그 산을 오르는 것은 불가능하다.

　→ We is impossible for us to climb the mountain.

④ 그들이 그 문제를 푸는 것은 어렵다.

　→ It is difficult for they to solve the problem.

⑤ 가난한 사람들을 도와주다니 그는 관대하다.

　→ It is generous of him to help the poor.

7. 다음 빈칸에 들어갈 말이 순서대로 짝지어진 것은? (4점)

> Last Saturday, I went to see my son's soccer game. It was exciting for me (A)_____ the game. But the other team player kicked my son's leg and broke it. It was very cruel (B)_____ to do such a thing.

① watching - for him

② watching - of him

③ watched - for him

④ to watch - of him

⑤ to watch - for him

[8-9] 다음 대화를 읽고 물음에 답하시오.

> G: Hi, Jinsu! We're in the same class again!
> B: Yeah! It's good to see you, Sora.
> 　(가)_____
> G: I've been great. How about you?
> B: I have been pretty busy. I have a piano competition next week.
> G: Oh! I didn't know you played the piano.
> B: Really? I've played the piano for 5 years.
> G: You must be good at it. Good luck in your competition!
> B: Thanks.

8. 위 대화의 (가)에 들어갈 말로 알맞은 것은? (3점)

① How far is it?

② How old are you?

③ How do you do?

④ How have you been?

⑤ How did you go there?

9. 위 대화의 내용과 일치하는 것은? (3점)

① Sora는 잘 지내지 못했다.

② Jinsu는 한가롭게 지낸 편이었다.

③ Jinsu는 다음 주에 피아노 경연 대회가 있다.

④ Sora도 피아노를 5년 이상 연습해 오고 있다.

⑤ Jinsu가 피아노 대회에서 우승할 것이 확실하다.

10. 다음 대화의 밑줄 친 ⓐ~ⓔ 중 흐름상 어색한 것은? (3점)

> G: ⓐAndy, how did the basketball game go?
> B: Our team lost.
> G: ⓑOh, I'm glad to hear that.
> B: It's okay. It was a great game.
> G: ⓒWhat was the score?
> B: It was 80 to 79. We lost by one point.
> G: ⓓThat was really close!
> B: Yeah. We played really well as team.
> G: ⓔThat's wonderful! I want to watch your next game.

① ⓐ   ② ⓑ   ③ ⓒ

④ ⓓ   ⑤ ⓔ

12. 다음 빈칸 (A)~(E)에 what이 들어갈 수 있는 경우를 〈보기〉에서 있는 대로 고른 것은? (3점)

> • I'll do (A)_____ I like most.
> • My dad bought me (B)_____ I wanted.
> • The bike is (C)_____ my son needs most.
> • The shop doesn't have (D)_____ I need to buy.
> • The thing (E)_____ I have to do is to clean my room.

① (A), (B)

② (A), (B), (D)

② (B), (C), (D)

④ (B), (D), (E)

⑤ (A), (B), (C), (D)

11. 다음 우리말이 자연스러운 문장이 되도록 〈보기〉의 단어들을 바르게 배열하여 완전한 영어 문장으로 쓰시오. (5점)

(1) 나를 위해 꽃을 가져오다니 넌 친절하구나.

> 보기
> flowers / you / me / it / kind / to / of / bring / is / for

정답: _____

(2) 오늘 네가 들었던 것을 나에게 얘기해 주렴.

> 보기
> heard / tell / you / me / what

정답: _____

13. 다음 대화의 흐름상, 알맞지 않은 말은? (3점)

> A: Amy, ⓐhow have you been?
> B: ⓑI've been great. How about you, Mike?
> A: ⓒPretty good. ⓓI have a bad cold.
> B: Oh, no! ⓔGet well soon.
> A: Thanks.

① ⓐ   ② ⓑ   ③ ⓒ

④ ⓓ   ⑤ ⓔ

14. 다음 글의 흐름으로 보아 빈칸에 들어갈 말로 가장 알맞은 것은? (4점)

> **My Best Group Project**
>
> My best group project was making a video to introduce our school. The name of our group was 'The Stars' and we had four members. First, we wrote a dialogue together. Then, we divided up the roles. I took the role of reporter. It was difficult for us to set the meeting time. But our video turned out to be great! I learned _____ _____.

① no smoke without fire

② no news is good news

③ blood is thicker than water

④ a good book is a great friend

⑤ many heads are better than one

15. 다음 대화의 빈칸에 들어갈 가장 알맞은 것을 고르시오. (3점)

> A: What is the homework?
> B: I don't know. I didn't hear _____.

① what the teacher said

② what the teacher says

③ which the teacher said

④ which the teacher says

⑤ that the teacher said

16. 다음 중 어법상 옳은 문장을 〈보기〉에서 있는 대로 고른 것은? (4점)

> **보기**
>
> ⓐ It is not easy for I to read this book.
> ⓑ It is impossible of you to win the game.
> ⓒ It was silly of him to give up the work.
> ⓓ It is important for them to eat healthy food.
> ⓔ It is very nice for you to come and help us.
> ⓕ It was smart for her to solve the math problem.
> ⓖ It was very rude for you to ignore his invitation.
> ⓗ It is very dangerous for kids to swim in this river.

① ⓐ, ⓒ, ⓔ

② ⓒ, ⓓ, ⓗ

③ ⓐ, ⓕ, ⓖ, ⓗ

④ ⓑ, ⓒ, ⓓ, ⓖ

⑤ ⓔ, ⓕ, ⓖ, ⓗ

James: Lily! Is that you? Long time no see.
Lily: James! It's been a long time. (ⓐ)
James: How have you been?
Lily: I've been good. How about you?
James: I've been really busy at school. (ⓑ)
Lily: It's wonderful. I've made many friends.
James: That's great! I'm happy to hear that.
   (ⓒ)
Lily: Thanks. Oh! I have to go to my piano
   lesson now. (ⓓ)
James: You still have my number, right? (ⓔ)
Lily: Yeah, I'll call you later. Have a good
   day!
James: You, too. Bye!

[경북 ○○중]

17. 위 대화의 ⓐ~ⓔ 중 주어진 문장이 들어갈 알맞은 곳을 고르시오. (3점)

How's your new school?

① ⓐ   ② ⓑ   ③ ⓒ

④ ⓓ   ⑤ ⓔ

[경북 ○○중]

18. 위 대화의 내용과 일치하지 <u>않는</u> 것을 고르시오. (4점)

① Lily hasn't seen James for a long time.

② Lily has a busy schedule at school.

③ Lily likes her new school life.

④ Lily will go to a piano lesson after the conversation.

⑤ Lily will make a phone call to James later.

Try the Marshmallow Challenge!

We need:
   20 sticks of spaghetti, 1 marshmallow, 1 meter of tape, 1 meter of string

Rule:
- Each team has four people.
- You have to build the tallest tower in your class.
- The marshmallow must be on top.
- The tower must stand ⓐby itself.
- The time limit for the challenge is 15 minutes.

The activity is good for:
- Building Relationships
- Solving Problems
- Thinking Creatively

[인천 ○○중]

19. 위 글의 내용과 일치하는 것은? (4점)

① 탑은 혼자 힘으로 15분 동안 지탱할 수 있어야 한다.

② 탑의 하단에 마시멜로우를 놓고, 20개의 스파게티를 연결하면 된다.

③ 이 활동을 통해 문제 해결 능력 및 창의적 사고를 기를 수 있다.

④ 4개의 팀으로 나누어 반에서 가장 높은 탑을 만드는 팀이 우승하게 된다.

⑤ 필요한 경우, 스파게티는 끊어서 사용하고 테이프와 줄로 연결할 수도 있다.

20. 위 글의 밑줄 친 ⓐ의 우리말 뜻은? (2점)

① 대신에 ② 대략
③ 스스로 ④ 서둘러
⑤ ~하는 도중에

[22-23] 다음 글을 읽고 물음에 답하시오.

Teacher's Feedback

Team A

You had ⓐmuch good ideas! You built the tower in a hurry, but everyone worked hard. Nice work!

Team B

It was wonderful ⓑthat you tried many times. I ⓒsure you learned from your mistakes. Finally, you ⓓmake a beautiful and tall tower. Good job!

Team C

You had good teamwork! You chose a good idea and improved on it. Also, I was deeply (A)_____ that everyone had a role. The tall tower looked ⓔstrongly.

22. 위 글의 밑줄 친 ⓐ~ⓔ 중 어법상 옳은 것은? (3점)

① ⓐ ② ⓑ ③ ⓒ
④ ⓓ ⑤ ⓔ

21. What is the purpose of the text above? (3점)

① 활동 설명
② 새 메뉴 홍보
③ 활동 결과 보고
④ 음식 조리법 안내
⑤ 진로 고민에 대한 조언

23. 위 글의 흐름으로 보아 빈칸 (A)에 들어갈 말로 가장 적절한 것은? (3점)

① tired
② bored
③ annoyed
④ confused
⑤ impressed

[24~30] 다음 글을 읽고 물음에 답하시오.

TEAM A

(가)_____

We had many good ideas. We talked about each idea (A)in detail. It was not easy for us to choose the best idea. Suddenly the teacher said, "Five minutes left." ⓐIn a hurry, we taped the sticks of spaghetti together. Then, we wrapped the string around them. The string got stuck to the tape and it was a big mess. With one second left, I put the marshmallow on top!

TEAM B

ⓑWe didn't spend much time on planning. All the members started building the tower right away. Our first tower looked like a tent. It wasn't very tall. We tried again. The next tower was tall but it couldn't stand by itself. After many tries, it was possible for us to build a beautiful and tall tower. It looked like the Leaning Tower of Pisa. ⓒWe finally made which we wanted!

TEAM C

We didn't try to choose the best idea. (나)_____, we took a good idea and improved on it. ⓓOne student said we needed a strong base. Another student suggested a triangle shape for the base. ⓔWe all agreed and divided up the roles such as time checker and tape cutter. We worked together as team. (다)_____, we built our tall tower!

24. 위 글의 (A)in detail의 의미와 반대되는 표현으로 적절한 것은? (4점)

① in brief
② at least
③ in advance
④ for instance
⑤ for the reason

25. 위 글의 (가)에 들어갈 말로 가장 알맞은 것은? (3점)

① Think before you act.
② Just do it.
③ We are one team.
④ Work together.
⑤ Believe your friends.

26. 위 글의 Team A, B, C의 활동 과정을 한 문장으로 가장 잘 표현한 것을 골라 Team A, B, C 순서대로 묶은 것은? (4점)

보기
ⓔ Just do it.
ⓕ Think before you act.
ⓖ We're one team.
ⓗ Act before you think.

① ⓔ － ⓖ － ⓗ
② ⓖ － ⓕ － ⓔ
③ ⓖ － ⓔ － ⓗ
④ ⓕ － ⓔ － ⓖ
⑤ ⓗ － ⓔ － ⓖ

27. 위 글의 내용과 일치하는 것은? (3점)

① Team A는 결국 탑을 만들지 못했다.

② Team A는 5분 만에 탑을 완성했다.

③ Team B의 첫 번째 탑은 스스로 서 있지 못했다.

④ Team B는 똑바로 서 있는 탑을 완성했다.

⑤ Team C는 삼각형 모양의 받침대를 만들었다.

28. 위 글에 대한 질문 중 본문의 내용에서 답을 찾을 수 없는 것은? (4점)

① What did Team A talk about in detail?

② What did Team B's final tower look like?

③ What problem did Team B's second tower have?

④ What did Team C do instead of choosing the best idea?

⑤ What shape did Team C agree on for the top of the tower?

29. 위 글의 ⓐ~ⓔ 중에서 어법상 어색한 것은? (3점)

① ⓐ　　　　② ⓑ　　　　③ ⓒ

④ ⓓ　　　　⑤ ⓔ

30. 위 글의 (나), (다)에 들어갈 말로 바르게 짝지어진 것은? (4점)

	(나)	(다)
①	For example	But
②	In the end	In addition
③	Instead	For example
④	Instead	In the end
⑤	Instead of	Instead

◎ 선택형 문항의 답안은 컴퓨터용 수정 싸인펜을 사용하여 OMR답안지에 바르게 표기하시오.
◎ 서술형 문제는 답을 답안지에 반드시 검정볼펜으로 쓰시오.
◎ 총 30문항 100점 만점입니다. 문항별 배점은 각 문항에 표시되어 있습니다.

[서울 ○○중]

1. 다음 단어의 영영 풀이로 어색한 것은? (3점)

① ancient: coming from long ago in the past
② climate: the situation in which someone or something lives works, etc.
③ population: a group of people or animals of a particular kind that live in a place
④ process: a series of things that are done in order to achieve a particular result
⑤ pollen: a fine powder produced by flowers that is needed to make seeds

[충북 ○○중]

2. 다음 문장의 밑줄 친 부분과 의미가 같은 것은? (3점)

Honey is a truly wonderful food.
Honey can <u>last</u> almost forever.

① This is the <u>last</u> homework to do.
② Where did you meet her <u>last</u>?
③ He is the <u>last</u> man to tell a lie.
④ The milk can <u>last</u> till the weekend.
⑤ I went there with my sister <u>last</u> winter.

[인천 ○○중]

3. 다음 대화의 빈칸에 들어갈 말로 가장 적절한 것은? (2점)

A: My neck hurts.
B: You should be more careful not to get text neck.
A: _____
B: Yes. You need to stretch your neck often.
A: Okay, I will. Thanks.

① How often do you work out?
② What's the problem with your neck?
③ Do you know how to prevent text neck?
④ Do you know how to stretch your neck?
⑤ Are you really worried about your text neck?

[경북 ○○중]

4. 다음 중 짝지어진 대화가 어색한 것은? (4점)

① A: How can I save energy?
　 B: You need to turn off the lights when you leave the room.
② A: Can you tell me how to solve this problem?
　 B: Well, I don't know.
③ A: Do you know how to do a team project well?
　 B: Yes. You can do a team project well by listening carefully to others' opinions.
④ A: Can you explain how to slow down global warming?
　 B: No, I can't. We need to save energy.
⑤ A: Do you know how to start this machine?
　 B: I'm sorry, I don't know.

5. 다음 밑줄 친 ⓐ~ⓔ 중 어법상 올바른 것은? (4점)

- 10 percent of the people ⓐspends some money on culture.
- One-third of the eggs ⓑwas cooked.
- Most of the members ⓒdoesn't agree with the new plan.
- One of the students ⓓwere late for school.
- Around half of the Columbia's population ⓔis under the age of 15.

① ⓐ   ② ⓑ   ③ ⓒ

④ ⓓ   ⑤ ⓔ

6. 다음 빈칸에 들어갈 말로 올바른 것은? (3점)

- This food (A)_____ by tomorrow.
- We (B)_____ environment.
- Many teens (C)_____ the movie.
- The traffic rules (D)_____.
- The milk (E)_____ by March 5.

① (A): is will delivered

② (B): should be protected

③ (C): will be loved

④ (D): should follow

⑤ (E): must be sold

7. 다음 우리말을 영어로 바르게 옮긴 것은? (4점)

벌 개체 수의 약 4분의 1 정도가 매년 죽는다.

① About one-four of the bee population dies every year.

② Around four first of the bee population die each year.

③ Around quarter of the bee population die each year.

④ About a quarter of the bee population dies every year.

⑤ About one-fourth of the bee population dies every years.

8. 다음 대화에 드러난 Brian의 심경으로 가장 적절한 것은? (3점)

Aram: Brian, how's your survey going?

Brian: I'm almost done. I surveyed 10 classmates about how green they are.

Aram: What was the result of it? You don't look like you are satisfied with it.

Brian: Well, it showed my friends are not so green. Three of them recycle plastic and only 10 percent of them use both sides of a sheet of paper. I think they should think about the environment more.

Aram: Umm. Sounds like a long way to go.

① proud   ② satisfied

③ scared   ④ peaceful

⑤ concerned

9. 괄호 안의 주어진 단어를 이용하여 문장을 완성할 때, 빈칸에 들어갈 올바른 단어를 각각 쓰시오. (4점)

Facts about Canada

(1) Half of the country _____(be) covered with forest.

(2) 20 percent of the people _____(speak) French.

[10–12] 다음 대화를 읽고 물음에 답하시오.

Minho: Linda, did you see the TV program, *The Sick Planet*?
Linda: Yes, I did. (1)_____ our planet.
Minho: Me, too. We should take action (2)_____.
Linda: You're right. Hey! (3)_____ participate in Earth Hour?
Minho: Earth Hour? What's that?
Linda: It's a world movement for the environment.
Minho: Sounds great! Do you know (4)_____ it?
Linda: Sure. We turn off our lights together for an hour.
Minho: That's so simple! So, when do we do it?
Linda: Since the first Earth Hour, which began on March 31, 2007, in Sydney, Australia, it has been held worldwide on the last Saturday of March every year.
Minho: Let us join it together next year.

10. 다음 대화를 통해 알 수 없는 질문은? (3점)

① Does Linda know how to take part in Earth Hour?
② Does Minho want to look up Earth Hour on the Internet?
③ Does Minho get to know the meaning of Earth Hour through Linda?
④ Are Linda and Minho worried about the Earth?
⑤ Does Minho think that it is so simple to turn off lights together for an hour?

11. 빈 칸에 알맞은 표현을 〈보기〉에서 골라 넣으시오. (4점)

보기
ⓐ I'm not sure
ⓑ I'm worried about
ⓒ how to participate in
ⓓ Why don't we
ⓔ to save the Earth

(1)_____ (2)_____ (3)_____
(4)_____

12. 위 대화의 내용과 일치하지 않는 것은? (3점)

① Who first invented Earth Hour?
② The boy is worried about the earth.
③ Linda watched *The Sick Planet* on TV.
④ The boy wants to participate in Earth Hour to save the earth.
⑤ To participate in Earth Hour, they have to turn off their lights for an hour.

13. 다음 중 어법상 옳은 문장을 고르시오.　(3점)

① Half of the bananas were rotten.

② A quarter of the people wants to take some rest.

③ 20% of the students skips breakfast.

④ One of the books are not mine.

⑤ Both he and his brother is very tall.

15. 다음 밑줄 친 ⓐ~ⓕ 중, 가리키는 대상이 같은 것끼리 짝지어진 것은?　(3점)

What is pollination? ⓐIt is moving pollen from one flower to another to make seeds. Pollen travels in many ways. Wind, water, and animals can carry ⓑit. Insects, birds and bats can take ⓒit between flowers, so the plants can make seeds and *reproduce. It is a very important part of the life cycle of plants.

What is pollen? ⓓIt is a fine yellow powder produced by flowers. ⓔIt is so tiny that ⓕit is best seen through a *microscope.

*reproduce 번식하다

**microscope 현미경

① ⓐ, ⓑ　　　　② ⓐ, ⓒ, ⓓ

③ ⓑ, ⓒ, ⓓ　　　④ ⓒ, ⓓ, ⓔ, ⓕ

⑤ ⓑ, ⓒ, ⓓ, ⓔ, ⓕ

14. 다음 〈보기〉에서 어법상 쓰임이 옳은 것은 모두 몇 개인가?　(4점)

보기

· Each basketball team has five players.

· Every students can borrow five books.

· The number of choices we can have are just two.

· About 20 percent of the students skips breakfast.

· A quarter of the money was spent on books.

· Most of the movies that I really loved are comedies.

· There are a number of languages spoken in the country.

① 2개　　　② 3개　　　③ 4개

④ 5개　　　⑤ 6개

16. 다음 글의 글쓴이의 주장으로 적절한 것은?　(3점)

How Green My Friends Are

I surveyed 10 classmates today. The survey was about how green they are. Most of them turn off the lights when they leave rooms. Four of them take a shower in less than 5 minutes. Half of them turn off the water when they brush their teeth. Three of them recycle plastic. Only 10 percent of them use both sides of a sheet of paper. I think my friends are not so green. They should think about the environment more.

① Let's protect our environment.

② Saving water is not difficult.

③ Learning how to recycle is easy.

④ Don't forget to turn off the lights.

⑤ We should brush our teeth after a meal.

[17~20] 다음 글을 읽고 물음에 답하시오.

Where have all the honey bees gone? It is really hard to see them these days. The bees are **(A)**[appearing / disappearing]! A lot of bees die every year. This is bad news for bees, but it's even **(B)**[worse / worst] news for people. Bees are very helpful to humans. (가)First, bees give us honey. Honey is a truly wonderful food. It is good for our health and tastes great. Honey can last almost forever. In fact, we can eat honey from ancient Egypt today! Second, bees help produce many crops such as apples and strawberries. These crops need the help of bees. Bees help in the process of pollination. Pollination is **(C)**[move / moving] pollen from one flower to another to make seeds. This is done by bees. And pollen is a fine yellow powder **(D)**[producing / produced] by flowers.

18. 위 글에서 다음의 영어 단어 뜻풀이 5개 중 4개에 해당하는 단어를 찾을 수 있다. 다음 중 위 글에서 찾을 수 없는 단어의 뜻풀이는? (4점)

① coming from long ago in the past

② a long, thin piece of wood, metal, or plastic

③ plants or plant products that are grown by farmers

④ a sweet substance collected by bees and used as food

⑤ small objects produced by a plant from which a new plant can grow

19. 위 글의 괄호 (A)~(D) 안에서 글의 흐름과 어법에 알맞은 것을 차례대로 짝지은 것은? (4점)

	(A)	(B)	(C)	(D)
①	appearing	worse	move	producing
②	appearing	worst	moving	producing
③	disappearing	worst	move	producing
④	disappearing	worse	moving	produced
⑤	disappearing	worse	move	produced

17. 위 글의 밑줄 친 (가) 문장을 <보기>와 같이 바꿀 때 괄호 안에 들어갈 알맞은 단어를 고르시오. (2점)

> **보기**
> First, bees give honey (   ) us.

① to   ② for

③ of   ④ at

⑤ in

20. 위 글에 언급된 내용이 아닌 것은? (3점)

① 꿀은 건강에 좋고 맛도 좋다.

② 요즘 꿀벌 보는 것은 정말 어렵다.

③ 모든 농작물은 결코 스스로 생산될 수 없다.

④ 고대 이집트 때의 꿀은 오늘 날에도 먹을 수 있다.

⑤ 벌은 수분 과정에 도움을 준다.

[경북 ○○중]

> Then what can we do to help ⓐunderline{our little yellow friends}? First, we can plant more flowers and trees. (A) This will (가)provide a good environment for ⓑbees to live in. (B) Also, trees help slow down global warming. (C) These chemicals are unhealthy for bees and ⓒpeople. (D) ⓓOur little friends need our help. Let's not let ⓔthem down! (E)

[경북 ○○중]

21. 위 글의 ⓐ~ⓔ 중 가리키는 대상이 다른 하나는?

(2점)

① ⓐ   ② ⓑ   ③ ⓒ

④ ⓓ   ⑤ ⓔ

[인천 ○○중]

22. 위 글의 밑줄 친 (가)와 바꿔 쓸 수 있는 것은? (3점)

① hurt   ② offer

③ steal   ④ prevent

⑤ describe

[경북 ○○중]

23. 위 글 앞에 나올 내용으로 가장 알맞은 것은? (3점)

① 벌을 지키는 방법

② 벌이 의사소통하는 방법

③ 벌에 쏘였을 때 응급 처치법

④ 벌이 수분 작용을 돕는 과정

⑤ 벌의 생존이 어려워진 이유

[경북 ○○중]

24. 위 글의 (A)~(E) 중 주어진 문장이 들어갈 알맞은 곳은?

(4점)

> Second, the use of harmful chemicals on crops must be stopped.

① (A)   ② (B)   ③ (C)

④ (D)   ⑤ (E)

[울산 ○○중]

25. What can we do to provide a good environment for bees? (답은 완전한 영어 문장으로 하나만 적을 것)

(5점)

정답: ＿＿＿＿＿＿＿＿＿＿＿＿＿

＿＿＿＿＿＿＿＿＿＿＿＿＿

[경기 ○○중]

26. 위 글의 제목으로 가장 적절한 것은? (4점)

① How to Protect Bees

② Trees: Bees' Sweet Home

③ The Best Environment for People

④ How Serious Is Global Warming?

⑤ Chemicals: What Is Needed on Crops

[27~30] 다음 글을 읽고 물음에 답하시오.

Bees are very **(A)**[helpful / harmful] to humans. First, bees ⓐgive us to honey. Honey is a ⓑtruly wonderful food. It is good for our health and tastes great. Honey can last almost forever. In fact, honey from **(B)**[ancient / modern] Egypt ⓒcan be eaten today! Second, bees ⓓhelp produce many crops such as apples and strawberries. These crops cannot be produced ⓔby themselves. They **(C)**[need / need not] the help of bees. Bees help in the process of pollination.

28. 위 글의 (A), (B), (C)에서 문맥상 알맞은 말이 바르게 짝지어진 것은? (4점)

	(A)	(B)	(C)
①	helpful	ancient	need
②	harmful	ancient	need
③	helpful	ancient	need not
④	harmful	modern	need not
⑤	helpful	modern	need not

29. 위 글의 밑줄 친 ⓐ~ⓔ 중 어법상 어색한 것은? (3점)

① ⓐ 　② ⓑ 　③ ⓒ

④ ⓓ 　⑤ ⓔ

27. 위 글의 제목으로 가장 알맞은 것은? (3점)

① What Bees Do for Humans

② Honey from Ancient Egypt

③ Honey for Our Health

④ How to Save the Bees

⑤ How to Grow Crops

30. 위 글의 내용과 일치하지 않는 것은? (3점)

① Bees provide honey for us.

② Honey is good for our health.

③ Honey cannot last for a long time.

④ Many crops need the help of bees.

⑤ Bees help in the process of pollination.

◎ 선택형 문항의 답안은 컴퓨터용 수정 싸인펜을 사용하여 OMR 답안지에 바르게 표기하시오.
◎ 서술형 문제는 답을 답안지에 반드시 검정 볼펜으로 쓰시오.
◎ 총 30문항 100점 만점입니다. 문항별 배점은 각 문항에 표시되어 있습니다.

[충북 ○○중]

1. 다음 밑줄 친 단어의 쓰임이 올바르지 <u>않은</u> 것은?
(3점)

① Bees can help to <u>produce</u> many crops.
② One of the reasons is <u>climate</u> change.
③ There are many <u>ancient</u> pyramids in Egypt.
④ The air <u>population</u> is getting worse these days.
⑤ We have no sugar, so let's use maple syrup <u>instead</u>.

[부산 ○○중]

2. 빈칸에 〈보기〉와 같은 형용사가 들어갈 수 <u>없는</u> 것은?
(3점)

> **보기**
>
> useful, helpful, harmful

① Smoking is _____ to your health.
② I found a new _____ for a plastic bottle.
③ Strong sunlight is very _____ to the skin.
④ This book has a lot of _____ information.
⑤ A dictionary is very _____ for studying languages.

[서울 마포구 ○○중]

3. 다음 단어들을 배열하여 우리말의 의미에 맞게 영작할 때, 6번째에 오는 단어는?
(4점)

> 약 1/4의 돈이 음식에 사용되었다.
> a, money, was, on, about, of, food, spent, quarter, the

① was ② spent ③ money
④ quarter ⑤ about

[경기 ○○중]

4. 다음 빈칸에 들어갈 말로 알맞은 것은?
(3점)

> A: _____
> B: You need to listen carefully to others' opinions.

① Why don't you do a team project?
② What kind of project do you like?
③ How can I do well for a team project?
④ When do you think you need to listen?
⑤ What do you do to listen to others' opinions?

[경북 ○○중]

5. 다음 글이 자연스러운 대화가 되도록 (A)~(E)를 바르게 배열한 것은?
(4점)

> (A) I'm worried about him.
> (B) Oh, I'm sorry to hear that.
> (C) Jane, what's the matter?
> (D) Don't worry. He'll be okay.
> (E) My brother broke his leg.

① (A)-(C)-(E)-(B)-(D)
② (C)-(E)-(B)-(A)-(D)
③ (E)-(A)-(C)-(D)-(B)
④ (C)-(A)-(B)-(D)-(E)
⑤ (E)-(B)-(C)-(A)-(D)

6. 다음 빈칸에 are가 들어갈 문장의 개수는? (4점)

- A quarter of the students _____ studying English.
- Half of the peach _____ rotten.
- 30 percent of the milk _____ left.
- Two-thirds of the country _____ covered with mountains.
- 40 percent of the people _____ from Korea.

① 1개 ② 2개 ③ 3개
④ 4개 ⑤ 5개

8. 빈칸 (A), (B)에 들어갈 말로 옳은 것은? (3점)

- Please wait. Your dish will ___(A)___ soon.
- You should ___(B)___ this cheese by May 31st.

	(A)	(B)
①	serve	sell
②	served	sold
③	serve	be sold
④	be served	sell
⑤	be served	be sold

7. 다음 문장 전환 중 올바른 것은? (3점)

① We should follow the rules.

→ The rules should follow by us.

② John will send the letter tomorrow.

→ The letter will be send tomorrow by John.

③ Mr. Lee could bring this box.

→ This box could be bought by Mr. Lee.

④ They might choose our idea.

→ Our idea might chosen by them.

⑤ The students must wear masks at school.

→ Masks must be worn at school by the students.

9. 다음 글에서 어법상 어색한 부분을 4군데 찾아 올바른 영어로 쓰시오. (6점)

Why are bees disappearing? One of the reason is climate change. Global warming has brought extreme hot and cold weather. Bees cannot survive in these conditions. The other reason is the harmful chemicals farmers use on crops. These chemicals kill only bad insects, but also good insects, like bees.

(1) 어색한 부분 : _____

올바르게 고친 표현 : _____

(2) 어색한 부분 : _____

올바르게 고친 표현 : _____

(3) 어색한 부분 : _____

올바르게 고친 표현 : _____

(4) 어색한 부분 : _____

올바르게 고친 표현 : _____

10. 다음 대화의 빈칸에 들어갈 말로 가장 알맞은 것은?

(3점)

> Minho: Linda, did you see the TV program, *The Sick Planet*?
>
> Linda: Yes, I did. I'm worried about our planet.
>
> Minho: Same here. We should take action to save the Earth.
>
> Linda: That's right. Hey! Why don't we _____?
>
> Minho: Earth Hour? What is that?
>
> Linda: It's a world movement for the environment.
>
> Minho: Sounds great. Do you know how to take part in it?
>
> Linda: Sure. We turn off our lights together for an hour.
>
> Minho: That's so simple! So, when do we do it?
>
> Linda: I don't know. It's different every year.
>
> Minho: Let's look it up on the Internet.

① save water at home

② reduce waste at home

③ separate trash at home

④ use public transportation

⑤ participate in the Earth Hour event

11. 다음 대화의 밑줄 친 ⓐ~ⓔ 중 흐름상 어색한 것은?

(3점)

> Emily: Lucas, did you know polar bears are endangered?
>
> Lucas: Yes, I did. ⓐI read about it in an article. It's because of global warming.
>
> Emily: You're right. ⓑTheir homes are melting away and their food is disappearing.
>
> Lucas: We should do something about it.
>
> Emily: ⓒDo you know how to speed up global warming?
>
> Lucas: ⓓWell, we can start by saving energy.
>
> Emily: That's right. ⓔWe need to turn the lights off when we leave the room.
>
> Lucas: Sounds great.

① ⓐ   ② ⓑ   ③ ⓒ

④ ⓓ   ⑤ ⓔ

12. 다음 중 어법상 어색한 문장은?

(3점)

① Half of the books were stolen.

② 30 percent of the students speak French.

③ More than 40 percent of the people opposes the policy.

④ A quarter of the oil is needed to run this machine.

⑤ Two-thirds of the planet is covered with water.

13. 다음 중 수동태로 바르게 바꾼 문장은? (3점)

① We should deliver the food.

   → The food should be delivered by us.

② My mom can drive this car.

   → This car can be drove by my mom.

③ Kate will send an email within 5 minutes.

   → An email will be send by Kate within 5 minutes.

④ You must follow the traffic rules.

   → The traffic rules must be followed to you.

⑤ He will play the piano this afternoon.

   → The piano would be played by him this afternoon.

14. 밑줄 친 부분이 어법상 적절하지 <u>않은</u> 것은? (3점)

① Half of the milk <u>was</u> spilled.

② 30 percent of the students <u>speak</u> Chinese.

③ A quarter of the money <u>was</u> spent on books.

④ 10 percent of the people <u>spends</u> some money on culture.

⑤ Around half of Cambodia's population <u>is</u> under the age of 15.

I surveyed 10 classmates today. The survey was about how ⓐ<u>green</u> my friends are. Seven of ten turn off lights when they leave rooms. Four of them take shower in less than 5 minutes. Half of them turn off the water when they brush their teeth. Three of them recycle plastic. Only 10 percent of them use both sides of sheet of paper. I think my friends are not so green. They should think about the environment more.

15. 위 글에서 학생들이 가장 많이 실천한 행동은? (3점)

① 방을 나갈 때 불끄기

② 종이 양면 사용하기

③ 5분 이하로 샤워하기

④ 플라스틱 재활용하기

⑤ 양치하는 동안 물 절약하기

16. 위 글의 밑줄 친 ⓐgreen의 의미와 같게 쓰인 것은? (3점)

① Serve with a <u>green</u> salad.

② The boy was dressed all in <u>green</u>.

③ Mr. <u>Green</u> is out of town this week.

④ The light changed from red to <u>green</u>.

⑤ To go <u>green</u>, you can use paper bags instead.

17. 다음 대화를 읽고 답할 수 <u>없는</u> 질문은? (4점)

G: Jinsu, did you know that polar bears are in danger?

B: Yes. I read about it in an article. It's because of global warming.

G: Right. Their homes are melting away and their food is disappearing.

B: We should do something about it.

G: Do you know how to slow down global warming?

B: Well, we can start by saving energy.

G: Right. We need to turn off the lights when we leave the room.

*G=girl, B=boy

① Which animal is in danger?

② What's happening to our food?

③ Why are polar bears' homes melting away?

④ What does the girl suggest to save energy?

⑤ What does the boy suggest to slow down global warming?

[18~21] 다음 글을 읽고 물음에 답하시오.

Why are bees (가)<u>disappearing</u>? (A) One of the reasons is climate change. Global warming has brought extremely hot and cold weather. (B) Bees cannot survive in these conditions. Another reason is the harmful chemicals farmers use on crops. (C) These chemicals kill not only bad insects, but also good insects, like bees. Then what can we do ⓐ<u>to help</u> our little yellow friends? First, we can plant more flowers and trees. (D) Also, trees help slow down global warming. Second, the use of harmful chemicals on crops must be stopped. (E) These chemicals are unhealthy for bees and people. Our little friends need our help. Let's not let them down!

18. 위 글에서 다음 주어진 문장이 들어갈 적절한 위치는? (3점)

This will provide a good environment for bees to live in.

① (A)　　② (B)　　③ (C)

④ (D)　　⑤ (E)

19. 위 글의 밑줄 친 (가)와 용법이 <u>다른</u> 것은? (2점)

① Look at the <u>sleeping</u> lion there.

② We can start by <u>saving</u> energy.

③ I heard the water <u>boiling</u> in the kettle.

④ Tom is <u>singing</u> so loudly in the classroom.

⑤ Look at those people <u>weeping</u> during the movie.

20. 위 글의 밑줄 친 ⓐ의 to부정사와 쓰임이 같은 것은?
(3점)

① He got up early <u>to</u> catch the train.
② Do you have time <u>to</u> help me write my book report?
③ We decided <u>to</u> stay home.
④ I told you <u>to</u> stop worrying about it.
⑤ The project was <u>to</u> develop technologies.

21. 위 글을 통해서 답을 할 수 있는 것은?   (3점)

① What chemicals are safe for bees?
② How do bees help other insects?
③ What is causing global warming?
④ How many farmers use chemicals on crops?
⑤ What are the reasons that bees are disappearing?

22. 위 글의 밑줄 친 ⓐ~ⓔ 중 설명이 옳지 않은 것은?
(4점)

① ⓐ는 '더 많은 꽃과 나무를 심는 것'을 의미한다.
② ⓑ는 'to slow'로 바꿔 쓸 수 있다.
③ ⓒ는 의미상 수동형인 'is must stopped'로 바꿔 써야 한다.
④ ⓓ는 'bees'를 의미한다.
⑤ ⓔ는 'disappoint them'의 의미이다.

23. 위 글의 밑줄 친 (A)to help와 어법상 쓰임이 같은 것은?
(3점)

① <u>To learn</u> English is fun.
② His dream is <u>to be</u> an actor.
③ I want <u>to have</u> a hamburger and Coke for lunch.
④ My mom made a promise <u>to buy</u> a watch for me.
⑤ You should study hard <u>to get</u> a good grade.

24. 위 글의 앞에 나올 내용으로 가장 적절한 것은? (3점)

① 벌에 쏘일 때의 대처 방법
② 여왕벌과 일벌의 역할
③ 벌들이 많이 거주하는 장소
④ 벌의 생존이 어려워진 이유
⑤ 벌이 서로 의사소통을 하는 방법

[22-24] 다음 글을 읽고 물음에 답하시오.

Then what can we do (A)<u>to help</u> our little yellow friends? First, we can plant more flowers and trees. ⓐ<u>This</u> will provide a good environment for bees to live in. Also, trees help ⓑ<u>slow</u> down global warming. Second, the use of harmful chemicals on crops ⓒ <u>must stop</u>. These chemicals are unhealthy for bees and people. ⓓ<u>Our little friends</u> need our help. Let's not ⓔ<u>let them down</u>!

(A)_____

Where have all the honey bees gone? ⓐIt is really hard to see them these days. The bees are disappearing! About a third of the bee population dies every year. This is bad news for bees, but it's ⓑeven worse news for people.

Bees are very (B)_____ to humans. First, ⓒbees give us honey. Honey is a truly wonderful food. It is good for our health and ⓓtastes great. Honey can ⓔlast almost forever. In fact, honey from ancient Egypt can be eaten today! Second, bees help produce many crops such as apples and strawberries. These crops cannot be produced by themselves. They need the help of bees. Bees help in the process of (C)_____.

Then, why are bees disappearing? One of the reasons is climate change. Global warming has brought extremely hot and cold weather. Bees cannot survive in these conditions. Another reason is the harmful chemicals such as pesticides* that farmers use on crops. These chemicals kill not only bad insects, but also good insects, like bees. Many experts also add that habitat loss and bee-diseases can be the reasons of bees' reduction.

*pesticide: 농약, 살충제

25. 위 글의 빈칸 (A)에 들어갈 제목으로 가장 적절한 것은? (4점)

① What is Pollination?
② Disappearing Honey Bees
③ How to Get Honey Bees
④ Honey Bees as Pollinators
⑤ Useful Honey Bees to Humans

26. 위 글의 빈칸 (B)에 들어갈 의미로 적절하지 <u>않은</u> 것은? (3점)

① useful   ② harmful
③ helpful   ④ beneficial
⑤ advantageous

27. 위 글의 빈칸 (C)에 들어갈 단어로 알맞은 것은? (3점)

① pollen   ② position
③ pollution   ④ pollination
⑤ population

28. 위 글의 밑줄 친 ⓐ~ⓔ 중 설명이 옳은 것은? (3점)

① ⓐ는 'the honey bee'를 의미한다.

② ⓑ는 비교급을 강조하는 부사로 '훨씬'의 의미로 해석된다.

③ ⓒ는 'bees give honey for us.'로 형식을 바꿔 쓸 수 있다.

④ ⓓ는 'tastes greatly'가 어법상 옳다.

⑤ ⓔ는 '맨 마지막의', '최후의'라는 의미로 사용되었다.

30. 위 글의 내용과 일치하지 않는 것은? (4점)

① 벌은 인간에게 매우 도움이 된다.

② 벌 개체 수의 약 3분의 1이 매년 죽는다.

③ 벌은 농작물들을 생산하는 데 도움을 준다.

④ 고대 이집트 때의 꿀을 오늘날에도 먹을 수 있다.

⑤ 사과와 딸기를 제외한 농작물들은 벌의 도움 없이도 스스로 생산할 수 있다.

29. 위 글을 읽고 나눈 대화 중 내용과 다른 것은? (4점)

① A: We can't find bees easily these days.

B: Right. Many bees are disappearing.

② A: Bees are exposed to many dangers.

B: I'm sorry to hear that.

③ A: Bees can't live in extreme weather conditions.

B: I agree. Bees are affected by climate change.

④ A: Farmers need to use more chemicals on crops.

B: Sure. Using them makes crops grow well.

⑤ A: Global warming is one of the causes of disappearing bees.

B: That's true.

3학년 영어 1학기 기말고사(3과) 1회

문항수 : 선택형(28문항) 서술형(1문항) 20 . . .

반	
이름	

점수

◎ 선택형 문항의 답안은 컴퓨터용 수정 싸인펜을 사용하여 OMR 답안지에 바르게 표기하시오.
◎ 서술형 문제는 답을 답안지에 반드시 검정 볼펜으로 쓰시오.
◎ 총 29문항 100점 만점입니다. 문항별 배점은 각 문항에 표시되어 있습니다.

[서울 강남구 ○○중]

1. 다음 중 빈칸에 필요 없는 단어는? (3점)

· I usually get _____ at 6 in the morning.
· My family got _____ last Saturday.
· Do you get _____ with your sister?
· You need to get _____ the No. 21 bus.

① up
② on
③ together
④ along
⑤ from

[울산 ○○중]

2. 다음 밑줄 친 부분을 바르게 해석하지 못한 것은? (4점)

① Let's get together in a few days. (모이다)
② They should get dressed quickly. (옷을 입다)
③ She got up late yesterday morning. (일어났다)
④ An old lady got on the bus. ([버스·기차에] 탔다)
⑤ He tries to get away with his friends. (~와 잘 지내다)

[서울 강남구 ○○중]

3. 다음 중 빈칸에 들어갈 말로 바르게 짝지은 것은? (3점)

· I'm (A)_____ to see her again.
· The movie was so (B)_____ that everyone fell asleep.

	(A)	(B)
①	surprised	bored
②	surprising	exciting
③	thrilled	scared
④	exciting	scared
⑤	excited	boring

[경북 ○○중]

4. 다음 대화의 빈칸에 들어갈 말로 알맞은 것은? (3점)

A: _____
B: Please put the cookies into the gift boxes.

① Can I ask you a favor?
② What do you want me to do?
③ Can you give me a hand?
④ Why did you make these cookies?
⑤ Where did you put the cookies?

[서울 마포구 ○○중]

5. 다음 대화가 자연스럽게 이어지도록 할 때, 주어진 문장이 들어갈 알맞은 위치는? (3점)

Can you give me a hand?

A: What are all these boxes and books for? (A)
B: I'm packing the books for the donation center. (B)
A: Sure. What do you want me to do? (C)
B: Please write the address on the boxes. (D)
A: No problem. (E)

① (A)
② (B)
③ (C)
④ (D)
⑤ (E)

[인천 ○○중]

Woman: Good morning. May I help you?
Tony: Hi, I'm here for the volunteer work.
Woman: Oh, you **(A)**[must / have to] be Tony.
Tony: That's right. What do you want me to do today?
Woman: Read this book for **(B)**[a / the] blind in the recording room.
Tony: No problem. Should I go in now?
Woman: Yes. Please go into Room 7.
Tony: Okay. Is there anything **(C)**[keeping / to keep] in mind?
Woman: Yes. Make sure you read slowly and clearly.
Tony: Okay. I'll do my best.

7. 위 대화의 괄호 (A), (B), (C)에 들어갈 말로 적절한 것은? (4점)

	(A)	(B)	(C)
①	must	a	keeping
②	must	the	to keep
③	must	the	keeping
④	have to	a	keeping
⑤	have to	the	to keep

[경북 ○○중]

8. 다음 대화의 밑줄 친 do[did] 중 그 쓰임이 다른 하나는? (3점)

A: What did you ⓐdo yesterday?
B: I ⓑdid my homework with my friends.
A: What was your homework?
B: It was drawing a poster and I ⓒdid my best.
A: What are you planning to ⓓdo tomorrow?
B: I'm going to watch a baseball game. I ⓔdo like watching a baseball game.

① ⓐ   ② ⓑ   ③ ⓒ
④ ⓓ   ⑤ ⓔ

[충북 ○○중]

6. What does the woman want Tony to do? (3점)

① She wants him to read a book fast and clearly.
② She wants him to read a book for the deaf.
③ She wants him to call his friends for the blind.
④ She wants him to read a book for the blind.
⑤ She wants him to learn how to read a book without any help.

[충북 ○○중]

9. 다음 우리말을 영어로 잘못 바꾼 것은? (4점)

① 화분에 물 주는 것을 확실히 해라.
   → Make sure you plant trees.
② TV 끄는 것을 확실히 해라.
   → Make sure you turn off the TV.
③ 문 잠그는 것을 확실히 해라.
   → Make sure you lock the door.
④ 개에게 먹이 주는 것을 확실히 해라.
   → Make sure you feed the dog.
⑤ 창문들을 닫는 것을 확실히 해라.
   → Make sure you close the windows.

10. 다음 문장의 밑줄 친 as와 쓰임이 같은 것은? (3점)

> <u>As</u> I was taking a picture, a light went on in my head. I thought, "I'm in the school art club."

① You'd better do <u>as</u> Mom asks.

② <u>As</u> it was late, I went to bed.

③ The kids used an old blanket <u>as</u> a tent.

④ The phone rang just <u>as</u> we were leaving.

⑤ <u>As</u> she has no car, she can't get there easily.

11. 다음 〈보기〉 문장이 글의 흐름상 (A)~(E) 중, 들어갈 가장 적절한 곳은?　(4점)

> 보기
>
> I suggested this idea at the next club meeting, and the members loved it.

> Many people like to take pictures in front of wall paintings. They make old neighborhoods bright and new. (A) Last month, I visited a village with wall paintings in Yeosu. (B) As I was taking a picture, a light went on in my head. (C) I thought, "I'm in the school art club. (D) Why don't we do wall paintings like these?" (E)

① (A)　　　② (B)　　　③ (C)

④ (D)　　　⑤ (E)

12. 다음 글을 읽고 'have'를 이용하여 쓴 문장 중 어법이 올바른 것은?　(3점)

> Some teachers at school give us advice. A says, "Be quiet in class!" B says, "Pick up trash on the ground!" C says, "Hand in the report on time!" D says, "Get along with your friends!" E says, "Read many books!" It's not easy to be a good student.

① A has us was quiet in class.

② B has us picked up trash on the ground.

③ C has us handed in the report on time.

④ D has us get along with our friends.

⑤ E has us reads many books.

13. 다음 중 어법에 맞는 문장 2개를 고른 것은?　(4점)

① I'm going to talking about my trip. I am really looking forward to giving great details.

② I'm going to read the book. I am looking forward to finding out what happens.

③ I'm going to go home next weekend. I am looking forward to see my dogs.

④ I'm going to painting my face. I am looking forward to having a cool design.

⑤ I'm going to make a mask. I'm looking forward to coloring it.

14. 다음 인터넷 기사에 대한 댓글이 바르지 <u>않은</u> 것은?
(3점)

> Yesterday Dream Middle School students planted 20 trees in the neighborhood park. They plan to plant trees every year.

① It was yesterday that they planted 20 trees.

② It was Dream Middle School students that planted trees in the neighborhood park.

③ It was 20 trees that they planted in the neighborhood park.

④ It was in the neighborhood park that they planted 20 trees.

⑤ It is every month that they plan to plant trees.

15. 다음 대화의 빈칸 (A)와 (B)에 들어갈 말이 바르게 연결된 것은?
(3점)

> Tony: What do you want me to do today?
> Woman: Please (A)_____.
> Tony: Okay, is there anything else?
> Woman: Yes. Make sure you (B)_____
> _____.

① A: giving the dog a bath
   B: brush the fur first

② A: to visit the nursing home
   B: take books with you

③ A: deliver meals to the elderly
   B: greet them politely

④ A: arranging the books on the table
   B: take out the garbage

⑤ A: go to the bookstore to get the magazines
   B: told the librarian "hello" for me

16. 다음 〈보기〉의 단어들을 우리말과 같은 뜻이 되도록 배열할 때 다섯 번째 오는 것은?
(4점)

> **보기**
> 그녀가 지난 주말에 심은 것은 바로 장미들이었어.
> → (planted / it / roses / weekend / she / was / that / last)

① she   ② roses

③ was   ④ weekend

⑤ that

[17–18] 다음 글을 읽고 물음에 답하시오.

> Many people like to take pictures in front of wall paintings. ⓐThey make old neighborhoods bright and new.
> Last month, I visited a village with wall paintings in Yeosu. As I was talking a picture, a light went on in my head. I thought, "I'm in the school art club. Why don't we do wall paintings like ⓑthese?" I suggested (A)this idea at the next club meeting, and the members loved it.
> We found a teen volunteer project on the Internet. The project was to do a wall painting in our neighborhood. We applied for ⓒit, and two weeks later, our club was selected!

17. 위 글의 밑줄 친 ⓐ~ⓒ가 가리키는 것으로 가장 적절하게 짝지은 것은? (4점)

　　　　ⓐ　　　　　　ⓑ　　　　　　ⓒ

① Many people - wall paintings - the Internet

② Many people - the members - the project

③ Wall paintings - wall paintings - the project

④ Wall paintings - the members - the project

⑤ Wall paintings - wall paintings - the Internet

We found a teen volunteer project on the Internet. The project was to do a wall painting in our neighborhood. We (가)apply it, and two weeks later, our club (나)select!

The day of the project finally came. The project manager had us meet at the painting site at 9 a.m. The wall was in very poor condition. There were strange writings and drawings on some parts. Other parts had old posters on them. We removed the posters first and (다)paint the writings and drawings with white paint.

The manager let us (A)_____ anything we wanted. We decided (B)_____ something cute (a)_____ the wall was near an elementary school. We divided into three groups and began (C)_____. I was in the group with Minsu and Jiwon. I chose my spot and started to paint my favorite movie character. Minsu (D)_____ some flowers and Jiwon did some background drawings.

* I=Homin

---

18. 위 글의 밑줄 친 (A)가 의미하는 것으로 가장 적절한 것은? (3점)

① taking pictures

② doing wall paintings

③ applying for the contest

④ joining the school art club

⑤ finding a teen volunteer project

---

19. 위 글의 We가 한 일이 아닌 것은? (4점)

① 그룹으로 나누어서 그리기

② 프로젝트 관리자가 원하는 것을 그리기

③ 벽의 한 부분에 있는 낡은 포스터 제거하기

④ 하얀색 페인트로 글들과 그림들 위에 덧칠하기

⑤ 벽에 영화 속 등장인물, 꽃들, 배경 그림들을 그리기

20. 위 글의 (A)~(D)에 들어갈 수 있는 단어의 형태가 <u>아</u>닌 것은? (4점)

① paint

② paints

③ to paint

④ painted

⑤ painting

21. 위 글에서 밑줄 친 (가), (나), (다)에 알맞은 형태로 짝지어진 것은? (3점)

(가)	(나)	(다)
① applied to	selected	painted out
② applied for	is selecting	painted over
③ applied to	was selected	painted out
④ applied to	selects	painted out
⑤ applied for	was selected	painted over

22. 위 글의 빈칸 (a)에 들어갈 단어가 사용된 문장을 고르면? (4점)

① Where have all the honey bees gone?

② That's exactly what I'm thinking of.

③ When I was young, my dream was to be a singer.

④ I'm pretty busy because I have to finish my homework.

⑤ Even if you are having a hard time now, I believe you will succeed someday.

23. 위 글의 내용을 바르게 이해한 학생들만을 있는 대로 고른 것은? (4점)

Kate: Homin's club members met near the middle school in the afternoon.

Mina: The condition of the wall was not good.

Brian: Homin's club members removed old posters and put new ones on the wall.

Yuna: The manager painted over old posters with green paint.

Peter: Homin's club members could paint the things that they wanted.

① Kate, Brian

② Mina, Yuna

③ Kate, Yuna, Peter

④ Mina, Peter

⑤ Kate, Mina, Brian, Yuna

24. 위 글의 내용과 일치하는 것은? (3점)

① 인터넷을 통해 지원한 다양한 클럽들이 모였다.

② 그림을 그릴 벽의 상태는 비교적 좋았다.

③ 우리가 원하는 것을 그릴 수 있었다.

④ 동네 분위기상 귀여운 그림은 어울리지 않았다.

⑤ 기존에 있던 벽화와 어울리는 그림을 그렸다.

[충북 ○○중]

Our club painted for about five hours. After we finished, we got together and shared the day's experiences. ⓐMinsu was very proud of his flower painting. ⓑHe said, "My flower is so real that a bee landed on it." ⓒI said, "Drawing on a wall was (A)_____ harder than drawing on paper."

ⓓWe all agreed that our wall painting wasn't perfect. ⓔBut it matters. We made our neighborhood a little brighter and happier. (B)We were proud of us. We didn't just paint pictures on a wall that day. It was a better tomorrow (C)_____ we painted.

27. 위 글의 빈칸 (A)에 들어가기에 <u>어색한</u> 것은? (3점)

① very　　　　② far

③ even　　　　④ still

⑤ much

[서울 강남구 ○○중]

25. 위 글의 밑줄 친 ⓐ~ⓔ 중 글의 흐름상 <u>어색한</u> 것은?

(4점)

① ⓐ　　　　② ⓑ　　　　③ ⓒ

④ ⓓ　　　　⑤ ⓔ

[충북 ○○중]

28. 위 글의 밑줄 친 (B)에서 어법상 <u>어색한</u> 것을 고쳐 다시 쓰시오. (4점)

→ _____

[서울 강남구 ○○중]

26. 위 글의 글쓴이가 느끼는 감정으로 알맞은 것은?

(3점)

① proud

② sad

③ disappointed

④ curious

⑤ upset

[서울 마포구 ○○중]

29. 위 글의 빈칸 (C)에 들어갈 알맞은 말은? (3점)

① when　　　　② what

③ which　　　　④ than

⑤ that

3학년 영어 1학기 기말고사(3과) 2회

반		점수	
이 름			

문항수 : 선택형(29문항) 서술형(1문항)　　20 ． ． ．

◎ 선택형 문항의 답안은 컴퓨터용 수정 싸인펜을 사용하여 OMR 답안지에 바르게 표기하시오.
◎ 서술형 문제는 답을 답안지에 반드시 검정 볼펜으로 쓰시오.
◎ 총 30문항 100점 만점입니다. 문항별 배점은 각 문항에 표시되어 있습니다.

1. 다음 빈칸에 공통으로 들어갈 단어는?　　(3점)

· My mom _____ me clean my room.
· The teachers _____ us study hard.

① have
② made
③ told
④ wanted
⑤ lets

2. 다음 중 단어와 영영풀이가 바르게 연결되지 않은 것은?　　(3점)

① stick – to take part in an activity
② mess – a very dirty or untidy condition
③ suggest – to mention something as a possibility
④ wrap – to cover something around something else
⑤ challenge – a new or difficult task that tests somebody's ability and skill

3. 다음 빈칸에 들어갈 수 <u>없는</u> 것은?　　(3점)

The teacher _____ us make mind maps about what we learned.

① let
② had
③ made
④ asked
⑤ helped

4. 다음 대화의 빈칸에 들어갈 말로 알맞은 것은? (3점)

A: It's time to go home.
B: Make sure you turn off the lights.
A: Okay, I will. _____
B: No, that's it. See you tomorrow.

① What time is it?
② Anything else?
③ I should go now.
④ How is everything?
⑤ Make sure you lock the doors.

5. 다음 밑줄 친 (A)와 바꿔 쓸 수 있는 문장은?　　(3점)

B: (A)What do you want me to do?
G: I want you to put the cookies in the gift boxes.

① What do you like to do?
② What can I do for you?
③ What's the matter with you?
④ How can I bake many cookies?
⑤ Why don't we help her make cookies?

[경기 ○○중]

Woman: Good morning. What can I do for you?

Tony: Hi. I'm here for the volunteer work.

Woman: Oh, you must be Tony.

Tony: That's right. (A)_____

Woman: Please read this book for the blind in the recording room.

Tony: No problem. Should I go in now?

Woman: Yes. Please go into Room 7.

Tony: Okay. Is there anything to keep in mind?

Woman: Yes. (B)Make sure you read slowly and clearly.

Tony: Okay. I'll do my best.

[경기 ○○중]

6. 위 대화의 빈칸 (A)에 들어가기에 가장 적절한 것은? (3점)

① I'll never give up!

② How have you been?

③ How long does the work take?

④ What do you want me to do today?

⑤ Let me tell you about the volunteer work.

[경기 ○○중]

7. 위 대화의 밑줄 친 (B)의 의도로 적절한 것은? (3점)

① 당부하기   ② 안부 묻기

③ 동의하기   ④ 보고하기

⑤ 허락 구하기

[경기 ○○중]

8. 다음 밑줄 친 it과 쓰임이 같은 것은? (2점)

It is boring to stay at home all weekend.

① It is Monday.

② It is in my bag.

③ It is impossible to eat all of this food.

④ It is too expensive, so I can't buy it.

⑤ It is too hot and humid here in summer.

[서울 마포구 ○○중]

9. 다음 문장의 밑줄 친 부분을 강조하는 구문으로 바꿀 때, 알맞은 것은? (4점)

I painted some roses in the garden on April 5th.

① It is some roses where I planted in the garden on April 5th.

② It was some roses that I planted in the garden on April 5th.

③ It were some roses that I planted in the garden on April 5th.

④ It is some roses that I planted were in the garden on April 5th.

⑤ It was some roses what I planted in the garden on April 5th.

10. What is the teacher talking about?　　(4점)

Teacher: Hello, class. Make groups of four people and sit around the tables. Today we're going to make bacon and egg sandwiches. Keep in mind two rules for our class. First, make sure you wash your hands before you start. Second, be careful when you use a knife. All right, let's start.

① Making friends in class.
② Making groups and sitting around the table.
③ How to wash hands before making food.
④ How to use a knife before making food.
⑤ Class rules before making sandwiches.

11. 다음 두 사람의 대화가 자연스럽도록 (A)~(C)를 바르게 배열한 것은?　　(3점)

B: What are all these boxes and books for?
 (A) Sure. What do you want me to do?
 (B) I'm packing the books for the donation center. Can you give me a hand?
 (C) Please write down the address on the boxes.
B: No problem.

① (A) - (B) - (C)
② (A) - (C) - (B)
③ (B) - (A) - (C)
④ (B) - (C) - (A)
⑤ (C) - (B) - (A)

12. 다음 중 짝지어진 대화가 <u>어색한</u> 것은?　　(3점)

① A: Make sure you close the windows.
　 B: Okay, I will.
② A: What do you want me to do?
　 B: Please take out the trash.
③ A: What do you think about the movie?
　 B: I think it's good. The acting is so great.
④ A: Is there anything to keep in mind?
　 B: Yes. Make sure you feed the dog.
⑤ A: I don't like raising pets. It takes a lot of time to take care of them.
　 B: I'm with you on that. They make us happy.

13. 다음 대화의 밑줄 친 ⓐ~ⓔ 중 문맥상 어휘 설명이 옳은 것은?　　(4점)

B: What are all these boxes and books for?
G: I'm ⓐpacking the books for the ⓑdonation center. Can you give me ⓒa hand?
B: Sure. What do you want me to do?
G: Please write the ⓓaddress on the boxes.
B: ⓔNo problem.

① ⓐ: remove or take out
② ⓑ: a person who performs voluntary work
③ ⓒ: physical assistance or help
④ ⓓ: give a speech to
⑤ ⓔ: Of course not.

14. 다음 중 우리말을 바르게 영작한 것은? (3점)

① 지배인은 민호가 그녀의 전화를 사용하게 했다.

→ The manager let Minho using her phone.

② 우리 할아버지는 내게 창문을 열게 하셨다.

→ My grandpa made me to open the window.

③ 치과의사는 내게 입을 벌리게 했다.

→ The dentist had me opened the mouth.

④ 엄마는 내게 매일 아침 7시에 일어나게 하신다.

→ My mom makes me get up at 7 every morning.

⑤ 나는 나의 개가 내 침대에서 자게 두었다.

→ I let sleep my dog on my bed.

15. 다음 중, It ~ that 쓰임이 나머지 넷과 성격이 <u>다른 한</u> 문장은? (4점)

① It was the vase that Jake broke yesterday.

② It was certain that I would pass the exam.

③ It was a novel that John borrowed from a library.

④ It was on the roof that the hen laid two eggs.

⑤ It was on the wall that he painted a big tree yesterday.

16. 다음 글에서 교사의 조언으로 언급되지 <u>않은</u> 것은? (3점)

> Some teachers at school give us advice. Ms. Brown says, "Be quiet in class!" Mr. Choi says, "Pick up trash on the ground!" Ms. Smith says, "Hand in the report on time!" Ms. Kim says, "Get along with your friends!" Mr. Green says, "Read many books!" It's not easy to be a good student.

① 수업 중에 조용히 하기

② 바닥에 떨어진 쓰레기 줍기

③ 보고서 제시간에 제출하기

④ 친구와 사이좋게 지내기

⑤ 많은 책을 구입하기

17. 다음 ⓐ~ⓕ 중 어법상 옳은 것을 있는 대로 고른 것은? (4점)

> ⓐ Daniel made his brother turn off the TV.
> ⓑ Ms. Kim has us get along with our friends.
> ⓒ My sister always helps me to clean the garden.
> ⓓ Has your girlfriend ever made you to do her homework?
> ⓔ I don't know why she let her little daughter buy a lot of clothes.
> ⓕ The teacher got the students memorize the poem.

① ⓐ, ⓑ

② ⓒ, ⓓ, ⓔ

③ ⓑ, ⓓ, ⓕ

④ ⓐ, ⓑ, ⓒ, ⓔ

⑤ ⓒ, ⓓ, ⓔ, ⓕ

18. 다음 〈보기〉의 that과 그 쓰임이 같은 것은? (3점)

보기

It was a bird <u>that</u> broke the window yesterday.

① Mina is looking for the pen <u>that</u> Jake lost yesterday.
② It was a lie <u>that</u> he graduated from high school.
③ I think <u>that</u> Korea is a beautiful country.
④ It was a novel <u>that</u> Mike borrowed from a library last week.
⑤ The only problem <u>that</u> I have is money.

19. 다음 밑줄 친 ⓐ∼ⓔ 중, 어법상 어색한 것은? (3점)

Hello, class. Today we're going to make bacon and egg sandwiches. Keep in mind three rules for our class. First, make sure you ⓐ<u>to wash</u> your hands ⓑ<u>before</u> you start. Second, ⓒ<u>be careful</u> when you use a knife. Lastly, remember ⓓ<u>to turn off</u> the gas stove ⓔ<u>when</u> you finish cooking.

① ⓐ   ② ⓑ   ③ ⓒ
④ ⓓ   ⑤ ⓔ

[20~26] 다음 글을 읽고 물음에 답하시오.

The manager let us paint ⓐ<u>anything</u> we wanted. We decided (A)<u>to paint</u> something ⓑ<u>cute</u> because the wall was near an elementary school. We divided into three groups and began painting. I was in the group with Minsu and Jiwon. I chose my spot and started to paint my favorite movie character. Minsu painted some flowers and Jiwon did some background drawings.

Our club painted for about five hours. After we finished, we got together and ⓒ<u>shared</u> the day's experiences. Minsu was very proud of his flower painting. He said, "My flower is so ⓓ<u>artificial</u> that a bee landed on it." I said, "Drawing on a wall was (B)_____ harder than drawing on paper."

We all agreed that our wall painting wasn't perfect. But it didn't matter. We made our neighborhood a little (C)_____. We were ⓔ<u>proud</u> of ourselves. We didn't just paint pictures on a wall that day. (가)<u>우리가 그린 것은 바로 더 나은 내일이었어.</u>

*I=Homin

20. 위 글의 ⓐ∼ⓔ 중 문맥상 어색한 것은? (4점)

① ⓐ   ② ⓑ   ③ ⓒ
④ ⓓ   ⑤ ⓔ

21. 위 글의 밑줄 친 (A)의 to paint와 용법이 같은 문장은 몇 개인가? (3점)

ⓐ My job is to teach students in middle school.
ⓑ It is important to be on time.
ⓒ I study hard to make my dream come true.
ⓓ I planned to take a train to Busan.
ⓔ There is something to tell you.

① 1개   ② 2개   ③ 3개
④ 4개   ⑤ 5개

22. 위 글의 빈칸 (B)에 들어갈 말로 알맞지 않은 것은? (3점)

① far   ② still
③ much   ④ a lot
⑤ more

23. 위 글의 빈칸 (C)에 들어갈 말로 가장 적절한 것은? (3점)

① upset and angry
② tired and worried
③ harder and worse
④ brighter and happier
⑤ darker and more nervous

24. 위 글의 밑줄 친 (가)의 우리말을 영어로 옮기시오. (eight words) (5점)

→ _____

25. 위 글을 통해서 알 수 있는 주인공의 심정으로 알맞은 것은? (3점)

① lonely
② shameful
③ disappointed
④ proud
⑤ nervous

26. 위 글의 내용과 일치하지 않는 것은? (4점)

① Homin painted his favorite movie character.
② Jiwon painted some background drawings.
③ Homin's club members shared the day's experiences after the volunteer work.
④ Minsu was proud of his flower painting.
⑤ Homin's club members perfectly painted pictures on a wall.

Hi. My name is Homin. This is ⓐme in front of the wall painting. The wings are so pretty, aren't ⓑthey? Many people like to take pictures in front of wall paintings. ⓒThey make old neighborhoods bright and new.

Last month, I visited a village with wall paintings in Yeosu. (A)As I was taking a picture, (B)a light went on in my head. I thought, "I'm in the school art club. Why don't we do wall paintings like these?" I suggested ⓓthis idea at the next club meeting, and the members loved it.

We found a teen volunteer project on the Internet. The project was to do a wall painting in our neighborhood. We applied for ⓔit, and two weeks later, our club was selected!

The day of the project finally came. The project manager had us meet at the painting site at 9 a.m. The wall was in very poor condition. There were strange writings and drawings on some parts. Other parts had old posters on them. We removed the posters first and painted over the writings and drawings with white paint.

27. 위 글의 ⓐ~ⓔ가 의미하는 것으로 어색한 것은?

(4점)

① ⓐ: 'Homin'
② ⓑ: 'the wings of the wall painting'
③ ⓒ: 'wall paintings'
④ ⓓ: 'visiting Yeosu'
⑤ ⓔ: 'the project'

28. 위 글의 밑줄 친 (A)As와 의미가 같은 것은? (3점)

① I will do it as I planned.
② As Tom grew older, he became wiser.
③ As it was a holiday, all banks were closed.
④ As a manager, I am in charge of this department.
⑤ We had a talk as we were waiting for them.

29. 위 글의 밑줄 친 (B)a light went on in my head의 뜻은? (4점)

① I left a light on.
② A light bulb hit my head.
③ A great idea occurred to me.
④ A lighting flashed over my head.
⑤ I turned on the flash of my camera.

30. 위 글의 내용과 일치하지 않는 것은? (3점)

① The school art club applied for the volunteer project.
② Old neighborhoods look better because of wall paintings.
③ While Homin was taking a picture, he came up with a good idea.
④ School art club members agreed to do a wall painting in their neighborhood.
⑤ Homin suggested painting for the art competition at the art club meeting.

◎ 선택형 문항의 답안은 컴퓨터용 수정 싸인펜을 사용하여 OMR답안지에 바르게 표기하시오.
◎ 서술형 문제는 답을 답안지에 반드시 검정볼펜으로 쓰시오.
◎ 총 30문항 100점 만점입니다. 문항별 배점은 각 문항에 표시되어 있습니다.

[경기 ○○중]

1. 다음 빈칸 (A)~(C)에 들어갈 말로 알맞은 것은? (3점)

· He (A)_____ to develop muscle.
· Drinking coffee keeps him (B)_____.
· It was a great (C)_____ to have the school so near.

	(A)	(B)	(C)
①	climb	awaken	character
②	exercise	awaken	object
③	exercises	awake	interest
④	work out	awake	condition
⑤	works out	awake	convenience

[경북 ○○중]

2. 다음 두 문장의 의미가 같도록 할 때, 빈칸에 들어갈 말로 알맞은 것은? (2점)

· The chair behind the tree is mine.
· The chair behind the tree _____ me.

① turns off   ② owes to
③ belongs to   ④ brushes off
⑤ stands for

[인천 ○○중]

3. 다음 중 밑줄 친 단어의 의미가 나머지 넷과 다른 것은? (3점)

① Since I was hungry, I had a whole pizza.
② She has written many books since she left college.
③ I couldn't call my friend since I didn't have my phone.
④ Since the sunlight was very strong, she had to wear her hat.
⑤ He is looking forward to the trip since he has never been to New Zealand.

[경기 ○○중]

4. 다음 밑줄 친 문장과 바꿔 쓸 수 있는 것을 <보기>에서 있는 대로 고른 것은? (4점)

A: I think reading books on a smartphone is good. We can read anytime.
B: You are absolutely right.

보기
ⓐ I don't agree.
ⓑ No doubt about it.
ⓒ I'm with you on that.
ⓓ That's exactly how I feel.
ⓔ I couldn't agree with you more.

① ⓒ, ⓓ   ② ⓐ, ⓑ, ⓓ
③ ⓒ, ⓓ, ⓔ   ④ ⓐ, ⓑ, ⓒ, ⓓ
⑤ ⓑ, ⓒ, ⓓ, ⓔ

5. 다음 중 우리말을 바르게 영작한 것은? (4점)

① 네가 더 높이 올라가면 올라갈수록, 더 멀리 본다.

　The higher you climb, the far you see.

② 그녀는 대학을 떠난 이후로 많은 책을 써왔다.

　She wrote many books since she left college.

③ 바빴기 때문에, 나는 친구를 도와줄 수가 없었다.

　As I was busy, I couldn't help my friend.

④ 네가 돈을 덜 쓰면 쓸수록, 더 많이 절약한다.

　The little you spend, the more you save.

⑤ 그는 그 사고 때문에 많이 달라졌다.

　He has changed a lot since the accident.

[6-7] 다음 대화를 읽고 물음에 답하시오.

> A: Hey, Anna. Why are you always drinking energy drinks?
> B: Because they help me ⓐstay awake.
> A: (A)_____, but they have a lot of caffeine.
> B: Well, they help me ⓑto focus on my studies.
> A: Did you know that ⓒtoo many caffeine can hurt your bones?
> B: Oh, I didn't know that.
> A: I think ⓓthat you should drink energy drinks ⓔless often.
> B: Maybe you're right. Thanks, Tom.

6. 위 대화의 흐름상, 빈칸 (A)에 들어갈 표현으로 적절하지 않은 것은? (3점)

① I don't agree

② I'm with you on that

③ You're totally right

④ You can say that again

⑤ That's exactly how I feel

7. 위 대화의 밑줄 친 ⓐ~ⓔ 중, 어법상 맞지 않는 것은? (3점)

① ⓐ　　② ⓑ　　③ ⓒ　　④ ⓓ　　⑤ ⓔ

[8-9] 다음 대화를 읽고 물음에 답하시오.

> A: What are all these boxes, Suji?
> B: They're items I ordered online.
> A: You like shopping on the Internet, don't you?
> B: Yes, I do. How do you feel about online shopping, Tony?
> A: I don't like it at all.
> B: Why?
> A: It's very difficult to know what an item actually looks like.
> B: Yes, it's true.
> A: It's also difficult to return an item if you don't like it.
> B: You're right, but I think it's very convenient.
> A: Well, convenience isn't everything.

8. 위 대화의 내용과 일치하지 않는 것은? (4점)

① Suji ordered items online.

② Suji likes online shopping.

③ Tony doesn't like online shopping.

④ Tony thinks returning an item that he buys online is easy.

⑤ Suji thinks online shopping is convenient.

9. 위 대화를 읽고 대답할 수 없는 질문은? (3점)

① What are they talking about?

② Where does this talk take place?

③ Where did Suji order items?

④ Why doesn't Tony like online shopping?

⑤ How does Suji feel about shopping on the Internet?

A: Brian, did you hear the news?

B: What news?

A: We can use smartphones during classes from next week.

B: Yes, I heard that.

A: (A)_____

B: I think it will be very useful. I can look up words I don't know.

A: Yeah. We can also find information on the Internet.

B: Right. It will be very (B)_____.

[경북 ○○중]

10. 위 대화의 빈칸 (A), (B)에 들어갈 말이 순서대로 연결된 것은? (3점)

	(A)	-	(B)
①	Do you agree with that?	-	scary
②	What do you think about it?	-	helpful
③	Did you give your opinion?	-	convenient
④	How do you feel about it?	-	useless
⑤	Do you have anything to say?	-	dangerous

[경북 ○○중]

11. What are they talking about? (2점)

① Internet usage etiquette

② Using smartphones in class

③ How to use smartphones

④ Using smartphones to find words

⑤ The bad things about smartphones

[서울 마포구 ○○중]

12. 다음 A의 고민에 대한 B의 조언을 〈조건〉에 맞게 완성하시오. (6점)

조건

• 주어진 ⓐ와 ⓑ의 단어를 모두 이용(어형 변화 가능)
• 각 문제 당 ⓐ에서 단어 2개, ⓑ에서 단어 2개 사용
• 필요시 단어 추가 가능
• 정답을 포함하는 문장 전체를 답안지에 적을 것

ⓐ little, much, well, hard
ⓑ spend, play, practice, save

(1) A: I want to save lots of money. What can I do?

B: The _____, the _____.

(2) A: I want to play soccer really well. What can I do?

B: The _____, the _____.

[서울 마포구 ○○중]

13. 다음 중 어법상 어색한 문장은? (3점)

① My mom gave me a pair of gloves.

② I found a pair of glasses on desk.

③ He packed three pair of jeans in his bag.

④ A detective was buying a pair of sneakers.

⑤ She bought two pairs of shoes for 20 dollars.

14. 다음 중 대화의 내용이 가장 자연스러운 것은? (3점)

① A: How do you feel about skipping breakfast?
　B: I think it's good. We can sleep more.
　A: I agree with you. Our brain may not work well.

② A: How do you feel about eating fast food?
　B: I think it's good. It is unhealthy and dangerous.
　A: I don't agree. Fast food has a lot of fat.

③ A: It's time to go home. Make sure you lock the doors.
　B: Okay, I will. Anything else?
　A: Okay. That's it. You should turn off the light. See you tomorrow.

④ A: How do you feel about reading books on a smartphone?
　B: I think it's good.
　A: I agree with you. It is not good for our eyes.

⑤ A: How do you feel about wearing school uniforms?
　B: I like it a lot. I don't need to worry about what to wear.
　A: I don't agree. Everybody looks the same.

15. 다음 글의 빈칸을 주어진 단어를 활용하여 〈조건〉에 맞게 완성하시오. **(6점)**

Dear Abby: I'm a middle school student who has been battling depression over the past few months. I didn't do well on a recent exam. I tried talking to my family, but ever since the loss of a beloved pet, my parents are having a difficult time emotionally, I don't want to trouble them even further. I feel trapped and lonely every day. Any advice would be greatly appreciated.

Lonely and Depressed in Incheon

Dear Lonely: The problem with depression is that, like any other untreated illness, it can grow worse. I'm recommending you two things to do right now.
(A) _____ you talk to your parents, _____ it is.
(B) _____ you are, _____ you get.

조건
• 주어진 단어를 어법에 맞게 변형할 수 있음.
• 비교급을 반드시 사용할 것.
• 어법과 철자의 오류가 없어야 함.

(A) _____ you talk to your parents, _____ it is. (soon, good)

(B) _____ you are, _____ you get. (positive, healthy)

16. 다음 대화를 읽고 질문에 알맞은 답을 고른 것은?

(2점)

Jun: You look excited. What happened to you?

Mira: I heard that we can use smartphones in class from next week.

Jun: Wow! I didn't expect it at all.

Mira: How do you feel about it?

Jun: I think it will be very helpful. I can take notes and search for the information on it.

Q: How does Jun feel about using a smartphone in class?

① It's cruel.

② It's helpful.

③ It's new but scary.

④ It's easy but unhealthy.

⑤ It's convenient but dangerous.

17. 다음 〈보기〉와 가장 관련 있는 글의 종류는? (4점)

보기

Our readers said ...

I felt sorry for Stanley. He was sent to a terrible place for something he didn't do.

- Jason Damon

I couldn't put this book down. Stanley's camp is full of adventures.   *- Minho Kim*

I don't think digging a hole builds character. How can it make a person better?

- Louis Alba

I think this book has one strong message: bad people never win.   *- Sophia white*

① poem   ② diary

③ review   ④ fairy tale

⑤ world history

[18~19] 다음 글을 읽고 물음에 답하시오.

The more Stanley dug, (A)_____ he became. It took less time to finish his hole each day. In his second week, as Stanley was finishing his hole, he saw something shiny in the dirt. Stanley's heart beat faster. He heard that anyone who found something interesting would (B)_____ the day off. He carefully picked up the shiny object and brushed off the dirt. It was a small gold tube. But it couldn't be real gold since it was too light. There were two letters, KB, at the bottom of the tube. What did KB stand (C)_____? Stanley's heart beat even faster.

18. 위 글의 빈칸 (A), (B), (C) 안에서 들어갈 말로 바르게 짝지어진 것은?

(3점)

	(A)	(B)	(C)
①	the strong	give	in
②	the strong	given	for
③	the stronger	be given	in
④	the stronger	be given	for
⑤	the strongest	be given	for

19. 위 글의 내용과 일치하지 <u>않는</u> 것은? (3점)

① 반짝이는 물건은 너무 가벼워서 진짜 금이 아닌 것 같았다.

② Stanley는 조심스럽게 반짝이는 물건을 주워서 흙을 털었다.

③ 흥미로운 것을 발견한 사람은 보상으로 금을 받는다고 했다.

④ 하루하루 지날수록 Stanley가 구덩이를 파는 데 시간이 덜 걸렸다.

⑤ Stanley는 구덩이 파는 것을 끝내 가고 있을 때 흙속에서 빛나는 물체를 보았다.

[20-21] 다음 글을 읽고 물음에 답하시오.

He heard that anyone who found something interesting would be given the day off. He carefully picked up the shiny <u>object</u> and brushed off the dirt. It was a small gold tube. But it couldn't be real gold since it was too light. These were two letters, KB, at the bottom of the tube. Stanley's heart beat even faster.

20. 위 글의 내용과 일치하지 <u>않는</u> 것은? (2점)

① 소년의 심장은 훨씬 더 빨리 뛰었다.

② 소년이 집어든 것은 작은 금색통이다.

③ 흥미로운 것을 발견한 날은 쉴 수 있다.

④ 너무 가벼웠지만 그것은 진짜 금이었다.

⑤ 통의 바닥에는 KB라는 글자가 있었다.

21. 위 글의 밑줄 친 object와 같은 의미로 쓰인 것은? (3점)

① Unidentified flying <u>object</u> is flying in the sky.

② There's no direct <u>object</u> in this sentence.

③ We were all too polite to <u>object</u> to the plan.

④ Now he had no <u>object</u> in life.

⑤ It is an <u>object</u> of study.

[22-30] 다음 글을 읽고 물음에 답하시오.

"Dig harder, Stanley! The harder you dig, the faster you'll finish!" yelled Mr. Sir. Stanley Yelnats couldn't dig any harder (가)<u>since</u> every single muscle hurt. He was thirsty and hungry. He wanted to go home. Unfortunately, Stanley's home for the next 18 months would be right here, at Camp Green Lake.

(A) However, Stanley didn't really steal a pair of sneakers. ⓐ<u>He</u> was just in the wrong place at the wrong time. One day, he was walking home from school. Suddenly, a pair of old sneakers fell from the sky. The sneakers hit ⓑ<u>him</u> on the head.

(B) ⓒ<u>He</u> started running with the sneakers to tell ⓓ<u>his</u> father (다)_____ happened. A few minutes later, the police stopped Stanley and (나)<u>running / asked / him / he / why / was</u> (그가 왜 달리고 있었는지를 그에게 물었다). Unfortunately for Stanley, the sneakers belonged to a famous baseball player, Clyde Livingstone. ⓔ<u>He</u> won the baseball championship several times. That was (라)_____ Stanley ended up at Camp Green Lake.

(C) Camp Green Lake was a terrible name. It wasn't green and there was no lake. Camp Green Lake was hot and full of sand. In fact, it wasn't even a camp. It was a place for bad boys. Then what was a good boy like Stanley doing here? He was sent to the camp for stealing a pair of sneakers.

22. 위의 주어진 글 다음에 이어질 글의 순서로 가장 적절한 것은? (3점)

① (A)-(C)-(B)

② (B)-(A)-(C)

③ (B)-(C)-(A)

④ (C)-(A)-(B)

⑤ (C)-(B)-(A)

23. 위 글의 밑줄 친 (가) 대신 사용할 수 있는 단어를 2개 고르면? (3점)

① as   ② unless

③ before   ④ though

⑤ because

24. 위 글의 (나)를 바르게 영작한 것은? (3점)

① why was he running him asked

② asked him why was he running

③ why he was running hims asked

④ asked him why he was running

⑤ why him was running he asked

25. 위 글에 나타난 Stanley의 심정은? (4점)

① relieved   ② grateful

③ pleased   ④ confident

⑤ depressed

26. 위 글을 읽고 대답할 수 없는 것은? (4점)

① How come Stanley couldn't dig any harder?

② Why was Camp Green Lake a terrible name?

③ How long did Stanley have to stay at Camp Green Lake?

④ What happened to Stanley when he was walking home from school?

⑤ Why did Stanley steal a pair of sneakers which belonged to a famous baseball player?

27. 위 글의 밑줄 친 ⓐ~ⓔ 중에서 가리키는 대상이 <u>다른</u> 것은? (3점)

① ⓐ   ② ⓑ   ③ ⓒ

④ ⓓ   ⑤ ⓔ

28. 위 글의 (B) 문단에서 빈칸 (다), (라)에 들어갈 알맞은 단어로 짝지어진 것은? (3점)

	(다)	(라)
①	who	why
②	why	when
③	who	when
④	what	why
⑤	what	who

29. According to the passage above, which of the following is true? (4점)

① Mr. Sir is very kind to Stanley.

② Stanley digs holes to develop his muscle.

③ Camp Green Lake is famous for its clear blue water.

④ Stanley is a bad boy because he stole a pair of sneakers.

⑤ Stanley will stay at Camp Green Lake for one and a half year.

30. 위 글을 읽고 빈칸 (A)~(C)에 들어갈 말로 알맞게 짝지어진 것은? (4점)

> Monday, August 5th
> Today, a pair of sneakers fell from the sky on my way home from school. I (A)_____ them up and started running home, but the police stopped me. (B)_____, I was sent to Camp Green Lake. Now, I'm in Group D. We have to dig one hole every day. The good news is that anyone who finds something interesting can get the (C)_____. I hope I can be the one.

	(A)	(B)	(C)
①	looked	Unfortunately	day off
②	looked	Fortunately	gold tube
③	raised	Unfortunately	gold tube
④	picked	Fortunately	shiny object
⑤	picked	Unfortunately	day off

3학년 영어 1학기 기말고사(4과) 2회

반		점수	
이름			

문항수 : 선택형(26문항) 서술형(4문항) 20 . . .

◎ 선택형 문항의 답안은 컴퓨터용 수정 싸인펜을 사용하여 OMR답안지에 바르게 표기하시오.
◎ 서술형 문제는 답을 답안지에 반드시 검정볼 펜으로 쓰시오.
◎ 총 30문항 100점 만점입니다. 문항별 배점은 각 문항에 표시되어 있습니다.

[서울 마포구 ○○중]

1. 다음 빈칸에 알맞은 단어를 〈보기〉에서 골라 쓸 때 사용되지 <u>않은</u> 것은? (4점)

보기
ⓐ afford   ⓑ appear   ⓒ assign
ⓓ beat   ⓔ raise

- My heart _____ at the news.
- Speak of the devil, and he will _____.
- He's poor. He can't _____ to buy a car.
- The teacher will _____ us some homework.

① ⓐ   ② ⓑ   ③ ⓒ
④ ⓓ   ⑤ ⓔ

[경북 ○○중]

2. 다음 밑줄 친 부분의 의미가 <u>어색한</u> 것은? (3점)

① What does KB <u>stand for</u>? (상징하다)
② <u>On my day off</u>, I usually read many books. (쉬는 날에)
③ He <u>ended up doing</u> all the work himself. (결국 하게 되었다)
④ I hope you'll <u>get along with</u> your classmates. (자랑스러워하다)
⑤ They <u>get together</u> and do volunteer work on Sunday. (모이다)

[서울 마포구 ○○중]

3. 다음 글의 밑줄 친 ⓐ~ⓔ의 의미가 바르게 짝지어진 것은? (3점)

> Stanley didn't really steal a pair of sneakers. He was just in the wrong place at the wrong time. One day, he was walking home from school. Suddenly, a pair of old sneakers ⓐ<u>fell from the sky</u>. The sneakers ⓑ<u>hit him on the head</u>.
> He started running with the sneakers to tell his father what happened. A few minutes later, the police stopped Stanley and asked him why he was running. ⓒ<u>Unfortunately</u> for Stanley, the sneakers ⓓ<u>belonged to</u> a famous baseball player, Clyde Livingstone. That was why Stanley ⓔ<u>ended up</u> at Camp Green Lake.

① ⓐ fell from the sky: 하늘로 던졌다
② ⓑ hit him on the head: 그의 머리를 때렸다
③ ⓒ Unfortunately: 다행히도
④ ⓓ belonged to: ~을 소유했다
⑤ ⓔ ended up: 결국 그만두었다

[경기 ○○중]

4. 다음 빈칸에 들어갈 말이 <u>다른</u> 것은? (3점)

① _____ I came home, it began to rain.
② He has changed a lot _____ the accident.
③ _____ she was not hungry, she didn't have lunch.
④ He left home in 2012 and hasn't come back _____.
⑤ She has written many books _____ she left college.

5. 다음 중 밑줄 친 since가 나머지와 <u>다른</u> 의미로 쓰인 것은? (3점)

① I had a whole pizza <u>since</u> I was hungry.

② He didn't go to school <u>since</u> it was a holiday.

③ Mr. Smith went to bed early <u>since</u> he was tired.

④ We couldn't go on a picnic <u>since</u> it rained a lot.

⑤ She has written many books <u>since</u> she left college.

6. 다음 우리말을 〈조건〉에 맞게 영어로 쓰시오. (4점)

> 비가 많이 왔기 때문에 우리는 소풍을 가지 않았다.
> (a picnic, since, a lot, on)

조건
1. 과거시제를 사용할 것
2. 괄호 안의 단어를 활용하여 11개의 단어로 문장을 완성할 것
3. 부정어를 쓸 경우 축약형으로 쓸 것

정답: _____

[7–8] 다음 대화를 읽고 물음에 답하시오.

> Tony: What are all these boxes, Suji?
> Suji: They're items I ordered online.
> Tony: You like shopping on the Internet, don't you?
> Suji: Yes, I do. How do you feel about the online shopping, Tony?
> Tony: I don't like it at all.
> Suji: Why?
> Tony: It's very difficult to know (A)_____.
> Suji: I agree with you.
> Tony: It's also difficult to return an item if you don't like it.
> Suji: You're right, but I think it's very convenient.
> Tony: Well, convenience isn't everything.

7. 위 대화의 내용과 일치하는 것은? (3점)

① Tony는 온라인 쇼핑을 매우 좋아한다.

② Suji는 온라인으로 상자를 하나만 주문했다.

③ Tony는 쇼핑에 있어서 편리함을 제일 중요하게 생각한다.

④ Tony는 마음에 들지 않으면 반품하기가 쉽지 않아서 온라인 쇼핑을 싫어한다.

⑤ Suji는 물건이 실제로 어떤지 알기가 어려워 온라인 쇼핑을 좋아하지 않는다.

8. 위 대화의 빈칸 (A)에 알맞은 것은? (3점)

① what an item actually looks like

② how an item actually looks like

③ how does an item actually looks like

④ what does an item actually looks like

⑤ what an item actually looks

[9-10] 다음 대화를 읽고 물음에 답하시오.

G: Brian, did you hear the news?
B: What news?
G: We can use smartphones during classes from next week.
B: Yes, I heard that.
G: How do you feel about it?
B: I think it will be very useful. I can (A)look up words I don't know.
G: Yeah. We can also find information on the Internet.
B: Right. It will be very helpful.

9. 위 대화의 (A)look up과 같은 뜻으로 쓰인 문장은?
(4점)

① They look up to him as their leader.
② Look up at the sky on some clear night.
③ At last things were beginning to look up.
④ Can you look up the opening time on the website?
⑤ Dogs look up to us. Cats look down on us. Pigs treat us as equals.

10. What are they talking about?
(3점)

① how to focus on their studies
② using smartphones during classes
③ finding news they don't know
④ looking up the words on the dictionary
⑤ how to use a computer during classes

11. 다음 독서 계획 내용 중 어색한 것은?
(3점)

① What is the title of the book?
   - Charlotte's Web
② How often will you read the book?
   - For two weeks
③ How long will you read it at a time?
   - 30 minutes
④ If you see a difficult word, what will you do?
   - Keep reading and guess its meaning
⑤ What activity would you like to do after reading the book?
   - Write a summary

[12-13] 다음 대화를 읽고 물음에 답하시오.

A: Hey, Jessica. Why are you always drinking energy drinks?
B: Because they help me stay ⓐawake.
A: (A)_____, but they have too ⓑmuch caffeine.
B: Well, they help me ⓒfocus on my studies.
A: Did you know that too much caffeine can ⓓhurt your bones?
B: Oh, I didn't know that.
A: I think you should drink energy drinks ⓔ more often.
B: Maybe you're right. Thanks, Tom.

12. 위 대화의 빈칸 (A)에 들어갈 말로 가장 적절한 것은?
(3점)

① I'd love to
② I don't think so
③ I'm with you on that
④ I don't agree with you
⑤ You are completely wrong

13. 위 대화의 밑줄 친 ⓐ~ⓔ 중 흐름상 어색한 표현은? (4점)

① ⓐ   ② ⓑ   ③ ⓒ

④ ⓓ   ⑤ ⓔ

14. 다음 대화의 흐름에 맞게 ⓐ~ⓒ를 알맞은 순서로 묶은 것은? (2점)

> B: Hi, Amy. Welcome to Korea.
> G: Long time no see, Minho. How have you been?
>
> ⓐ I came here by subway.
> ⓑ How do you feel about the subway in Korea?
> ⓒ Great. How did you come here from the airport?
>
> G: I think it's very clean.

① ⓐ-ⓑ-ⓒ   ② ⓑ-ⓐ-ⓒ

③ ⓑ-ⓒ-ⓐ   ④ ⓒ-ⓐ-ⓑ

⑤ ⓒ-ⓑ-ⓐ

15. 다음 단어를 (1), (2)에 모두 사용하여 제시된 우리말에 맞는 영어 문장을 완성하시오. (4점)

> since

(1) 나는 나의 폰을 갖고 있지 않았기 때문에, 친구에게 전화를 할 수 없었다.

→ _____, I couldn't call my friend.

(2) 그가 여기 온 이후로 3년이 지났다.

→ It has been three years _____
_____.

16. 다음 밑줄 친 ⓐ~ⓕ 중 어법상 어색한 것을 있는 대로 고른 것은? (3점)

> Summer is Coming!
> Come to Our Bakdal Swimming Pool.
>
> When you feel hungry, enjoy your meal with "Bakdal hamburger." It ⓐcan cook in 3 minutes. It ⓑcan also be delivered to your table.
>
> Our pool is full of adventures! It ⓒwill be loved by many teens. This camera ⓓcan be used in water. You ⓔcan take pictures anywhere. Be careful with the summer's sun. Your skin ⓕmust be protected from the sun.

① ⓐ   ② ⓔ

③ ⓐ, ⓔ   ④ ⓑ, ⓒ, ⓓ, ⓕ

⑤ ⓒ, ⓓ, ⓔ, ⓕ

17. 다음 우리말을 〈조건〉에 맞게 영어로 쓰시오. (4점)

> 우리가 높이 오르면 오를수록, 더 추워진다.
> (high, climb, cold, become)

조건
1. The+비교급, the+비교급 표현을 사용할 것.
2. 현재시제로 쓸 것.
3. 괄호 안의 단어를 활용하여 8개의 단어로 문장을 완성할 것.

정답: _____ _____ _____ _____

_____ _____ _____ _____

Stanley didn't really steal a pair of sneakers. He was just in the wrong place at the wrong time. One day, he was walking home from school. Suddenly, a pair of old sneakers fell from the sky. The sneakers hit him on the head.

He started running with the sneakers to tell his father what happened. A few minutes later, the police stopped Stanley and asked him (A)(he / running / why / was). Unfortunately for Stanley, the sneakers belonged to a famous baseball player, Clyde Livingstone. That was (B)_____ Stanley ended up at Camp Green Lake.

[충북 ○○중]

19. 위 글의 빈칸 (B)에 들어갈 말로 가장 알맞은 것은? (3점)

① which　　　　② why

③ where　　　　④ when

⑤ who

[서울 강남구 ○○중]

20. 위 글의 내용에 의하면 'a pair of sneakers'는 누구의 것인가? (2점)

① Stanley

② Stanley's father

③ a police officer

④ a baseball player

⑤ a famous singer

[울산 ○○중]

18. 위 글의 괄호 (A)를 어순에 맞게 배열한 것은? (3점)

① why was he running

② why he was running

③ why running he was

④ he was running why

⑤ he why was running

[울산 ○○중]

21. 위 글의 내용과 일치하지 <u>않는</u> 것은? (3점)

① Stanley는 운동화를 훔치지 않았다.

② 운동화가 Stanley의 머리에 맞았다.

③ 운동화는 유명한 야구선수의 것이었다.

④ Stanley는 결국 운동화를 갖게 되었다.

⑤ Stanley는 잘못된 시간에 잘못된 장소에 있었다.

Stanley was assigned to Group D in the camp. There were six other boys in Stanley's group. They all had cool names like X-Ray, Zigzag and Zero. Each boy had to dig one hole every day. It had to be about 150cm deep and 150cm (A)_____. Mr. Sir said, "You are digging (가)to build character."

@스탠리가 땅을 더 많이 팔수록, 그는 더 강해졌다. It took (B)_____ time to finish his hole each day. In his second week, as Stanley was finishing his hole, he saw something shiny in the dirt. Stanley's heart beat faster. He heard that anyone who found something interesting would be given the day off. He carefully picked up the (C)_____ object and brushed off the dirt. It was a small gold tube. But it couldn't be real gold since it was too (D)_____. There were two letters, KB, at the bottom of the tube. What did KB stand for? Stanley's heart beat even (E)_____.

23. 위 글을 읽고 대답할 수 없는 질문은? (3점)

① What did KB stand for?

② Who can have the day off?

③ Why did Stanley's heart beat faster?

④ How many boys were there in Stanley's group?

⑤ When did Stanley see something shiny in the dirt?

24. 위 글의 의미상 (A)~(E)에 들어갈 수 없는 것은? (4점)

① (A) wide

② (B) less

③ (C) shiny

④ (D) light

⑤ (E) slower

22. Which question can NOT be answered? (4점)

① How many boys were in the camp?

② How big did their holes have to be?

③ Which group was Stanley assigned to?

④ What did each boy have to do every day?

⑤ When did Stanley find the shiny gold tube?

25. 위 글의 밑줄 친 (가)to build와 쓰임이 같은 것은? (3점)

① It's time to go to bed.

② Suwon has no pen to write with.

③ She waited to buy a movie ticket.

④ I have a lot of friends to help me.

⑤ Yiseong wants to send this letter to her.

26. 위 글의 우리말 ⓐ와 같은 뜻이 되도록 빈칸을 채우시오. (5점)

The _____, the _____.

28. 위 글의 흐름상 빈칸 (a)에 들어갈 알맞은 단어는? (3점)

① In fact
② Finally
③ Fortunately
④ Instead
⑤ On the other hand

29. 위 글의 빈칸 (가), (나), (다)에 들어갈 말로 바르게 짝지어진 것은? (4점)

	(가)	(나)	(다)
①	since	Unfortunately	even
②	so	Loudly	far
③	so	Happily	ever
④	before	Easily	still
⑤	before	Loudly	ever

[27-30] 다음 글을 읽고 물음에 답하시오.

"Dig harder, Stanley! The harder you dig, the faster you'll finish!" yelled Mr. Sir.

Stanley Yelnats couldn't dig any harder (가)_____ every single muscle hurt. He was thirsty and hungry. He wanted to go home. (나)_____ Stanley's home for the next 18 months would be right here, at Camp Green Lake.

Camp Green Lake was a terrible name. (A) It wasn't green and there was no lake. Camp Green Lake was hot and full of sand. (B) (a)_____, it wasn't (다)_____ a camp. (C) It was a place for bad boys. (D) He was sent to the camp for stealing a pair of sneakers. (E)

27. 위 글의 (A)~(E) 중 다음 문장이 들어가기에 가장 적절한 곳은? (3점)

Then what was a good boy like Stanley doing here?

① (A)   ② (B)   ③ (C)
④ (D)   ⑤ (E)

30. 위 글의 Camp Green Lake에 대한 설명과 일치하는 것은? (4점)

① There is no sand in Camp Green Lake.
② It is a popular camp for boys and girls.
③ It is a place for good boys like Stanley.
④ Stanley will be there for the next 18 months.
⑤ Boys often come to Camp Green Lake to swim in the lake.

정답 및 해설

Lesson 1 (중간)

01 ⑤	02 ⑤	03 ③	04 ②	05 ④	06 ④	07 ②
08 ②	09 ②	10 ④	11 ②	12 ①	13 ⑤	14 ②
15 ②	16 ③	17 ④	18 ①	19 ②	20 ②	21 ②
22 ③	23 ①	24 ⑤	25 like		26 ④	27 ③
28 ④	29 ⑤	30 ①				

01 different는 형용사로 '다른'이라는 뜻을 갖는다. ⓐ에는 명사형인 difference가, ⓑ에는 부사형인 differently가 들어가야 어법상 적절하다.

02 planet은 '행성'이라는 뜻을 가진 단어이다. '식물로부터 생성된 새로운 식물이 자랄 수 있는 작고 단단한 물체'라는 영영 풀이가 가리키는 것은 seed(씨앗)이다.

03 ③에서 quickly는 명사 shower를 수식하기 때문에 부사형인 아닌 형용사형인 quick이 되어야 어법상 적절하다.

04 ① that → what / ③ That → What / ④ which → what / ⑤ what → which로 고쳐야 어법상 적절한 문장이 된다.

05 ④ It's been a long time.은 "오래간만이다."라는 뜻으로, 어떻게 지냈냐는 태민이의 질문에 대한 대답으로 적절하지 않다.

06 위 대화에서 태민이는 5년 동안 피아노를 연주해 왔다고 ("I've played the piano for 5 years.") 언급했다.

07 위 대화에서 태민이가 피아노 대회에 나간다고 했으므로 그에 대한 Jenny의 반응으로 가장 적절한 것은 ② Good luck in your competition.(대회에서 잘 되길 바랄게.)이다.

08 위 글에 따르면, Andy의 팀은 1점차로 졌다고("It was 80 to 79.") 언급되어 있다.

09 G의 말에 대해 B의 반응이 "그걸 들어 기쁘다."였다. 따라서 G가 할 말로 적절하지 않은 것은 ② I dropped my new smartphone.(내 스마트폰을 떨어뜨렸어.)이다.

10 ⓐ stick → sticks / ⓑ have → has / ⓒ the taller → the tallest / ⓔ Creativity→ Creatively로 고쳐야 어법상 적절한 문장이 된다.

11 위 글의 내용에 따르면, 규칙은 총 다섯 가지가 언급되어 있다.

12 ⓒ by oneself → by itself / ⓔ for us build → for

13 ⓐ of → for / ⓑ for he → for him / ⓓ for → of / ⓔ of his → of him으로 고쳐야 어법상 적절한 문장이 된다.

us to build로 고쳐야 어법상 적절한 문장이 된다.

14 <보기>의 문장에서 쓰인 what은 관계대명사 역할을 한다. ②의 what은 의문사 역할을 한다.

15 ②에는 for가 들어가야 어법상 적절하다. 나머지 빈칸에는 모두 of가 들어가야 어법상 적절하다.

16 위 글은 친구들과 조별 과제를 통해 혼자 하는 것보다 더 나은 결과를 만들어냈다고 이야기하고 있다. 따라서 빈칸에 들어갈 내용으로 가장 적절한 것은 ③ two heads are better than one(두 사람이 한 사람보다 낫다)이다.

17 ⓓgot stuck은 '막혔다', '걸렸다'라는 뜻으로 사용되었다.

18 화자와 친구들은 급해서 스파게티 면을 테이프로 붙였다 (we taped the sticks of spaghetti together.')고 언급되어 있다.

19 (가)it는 가주어로서 뒤에 이어 나오는 to부정사 구문을 대신한다. 따라서 이와 같이 가주어 구문으로 사용되지 않은 것은 ② It was not very cold yesterday.(어제는 별로 춥지 않았다.)이다.

20 선생님은 조별 과제를 하고 있는 학생들에게 "5분 남았다"("Five minutes left.")라고 말했다.

21 (가)must는 '~해야 한다'라는 의무를 나타내는 조동사이다. must가 이와 같은 의미로 쓰인 문장은 ② I must buy a ticket for the show.(쇼를 보기 위해선 표를 구매해야 한다)이다.

22 ⓒby itself은 '스스로'라는 뜻으로 사용되었다.

23 위 글에서는 활동의 실제 사례에 대해서는 언급된 바 없다.

24 ⓔthat은 the thing which의 의미를 가진 what으로 바꿔 써야 어법상 적절하다.

25 (가)에는 '~처럼 보이다'라는 뜻을 가진 look like가 들어가야 문맥상 적절하다.

26 ⓔ누가 먼저 탑을 만들기 시작했는지에 대해서는 언급되지 않았다.

27 ⓐto choose는 to부정사의 명사적 용법으로 사용되었다. 이와 같이 명사적 용법으로 쓰인 문장은 ③ My best group project was to make a video.(내 조별 과제는 동영상을 만드는 것이었다.)

28 C조는 삼각형 모양으로 탑의 기반을 만들었다.

29 (A) develop 발전시키다 (B) share 공유하다

30 우리는 모두 동의했고 테이프 자르는 사람과 시간을 확인하는 사람 등으로 역할을 나누었다('We all agreed and divided up the roles such as time checker and tape cutter.')라고 언급된 바 있다.

Lesson 1 (중간)

2회

```
01 ③  02 ①  03 ②  04 ③  05 ①  06 ⑤  07 ④
08 ④  09 ③  10 ②
```
11 (1) It is kind of you to bring flowers for me.
　 (2) Tell me what you heard today.
```
12 ⑤  13 ③  14 ⑤  15 ①  16 ②  17 ②  18 ②
19 ③  20 ③  21 ①  22 ②  23 ⑤  24 ①  25 ①
26 ④  27 ⑤  28 ⑤  29 ③  30 ④
```

01 donation은 '기부'란 뜻을 가진 단어로 '개인 또는 기관을 돕기 위해 무언가를 주는 것'이라는 영영풀이에 알맞은 단어다.

02 hard는 '열심히' 또는 '열심히 하는'이라는 형용사적 의미와 부사적 의미를 함께 쓰는 단어이다. hardly는 '거의 ~않는'이라는 뜻을 가진 단어로 hard의 부사형이 아니다. 나머지 단어들의 관계는 형용사와 부사의 관계이다.

03 ① for → of / ③ his → him / ④ of → for / ⑤ of → for로 고쳐야 어법상 적절한 문장이 된다.

04 ⓒwhat은 the thing which의 뜻으로 쓰인 관계대명사이다. 나머지는 모두 의문사 역할을 하는 what이다.

05 "좋은 소식 있니?"라는 문장이 들어가기에 가장 적절한 곳은 Cathy에게 신나 보인다고 말하고 있는 (A)이다.

06 ① That → It / ② for → of / ③ We → It / ④ they → them으로 고쳐야 어법상 적절한 문장이 된다.

07 (A) 가주어 it이 쓰인 문장이므로 to watch가 되어야 한다. (B) 사람의 성격이나 태도를 나타내는 형용사 뒤에는 'of+목적격' 형태로 의미상의 주어를 쓴다.

08 오랜만에 만난 사람에게 안부를 물을 때 "How have you been?"이라는 표현을 쓸 수 있다.

09 진수는 다음 주에 피아노 대회를 나간다고("I have a piano competition next week.") 언급한 바 있다.

10 농구 시합에서 졌다는 Andy에게 ⓑOh, I'm glad to hear that.(그 말을 들어 기쁘다.)이라고 말하는 것은 대화의 흐름상 자연스럽지 않다.

11 (1) to부정사의 의미상의 주어는 'for/of+목적격' 형태로 to부정사 앞에 위치하며 to부정사를 행하는 주체를 나타낸다. 「It+is/was+형용사+for/of+목적격+to부정사 ~.」의 형태로 자주 쓰며, 이때 It은 가주어이고 to부정사 (구)가 진주어이다. (2) 관계대명사 what은 선행사를 포함하는 관계대명사로 두 문장을 연결하는 역할을 하며, 명사절을 이끌어 '~하는 것'으로 해석된다. 관계대명사 what이 이끄는 절은 문장에서 주어, 목적어, 보어 역할을 할 수 있다.

12 (E) 앞에 the thing이라는 선행사가 있기 때문에 관계대명사 what 대신 which[that]를 쓰는 것이 어법상 적절하다.

13 상대방이 안부를 물어봤을 때 감기가 걸렸다고 이야기했으므로 ⓒPretty good.(꽤 좋아.)이라는 문장은 대화 흐름상 자연스럽지 않다.

14 위 글은 친구들과 조별과제를 통해 혼자 하는 것보다 더 나은 결과를 만들어냈다고 이야기하고 있다. 따라서 빈칸에 들어갈 내용으로 가장 적절한 것은 ⑤ many heads are better than one.(여러 명이 혼자 하는 것보다 낫다)이다.

15 위 글에서 선생님이 하신 말씀을 듣지 못했다는 내용이므로 빈칸에는 ① what the teacher said가 들어가야 문맥상 적절하다.

16 ⓐ for I → for me / ⓑ of → for / ⓔ for → of / ⓕ for → of / ⓖ for → of로 고쳐야 어법상 적절한 문장이 된다.

17 "새 학교 생활은 어떠니?"라는 문장이 들어가기에 가장 적절한 곳은 James가 전학간 Lily에게 질문하는 곳인 ⓑ이다.

18 Lily가 학교에서 바쁜 일정을 보내고 있는지에 대해서는 언급된 바 없다.

19 글의 후반부에 언급된 것처럼, 이 활동은 문제 해결 능력(Solving Problems) 및 창의적 사고(Thinking Creatively)를 기르는 데 좋다.

20 by oneself는 '~ 스스로'라는 뜻으로 이 경우에는 '(타워) 스스로'라는 뜻으로 사용되었다.

21 위 글의 목적은 스파게티로 탑을 쌓는 활동에 대해서 설명하는 것이다.

22 ⓐ many / ⓒ was sure / ⓓ made / ⓔ strong으로 고쳐야 어법상 적절한 문장이 된다.

23 impressed: 감명을 받은, 인상 깊게 생각하는

24 in detail은 '자세히', '상세하게'라는 뜻으로 사용된다. 따라서 이와 반대되는 뜻으로 사용되는 표현은 ① in brief(간략하게)이다.

25 A조는 좋은 아이디어가 많아서 탑을 쌓는 활동을 하기 전에 서로의 아이디어에 대해서 상세하게 이야기를 나눴다고 언급되어 있다. 따라서 (가)에 들어갈 말로 가장 적절한 것은 ① Think before you act.(행동하기 전에 생각하라.)이다.

26 A조는 실제로 행동하기 전에 아이디어를 모으고 이야기를 많이 나누었으므로 Think before you act.가, B조는 아이디어를 짜기 전에 미리 행동을 시작했으므로 'Just do it.'이, C조는 팀으로 함께 일했으므로 'We're one team.'이 제목으로 이어져야 자연스럽다.

27 세 번째 문단에서 C조는 한 학생이 삼각형 모양을 제안했고 거기에 동의('Another student suggested a triangle shape for the base. We all agreed')했다고 언급했다.

28 C조가 탑의 꼭대기를 무슨 모양으로 하기로 동의했는지에 대해서는 위 글에서 언급되어 있지 않다.

29 ⓒwhich는 the thing which의 의미로 사용되는 관계대명사 what으로 바꿔 써야 어법상 적절하다.

30 (나) Instead 대신에 (다) In the end 마침내, 결국

Lesson 2 (중간)

> **01** ② **02** ④ **03** ③ **04** ④ **05** ⑤ **06** ⑤ **07** ④
> **08** ⑤ **09** (1) is (2) speak **10** ②
> **11** (1) ⓑ (2) ⓔ (3) ⓓ (4) ⓒ **12** ① **13** ① **14** ③
> **15** ⑤ **16** ① **17** ① **18** ② **19** ④ **20** ③ **21** ①
> **22** ② **23** ⑤ **24** ③
> **25** We can plant more flowers and trees.
> **26** ① **27** ① **28** ① **29** ① **30** ③

01 climate은 '기후'라는 뜻을 가진 단어이다.

02 주어진 문장에서 last는 '지속하다', '지속되다'라는 뜻으로 사용되었다. 이와 같은 의미로 사용된 문장은 ④ The milk can last till the weekend.(우유는 주말까지 먹을 수 있다)이다.

03 A의 말에 대한 B의 대답이 "넌 목을 자주 스트레칭할 필요가 있어."이다. 따라서 A의 말로 가장 적절한 것은 ③ Do you know how to prevent text neck?이다.

04 어떻게 지구 온난화를 늦출 수 있는지 설명해 달라는 A의 질문에 대해 "아니, 우리는 에너지를 아껴야 해."라는 B의 대답은 흐름상 적절하지 않다.

05 ⓐ spend / ⓑ were / ⓒ don't / ⓓ was로 고쳐야 어법상 적절한 문장이 된다.

06 (A) will be / (B) should protect / (C) will love / (D) should be followed가 들어가는 것이 어법상 적절하다.

07 a quarter of ~는 '~의 4분의 1'이라는 뜻이다. 따라서 주어진 우리말은 About a quarter of the bee population dies every year. 또는 About one-fourth of the bee population dies every year.라고 영작할 수 있다.

08 위 대화에서 Brian은 친구들을 대상으로 얼마나 환경 보

호를 잘하는지 조사했고 그 결과에 대해 만족스럽지 않아 보인다고("You don't look like you are satisfied with it.") 한다. 따라서 Brian의 심정으로 가장 적절한 것은 ⑤ concerned(걱정스러운)이다.

09 주어가 「half/all/most/some/part/분수/퍼센트+of+명사」의 형태인 경우, 동사는 명사의 수에 일치시킨다. of 뒤의 명사가 단수 명사이면 동사의 단수형을 쓰고, of 뒤의 명사가 복수 명사이면 동사의 복수형을 쓴다.

10 민호가 지구의 시간(Earth Hour)에 대해서 조사하기를 원하는지에 대해서는 위 대화에서 언급되지 않았다.

11 (1) I'm worried about ~에 대해서 걱정하다
(2) to save the Earth 지구를 지키기 위해
(3) Why don't we ~? 우리 ~하는 것 어때?
(4) how to participate in ~에 참여하는 방법

12 누가 지구의 시간을 처음 만들었는지는 위 대화에서 언급되지 않았다.

13 ② wants → want / ③ skips → skip / ④ are → is / ⑤ is → are로 고쳐야 어법상 적절한 문장이 된다.

14 students → student / are → is / skips → skip으로 고쳐야 어법상 적절한 문장이 된다.

15 ⓐ는 pollination을 가리키며 나머지는 모두 pollen을 가리킨다.

16 글의 후반부에 'I think my friends are not so green. They should think about the environment more.' 라고 말한 것으로 미루어 보아, 글쓴이가 하고자 하는 말은 ① Let's protect our environment.(환경을 보호하자) 이다.

17 동사 give를 쓸 경우 목적어로 간접 목적어(~에게)+직접 목적어(~을/를) 순으로 쓸 수 있다. 직접 목적어가 앞에 올 경우에는 전치사 to를 간접 목적어 앞에 붙여 써도 같은 의미의 문장이 된다.

18 'a long, thin piece of wood, metal, or plastic.'이라는 영영 풀이가 가리키는 것은 stick(막대기)이다. ① ancient, ③ crops, ④ honey, ⑤ seed를 가리킨다.

19 (A) disappear 사라지다 (B) worse 더 나쁜 (C) moving 옮기는 것(동명사) (D) (which is) produced a fine yellow powder를 수식하는 관계대명사절

20 모든 농작물은 결코 스스로 생산될 수 있는지 없는지에 대해서는 위 글에서 언급되어 있지 않다.

21 ⓒ는 사람들(people)을, 나머지는 모두 벌들(bees)을 가리킨다.

22 (가)provide는 '제공하다'라는 뜻으로 사용되었다. 이와 바꿔 쓸 수 있는 단어는 ② offer(제공하다)이다.

23 위 글에서는 점점 사라지고 있는 벌들을 돕기 위한 방법들을 설명하고 있다. 따라서 위 글의 앞에 나올 내용으로 가장 적절한 것은 ⑤ '벌의 생존이 어려워진 이유'이다.

24 '두 번째로, 작물에 해로운 화학 물질의 사용은 반드시 멈춰져야 한다.'라는 문장이 들어가기에 가장 적절한 것은 화학 물질이 벌과 사람에게 해롭다고 설명하고 있는 문장 앞인 (C)이다.

25 위 글에서는 사라지고 있는 벌들을 돕기 위해서 더 많은 꽃과 나무를 심거나, 새로운 화학물질을 사용하지 않는 등의 방법을 제시하였다.

26 위 글에서는 점점 사라지고 있는 벌들을 돕기 위한 방법들을 제시하고 있다. 따라서 위 글의 제목으로 가장 적절한 것은 ① How to Protect Bees(벌을 보호하는 방법)이다.

27 위 글에서는 왜 벌들이 인간에게 유용하고 도움을 주는 존재인지에 대해서 설명하고 있다. 따라서 위 글의 제목으로 가장 적절한 것은 ① What Bees Do for Humans(벌들이 인간을 위해 하는 일)이다.

28 (A) helpful 도움을 주는, (B) ancient 옛날의, 고대의, (C) need 필요로 하다

29 ⓐ 동사 give를 쓸 경우 목적어로 간접 목적어(~에게)+직접 목적어(~을/를) 순으로 쓸 수 있다. 직접 목적어가 앞에 올 경우에는 전치사 to를 간접 목적어 앞에 붙여 써도 같은 의미의 문장이 된다. 따라서 ⓐgive honey to us가 되어야 어법상 적절하다.

30 위 글에 따르면 꿀을 영원히 지속될 수 있다고('Honey can last almost forever') 언급되어 있다.

Lesson 2 (중간)

01 ④	**02** ②	**03** ③	**04** ③	**05** ②	**06** ②	**07** ⑤
08 ④						

09 (1) reason → reasons (2) extreme → extremely
　　(3) The other → Another (4) only → not only

10 ⑤	**11** ③	**12** ③	**13** ①	**14** ④	**15** ①	**16** ⑤
17 ②	**18** ④	**19** ②	**20** ①	**21** ⑤	**22** ③	**23** ③
24 ④	**25** ②	**26** ②	**27** ④	**28** ②	**29** ④	**30** ⑤

01 population은 '인구'라는 뜻을 지닌다. 문맥상 pollution(오염)이 들어가야 자연스럽다.

02 ②에는 형용사가 아니라 명사가 들어가야 어법상 적절하다.

03 주어진 우리말을 영작하면, 'About a quarter of the money was spent on food.'가 된다.

04 위 대화의 문맥상, ③ How can I do well for a team project?(내가 조별 과제를 어떻게 하면 잘할 수 있을까?)라는 문장이 들어가야 한다.

05 A가 B(Jane)에게 무슨 일이냐고 묻자, B는 남동생이 다리를 다쳤다고 이야기한다. 이에 A는 그 말을 들어 유감이라고 말하자, B는 남동생이 걱정 된다고 대답한다. 이에 A는 걱정 말라고 이야기하면서 그가 괜찮을 것이라고 대답하는 순서로 이어지는 것이 대화의 흐름상 가장 자연스럽다.

06 빈칸 맨위에서부터 are, is, is, is, are가 들어가야 어법상 적절하다.

07 ① should follow → should be followed / ② send → sent / ③ bought → brought / ④ might chosen → might be chosen으로 고쳐야 어법상 적절한 문장이 된다.

08 (A) 주어가 Your dish이기 때문에 동사는 수동태인 be served가 되어야 한다. (B) 조동사 should가 쓰였기 때문에 동사원형인 sell을 써야 어법상 적절하다.

09 (1) one of + 복수 명사 (2) 형용사를 수식할 때는 부사를 쓴다. (3) Another 또 다른 (4) not only A but also B A 뿐만 아니라 B도 역시

10 위 대화에서 민호가 지구를 지키기 위해 행동에 나서야 한다고 말했고 이에 Linda는 동의했다. 따라서 빈칸에 들어갈 말로 가장 적절한 것은 ⑤ participate in the Earth Hour event이다.

11 ⓒspeed up은 '가속화시키다'라는 의미로, 지구 온난화를 늦추거나 막을 방법에 대해서 이야기하고 있는 위 대화의 내용과 어울리지 않는다.

12 주어 More than 40 percent of the people을 복수 취급하기 때문에 ③ opposes를 oppose로 고쳐야 어법상 적절한 문장이 된다.

13 ② drove → driven / ③ send → sent / ④ to → by / ⑤ would → will로 고쳐야 어법상 적절한 문장이 된다.

14 10 percent of the people을 복수 취급하기 때문에 ④ spends는 spend로 고쳐야 어법상 적절한 문장이 된다.

15 10명 중 7명의 학생들이 방을 나갈 때 불을 끈다('Seven of ten turn off lights when they leave rooms.')고 언급되어 있다.

16 ⓐgreen은 '환경 친화적인'이라는 뜻으로 사용되었다. / ① 초록의, ② 초록색, ③ 고유명사, ④ 초록색

17 ② What's happening to our food?(우리의 식량에 무슨 일이 벌어지고 있는가?)라는 내용은 위 대화에서 언급되어 있지 않다.

18 '이것은 벌들이 살기에 좋은 환경을 제공할 것이다'라는 문장이 들어가기에 가장 적절한 곳은 나무와 꽃을 심어야

한다고 주장하고 있는 (D)이다.

19 (가)disappearing은 현재분사로, 문장 내에서 현재 진행형을 만드는 동사로 사용되었다. ② We can start by saving energy.에서 saving은 동사와 명사가 결합된 동명사이다.

20 ⓐto help는 to부정사의 부사적 용법(~하기 위해)으로 사용되었다. 이와 쓰임이 같은 문장은 ① He got up early to catch the train.(그는 열차를 타기 위해 일찍 일어났다.)이다.

21 위 글에서는 벌들이 사라지는 이유로 지구 온난화와 해로운 화학물질의 사용을 예시로 들었다.

22 ⓒ는 의미상 수동형인 'must be stopped'로 바꿔 써야 한다.

23 (A)to help는 to부정사의 부사적 용법(~하기 위해)으로 사용되었다. 이와 쓰임이 같은 문장은 ⑤ You should study hard to get a good grade.(좋은 성적을 받기 위해선 공부를 열심히 해야 한다.)이다.

24 위 글에서는 점점 사라지고 있는 벌들을 도울 수 있는 방법에 대해서 설명하고 있다. 따라서 위 글의 앞에 나올 내용으로 가장 적절한 것은 ④ '벌의 생존이 어려워진 이유'이다.

25 위 글에서는 벌들이 인간에게 도움이 된다고 이야기하면서 벌들이 사라지는 이유에 대해서 설명하고 있다. 따라서 위 글의 빈칸에 들어갈 제목으로 가장 적절한 것은 ② Disappearing Honey Bees(사라지고 있는 꿀벌들)이다.

26 두 번째 문단에서는 벌들이 인간에게 꿀이나 작물을 기르게 하는 등의 도움을 준다는 내용에 대해서 이야기하고 있다. 따라서 빈칸에 들어갈 단어로 가장 적절하지 않은 것은 ② harmful(해로운)이다.

27 위 글에서는 꿀벌이 꽃가루를 옮기는 pollination(수분 작용)에 대해서 이야기하고 있다.

28 ⓑeven은 비교급을 강조하는 의미로 사용되었다.

29 위 글에서는 농부들이 작물에 화학물질을 사용하는 것을 꿀벌들이 사라지고 있는 이유로 보았기 때문에, 화학물질을 더 사용해야 한다는 주장은 적절하지 않다.

30 사과와 딸기 뿐만 아니라 다른 많은 종류의 작물들도 꿀벌의 수분 작용이 필요하다고('bees help produce many crops such as apples and strawberries. These crops cannot be produced by themselves.') 언급되어 있다.

Lesson 3 (기말)

01 ⑤	**02** ⑤	**03** ⑤	**04** ②	**05** ②	**06** ④	**07** ②
08 ⑤	**09** ①	**10** ④	**11** ⑤	**12** ④	**13** ②, ⑤	
14 ⑤	**15** ③	**16** ①	**17** ③	**18** ②	**19** ②	**20** ②
21 ⑤	**22** ④	**23** ④	**24** ③	**25** ⑤	**26** ①	**27** ①
28 We were proun of ourselves.					**29** ⑤	

01 위에서부터 순서대로 get up 일어나다 / got together 모였다 / get along with ~와 잘 지내다 / get on ~을 타다

02 get away with는 '치우다, 모면하다'라는 뜻을 갖는다. '~와 잘 지내다'라는 단어는 'get along with'이다.

03 (A) excited 신난, 흥분한 (B) boring 지루하게 하는

04 A의 말에 대한 B의 대답이 "선물 상자에 쿠키를 넣어주렴."이다. 따라서 A가 한 말로 가장 적절한 것은 상대방에게 도움을 주고자 할 때 구체적으로 필요로 하는게 무엇인지 묻는 표현인 ② What do you want me to do?(제가 무엇을 하길 바라세요?)이다.

05 "Can you give me a hand?"는 "저를 좀 도와주시겠어요?"라는 의미로 상대방에게 도움을 요청할 때 쓰는 표현이다. 따라서 위 대화에서는 (B)에 들어가는 것이 흐름상 가장 자연스럽다.

06 위 글에서 여성 화자는 Tony에게 "Read this book for the blind in the recording room."(녹음실에서 시각 장애인분들을 위한 이 책을 읽어주세요.)라고 요청했다.

07 (A) must ~임에 틀림 없다 (B) the+형용사 ~한 사람들 (cf. the blind 시각 장애인) (C) anything을 수식할 수 있는 것은 to부정사형인 to keep이다.

08 ⓔdo는 일반동사 앞에서 동사를 강조할 때 쓰는 표현이다.

09 plant는 '심다'라는 뜻을 갖는 동사이다. '물을 주다'라는 동사는 'water'이다.

10 밑줄 친 as는 '~할 때, ~하는 동안'의 뜻으로 시간의 부사절을 이끄는 접속사로 쓰였다.

11 "난 다음 동아리 모임에서 이 아이디어를 제안했고 회원들은 그것을 마음에 들어했다."라는 문장이 들어가기에 가장 적절한 곳은 화자가 "Why don't we do wall paintings like these?"라고 말하고 있는 (E)이다.

12 사역동사 have는 목적보어로 동사원형(능동) 또는 과거분사형(수동)을 취한다. 따라서 ④ D has us get along with our friends.(D는 우리가 친구들과 잘 지내도록 한다.)가 어법상 가장 적절하다.

13 "I'm going to ~"는 미래에 어떤 일을 할 것이라는 표현으로 to 뒤에 동사원형을 취한다. "look forward to ~"

는 '~를 기대하다, 고대하다'라는 뜻으로 전치사 to 뒤에 명사 혹은 동명사형을 취한다.

14 위 글에 따르면 학생들은 매년 나무를 심기로 계획했다고 언급되어 있다.

15 Tony가 여인에게 뭘 하기를 바라느냐고 물어봤으므로 (A)에는 deliver meals to the elderly(어르신에게 식사를 배달하라)를, (B)에는 Make sure라는 표현이 사용되었으므로 greet them politely(예의 바르게 인사하라)가 들어가야 문맥상 자연스럽다.

16 주어진 우리말을 영작하면 'It was roses that she planted last weekend.'라는 문장이 된다.

17 ⓐ 대명사 They는 앞에서 언급된 복수 명사인 wall paintings를 가리킨다. ⓑ these 역시 여수에 있는 wall paintings를 가리킨다. ⓒ it은 앞에서 언급된 단수명사인 a teen volunteer project를 가리킨다.

18 (A)this idea는 앞에서 언급한 "Why don't we do wall paintings like these?"에서 벽화를 그리는 것을 의미한다.

19 위 글에 따르면, 프로젝트 관리자는 학생들이 원하는 그림을 그리게 해주었다고 언급되어 있다.

20 (A) paint, (B) to paint, (C) painting[to paint], (D) painted가 들어가야 어법상 적절하다.

21 (가) apply for ~에 지원하다 (나) select 선택하다 (다) paint over ~ 위에 그림을 그리다

22 문맥상 (a)에는 because(~이기 때문에)가 들어간다.

23 위 글에 따르면, 벽화를 그리기 전에 벽에는 글씨들과 그림들, 그리고 오래된 포스터들이 있어서 상태가 좋지 않았다. 또한 호민이의 동아리는 프로젝트 관리자가 원하는 그림을 그릴 수 있게 해주었기 때문에 원하는 그림을 그렸다.

24 마지막 문단에 언급되어 있듯이, 프로젝트 관리자는 원하는 그림을 그릴 수 있게 해주었다('The manager let us paint anything we wanted.').

25 동아리 회원들이 벽화를 그리고 난 다음 그것이 완벽하다고 생각하지는 않았지만 그건 중요하지 않다고 이야기하고 있으므로 ⓔBut it matters.(그건 중요하다.)는 문맥상 자연스럽지 않다.

26 글쓴이는 자원봉사활동으로 벽화를 그렸고 그것이 마을을 더 밝고 행복하게 만들었기 때문에 그 사실에 대해서 뿌듯해 하고 있다.

27 비교급을 강조할 때, 비교급 앞에 much, still, even, far, a lot 등의 부사(구)를 쓰며 '(…보다) 훨씬 더 ~한'이라는 의미를 갖는다. very는 원급의 형용사(또는 부사)를 수식하며, 비교급은 수식하지 않는다.

28 전치사 of의 목적어가 주어와 동일인이므로 재귀대명사를 써야 한다.

29 It ~ that 강조 구문은 강조하고자 하는 부분을 it is/was와 that 사이에 넣고, 나머지 부분을 that 뒤에 써서 나타낸다. '…한 것은 바로 ~이다/이었다'라고 해석한다.

Lesson 3 (기말)

01 ②	02 ①	03 ④	04 ②	05 ②	06 ④	07 ①
08 ③	09 ②	10 ⑤	11 ①	12 ⑤	13 ③	14 ④
15 ②	16 ⑤	17 ④	18 ④	19 ①	20 ④	21 ③
22 ⑤	23 ④					

24 It was a better tomorrow that we painted.

25 ④	26 ⑤	27 ④	28 ⑤	29 ③	30 ⑤

01 위 문장들에서는 목적보어로 동사원형을 취하는 사역동사 중에 단수 주어와 복수 주어일 경우 쓸 수 있는 과거형 ② made가 들어가는 것이 어법상 가장 적절하다.

02 stick은 '막대기' 혹은 '찌르다'라는 뜻을 갖는 단어이다. '어떤 행동에 참여하다'라는 영영 풀이가 가리키는 단어는 participate이다.

03 동사 ask는 목적보어로 to부정사를 취한다.

04 위 글에서 집에 갈 때 불을 끄라는 B의 말에 대해 A가 ② Anything else?(또 다른 건?)이라고 물어보는 것이 대화 흐름상 가장 자연스럽다.

05 "What do you want me to do?"는 '내가 무엇을 하길 원하니?'라는 뜻으로 상대방에게 도움을 주고자 할 때 그 사람이 구체적으로 필요로 하는 도움이 무엇인지 묻는 표현이다. 이와 바꿔 쓸 수 있는 표현으로는 ② What can I do for you? 등이 있다.

06 위 대화에 따르면, Tony는 봉사활동을 하러 갔으므로 빈칸에 들어갈 말로 가장 적절한 것은 상대방에게 도움을 주고자 할 때 그 사람이 구체적으로 필요로 하는 도움이 무엇인지 묻는 ④ What do you want me to do today?이다.

07 "make sure+주어+동사 ~"는 '반드시 ~하다'라는 뜻으로 상대방이 어떤 일을 잊지 않고 꼭 할 것을 당부할 때 사용할 수 있는 표현이다.

08 밑줄 친 It은 가주어 역할을 하는 it으로, 뒤에 나오는 to부정사가 이끄는 구문을 대신한다.

09 It ~ that 강조 구문은 강조하고자 하는 부분을 It is/was와 that 사이에 넣고, 나머지 부분을 that 뒤에 써서 나타낸다. '…한 것은 바로 ~이다/이었다'라고 해석한다.

10 선생님이 "Keep in mind two rules for our class.

(이 수업에서 두 가지 규칙을 명심하세요.)"라고 언급한 바 있다.

11 B가 이 상자들은 무엇이냐고 묻자, A는 기부하려고 책을 포장하고 있다고 말하면서 도움을 요청한다. B는 무엇을 하면 되냐고 묻자, A는 상자에 주소를 써달라고 부탁한다. 이에 B는 문제 없다고 대답하는 순서로 이어지는 것이 대화 흐름상 가장 적절하다.

12 돌보는 시간이 많이 들기 때문에 반려동물을 기르는 것을 좋아하지 않는다는 A의 말에 대해 B가 동의한다고 말한 후 반려동물이 우리를 행복하게 해준다고 말하는 것은 대화 흐름상 적절하지 않다.

13 ⓐpack 포장하다 / ⓑdonation 기부 / ⓓaddress 주소 / ⓔNo problem. "문제 없어."

14 ① using → use / ② to open → open / ③ opened → open / ⑤ let sleep my dog → let my dog sleep 으로 고쳐야 어법상 적절한 문장이 된다.

15 ② It was certain that I would pass the exam.은 '내가 시험에 통과할 것이라는 것은 확실했다'라는 뜻으로 접속사 that으로 연결된 문장이다. 나머지는 모두 It ~ that 강조 구문이다.

16 위 글에서 선생님이 많은 책을 구입하라는 조언은 언급된 바 없다.

17 ⓓ to do → do / ⓕ memorize → to memorize로 고쳐야 어법상 적절한 문장이 된다.

18 <보기> 문장은 It ~ that 강조 구문이다. 이와 쓰임이 같은 문장은 ④ It was a novel that Mike borrowed from a library last week.(Mike가 지난주 도서관에서 빌린 것은 소설책이었다.)이다.

19 ⓐto wash는 wash로 고쳐야 어법상 적절한 문장이 된다.

20 ⓓartificial(인공적인)은 real(진짜의)로 바꿔야 문맥상 적절하다.

21 (A)to paint는 to부정사의 명사적 용법이다. 따라서 이와 용법이 같은 것은 ⓐ, ⓑ, ⓓ이다. ⓒ는 부사적 용법, ⓔ는 형용사적 용법이 사용된 문장이다.

22 비교급을 강조할 때, 비교급 앞에 much, still, even, far, a lot 등의 부사(구)를 쓰며 '(...보다) 훨씬 더 ~ 한'이라는 의미를 갖는다. 이때 harder는 hard의 비교급이므로 more는 쓸 수 없다.

23 위 글의 문맥상 벽화로 인해 마을이 더 밝아지고 행복해졌다(brighter and happier)는 말이 들어가야 자연스럽다.

24 It ~ that 강조 구문을 이용해 'It was a better tomorrow that we painted.'라고 영작할 수 있다.

25 위 글에서 화자는 자원봉사활동으로 벽화를 그렸고 그것이 마을을 더 밝고 행복하게 만들었기 때문에 그 사실에 대해서 자랑스러워하고 있다.

26 호민이의 그림 동아리가 완벽하게 벽화를 그리지는 않았다고 언급되어 있다.

27 ⓓthis idea는 벽화를 그리는 것을 의미한다.

28 (A)As는 '~할 때, ~하는 동안'의 뜻으로 시간의 부사절을 이끄는 접속사로 쓰였다. 따라서 이와 쓰임이 같은 것은 ⑤ We had a talk as we were waiting for them.(그들을 기다리는 동안 우리는 이야기를 나누었다.)이다.

29 a light went on in my head는 '내 머릿속에 좋은 생각이 떠올랐다'라는 뜻의 관용적 표현이다.

30 호민이는 미술 동아리 모임에서 미술대회에 참가하는 것이 아니라 봉사활동으로 벽화를 그리는 것을 제안했다.

Lesson 4 (기말) 1회

01 ⑤	**02** ③	**03** ②	**04** ⑤	**05** ③	**06** ①	**07** ③
08 ④	**09** ②	**10** ②	**11** ②			

12 (1) less you spend / more you save
(2) harder you practice / better you play

13 ③   **14** ⑤

15 (A) The sooner, the better
(B) the more positive, the healthier

16 ②	**17** ③	**18** ④	**19** ③	**20** ④	**21** ①	**22** ④
23 ①, ⑤		**24** ④	**25** ⑤	**26** ⑤	**27** ⑤	**28** ④
29 ⑤	**30** ⑤					

01 (A) work out 운동하다 (B) awake 깨어 있는 (C) convenience 편리함

02 belong to ~의 것이다

03 ② since는 '~한 이래로'라는 뜻으로 사용되었다. 나머지 since는 모두 '~이기 때문에'라는 뜻으로 사용되었다.

04 밑줄 친 문장은 상대방의 의견에 동의를 나타내는 표현이다. 이와 같은 표현으로는 "No doubt about it.", "I'm with you on that.", "That's exactly how I feel.", "I couldn't agree with you more." 등이 있다.

05 ① the far → the farther / ② wrote → has written / ④ The little → the less / ⑤ since → due to로 고쳐야 어법상 적절한 문장이 된다.

06 문맥상 (A)에는 상대방의 의견에 동의하는 표현이 들어가야 한다.

07 카페인은 셀 수 없는 명사이기 때문에 ⓒtoo many를 too

much로 고쳐야 어법상 적절한 문장이 된다.

08 Tony(A)는 온라인으로 사는 물건을 반품하는 것이 어렵 다고 생각한다.

09 ② Where does this talk take place?(이 대화는 어디 에서 하고 있는가?)에 대해서는 위 글에서 언급되어 있지 않다.

10 위 대화에서는 수업 시간에 핸드폰을 사용할 수 있게 된 것 에 대해서 이야기를 나누고 있다. A는 B에게 (A) What do you think about it?라고 묻고, 이에 대해 B는 (B) helpful이라고 대답하는 것이 문맥상 가장 적절하다.

11 위 대화에서는 수업 시간에 핸드폰을 사용할 수 있게 된 것 에 대해서 이야기를 나누고 있다.

12 「The+비교급(+주어+동사) ~, the+비교급(+주어+동 사) ...」의 어순으로 '~할수록, (점점) 더 …하다'라는 뜻 이다. '주어 + 동사'를 생략하고 쓰기도 한다.

13 ③ three pair → three pairs로 고쳐야 어법상 적절한 문 장이 된다.

14 A가 교복을 입는 것에 대해서 어떻게 생각하냐고 묻자, B 는 무엇을 입을지 걱정하지 않아도 되기 때문에 좋다고 생 각한다. 이에 A는 모든 학생들이 다 똑같아 보여서 싫다고 이야기하는 대화가 문맥상 가장 자연스럽다.

15 「The+비교급(+주어+동사) ~, the+비교급(+주어+동 사) ...」의 어순으로 '~할수록, (점점) 더 …하다'라는 뜻 이다. '주어 + 동사'를 생략하고 쓰기도 한다.

16 Jun의 마지막 말에 따르면, Jun은 수업 도중에 핸드폰을 사용하는 것이 공부에 도움이 될 것이라고 생각한다.

17 위 글에서는 독자들이 읽은 책에 대해서 코멘트를 남기고 있다. 따라서 위 글의 종류는 ③ review(논평)이다.

18 (A) the+비교급 구문으로 the stronger는 '(더 파면 팔 수록) 더 강해진다'라는 의미이다. (B) 흥미로운 것을 발 견해내는 사람이 하루 휴식을 받게 되는 것이므로 수동형 인 be given이 적절하다. (C) stand for 상징하다, 의미 하다

19 흥미로운 것을 발견해내는 사람은 하루 휴식을 받게 된다 고 언급되어 있다.

20 Stanley가 집어든 것이 너무 가볍기 때문에 진짜 금이 아 닐 것('But it couldn't be real gold since it was too light.')이라고 언급되어 있다.

21 위 글의 밑줄 친 object는 '물체'라는 의미로 사용되었다. 이와 같은 의미로 쓰인 문장은 ① Unidentified flying object is flying in the sky.(미확인 비행물체가 하늘을 날고 있다.)이다.

22 첫 문단의 마지막 문장에 Camp Green Lake가 언급되

어 있으므로 Camp Green Lake를 소개하는 (C)문단이 바로 뒤에 온다. 그 후 왜 Stanley가 캠프에 오게 되었는 지 설명하고 있는 (A)문단과 (B)문단 순서로 이어지는 것 이 글의 흐름상 가장 적절하다.

23 (가)since는 '~이기 때문에'라는 뜻으로 사용되었다. 따 라서 since와 바꿔 쓸 수 있는 단어는 as, because이다.

24 의문사 why를 이용한 간접의문문을 만들 때, 'why+주 어+동사' 순으로 쓴다. / ask+간접 목적어(~에게)+ 직접 목적어(~을/를) ~에게 …를 물어보다

25 위 글에 따르면, Stanley는 자신이 하지 않은 잘못으로 인 해 교정 캠프에 끌려갔다. 따라서 Stanley의 심정으로 가 장 적절한 것은 ⑤ depressed(우울한)이다.

26 위 글에 따르면, 운동화를 Stanley가 훔친 것이 아니라 하 늘에서 떨어졌고 Stanley가 그것을 발견했다.

27 ⓔHe는 Clyde Livingstone을 가리킨다.

28 (다) what happened 무슨 일이 일어났는지 (라) That was why ~ 그것이 ~한 이유였다

29 Stanley는 18개월 동안 캠프에서 지내게 될 것이라고 언 급되어 있다.

30 (A) pick up 집어들다 (B) Unfortunately 운이 나쁘게 도 (C) day off 하루 휴가

Lesson 4 (기말) 〔2회〕

01 ⑤ **02** ④ **03** ② **04** ① **05** ⑤
06 We didn't go on a picnic since it rained a lot.
07 ④ **08** ① **09** ④ **10** ② **11** ② **12** ③ **13** ⑤
14 ④
15 (1) Since I didn't have my phone
　　 (2) since he came here
16 ①
17 The higher we climb, the colder it becomes.
18 ② **19** ② **20** ④ **21** ④ **22** ① **23** ① **24** ⑤
25 ③ **26** more Stanley dug, stronger he became
27 ④ **28** ① **29** ① **30** ④

01 위에서부터 순서대로 ⓓbeat(뛰다), ⓑ appear(나타나 다), ⓐ afford(~할 여유가 있다), ⓒ assign(부과하다) 이 들어가야 문맥상 적절하다.

02 get along with ~와 잘 지내다

03 ⓐ 하늘에서 떨어졌다 / ⓒ 운이 나쁘게도 / ⓓ ~에게 속 했다 / ⓔ 결국 ~가 되었다

04 ①은 when이나 as, 나머지 빈칸에는 since가 들어가는

것이 문맥상 적절하다.

05 ⑤ since는 '~ 이래로'라는 뜻으로 사용되었다. 나머지는 모두 '~ 때문에'라는 뜻으로 사용되었다.

06 go on a picnic 소풍을 가다 / since ~ 때문에

07 Tony는 물건이 마음에 들지 않으면 반품하기도 힘들다 ('It's also difficult to return an item if you don't like it.')고 언급한 바 있다.

08 의문사 what을 사용해 간접 의문문(의문사+주어+동사)인 what an item actually looks like을 쓸 수 있다.

09 (A)look up은 '(정보를) 찾아보다'라는 뜻을 가진 숙어이다. 이와 같은 뜻으로 쓰인 문장은 ④ Can you look up the opening time on the website?(웹사이트에서 문을 여는 시간을 찾아볼 수 있니?)이다.

10 위 대화에서는 수업 시간에 핸드폰을 사용하는 것이 허용된 것에 대해서 이야기하고 있다.

11 "How often ~?"은 빈도를 물어보는 질문이다. 따라서 For two weeks(2주 동안)라는 대답은 적절하지 않다.

12 에너지 드링크가 깨어 있게 도와준다는 B의 말에 대해 A가 동의하고 있으므로 동의를 나타내는 표현인 ③ I'm with you on that이 가장 적절하다.

13 에너지 드링크를 덜 먹으라고 조언하고 있기 때문에 ⓔ more를 less로 바꿔 써야 한다.

14 G가 어떻게 지냈냐고 물어봤으므로 이에 대해 B는 잘 지냈다고 대답하면서 공항에서 여기까지 어떻게 왔냐고 묻는다. 이에 G는 지하철을 타고 왔다고 대답하고, B는 한국의 지하철이 어떠냐고 묻자 G가 지하철이 깨끗하다고 대답하는 순서로 이어지는 것이 흐름상 가장 자연스럽다.

15 since는 '~ 이래로'라는 의미로 쓰이거나 '~ 때문에'라는 뜻으로 쓰이기도 한다.

16 주어가 박달버거이기 때문에 동사 ⓐcan cook은 can be cooked가 되는 것이 어법상 적절하다.

17 「The +비교급(+주어+동사) ~, the+비교급(+주어+동사) …」의 어순으로 '~할수록, (점점) 더 …하다'라는 뜻이다. '주어 + 동사'를 생략하고 쓰기도 한다.

18 의문사 why가 쓰인 간접 의문문이므로 의문사+주어+동사 순인 why he was running이 들어가야 한다.

19 That was why ~. 그것이 ~한 이유였다.

20 위 글에 따르면 하늘에서 떨어진 운동화는 유명한 야구 선수의 것이었다.

21 위 글에 따르면, 하늘에서 떨어진 운동화는 Stanley의 것이 아니었기 때문에 운동화를 갖지는 않았다.

22 ① How many boys were in the camp?(캠프에는 몇 명의 소년들이 있었는가?)에 대해서는 위 글에서 언급된 바 없다.

23 ① What did KB stand for?(KB는 무엇을 의미하는가?)라는 질문에 대한 대답은 위 글에서 언급 되지 않았다.

24 문맥상 (E) slower는 faster가 되어야 적절하다.

25 (가)to build는 to부정사의 부사적 용법으로 사용되었다. 따라서 이와 쓰임이 같은 것은 ③ She waited to buy a movie ticket.(그녀는 영화 티켓을 사기 위해 기다렸다.)이다.

26 「The +비교급(+주어+동사) ~, the+비교급(+주어+동사) …」의 어순으로 '~할수록, (점점) 더 …하다'라는 뜻이다. '주어 + 동사'를 생략하고 쓰기도 한다.

27 '그렇다면 Stanley 같이 착한 소년이 여기서 무엇을 하고 있었던 걸까?'라는 문장이 들어가기에 가장 적절한 곳은 Stanley가 교정 캠프에 오게 된 이유를 설명하고 있는 (D)이다.

28 In fact 사실은

29 (가) since ~ 때문에 (나) Unfortunately 운이 나쁘게도 (다) even 심지어

30 이제 18개월 간 Stanley의 집은 바로 여기, 캠프 그린 레이크일 것이다.('Stanley's home for the next 18 months would be right here, at Camp Green Lake.'고 언급되어 있다.

MEMO